Chapter 1: Writing Processes
Learning by Doing: Analyzing Audience

Chapter 2: Reading Processes
Learning by Doing: Reading Online

Chapter 3: Critical Thinking Processes
Learning by Doing: Analyzing Logic

Chapter 4: Recalling an Experience
Learning from Other Writers: Howie Chackowicz,
The Game Ain't Over 'til the Fatso Man Sings [AUDIO]
Learning by Doing: Recalling from Photographs

Chapter 5: Observing a Scene
Learning from Other Writers: Multiple
Photographers, *Observing the* Titanic: *Past
and Present* [VISUAL ESSAY]
Learning by Doing: Scenes from the News

Chapter 6: Comparing and Contrasting
Learning from Other Writers: *National Geographic*
Editors, *Hurricane Katrina Pictures: Then & Now,
Ruin & Rebirth* [VISUAL ESSAY]
Learning by Doing: Comparing and Contrasting
Experience of a Major Event

Chapter 7: Taking a Stand
Learning from Other Writers: UNICEF Editors,
Dirty Water Campaign [VIDEO]
Learning by Doing: Writing Your Representative

Chapter 8: Evaluating and Reviewing
Learning from Other Writers: *Consumer Reports*
Editors, *Best Buttermilk Pancakes* [VIDEO]
Learning by Doing: Evaluating Film

Chapter 9: Sup̄̄̄̄̄ Sources
Learning from Ot̄̄̄̄
[TEXT, AUDIO, VIDEO]
Cary Tennis, *Why Am I Obsessed wi̅̅̅*
Karen Sternheimer, *Celebrity Relationships: Whȳ̄
We Care?*
Tom Ashbrook and Ty Burr, *The Strange Power
of Celebrity*
Timothy J. Bertoni and Patrick D. Nolan, *Dead Men
Do Tell Tales*
Learning by Doing: Finding Credible Sources

**Chapter 10: Responding to Visual
Representations**
Learning from Another Writer: Shannon Kintner,
Charlie Living with Autism [STUDENT VISUAL ESSAY]
Learning by Doing: Analyzing the Web Site for Your
Campus

Chapter 11: Writing Online
Learning by Doing: Exploring Your CMS or LMS
Learning from Another Writer: Portland State
University Writing Center, *Sample E-mail to
an Instructor* [VIDEO TUTORIAL]
Learning by Doing: Tracking Your Time Online

Chapter 12: Strategies for Generating Ideas
Learning by Doing: Brainstorming from a Video

**Chapter 13: Strategies for Stating a Thesis
and Planning**
Learning by Doing: Analyzing a Thesis

Chapter 14: Strategies for Drafting
Learning by Doing: Identifying Topic Sentences
Learning by Doing: Identifying Transitions

Chapter 15: **Strategies for Revising and Editing**
Learning by Doing: Editing Sentences

Chapter 16: **Planning Your Research Project**
Learning by Doing: Narrowing Online Research

Chapter 17: **Working with Sources**
Learning by Doing: Practicing with Online Sources

Chapter 18: **Finding Sources**
Learning by Doing: Comparing Google and Database Searches

Chapter 19: **Evaluating Sources**
Learning by Doing: Evaluating Online Sources

Chapter 20: **Integrating Sources**
Learning by Doing: Quoting and Paraphrasing Accurately

Chapter e-1: **Families**
Amy Tan, *Mother Tongue* [TEXT]
Richard Rodriguez, *Public and Private Language* [TEXT]
StrategyOne Editors, *Once a Mother, Always a Mother* [INFOGRAPHIC]
GOOD/Column Five Editors, *Paternity Leave around the World* [INFOGRAPHIC]

Chapter e-2: **Men and Women**
Robert Jensen, *The High Cost of Manliness* [TEXT]
Julie Zeilinger, *Guys Suffer from Oppressive Gender Roles Too* [TEXT]
Deborah Tannen, *Who Does the Talking Here?* [TEXT]
Jed Conklin, *Boxing Beauties* [VISUAL ESSAY]

Chapter e-3: **Popular Culture**
Stephen King, *Why We Crave Horror Movies* [TEXT]
Gerard Jones, *Violent Media Is Good for Kids* [TEXT]
Chuck Klosterman, *My Zombie, Myself: Why Modern Life Feels Rather Undead* [TEXT]
Brad Shoup, *"Harlem Shake" vs. History: Is the YouTube Novelty Hits Era That Novel?* [TEXT]

Chapter e-4: **Digital Living**
Elizabeth Stone, *Grief in the Age of Facebook* [TEXT]
Libby Copeland, *Is Facebook Making Us Sad?* [TEXT]
Sherry Turkle, *How Computers Change the Way We Think* [TEXT]
Off Book Editors, *Generative Art – Computers, Data, and Humanity* [VIDEO]

Chapter e-5: **Explorations on Living Well**
Juliet Schor, *The Creation of Discontent* [TEXT]
Llewellyn H. Rockwell Jr., *In Defense of Consumerism* [TEXT]
Sarah Adams, *Be Cool to the Pizza Dude* [AUDIO AND TEXT]
Brent Foster, *Highway Angel* [VIDEO]

The Concise Bedford
Guide *for* Writers

THE
Concise Bedford
Guide *for* Writers

X. J. Kennedy
Dorothy M. Kennedy
Marcia F. Muth

BEDFORD/ST. MARTIN'S

Boston ◆ New York

For Bedford/St. Martin's

Publisher: Leasa Burton
Developmental Editor: Regina Tavani
Senior Editor: Martha Bustin
Senior Production Editor: Gregory Erb
Senior Production Supervisor: Steven Cestaro
Executive Marketing Manager: Molly Parke
Editorial Assistant: Brenna Cleeland
Copy Editor: Hilly van Loon
Indexer: Constance A. Angelo
Photo Researcher: Naomi Kornhauser
Senior Art Director: Anna Palchik
Text Design: Lisa Buckley
Cover Design: Marine Miller
Cover Photo: By Fuse courtesy of gettyimages®
Composition: Graphic World, Inc.
Printing and Binding: RR Donnelley and Sons

President, Bedford/St. Martin's: Denise B. Wydra
Editorial Director, English and Music: Karen S. Henry
Director of Marketing: Karen R. Soeltz
Production Director: Susan W. Brown
Director of Rights and Permissions: Hilary Newman

Manufactured in the United States of America.

8 7 6 5 4 3
f e d c b a

For information, write: Bedford/St. Martin's, 75 Arlington Street, Boston, MA 02116
(617-399-4000)

ISBN 978-1-4576-4876-2

Acknowledgments

Preface

TO THE INSTRUCTOR

The *Concise Bedford Guide for Writers* is drawn from the tradition of *The Bedford Guide for College Writers*, now in its tenth edition. This new compact text retains all of the features that have made the original text the enduring success that it is, including clear and succinct instruction, thorough coverage with a flexible organization, and frequent opportunities for active learning—and it does so at nearly half the size. The streamlined rhetoric introduces students to commonly assigned writing situations and strategies, while a succinct research manual covers the essentials of college-level research and documentation. The reader, located entirely online, takes advantage of all that the Web has to offer, giving students access not only to essays by well-known authors but also to innovative, engaging multimodal texts to develop visual literacy. Like its related texts, *The Concise Bedford Guide* has been designed with one overarching goal: to help students become the confident, resourceful, and *independent* writers they will need to be.

The belief that students learn by doing has shaped *The Bedford Guide* tradition from the beginning. This text therefore includes an exceptional number of opportunities for practice and self-assessment. Class-tested, hands-on "Learning by Doing" activities and assignments, located both in print and online, give students frequent opportunities to apply what they have learned and become comfortable with each step in the process as they go along.

Despite its compact size, *The Concise Bedford Guide* gives students all they need to write well in a single, flexible, interactive product. The online reader is thoroughly integrated with the book's writing situations and process-oriented strategies, while grammar and usage instruction in the Quick Editing Guide is complemented by adaptive online *LearningCurve* exercises—available as part of the e-book or free to package with the print book. In addition to the research manual, the text contains sample MLA and APA student papers and a helpful Quick Format Guide and Quick Research Guide in the appendices. *The Concise Bedford Guide* gives students the tools they need to succeed as writers.

Most important, the book focuses on building transferable skills. Recognizing that the college composition course may be one of a student's last classes with in-depth writing instruction, we have made every effort to ensure that *The Concise Bedford Guide* develops writers able to meet future challenges. It offers supportive step-by-step guidance, "Why Writing Matters" features, and varied end-of-chapter "Additional Writing Assignments." These and other features prepare students to apply what they have learned in other courses and in the workplace, meeting whatever rhetorical challenges lie ahead, in college and in life.

Bedford Integrated Media

e-Pages connect with students and build writing and critical thinking skills

The Concise Bedford Guide comes with Bedford Integrated Media: e-Pages that give the book a rich array of assignable, multimodal content. These materials extend the book's focus on active learning and transferable skills into the online environment. They also expand alternatives for class-specific activities, such as using the e-Pages research cluster on celebrity culture (Chapter 9) to improve working with sources. Two types of e-Pages accompany the book and take advantage of all the Web can do:

- **Readings.** Multimodal readings in e-Pages include videos, audio segments, interviews, infographics, and visual essays. Each is contextualized by a headnote and accompanied by critical reading and thinking questions. Students type their answers into response boxes that report to their instructor's gradebook. In Chapters 4 to 11 ("Recalling an Experience" through "Writing Online"), one e-Pages reading per chapter is featured as part of "Learning from Other Writers." The e-Pages reading topics in these chapters include campaign video from UNICEF on their clean drinking water initiative, *National Geographic's Hurricane Katrina Pictures: Then & Now, Ruin & Rebirth* (visual essay), a sociologist's explanation of the American obsession with celebrity relationships (video), and from NPR's *This American Life*, a story of school, relationships, and mistaken perceptions (audio segment).

  "A Writer's Reader" offers twenty readings, many of them multimodal, organized thematically. Classic essays such as Amy Tan's "Mother Tongue" are paired alongside innovative examples of multimodal composition, such as a photo essay on women boxers and an infographic evaluating paternity leave policies around the world.

- **Assignments and activities.** Assignment questions accompanying the readings encourage both critical reading and thinking. Online "Learning by Doing" activities encourage students to explore topics such as analyzing audience, reading online, recalling from photographs, and finding credible sources. For a complete list of e-Pages content, turn to the front of the book.

Students access e-Pages materials through the Bedford Integrated Media page for *The Concise Bedford Guide for Writers* at **bedfordstmartins.com /concisebedguide**. They receive automatic access to e-Pages with the purchase of a new book. (Students who do not buy a new book can purchase access at this same site.) The e-Pages format makes it easy for instructors to see and evaluate what students are doing and gives new options for readings and assignments.

Instructors receive log-in information in a separate e-mail with access to all of the resources in Bedford Integrated Media. You can also log in or request access information at the book's media page.

:e National Geographic Editors   **Visual Essay**

Hurricane Katrina Pictures: Then & Now, Ruin & Rebirth

National Geographic compiled a series of images showing how New Orleans has recovered since the immediate aftermath of Hurricane Katrina, which hit the area in 2005. To view the photos, go to Chapter 6: **bedfordstmartins .com/concisebedguide**.

Everything You Need

Part One: A College Writer's Processes

The first part of the book introduces students to the interconnected processes of writing (Chapter 1), reading (Chapter 2), and critical thinking (Chapter 3). The instruction is complemented by several examples of student writing, including a critical reading response in Chapter 2, "Reading Processes."

Part Two: A Writer's Situations

In Part Two, six core chapters—each including three sample readings (one by a student, one by a professional writer, and one multimodal online selection)—guide students through a full range of common first-year writing assignments. The rhetorical situations covered include recalling an experience (Chapter 4), observing a scene (Chapter 5), comparing and contrasting (Chapter 6), taking a stand (Chapter 7), evaluating and reviewing (Chapter 8), and supporting a position with sources (Chapter 9). The part concludes with two chapters that cover increasingly common writing situations: responding to visual representations (Chapter 10) and writing online (Chapter 11). "Why Writing Matters" features, readings, visuals, "Responding to an Image" chapter openers for class discussion and journal writing, and "Additional Writing Assignments" make these chapters both useful and interesting for students.

Part Three: A Writer's Strategies

Part Three is a convenient resource offering practical advice for the stages of common writing processes: generating ideas (Chapter 12), stating a thesis and planning (Chapter 13), drafting (Chapter 14), and revising and editing (Chapter 15), each concluding with a reflective "Learning by Doing" activity. Marginal annotations strategically placed earlier in the book guide students to these chapters, which collectively serve as a writer's toolbox.

Part Four: A Writer's Research Manual

Part Four offers a remarkably comprehensive guide to source-based writing, detailing all the essential steps for print and electronic research. Informed by a survey of academic librarians, this manual reflects current best practices in planning a research project (Chapter 16), working with sources (Chapter 17), finding sources (Chapter 18), evaluating sources (Chapter 19), and integrating sources (Chapter 20).

Appendices

In the appendices, a "Quick Format Guide" illustrates academic document design. Next, a "Quick Research Guide" conveniently—and briefly—reviews how to find, evaluate, integrate, cite, and document sources. Then a "Quick Editing Guide" gives special attention to the most troublesome grammar and editing problems. Finally, two sample student research papers—one using MLA documentation and the other using APA documentation—conclude the appendices.

ⓔ A Writer's Reader

Located entirely online in the book's e-Pages, this thematic reader offers twenty selections that take advantage of all that the Web can do. The selections are arranged around five themes that provide a meaningful context for students: families, men and women, popular culture, digital living, and explorations on living well. Each thematic group includes two paired text essays as well as two multimodal pieces—such as a photo essay on female boxers and a video interview with artists who allow computers to make key decisions about their creations. Apparatus that encourages critical thinking and writing accompanies each reading. A rhetorical table of contents (pp. xxviii–xxx) shows how selections can coordinate with and illustrate Part 2, "A Writer's Situations." A biographical headnote and a brief prereading tip or question introduce each reading. Each selection is followed by questions on meaning, writing strategies, critical reading, vocabulary, and connections to other selections; journal prompts; and suggested writing assignments, one personal and the other analytical. These questions, which students complete and submit online, lead them from reading carefully for both thematic and rhetorical elements to applying new strategies and insight in their own writing.

You Get More Choices for *The Concise Bedford Guide for Writers*

Bedford/St. Martin's offers resources and format choices that help you and your students get even more out of the book and your course. To learn more about or order any of the following products, contact your Bedford/St. Martin's sales representative, e-mail sales support (sales_support@bfwpub.com), or visit the Web site at bedfordstmartins.com/concisebedguide/catalog.

Let Students Choose Their Format

Bedford/St. Martin's offers a range of affordable formats, allowing students to choose the one that works for them. For details, visit bedfordstmartins.com/bedguide/catalog/formats.

- *Bedford e-Book to Go* A portable, downloadable e-book at about half the price of the print book
- *Other popular e-book formats* For details, visit bedfordstmartins.com/ebooks

Choose the Flexible *Bedford e-Portfolio*

Students can collect, select, and reflect on their coursework and personalize and share their e-Portfolio for any audience—instructors, peers, potential employers, or family and friends. Instructors can provide as much or as little structure as they see fit. Rubrics and learning outcomes can be aligned to student work, so instructors and programs can gather reliable and useful assessment data. Every *Bedford e-Portfolio* comes pre-loaded with *Portfolio Keeping* and *Portfolio Teaching*, by Nedra Reynolds and Elizabeth Davis. *Bedford e-Portfolio* can be purchased separately or packaged with the print book at a significant discount. An activation code is required. To order *e-Portfolio* with the print book, use ISBN 978-1-4576-7625-3. For more details, visit bedfordstmartins.com/eportfolio.

Watch Peer Review Work

Eli Review lets instructors scaffold their assignments in a clearer, more effective way for students—making peer review more visible and teachable. Because teachers get real-time analytics about how well students have met criteria in a writing task *and* about how helpful peer comments have been, they can intervene in real time to teach how to give good feedback and how to shape writing to meet criteria. When students can instantly see which comments are endorsed by their teacher and how their feedback has been rated by their peers, they're motivated to give the best reviews, get the best ratings, think like writers, and revise with a plan. *Eli Review* can be purchased separately or packaged with the print book at a significant discount. An activation code is required. To order *Eli Review* with the print book, use ISBN 978-1-4576-7610-9. For details, visit bedfordstmartins.com/eli.

Select Value Packages

Add value to your text by packaging one of the following resources with *The Concise Bedford Guide* at a significant discount. To learn more about package options for any of the following products, contact your Bedford/St. Martin's sales representative or visit bedfordstmartins.com/concisebedguide/catalog.

LearningCurve for Readers and Writers, Bedford/St. Martin's adaptive quizzing program, quickly learns what students already know and helps them practice what they don't yet understand. Game-like quizzing motivates students to engage with their course, and reporting tools help teachers discern their students' needs. *LearningCurve for Readers and Writers* can be packaged with *The Concise Bedford Guide* at a significant discount. An activation code is required. To order *LearningCurve* packaged with the print book, use ISBN 978-1-4576-7650-5. For details, visit bedfordstmartins.com /englishlearningcurve.

VideoCentral is a growing collection of videos for the writing class that captures real-world, academic, and student writers talking about how and why they write. Writer and teacher Peter Berkow interviewed hundreds of people — from Michael Moore to Cynthia Selfe — to produce over 140 brief videos about topics such as revising and getting feedback. *VideoCentral* can be packaged with *The Concise Bedford Guide for Writers* at a significant discount. An activation code is required. To order *VideoCentral* packaged with the print book, use ISBN 978-1-4576-7589-8.

i-series is a popular series presenting multimedia tutorials in a flexible format — because there are things you cannot do in a book.

- *ix visual exercises* helps students put into practice key rhetorical and visual concepts. To order *ix visual exercises* packaged with the print book, use ISBN 978-1-4576-7598-0.

- *i-claim: visualizing argument* offers a new way to see argument — with 6 tutorials, an illustrated glossary, and over 70 multimedia arguments. To order *i-claim: visualizing argument* packaged with the print book, use ISBN 978-1-4576-7633-8.

Portfolio Keeping, **Third Edition,** by Nedra Reynolds and Elizabeth Davis, provides all the information students need to use the portfolio method in a writing course. *Portfolio Teaching,* a companion guide for instructors, provides the practical information instructors and writing program administrators need to use the portfolio method effectively in a writing course. To order *Portfolio Keeping* packaged with the print book, use ISBN 978-1-4576-7582-9.

Try *Re:Writing 2* for Fun

bedfordstmartins.com/rewriting

What's the fun of teaching writing if you can't try something new? The best collection of free writing resources on the Web, *Re:Writing 2* gives you and your students even more ways to think, watch, practice, and learn about writing concepts. Listen to Nancy Sommers on using a teacher's comments to revise. Try a logic puzzle. Consult our resources for writing centers. All free for the fun of trying it. Visit bedfordstmartins.com/rewriting.

Instructor Resources

bedfordstmartins.com/concisebedguide/catalog

You have a lot to do in your course. Bedford/St. Martin's wants to make it easy for you to find the support you need — and to get it quickly.

Practical Suggestions for Teaching with The Concise Bedford Guide for Writers is available in PDF that can be downloaded from the Bedford/St. Martin's online catalog. In addition to chapter overviews and teaching tips, the Instructor's Manual includes sample syllabi, correlations to the Council of Writing Program Administrators' Outcomes Statement, and classroom activities.

TeachingCentral offers the entire list of Bedford/St. Martin's print and online professional resources in one place. You will find landmark reference works, sourcebooks on pedagogical issues, award-winning collections, and practical advice for the classroom — all free for instructors at bedfordstmartins.com/teachingcentral.

Bits collects creative ideas for teaching a range of composition topics in an easily searchable blog format. A community of teachers — leading scholars, authors, and editors — discuss revision, research, grammar and style, technology, peer review, and much more. Take, use, adapt, and pass the ideas around. Then, come back to the site to comment or share your own suggestion. Visit bedfordbits.com.

Thanks and Appreciation

Many individuals contributed significantly to *The Concise Bedford Guide for Writers*, and we extend our sincerest thanks to all of them.

Editorial Advisory Board

As we began to prepare the new edition of *The Bedford Guide for College Writers*, we assembled an editorial advisory board to respond to the many significant changes we planned and to share ideas about how to make the book more useful to both students and teachers. These dedicated instructors responded thoroughly and insightfully to new features of the text, answered innumerable questions, and suggested many ideas, activities, and assignments. They also submitted student papers and in ways large and small helped to shape all the versions of the book, including the new *Concise Bedford Guide for Writers*. We are extremely grateful to each one of them:

- Kathleen Beauchene, Community College of Rhode Island
- Vicki Besaw, College of Menominee Nation
- Thomas Eaton, Southeast Missouri State University
- Sonia Feder-Lewis, Saint Mary's University of Minnesota
- Audrey Hillyer, University of Southern Indiana
- Beth Koruna, Columbus State Community College
- Tracy Kristo, Anoka-Ramsey Community College
- Kathryn Lane, Northwestern Oklahoma State University
- Leigh Martin, Community College of Rhode Island
- Anna McKennon, Fullerton College

- Terry Novak, Johnson and Wales University
- Arthur L. Schuhart, Northern Virginia Community College–Annandale
- Dana Waters, Dodge City Community College

Reviewers

The following instructors reviewed the initial table of contents for *The Concise Bedford Guide for Writers* and offered invaluable insight and suggestions. We extend our sincerest thanks to all of them for lending their helpful guidance as we developed this new text.

- Susanne Bentley, Great Basin College
- Lucas Brown, North Idaho College
- Sonia Feder-Lewis, Saint Mary's University of Minnesota
- Anissa Graham, University of North Alabama
- Peter Huk, University of California Santa Barbara
- Alison Klaum, University of Delaware
- Todd McCann, Bay de Noc Community College
- Cara Rodriguez, Casper College
- Laurie Sherman, Community College of Rhode Island

Other Colleagues

We also extend our gratitude to instructors across the country who took time and care to review for the tenth edition of *The Bedford Guide for College Writers with Reader, Research Manual, and Handbook*. Their thoughtful feedback and suggestions also informed the development of this text. For this we thank

- Jacob Agatucci, Central Oregon Community College
- Jennifer Aly, University of Hawaii Maui College
- Laura Ballard, Mesa Community College
- Norman Bates, Cochise College
- Sean Bernard, University of La Verne
- Laura Caudill, Sullivan University
- Donna Craine, Front Range Community College
- Andrea Deacon, University of Wisconsin–Stout
- Sharon Derry, Sierra College
- Marcia Dinneen, Bridgewater State College
- Kimberly Fangman, Southeast Community College

- Dwedor Ford, Winston-Salem State University
- Anissa Graham, University of North Alabama
- Letizia Guglielmo, Kennesaw State University
- Russell Hall, Penn State Behrend
- Alexis Hart, Virginia Military Institute
- Jane Holwerda, Dodge City Community College
- Peter Huk, University of California Santa Barbara
- Sarah Hutton, University of Massachusetts–Amherst
- Diane Jakacki, Georgia Institute of Technology
- Saiyeda Khatun, Johnson & Wales University
- Karla Saari Kitalong, Michigan Technological University
- Lynn Lampert, California State University–Northridge
- Ellen Leonard, Springfield Technical Community College
- John Lusk, St. Clair County Community College
- Todd McCann, Bay College
- Linda McHenry, Fort Hays State University
- Lanell Mogab, Clinton Community College
- Susan Perry, Greenville Technical College
- Sheryl Ruszkiewicz, Baker College of Allen Park
- Laura Saunders, Simmons College
- Laurie Sherman, Community College of Rhode Island
- Tammy Sugarman, Georgia State University
- Anthony Vannella, San Antonio College
- Laura Wind, Northeastern University

Contributors

The Concise Bedford Guide for Writers could not have been completed without the help of numerous individuals. Special thanks go to Dana Waters (Dodge City Community College) for developing the book's instructor's manual, *Practical Suggestions.* Jennifer Krisuk (Dodge City Community College) contributed to the manual a section on teaching writing with tablets. Stefanie Wortman and Wendy Perkins wrote excellent apparatus for the new reading selections. Art researcher Naomi Kornhauser helped us by finding eye-catching and thought-provoking photographs and other images. She also cleared permissions for the art. Caryn Burtt efficiently cleared text permissions under the able guidance of Kalina Ingham. Shannon Walsh contributed tremendously to the e-Pages and especially to "A Writer's Reader." Kate Mayhew helped us with expert e-Pages research. Candace Rardon was our special student consultant on many matters concerning student writing and brought her great energy and valuable perspective to the project.

We thank very talented and patient graphic designer Lisa Buckley for the text's attractive design. Anna Palchik, senior art director, also played a crucial role in the design.

We gratefully acknowledge the contribution of photographer David L. Ryan. His beautiful and unusual photographs of urban bathers, boats, commuters, and playing fields appear at the beginnings of Parts One through Four and on pages A-81–A-82. We are honored to feature these works, and we thank the artist for letting us include them.

Student Writers

This text includes the writings of the following student writers, who graciously shared their work with us: Richard Anson, Cristina Berrios, Linn Bourgeau, Betsy Buffo, Joseph Cauteruccio Jr., Heather Church, Olof Eriksson, Elizabeth Erion, Alea Eyre, Marjorie Lee Garretson, Sarah E. Goers, Jacob Griffin, Stephanie Hawkins, Alley Julseth, Cindy Keeler, Heidi Kessler, Shannon Kintner, Melissa Lamberth, Jenny Lidington, Abigail Marchand, Schyler Martin, Daniel Matthews, Angela Mendy, Jennifer Miller, Susanna Olsen, Shari O'Malley, Candace Rardon, Robert G. Schreiner, Rachel Steinhaus, Joshua Tefft, Leah Threats, Joel Torres, Donna Waite, Arthur Wasilewski, Christopher Williams, and Carrie Williamson.

Editorial

At Bedford/St. Martin's three individuals merit special recognition. President of Bedford/St. Martin's Denise B. Wydra (also a former editor of *The Bedford Guide*) first proposed the idea of a concise text for *The Bedford Guide* family and contributed invaluable suggestions as we developed it. We greatly value the guidance of Editorial Director Karen S. Henry, who has helped sustain the other versions of *The Bedford Guide* through many editions and who has provided perceptive advice at crucial points in the development of *The Concise Bedford Guide*. Publisher Leasa Burton likewise offered vital insight and suggestions during the course of the text's development, especially with regard to its integrated media.

The editorial effort behind the development of *The Bedford Guide for College Writers* is truly a team endeavor. Marcia F. Muth assumed a major authorial role in the seventh edition, answering needs expressed by users with many exciting new features. She has continued in that role with her work on *The Concise Bedford Guide*, developing the book's contents and features with creativity and dedication. Associate Editor Regina Tavani performed helpful market research in the early stages of the text's planning and thoughtfully guided the book through development and production. Senior Editor

Martha Bustin brought helpful insight and suggestions from her work developing *The Bedford Guide*. Editorial assistant Brenna Cleeland joined the team when the book was in its final stages and lent her efficient help to ongoing work on the print and electronic ancillaries. Kimberly Hampton guided the production of the electronic resources, bringing creativity and energy to the development of the e-book, e-Pages, and other parts of the book's ancillary package.

Other members of the Bedford/St. Martin's staff contributed greatly to *The Concise Bedford Guide*. Many thanks and heartfelt appreciation go to Gregory Erb, who, with an exacting eye, great patience, and good humor, shepherded the book through production. Under Greg's care, the production process could not have gone more smoothly. Sue Brown, Elise Kaiser, and Elizabeth Schaaf helped immensely with production's "big picture" issues. Marine Bouvier Miller created the lovely design of the book's cover. Molly Parke skillfully coordinated the marketing of the book and offered much good advice based on feedback from the field. Karen Melton Soeltz and Jane Helms also offered valuable marketing advice. The book's promotion was ably handled by Mike Paparisto. Pelle Cass generously contributed to the pages (located after the appendices) about the book's four part-opening photographs and about key correspondences between the work of writers and photographers.

Marcia Muth is especially grateful to the School of Education and Human Development at the University of Colorado Denver for sponsoring her writing workshops. She also thanks CU Online for its many creative suggestions about online instruction, especially those presented at Web Camp and in *The CU Online Handbook: Teach Differently: Create and Collaborate*. Special appreciation also goes to Mary Finley, University Library at California State University Northridge, and Rodney Muth, University of Colorado Denver, for ongoing expert advice. Finally, we once again thank our friends and families for their unwavering patience, understanding, and encouragement.

Contents

Preface: To the Instructor   vii

Rhetorical Contents   xxviii

Selected Visual Contents   xxxi

Features of *The Concise Bedford Guide* Correlated to WPA Outcomes   xxxiii

How to Use *The Concise Bedford Guide for Writers*   xl

Part One   A College Writer's Processes   2

Introduction: Meeting College Expectations   5

1. Writing Processes   6

Writing, Reading, and Critical Thinking   6

A Process of Writing   7

Getting Started   7

Generating Ideas   7

Learning by Doing Reflecting on Ideas   8

Planning, Drafting, and Developing   8

Learning by Doing Reflecting on Drafts   10

Revising and Editing   10

Learning by Doing Reflecting on Finishing   11

Purpose and Audience   11

Writing for a Reason   11

Learning by Doing Considering Purpose   12

Writing for Your Audience   12

Learning by Doing Analyzing Audience   e

Learning by Doing Considering Audience   14

Targeting a College Audience   15

Learning by Doing Considering a College Audience   15

Additional Writing Activities   16

2. Reading Processes   17

A Process of Critical Reading   17

Learning by Doing Describing Your Reading Strategies   18

Getting Started   18

Preparing to Read   19

Learning by Doing Preparing to Read   20

Responding to Reading   20

Learning by Doing Annotating a Passage   22

Learning by Doing Responding in a Reading Journal   23

Learning from Another Writer: Reading Summary and Response   24

■ **Student Summary and Response: Olof Eriksson,** The Problems with Masculinity   24

Reading on Literal and Analytical Levels   25

Learning by Doing Reading Analytically   27

Generating Ideas from Reading   27

Learning from Another Writer: Critical Reading and Response   29

■ **Student Critical Reading Response: Alley Julseth,** Analyzing "The New Literacy"   30

Learning by Doing Reading Critically   31

■ **Michael Shermer,** The Science of Righteousness   32

Reading Online and Multimodal Texts   33

Learning by Doing Reading Online   e

Learning by Doing Reading a Web Site   35

Additional Writing Activities   35

3. Critical Thinking Processes   37

A Process of Critical Thinking   37

Getting Started   38

Learning by Doing Thinking Critically to Solve a

Campus Problem   38

Learning by Doing Thinking Critically to Explore an Issue   38

Applying Critical Thinking to Academic Problems   39

Learning by Doing Thinking Critically to Respond to an Academic Problem   39

Supporting Critical Thinking with Evidence   40

Types of Evidence   41

Learning by Doing Looking for Evidence   43

Testing Evidence   43

Using Evidence to Appeal to Your Audience   44

Logical Appeal (Logos)   44

Emotional Appeal (Pathos)   44

Ethical Appeal (Ethos)   45

Learning by Doing Identifying Types of Appeals   45

Learning from Another Writer: Rhetorical Analysis   45

■ **Student Rhetorical Analysis: Richard Anson,** Young Americans and Media News   46

Presenting Your Critical Thinking   47

Learning by Doing Testing Logical Patterns   51

Learning by Doing Analyzing Logic   ℮

Avoiding Faulty Thinking   52

Learning by Doing Analyzing Reasoning   52

■ **David Rothkopf,** A Proposal to Draft America's Elderly   53

Additional Writing Activities   54

Part Two A Writer's Situations   56

Introduction: Writing in College   59

4. Recalling an Experience   60

Learning from Other Writers   62

■ **Russell Baker,** The Art of Eating Spaghetti   62

■ **Student Essay: Robert G. Schreiner,** What Is a Hunter? 65

■ **Howie Chackowicz,** The Game Ain't Over 'til the Fatso Man Sings *[Audio]* ℮ and 68

Learning by Writing   69

The Assignment: Recalling a Personal Experience   69

Learning by Doing Recalling from Photographs   ℮

Generating Ideas   70

Learning by Doing Creating Your Writing Space   72

Planning, Drafting, and Developing   72

Learning by Doing Stating the Importance of Your Experience   72

Learning by Doing Selecting and Arranging Events   73

Revising and Editing   74

Learning by Doing Appealing to the Senses   75

Additional Writing Assignments   76

5. Observing a Scene   80

Learning from Other Writers   82

■ **Eric Liu,** The Chinatown Idea   82

■ **Student Essay: Alea Eyre,** Stockholm   85

■ **Multiple Photographers,** Observing the *Titanic*: Past and Present *[Visual Essay]* ℮ and 87

Learning by Writing   88

The Assignment: Observing a Scene   88

Learning by Doing Scenes from the News   ℮

Generating Ideas   90

Learning by Doing Enriching Sensory Detail   92

Planning, Drafting, and Developing   92

Learning by Doing Experimenting with Organization   93

Revising and Editing   94

Learning by Doing Strengthening Your Main Impression   94

Additional Writing Assignments   96

6. Comparing and Contrasting 99

Learning from Other Writers 101

- **David Brooks,** The Opportunity Gap 101
- **Student Essay: Jacob Griffin,** Karate Kid vs. Kung Fu Panda: A Race to the Olympics 104
- *National Geographic* **Editors,** Hurricane Katrina Pictures: Then & Now, Ruin & Rebirth *[Visual Essay]* e and 107

Learning by Writing 108

The Assignment: Comparing and Contrasting 108

Learning by Doing Comparing and Contrasting Experience of a Major Event e

Generating Ideas 109

Learning by Doing Making a Comparison-and-Contrast Table 110

Planning, Drafting, and Developing 111

Learning by Doing Pinpointing Your Purpose 111

Learning by Doing Building Cohesion with Transitions 113

Revising and Editing 114

Additional Writing Assignments 116

7. Taking a Stand 119

Learning from Other Writers 121

- **Suzan Shown Harjo,** Last Rites for Indian Dead 121
- **Student Essay: Marjorie Lee Garretson,** More Pros Than Cons in a Meat-Free Life 124
- **UNICEF Editors,** Dirty Water Campaign *[Video]* e and 127

Learning by Writing 127

The Assignment: Taking a Stand 127

Learning by Doing Writing Your Representative e

Generating Ideas 129

Learning by Doing Asking Your Question 130

Learning by Doing Supporting a Claim 136

Planning, Drafting, and Developing 137

Learning by Doing Refining Your Plans 138

Learning by Doing Making Columns of Appeals 139

Revising and Editing 140

TAKE ACTION Strengthening Support for a Stand 142

Recognizing Logical Fallacies 143

Additional Writing Assignments 145

8. Evaluating and Reviewing 148

Learning from Other Writers 150

- **Scott Tobias,** The Hunger Games 150
- **Student Essay: Elizabeth Erion,** Internship Program Falls Short 153
- *Consumer Reports* **Editors,** Best Buttermilk Pancakes *[Video]* e and 155

Learning by Writing 155

The Assignment: Writing an Evaluation 155

Learning by Doing Evaluating Film e

Generating Ideas 157

Learning by Doing Developing Criteria 159

Planning, Drafting, and Developing 159

Learning by Doing Stating Your Overall Judgment 159

Learning by Doing Supporting Your Judgments 160

Revising and Editing 160

Additional Writing Assignments 162

9. Supporting a Position with Sources 166

Learning from Other Writers 168

- **Jake Halpern: The Popular Crowd** 168
- **Student Essay: Abigail Marchand,** The Family Dynamic 171
- **Research Cluster: Celebrity Culture** *[Text, Audio, and Video]* e and 173
  - **Cary Tennis,** Why Am I Obsessed with Celebrity Gossip?
  - **Karen Sternheimer,** Celebrity Relationships: Why Do We Care?
  - **Tom Ashbrook and Ty Burr,** The Strange Power of Celebrity

■ **Timothy J. Bertoni and Patrick D. Nolan,** Dead Men *Do* Tell Tales

Learning by Writing   174

The Assignment: Supporting a Position with Sources   174

Learning by Doing Finding Credible Sources   🄴

Generating Ideas   176

Learning by Doing Selecting Reliable Sources   178

Planning, Drafting, and Developing   178

Learning by Doing Connecting Evidence and Thesis   179

The Academic Exchange   182

Revising and Editing   189

Learning by Doing Launching Your Sources   190

Learning by Doing Checking Your Presentation of Sources   193

TAKE ACTION Integrating Source Information Effectively   194

Additional Writing Assignments   196

10. Responding to Visual Representations   200

Using Strategies for Visual Analysis   201

Learning by Doing Analyzing the Web Site for Your Campus   🄴

Level One: Seeing the Big Picture   202

Source, Purpose, and Audience   202

Prominent Element   202

Focal Point   204

Learning by Doing Seeing the Big Picture   204

Level Two: Observing the Characteristics of an Image   204

Cast of Characters   205

Story of the Image   205

Design and Arrangement   205

Artistic Choices   206

Learning by Doing Observing Characteristics   211

Level Three: Interpreting the Meaning of an Image   211

General Feeling or Mood   211

Sociological, Political, Economic, or Cultural Attitudes   213

Language   214

Signs and Symbols   215

Themes   215

Learning by Doing Interpreting Meaning   216

Learning from Another Writer: Visual Analysis   216

■ **Student Analysis of an Advertisement: Rachel Steinhaus, "Life, Liberty, and the Pursuit"**   216

Learning by Writing   219

The Assignment: Analyzing a Visual Representation   219

Generating Ideas   219

Planning, Drafting, and Developing   220

Revising and Editing   221

Learning from Another Writer: Visual Essay   222

■ **Student Visual Essay: Shannon Kintner, Charlie Living with Autism**   🄴 and 222

Additional Writing Assignments   225

11. Writing Online   227

Getting Started   228

Learning by Doing Identifying Online Writing Expectations   228

Learning by Doing Tracking Your Time Online   🄴

Learning by Doing Exploring Your CMS or LMS   🄴

Class Courtesy   228

Online Ethics   229

Learning by Doing Making Personal Rules   230

Common Online Writing Situations   231

Messages to Your Instructor   231

Learning by Doing Finding a College Voice   232

Learning from Other Writers: Messages to Your Instructor   232

■ **Portland State University Writing Center,** Sample E-mail to an Instructor *[Video Tutorial]*   🄴 and 233

Learning by Doing Contacting Your Instructor   234

Online Profile 234
Learning by Doing Posting a Personal Profile 234
Learning by Doing Introducing a Classmate 235
Online Threaded Discussions or Responses 235
Learning from Other Writers: Threaded Discussion 235
Learning by Doing Joining a Threaded Discussion 238

File Management 238
Learning by Doing Preparing a Template 238
Learning by Doing Organizing Your Files 239

Additional Writing Assignments 242

Part Three A Writer's Strategies 244

Introduction: Expanding Your Resources 247

12. Strategies for Generating Ideas 248

Finding Ideas 248
Building from Your Assignment 249
Learning by Doing Building from Your Assignment 250
Brainstorming 250
Learning by Doing Brainstorming from a Video e
Learning by Doing Brainstorming 251
Freewriting 251
Learning by Doing Freewriting 252
Doodling or Sketching 252
Learning by Doing Doodling or Sketching 254
Mapping 254
Learning by Doing Mapping 254
Imagining 255
Learning by Doing Imagining 256
Asking a Reporter's Questions 256
Learning by Doing Asking a Reporter's Questions 257
Seeking Motives 257
Learning by Doing Seeking Motives 258
Keeping a Journal 259
Learning by Doing Keeping a Journal 260

Getting Ready 260
Setting Up Circumstances 260
Preparing Your Mind 261
Learning by Doing Reflecting on Generating Ideas 261

13. Strategies for Stating a Thesis and Planning 262

Shaping Your Topic for Your Purpose and Your Audience 262
Learning by Doing Considering Purpose and Audience 263

Stating and Using a Thesis 263
Learning by Doing Analyzing a Thesis e
Learning by Doing Identifying Theses 264
How to Discover a Working Thesis 264
Learning by Doing Discovering a Thesis 266
How to State a Thesis 266
Learning by Doing Examining Thesis Statements 269
How to Improve a Thesis 269
TAKE ACTION Building a Stronger Thesis 270
How to Use a Thesis to Organize 271
Learning by Doing Using a Thesis to Preview 272

Organizing Your Ideas 272
Grouping Your Ideas 272
Learning by Doing Clustering 275
Outlining 275
Learning by Doing Moving from Outline to Thesis 279
Learning by Doing Responding to an Outline 281
Learning by Doing Outlining 283
Learning by Doing Reflecting on Planning 283

14. Strategies for Drafting 284

Making a Start Enjoyable 284
Restarting 285
Paragraphing 285
Using Topic Sentences 286
Learning by Doing Identifying Topic Sentences e
Learning by Doing Shaping Topic Sentences 289

Writing an Opening   290

Writing a Conclusion   292

  Learning by Doing Opening and Concluding   294

Adding Cues and Connections   295

  Learning by Doing Identifying Transitions   e

  Learning by Doing Identifying Transitions   299

  Learning by Doing Reflecting on Drafting   299

15. Strategies for Revising and Editing   300

Re-viewing and Revising   300

  Revising for Purpose and Thesis   301

  Revising for Audience   302

  Learning by Doing Editing Sentences   e

  Revising for Structure and Support   303

  Learning by Doing Tackling Macro Revision   304

  Working with a Peer Editor   304

  Questions for a Peer Editor   305

  Meeting with Your Instructor   306

  Decoding Your Instructor's Comments   306

Revising for Emphasis, Conciseness, and Clarity   308

  Stressing What Counts   308

  Cutting and Whittling   309

  Keeping It Clear   310

  Learning by Doing Tackling Micro Revision   311

Editing and Proofreading   313

  Editing   314

  Proofreading   315

  Learning by Doing Editing and Proofreading   316

  Learning by Doing Reflecting on Revising and Editing   317

Part Four A Writer's Research Manual   318

Introduction: Investigating Questions   321

16. Planning Your Research Project   322

Beginning Your Inquiry   324

The Assignment: Writing from Sources   324

  Learning by Doing Reflecting on Research   324

Asking a Research Question   324

  Exploring Your Territory   325

  Turning a Topic into a Question   326

  Learning by Doing Polling Your Peers   328

  Surveying Your Resources   329

  Learning by Doing Narrowing Online Research   e

  Using Keywords and Links   330

  Learning by Doing Proposing Your Project   330

Managing Your Project   330

  Recording Information   330

  Starting a Research Archive   331

  Learning by Doing Interviewing a Researcher   332

17. Working with Sources   333

Drawing the Details from Your Sources   334

  Starting a Working Bibliography   334

  Learning by Doing Teaming Up for Source "Warm-Ups"   335

  Learning by Doing Practicing with Online Sources   e

Capturing Information in Your Notes   335

  Source Navigator Article in a Print Magazine   336

  Source Navigator Article in a Scholarly Journal from a Database   338

  Source Navigator Book   340

  Source Navigator Page from a Web Site   342

  Quoting   345

  Sample Quotations, Paraphrase, and Summary (MLA Style)   346

  Paraphrasing   347

  Summarizing   347

  Mixing Methods   347

  Learning by Doing Capturing Information from Sources   348

Developing an Annotated Bibliography   349

  Learning by Doing Writing an Annotation   350

18. Finding Sources 351

Searching the Internet 352

Finding Recommended Internet
Resources 352

Selecting Search Engines 353

Learning by Doing Comparing Web
Searches 354

Learning by Doing Comparing Google and
Database Searches e

Conducting Advanced Electronic
Searches 354

Finding Specialized Online Materials 356

Searching the Library 356

Learning by Doing Reflecting on Your Library
Orientation Session 357

Learning by Doing Brainstorming for Search
Terms 360

Searching Library Databases 360

Learning by Doing Comparing Databases 365

Learning by Doing Comparing Google and
Database Searches 366

Using Specialized Library Resources 366

19. Evaluating Sources 368

Evaluating Library and Internet
Sources 368

Learning by Doing Evaluating Your
Sources 370

Learning by Doing Evaluating Online
Sources e

Who Is the Author? 372

Who Else Is Involved? 372

What Is the Purpose? 373

When Was the Source Published? 374

Where Did You Find the Source? 374

Why Would You Use This Source? 374

How Would This Source Contribute to Your
Paper? 374

Learning by Doing Adding Useful Sources 375

Reconsidering Purpose and Thesis 375

20. Integrating Sources 376

Using Sources Ethically 376

Capturing, Launching, and Citing
Evidence 379

Quoting and Paraphrasing Accurately 379

Learning by Doing Quoting and Paraphrasing
Accurately e

Summarizing Concisely 381

Avoiding Plagiarism 383

Launching Source Material 384

TAKE ACTION Integrating and Synthesizing
Sources 386

Learning by Doing Connecting Your
Sources 387

Citing Each Source Clearly 387

Synthesizing Ideas and Sources 387

Learning by Doing Launching and Citing Your
Sources 388

Learning by Doing Synthesizing Your
Sources 388

Appendices and Other Resources

Introduction: Turning to References 389

Quick Format Guide A-1

A. Following the Format for an Academic
Paper A-1

B. Integrating and Crediting Visuals A-8

C. Preparing a Document Template A-13

D. Solving Common Format Problems A-13

E. Designing Other Documents for Your
Audience A-14

F. Organizing a Résumé and an Application
Letter A-17

Quick Research Guide A-20

A. Defining Your Quest A-21

B. Searching for Recommended
Sources A-24

C. Evaluating Possible Sources A-26

D. Capturing, Launching, and Citing Evidence Added from Sources   A-28

E. Citing and Listing Sources in MLA or APA Style   A-32

Quick Editing Guide   A-39

A. Editing for Common Grammar Problems   A-40

B. Editing to Ensure Effective Sentences   A-49

TAKE ACTION Improving Sentence Style   A-50

TAKE ACTION Improving Sentence Clarity   A-51

C. Editing for Common Punctuation Problems   A-53

D. Editing for Common Mechanics Problems   A-56

A Sample MLA Research Paper   A-59

Candace Rardon, Meet Me in the Middle: The Student, the State, and the School   A-60

A Sample APA Research Paper   A-68

Jenny Lidington, Sex Offender Lists: A Never-Ending Punishment   A-69

About the Part Opening Photographs   A-81

Index   I-1

Correction Symbols

Proofreading Symbols

e A Writer's Reader

Introduction: Reading to Write

e-1 Families

PAIRED ESSAYS

■ **Amy Tan,** Mother Tongue *[Text]* e
A Chinese American writer examines the effects of her mother's imperfect English on her own experience as a daughter and a writer.

■ **Richard Rodriguez,** Public and Private Language *[Text]* e
The author, the son of Spanish-speaking Mexican American parents, recounts the origin of his complex views of bilingual education.

■ **StrategyOne Editors,** Once a Mother, Always a Mother *[Infographic]* e
According to a recent survey, today's grandmothers are often key figures in the raising and nurturing of their grandchildren.

■ **GOOD/Column Five Editors,** Paternity Leave around the World *[Infographic]* e
Parental leave policies in the U.S., which make it difficult for new fathers to take time off work, are compared with policies in other countries.

e-2 Men and Women

PAIRED ESSAYS

■ **Robert Jensen,** The High Cost of Manliness *[Text]* e
The author calls for abandoning the prevailing definition of masculinity, arguing that it is "toxic" to both men and women.

■ **Julie Zeilinger,** Guys Suffer from Oppressive Gender Roles Too *[Text]* e
Men may pay too high a price in hiding emotions and shoehorning themselves into society's tough, narrow, masculine stereotypes.

■ **Deborah Tannen,** Who Does the Talking Here? *[Text]* e
Studies show that men talk more at work and in public, while women talk more at home, using talk as "the glue that holds a relationship together."

■ **Jed Conklin,** Boxing Beauties *[Visual Essay]* e
Taken at the Olympic Team Trials in London 2012, this series of photographic portraits honors members of the U.S. women's boxing team.

e-3 Popular Culture

┌ PAIRED ESSAYS

■ **Stephen King,** Why We Crave Horror Movies *[Text]* e

The author examines the appeal of scary movies, watched to reaffirm normalcy and to acknowledge and quell the suppressed, uncivilized "worst in us."

■ **Gerard Jones,** Violent Media Is Good for Kids *[Text]* e

Violent stories and characters can have an empowering effect, helping some people pull themselves out of "emotional traps," └ the author argues.

■ **Chuck Klosterman,** My Zombie, Myself: Why Modern Life Feels Rather Undead *[Text]* e

The current zombie craze could symbolize our fear that we will be consumed by the Internet and by e-mails and texts that just keep coming at us.

■ **Brad Shoup,** "Harlem Shake" vs. History: Is the YouTube Novelty Hits Era That Novel? *[Multimodal Essay]* e

To the dismay of music purists, *Billboard* now factors YouTube streams into its Hot 100 list, but the list has always contained plenty of goofy songs.

e-4 Digital Living

┌ PAIRED ESSAYS

■ **Elizabeth Stone,** Grief in the Age of Facebook *[Text]* e

Reactions to the tragic death of a talented young woman lead the author to consider the emerging practices of online mourning.

■ **Libby Copeland,** Is Facebook Making Us Sad? *[Text]* e

Facebook can lead to depression and "presentation anxiety," if we compare ourselves unfavorably with friends who └ appear to have perfect, fun-filled lives.

■ **Sherry Turkle,** How Computers Change the Way We Think *[Text]* e

A psychologist explores the effect of online chat, PowerPoint slides, word processors, and simulation games on our "habits of mind."

■ **Off Book Editors,** Generative Art – Computers, Data, and Humanity *[Video]* e

Three innovative creators discuss how they allow computers to make some key decisions about their creations.

e-5 Explorations on Living Well

┌ PAIRED ESSAYS

■ **Juliet Schor,** The Creation of Discontent *[Text]* e

The author questions whether luxury and consumerism lead to happiness, as promised, or whether the opposite is true.

■ **Llewellyn H. Rockwell Jr.,** In Defense of Consumerism *[Text]* e

The author sees consumerism as beneficial └ and argues that it has many positive effects.

■ **Sarah Adams,** Be Cool to the Pizza Dude *[Audio and Text]* e

The author uses one simple rule to illuminate the principles she follows in everyday life.

■ **Brent Foster,** Highway Angel *[Video]* e

The author profiles Thomas Weller, a man who rides his "search and rescue" car along San Diego's highways, helping stranded motorists for free.

RHETORICAL CONTENTS

*(Essays listed in order of appearance; * indicates student essays)*

Analyzing a Subject

* Olof Eriksson • The Problems with Masculinity 24
* Alley Julseth • Analyzing "The New Literacy" 30
Michael Shermer • The Science of Righteousness 32
* Richard Anson • Young Americans and Media News 46
David Brooks • The Opportunity Gap 101
* Marjorie Lee Garretson • More Pros Than Cons in a Meat-Free Life 124
Jake Halpern • The Popular Crowd 168
* Abigail Marchand • The Family Dynamic 171
Celebrity Culture *[Text, Audio, and Video]* 🄴 and 173
StrategyOne • Once a Mother, Always a Mother *[Infographic]* 🄴
Robert Jensen • The High Cost of Manliness *[Text]* 🄴
Julie Zeilinger • Guys Suffer from Oppressive Gender Roles Too *[Text]* 🄴
Deborah Tannen • Who Does the Talking Here? *[Text]* 🄴
Stephen King • Why We Crave Horror Movies *[Text]* 🄴
Gerard Jones • Violent Media Is Good for Kids *[Text]* 🄴
Chuck Klosterman • My Zombie, Myself *[Text]* 🄴
Brad Shoup • "Harlem Shake" vs. History *[Text]* 🄴
Elizabeth Stone • Grief in the Age of Facebook *[Text]* 🄴
Libby Copeland • Is Facebook Making Us Sad? *[Text]* 🄴

Analyzing Processes

Richard Rodriguez • Public and Private Language *[Text]* 🄴
Elizabeth Stone • Grief in the Age of Facebook *[Text]* 🄴
Sherry Turkle • How Computers Change the Way We Think *[Text]* 🄴

Juliet Schor • The Creation of Discontent *[Text]* 🄴
Llewellyn H. Rockwell Jr. • In Defense of Consumerism *[Text]* 🄴

Analyzing Visuals

Observing the *Titanic:* Past and Present *[Visual Essay]* 🄴 and 87
National Geographic • Hurricane Katrina Pictures *[Visual Essay]* 🄴 and 107
Scott Tobias • The Hunger Games 150
*Rachel Steinhaus • "Life, Liberty, and the Pursuit" 216
* Shannon Kintner • Charlie Living with Autism 🄴 and 222
Jed Conklin • Boxing Beauties *[Visual Essay]* 🄴
Stephen King • Why We Crave Horror Movies *[Text]* 🄴
Gerard Jones • Violent Media Is Good for Kids *[Text]* 🄴
Brad Shoup • "Harlem Shake" vs. History *[Text]* 🄴
Off Book • Generative Art *[Video]* 🄴

Arguing

David Rothkopf • A Proposal to Draft America's Elderly 53
David Brooks • The Opportunity Gap 101
National Geographic • Hurricane Katrina Pictures *[Visual Essay]* 🄴 and 107
Suzan Shown Harjo • Last Rites for Indian Dead 121
* Marjorie Lee Garretson • More Pros Than Cons in a Meat-Free Life 124
UNICEF • Dirty Water Campaign *[Video]* 🄴 and 127
*Elizabeth Erion • Internship Program Falls Short 153
Jake Halpern • The Popular Crowd 168
* Abigail Marchand • The Family Dynamic 171
Celebrity Culture *[Text, Audio, and Video]* 🄴 and 173

🄴 For readings that go beyond the printed page, see **bedfordstmartins.com/concisebedguide**

* Rachel Steinhaus • "Life, Liberty, and the Pursuit" 216

Julie Zeilinger • Guys Suffer from Oppressive Gender Roles Too *[Text]* e

Chuck Klosterman • My Zombie, Myself *[Text]* e

Sherry Turkle • How Computers Change the Way We Think *[Text]* e

Juliet Schor • The Creation of Discontent *[Text]* e

Llewellyn H. Rockwell Jr. • In Defense of Consumerism *[Text]* e

Sarah Adams • Be Cool to the Pizza Dude *[Audio and Text]* e

Comparing and Contrasting

Michael Shermer • The Science of Righteousness 32

Observing the *Titanic:* Past and Present *[Visual Essay]* e and 87

David Brooks • The Opportunity Gap 101

* Jacob Griffin • Karate Kid vs. Kung Fu Panda: A Race to the Olympics 104

National Geographic • Hurricane Katrina Pictures *[Visual Essay]* e and 107

Scott Tobias • The Hunger Games 150

Richard Rodriguez • Public and Private Language *[Text]* e

Good/Column Five • Paternity Leave around the World *[Infographic]* e

Julie Zeilinger • Guys Suffer from Oppressive Gender Roles Too *[Text]* e

Deborah Tannen • Who Does the Talking Here? *[Text]* e

Chuck Klosterman • My Zombie, Myself *[Text]* e

Brad Shoup • "Harlem Shake" vs. History *[Text]* e

Defining

* Olof Eriksson • "The Problems with Masculinity" 24

Michael Shermer • The Science of Righteousness 32

* Robert G. Schreiner • What Is a Hunter? 65

Richard Rodriguez • Public and Private Language *[Text]* e

Robert Jensen • The High Cost of Manliness *[Text]* e

Chuck Klosterman • My Zombie, Myself *[Text]* e

Brad Shoup • "Harlem Shake" vs. History *[Text]* e

Describing

Russell Baker • The Art of Eating Spaghetti 62

* Robert G. Schreiner • What Is a Hunter? 65

Howie Chackowicz • The Game Ain't Over 'til the Fatso Man Sings *[Audio]* e and 68

Eric Liu • The Chinatown Idea 82

* Alea Eyre • Stockholm 85

*Jacob Griffin • Karate Kid vs. Kung Fu Panda: A Race to the Olympics 104

Brent Foster • Highway Angel *[Video]* e

Dividing and Classifying

Michael Shermer • The Science of Righteousness 32

Richard Rodriguez • Public and Private Language *[Text]* e

Robert Jensen • The High Cost of Manliness *[Text]* e

Evaluating and Reviewing

* Alley Julseth • Analyzing "The New Literacy" 30

Michael Shermer • The Science of Righteousness 32

* Richard Anson • Young Americans and Media News 46

Scott Tobias • The Hunger Games 150

*Elizabeth Erion • Internship Program Falls Short 153

Consumer Reports • Best Buttermilk Pancakes *[Video]* e and 155

Robert Jensen • The High Cost of Manliness *[Text]* e

Stephen King • Why We Crave Horror Movies *[Text]* e

Gerard Jones • Violent Media Is Good for Kids *[Text]* e

Sherry Turkle • How Computers Change the Way We Think *[Text]* e

Explaining Causes and Effects

Michael Shermer • The Science of Righteousness 32

David Brooks • The Opportunity Gap 101

Jake Halpern • The Popular Crowd 168

Celebrity Culture *[Text, Audio, and Video]* e and 173

Amy Tan • Mother Tongue *[Text]* e

Stephen King • Why We Crave Horror Movies *[Text]* e

Gerard Jones • Violent Media Is Good for Kids
[Text] e

Libby Copeland • Is Facebook Making Us Sad?
[Text] e

Sherry Turkle • How Computers Change the Way
We Think [Text] e

Juliet Schor • The Creation of Discontent [Text] e

Llewellyn H. Rockwell Jr. • In Defense of Consumerism [Text] e

Giving Examples

David Rothkopf • A Proposal to Draft America's
Elderly   53

Howie Chackowicz • The Game Ain't Over 'til the
Fatso Man Sings [Audio] e and 68

* Marjorie Lee Garretson • More Pros Than Cons
in a Meat-Free Life   124

*Elizabeth Erion • Internship Program Falls
Short   153

Consumer Reports • Best Buttermilk Pancakes
[Video] e and 155

Robert Jensen • The High Cost of Manliness
[Text] e

Deborah Tannen • Who Does the Talking Here?
[Text] e

Brad Shoup • "Harlem Shake" vs. History
[Text] e

Elizabeth Stone • Grief in the Age of Facebook
[Text] e

Juliet Schor • The Creation of Discontent
[Text] e

Llewellyn H. Rockwell Jr. • In Defense of Consumerism [Text] e

Sarah Adams • Be Cool to the Pizza Dude [Audio
and Text] e

Interviewing a Subject

Amy Tan • Mother Tongue [Text] e

Elizabeth Stone • Grief in the Age of Facebook
[Text] e

Brent Foster • Highway Angel [Video] e

Observing a Scene

Eric Liu • The Chinatown Idea   82

*Alea Eyre • Stockholm   85

Observing the Titanic: Past and Present [Visual
Essay] e and 87

* Shannon Kintner • Charlie Living with Autism
[Student Visual Essay] e and 222

Recalling an Experience

Russell Baker • The Art of Eating Spaghetti   62

* Robert G. Schreiner • What Is a Hunter?   65

Howie Chackowicz • The Game Ain't Over 'til the
Fatso Man Sings [Audio] e and 68

Eric Liu • The Chinatown Idea   82

* Alea Eyre • Stockholm   85

Amy Tan • Mother Tongue [Text] e

Richard Rodriguez • Public and Private Language
[Text] e

Elizabeth Stone • Grief in the Age of Facebook
[Text] e

Supporting a Position with Sources

David Brooks • The Opportunity Gap   101

Suzan Shown Harjo • Last Rites for Indian
Dead   121

Jake Halpern • The Popular Crowd   168

* Abigail Marchand • The Family Dynamic   171

Celebrity Culture [Text, Audio, and Video] e and 173

StrategyOne • Once a Mother, Always a Mother
[Infographic] e

Good/Column Five • Paternity Leave around the
World [Infographic] e

Deborah Tannen • Who Does the Talking Here?
[Text] e

Brad Shoup • "Harlem Shake" vs. History [Text] e

Sherry Turkle • How Computers Change the Way
We Think [Text] e

Taking a Stand

David Rothkopf • A Proposal to Draft America's
Elderly   53

David Brooks • The Opportunity Gap   101

Suzan Shown Harjo • Last Rites for Indian
Dead   121

* Marjorie Lee Garretson • More Pros Than Cons
in a Meat-Free Life   124

UNICEF • Dirty Water Campaign [Video] e and
127

*Elizabeth Erion • Internship Program Falls
Short   153

Julie Zeilinger • Guys Suffer from Oppressive
Gender Roles Too [Text] e

Juliet Schor • The Creation of Discontent [Text] e

Llewellyn H. Rockwell Jr. • In Defense of Consumerism [Text] e

Sarah Adams • Be Cool to the Pizza Dude [Audio
and Text] e

SELECTED VISUAL CONTENTS

For names of photographers, artists, and illustrators, see pages A-78–A-79.

Advertisements and Public Service Announcements

UNICEF Tap Project on the need for clean water, 127
No Swearing sign, 198
Shark Warning sign, 198
Figure 10.1 PSA, Act Against Violence, 207
Figure 10.6 Volkswagen advertisement, 207
Figure 10.7 Chevrolet advertisement, 208
Figure 10.12 PSA of bear, Americans for National Parks, 213
Figure 10.13 PSA with wordplay, "toLEARNce," 214
Figure 10.14 Anti-smoking billboard, 214
Figure 10.15 Anti-drunk-driving poster, 215

Document Design

Figure 10.8 "Stairway" type design, 209
Figure 10.9 Type as cultural cliché, 210
Formal outline, 83, 280
MLA first page, A-2
MLA Works Cited, A-3
APA title page, A-4
APA Abstract, A-4
APA first page, A-5
APA References, A-6
MLA and APA table formats, A-9–A-10
Typefaces, A-14
List formats, A-15
Heading levels, A-16

Journal Questions and Visual Assignments

Series of four aerial photographs, 4–5, 56–57, 244–45, 318–19. See journal questions about these photographs on the last two pages of the appendices.
Group of women sharing dinner, 77
Hikers in silhouette, 78
Times Square crowd, 78
Concert, 79
Airport, 79
* Baseball player making catch, 80
Observing the Titanic [*e-Pages visual essay*], e and 85–86
View from bicycle, 97

Server at party, 98
Climbers on Mt. Rushmore, 98
* Couple at Woodstock, 99
Hurricane Katrina Pictures: Then & Now, Ruin & Rebirth [*e-Pages visual essay*], e and 107
Photographs from *What the World Eats*, by Peter Menzel, 117–118
* Protest against education cutbacks, 119
Patient overlooking fundraising walk, 146
Family reading, 146
Cell phone tower disguised as tree, 147
* Judging giant pumpkins, 148
Church at Auvers-sur-Oise (photo), 164
The Church at Auvers-sur-Oise by Vincent van Gogh, 164
Office with cubicles, 165
Office with open plan, 165
Contestant in child beauty pageant, 197
No Swearing sign, 198
Shark Warning sign, 198
Gamblers in Las Vegas, 199
Charlie Living with Autism [*e-Pages visual essay*], e and 222–24
Once a Mother, Always a Mother [*e-Pages infographic*], e
Paternity Leave around the World [*e-Pages infographic*], e
Boxing Beauties [*e-Pages visual essay*], e

Other Images

Aerial photo of fountain and bathers, 2–3
Aerial photo of rowboats tied to dock, 56–57
Lady Macbeth, 63
Soccer player, 71
* Baseball player making catch, 80
Market in New York City's Chinatown, 84
Emergency room, 89
Elvis impersonators, 91
View from bicycle, 97
Server at party, 98
Climbers on Mt. Rushmore, 98
Couple at Woodstock, 99
Protest against education cutbacks, 119
Funeral procession for reburial of Native American remains, 122

Joan of Arc, 128
Patient overlooking fundraising walk, 146
Family reading, 146
Cell phone tower disguised as tree, 147
Judging giant pumpkins, 148
Map of Panem (V. Arrow), 151
Red carpet at Academy Awards, 174
Contestant in child beauty pageant, 197
Figure 10.2 Batman at a donut shop, 203
Figure 10.10 Future Open sign, 210
Figure 10.11 Amusement park ride at sunset, 212
Figure 19.1: Screenshots from the American Society
   for the Prevention of Cruelty to Animals (ASPCA)
   Web site, 371

Pairs, Series, and Collages

Series of four aerial photographs, 4–5, 56–57, 244–
   45, 318–19
Recalled experiences, 58
Observing the Titanic *[e-Pages visual essay]*, e and 85–86
Couple at Woodstock, 1969 and 2009, 116
Karate and Kung fu, 122
*Hurricane Katrina Pictures: Then & Now, Ruin & Rebirth
   [e-Pages visual essay]*, e and 124
Photographs from *What the World Eats*, by Peter Men-
   zel, 134–35
Church at Auvers-sur-Oise; *The Church at Auvers-sur-
   Oise* by Vincent van Gogh, 164

Office with cubicles; office with open plan, 164
Students consulting sources, 166
Charlie Living with Autism [e-Pages visual essay], e and
   222–24
Boxing Beauties [e-Pages visual essay], e

Representations of Data and Processes

Heat maps of Web pages from eye-tracking studies,
   34
Line graph, Annual rise in cost of attending college,
   A-62
Table samples, A-9–A-10
Figure A.1 Diagram of wastewater treatment, A-11
Figure A.2 Comparative line graph on food allergies,
   A-11
Figure A.3 Bar graph on binge drinking, A-12
Figure A.4 Pie chart on household energy use, A-12

Videos

Dirty Water Campaign, e and 127
Best Buttermilk Pancakes, e and 155
Celebrity Relationships: Why Do We Care?, e and
   173
Sample E-mail to an Instructor, e and 233
Generative Art – Computers, Data, and
   Humanity, e
Highway Angel, e

---

* Indicates an accompanying "Responding to an Image" activity

FEATURES OF *THE CONCISE BEDFORD GUIDE* AND ANCILLARIES

Correlated to the Writing Program Administrators (WPA) Outcomes Statement

WPA Goals and Learning Outcomes	Support in *The Concise Bedford Guide*
Rhetorical Knowledge: Student Outcomes	
Focus on a purpose	■ Purpose and Audience (pp. 11–15) ■ Chs. 4–10, including thesis development and revision ■ Ch. 13: Strategies for Stating a Thesis and Planning (pp. 262–63) ■ Ch. 15: Strategies for Revising and Editing with revision for purpose, thesis, and audience (pp. 301–2) ■ Re:Writing: Visualizing Purpose tutorial ■ *VideoCentral**: videos on rhetorical purpose *For instructors* The following ancillary contains helpful tips, strategies, and resources for teaching purpose, as well as for the other topics considered throughout this chart. ■ *Practical Suggestions for Teaching with The Concise Bedford Guide for Writers*
Respond to the needs of different audiences	■ Writing for Your Audience and Targeting a College Audience (pp. 12–16) ■ Using Evidence to Appeal to Your Audience (pp. 44–45) ■ Chs. 4–9, with situational consideration of audience and Peer Response questions ■ Attention to writing for specific audiences such as Messages to Your Instructor (pp. 231–34), Online Threaded Discussions (pp. 235–38), and research (p. 324) ■ Shaping Your Topic for Your Purpose and Audience (pp. 262–63) ■ Revising for Audience (pp. 302–3), Working with a Peer Editor (pp. 304–6), and Meeting with Your Instructor (p. 306) ■ Re:Writing: Visualizing Audience tutorial
Respond appropriately to different kinds of rhetorical situations	■ Part Two: A Writer's Situations (pp. 56–243) with detailed advice on responding to varied rhetorical situations from recalling an experience to supporting a position with sources ■ Chs. 4–11 with opening "Why Writing Matters" and Chs. 16–20 with "Why Research Matters" feature illustrating college, workplace, and community situations (e.g., pp. 61 and 167) ■ Re:Writing: Visualizing Context tutorial ■ e-Pages: Learning by Doing activities for Part Two

This resource is available packaged with the print book. See the preface for details.

WPA Goals and Learning Outcomes	Support in *The Concise Bedford Guide*
Rhetorical Knowledge: Student Outcomes	
Use conventions of format and structure appropriate to the rhetorical situation	■ Examples of effective structure in Part Two (see sample annotations, pp. 121–24) ■ Ch. 11 on file management and templates (pp. 238–41) ■ Quick Format Guide ■ Quick Research Guide ■ Re:Writing: Sample student writing
Adopt appropriate voice, tone, and level of formality	■ Purpose and audience coverage (pp. 11–15 and throughout) ■ Facing the Challenge: Finding Your Voice (pp. 175–76) and Join the Academic Exchange (pp. 180 and 182–86)
Understand how genres shape reading and writing	■ Part Two: A Writer's Situations (pp. 56–243) with professional and student essays, guided writing advice, and opening and closing images for analysis for a variety of rhetorical situations ■ Why Writing Matters sections opening Chs. 4–11 and Chs. 16–20 with applications in college, at work, in the community (e.g., p. 167). ■ *A Writer's Reader* with 20 readings in five thematic groups ■ *A Writer's Research Manual* (pp. 318–88) and Quick Research Guide (pp. A-20–A-38) ■ Re:Writing: Sample student writing
Write in several genres	■ Rhetorical strategies for varied situations in Part Two, including student and professional examples, Why Writing Matters, Facing the Challenge, and Discovery, Revision, and Editing checklists ■ *A Writer's Research Manual* (pp. 318–88) and Quick Research Guide (pp. A-20–A-38)
Use writing and reading for inquiry, learning, thinking, and communicating	■ Part One: writing, reading, and critical thinking processes ■ Parts Two, Three, and Four emphasizing the connection between reading and writing ■ *A Writer's Reader* with 20 readings grouped thematically ■ Critical reading apparatus in Part Two: A Writer's Situations (e.g., pp. 62, 65) and in *A Writer's Reader* (e-Pages) ■ Re:Writing: Reading Critically video *For instructors:* ■ *Practical Suggestions for Teaching with The Concise Bedford Guide for Writers*, Ch. 3, Teaching Critical Thinking and Writing ■ *Teaching Composition: Background Readings:* Ch. 1, Teaching Writing: Key Concepts, Philosophies, Frameworks, and Experiences

* This resource is available packaged with the print book. See the preface for details.

WPA Goals and Learning Outcomes	Support in *The Concise Bedford Guide*
Critical Thinking, Reading, and Writing: Student Outcomes	
Understand a writing assignment as a series of tasks, including finding, evaluating, analyzing, and synthesizing appropriate primary and secondary sources	▪ Chs. 4–10 breaking writing assignments into guided tasks ▪ Ch. 9: Supporting a Position with Sources ▪ Ch. 16: Planning Your Research Project ▪ Ch. 17: Working with Sources, including capturing information and developing an annotated bibliography ▪ Chs. 18–20 on finding, evaluating, integrating, and synthesizing sources (pp. 351–88) ▪ Quick Research Guide ▪ e-Pages: Additional Learning by Doing activity on finding and evaluating credible sources ▪ *VideoCentral**: Videos on integrating sources ▪ Visual and Source Activity options in Part 1; Visual and Source Assignment options in Parts 2 and 3.
Integrate students' own ideas with those of others	▪ *A Writer's Reader* with journal prompts, writing suggestions, and paired essays ▪ Ch. 9: Supporting a Position with Sources (pp. 166–99) ▪ Chs. 18–20 on finding, evaluating, integrating and synthesizing sources (pp. 351–88) ▪ Quick Research Guide ▪ Re:Writing: Research and documentation advice and models
Understand the relationships among language, knowledge, and power	▪ Purpose and Audience (pp. 11–15) and audience analysis throughout ▪ Selections in *A Writer's Reader* on language and literacy by Tan, Rodriguez, Tannen, and others ▪ Re:Writing: Why Writing Matters video *For instructors:* ▪ *Teaching Composition: Background Readings:* Ch. 4, Issues in Writing Pedagogy: Institutional Politics and the Other
Be aware that it usually takes multiple drafts to create and complete a successful text	▪ Ch. 1: Writing Processes (pp. 6–16) with process overview ▪ Chs. 4–10 with situation-specific process guidance ▪ Part Three writing processes in detail ▪ *Portfolio Keeping,* Third Edition,* discussing portfolio keeping as a reflection of writing processes *For instructors:* ▪ *Teaching Composition: Background Readings:* Ch. 2, Thinking about the Writing Process

WPA Goals and Learning Outcomes	Support in *The Concise Bedford Guide*
Processes: Student Outcomes	
Develop flexible strategies for generating ideas, revising, editing, and proofreading	▪ Ch. 1: A Writer's Processes with an overview of generating ideas, planning, drafting, developing, revising, editing, and proofreading (pp. 6–16) ▪ Part Two with situation-specific process strategies ▪ Part Three: A Writer's Strategies with detailed coverage of writing processes (pp. 244–317) ▪ Re:Writing: Getting Started video *For instructors:* ▪ *Teaching Composition: Background Readings:* Revising a Draft (pp. 195–246); Ch. 3, Responding to and Evaluating Student Writing
Understand writing as an open process that permits writers to use later invention and rethinking to revise their work	▪ Ch. 13: Strategies for Revising and Editing ▪ Revision coverage with examples in every Part Two chapter ▪ Recurring presentation of a flexible and recursive process of writing (pp. 7–11) ▪ Re:Writing: Revising video ▪ *Portfolio Keeping,* Third Edition*, discussing portfolio keeping as a reflection of writing processes *For instructors:* ▪ *Teaching Composition: Background Readings:* Ch. 2, Thinking about the Writing Process
Understand the collaborative and social aspects of writing processes	▪ Learning by Doing features including collaborative activities (e.g., pp. 136, 138, 159) and Peer Response guidelines (Part Two and pp. 304–6) ▪ Part Two: Additional Writing Assignments with collaborative options (e.g., pp. 116–17) ▪ *Portfolio Keeping,* Third Edition*, Ch. 5, Keeping Company and Working with Others, addressing community and peer response *For instructors:* ▪ *Practical Suggestions for Teaching with The Concise Bedford Guide for Writers,* Ch. 2, Creating a Writing Community
Learn to critique their own and others' works	▪ Ch. 15: Strategies for Revising and Editing with peer-editing advice (pp. 304–6) ▪ Peer Response sections for each chapter in Part Two ▪ Self-assessment Take Action charts (e.g., p. 142) ▪ *Portfolio Keeping,* Third Edition*, Ch. 5, Keeping Company and Working with Others, addressing community and peer response *For instructors:* ▪ *Practical Suggestions for Teaching with The Concise Bedford Guide for Writers,* Ch. 2, Creating a Writing Community

* This resource is available packaged with the print book. See the preface for details.

WPA Goals and Learning Outcomes	Support in *The Concise Bedford Guide*
Processes: Student Outcomes	
Learn to balance the advantages of relying on others with the responsibility of doing their part	■ Face-to-face and online individual, paired, small-group, and whole-class "Learning by Doing" activities throughout ■ Ethical explorations in Ch. 3: Critical Thinking Processes, Ch. 9: Supporting a Position with Sources, Ch. 11: Writing Online, Ch. 20: Integrating Sources, and the Quick Research Guide ■ *Portfolio Keeping,* Third Edition*, Ch. 5, Keeping Company and Working with Others, addressing community and peer response *For instructors:* ■ *Practical Suggestions for Teaching with The Concise Bedford Guide for Writers,* Ch. 2, Creating a Writing Community
Use a variety of technologies to address a range of audiences	■ Visual Activities in Part 1, which also includes Reading Online and Multimodal Texts in Ch. 2 ■ Visual Assignment options in Part 2 (Chs. 4–11) ■ Ch. 10: Responding to Visual Representations ■ Ch. 11: Writing Online ■ *A Writer's Research Manual* with online strategies throughout (pp. 318–88) ■ Quick Research Guide, including Searching for Recommended Sources (pp. A-24–A-26) ■ Quick Format Guide, including a section on integrating and crediting visuals (pp. A-8–A-12) ■ *ix visualizing composition**: Interactive assignments and guided analysis offer practice with multimedia texts ■ e-Pages: Multimodal readings that integrate audio, video, visuals, and text *For instructors:* ■ *Practical Suggestions for Teaching with The Concise Bedford Guide for Writers,* Ch. 11, Writing Online ■ *Teaching Composition: Background Readings:* Teaching Writing with Computers (pp. 305–37); Teaching Visual Literacy (pp. 337–76)
Learn common formats for different kinds of texts	■ Advice on various types of assignments in Part Two and Part Three ■ Quick Format Guide with MLA and APA paper and table formats, sample tables and figures, a résumé, and an application letter ■ *ix visualizing composition**: Interactive assignments and guided analysis for practice with multimedia texts *For instructors:* ■ *Teaching Composition: Background Readings:* Teaching Visual Literacy (pp. 337–76)

WPA Goals and Learning Outcomes	Support in *The Concise Bedford Guide*
Knowledge of Conventions	
Develop knowledge of genre conventions ranging from structure and paragraphing to tone and mechanics	■ Part Two: A Writer's Situations ■ Part Three: A Writer's Strategies, including chapters on planning, drafting, and revising and editing ■ Re:Writing: Why Proofreading Matters video
Practice appropriate means of documenting their work	■ Options for source-based activities (Chs. 1–3) and assignments (Chs. 4–11) concluding each chapter ■ Ch. 9: Supporting a Position with Sources (pp. 166–99), including The Academic Exchange (pp. 182–83) ■ Take Action self-assessment and revision charts on Integrating Source Information Effectively (p. 194), Integrating and Synthesizing Sources (p. 386) ■ Chs. 17–20 on working with, finding, evaluating, integrating, and synthesizing sources, including annotated bibliographies (pp. 349–50) ■ Source Navigators (pp. 336–43) ■ Quick Research Guide (pp. A-20–A-38) ■ Sample student papers in MLA and APA styles (pp. A-59–A-76) ■ Re:Writing: *The Bedford Bibliographer* for help in collecting sources and creating bibliography; exercises on MLA and APA style
Control such surface features as syntax, grammar, punctuation, and spelling	■ Quick Editing Guide with Editing Checklist (pp. A-39–A-40) and two Take Action charts (pp. A-50–A-51) ■ Part Two revising and editing advice, including cross-references to relevant topics in the Quick Editing Guide ■ Ch. 15: Strategies for Revising and Editing ■ Re:Writing: Take Action charts ■ LearningCurve exercises on grammar and usage *For instructors:* ■ *Practical Suggestions for Teaching with The Concise Bedford Guide for Writers,* Ch. 4, Providing Support for Underprepared Students

* This resource is available packaged with the print book. See the preface for details.

WPA Goals and Learning Outcomes	Support in *The Concise Bedford Guide*
Composing in Electronic Environments	
Use electronic environments for drafting, reviewing, revising, editing, and sharing texts	■ Ch. 11: Writing Online, including course or learning management systems ■ Additional Writing Assignments in Parts Two and Three with online options ■ Ch. 15: Strategies for Revising and Editing ■ Learning by Doing activities with many online options ■ *Portfolio Keeping*, Third Edition*, discussion of electronic presentation of portfolios ■ e-Pages: Learning by Doing: Becoming Familiar with Your Course Management System ■ e-Pages: Questions with each essay that students can answer online *For instructors:* ■ *Practical Suggestions for Teaching with The Concise Bedford Guide for Writers:* Chs. 5 and 6, Teaching Writing Online and Assessing Student Writing ■ *Teaching Composition: Background Readings:* Teaching Writing with Computers (pp. 305–37)
Locate, evaluate, organize, and use research material collected from electronic sources	■ Reading Online and Multimodal Texts, pp. 33–35 ■ Ch. 9: Supporting a Position with Sources including e-Pages Research Cluster ■ Chs. 17–20 on working with, finding, evaluating, and integrating sources, including annotated bibliographies (pp. 349–50) ■ Quick Research Guide ■ Re:Writing: *The Bedford Bibliographer* for help in collecting sources and creating bibliography; research checklists *For instructors:* ■ *Practical Suggestions for Teaching with The Concise Bedford Guide for Writers:* Chs. 5 and 6, Teaching Writing Online, and Assessing Student Writing ■ *Teaching Composition: Background Readings:* Teaching Writing with Computers (pp. 305–37)
Understand and exploit the differences in the rhetorical strategies and in the affordances available for both print and electronic composing processes and texts	■ Ch. 11: Writing Online ■ Part Three: A Writer's Strategies ■ Reading Online and Multimodal Texts, pp. 33–35 ■ *A Writer's Reader,* Ch. e-4: Digital Living, including four provocative selections ■ Re:Writing: tutorial on Web design ■ e-Pages: Multimodal readings that integrate audio, video, text, and visuals *For instructors:* ■ *Practical Suggestions for Teaching with The Concise Bedford Guide for Writers,* Teaching Writing Online ■ *Teaching Composition: Background Readings:* Teaching Writing with Computers (pp. 305–37)

How to Use *The Concise Bedford Guide for Writers*

Just as you may be unsure of what to expect from your writing course, you may be unsure of what to expect from your writing textbook. You may even be wondering how any textbook can improve your writing. In fact, a book alone can't make you a better writer, but practice can, and *The Concise Bedford Guide for Writers* is designed to make your writing practice effective and productive. This text offers help — easy to find and easy to use — for writing essays most commonly assigned in college.

Underlying *The Concise Bedford Guide* is the idea that writing is a necessary and useful skill beyond the writing course. The skills you will learn throughout this book are transferable to other areas of your life — future courses, jobs, and community activities — making *The Concise Bedford Guide* both a time-saver and a money-saver. The following sections describe how you can get the most out of this text.

Finding Information in *The Concise Bedford Guide*

In *The Concise Bedford Guide,* it is easy to find what you need when you need it. Each of the tools described here directs you to useful information — fast.

Brief List of Contents. Open the book to the inside front cover. At a glance you can see a list of the topics in *The Concise Bedford Guide.* If you are looking for a specific chapter, this brief list of contents is the quickest way to find it.

List of e-Pages Contents. Facing the inside front cover you will find a list of readings and writing activities available online at **bedfordstmartins .com/concisebedguide**. Included exclusively in the e-Pages is the book's thematic reader, which features twenty carefully selected essays. Many selections both in the reader portion of the e-Pages and elsewhere are multimodal and include videos, audio segments, infographics, and visual essays. The e-Pages also feature online assignments, such as interactive versions of the "Learning by Doing" activities and critical reading and thinking questions about the e-Pages readings. The e-Pages extend this book into the online environment, giving you a rich array of integrated multimodal content.

Contents

Preface: To the Instructor   vii

Rhetorical Contents   xxviii

Selected Visual Contents   xxxi

Features of *The Concise Bedford Guide*
Correlated to WPA Outcomes   xxxiii

How to Use *The Concise Bedford Guide
for Writers*   xl

**Part One   A College Writer's
Processes** 2

Introduction: Meeting College Expectations   5

1. Writing Processes 6

Writing, Reading, and Critical Thinking   6

A Process of Writing   7

  Getting Started   7

  Generating Ideas   7

  Learning by Doing Reflecting on Ideas   8

  Planning, Drafting, and Developing   8

  Learning by Doing Reflecting on Drafts   10

  Revising and Editing   10

  Learning by Doing Reflecting on Finishing   11

Purpose and Audience   11

  Writing for a Reason   11

  Learning by Doing Considering Purpose   12

  Writing for Your Audience   12

  Learning by Doing Analyzing Audience   ℮

  Learning by Doing Considering Audience   14

  Targeting a College Audience   15

  Learning by Doing Considering a College
  Audience   15

Additional Writing Activities   16

2. Reading Processes 17

A Process of Critical Reading   17

  Learning by Doing Describing Your Reading
  Strategies   18

  Getting Started   18

  Preparing to Read   19

  Learning by Doing Preparing to Read   20

  Responding to Reading   20

  Learning by Doing Annotating a Passage   22

  Learning by Doing Responding in a Reading
  Journal   23

Learning from Another Writer: Reading
Summary and Response   24

  ■ **Student Summary and Response: Olof Eriksson,** The Problems with Masculinity   24

Reading on Literal and Analytical Levels   25

  Learning by Doing Reading Analytically   27

  Generating Ideas from Reading   27

Learning from Another Writer: Critical
Reading and Response   29

  ■ **Student Critical Reading Response: Alley
  Julseth,** Analyzing "The New Literacy"   30

  Learning by Doing Reading Critically   31

  ■ **Michael Shermer,** The Science of
  Righteousness   32

Reading Online and Multimodal Texts   33

  Learning by Doing Reading Online   ℮

  Learning by Doing Reading a Web Site   35

Additional Writing Activities   35

3. Critical Thinking Processes 37

A Process of Critical Thinking   37

  Getting Started   38

  Learning by Doing Thinking Critically to Solve a

℮ For readings that go beyond the printed page, see **bedfordstmartins.com/concisebedguide**   xix

Detailed List of Contents. Beginning on p. xix, the longer, more detailed list of contents breaks down the topics covered within each chapter of the book. Use this list to find a specific part of a chapter. For example, if you have been asked to read Olof Eriksson's paper, "The Problems with Masculinity," a quick scan of the detailed contents will show you that it begins on page 24.

Rhetorical List of Contents. This list, beginning on page xxviii, includes all the readings in *The Concise Bedford Guide,* organized by writing strategy or situation, such as "Explaining Causes and Effects," or "Evaluating and Reviewing." Use this list to locate examples of the kind of writing you are doing and to see how other writers have approached their material.

Selected List of Visuals. On page xxxi is a list of many of the photographs or other visual images in *The Concise Bedford Guide,* arranged by type, genre, or purpose. This list can help you locate photographs, such as an advertisement or visual essay, to analyze or compare in your writing. In our increasingly visual age, knowing how to read and analyze visuals and then to write about them is a particularly valuable skill.

Locator Guide. If you find yourself stuck at any stage of the writing process, open the book to the page facing the inside back cover. There you will find the page numbers of Learning by Doing activities, self-assessment Take Action flowcharts, and other resources. If you are having trouble writing an opening to your paper, for example, this Locator Guide makes it easy for you to turn to the right place at the right time.

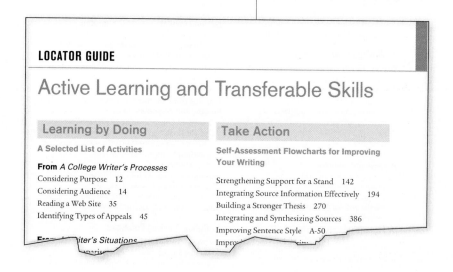

LOCATOR GUIDE

Active Learning and Transferable Skills

Learning by Doing
A Selected List of Activities

From *A College Writer's Processes*
Considering Purpose   12
Considering Audience   14
Reading a Web Site   35
Identifying Types of Appeals   45

From *A Writer's Situations*

Take Action
Self-Assessment Flowcharts for Improving Your Writing

Strengthening Support for a Stand   142
Integrating Source Information Effectively   194
Building a Stronger Thesis   270
Integrating and Synthesizing Sources   386
Improving Sentence Style   A-50

Alternating pattern of organization, 113
Analysis
    in critical reading, 26, 26 (fig.)
    in critical thinking processes, 37–38, 40, 52–54
    of readers' points of view, 137
    of writing strategies, 29
Annotated bibliography, 349–50
Annotation
    of critical reading, 21–23
    writing, 350
Antecedent, A-46–48
APA style, 334–44, A-36–38
    academic paper format, 389, A-4–6
    annotated bibliography entries, 349–50

Index. *The Concise Bedford Guide*'s index is an in-depth list of the book's contents in alphabetical order. Turn to page I-1 when you want to find the information available in the book for a particular topic. This example shows you all the places to look for help with analyzing material, a common assignment in college.

Marginal Cross-References. You can find additional information quickly by using the references in the margins—notes on the sides of each page that tell you where to turn in the book or online. For online resources, visit **bedfordstmartins.com/concisebedguide** for more help or for other activities related to what you are reading.

Color-Coded Pages. Several sections of *The Concise Bedford Guide* are color-coded to make them easy to find.

- "Quick Format Guide" (pp. A-1–A-19). If you need help formatting your paper, turn to this section at the back of the book, which is designated with yellow-edged pages.

- "Quick Research Guide" (pp. A-20–A-38). If you need fast help with research processes, sources, or the basics of MLA or APA style, turn to this section at the back of the book, which is designated with orange-edged pages.

- "Quick Editing Guide" (pp. A-39–A-58). If you need help as you edit your writing, turn to this section at the back of the book, which is designated with blue-edged pages.

- "A Sample MLA Research Paper" (pp. A-59–A-67). If you want to see how to apply MLA guidelines as you prepare your research paper, turn to the sample student paper, which is designated with green-edged pages.

- "A Sample APA Research Paper" (pp. A-68–A-76). If you want to see how to apply APA guidelines as you prepare your research paper, turn to the sample student paper, which is designated with turquoise-edged pages.

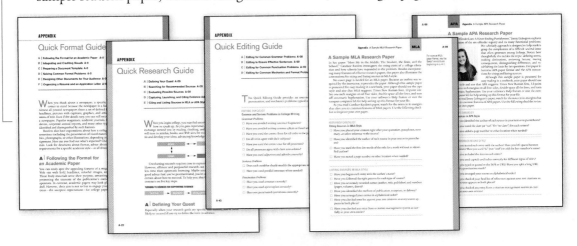

Becoming a Better Writer by Using *The Concise Bedford Guide*

The Concise Bedford Guide includes readings, checklists, activities, and other features that will help you to improve your writing and to do well in college and on the job.

Model Readings and e-Pages. *The Concise Bedford Guide* is filled with examples of both professional and student essays, located on the beige pages in Part Two. All these essays are accompanied by informative notes about the author, pre-reading questions, definitions of difficult words, questions for thinking more deeply about the reading, and suggestions for writing.

Reading Annotations. Student essays include questions in the margins to spark your imagination and your ideas as you read. Professional essays in Part Two: A Writer's Situations include annotations to point out notable features, such as the thesis and supporting points.

The Concise Bedford Guide also includes e-Pages with texts, multimodal readings (such as videos, audio segments, and infographics), and online assignments (such as critical thinking and reading questions and "Learning by Doing" activities). The e-Pages are marked in the main Contents and in the book pages with this icon: 🄴. To access them, visit **bedfordstmartins.com/concisebedguide**.

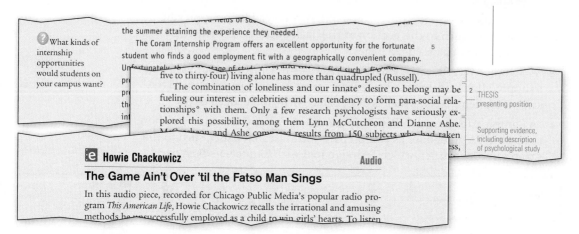

the summer attaining the experience they needed.

The Coram Internship Program offers an excellent opportunity for the fortunate student who finds a good employment fit with a geographically convenient company. Unfortunately   5

🄴 **Howie Chackowicz**   **Audio**

The Game Ain't Over 'til the Fatso Man Sings

In this audio piece, recorded for Chicago Public Media's popular radio program *This American Life*, Howie Chackowicz recalls the irrational and amusing methods he unsuccessfully employed as a child to win girls' hearts. To listen

(margin note, left:) ❓ What kinds of internship opportunities would students on your campus want?

(text fragment:) five to thirty-four) living alone has more than quadrupled (Russell).

The combination of loneliness and our innate° desire to belong may be fueling our interest in celebrities and our tendency to form para-social relationships° with them. Only a few research psychologists have seriously explored this possibility, among them Lynn McCutcheon and Dianne Ashe. McCutcheon and Ashe compared results from 150 subjects who had taken

(margin notes, right:) 2 THESIS presenting position

Supporting evidence, including description of psychological study

Clear Assignments. In Chapters 4 to 10, the "Learning by Writing" section presents the assignment for the chapter and guides you through the process of writing that type of essay. The "Facing the Challenge" section in each of these chapters helps you through the most complicated step in the assignment.

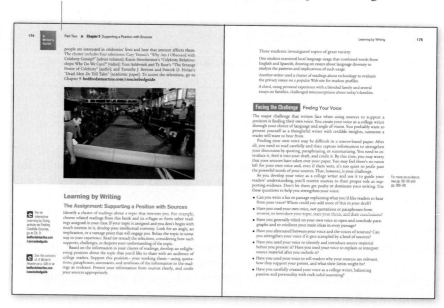

"Learning by Doing." These activities are designed to let you practice and apply what you are learning to your own writing. They encourage you to make key concepts your own so that you will be able to take what you have learned and apply it in other writing situations and contexts in college and in the workplace.

> **Learning by Doing** 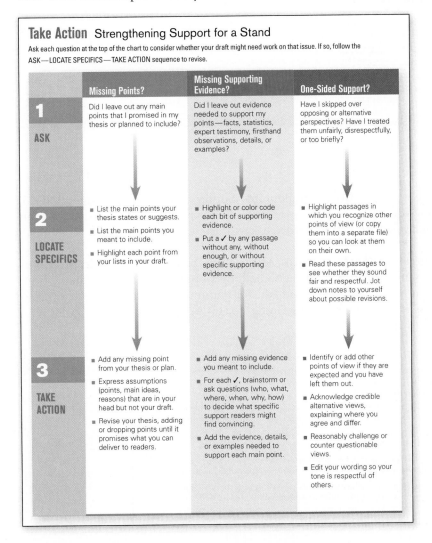 Selecting Reliable Sources
>
> When you choose your own sources, evaluate them to be sure they are reliable choices that your audience will respect. When your sources are assigned, assess their strengths, weaknesses, and limitations to use them effectively. Bring your articles, essays, and other sources to a small-group evaluation session. Using the checklist in C3 in the Quick Research Guide (pp. A-27–A-28), discuss your common sources or a key source selected by each writer in the group. Look for points that you might mention in a paper to bolster a source's credibility with readers (for example, the author's professional affiliation). Look as well for limitations that might restrict what a source can support.

"Take Action" Charts. These flowcharts focus on common writing challenges. They help you to ask the right questions of your draft and to take active steps to revise effectively. They are a powerful tool in helping you become an independent writer, able to assess what you have written and improve it on your own.

Take Action Strengthening Support for a Stand

Ask each question at the top of the chart to consider whether your draft might need work on that issue. If so, follow the ASK — LOCATE SPECIFICS — TAKE ACTION sequence to revise.

	Missing Points?	**Missing Supporting Evidence?**	**One-Sided Support?**
1 ASK	Did I leave out any main points that I promised in my thesis or planned to include?	Did I leave out evidence needed to support my points—facts, statistics, expert testimony, firsthand observations, details, or examples?	Have I skipped over opposing or alternative perspectives? Have I treated them unfairly, disrespectfully, or too briefly?
2 LOCATE SPECIFICS	■ List the main points your thesis states or suggests. ■ List the main points you meant to include. ■ Highlight each point from your lists in your draft.	■ Highlight or color code each bit of supporting evidence. ■ Put a ✔ by any passage without any, without enough, or without specific supporting evidence.	■ Highlight passages in which you recognize other points of view (or copy them into a separate file) so you can look at them on their own. ■ Read these passages to see whether they sound fair and respectful. Jot down notes to yourself about possible revisions.
3 TAKE ACTION	■ Add any missing point from your thesis or plan. ■ Express assumptions (points, main ideas, reasons) that are in your head but not your draft. ■ Revise your thesis, adding or dropping points until it promises what you can deliver to readers.	■ Add any missing evidence you meant to include. ■ For each ✔, brainstorm or ask questions (who, what, where, when, why, how) to decide what specific support readers might find convincing. ■ Add the evidence, details, or examples needed to support each main point.	■ Identify or add other points of view if they are expected and you have left them out. ■ Acknowledge credible alternative views, explaining where you agree and differ. ■ Reasonably challenge or counter questionable views. ■ Edit your wording so your tone is respectful of others.

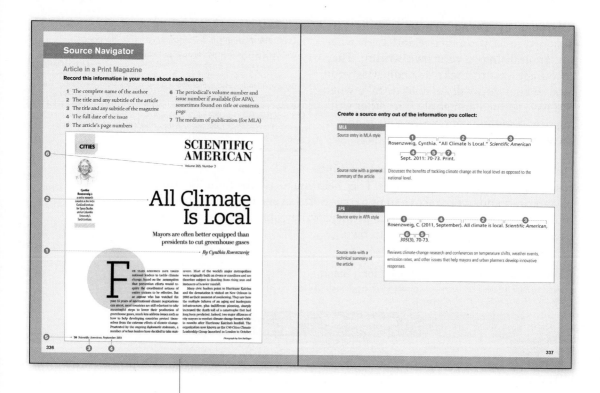

Resources for Crediting Sources. Source Navigators, on pages 336–43, show you where to look in several major types of sources so that you can quickly find the details needed to credit these sources correctly.

Helpful Checklists. Easy-to-use checklists help you to consider your purpose and audience, discover something to write about, get feedback from a peer, revise your draft, and edit for grammatical correctness, using references to the "Quick Editing Guide" (pages A-39–A-58).

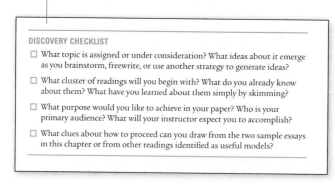

DISCOVERY CHECKLIST

☐ What topic is assigned or under consideration? What ideas about it emerge as you brainstorm, freewrite, or use another strategy to generate ideas?

☐ What cluster of readings will you begin with? What do you already know about them? What have you learned about them simply by skimming?

☐ What purpose would you like to achieve in your paper? Who is your primary audience? What will your instructor expect you to accomplish?

☐ What clues about how to proceed can you draw from the two sample essays in this chapter or from other readings identified as useful models?

Why Writing Matters. You will apply the writing skills that you learn using *The Concise Bedford Guide* to writing in other college courses, at your job, and in your community. Sections at the beginning of Chapters 4 through 11 consider why each type of writing that you do in this course will be relevant and helpful to you, wherever your path ahead takes you. Similar sections begin Chapters 16 through 20, considering the relevance of research stages and activities.

Why Taking a Stand Matters

In a College Course

- You take a stand in an essay or exam when you respond, pro or con, to a statement such as "The Web, like movable type for printing, is an invention that has transformed human communication."
- You take a stand when you write research papers that support your position on juvenile sentencing, state support for higher education, or tax breaks for new home buyers.

In the Workplace

- You take a stand when you persuade others that your case report supports a legal action that will benefit your clients or that your customer-service initiative will attract new business.

In Your Community

- You take a stand when you write a letter to the editor appealing to voters to support a local bond issue.

When have you taken a stand in your writing? In what circumstances are you likely to do so again?

The Concise Bedford
Guide for Writers

A COLLEGE WRITER'S PROCESSES

A College Writer's Processes Contents

1 **Writing Processes**   6

2 **Reading Processes**   17

3 **Critical Thinking Processes**   37

Introduction: Meeting College Expectations

As a college writer you probably wrestle with the question, What should I write? You may feel you have nothing to say or nothing worth saying. Maybe your difficulty lies in understanding the requirements of your writing situation, finding a topic, or uncovering information about it. Perhaps you, like many other college writers, have convinced yourself that professional writers have some special way of discovering ideas for writing. But they have no magic. In reality, what they have is experience and confidence, the products of lots of practice writing.

In *The Concise Bedford Guide*, we want you to become a better writer by actually writing. To help you do so, we'll give you a lot of practice as well as useful advice to help you build your skills and confidence. Because writing and learning to write are many-faceted tasks, each part of this book is devoted to a different aspect of writing. Together, these four parts contribute to a seamless whole, much like the writing process itself.

Part One introduces writing, reading, and thinking critically — essential processes for meeting college expectations. Your college instructors will expect you to show how you have grown as a writer, a reader, and a thinker. More specifically, they will want you to write thoughtful, purposeful papers, appropriately directed to your audience. They will want you not only to rely on your own ideas but also to read the writings of others and to ask questions about what you read. And they will expect you to think critically and to state your points clearly as you write, integrating and supporting your own ideas with those drawn from your reading. The first part of this book briefly introduces the processes — writing, reading, and thinking critically — that will help you meet these essential academic expectations.

For information and journal questions about the Part One photograph, see the last two pages of the Appendices.

1 Writing Processes

You are already a writer with long experience. In school you have taken notes, written book reports and term papers, answered exam questions, perhaps kept a journal. In the community or on the job you've composed letters and e-mails. You've sent text messages or tweets to friends, made lists, maybe even written songs or poetry. All this experience is about to pay off as you tackle college writing, learning by doing.

In this book our purpose is to help you to write better, deeper, clearer, and more satisfying papers than you have ever written before and to learn to do so by actually writing. Throughout the book we'll give you a lot of practice—in writing processes, patterns, and strategies—to build confidence. And we'll pose various writing situations and say, "Go for it!"

Writing, Reading, and Critical Thinking

In college you will expand what you already know about writing. You may be asked not only to recall an experience but also to reflect upon its significance. Or you may go beyond summarizing positions about an issue to present your own position or propose a solution. Above all, you will read and think critically—not just stacking up facts but analyzing what you discover, deciding what it means, and weighing its value. As you read—and write—actively, you will engage with the ideas of others, analyzing and judging those ideas. You will use criteria—models, conventions, principles, standards—to assess or evaluate what you are doing.

For more on reading critically, see Ch. 2. For more on thinking critically, see Ch. 3.

WRITER'S CHECKLIST

☐ Have you achieved your purpose?

☐ Have you considered your audience?

☐ Have you clearly stated your point as a thesis or unmistakably implied it?

☐ Have you supported your point with enough reliable evidence to persuade your audience?

☐ Have you arranged your ideas logically so that each follows from, supports, or adds to the one before it?

☐ Have you made the connections among ideas clear to a reader?

☐ Have you established an appropriate tone?

In large measure, learning to write well is learning what questions to ask as you write. For that reason, we include questions, suggestions, and activities to help you accomplish your writing tasks and reflect on your own processes as you write, read, and think critically.

A Process of Writing

Writing can seem at times an overwhelming drudgery, worse than scrubbing floors; at other moments, it's a sport full of thrills—like whizzing downhill on skis, not knowing what you'll meet around a bend. Unpredictable as the process may seem, nearly all writers do similar things:

- They generate ideas.
- They plan, draft, and develop their papers.
- They revise and edit.

These three activities form the basis of most effective writing processes, and they lie at the heart of each writing situation in this book.

For full chapters on stages of the writing process, see Chs. 12–15.

For a variety of writing situations, see Part 2, especially Chs. 4–9.

Getting Started

Two considerations—what you want to accomplish as a writer and how you want to appeal to your audience—will shape the direction of your writing. Clarifying your purpose and considering your audience are likely to increase your confidence as a writer. Even so, your writing process may take you in unexpected directions, not necessarily in a straight line. You can skip around, work on several parts at a time, test a fresh approach, circle back over what's already done, or stop to play with a sentence until it clicks.

Generating Ideas

The first activity in writing—finding a topic and something to say about it—is often the most challenging and least predictable. The chapter section called "Generating Ideas" is filled with examples, questions, checklists, and visuals designed to trigger ideas that will help you begin the writing assignment.

Discovering What to Write About. You may get an idea while texting friends, riding your bike, or staring out the window. Sometimes a topic lies near home, in a conversation or an everyday event. Often, your reading will

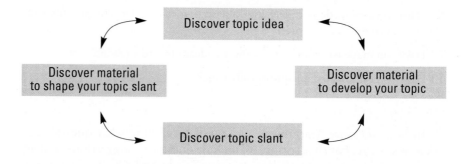

raise questions that call for investigation. Even if an assignment doesn't appeal to you, your challenge is to find a slant that does. Find it, and words will flow—words to engage readers and accomplish your purpose.

Discovering Material. To shape and support your ideas, you'll need facts and figures, reports and opinions, examples and illustrations. How do you find supporting material that makes your slant on a topic clear and convincing? Luckily you have many sources at your fingertips. You can recall your experience and knowledge, observe things around you, talk with others who are knowledgeable, read enlightening materials that draw you to new approaches, and think critically about all these sources.

For a discussion on writing processes in online classes, see pp. 235–37.

Learning by Doing 🖍 Reflecting on Ideas

Think over past writing experiences at school or work. How do you get ideas? Where do they come from? Where do you turn for related material? What are your most reliable sources of inspiration and information? Share your experiences with others in class or online, noting any new approaches you would like to try.

✳Planning, Drafting, and Developing

Next you will plan your paper, write a draft, and develop your ideas further. The sections titled "Planning, Drafting, and Developing" will help you through these stages for the assignment in that chapter.

Planning. Having discovered a burning idea to write about (or at least a smoldering one) and some supporting material (but maybe not enough yet), you will sort out what matters most. If you see one main point, or thesis, test various ways of stating it, given your purpose and audience:

MAYBE   Parking in the morning before class is annoying.

OR   Campus parking is a big problem.

Next arrange your ideas and material in a sensible order that will clarify your point. For example, you might group and label your ideas, make an outline, or analyze the main point, breaking it down into parts:

> Parking on campus is a problem for students because of the long lines, inefficient entrances, and poorly marked spaces.

But if no clear thesis emerges quickly, don't worry. You may find one while you draft — that is, while you write an early version of your paper.

Drafting. As your ideas begin to appear, welcome them and lure them forth so they don't go back into hiding. When you take risks at this stage, you'll probably be surprised and pleased at what happens, even though your first version will be rough. Writing takes time; a paper usually needs several drafts and maybe a clearer introduction, stronger conclusion, more convincing evidence, or even a fresh start.

Developing. Weave in explanations, definitions, examples, details, and varied evidence to make your ideas clear and persuasive. For example, you may define an at-risk student, illustrate the problems of single parents, or

For help developing a main point, go to the interactive "Take Action" charts in Re:Writing at **bedfordstmartins.com /concisebedguide.**

For advice on using a few sources, see the Quick Research Guide, pp. A-20–A-38.

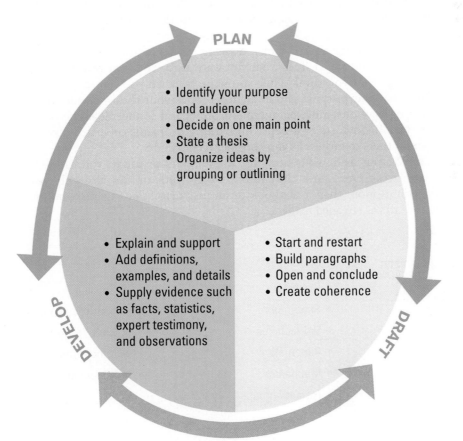

Processes for Planning, Drafting, and Developing

supply statistics about hit-and-run accidents. If you need specific support for your point, use strategies for developing ideas—or return to those for generating ideas. Work in your insights if they fit.

Learning by Doing 🔲 Reflecting on Drafts

Reflect on your past writing experiences. How do you usually plan, draft, and develop your writing? How well do your methods work? How do you adjust them to the situation or type of writing you're doing? Which part of producing a draft do you most dread, enjoy, or wish to change? Why? Write down your reflections, and then share your experiences with others in class or online.

Revising and Editing

You might be tempted to relax once you have a draft, but for most writers, revising begins the work in earnest. Each "Revising and Editing" section provides checklists as well as suggestions for working with a peer.

Revising. Revising means both reseeing and rewriting, making major changes so your paper does what you want it to. You may revise what you know and what you think while you write or when you reread. You might reconsider your purpose and audience, rework your thesis, decide what to put in or leave out, move paragraphs around, and connect ideas better. Perhaps you'll add costs to a paper on parking problems or switch attention from mothers to fathers as you consider teen parents.

If you put aside your draft for a few hours or a day, you can reread it with fresh eyes and a clear mind. Other students can also help you—sometimes more than a textbook or an instructor can—by responding to your drafts as engaged readers.

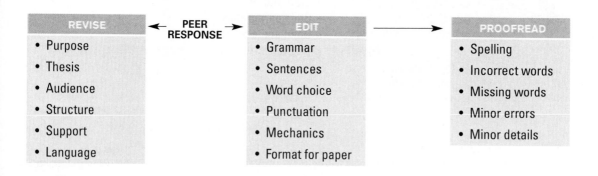

REVISE	PEER RESPONSE	EDIT		PROOFREAD
• Purpose		• Grammar		• Spelling
• Thesis		• Sentences		• Incorrect words
• Audience		• Word choice		• Missing words
• Structure		• Punctuation		• Minor errors
• Support		• Mechanics		• Minor details
• Language		• Format for paper		

Editing. Editing means refining details, improving wording, and correcting flaws that may stand in the way of your readers' understanding and enjoyment. Don't edit too early, though, because you may waste time on parts that you later revise out. In editing, you usually make these repairs:

For editing advice, see the Quick Editing Guide, pp. A-39–A-58. For format advice, see the Quick Format Guide, pp. A-1–A-19.

- Drop unnecessary words; choose lively and precise words.
- Replace incorrect or inappropriate wording.
- Rearrange words in a clearer, more emphatic order.
- Combine short, choppy sentences, or break up long, confusing ones.
- Refine transitions for continuity of thought.
- Check grammar, usage, punctuation, and mechanics.

Proofreading. Finally you'll proofread, taking a last look, checking correctness, and catching doubtful spellings or word-processing errors.

Learning by Doing 🖋 Reflecting on Finishing

Think over past high-pressure writing experiences: major papers at school, reports at work, or personal projects such as a blog or Web site. What steps do you take to rethink and refine your writing before submitting or posting it? What prompts you to make major changes? How do you try to satisfy concerns or quirks of your main reader or a broader audience? Work with others in class or online to collect and share your best ideas about wrapping up writing projects.

Purpose and Audience

At any moment in the writing process, two questions are worth asking:

WHY AM I WRITING?   WHO IS MY AUDIENCE?

Writing for a Reason

Like most college writing assignments, every assignment in this book asks you to write for a definite reason. For example, you'll recall a memorable experience in order to explain its importance for you; you'll take a stand on a controversy in order to convey your position and persuade readers to respect it. Be careful not to confuse the sources and strategies

For more on using your purpose for planning, see pp. 262–68, and for revising, see pp. 301–2.

you apply in these assignments with your ultimate purpose for writing. "To compare and contrast two things" is not a very interesting purpose; "to compare and contrast two Web sites *in order to explain which is more reliable*" implies a real reason for writing. In most college writing, your purpose will be to explain something to your readers or to convince them of something.

To sharpen your concentration on your purpose, ask yourself from the start: What do I want to do? And, in revising, Did I do what I meant to do? These practical questions will help you slice out irrelevant information and remove other barriers to getting your paper where you want it to go.

Learning by Doing Considering Purpose

Imagine that you are in the following writing situations. For each, write a sentence or two summing up your purpose as a writer.

1. The instructor in your psychology course has assigned a paragraph about the meanings of three essential terms in your readings.
2. You're upset about a change in financial aid procedures and plan to write a letter asking the financial aid director to remedy the problem.
3. You're starting a blog about your first year at college so your extended family can envision the environment and share your experiences.
4. Your supervisor wants you to write an article about the benefits of a new company service for the customer newsletter.
5. Your Facebook profile seemed appropriate last year, but you want to revise it now that you're attending college and have a job with future prospects.

Writing for Your Audience

For an interactive Learning by Doing activity on analyzing audience, go to Ch. 1: **bedfordstmartins .com/concisebedguide**.

Your audience, or your readers, may or may not be defined in your assignment. Consider the following examples:

ASSIGNMENT 1	Discuss the advantages and disadvantages of homeschooling.
ASSIGNMENT 2	In a letter to parents of school-aged children, discuss the advantages and disadvantages of homeschooling.

If your assignment defines an audience, as the second example does, you need to think about how to approach those readers and what to assume about their views. For example, what points would you include in a discussion aimed at parents? How would you organize your ideas? Would you discuss advantages or disadvantages first? On the other hand, how might your approach differ if the assignment read this way?

For more on planning for your readers, see pp. 262–63. For more on revising for them, see pp. 302–3.

ASSIGNMENT 3	In a newsletter article for teachers, discuss the advantages and disadvantages of homeschooling.

Audience Characteristics and Expectations

	General Audience	College Instructor	Work Supervisor	Campus Friend
Relationship to You	Imagined but not known personally	Known briefly in a class context	Known for some time in a job context	Known in campus and social contexts
Reason for Reading Your Writing	Curious attitude and interest in your topic assumed	Professional responsibility for your knowledge and skills	Managerial interest in and reliance on your job performance	Personal interest based on shared circumstances
Knowledge About Your Topic	Level of awareness assumed and gaps addressed with logical presentation	Well informed about college topics but wants to see what you know	Informed about the business and expects reliable information from you	Friendly but may or may not be informed beyond social interests
Forms and Formats Expected	Essay, article, letter, report, or other format	Essay, report, research paper, or other academic format	Memo, report, Web page, e-mail, or letter using company format	Notes, blog entries, social networking, or other informal messages
Language and Style Expected	Formal, using clear words and sentences	Formal, following academic conventions	Appropriate for advancing you and the company	Informal, using abbreviations, phrases, and slang
Attitude and Tone Expected	Interested and thoughtful about the topic	Serious and thoughtful about the topic and course	Respectful, showing reliability and work ethic	Friendly and interested in shared experiences
Amount of Detail Expected	Sufficient detail to inform or persuade the reader you envision	Enough sound or research-based evidence to support your thesis	General or technical information as needed	Much detail or little, depending on the topic

Audiences may be identified by characteristics, such as role (parents) or occupation (teachers), that suggest values to which a writer might appeal. As the chart above suggests, you can analyze preferences, biases, and concerns of readers to engage and influence them more successfully. When you consider what readers know, believe, and value, you can aim your writing toward them with a better chance of hitting your mark.

AUDIENCE CHECKLIST

☐ Who are your readers? What is their relationship to you?

☐ What do they know about this topic? What do you want them to learn?

☐ How much detail will they want to read about this topic?

☐ What objections are they likely to raise as they read? How can you anticipate and overcome their objections?

☐ What is likely to convince them? What's likely to offend them?

☐ What tone and style would most effectively influence them?

Learning by Doing 👆 Considering Audience

Read the following notices directed to subscribers of two magazines, *Zapped!* and *works & conversations*. Examine the style, tone, language, sequence of topics, or other features of each appeal. Write two short paragraphs—one about each notice—explaining what you can conclude about the letter's target audience and its appeal to that audience.

Zapped! misses you.

Dear Dan Morrison,

All last year, *Zapped!* magazine made the trek to 5 Snowden Lane and it was always a great experience. You took great care of *Zapped!*, and *Zapped!* gave you hours of entertainment, with news and interviews from the latest indie bands, honest-as-your-momma reviews of musical equipment, and your first glimpse of some of the finest graphic serials being published today.

But, Dan, we haven't heard from you and are starting to wonder what's up. Don't you miss *Zapped!*? One thing's for sure: *Zapped!* misses you.

We'd like to re-establish the relationship: if you renew your subscription by March 1, you'll get 20% off last year's subscription price. That's only $24 for another year of great entertainment. Just fill out the other side of this card and send it back to us; we'll bill you later.

Come on, Dan. Why wait?

Thanks,

Carly Bevins

Carly Bevins
Director of Sales

Figure 1.1 Renewal Letter from *Zapped!*

works & CONVERSATIONS

What's Something Worth That You Get For Free?

A friend suggested, "Charge $20 per issue. People will value it more." There's something true about that. So how can what we do be valued if no money is charged? Of course, the magazine is not really free. What you're receiving has been paid for by others—both in dollars and effort.

We don't sell ads, either. We found something refreshing about creating an ad-free space.

We live in a transactional time, in an if-then culture deeply accustomed to the conditional. The gift economy then, is a whisper in the ear of the collective, a whisper insisting against the odds that there is another way of encountering this world and each other: through generosity.

We participate in a quiet, no-strings revolution where each act serves as its own catalyst—and as a movement from isolation to community, from scarcity to abundance. That's the spirit in which *works & conversations* is offered. We count on support from like-minded and like-hearted read-

ers, and produce the magazine in the spirit of a gift. It comes to you through an invisible circle of giving. We are grateful to, and much encouraged by, the generosity that has been shown by readers.

If you are paying this forward in some way other than with a financial contribution, we'd love to hear about it. Please send us a note at the address below or by email to rwhit@jps.net.

Thank you for your readership.
—servicespace.org volunteers

If you wish to help pay-it-forward with a financial contribution you can...

•Donate online at:
http://www.conversations.org/?op=donate

•Or send a check payable to "works & conversations" at: works & conversations
P. O. Box 5008
Berkeley, CA 94705

works & conversations

70

Figure 1.2 Appeal to Readers of *works & conversations*

Targeting a College Audience

Many of your college assignments, like Assignment 1 on page 12, may assume that you are addressing general college readers, represented by your instructor and possibly your classmates. Such readers typically expect clear, logical writing with supporting evidence to explain or persuade. Of course, the format, approach, or evidence may differ by field. For example, biologists might expect the findings from your experiment while literature specialists might look for relevant quotations from the novel you're analyzing.

COLLEGE AUDIENCE CHECKLIST

☐ How has your instructor advised you to write for readers? What criteria related to audience will be used for grading your papers?

☐ What do the assigned readings in your course assume about an audience? Has your instructor recommended models or sample readings?

☐ What topics, issues, and problems intrigue readers in the course area? What puzzles do they want to solve? How do they want to solve them?

☐ How is writing in the course area commonly organized? For example, do writers tend to follow a persuasive pattern — introducing the issue, stating an assertion or a claim, backing the claim with logical points and supporting evidence, acknowledging other views, and concluding? Or do they use conventional headings — perhaps *Abstract, Introduction, Methodology, Findings,* and *Discussion*?

☐ What evidence typically supports ideas or interpretations — facts and statistics, quotations from texts, summaries of research, references to authorities or prior studies, experimental findings, observations, or interviews?

☐ What style, tone, and level of formality do writers in the field use?

Learning by Doing 🎯 Considering a College Audience

Use the checklist above to examine reading or writing assignments for another course. What are some prominent features of writing in the area? Which of these might be expected in student papers? How would your college paper differ from writing on the same topic for another audience (perhaps a letter to the editor, newspaper article, consumer brochure, summary for young students, or Web page)?

Additional Writing Activities

1. Write a few paragraphs or an online posting about your personal goals as a writer during this class. What do you already do well as a writer? What do you need to improve? What do you hope to accomplish? How might you benefit, in college or elsewhere, from improving your writing?

2. **Source Activity.** Select a passage from a textbook or reading assigned in a course. Rewrite the passage for a nonacademic audience (such as readers of a specific magazine or newspaper, visitors to a certain Web site, or interested amateurs).

3. **Source Activity.** Find a nonacademic article, pamphlet, or Web page. Try your hand at rewriting a passage as a college textbook or reading in the field might present the material. Then write an informal paragraph explaining why this task was easy, challenging, or impossible.

4. **Visual Activity.** Working with classmates, examine an academic and a nonacademic resource (such as those for questions 2 and 3 above). Compare and contrast physical features such as page layout, arrangement of text and space, images, color, type size and font, section divisions, and source credits. Write a paragraph about each resource, explaining how its features serve its purpose and appeal to its audience.

Reading Processes

2

What's so special about college reading? Don't you just pick up the book, start on the first page, and keep going as you have ever since you met *The Cat in the Hat*? Reading from beginning to end works especially well when you are eager to find out what happens next, as in a thriller, or what to do next, as in a cookbook. On the other hand, much of your college reading is complicated. Dense, challenging material often requires closer, slower reading and deeper thinking — in short, a process for reading critically.

A Process of Critical Reading

Reading critically means approaching whatever you read in an active, questioning manner. This essential college-level skill changes reading from a spectator sport to a contact sport. You no longer sit in the stands, watching graceful skaters glide by. Instead, you charge right into a rough-and-tumble hockey game, gripping your stick and watching out for your teeth.

Critical reading, like critical thinking, is not an activity reserved for college courses. It is a continuum of strategies that thoughtful people use every day to grapple with new information, to integrate it with existing knowledge, and to apply it to problems in daily life:

For more on critical thinking, see Ch. 3.

- They get ready to do their reading.
- They respond as they read.
- They read on literal and analytical levels.

Building your critical reading skills can bring many benefits, especially if you aren't a regular reader. You'll open the door to information you've never encountered and to ideas unlikely to come up with friends. For this course alone, you will be prepared to evaluate strengths and weaknesses of essays by professionals, students, and classmates. If you research a topic, you will be ready to figure out what your sources say, what they assume and imply, whether they are sound, and how you might use them to help make your point. In addition, you can apply your expanded skills in other courses, your job, and your community.

Many instructors help you develop your skills, especially once you realize that they want to improve your critical reading, not complicate your life. Some prepare you by previewing a reading so you learn its background or structure. Others supply reading questions so you know what to look for or give motivational credit for reading responses. Still others may share their own reading processes with you, revealing what they read first (maybe the opening and conclusion) or how they might decide to skip a section (such as Methods in a report whose conclusions they want first).

In the end, however, making the transition to college reading requires your time and energy—and both will be well spent. Once you build your skills as a critical reader, you'll save time by reading more effectively, and you'll save energy by improving both your reading and your writing.

Learning by Doing 📷 Describing Your Reading Strategies

Briefly describe your reading strategies in different situations. For example, how do you read a magazine, newspaper, or popular novel? What's different about reading the material assigned in college? What techniques do you use for reading assignments? Working with others in class or online, collect your best ideas about how to cope effectively, especially in classes with lots of reading.

Scene from *Hansel and Gretel*, a Grimm's fairy tale.

Getting Started

College reading is active reading. Your instructors expect you to do far more than recognize the words on the page. They want you to read their assignments critically and then to think and write critically about what you have read. Many offer pointers about readings: they want to help you find a trail through the text so you won't get lost as you read.

- If you know the old tale of Hansel and Gretel, you'll recall those resourceful children who dropped crumbs as they walked so that they could retrace their steps through the deep, dark woods. If so, you are interacting with this book, bringing to it your memories and experience. You won't stop to puzzle over woods, trails, and crumbs. You'll just keep reading.

■ If you have never met Hansel and Gretel, you may have to stop and puzzle out how they might connect to the reading process.

Many readers—even college professors—feel lost when they begin complex texts about something new. However, experienced critical readers hike through the intellectual woods with confidence because they know how to use many reading strategies. You can learn and practice such strategies, too, following the trail of bread crumbs left by other writers and dropping them for your readers as well.

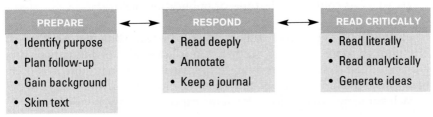

Preparing to Read

Before you read, think ahead about how to approach the reading process—how to make the most of the time you spend reading.

Thinking about Your Purpose. When you begin to read, ask questions like these about your immediate purpose:

■ What are you reading?

■ Why are you reading? What do you want to do with the reading?

■ What does your instructor expect you to learn from the reading?

■ Do you need to memorize details, find main points, or connect ideas?

■ How does this reading build on, add to, contrast with, or otherwise relate to other reading assignments in the course?

Planning Your Follow-Up. When you are required to read or to select a reading, ask yourself what your instructor expects to follow it:

■ Do you need to be ready to discuss the reading during class?

■ Will you need to mention it or analyze it during an examination?

■ Will you need to write about it or its topic?

■ Do you need to find its main points? Sum it up? Compare it? Question it? Spot its strengths and weaknesses? Draw useful details from it?

Gaining Background. Knowing a reading's context, approach, or frame of reference can help you predict where the reading is likely to go and how it relates to other readings. Begin with your available resources:

- Do the syllabus, schedule, and class notes reveal why your instructor assigned the reading? What can you learn from reading questions, tips about what to watch for, or connections with other readings?
- Does your reading have a book jacket or preface, an introduction or abstract that sums it up, or reading pointers or questions?
- Does any enlightening biographical or professional information about the author accompany the reading?
- Can you identify or speculate about the reading's original audience based on its content, style, tone, or publication history?

Skimming the Text. Before you actively read a text, skim it—quickly read only enough to introduce yourself to it. If it has a table of contents or subheadings, read those first to figure out what it covers and how it is organized. Read the first paragraph and then the first (or first and last) sentence of each paragraph that follows. Read the captions of any visuals.

Learning by Doing 🔟 Preparing to Read

Select a reading from this book or its e-Pages, and try out a few strategies for preparing to read. Then sum up which strategies worked, which didn't, and whether you feel prepared to read the selection critically. Discuss your experience with others in class or online.

Responding to Reading

You may be accustomed to reading simply for facts or main ideas. However, critical reading is far more active than fact hunting. It requires responding, questioning, and challenging as you read.

Reading Deeply. College assignments often require more concentration than other readings do. Use these questions to dive below the surface:

- How does the writer begin? What does the opening paragraph or section reveal about the writer's purpose and point? How does the writer prepare readers for what follows?
- How might you trace the progression of ideas in the reading? How do headings, previews of what's coming up, summaries of what's gone before, and transitions signal the organization?
- Are difficult or technical terms defined in specific ways? How might you highlight, list, or record such terms so that you master them?
- How might you record or recall the details in the reading? How could you track or diagram interrelated ideas to grasp their connections?

- How do word choice, tone, and style alert you to the complex purpose of a reading that is layered or indirect rather than straightforward?

- Does the reading include figurative or descriptive language, references to other works, or recurring themes? How do these enrich the reading?

- Can you answer any reading questions in your textbook, assignment, study guide, or syllabus? Can you restate headings in question form to create your own questions and then supply the answers? For example, change "Major Types of X" to "What are the major types of X?"

Annotating the Text. Writing notes on the page (or on a copy if the material is not your own) is a useful way to trace the author's points, question them, and add your own comments as they pop up. The following passage ends the introduction of "The New Science of Siblings," written by Jeffrey Kluger (with reporting by Jessica Carsen, Wendy Cole, and Sonja Steptoe) and featured as the cover story in the July 10, 2006, *Time* (pp. 47–48). Notice how one writer annotated this passage:

For more on evaluating what you read, see section C in the Quick Research Guide, pp. A-26–A-28.

For a Critical Reading Checklist, see pp. 28–29.

Key point — both obvious and surprising

Good quote — from UC Davis authority

Sums up past studies but new to me

Not exactly! My sister's definitely a striver, but I'm no rebel

Wow — global research!

Have to go for the drama — competition and favorites!!

Our spouses arrive comparatively late in our lives; our parents eventually leave us. Our siblings may be the only people we'll ever know who truly qualify as partners for life. "Siblings," says family sociologist Katherine Conger of the University of California, Davis, "are with us for the whole journey."

Within the scientific community, siblings have not been wholly ignored, but research has been limited mostly to discussions of birth order. Older sibs were said to be strivers; younger ones rebels; middle kids the lost souls. The stereotypes were broad, if not entirely untrue, and the discussion mostly ended.

But all that's changing. At research centers in the United States, Canada, Europe, and elsewhere, investigators are launching a wealth of new studies into the sibling dynamic, looking at ways brothers and sisters steer one another into—or away from—risky behavior; how they form a protective buffer against family upheaval; how they educate one another about the opposite sex; how all siblings compete for family recognition and come to terms—or blows—over such impossibly charged issues as parental favoritism.

Scary — I never thought of my sister this way!

Cousins= example — pulled together when parents split

When you annotate a reading, don't passively highlight big chunks of text. Instead, respond actively using pen or pencil or adding a comment to a file. Next, read slowly and carefully so that you can follow what the reading says and how it supports its point. Record your own reactions, not what you think you are supposed to say:

- Jot down things you already know or have experienced to build your own connection to the reading.

- Circle key words, star or check ideas when you agree or disagree, add arrows to mark connections, or underline key points, ideas, or definitions to learn the reading's vocabulary.

- Add question marks or questions about meaning or implications.

- Separate main points from supporting evidence and detail. Then you can question a conclusion, or challenge the evidence that supports it. (Main points often open a section or paragraph, followed by supporting detail, but sometimes this pattern is reversed.)

- React to quotable sentences or key passages. If they are hard to understand, restate them in your own words.

- Talk to the writer—maybe even talk back. Challenge weak points, respond with your own thoughts, draw in other views, or boost the writer's persuasive ideas.

- Sum up the writer's main point, supporting ideas, and notable evidence or examples.

- Consider how the reading appeals to your head, heart, or conscience.

Learning by Doing 🔳 Annotating a Passage

For a sample annotated passage, see p. 21.

Annotate the following passage. It opens the summary of findings for the survey "How Mobile Devices Are Changing Community Information Environments" (Pew Internet & American Life Project, *2011 State of the News Media Report*).

Local news is going mobile. Nearly half of all American adults (47%) report that they get at least some local news and information on their cellphone or tablet computer.   1

What they seek out most on mobile platforms is information that is practical and in real time: 42% of mobile device owners report getting weather updates on their phones or tablets; 37% say they get material about restaurants or other local businesses. These consumers are less likely to use their mobile devices for news about local traffic, public transportation, general news alerts or to access retail coupons or discounts.   2

One of the newest forms of on-the-go local news consumption, mobile applications are just beginning to take hold among mobile device owners.   3

Compared with other adults, these mobile local news consumers are younger, live in higher income households, are newer residents of their communities, live in nonrural areas, and tend to be parents of minor children. Adults who get local news and information on mobile devices are more likely than others to feel they can have an impact on their communities, more likely to use a variety of media platforms, feel more plugged into the media   4 environment than they did a few years ago, and are more likely to use social media:

- 35% of mobile local news consumers feel they can have a big impact on their community (vs. 27% of other adults)
- 65% feel it is easier today than five years ago to keep up with information about their community (vs. 47% of nonmobile connectors)
- 51% use six or more different sources or platforms monthly to get local news and information (vs. 21%)
- 75% use social network sites (vs. 42%)
- 15% use Twitter (vs. 4%)

Tablets and smartphones have also brought with them news applications or "apps." One-quarter (24%) of mobile local news consumers report having an app that helps them get information or news about their local community. That equates to 13% of all device owners and 11% of the total American adult population. Thus while nearly 5 in 10 get local news on mobile devices, just 1 in 10 use apps to do so. Call it the app gap.

5

Keeping a Reading Journal. A reading journal is an excellent place to record not just what you read but how you respond to it. As you read actively, you will build a reservoir of ideas for follow-up writing. Use a special notebook or an easy-to-sort research file to address questions like these:

For advice on keeping a writer's journal, see Ch. 12.

- What is the subject of the reading? What is the writer's stand?
- What does the writer take for granted? What assumptions does he or she begin with? Where are these stated or suggested?
- What are the writer's main points? What evidence supports them?
- Do you agree with what the writer has said? Do his or her ideas clash with your ideas or question something you take for granted?
- Has the writer told you more than you wanted to know or failed to tell you something you wish you knew?
- What conclusions can you draw from the reading?
- Has the reading opened your eyes to new ways of viewing the subject?

Learning by Doing 🎯 Responding in a Reading Journal

Return to the passage that you annotated on pages 22–23. Write a brief journal entry about this passage. Concentrate on two points: what the passage says and how you respond.

Learning from Another Writer: Reading Summary and Response

For another reading response on both literal and analytical levels, see pp. 29–31.

Olof Eriksson's instructor asked students to write a one-page reading response, including a summary and a personal response, before writing each assigned essay. Your instructor may also ask you to keep a reading journal or to submit or post online your responses to readings. Your assignment might require brief features such as these:

- **Summary:** a short statement in your own words of the reading's main points (without your opinion, evaluation, or judgment).
- **Paraphrase:** a restatement of a passage using your own words and sentences.

For more on citing sources, see E1–E2 in the Quick Research Guide, pp. A-32–A-38.

- **Quotation:** a noteworthy expression or statement in the author's exact words, presented in quotation marks and correctly cited.
- **Personal response:** a statement and explanation of your reaction to the reading.
- **Critique:** your evaluation of the strengths or weaknesses of the reading.
- **Application:** a connection between the reading and your experience.
- **Question:** a point of curiosity or uncertainty that you wish the writer had covered.

Olof Eriksson   **Student Summary and Response**

The Problems with Masculinity

To read Jensen's essay, go to Ch. e-2: **bedfordstmartins.com /concisebedguide**.

Robert Jensen writes in his essay "The High Cost of Manliness" about masculinity 1
and how our culture creates expectations of certain traits from the males in our society. He strongly opposes this view of masculinity and would prefer that sociological constructs like masculinity and femininity were abolished. As examples of expected traits, he mentions strength and competition. Males are supposed to take what they want and avoid showing weaknesses. Then Jensen points out negative consequences of enforcing masculinity, things like rape and men having trouble showing vulnerability. He counters the argument of differences in biology between males and females by pointing out that we do not know how much comes from biology and how much comes from culture, but that both certainly matter and we should do what we can. He is also concerned about giving positive attributes to masculinity, as that effectively tells us they only belong with males. He ends by observing that we are facing challenges now that cannot be met with the current view of masculinity.

I agree with what Jensen says, and I find it a problem today that the definition 2
of masculinity is so closely connected to competition and aggression. Even so, I

find that my own definition of masculinity is very close to the general one. I would say it is to be strong and determined, always winning. I'm sure most people have a similar idea of what it is, even as most people would disagree logically. That is why we need to make an effort to change our culture, just as Jensen argues. If we can either abolish masculinity and femininity or simply change them into a lot more neutral and closely related terms, then we will be a lot closer to real equality between the genders. This change will not only help remove most of the negative impacts Jensen brought up but also help pave a better way for future generations, reducing their problems.

Works Cited

Jensen, Robert. "The High Cost of Manliness." *The Bedford Guide for College Writers.* 10th ed. Ed. X. J. Kennedy, Dorothy M. Kennedy, and Marcia F. Muth. Boston: Bedford, 2014. 534–38. Print.

Questions to Start You Thinking

Meaning

1. According to Eriksson, what is Jensen's topic and Jensen's position on this topic? Where does Eriksson present this information?

2. What is Eriksson's personal response to the essay? Where does he present his views?

Writing Strategies

3. How does Eriksson consider his audience as he organizes and develops his summary and response?

4. What kinds of material from the essay does Eriksson use to develop his summary?

Reading on Literal and Analytical Levels

Educational expert Benjamin S. Bloom identified six levels of cognitive activity: knowledge, comprehension, application, analysis, synthesis, and evaluation.[1] (A recent update recasts *synthesis* as *creating* and moves it above evaluation to the highest level.) Each level acts as a foundation for the next. Each also demands higher thinking skills than the previous one. Experienced readers, however, jump among these levels, gathering information and insight as they occur.

---

[1]Benjamin S. Bloom et al., *Taxonomy of Educational Objectives, Handbook 1: Cognitive Domain* (New York: McKay, 1956). See also the update in David R. Krathwohl, "A Revision of Bloom's Taxonomy: An Overview," *Theory into Practice* 41.4 (2002): 212–218.

The first three levels are literal skills, building blocks of thought. The last three levels—analysis, synthesis, and evaluation—are analytical skills that your instructors especially want you to develop. To read critically, you must engage with a reading on both literal and analytical levels. Suppose you read in your history book a passage about Franklin Delano Roosevelt (FDR), the only American president elected to four consecutive terms.

Knowing. Once you read the passage, even if you have little background in American history, you can decode and recall the information it presents about FDR and his four terms in office.

Comprehending. To understand the passage, you need to know that a term for a U.S. president is four years and that *consecutive* means "continuous." Thus FDR was elected to serve for sixteen years.

Applying. To connect this knowledge to what you already know, you think of other presidents—George Washington, who served two terms; Grover Cleveland, who served two terms but not consecutively; Jimmy Carter, who served one term; the second George Bush, who served two terms. Then you realize that four terms are quite unusual. In fact, the Twenty-second Amendment to the Constitution, ratified in 1951, now limits a president to two terms.

Analyzing. You can scrutinize FDR's four terms from various angles, selecting a principle for analysis that suits your purpose. Then you can use this principle to break the information into its components or parts. For example, you might analyze FDR's tenure in relation to that of other presidents. Why has FDR been the only president elected to serve four terms? What circumstances contributed to three reelections?

Literal and Analytical Reading Skills
The information in this figure is adapted from Benjamin S. Bloom et al., *Taxonomy of Educational Objectives, Handbook 1: Cognitive Domain* (New York: McKay, 1956).

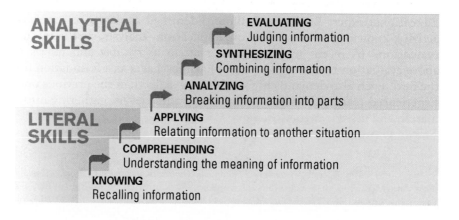

Synthesizing. To answer your questions, you may read more or review past readings. Then you begin synthesizing—creating a new approach or combination by pulling together facts and opinions, identifying evidence accepted by all or most sources, examining any controversial evidence, and drawing conclusions that reliable evidence seems to support. For example, you might logically conclude that the special circumstances of the Great Depression and World War II contributed to FDR's four terms, not that Americans reelected him out of pity because he had polio.

Evaluating. Finally, you evaluate the significance of your new knowledge for understanding Depression-era politics and assessing your history book's approach. You might ask yourself, Why has the book's author chosen to make this point? How does it affect the rest of the discussion? And you may also have concluded that FDR's four-term presidency is understandable in light of the events of the 1930s and 1940s, that the author has mentioned this fact to highlight the era's unique political atmosphere, and that, in your opinion, it is evidence neither for nor against FDR's excellence as a president.

Learning by Doing 🎨 Reading Analytically

Think back to something you have read recently that helped you make a decision, perhaps a newspaper or magazine article, an electronic posting, or a college brochure. How did you analyze what you read, breaking the information into parts? How did you synthesize it, combining it with what you already knew? How did you evaluate it, judging its significance for your decision?

Generating Ideas from Reading

Like flints that strike each other and cause sparks, readers and writers provoke one another. For example, when your class discusses an essay, you may be surprised by the range of insights your classmates report. Of course, they may be equally surprised by what you see. Above all, reading is a dynamic process. It may change your ideas instead of support them. Here are suggestions for unlocking the potential of a good text.

For more on generating ideas, see Ch. 12.

Looking for Meaty Pieces. Spur your thinking about current topics by browsing through essay collections or magazines in the library or online. Try *Atlantic, Harper's, New Republic, Commentary,* or special-interest magazines such as *Architectural Digest* or *Scientific American.* Check editorials and op-ed columns in your local newspaper, the *New York Times,* or the *Wall Street Journal.* Search the Internet on intriguing topics (such as silent-film technology) or issues (such as homeless children). Look for meaty, not superficial, articles written to inform and convince, not entertain or amuse.

Logging Your Reading. For several days keep a log of the articles that you find. Record the author, title, and source for each promising piece so that you can easily find it again. Briefly note the subject and point of view as well, so you can identify a range of possibilities.

Recalling Something You Have Already Read. What have you read lately that started you thinking? Return to a reading—a chapter in a history book, an article for sociology, a research report for biology.

Paraphrasing and Summarizing Complex Ideas. Do you feel overwhelmed by challenging reading? If so, read slowly and carefully. Try two common methods of recording and integrating ideas from sources into papers.

For more on paraphrase and summary, see Ch. 9 and D4–D5 in the Quick Research Guide, pp. A-29–A-30.

- Paraphrase: restate an author's complicated ideas fully but in your own language, using different wording and different sentence patterns.
- Summarize: reduce an author's main point to essentials, using your own clear, concise, and accurate language.

Accurately recording what a reading says can help you grasp its ideas, especially on literal levels. Once you understand what it says, you can agree, disagree, or question.

Reading Critically. Instead of just soaking up what a reading says, try a conversation with the writer. Criticize. Wonder. Argue back. Demand convincing evidence. Use the following checklist to get started.

CRITICAL READING CHECKLIST

☐ What problems and issues does the author raise?

☐ What is the author's purpose? Is it to explain or inform? To persuade? To amuse? In addition to this overall purpose, is the author trying to accomplish some other agenda?

☐ How does the author appeal to you as a reader? Where do you agree and disagree? Where do you want to say "Yeah, right!" or "I don't think so!"?

☐ How does this piece relate to your own experiences or thoughts? Have you encountered anything similar? Does the topic or approach engage you?

☐ Are there any important words or ideas that you don't understand? If so, do you need to reread or turn to a dictionary or reference book?

☐ What is the author's point of view? What does the author assume or take for granted? Where does the author reveal these assumptions? Do they make the selection seem weak or biased?

☐ Which statements are facts, verifiable by observation, firsthand testimony, or research? Which are opinions? Does one or the other dominate?

☐ Is the writer's evidence accurate, relevant, and sufficient? Is it persuasive?

For more on facts and opinions, see pp. 40–42.

For more on evaluating evidence, see C1–C3 in the Quick Research Guide, pp. A-26–A-28.

Analyzing Writing Strategies. Reading widely and deeply can reveal what others say and how they shape and state it. For some readings in this book, notes in the margin identify key features such as the introduction, thesis statement or main idea, major points, and supporting evidence. Ask questions such as these to help you identify writing strategies:

WRITING STRATEGIES CHECKLIST

☐ How does the author introduce the reading and try to engage the audience?

☐ Where does the author state or imply the main idea or thesis?

☐ How is the text organized? What main points develop the thesis?

☐ How does the author supply support — facts, data, statistics, expert opinions, experiences, observations, explanations, examples, other information?

☐ How does the author connect or emphasize ideas for readers?

☐ How does the author conclude the reading?

☐ What is the author's tone? How do the words and examples reveal the author's attitude, biases, or assumptions?

Learning from Another Writer: Critical Reading and Response

Alley Julseth was asked to read an essay on both literal and analytical levels. Her critical reading analysis presents a thoughtful personal response to Clive Thompson's "The New Literacy."

Alley Julseth   **Student Critical Reading Response**

Analyzing "The New Literacy"

For another reading
response, see
pp. 24–25.

Being part of a generation that spends an immense amount of time online, I find [1] it rather annoying to hear that youth today are slowly diminishing the art of writing. Because Facebook and Twitter have limited character space, I do use abbreviations such as s.m.h. (shaking my head), "abt" (about), and "u" (you). However, my simplistic way of writing informally for online media has no correlation with my formal writing. In "The New Literacy" essay, Clive Thompson indicates that this lack of correlation seems to be the case with many more students.

Thompson explores the idea that the advancing media is changing the way [2] students write. After citing Professor Sutherland blaming technology for "bleak, bald, sad shorthand" (qtd. in Thompson 584), he goes on to describe the Stanford Study of Writing, conducted by writing professor Andrea Lunsford. She studied over 14,000 examples of student writing from academic essays to e-mails and chats. From these samples, she learned that "young people today write far more than any generation before them" (585). I completely agree with this point based on the large volume I write socializing on the Internet. I believe that the time I spend online writing one-dimensional phrases does not weaken my formal writing as a student.

Thompson goes on to explain that the new way of writing on the Internet is [3] actually more similar to the Greek tradition of argument than to the essay and letter-writing tradition of the last half century. Lunsford concluded that "the students were remarkably adept at what rhetoricians call *kairos* — assessing their audience and adapting their tone and technique to get their point across" (585). Their Internet writing is like a conversation with another person.

I find this conclusion interesting. As I advance in my writing as a student, I [4] remember being taught as a child that there is a distinct line between writing an essay that is due to a teacher and writing a letter to a friend. Although the two are different, there are similarities as well. The nice thing about writing on the Internet is that I can choose what I write about and how I say it. When I'm writing to a friend, sticking to the point isn't exactly the goal, but I do get my main point across. However, I never write a formal essay unless it is assigned. Like the Stanford students, I do not look forward to writing an essay simply for the grade. Writing for a prompt I did not choose does not allow me to put my full-hearted passion into the essay. When I was younger, I wrote essays that were more bland and straight to the point. As I write now, I try to think as though I am reading to a room full of people, keeping my essay as interesting as I can.

Thompson ends his piece on the importance of good teaching. This importance is [5] true; teaching is the way students learn how to draw that line between formal and informal writing and how to write depending on audience. I appreciate and completely agree with Thompson's essay. I feel that he describes the younger generation very well. He is pushing away what high-brow critics say, and he is saying we are almost inventing a new way of writing.

Works Cited

Thompson, Clive. "The New Literacy." *The Bedford Guide for College Writers*. 10th ed. Ed. X. J. Kennedy, Dorothy M. Kennedy, and Marcia F. Muth. Boston: Bedford, 2014. 584–87. Print.

Questions to Start You Thinking

Meaning

1. According to Julseth, what is the issue that Thompson raises, and what is his position on this topic? Where does Julseth present this information?

2. What are Julseth's main points in her analysis?

3. How does Julseth apply this reading to her own life?

Writing Strategies

4. How has Julseth demonstrated both literal and critical reading responses?

5. How does Julseth develop her analysis? What kinds of material does she draw from the essay?

Learning by Doing 🎦 Reading Critically

Using the advice in this chapter, critically read the following *Scientific American* essay, written by the author of *The Believing Brain*. First, add your own notes and comments in the margin, responding on both literal and analytical levels. Second, add notes about writing strategies. (Sample annotations are supplied to help you get started.) Finally, write a brief summary of the reading and your own well-reasoned conclusions about it.

For a sample annotated passage, see p. 21.

Michael Shermer

The Science of Righteousness

Which of these two narratives most closely matches your political perspective? 1

Once upon a time people lived in societies that were unequal and oppressive, 2
*where the rich got richer and the poor got exploited. Chattel slavery, child labor,
economic inequality, racism, sexism and discriminations of all types abounded
until the liberal tradition of fairness, justice, care and equality brought about a free
and fair society. And now conservatives want to turn back the clock in the name of
greed and God.*

Once upon a time people lived in societies that embraced values and tradition, 3
*where people took personal responsibility, worked hard, enjoyed the fruits of their
labor and through charity helped those in need. Marriage, family, faith, honor, loyalty, sanctity, and respect for authority and the rule of law brought about a free and
fair society. But then liberals came along and destroyed everything in the name of
"progress" and utopian social engineering.*

Although we may quibble over the details, political science research 4
shows that the great majority of people fall on a left-right spectrum with
these two grand narratives as bookends. And the story we tell about ourselves reflects the ancient tradition of "once upon a time things were bad,
and now they're good thanks to our party" or "once upon a time things
were good, but now they're bad thanks to the other party." So consistent
are we in our beliefs that if you hew to the first narrative, I predict you read
the *New York Times*, listen to progressive talk radio, watch CNN, are prochoice and anti-gun, adhere to separation of church and state, are in favor
of universal health care, and vote for measures to redistribute wealth and
tax the rich. If you lean toward the second narrative, I predict you read the
Wall Street Journal, listen to conservative talk radio, watch Fox News, are
pro-life and anti-gun control, believe America is a Christian nation that
should not ban religious expressions in the public sphere, are against universal health care, and vote against measures to redistribute wealth and tax
the rich.

Why are we so predictable and tribal in our politics? In his remarkably 5
enlightening book, *The Righteous Mind: Why Good People Are Divided by Politics
and Religion* (Pantheon, 2012), University of Virginia psychologist Jonathan
Haidt argues that to both liberals and conservatives, members of the other
party are not just wrong; they are righteously wrong—morally suspect and
even dangerous. "Our righteous minds made it possible for human beings,"
Haidt argues, "to produce large cooperative groups, tribes, and nations
without the glue of kinship. But at the same time, our righteous minds
guarantee that our cooperative groups will always be cursed by moralistic
strife." Thus, he shows, morality binds us together into cohesive groups but
blinds us to the ideas and motives of those in other groups.

The evolutionary Rubicon that our species crossed hundreds of thou-   6 *Rubicon??*
sands of years ago that led to the moral hive mind was a result of "shared in-
tentionality," which is "the ability to share mental representations of tasks
that two or more of [our ancestors] were pursuing together. For example,
while foraging, one person pulls down a branch while the other plucks the
fruit, and they both share the meal." Chimps tend not to display this behavior, Haidt says, but "when early humans began to share intentions, their
ability to hunt, gather, raise children, and raid their neighbors increased ex-
ponentially. Everyone on the team now had a mental representation of the
task, knew that his or her partners shared the same representation, knew
when a partner had acted in a way that impeded success or that hogged the
spoils, and reacted negatively to such violations." Examples of modern political violations include Democrat John Kerry being accused of being a "flip-
flopper" for changing his mind and Republican Mitt Romney declaring
himself "severely conservative" when it was suggested he was wishy-washy in
his party affiliation.

Our dual moral nature leads Haidt to conclude that we need both liberals   7
and conservatives in competition to reach a livable middle ground. As philosopher John Stuart Mill noted a century and a half ago: "A party of order or
stability, and a party of progress or reform, are both necessary elements of a
healthy state of political life."

Reading Online and Multimodal Texts

Traditionally, a literate person was someone who could read and write.
That definition remains current, but online technologies have vastly increased the complexity of reading and writing. Multimodal texts now
combine written materials with images, sounds, and motions. Such
texts cannot be confined to the fixed form of a printed page and may be
randomly or routinely updated. They also may be accessed flexibly as a
reader wanders through sites and follows links rather than paging
through the defined sequence of a bound book. More innovations,
unimaginable now, might well emerge even before you graduate from
college.

Learning to read and write effectively has likewise increased in complexity. Many people simply assume that a reader's eye routinely moves from
left to right, from one letter or word to the next. However, eye-movement
studies show that readers actually jump back and forth, skip letters and
words, and guess at words the eye skips. Online readers also may jump

e For an
interactive
Learning by Doing
activity on reading
online, go to Ch. 2:
**bedfordstmartins
.com/concisebedguide**.

For more on
responding to images,
see Ch. 10.

from line to line or chunk to chunk, scanning the page (see heat maps below). In addition, multimodal texts may draw the eye to, or from, the typical left-to-right, top-to-bottom path with an image. Analyzing the meaning or impact of an image may require "reading" its placement and arrangement.

What might these changes mean for you as a reader and writer? Your critical reading skills are likely to be increasingly useful. The essential challenge of deep, thoughtful reading applies to graphic novels, blogs, photo essays, and YouTube videos just as it applies to printed books, articles, and essays. In fact, some might argue that texts using multiple components and appealing to multiple senses require even more thorough scrutiny to grasp what they are saying and how they are saying it. Here are some suggestions about how you might apply your critical skills in these new contexts:

- Concentrate on your purpose to stay focused when you read online or multimodal texts, especially if those texts tug you further and further away from your original search or material.

- Create an online file, reading journal, research journal, or writer's blog so that you have a handy location for responding to new materials.

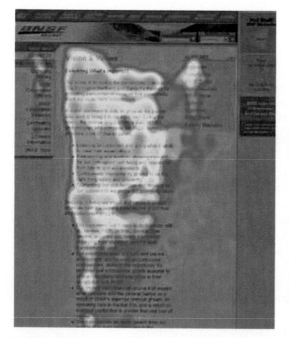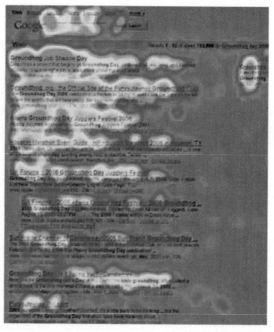

Heat maps from eye-tracking studies showing how people scan online pages in an F-shaped pattern.

- Bookmark meaty online readings, sites, or multimodal texts so you can easily return to examine their details. Consider what you see or hear, what the material suggests, and how it appeals to you.

- Read features and effects of visual or multimodal texts as carefully as you read words in print texts. Observe composition, symmetry, sequence, shape, color, texture, brightness, and other visual components.

- Listen for the presence and impact of audio characteristics such as sound effects (accuracy, clarity, volume, timing, emotional power), speech (pitch, tone, dialect, accent, pace), and music (instrumentation, vocals, melody, rhythm, harmony, musical roots, cuts, remix decisions).

- Examine visual or multimodal materials critically — analyzing components, synthesizing varied information, and evaluating effects.

- Evaluate research material that presents evidence to support your points or to challenge other views so that you rely on trustworthy sources.

- Secure any necessary permission to add someone else's visual or other material to your text and to credit your source appropriately.

- Generate even more ideas by rereading this chapter and thinking about how you could apply the skills presented here in new situations.

Learning by Doing 🗝 Reading a Web Site

Working with a small group — on a laptop in class, at the computer lab, or online — examine a Web site about a topic you might want to investigate. Critically "read" and discuss the site's text, images, organization, and other features that might persuade you that it would or would not be a reliable source.

Additional Writing Activities

1. **Source Activity.** Select a print or e-Pages essay from this book. Annotate the reading, marking both its key ideas and your own reactions to it. Review the text and your annotations, and then write two paragraphs, one summarizing the reading and the other explaining your personal response to it.

2. **Source Activity.** Follow up on Activity 1, working with others who have responded to the same essay. Share your summaries, noting the strengths of each. Then develop a collaborative summary that briefly and fairly presents the main points of the reading. (You can merge your existing summaries or

For the contents of *A Writer's Reader,* see pp. xxvi–xxvii or go to **bedfordstmartins.com /concisebedguide**.

make a fresh start.) When you finish the group summary, decide which methods of summarizing work best.

3. **Source Activity.** Follow up on Activity 1 by adding a critical reading analysis and response.

4. **Source Activity.** Select a passage from the textbook or readings for another course you are taking or have taken. Annotate the passage, and make some notes using the Critical Reading Checklist and the Writing Strategies Checklist (pp. 28–29) as guides. Pay special attention to the reading's purpose and its assumptions about its audience. Write a paragraph or two about your critical examination of the passage.

5. **Visual Activity.** Select a multimodal e-Pages selection, Web page, blog entry, YouTube video, photo from an online gallery, or another brief online text. "Read" this text critically, adapting reading processes and skills from this chapter. Write a short summary and response, including a link or a printout of the page or section to which you have responded.

Critical Thinking Processes

3

Critic, from the Greek word *kritikos,* means "one who can judge and discern"—in short, someone who thinks critically. College will have given you your money's worth if it leaves you better able to judge and discern—to determine what is more and less important, to make distinctions and recognize differences, to generalize from specifics, to draw conclusions from evidence, to grasp complex concepts, to choose wisely. The effective thinking that you will need in college, on the job, and in daily life is active and purposeful, not passive and ambling. It is critical thinking.

A Process of Critical Thinking

Critical thinking, like critical reading, draws on a cluster of intellectual strategies and skills.

For more on critical reading, see Ch. 2.

Critical Thinking Skill	Definition	Applications for Readers	Applications for Writers
Analysis	Breaking down information into its parts and elements	Analyzing the information in articles, reports, and books to grasp the facts and concepts they contain	Analyzing events, ideas, processes, and structures to understand them and explain them to readers
Synthesis	Putting together elements and parts to form new wholes	Synthesizing information from several sources, examining implications, and drawing conclusions supported by reliable evidence	Synthesizing source materials with your own thoughts in order to convey the unique combination to others
Evaluation	Judging according to standards or criteria	Evaluating a reading by determining standards for judging, applying them to the reading, and arriving at a conclusion about its value, significance, or credibility	Evaluating something in writing by convincing readers that your standards are reasonable and that the subject either does or does not meet those standards

These three activities—analysis, synthesis, and evaluation—are the core of critical thinking. They are not new to you, but applying them rigorously in college-level reading and writing may be. When you approach college reading and writing tasks, instructors will expect you (and you should expect yourself) to think, read, write, and think some more.

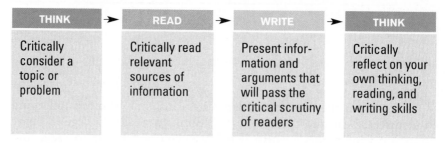

THINK	READ	WRITE	THINK
Critically consider a topic or problem	Critically read relevant sources of information	Present information and arguments that will pass the critical scrutiny of readers	Critically reflect on your own thinking, reading, and writing skills

Getting Started

You use critical thinking every day to explore problems step by step and reach solutions. Suppose you don't have enough money both to pay your tuition and to buy the car you need. First, you might pin down the causes of your financial problem. Next, you might examine your options to find the best solution, as shown in the graphic on page 39.

Learning by Doing Thinking Critically to Solve a Campus Problem

With classmates, identify a common problem for students at your college—juggling a busy schedule, parking on campus, making a class change, joining a social group, or some other issue. Working together, use critical thinking to explore the problem and identify possible solutions.

You can follow the same steps to examine many types of issues, helping you analyze a situation or dilemma, creatively synthesize to develop alternatives, and evaluate a possible course of action.

Learning by Doing Thinking Critically to Explore an Issue

You have worked hard on a group presentation that will be a major part of your grade—and each member of the group will get the same grade. Two days before the project is due, you discover that one group member has plagiarized heavily from sources well known to your instructor. Working together with classmates, use critical thinking to explore your problem and determine what you might do.

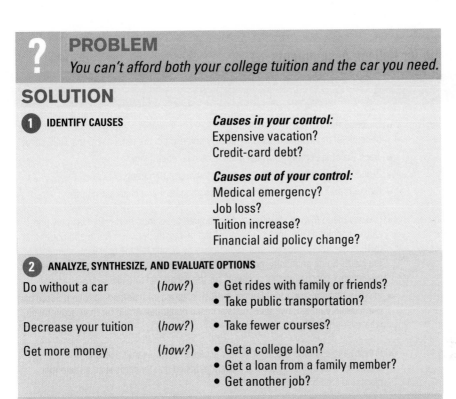

? **PROBLEM**
You can't afford both your college tuition and the car you need.

SOLUTION

1 IDENTIFY CAUSES

Causes in your control:
Expensive vacation?
Credit-card debt?

Causes out of your control:
Medical emergency?
Job loss?
Tuition increase?
Financial aid policy change?

2 ANALYZE, SYNTHESIZE, AND EVALUATE OPTIONS

Do without a car   (*how?*)   • Get rides with family or friends?
                                         • Take public transportation?

Decrease your tuition   (*how?*)   • Take fewer courses?

Get more money   (*how?*)   • Get a college loan?
                                         • Get a loan from a family member?
                                         • Get another job?

3 REACH A LOGICAL CONCLUSION

Apply for a short-term loan through the college for tuition.

Critical Thinking in Action

Applying Critical Thinking to Academic Problems

As you grapple with academic problems and papers, you'll be expected to use your critical thinking skills—analyzing, synthesizing, and evaluating—as you read and write. You may simply dive in, using each skill as needed. However, the very wording of an assignment or examination question may alert you to a skill that your instructor expects you to use, as the first sample assignment in each set illustrates in the chart below.

Learning by Doing 🖐 Thinking Critically to Respond to an Academic Problem

Working with a classmate or small group, select a sample assignment (not already explained) from the table above or from one of your classes. Explain how you would approach the assignment to demonstrate your critical thinking. Share your strategies for tackling college assignments.

Using Critical Thinking for College Assignments

Critical Thinking Skill	Sample College Writing Assignments
Analysis: breaking into parts and elements based on a principle	■ Describe the immediate causes of the 1929 stock market crash. (Analyze by using the principle of immediate causes to identify and explain the reasons for the 1929 crash.) ■ Trace the stages through which a bill becomes federal law. ■ Explain and illustrate the three dominant styles of parenting. ■ Define *romanticism,* identifying and illustrating its major characteristics.
Synthesis: combining parts and elements to form new wholes	■ Discuss the following statement: High-minded opposition to slavery was only one cause, and not a very important one, of the animosity between North and South that in 1861 escalated into civil war. (Synthesize by combining the causes or elements of the North-South animosity, going beyond the opposition to slavery, to form a new whole: your conclusion that accounts for the escalation into civil war.) ■ Imagine that you are a trial lawyer in 1921, charged with defending Nicola Sacco and Bartolomeo Vanzetti, two anarchists accused of murder. Argue for their acquittal on whatever grounds you can justify.
Evaluation: judging according to standards or criteria	■ Present and evaluate the most widely accepted theories that account for the disappearance of the dinosaurs. (Evaluate, based on standards such as scientific merit, the credibility of each theory.) ■ Defend or challenge the idea that houses and public buildings should be constructed to last no longer than twenty years. ■ Contrast the models of the solar system advanced by Copernicus and by Kepler, showing how the latter improved on the former.

Supporting Critical Thinking with Evidence

As you write a college paper, you try to figure out your purpose, position, and strategies for getting readers to follow your logic and accept your points. Your challenge, of course, is not just to think clearly but to demonstrate your thinking to others, to persuade them to pay attention to what you say. And sound evidence is what critical readers want to see.

For advice on using a few sources, see the Quick Research Guide, pp. A-20–A-38.

Sound evidence supports your main idea or thesis, convincing readers by substantiating your points. It also bolsters your credibility as a writer, demonstrating the merit of your position. When you write, you need to marshal enough appropriate evidence to clarify, explain, and support your ideas. Then you need to weave claims, evidence, and your own interpretations together into a clearly reasoned explanation or argument.

Types of Evidence

What is evidence? It is anything that demonstrates the soundness of a claim. Facts, statistics, expert testimony, and firsthand observations are four reliable forms of evidence. Other evidence might include examples, illustrations, details, and opinions. Depending on the purpose of your assignment, some kinds of evidence weigh more heavily than others. For example, readers might appreciate your memories of livestock care on the farm in an essay recalling your childhood summers. However, they would probably discount your memories in an argumentative paper about ethical agricultural methods unless you could show that your memories are representative or that you are an expert on the subject. Personal experience may strengthen an argument but generally is not sufficient as its sole support. If you are in doubt about the type of evidence an assignment requires, ask your instructor whether you should use sources or rely on personal experience and examples.

For more on using evidence in a paper that takes a stand, see pp. 133–38.

Facts. Facts are statements that can be verified objectively, by observation or by reading a reliable account. They are usually stated dispassionately: "If you pump the air out of a five-gallon varnish can, it will collapse." Of course, we accept many of our facts based on the testimony of others. For example, we believe that the Great Wall of China exists, although we may never have seen it with our own eyes.

Sometimes people say facts are true statements, but truth and sound evidence may be confused. Consider the truth of these statements:

The tree in my yard is an oak.	*True* because it can be verified
A kilometer is 1,000 meters.	*True* using the metric system
The speed limit on the highway is 65 miles per hour.	*True* according to law
Fewer fatal highway accidents have occurred since the new exit ramp was built.	*True* according to research studies
My favorite food is pizza.	*True* as an opinion
More violent criminals should receive the death penalty.	*True* as a belief
Murder is wrong.	*True* as a value judgment

Some would claim that each statement is true, but when you think critically, you should avoid treating opinions, beliefs, judgments, or personal experience as true in the same sense that verifiable facts and events are true.

Statistics. Statistics are facts expressed in numbers. What portion of American children are poor? According to statistics from the U.S. Census Bureau, 13.2 million children (or 18.2 percent of all children) lived in poverty in 2008 compared with 16.4 million (or 22.5 percent) in 2011. Clear as such figures seem, they may raise complex questions. For example, how significant is the increase in the poverty rate over three years? Has the percentage fluctuated or steadily increased? What percentage of children were poor over longer terms such as fifteen years or twenty?

Most writers, without trying to be dishonest, interpret statistics to help their causes. The statement "Fifty percent of the populace have incomes above the poverty level" might substantiate the fine job done by the government of a developing nation. Putting the statement another way—"Fifty percent of the populace have incomes below the poverty level"—might use the same statistic to show the inadequacy of the government's efforts.

Even though a writer is free to interpret a statistic, statistics should not be used to mislead. On the wrapper of a peanut candy bar, we read that a one-ounce serving contains only 150 calories. The claim is true, but the bar weighs 1.6 ounces. Gobble it all—more likely than eating 62 percent of it—and you'll ingest 240 calories, a heftier snack than the innocent statistic on the wrapper suggests. Because abuses make some readers automatically distrustful, use figures fairly when you write, and make sure they are accurate. If you doubt a statistic, compare it with figures reported by several other sources. Distrust a statistical report that differs from every other report unless it is backed by further evidence.

Expert Testimony. By "experts," we mean people with knowledge gained from study and experience in a particular field. The test of an expert is whether his or her expertise stands up to the scrutiny of others who are knowledgeable in that field. The views of Peyton Manning on how to play offense in football carry authority. So do the views of economist and former Federal Reserve chairman Alan Greenspan on what causes inflation. However, Manning's take on the economy or Greenspan's thoughts on football might not be authoritative. Also consider whether the expert has any bias or special interest that would affect reliability. Statistics on cases of lung cancer attributed to smoking might be better taken from government sources than from the tobacco industry.

Firsthand Observation. Firsthand observation is persuasive. It can add concrete reality to abstract or complex points. You might support the claim "The Meadowfield waste recycling plant fails to meet state guidelines" by recalling your own observations: "When I visited the plant last January, I was struck by the number of open waste canisters and by the lack of protective gear for the workers who handle these toxic materials daily."

As readers, most of us tend to trust the writer who declares, "I was there. This is what I saw." Sometimes that trust is misplaced, however, so always be wary of a writer's claim to have seen something that no other evidence supports. Ask yourself, Is this writer biased? Might the writer have (intentionally or unintentionally) misinterpreted what he or she saw? Of course, your readers will scrutinize your firsthand observations, too; take care to reassure them that your observations are unbiased and accurate.

Few people save some of a candy bar to eat later.

For more on observation, see Ch. 5.

Learning by Doing 🎥 Looking for Evidence

Using the issue you explored for the activity on page 38, what would you need to support your identification, explanation, or solution of the problem? Working with classmates, identify the kinds of evidence that would be most useful. Where or how might you find such evidence?

For more on selecting evidence to persuade readers, see pp. 136–37.

Testing Evidence

As both a reader and a writer, always critically test and question evidence to see whether it is strong enough to carry the weight of the writer's claims.

For advice on evaluating sources of evidence, see C in the Quick Research Guide, pp. A-26–A-28.

EVIDENCE CHECKLIST

☐ Is it accurate?
- Do the facts and figures seem accurate based on what you have found in published sources, reports by others, or reference works?
- Are figures or quoted facts copied correctly?

☐ Is it reliable?
- Is the source trustworthy and well regarded?
- Does the source acknowledge any commercial, political, advocacy, or other bias that might affect the quality of its information?
- Does the writer supplying the evidence have appropriate credentials or experience? Is the writer respected as an expert in the field?
- Do other sources agree with the information?

☐ Is it up-to-date?
- Are facts and statistics — such as population figures — current?
- Is the information from the latest sources?

☐ Is it to the point?
- Does the evidence back the exact claim made?
- Is the evidence all pertinent? Does any of it drift from the point to interesting but irrelevant evidence?

☐ Is it representative?
- Are examples typical of all the things included in the writer's position?
- Are examples balanced? Do they present the topic or issue fairly?
- Are contrary examples acknowledged?

☐ Is it appropriately complex?
- Is the evidence sufficient to account for the claim made?
- Does it avoid treating complex things superficially?
- Does it avoid needlessly complicating simple things?

For information on mistakes in thinking, see pp. 51–52 and pp. 143–44.

☐ Is it sufficient and strong enough to back the claim and persuade readers?
- Are the amount and quality of the evidence appropriate for the claim and for the readers?
- Is the evidence aligned with the existing knowledge of readers?
- Does the evidence answer the questions readers are likely to ask?
- Is the evidence vivid and significant?

Using Evidence to Appeal to Your Audience

For more on appeals, see pp. 138–40.

One way to select evidence and to judge whether it is appropriate and sufficient is to consider the types of appeals — logical, emotional, and ethical. Most effective arguments work on all three levels, using all three types of appeals with evidence that supports all three.

Logical Appeal (Logos)

When writers use a logical appeal (*logos,* or "word" in Greek), they appeal to the reader's mind or intellect. This appeal relies on evidence that is factual, objective, clear, and relevant. Critical readers expect to find logical evidence that supports major claims and statements.

> Example: If a writer were arguing for term limits for legislators, she wouldn't want to base her argument on the evidence that some long-term legislators were or weren't reelected (irrelevant) or that the current system is unfair to young people who want to get into politics (illogical). Instead, she might argue that the absence of term limits encourages corruption, using evidence of legislators who repaid lobbyists for campaign contributions with key votes.

Emotional Appeal (Pathos)

When writers use an emotional appeal (*pathos,* or "suffering" in Greek), they appeal to the reader's heart. They choose language, facts, quotations, examples, and images that evoke emotional responses. Of course, convincing writing does touch readers' hearts as well as their minds. Without this heartfelt tug, a strict logical appeal may seem cold and dehumanized.

> Example: If a writer opposed hunting seals for their fur, he might combine statistics about the number of seals killed each year and the overall population decrease with a vivid description of baby seals being slaughtered.

Some writers use emotional words and sentimental examples to manipulate readers — to arouse their sympathy, pity, or anger in order to convert them without much logical evidence—but dishonest emotional appeals may alienate readers.

> Example: Instead of basing an argument against a political candidate on pitiful images of scrawny children living in roach-infested squalor, a good writer would report the candidate's voting record on issues that affect children.

Ethical Appeal (Ethos)

When writers use an ethical appeal (*ethos,* or "character" in Greek), they call on the reader's sense of fairness and trust. They select and present evidence in a way that will make the audience trust them, respect their judgment, and believe what they have to say. The best logical argument in the world falls flat when readers don't take the writer seriously. How can you use an ethical appeal to establish your credibility as a writer? First you need to establish your credentials in the field through experience, reading, or interviews that helped you learn about the subject.

> Example: If you are writing about water quality, tell your readers about the odor, taste, and color of your local water. Identify medical or environmental experts you contacted or whose reports you read.

Demonstrate your knowledge through the information you present, the experts and sources you cite, and the depth of understanding you convey. Establish a rapport with readers by indicating values and attitudes that you share with them and by responding seriously to opposing arguments. Finally, use language that is precise, clear, and appropriate in tone.

Learning by Doing 📷 Identifying Types of Appeals

Bring to class or post links for the editorial or opinion page from a newspaper, newsmagazine, or blog with a strong point of view. Read some of the pieces, and identify the types of appeals used by each author to support his or her point. With classmates, evaluate the effectiveness of these appeals.

Learning from Another Writer: Rhetorical Analysis

Richard Anson was asked to read an outside selection critically and then write a brief rhetorical analysis to identify the reading's audience and its writer's logical, emotional, and ethical appeals to that audience. Because his class was analyzing the 2012 presidential election campaign, Anson found an essay with a historical perspective on the involvement of young adults in current events.

Richard Anson   **Student Rhetorical Analysis**

Young Americans and Media News

In a world where young adults may be more interested in *American Idol* than in who is running for president, it is critical to take a step back and look at the factors involved prior to the presidential elections of 2008 and 2012. Stephen Earl Bennett has done just that in "Young Americans' Indifference to Media Coverage of Public Affairs," an essay that appeared in *PS: Political Science & Politics*, a journal that focuses on contemporary politics and the teaching thereof. Being featured in this journal, as well as being a Fellow of the Center for the Study of Democratic Citizenship at the University of Cincinnati, easily establishes Bennett's trustworthy character or ethos.   1

Given where the article was published, it is safe to say that he is trying to reach an audience of professors in the field of political science and possibly policy makers as well. With this assumption, however, Bennett makes an error. His essay focuses solely on facts and numbers and not at all on the audience's emotions. A reader would be hard-pressed to find any appeals to emotion (pathos) in his essay at all and could liken it to an instruction manual on American youth's indifference to current events. Professors may be more likely to respond to the logical appeal (logos) of facts and numbers than some other readers, but they are still human, and few humans enjoy reading instruction manuals for fun. For example, Bennett starts off with "Although young Americans are normally less engaged in politics than their elders (Converse with Niemi 1971), today's youth are more withdrawn from public affairs than earlier birth cohorts were when they were young (Bennett 1997)" (Bennett 1). In this first sentence alone, Bennett is citing from two other sources, one of which happens to be his own. There is nothing wrong with jumping right in, but this is a little over the top and very dry for an introduction.   2

The idea that more people vote for *American Idol* than their own president in the leading democratic nation in the world is just pathetic. There's no other way to describe it. On this point, Bennett agrees with other readings discussed in class. He also agrees that current affairs and news need to be more widely taught in schools across the nation and that something needs to be done to attract American youth to the news. The Bennett article was published in 1998, and maybe the interest of young voters in the 2008 and 2012 presidential elections shows that Americans have started listening.   3

Works Cited

Bennett, Stephen Earl. "Young Americans' Indifference to Media Coverage of Public Affairs." *PS: Political Science & Politics* 31.3 (1998): 535–41. *General OneFile.* Web. 15 Nov. 2012.

Questions to Start You Thinking

Meaning

1. According to Anson, what position about the political engagement of young people does Bennett take?

2. What is Anson's position about Bennett's article?

Writing Strategies

3. Why do you think that Anson begins with information about the article and its author instead of a summary of Bennett's main points?

4. Why do you think that Anson decided to arrange his discussion of the three appeals — ethos, pathos, and logos — in that order?

Presenting Your Critical Thinking

Why do you have to worry about critical thinking? Isn't it enough just to tell everybody else what you think? That tactic probably works fine when you casually debate with your friends. After all, they already know you, your opinions, and your typical ways of thinking. They may even find your occasional rant entertaining. Whether they agree or disagree, they probably tolerate your ideas because they are your friends.

For more on taking a stand, see Ch. 7; for more on evaluation, see Ch. 8; and for more on supporting a position, see Ch. 9.

When you write a paper in college, however, you face a different type of audience, one that expects you to explain what you assume, what you advocate, and why you hold that position. That audience wants to learn the specifics — reasons you find compelling, evidence that supports your view, and connections that relate each point to your position. Because approaches and answers to complex problems may differ, your college audience expects reasoning, not emotional pleading or bullying or preaching.

How you reason and how you present your reasoning are important parts of gaining the confidence of college readers. College papers typically develop their points based on logic, not personal opinions or beliefs. Most are organized logically, often as a series of reasons, each making a claim, a statement, or an assertion that is backed up with persuasive supporting evidence. Your assignment or your instructor may recommend ways such as the following for showing your critical thinking.

Reasoning Deductively or Inductively. When you state a *generalization,* you present your broad general point, viewpoint, or conclusion.

For more about the statement-support pattern, see A in the Quick Research Guide, pp. A-21–A-24.

> The admissions requirements at Gerard College are unfair.

On the other hand, when you supply a *particular,* you present an instance, a detail, an example, an item, a case, or other specific evidence to demonstrate that a general statement is reasonable.

DEDUCTIVE PATTERN

FIRST: Broad generalization or conclusion. **THEN:** Details, examples, facts, and supporting particulars.

FIRST: Particulars, details, examples, facts. **THEN:** Concluding generalization.

INDUCTIVE PATTERN

A Gerard College application form shows the information collected by the admissions office. Under current policies, standardized test scores are weighted more heavily than better predictors of performance, such as high school grades. Qualified students who do not test well often face a frustrating admissions process, as Irma Lang's situation illustrates.

Your particulars consist of details that back up your broader point; your generalizations connect the particulars so that you can move beyond isolated, individual cases.

Most college papers are organized *deductively*. They begin with a general statement (often a thesis) and then present particular cases to support or apply it. Readers like this pattern because it reduces mystery; they learn right away what the writer wants to show. Writers like this pattern because it helps them state up front what they want to accomplish (even if they have to figure some of that out as they write and state it more directly as they revise). Papers organized deductively sacrifice suspense but gain directness and clarity.

For more about thesis statements, see Ch. 13.

On the other hand, some papers are organized *inductively*. They begin with the particulars—a persuasive number of instances, examples, or details—and lead up to the larger generalization that they support. Because readers have to wait for the generalization, this pattern allows them time to adjust to an unexpected conclusion that they might initially reject. For this reason, writers favor this pattern when they anticipate resistance from their audience and want to move gradually toward the broader point.

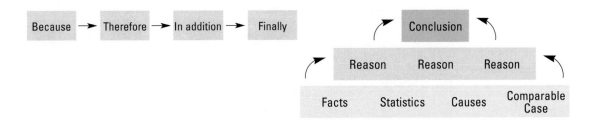

Building Sequences and Scaffolds. You may use several strategies for presenting your reasoning, depending on what you want to show and how you think you can show it most persuasively. You may develop a line of reasoning, a series of points and evidence, running one after another in a sequence or building on one another to support a persuasive scaffold.

Developing Logical Patterns. The following patterns are often used to organize reasoning in college papers. They can help show relationships but don't automatically prove them. In fact, each has advantages but may also have disadvantages, as the sample strengths and weaknesses illustrate.

> *Pattern:* Least to Most
> *Advantage:* Building up to the best points can produce a strong finish.
> *Disadvantage:* Holding back on strong points makes readers wait.

> *Pattern:* Most to Least
> *Advantage:* Beginning with the strongest point can create a forceful opening.
> *Disadvantage:* Tapering off with weaker points may cause readers to lose interest.

LEAST TO MOST PATTERN

Least persuasive → More persuasive → Most persuasive →

MOST TO LEAST PATTERN

Most persuasive → Less persuasive → Least persuasive →

> *Pattern:* Comparison and Contrast
> *Advantage:* Readers can easily relate comparable points about things of like kind.
> *Disadvantage:* Some similarities or differences don't guarantee or prove others.

For more on comparison and contrast, see Ch. 6.

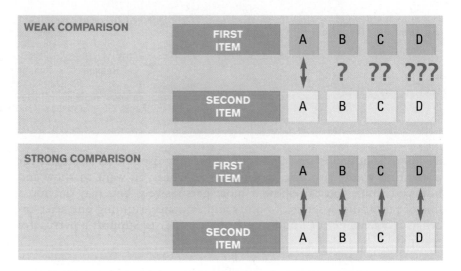

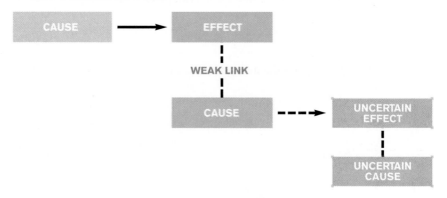

Pattern: Cause and Effect

Advantage: Tracing causes or effects can tightly relate and perhaps predict events.

Disadvantage: Weak links can call into question all relationships in a series of events.

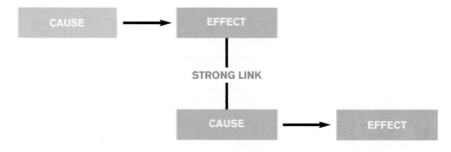

	Sound Reasoning	Weak Reasoning
Comparisons	Comparison that uses substantial likeness to project other similarities: Like the third graders in the innovative reading programs just described, the children in this town also could become better readers.	Inaccurate comparison that relies on slight or superficial likenesses to project other similarities: Like kittens eagerly stalking mice in the fields, young readers should gobble up the tasty tales that were the favorites of their grandparents.
Causes and Effects	Causal analysis that relies on well-substantiated and specific connections relating events and outcomes: City water reserves have suffered from below-average rainfall, above-average heat, and steadily increasing consumer demand.	Faulty reasoning that oversimplifies causes, confuses them with coincidences, or assumes a first event must cause a second: One cause—and one alone—accounts for the ten-year drought that has dried up local water supplies.
Reasons	Logical reasons that are supported by relevant evidence and presented with fair and thoughtful consideration: As the recent audit indicates, all campus groups that spend student activity fees should prepare budgets, keep clear financial records, and substantiate expenses.	Faulty reasons that rely on bias, emotion, or unrelated personal traits or that accuse, flatter, threaten, or inspire fear: All campus groups, especially the arrogant social groups, must stop ripping off the average student's fees and threatening to run college costs sky high.
Evidence	Evidence that is accurate, reliable, current, relevant, fair, and sufficient to persuade readers: Both the statistics from international agencies and the accounts of Sudanese refugees summarized earlier suggest that, while a fair immigration policy needs to account for many complexities, it should not lose sight of compassion.	Weak evidence that is insufficient, dated, unreliable, slanted, or emotional: As five-year-old Lannie's frantic flight across the Canadian border in 1988 proves, refugees from all the war-torn regions around the world should be welcomed here because this is America, land of the free.
Conclusions	Solid conclusions that are based on factual evidence and recognize multiple options or complications: As the recent campus wellness study has demonstrated, college students need education about healthy food and activity choices.	Hasty conclusions that rely on insufficient evidence, assumptions, or simplistic two-option choices: The campus health facility should refuse to treat students who don't eat healthy foods and exercise daily.

Learning by Doing 🔲 Testing Logical Patterns

Continuing with the issue and possible evidence you explored for the activities on pages 38 and 43, work with classmates to figure out several patterns you could use to present your evidence to an audience of people who could help to solve the problem or address the issue. What would be the advantages or disadvantages of each pattern, given your issue, audience, and possible evidence?

For an interactive Learning by Doing activity on analyzing logic, go to Ch. 3: **bedfordstmartins .com/concisebedguide**.

For specific logical fallacies, see pp. 143–44.

Avoiding Faulty Thinking

Common mistakes in thinking can distort evidence or lead to wrong conclusions. How can you avoid such mistakes as you write or spot them as you read? A good strategy is to look carefully at the ways in which you (or the author of a reading) describe events, relate ideas, identify reasons, supply evidence, and draw conclusions.

Use the following questions to help you refine your reasoning as you plan, draft, or revise a college paper:

LOGICAL REASONING CHECKLIST

☐ Have you reviewed your assignment or syllabus, looking for advice or requirements about the kind of reasoning or evidence expected?

☐ Have you developed your reasoning on a solid foundation? Are your initial assumptions sound? Do you need to identify, explain, or justify them?

☐ Is your thesis or position stated clearly? Are its terms explained or defined?

☐ Have you presented your reasons for thinking your thesis is sound? Have you arranged them in a sequence that will make sense to your audience? Have you used transitions to introduce and connect them so readers can't miss them?

☐ Have you used evidence that your audience will respect to support each reason you present? Have you favored objective, research-based evidence (facts, statistics, and expert testimony that others can substantiate) rather than personal experiences or beliefs that others cannot or may not share?

☐ Have you explained your evidence so that your audience can see how it supports your points and applies to your thesis? Have you used transitions to specify relationships for readers?

☐ Have you enhanced your own credibility by acknowledging, rather than ignoring, other points of view? Have you integrated or countered these views?

☐ Have you adjusted your tone and style so you come across as reasonable and fair-minded? Have you avoided arrogant claims about proving (rather than showing) points?

☐ Have you credited any sources as expected by academic readers?

▬▬▬▬

Learning by Doing 🔲 Analyzing Reasoning

Analyze the following newspaper column, which uses irony to make its case. Identify its stated and actual position, its sequence of reasons or points, its supporting evidence, and its methods of appealing to readers. The column by David Rothkopf, author of *Power, Inc.*, appeared in the *Denver Post* on August 23, 2012.

David Rothkopf

A Proposal to Draft America's Elderly

I t is sadly apparent to those who travel this great country—when they see   1
along the highways aging bikers with long grey ponytails or on the beaches men who are long past the age when they should be seen in Speedos or at political rallies, where they quake in fear over competing claims about retirement benefits—that the elderly are not only an eyesore but also a growing threat to our society because of their cost, the speed at which they drive, and because, absent real work to do or support from their impoverished government, they could easily turn to crime or worse, turn to us, their relatives, and seek to move into our basement or family rooms.

I think it is agreed by all Americans that this prodigious number of bur-   2
densome old folks visible to all as they conduct their morning mall walks or take up valuable bench space in public parks are—given the present deplorable state of the nation—a source of great unease, debate and public dissension and therefore whoever could find a fair, cheap, and easy method of making these chronologically challenged Americans sound and useful members of the commonwealth would earn the gratitude of the public to such a degree that he would have a statue erected in his honor.

The great advantage to my program is instantly apparent to anyone   3
who hears it, even those with profound intellectual deficits like reality-show contestants and members of Congress: It solves not only the greatest problem the country faces—that of ensuring care for the elderly—but it also does so instantly and in such a sweeping nature that it might once again reknit the rent fabric of our polity and restore unity to a fractured, hurting society.

The aforementioned program is the draft, nationwide conscription, and   4
my proposal is that we institute mandatory military service for all Americans over 65.

Can you think of a single proposal that so directly addresses the shared   5
concerns of an aging nation for its oldest citizens while at the same time guaranteeing the public care for those seniors sought by Democrats and providing for the strengthened national defense so important to all Republicans? One that helps trim our fiscal deficit and eliminate the retirement health-care deficit altogether?

This approach would immediately place our elderly into the care of the   6
government via an institution, the military, which is accustomed to providing for every need of its members and has a long history of putting into productive use those whom age also renders nearly impossible to deal with: teenagers.

? What tone does the writer use to introduce his argument?

? Do all Americans agree with the writer? Why does the writer claim that they do?

? Is this a serious proposal? How do you know that?

? How persuasive are the benefits that the writer identifies?

Second, because every older American would be in the military, we would 7
actually have no need at all for Medicare.

Third, because the nature of modern warfare is increasingly limited to 8
electronic, cyber, drone-based or other joystick-driven activities, the physical
limitations of many older Americans should not be a problem.

Fourth, because it is unavoidable that conflicts do occur, were we to field 9
an army of the elderly, we would eliminate war's greatest tragedy: the un-
timely death of the young who have historically been called upon to fight.
This would have the added benefit of significantly reducing the health-care
and Social Security costs these honored dead might otherwise have incurred,
especially those associated with the last six months of life.

The program would get aging drivers off the roads. Similarly, programs 10
like "Don't Ask, Don't Tell" would be unnecessary, as most members of the
military won't remember what the question was in the first place.

Supposing that there are 40 million Americans over the age of 65, and 11
48 million on Medicare, this would clearly both largely remove the problems associated with that failing program and, at the same time, provide
a large pool of people for military service. While there are currently 73
million people between the ages of 18 and 49 and thus eligible for military service, it must be remembered that a draft would bring far more
people into service than the approximately 2.25 million Americans in active or reserve service today.

What other
ideas might be
proposed?

Given the obvious merits of such a program, I think it is fair to ask 12
that no man or woman take issue with it unless he or she has a superior
idea.

Additional Writing Activities

1. List your main reasons (and some supporting details) for and against
   doing something: going somewhere, joining something, buying something, or the like. Then outline one presentation directed to someone
   who would agree with you and another directed to someone who would
   disagree. Do your two plans differ? If so, how and why?

2. Working with a group, survey several opinion pieces. Refer to Presenting
   Your Critical Thinking (pp. 47–51) to help you identify the patterns the
   writers use to present their views. Then speculate about why they chose to
   organize as they did.

3. Divide a page into three columns, or create a table in a file. Label each
   column with a type of appeal: logical, emotional, ethical. Pick a specific
   local issue about which you have a definite view, and identify a specific

audience that you might be able to persuade to agree with, or at least consider, your position. Start filling in the columns with persuasive evidence that supports your view. Discuss your table with one or two classmates to decide what evidence would most effectively appeal to your audience.

4. **Source Activity.** Select an editorial, opinion column, or brief blog entry that takes a clear stand on an issue. Analyze its stand, main points, evidence, and appeals to readers. Write a paragraph explaining how it makes its case. Then write a second paragraph stating and justifying your judgment about how well it succeeds.

5. If you disagree with the opinion piece that you analyzed in Activity 4, write a paragraph or two explaining and supporting your own point of view.

6. **Visual Activity.** Select a Web page, a powerful photo, a cartoon, a graphical display of information, or another text that uses an image to help make its point about an issue. Adapt the critical thinking skills in this chapter to analyze this visual text, examining its evidence and its appeals to viewers. Write a paragraph or two explaining how it makes its case, including a link to the item or a printout.

A WRITER'S SITUATIONS

PART TWO

A Writer's Situations Contents

4 **Recalling an Experience**   60

5 **Observing a Scene**   80

6 **Comparing and Contrasting**   99

7 **Taking a Stand**   119

8 **Evaluating and Reviewing**   148

9 **Supporting a Position with Sources**   166

10 **Responding to Visual Representations**   200

11 **Writing Online**   227

Introduction: Writing in College

The chapters in Part Two form the core of *The Concise Bedford Guide*. Each presents a writing situation and then guides you as you write a paper in response. You'll develop skills in recalling, observing, comparing and contrasting, taking a stand, evaluating and reviewing, and supporting a position with sources. In addition, two final chapters lead you through common situations that most students encounter — writing about visuals and writing online.

For information and journal questions about the Part Two photograph, see the last two pages of the Appendices.

The first six writing assignments are arranged roughly in order of increasing complexity — that is, according to the level of critical reading and thinking required. Some require analysis — breaking something down into its components to understand it better. Others require synthesis — combining information from various sources with your own ideas and conclusions in order to achieve a new perspective. The complex task of evaluating draws on several critical strategies, establishing criteria for judging and then analyzing your subject to see how well it meets your standards. Taken together, these chapters present many of the writing situations you will meet in other college courses and in your career. Their advice and your experience as a writer will act as resources when you meet unfamiliar writing situations or need to marshal appropriate evidence as you write.

Recalling an Experience

Responding to an Image

Look carefully at one of the photographs in the grid. In your view, when was this photograph taken? Who might the person or people be? Where are they, and why are they there? What are they doing? What relationships and emotions does the picture suggest with its focal point and arrangement? Write about an experience the image helps you recall or about a possible explanation of events in this picture. Use vivid detail to convey what happened to you or what might have happened to the people in the picture.

Writing from recall is writing from memory, a writer's richest—and handiest—resource. Recall is clearly necessary when you write of a personal experience, a favorite place, a memorable person. Recall also helps you probe your memories of specific events. For example, in a literacy narrative you might examine the significance of your experiences learning to read or write. On the other hand, in a reflection you might begin with an incident that you recall and then explore the ideas that evolve from it.

Even when an instructor hands you a subject that seems to have nothing to do with you, your memory is the first place to look. Suppose you have to write a psychology paper about how advertisers prey on consumers' fears. Begin with what you remember. What ads have sent chills down your back? What ads have suggested that their products could save you from a painful social blunder, a lonely night, or a deadly accident? All by itself, memory may not give you enough to write about, but you will rarely go wrong if you start by jotting down something remembered.

Why Recalling an Experience Matters

In a College Course
- You recall your experiences of visiting or living in another region or country to add authority to your sociology paper on cultural differences.
- You recall and record both routine and unusual events in the reflective journal you keep during your internship or clinical experience.

In the Workplace
- You recall past successes, failures, or customer comments to provide compelling reasons for adopting your proposals for changing a product or service.

In Your Community
- You recall your own experiences taking standardized tests to add impact to your appeal to the local school board to change the testing program at your child's school.

When have you recalled experiences in your writing? What did these recollections add to your writing? In what situations might you rely on recollection again in future writing?

Learning from Other Writers

Here are two samples of good writing from recall—one by a professional writer, one by a college student. To help you begin to analyze the first reading, look at the notes in the margin. They identify features such as the main idea, or thesis, and the first of the main events that support it in a paper written from recall.

As You Read These Recollections

For another essay that recalls an experience, read "Mother Tongue" by Amy Tan in Ch. e-1: **bedfordstmartins.com /concisebedguide**.

As you read these essays, ask yourself the following questions:

1. Is the perspective of the essay primarily that of a child or an adult? Why do you think so?

2. What does the author realize after reflecting on the events recalled? Does the realization come soon after the experience or later, when the writer examines the events from a more mature perspective?

3. How does the realization change the individual?

Russell Baker

The Art of Eating Spaghetti

In this essay from his autobiography *Growing Up* (1982), columnist Russell Baker recalls being sixteen in urban Baltimore and wondering what to do with his life.

Introduction

The only thing that truly interested me was writing, and I knew that sixteen-year-olds did not come out of high school and become writers. I thought of writing as something to be done only by the rich. It was so obviously not real work, not a job at which you could earn a living. Still, I had begun to think of myself as a writer. It was the only thing for which I seemed to have the smallest talent, and, silly though it sounded when I told people I'd like to be a writer, it gave me a way of thinking about myself which satisfied my need to have an identity. 1

THESIS stating main idea

The notion of becoming a writer had flickered off and on in my head since the Belleville days, but it wasn't until my third year in high school that the possibility took hold. Until then I'd been bored by everything associated with English courses. I found English grammar dull and baffling. I hated the assignments to turn out "compositions," and went at them like heavy labor, turning out leaden, lackluster paragraphs that were agonies for teachers to read and for me to write. The classics thrust on me to read seemed as deadening as chloroform. 2

Major event 1

When our class was assigned to Mr. Fleagle for third-year English I anticipated another grim year in that dreariest of subjects. Mr. Fleagle was notorious among City students for dullness and inability to inspire. He was said to be stuffy, dull, and hopelessly out of date. To me he looked to be sixty or sev- 3

Lady Macbeth, played by Maria Guleghina, Royal Opera House, London.

enty and prim to a fault. He wore primly severe eyeglasses, his wavy hair was primly cut and primly combed. He wore prim vested suits with neckties blocked primly against the collar buttons of his primly starched white shirts. He had a primly pointed jaw, a primly straight nose, and a prim manner of speaking that was so correct, so gentlemanly, that he seemed a comic antique.

I anticipated a listless,° unfruitful year with Mr. Fleagle and for a long time was not disappointed. We read *Macbeth*. Mr. Fleagle loved *Macbeth* and wanted us to love it too, but he lacked the gift of infecting others with his own passion. He tried to convey the murderous ferocity of Lady Macbeth one day by reading aloud the passage that concludes

> . . . I have given suck, and know
> How tender 'tis to love the babe that milks me.
> I would, while it was smiling in my face,
> Have plucked my nipple from his boneless gums. . . .

The idea of prim Mr. Fleagle plucking his nipple from boneless gums was too much for the class. We burst into gasps of irrepressible snickering. Mr. Fleagle stopped.

"There is nothing funny, boys, about giving suck to a babe. It is the — the very essence of motherhood, don't you see."

He constantly sprinkled his sentences with "don't you see." It wasn't a question but an exclamation of mild surprise at our ignorance. "Your

4

Support for major event 1

5

6

---

listless: Lacking energy or enthusiasm.

pronoun needs an antecedent, don't you see," he would say, very primly. "The purpose of the Porter's scene, boys, is to provide comic relief from the horror, don't you see."

Late in the year we tackled the informal essay. "The essay, don't you see, is the . . ." My mind went numb. Of all forms of writing, none seemed so boring as the essay. Naturally we would have to write informal essays. Mr. Fleagle distributed a homework sheet offering us a choice of topics. None was quite so simpleminded as "What I Did on My Summer Vacation," but most seemed to be almost as dull. I took the list home and dawdled until the night before the essay was due. Sprawled on the sofa, I finally faced up to the grim task, took the list out of my notebook, and scanned it. The topic on which my eye stopped was "The Art of Eating Spaghetti."

This title produced an extraordinary sequence of mental images. Surging up out of the depths of memory came a vivid recollection of a night in Belleville when all of us were seated around the supper table—Uncle Allen, my mother, Uncle Charlie, Doris, Uncle Hal—and Aunt Pat served spaghetti for supper. Spaghetti was an exotic treat in those days. Neither Doris nor I had ever eaten spaghetti, and none of the adults had enough experience to be good at it. All the good humor of Uncle Allen's house reawoke in my mind as I recalled the laughing arguments we had that night about the socially respectable method for moving spaghetti from plate to mouth.

Suddenly I wanted to write about that, about the warmth and good feeling of it, but I wanted to put it down simply for my own joy, not for Mr. Fleagle. It was a moment I wanted to recapture and hold for myself. I wanted to relive the pleasure of an evening at New Street. To write it as I wanted, however, would violate all the rules of formal composition I'd learned in school, and Mr. Fleagle would surely give it a failing grade. Never mind. I would write something else for Mr. Fleagle after I had written this thing for myself.

When I finished it the night was half gone and there was no time left to compose a proper, respectable essay for Mr. Fleagle. There was no choice next morning but to turn in my private reminiscence° of Belleville. Two days passed before Mr. Fleagle returned the graded papers, and he returned everyone's but mine. I was bracing myself for a command to report to Mr. Fleagle immediately after school for discipline when I saw him lift my paper from his desk and rap for the class's attention.

"Now, boys," he said, "I want to read you an essay. This is titled 'The Art of Eating Spaghetti.'"

And he started to read. My words! He was reading *my words* out loud to the entire class. What's more, the entire class was listening. Listening attentively. Then somebody laughed, then the entire class was laughing, and not in contempt and ridicule, but with openhearted enjoyment. Even Mr. Fleagle stopped two or three times to repress a small prim smile.

I did my best to avoid showing pleasure, but what I was feeling was pure ecstasy at this startling demonstration that my words had the power to make

7

8

9

10

11

12

13

reminiscence: Memory.

people laugh. In the eleventh grade, at the eleventh hour as it were, I had discovered a calling. It was the happiest moment of my entire school career. When Mr. Fleagle finished he put the final seal on my happiness by saying, "Now that, boys, is an essay, don't you see. It's—don't you see—it's of the very essence of the essay, don't you see. Congratulations, Mr. Baker."

For the first time, light shone on a possibility. It wasn't a very heartening possibility, to be sure. Writing couldn't lead to a job after high school, and it was hardly honest work, but Mr. Fleagle had opened a door for me. After that I ranked Mr. Fleagle among the finest teachers in the school.

14 | Conclusion restating thesis

Questions to Start You Thinking

Meaning

1. In your own words, state what Baker believes he learned in the eleventh grade about the art of writing. What incidents or statements help identify this lesson for readers? What lesson, if any, did you learn from the essay?

2. Why do you think Baker included this event in his autobiography?

3. Have you ever changed your mind about something you had to do, as Baker did about writing? Or about a person, as he did about Mr. Fleagle?

Writing Strategies

4. What is the effect, in paragraph 3, of Baker's repetitions of the words *prim* and *primly*? What other devices does he use to characterize Mr. Fleagle vividly? Why do you think Baker uses so much space to portray his teacher?

5. What does the quotation from *Macbeth* add to Baker's account? Had the quotation been omitted, what would have been lost?

6. How does Baker organize the essay? Why does he use this order?

Robert G. Schreiner   Student Essay

What Is a Hunter?

In this college essay, Robert G. Schreiner uses vivid details to bring to life a significant childhood event.

What is a hunter? This is a simple question with a relatively straightforward answer. A hunter is, according to *Webster's New Collegiate Dictionary*, a person who hunts game (game being various types of animals hunted or pursued for various reasons). However, a second question is just as simple but without such a straightforward answer: What characteristics make up a hunter? As a child, I had always considered the most important aspect of the hunter's person to be his ability to use a rifle, bow, or whatever weapon was appropriate to the type of hunting being done. Having many relatives in rural areas of Virginia and Kansas, I had been exposed to rifles a great deal. I had done extensive target shooting and considered myself to be quite proficient in the use of firearms. I had never been hunting, but I had always thought that since I could fire a rifle accurately I would make a good hunter.

One Christmas holiday, while we were visiting our grandparents in Kansas, my   2
grandfather asked me if I wanted to go jackrabbit hunting with him. I eagerly accepted, anxious to show off my prowess° with a rifle. A younger cousin of mine also wanted to come, so we all went out into the garage, loaded two .22 caliber rifles and a 20-gauge shotgun, hopped into the pickup truck, and drove out of town. It had snowed the night before, and to either side of the narrow road swept six-foot-deep powdery drifts. The wind twirled the fine crystalline snow into whirling vortexes° that bounced along the icy road and sprayed snow into the open windows of the pickup. As we drove, my grandfather gave us some pointers about both spotting and shooting jackrabbits. He told us that when it snows, jackrabbits like to dig out a hollow in the top of a snowdrift, usually near a fencepost, and lie there soaking up the sunshine. He told us that even though jackrabbits are a grayish brown, this coloration is excellent camouflage in the snow, for the curled-up rabbits resemble rocks. He then pointed out a few rabbits in such positions as we drove along, showing us how to distinguish them from exposed rocks and dirt. He then explained that the only way to be sure that we killed the rabbit was to shoot for the head and, in particular, the eye, for this was on a direct line with the rabbit's brain. Since we were using solid point bullets, which deform into a ball upon impact, a hit anywhere but the head would most likely only wound the rabbit.

My grandfather then slowed down the pickup and told us to look out for the   3
rabbits hidden in the snowdrifts. We eventually spotted one about thirty feet from the road in a snow-filled gully. My cousin wished to shoot the first one, so he hopped out of the truck, balanced the .22 on the hood, and fired. A spray of snow erupted about a foot to the left of the rabbit's hollow. My cousin fired again, and again, and again, the shots pockmarking the slope of the drift. He fired once more and the rabbit bounced out of its hollow, its head rocking from side to side. He was hit. My cousin eagerly gamboled into the snow to claim his quarry.° He brought it back holding it by the hind legs, proudly displaying it as would a warrior the severed head of his enemy. The bullet had entered the rabbit's right shoulder and exited through the neck. In both places a thin trickle of crimson marred the gray sheen of the rabbit's pelt. It quivered slightly and its rib cage pulsed with its labored breathing. My cousin was about to toss it into the back of the pickup when

How does the writer convey his grandfather's definition of hunting?

---

prowess: Superior skill.   **vortex:** Rotation around an axis, as in a whirlwind.
quarry: Prey.

my grandfather pointed out that it would be cruel to allow the rabbit to bleed slowly to death and instructed my cousin to bang its head against the side of the pickup to kill it. My cousin then proceeded to bang the rabbit's head against the yellow metal. Thump, thump, thump, thump; after a minute or so my cousin loudly proclaimed that it was dead and hopped back into the truck.

The whole episode sickened me to some degree, and at the time I did not know why. We continued to hunt throughout the afternoon, and feigning boredom, I allowed my cousin and grandfather to shoot all of the rabbits. Often, the shots didn't kill the rabbits outright so they had to be killed against the pickup. The thump, thump, thump of the rabbits' skulls against the metal began to irritate me, and I was strangely glad when we turned around and headed back toward home. We were a few miles from the city limits when my grandfather slowed the truck to a stop, then backed up a few yards. My grandfather said he spotted two huge "jacks" sitting in the sun in a field just off the road. He pointed them out and handed me the .22, saying that if I didn't shoot something the whole afternoon would have been a wasted trip for me. I hesitated and then reluctantly accepted the rifle. I stepped out onto the road, my feet crunching on the ice. The two rabbits were about seventy feet away, both sitting upright in the sun. I cocked and leveled the rifle, my elbow held almost horizontal in the military fashion I had learned to employ. I brought the sights to bear on the right eye of the first rabbit, compensated° for distance, and fired. There was a harsh snap like the crack of a whip and a small jolt to my shoulder. The first rabbit was gone, presumably knocked over the side of the snowdrift. The second rabbit hadn't moved a muscle; it just sat there staring with that black eye. I cocked the rifle once more and sighted a second time, the bead of the rifle just barely above the glassy black orb that regarded me so passively. I squeezed the trigger. Again the crack, again the jolt, and again the rabbit disappeared over the top of the drift. I handed the rifle to my cousin and began making my way toward the rabbits. I sank into powdery snow up to my waist as I clambered to the top of the drift and looked over.

On the other side of the drift was a sight that I doubt I will ever forget. There was a shallow, snow-covered ditch on the leeward side of the drift and it was into this ditch that the rabbits had fallen, at least what was left of the rabbits. The entire ditch, in an area about ten feet wide, was spattered with splashes of crimson blood, pink gobbets of brain, and splintered fragments of bone. The twisted corpses of the rabbits lay in the bottom of the ditch in small pools of streaming blood. Of both the rabbits, only the bodies remained, the heads being completely gone. Stumps of vertebrae protruded obscenely from the mangled bodies, and one rabbit's hind legs twitched spasmodically. I realized that my cousin must have made a mistake and loaded the rifle with hollowpoint explosive bullets instead of solid ones.

4　Why do you think that the writer reacts as he does?

5

compensate: Counterbalance.

I shouted back to the pickup, explaining the situation, and asked if I should   6
bring them back anyway. My grandfather shouted back, "No, don't worry about it,
just leave them there. I'm gonna toss these jacks by the side of the road anyway;
jackrabbits aren't any good for eatin'."

Looking at the dead, twitching bodies I thought only of the incredible waste of   7
life that the afternoon had been, and I realized that there was much more to being
a hunter than knowing how to use a rifle. I turned and walked back to the pickup,
riding the rest of the way home in silence.

❓ Why do you
think the writer
returns in silence?

Questions to Start You Thinking

Meaning

1. Where in the essay do you first begin to suspect the writer's feelings
   about hunting? What in the essay or in your experience led you to this
   perception?

2. How would you characterize the writer's grandfather? How would you
   characterize his cousin?

3. How did the writer's understanding of himself change as a result of this
   hunting experience?

Writing Strategies

4. How might the essay be strengthened or weakened if the opening paragraph were cut out? Without this paragraph, how would your understanding of the author and his change be different?

5. Would Schreiner's essay be more or less effective if he explained in
   the last paragraph what he means by "much more to being a
   hunter"?

6. What are some of Schreiner's memorable images?

7. Using highlighters or marginal notes, identify the essay's introduction,
   thesis, major events, support for each event, and conclusion. How effective is the organization of this essay?

e **Howie Chackowicz**   **Audio**

The Game Ain't Over 'til the Fatso Man Sings

In this audio piece, recorded for Chicago Public Media's popular radio program *This American Life*, Howie Chackowicz recalls the irrational and amusing
methods he unsuccessfully employed as a child to win girls' hearts. To listen
to the selection, go to Chapter 4: **bedfordstmartins.com/concisebedguide**.

Learning by Writing

The Assignment: Recalling a Personal Experience

Write about one specific experience that changed how you acted, thought, or felt. Use your experience as a springboard for reflection. Your purpose is not merely to tell an interesting story but to show your readers — your instructor and your classmates — the importance of that experience for you.

We suggest you pick an event that is not too personal, too subjective, or too big to convey effectively to others. Something that happened to you or that you observed, an encounter with a person who greatly influenced you, a decision that you made, or a challenge or an obstacle that you faced will be easier to recall (and to make vivid for your readers) than an interior experience like a religious conversion or falling in love.

These students recalled experiences heavy and light:

One writer recalled guitar lessons with a teacher who at first seemed harsh but who turned out to be a true friend.

Another student recalled a childhood trip when everything went wrong and she discovered the complexities of change.

Another recalled competing with a classmate who taught him a deeper understanding of success.

For an interactive Learning by Doing activity on recalling from photographs, go to Ch. 4: **bedfordstmartins .com/concisebedguide**.

Facing the Challenge · Writing from Recall

The major challenge writers confront when writing from recall is to focus their essays on a main idea. When writing about a familiar — and often powerful — experience, it is tempting to include every detail that comes to mind and equally easy to overlook familiar details that would make the story's relevance clearer to the reader.

When you are certain of your purpose in writing about a particular event — what you want to show readers about your experience — you can transform a laundry list of details into a narrative that connects events clearly around a main idea. You can select details that work together to convey the significance of your experience. To help you decide what to show your readers, respond to each of these questions in a few sentences:

- What was important to you about the experience?
- What did you learn from it?
- How did it change you?
- How would you reply to a reader who asked "So what?"

Once you have decided on your main point about the experience, you should select the details that best illustrate that point and show readers why the experience was important to you.

Generating Ideas

For more on each strategy for generating ideas in this section or for additional strategies, see Ch. 12.

You may find that the minute you are asked to write about a significant experience, the very incident will flash to mind. Most writers, though, will need a little time for their memories to surface. Often, when you are busy doing something else — observing the scene around you, talking with someone, reading about someone else's experience — the activity can trigger a recollection. When a promising one emerges, write it down. Perhaps, like Russell Baker, you found success when you ignored what you thought you were supposed to do in favor of what you really wanted to do. Perhaps, like Robert Schreiner, you learned from a painful experience.

Try Brainstorming. When you brainstorm, you just jot down as many ideas as you can. You can start with a suggestive idea — *disobedience, painful lesson, childhood, peer pressure* — and list whatever occurs through free association. You can also use the questions in the following checklist:

DISCOVERY CHECKLIST

☐ Did you ever break an important rule or rebel against authority? What did you learn from your actions?

☐ Did you ever succumb to peer pressure? What were the results of going along with the crowd? What did you learn?

☐ Did you ever regard a person in a certain way and then have to change your opinion of him or her? What produced this change?

☐ Did you ever have to choose between two equally attractive alternatives? How might your life have been different if you had chosen differently?

☐ Have you ever been appalled by witnessing an act of prejudice or insensitivity? What did you do? Do you wish you had done something different?

Try Freewriting. Devote ten minutes to freewriting — simply writing without stopping. If you get stuck, write "I have nothing to say" over and over, until ideas come. They will come. After you finish, you can circle or draw lines between related items, considering what main idea connects events.

Try Doodling or Sketching. As you recall an experience such as breaking your arm during a soccer tournament, try sketching whatever helps you recollect the event and its significance. Turn doodles into words by adding comments on main events, notable details, and their impact on you.

Try Mapping Your Recollections. Identify a specific time period such as your birthday last year, the week when you decided to enroll in college, or a time when you changed in some way. On a blank page, on movable sticky notes, or

in a computer file, record all the details you can recall about that time—people, statements, events, locations, and related physical descriptions.

Try a Reporter's Questions. Once you recall an experience you want to write about, ask "the five **W**'s and an **H**" that journalists find useful.

- **W**ho was involved?
- **W**hat happened?
- **W**here did it take place?
- **W**hen did it happen?
- **W**hy did it happen?
- **H**ow did the events unfold?

Any question might lead to further questions—and to further discovery.

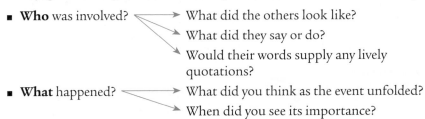

- **Who** was involved?
  - What did the others look like?
  - What did they say or do?
  - Would their words supply any lively quotations?
- **What** happened?
  - What did you think as the event unfolded?
  - When did you see its importance?

Consider Sources of Support. Because your memory both retains and drops details, you may want to check your recollections of an experience. Did you keep a journal at the time? Do your memories match those of a friend or relative who was there? Was the experience (big game, new home,

birth of a child) a turning point that you or your family would have photo-
graphed? Was it sufficiently public (such as a community catastrophe) or
universal (such as a campus event) to have been recorded in a newspaper? If
so, these resources can remind you of forgotten details or angles.

Learning by Doing Creating Your Writing Space

If you are online, in a computer lab, or on your laptop, begin your first writing assignment right now by creating your electronic writing space. Open,
label, and save a file for generating ideas. Systematically label your writing
files for submission as directed or with your name, course, assignment, and
writing stage, draft number, or date so that their sequence is clear: Marcus
Recall Ideas 9-14-13 or Chung W110 Recall 1. Store the first file to a course
folder or a subfolder for each assignment. If you are in a face-to-face class,
label a new page in your notebook so that your ideas are easy to find. Now
use your new file or your notebook to brainstorm, freewrite, or try another
strategy for generating ideas.

Planning, Drafting, and Developing

For more strategies for
planning and drafting
papers, see Chs. 13
and 14.

Now, how will you tell your story? If the experience is still fresh in your
mind, you may be able simply to write a draft, following the order of
events. If you want to plan before you write, here are some suggestions.

For more on stating
a thesis, see
pp. 263–72.

Start with a Main Idea, or Thesis. Jot down a few words that identify the
experience and express its importance to you. Next, begin to shape these
words into a sentence that states its significance — the main idea that you
want to convey to a reader. If you aren't certain yet about what that idea is,
just begin writing. You can work on your thesis as you revise.

For help developing
effective thesis
statements, go to the
interactive "Take
Action" charts in
Re:Writing at
**bedfordstmartins.com
/concisebedguide**.

TOPIC IDEA + SLANT	reunion in Georgia + really liked meeting family
WORKING THESIS	When I went to Georgia for a family reunion, I enjoyed meeting many relatives.

Learning by Doing Stating the Importance of Your Experience

For examples of time
markers and other
transitions, see
pp. 295–99.

Work up to stating your thesis by completing these two sentences: The most
important thing about my experience is _____. I want to share this
so that my readers _____. Exchange sentences with a classmate or
a small group, either in person or online. Ask each other questions to
sharpen ideas about the experience and express them in a working thesis.

Establish Your Chronology. Retelling an experience is called *narration,* and the simplest way to organize is chronologically—relating the essential events in the order in which they occurred. On the other hand, sometimes you can start an account of an experience in the middle and then, through *flashback,* fill in whatever background a reader needs to know.

Richard Rodriguez, for instance, begins *Hunger of Memory* (Boston: David R. Godine, 1982), a memoir of his bilingual childhood, with an arresting sentence:

> I remember, to start with, that day in Sacramento, in a California now nearly thirty years past—when I first entered a classroom, able to understand about fifty stray English words.

The opening hooks our attention. In the rest of his essay, Rodriguez fills us in on his family history, on the gulf he came to perceive between the public language (English) and the language of his home (Spanish).

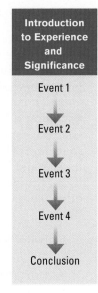
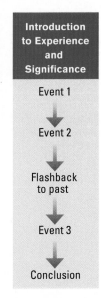

For a selection from *Hunger of Memory,* go to "Public and Private Language" in Ch. e-1: **bedfordstmartins.com /concisebedguide**.

Learning by Doing Selecting and Arranging Events

Open a new file, or start a new page in your notebook. List the main events in the order in which they occurred during the experience you plan to write about. Next, sum up the main idea you want to convey to readers. Then decide whether each event in your list supports that main idea. Drop unrelated events, or refine your main idea to reflect the importance of the events more accurately. Exchange files or pages with a classmate, and test each other's sequence of events against the main idea. Note clear connections and engaging events. Add question marks and comments if you notice shifts, gaps, irrelevant events, or missing connections. Use these comments to improve your selection of events and the clarity of your main idea.

Show Your Audience What Happened. How can you make your recollections come alive for your readers? Return to Baker's account of Mr. Fleagle teaching *Macbeth,* Schreiner's depiction of his cousin putting the wounded rabbits out of their misery, or Chackowicz's experiences. These writers have not merely told us what happened; they have *shown* us, by creating scenes that we can see in our mind's eye.

As you tell your story, zoom in on at least two or three specific scenes. Show your readers exactly what happened, where it occurred, what was said, who said it. Use details and words that appeal to all five senses—sight, sound, touch, taste, smell. Carefully position any images you include to clarify visual details for readers. (Be sure that your instructor approves such additions.)

For help supporting a thesis, go to the interactive "Take Action" charts in Re:Writing at **bedfordstmartins.com /concisebedguide**.

Revising and Editing

For more on adding visuals, see B in the Quick Format Guide, pp. A-8–A-12.

After you have written an early draft, put it aside for a few days — or hours if your deadline is looming. Then read it over carefully. Try to see it through the eyes of a reader, noting both pleasing and confusing spots. Revise to express your thoughts and feelings clearly and strongly to your readers.

For more revising and editing strategies, see Ch. 15.

Focus on a Main Idea, or Thesis. As you read over the essay, return to your purpose: What was so important about this experience? Why is it so memorable? Will readers see why it was crucial in your life? Will they understand how your life has been different ever since? Be sure to specify a genuine difference, reflecting the incident's real impact on you. In other words, revise to keep your essay focused on a single main idea or thesis.

WORKING THESIS	When I went to Georgia for a family reunion, I enjoyed meeting many relatives.
REVISED THESIS	Meeting my Georgia relatives showed me how powerfully two values — generosity and resilience — unite my family.

Peer Response 👥 Recalling an Experience

Have a classmate or friend read your draft and suggest how you might present the main idea about your experience more clearly and vividly. Ask your peer editor questions such as these about writing from recall:

For general questions for a peer editor, see p. 305.

- What do you think the writer's main idea or thesis is? Where is it stated or clearly implied? Why was this experience significant?

- What emotions do people in the essay feel? How did *you* feel as a reader?

- Where does the essay come alive? Underline images, descriptions, and dialogue that seem especially vivid.

- If this paper were yours, what is the one thing you would be sure to work on before handing it in?

Add Concrete Detail. Ask whether you have made events come alive for your audience by recalling them in sufficient concrete detail. Be specific enough that your readers can see, smell, taste, hear, and feel what you experienced. Make sure that all your details support your main idea or thesis. Notice again Robert Schreiner's focus in his second paragraph on the world outside his own skin: his close recall of the snow, of his grandfather's pointers about the habits of jackrabbits and the way to shoot them.

Learning by Doing 🖿 Appealing to the Senses

Working online or in person with a classmate, exchange short passages from your drafts. As you read each other's paragraphs, highlight the sensory details—sights, sounds, tastes, sensations, and smells that bring a description to life. Then jot down the sense to which each detail appeals in the margin or in a file comment. Return each passage to the writer, review the notes about yours, and decide whether to strengthen your description with more—or more varied—details.

Follow a Clear Sequence. Reconsider the order of events, looking for changes that make your essay easier for readers to follow. For example, if a classmate seems puzzled about the sequence of your draft, make a rough outline or list of main events to check the clarity of your arrangement. Or add more transitions to connect events and clarify where your account is going.

For more on outlining, see pp. 275–83.

For more on transitions, see pp. 295–99.

Revise and rewrite until you've related your experience and its impact as well as you can. Here are some useful questions about revising your paper:

REVISION CHECKLIST

- ☐ Where have you shown why this experience was important and how it changed your life?

- ☐ How have you engaged readers so they will keep reading? Will they find your paper dramatic, instructive, or revealing? Will they see and feel your experience?

- ☐ Why do you begin your narration as you do? Is there another place in the draft that would make a better beginning?

- ☐ If the events are not in chronological order, how have you made the organization easy for readers to follow?

- ☐ In what ways does the ending provide a sense of finality?

- ☐ Do you stick to a point? Is everything relevant to your main idea or thesis?

- ☐ If you portray any people, how have you made their importance clear? Which details make them seem real, not just shadowy figures?

- ☐ Does any dialogue sound like real speech? Read it aloud. Try it on a friend.

After you have revised your recall essay, edit and proofread it. Carefully check the grammar, word choice, punctuation, and mechanics—and then correct any problems you find. Here are some questions to get you started:

For more editing and proofreading strategies, see pp. 313–17.

For more help, find the relevant checklists in the Quick Editing Guide beginning on p. A-39. Turn also to the Quick Format Guide beginning on p. A-1.

EDITING CHECKLIST

☐ Is your sentence structure correct? Have you avoided writing fragments, comma splices, or fused sentences?   A1, A2

☐ Have you used correct verb tenses and forms throughout? When you present a sequence of past events, is it clear what happened first and what happened next?   A3

☐ When you use transitions and other introductory elements to connect events, have you placed any needed commas after them?   C1

☐ In your dialogue, have you placed commas and periods before (inside) the closing quotation mark?   C3

☐ Have you spelled everything correctly, especially the names of people and places? Have you capitalized names correctly?   D1, D2

Also check your paper's format using the Quick Format Guide. Follow the style expected by your instructor for features such as the heading, title, running head, page numbers, margins, and paragraph indentation.

When you have made all the changes you need to make, save your file, print out a clean copy of your paper or attach the file — and submit it.

Additional Writing Assignments

1. Choose a person outside your immediate family who had a marked effect on your life, either good or bad. Jot down ten details that might show what that person was like: physical appearance, way of talking, habits, or memorable incidents. Then look back at "The Art of Eating Spaghetti" to identify the kinds of detail Baker uses to portray Mr. Fleagle, noting any you might add to your list. Write your paper, including details to help readers experience the person's impact on you.

2. Recall a place you were fond of — your grandma's kitchen, a tree house, a library, a locker room, a vacation retreat. What made it different from other places? Why was it important? What do you feel when you remember it? Write a paper that uses specific, concrete details to explain to your audience why this place was memorable. If you have a photograph of the place, look at it to jog your memory, and consider adding it to your paper.

3. Write a paper or a podcast text to recall a familiar ceremony, ritual, or observation, perhaps a holiday, a rite of passage (confirmation, bar or bat

mitzvah, college orientation, graduation), a sporting event, a family custom. How did the tradition originate? Who takes part? How has it changed over the years? What does it add to the lives of those who observe it? Share with your audience the importance of the tradition to you.

4. Recall how you learned to read, write, or see how literacy could shape or change your life. What early experiences with reading or writing do you recall? How did these experiences affect you? Were they turning points for you? Write an essay about the major events in your literacy story—your personal account of your experiences learning to read or write—so that your audience understands the impact of those events on you. If you wish, address a specific audience—such as students or a teacher at your old school, a younger relative, your own children (real or future), or a person involved in your experience.

5. **Source Assignment.** Respond to one of the preceding assignments by supplementing your recollections with information from a source. You might turn to a personal source (family record, photograph, relative's account) or a published account (newspaper story reporting an event, article about a tradition, essay recalling an experience). Jot down relevant details from your source, or write a brief summary of it. Integrate this information in your essay, and be sure to cite your source.

6. **Visual Assignment.** Examine the images on the next two pages. What do you recall about an experience in a similar social, natural, or urban environment? What events took place there? How did you react to those events? What was their importance to you? How did the experience change you, your ideas, or your decisions? Write an essay that briefly recalls your experience and then reflects on its importance or consequences for you. Add your own photo to your text, if you wish.

5 Observing a Scene

Ryan Raburn of the Detroit Tigers saves a home run by catching a fly ball in the eighth inning against the Pittsburgh Pirates on June 24, 2012, at PNC Park in Pittsburgh, Pennsylvania.

Responding to an Image

This scene might look and feel quite different to different observers, depending on their vantage points, emotions, and experiences. In this image, what prominent element attracts your attention? Who are the observers? Which details might be important for them? Although visual details are central, what other senses and emotions might come into play?

Most writers begin to write by recalling what they know. Then they look around and add what they observe. Some writing consists almost entirely of observation—a reporter's eyewitness account of a fire, a clinical report by a nurse detailing a patient's condition, a scientist's account of a laboratory experiment, a traveler's blog or photo essay. In fact, observation plays a large role in any writing that describes a person, place, or thing. Observation also provides support, details to make a point clear or convincing. For example, a case study might report information from interviews and analyze artifacts—whether ancient bowls, new playground equipment, or decades of airport records. However, to make its abstractions and statistics more vivid, it also might integrate compelling observation.

If you need more to write about, open your eyes—and your other senses. Take in what you can see, hear, smell, touch, and taste. As you write, report your observations in concrete detail. Of course, you can't record everything your senses bring you. You must be selective based on what's important and relevant for your purpose and audience. To make a football game come alive for readers of your college newspaper, you might mention the overcast cold weather and the spicy smell of bratwurst. But if your purpose is primarily to explain which team won and why, you might stress the muddy playing field, the most spectacular plays, and the players who scored.

Why Observing a Scene Matters

In a College Course

- You observe and report compelling information from field trips in sociology, criminal justice, or anthropology as well as impressions of a play, a concert, an exhibit, or a historical site for a humanities class.
- You observe clinical practices in health or education, habitats for plants and animals, the changing night sky, or lab experiments to report accurate information and to improve your own future practice.

In the Workplace

- You observe and analyze to lend credibility to your case study as a nurse, teacher, or social worker or to your site report as an engineer or architect.

In Your Community

- You observe, photograph, and report on hazards (a dangerous intersection, a poorly lighted park, a run-down building), needs (a soccer arena, a performing arts center), or disasters (an accident, a crime scene, a flood) to motivate action by authorities or fellow citizens.

When have you included observations in your writing? How did these observations contribute to your writing? In what situations might you use observation in future writing?

Learning from Other Writers

Here are two essays by writers who observe their surroundings and reflect on their observations. As you begin to analyze the first reading, look at the notes in the margin. They identify features such as the main impression created in the observation and stated in the thesis, the first of the locations observed, and the supporting details that describe the location.

For another essay on multicultural identity, read "Public and Private Language" by Richard Rodriguez in Ch. e-1: **bedfordstmartins.com /concisebedguide**.

As You Read These Observations

As you read these essays, ask yourself the following questions:

1. What does the writer observe? Places? People? Behavior? Things?

2. What senses does each writer rely on? What sensory images does each develop? Find some striking passages in which the writer reports observations. What makes these passages memorable to you?

3. Why does the writer use observation? What conclusion does the writer draw from reflecting on the observations?

Eric Liu

The Chinatown Idea

Eric Liu is an educator, lecturer, and author of *Guiding Lights* (2004), a book about mentorship. In this selection from *The Accidental Asian* (1998), he describes a childhood visit to Chinatown in New York City.

Introduction

Another family outing, one of our occasional excursions to the city. It was a Saturday. I was twelve. I remember only vaguely what we did during the day — Fifth Avenue, perhaps, the museums, Central Park, Carnegie Hall. But I recall with precision going to Chinatown as night fell.   1

Vantage point 1

We parked on a side street, a dim, winding way cluttered with Chinese placards° and congested with slumbering Buicks and Chevys. The license plates — NEW YORK, EMPIRE STATE — seemed incongruous here, foreign. We walked a few blocks to East Broadway. Soon we were wading through thick crowds on the sidewalk, passing through belts of aroma: sweat and breath, old perfume, spareribs. It was late autumn and chilly enough to numb my cheeks, but the

Supporting detail

bustle all around gave the place an electric warmth. Though it was evening, the scene was lit like a stage, thanks to the aluminum lamps hanging from every produce stand. Peddlers lined the street, selling steamed buns and chicken feet and imitation Gucci bags. Some shoppers moved along slowly. Others stopped at each stall, inspecting the greens, negotiating the price of fish, talking loudly. I strained to make sense of the chopped-off twangs of   2

placards: Posters, signs.

Cantonese coming from every direction, but there were more tones than I knew: my ear was inadequate; nothing was intelligible.

This was the first time I had been in Chinatown after dark. Mom held Andrea's hand as we walked and asked me to stay close. People bumped us, brushed past, as if we were invisible. I felt on guard, alert. I craned my neck as we walked past a kiosk° carrying a Chinese edition of *Playboy*. I glanced sidelong at the teenage ruffians on the corner. They affected an air of menace with their smokes and leather jackets, but their feathery almost-mustaches and overpermed hair made them look a bit ridiculous. Nevertheless, I kept my distance. I kept an eye on the sidewalk, too, so that I wouldn't soil my shoes in the streams of putrid° water that trickled down from the alleyways and into the parapet° of trash bags piled up on the curb.

3

— Supporting detail

I remember going into two stores that night. One was the Far Eastern Bookstore. It was on the second floor of an old building. As we entered, the sounds of the street fell away. The room was spare and fluorescent. It looked like an earnest community library, crowded with rows of chest-high shelves. In the narrow aisles between shelves, patrons sat cross-legged on the floor, reading intently. If they spoke at all it was in a murmur. Mom and Dad each found an absorbing book. They read standing up. My sister and I, meanwhile, wandered restlessly through the stacks, scanning the spines for stray English words or Chinese phrases we might recognize. I ended up in children's books and leafed through an illustrated story about the three tigers. I couldn't read it. Before long, I was tugging on Dad's coat to take us somewhere else.

4

The other shop, a market called Golden Gate, I liked much more. It was noisy. The shoppers swarmed about in a frenzy. On the ground level was an emporium° of Chinese nonperishables: dried mushrooms, spiced beef, seaweed, shredded pork. Open crates of hoisin sauce° and sesame chili paste. Sweets, like milky White Rabbit chews, coconut candies, rolls of sour "haw flakes." Bags of Chinese peanuts, watermelon seeds. Down a narrow flight of stairs was a storehouse of rice cookers, ivory chopsticks, crockery, woks that hung from the wall. My mother carefully picked out a set of rice bowls and serving platters. I followed her to the long checkout line, carrying a basket full of groceries we wouldn't find in Poughkeepsie. I watched with wonder as the cashier tallied up totals with an abacus.

5

THESIS
stating main impression

We had come to this store, and to Chinatown itself, to replenish our supply of things Chinese: food and wares, and something else as well. We had ventured here from the colorless outer suburbs to touch the source, to dip into a pool of undiluted Chineseness. It was easier for my parents, of course, since they could decode the signs and communicate. But even I, whose bond to his ancestral culture had frayed down to the inner cord of *appetite* — even I could feel somehow fortified by a trip to Chinatown.

6

kiosk: Booth.   **putrid:** Rotten; decaying.   **parapet:** Wall, as on a castle.   **emporium:** Marketplace.   **hoisin sauce:** A sweet brown sauce that is a popular Chinese condiment.

Yet we knew that we couldn't stay long—and that we didn't really want   7
to. We were Chinese, but we were still outsiders. When any peddler addressed
us in Cantonese, that became obvious enough. They seemed so familiar and
so different, these Chinatown Chinese. Like a reflection distorted just so.
Their faces were another brand of Chinese, rougher-hewn. I was fascinated by
them. I liked being connected to them. But was it because of what we
shared—or what we did not? I began that night to distinguish between my
world and theirs.

Conclusion drawn
from observation

It was that night, too, as we were making our way down East Broadway,   8
that out of the blur of Chinese faces emerged one that we knew. It was Po-
Po's° face. We saw her just an instant before she saw us. There was surprise in
her eyes, then hurt, when she peered up from her parka. Everyone hugged
and smiled, but this was embarrassing. Mom began to explain: we'd been up-
town, had come to Chinatown on a whim, hadn't wanted to barge in on her
unannounced. Po-Po nodded. We made some small talk. But the realization
that her daily routine was our tourist's jaunt,° that there was more than just
a hundred miles between us, consumed the backs of our minds like a flame
to paper. We lingered for a minute, standing still as the human current
flowed past, and then we went our separate ways.

Afterward, during the endless drive home, we didn't talk about bumping   9
into Po-Po. We didn't talk about much of anything. I looked intently through
the window as we drove out of Chinatown and sped up the FDR Drive, then
over the bridge. Manhattan turned into the Bronx, the Bronx into Yonkers,
and the seams of the parkway clicked along in soothing intervals as we cruised
northward to Dutchess County. I slipped into a deep, open-mouthed slumber,

Po-Po: The narrator's grandmother.   **jaunt:** Trip, outing.

not awakening until we were back in Merrywood, our development, our own safe enclave. I remember the comforting sensation of being home: the sky was clear and starry, the lawn a moon-bathed carpet. We pulled into our smooth blacktop driveway. Silence. It was late, perhaps later than I'd ever stayed up. Still, before I went to bed, I made myself take a shower.

Questions to Start You Thinking

Meaning

1. Why do Liu and his family go to Chinatown?

2. How do Liu and his family feel when they encounter Po-Po? What observations and descriptions lead you to that conclusion?

3. What is the significance of the last sentence? How does it capture the essence of Liu's Chinatown experience?

Writing Strategies

4. In which paragraphs or sections does the writer's use of sensory details capture the look, feel, or smell of Chinatown? In general, how successfully has Liu included various types of observations and details?

5. How does Liu organize his observations? Is this organization effective? Why or why not?

6. Which of the observations and events in this essay most clearly reveal that Liu considers himself to be a "tourist"?

Alea Eyre   **Student Essay**

Stockholm

For her first-year composition class, Alea Eyre records her introduction to an unfamiliar location.

1 The amount of noise and movement bustling around me was almost electrifying. As soon as I stepped off the plane ramp, I was enveloped into a brand new world. I let all my heightened senses work together to take in this new experience. Fear and elation collided in my head as I navigated this new adventure by myself. I was thirteen years old and just taking the final steps of a lonely twenty-six-hour journey across the world from Hawaii to Sweden.

When have you had similar surprises in a new environment?

2 I had never seen so many white folks in one place. Hundreds crowded and rushed to be somewhere. The busy airport felt like a culture shock but not in a bad way. Blonde hair whipped past me, snuggled in caps and scarves. Skin tucked in coats and jeans appeared so shockingly white it almost blinded me. Delicate yet tall and sturdy people zipped around me as if they had to attend to an emergency.

3 A music-like language danced around my ears, exciting me as I drew closer to the baggage claim. The sound was so familiar yet seemed so distant. I had heard it

inconsistently since childhood with the coming and going of my three half sisters. It unfurled off native speakers' tongues, rising and falling in artistic tones. For the past few months, I had studied my Swedish language book diligently, attempting to match my untrained tongue to the rolling R's and foreign sounds. On paper, the language looked silly, complicated, and unpronounceable. When spoken correctly, it sounded magical and delighted the ears. As I walked swiftly, trying to keep up with the general pace of this international airport, my ears stayed perked up, catching bits and pieces of conversations.

? What kinds of places does this building bring to mind?

The building was cavernous and had modern wooden architecture that accentuated every corner. Floor to ceiling windows brightened each area, letting in ample light and a view of the dreary early spring surroundings. I felt my eyes widen as I viewed the melting, slushy brown snow and bright green grass peeking up beneath it. Endless birch trees spread before me, and vibrant flowers dotted their roots. Everything inside and out felt so clean and new; even all of the people looked fresh and well dressed. The true Europeans that I had read about for so long were now displayed up close. Pale as they were, none of them looked as if they were sick, overweight, or druggies. I was taken aback, used to the vivid rainbow of shapes, colors, sizes, and overall variety of my Honolulu neighborhood. Every race and social class crammed into the concrete blocks of apartments in my hometown. Everything there felt dirty and unpredictable, but here in Stockholm, everything felt like a lily-white world.   4

? When have you been observed as well as observer?

As I neared the head of the line at customs, sets of eyes from every direction lingered on me. I was still a child, traveling by myself and sticking out against the array of white with my thick dark hair and almond-colored skin. I figured that my features kept them guessing. I was obviously not white, black, or Middle Eastern, but a mix of many different races and cultures that were completely foreign to them. Even back home, people could never guess what my blood combination was. I soon learned that Sweden has extremely strict immigration rules, and hardly anybody can get in. The country took in some Middle Eastern refugees during past wars, but other than that, blonde-haired blue-eyed Swedes turn up around every corner.   5

With my passport stamped and luggage in tow, I descended down a steep escalator, sandwiched in among a family of five. Listening intently to the lilt of their language, I tried to pick up on what they were discussing. Only able to translate a few simple words, I felt discouraged. Exhaustion was creeping up on me both mentally and physically as the initial adrenaline started to wear off. The flights to get here were lengthy and cramped, while the layovers were stressful and rushed. Jet lag settled in and clouded my already foggy head. I needed the luxury of rejuvenating sleep as soon as possible.   6

Finally, the escalator neared the ground floor. I surveyed the crowd anxiously, winding my way through the masses of people. My sister was supposed to be here somewhere, ready to begin a five-month-long period of dealing with my adolescent   7 hormones. I came here to live and learn, go to a Swedish school, and be immersed in a foreign culture. I spotted her, all the way at the end of the floor, near the sets of doors that led to this new world. She stood there, completely still and silent, but smiling and relieved that I actually made it. Her belly filled out the coat she wore, blossoming with her first child. Her hair was long and silky, and her eyes bright and earnest. She glowed with happiness, now looking like a mother. I fell into her arms, feeling ecstatic after not seeing her for years. We left the airport together, beaming as we walked through the crisp, freezing air. As we neared the car, I reached down and touched the melting snow. My virgin hands explored this new texture, and my nerves tingled. Feeling content, I slid into the car and prepared myself for the exciting journey ahead of me.

> ❓ How have you responded to the sights, sounds, and emotions that the writer has described?

Questions to Start You Thinking

Meaning

1. What is Eyre's response to the scene at the Stockholm airport?

2. What is the point of the overall impression Eyre creates? What does that impression reveal about her?

3. In paragraph 7, what does Eyre mean when she says she prepared herself "for the exciting journey ahead"?

Writing Strategies

4. How does contrasting Honolulu and Stockholm contribute to the vivid impression of the scene Eyre observes?

5. Which sense does Eyre use most effectively? Point to a few examples that support your choice.

6. How does Eyre convey motion and movement? What does this activity contribute to her observation?

7. Using highlighters or marginal notes, identify the essay's introduction, thesis, major vantage points for observation, details supporting each part of the observation, and conclusion. How effective is this organization?

ⓔ Multiple Photographers   **Visual Essay**

Observing the *Titanic*: Past and Present

On its maiden voyage in 1912, the *Titanic* hit an iceberg and sank within three hours, killing more than 1,500 people on board. The wreck was discovered in 1985 by Robert Ballard, at a depth of two miles beneath the Atlantic's surface, and has been visited by many, including filmmaker James

Cameron. To click through a series of photos that contrasts images of the ship when it was first built with images of its remains, go to Chapter 5: **bedfordstmartins.com/concisebedguide**.

The *Titanic*, 1912.

Learning by Writing

The Assignment: Observing a Scene

For an interactive Learning by Doing activity on scenes from the news, go to Ch. 5: **bedfordstmartins .com/concisebedguide**.

Observe a place near your campus, home, or job and the people who frequent it. Then write a paper that describes the place, the people, and their actions so as to convey the spirit of the place and offer some insight into its impact on the people.

This assignment is meant to start you observing closely enough that you go beyond the obvious. Go somewhere nearby, and station yourself where you can mingle with the people there. Open all your senses so that you see, smell, taste, hear, and feel. Jot down what you immediately notice, especially the atmosphere and its effect on the people there. Take notes describing the location, people, actions, and events you see. Then use your observations to convey the spirit of the scene. What is your main impression of the place? Of the people there? Of the relationship between people and place? Your purpose is not only to describe the scene but also to express thoughts and feelings connected with what you observe.

Three student writers wrote about these observations:

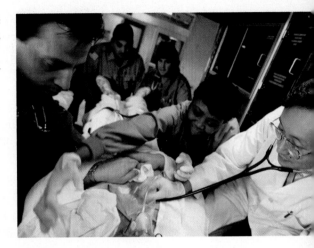

> One student, who works nights in the emergency room, observed the scene and the community that abruptly forms when an accident victim arrives: medical staff, patient, friends, and relatives.
>
> Another observed a bar mitzvah celebration that reunited a family for the first time in many years.
>
> Another observed the activity in the bleachers in a baseball stadium before, during, and after a game.

When you select the scene you wish to observe, find out from the person in charge whether you'll need to request permission to observe there, as you might at a school, business, or other restricted or privately owned site.

Facing the Challenge   Observing a Scene

The major challenge writers face when writing from observation is to select compelling details that convey an engaging main impression of a scene. As we experience the world, we are bombarded by sensory details, but our task as writers is to choose those that bring a subject alive for readers. For example, describing an oak as "a big tree with green leaves" is too vague to help readers envision the tree or grasp its unique qualities. Consider:

- What colors, shapes, and sizes do you see?
- What tones, pitches, and rhythms do you hear?
- What textures, grains, and physical features do you feel?
- What fragrances and odors do you smell?
- What sweet, spicy, or other flavors do you taste?

After recording the details that define the scene, ask two more questions:

- What overall main impression do these details establish?
- Which specific details will best show the spirit of this scene to a reader?

Your answers will help you decide which details to include in your paper.

Generating Ideas

For more on each strategy for generating ideas in this section or for additional strategies, see Ch. 12.

Although setting down observations might seem cut-and-dried, to many writers it is true discovery. Here are some ways to generate such observations.

Brainstorm. First, you need to find a scene to observe. What places interest you? Which are memorable? Start brainstorming — listing rapidly any ideas that come to mind. Here are a few questions to help you start your list:

DISCOVERY CHECKLIST

☐ Where do people gather for some event or performance (a stadium, a church, a theater, an auditorium)?

☐ Where do people meet for some activity (a gym, a classroom)?

☐ Where do crowds form while people are getting things or services (a shopping mall, a dining hall or student union, a dentist's waiting room)?

☐ Where do people pause on their way to yet another destination (a light-rail station, a bus or subway station, an airport, a restaurant on the toll road)?

☐ Where do people go for recreation or relaxation (an arcade, a ballpark)?

☐ Where do people gather (a fire, a party, a wedding, a graduation, an audition)?

Get Out and Look. If nothing on your list strikes you as compelling, plunge into the world to see what you see. Visit a city street or country hillside, a campus building or practice field, a contest, a lively scene — a mall, an airport, a fast-food restaurant, a student hangout — or a scene with only a few people sunbathing, walking dogs, or tossing Frisbees. Observe for a while, and then mix and move to gain different views.

Record Your Observations. Alea Eyre's essay "Stockholm" began with some notes about her vivid memories of her trip. She was able to mine those memories for details to bring her subject to life.

Your notes on a subject — or tentative subject — can be taken in any order or methodically. To draw up an "observation sheet," fold a sheet of paper in half lengthwise. Label the left column "Objective," and impartially list what you see, like a zoologist looking at a new species of moth. Label the right column "Subjective," and list your thoughts and feelings about what you observe. The quality of your paper will depend in large part on the truthfulness and accuracy of your observations. Your objective notes will trigger more subjective ones.

Elvis impersonators gather to audition in a Las Vegas contest.

Objective

The ticket holders form a line on the weathered sidewalk outside the old brick hall, standing two or three deep all the way down the block.

Groups of friends talk, a few couples hug, and some guys burst out in staccato laughter as they joke.

Everyone shuffles forward when the doors open, looking around at the crowd and edging toward the entrance.

Subjective

This place has seen concerts of all kinds — you can feel the history as you wait, as if the hall protects the crowds and the music.

The crowd seems relaxed and friendly, all waiting to hear their favorite group.

The excitement and energy grow with the wait, but it's the concert ritual — the prelude to a perfect night.

Include a Range of Images. Have you captured not just sights but sounds, textures, odors? Have you observed from several vantage points or on several occasions to deepen your impressions? Have you added sketches or doodles to your notes, perhaps drawing the features or shape of the place? Can you begin writing as you continue to observe? Have you noticed how other writers use *images*, evoking sensory experience, to record what they sense? In the memoir *Northern Farm* (New York: Rinehart, 1948), naturalist Henry Beston describes a remarkable sound: "the voice of ice," the midwinter sound of a whole frozen pond settling and expanding in its bed.

> Sometimes there was a sort of hollow oboe sound, and sometimes a groan with a delicate undertone of thunder. . . . Just as I turned to go, there came from below one curious and sinister crack which ran off into a sound like the whine of a giant whip of steel lashed through the moonlit air.

Learning by Doing 🗨 Enriching Sensory Detail

Review the detail in your observation notes. Because observers often note first what they see, mark references to other senses by underlining sounds, circling smells, and boxing textures or by adding different color highlights to your file. (Mark taste, too, if appropriate.) Compare your coverage with that of a classmate or small group, either in class or online. Add more variety from memory, or list what you want to observe when you return to the scene to listen, sniff, taste, or touch. (You can also use this activity to analyze sensory details in paragraphs from the two essays opening this chapter.)

For more strategies for planning and drafting, see Chs. 13 and 14.

Planning, Drafting, and Developing

After recording your observations, look over your notes, circling whatever looks useful. Maybe you can rewrite your notes into a draft, throwing out details that don't matter, leaving those that do. Maybe you'll need a plan to help you organize all the observations, laying them out graphically or in a simple scratch outline.

For more on stating a thesis, see pp. 263–72.

Start with a Main Impression or Thesis. What main insight or impression do you want to convey? Answering this question will help you decide which details to include, which to omit, and how to avoid a dry list of facts.

For help developing effective thesis statements, go to the interactive "Take Action" charts in Re:Writing at **bedfordstmartins.com /concisebedguide**.

PLACE OBSERVED	Smalley Green after lunch
MAIN IMPRESSION	relaxing activity is good after a morning of classes
WORKING THESIS	After their morning classes, students have fun relaxing on Smalley Green with their dogs and Frisbees.

Organize to Show Your Audience Your Point. How do you map out a series of observations? Your choice depends on your purpose and the main impression you want to create. Whatever your choice, add transitions—words or phrases to guide the reader from one vantage point, location, or idea to the next. Consider options such as those shown on the next page.

As you create your "picture," you bring a place to life using the details that capture its spirit. If your instructor approves, consider whether adding a photograph, sketch, diagram, or other illustration—with a caption— would enhance your written observation.

For more organization strategies, see pp. 270–71.

For transitions that mark place or direction, see p. 297.

Learning by Doing 🎯 Experimenting with Organization

Take a second look at the arrangement of the details in your observation. Select a different yet promising sequence, and test it by outlining your draft (or reorganizing another file) in that order. Ask classmates for reactions as you consider which sequence most effectively conveys your main impression.

SPATIAL MOVEMENT	top ↓ bottom	left ↓ right	near ↓ far	center ↓ edge

PROMINENT FEATURES	least: Sunday suit, light blue blouse, dramatic flowered hat ↓ most: Grandma's sharp eyes, spotting the best in others

SPECIFIC DETAILS TO GENERAL IMPRESSION	souvenir sellers calling, small waves slapping tour boats, and pungent fish frying on Fisherman's Wharf ↓ In all this commotion, a visitor sees the wharf's vitality.

COMMON AND ORDINARY TO UNUSUAL FEATURES	mounds of bright leaves, crisp fall air, children bouncing ↓ the sheer joy of every moment at the playground across from the pediatric cancer center

Sequential Organization of Details

Revising and Editing

For more revising and editing strategies, see Ch. 15.

Your revising, editing, and proofreading will be easier if you have accurate notes on your observations. But what if you don't have enough detail for your draft? If you have doubts, go back to the scene to take more notes.

Focus on a Main Impression or Thesis. As you begin to revise, have a friend read your observation, or read it yourself as if you had never seen the place you observed. Note gaps that would puzzle a reader, restate the spirit of the place, or sharpen the description of the main impression you want to convey in your thesis.

WORKING THESIS   After morning classes, students have fun relaxing on Smalley Green with their dogs and Frisbees.

REVISED THESIS   When students, dogs, and Frisbees accumulate on Smalley Green after lunch, they show how much campus learning takes place outside of class.

Learning by Doing 🐣 Strengthening Your Main Impression

Complete these two sentences: The main impression that I want to show my audience is _____ . The main insight that I want to share is _____ . Exchange sentences with a classmate or small group, and then each read aloud that draft while the others listen for the impression and insight the writer wants to convey. After each reading, discuss revision options with the writer—cuts, additions, changes—to strengthen that impression.

For help supporting a thesis, go to the interactive "Take Action" charts in Re:Writing at **bedfordstmartins.com /concisebedguide**.

Add Relevant and Powerful Details. Next, check your selection of details. Does each detail contribute to your main impression? Should any details be dropped or added? Should any be rearranged so that your organization, moving point to point, is clearer? Could any observations be described more vividly, powerfully, or concretely? Could any vague words such as *very, really, great,* or *beautiful* be replaced with more specific words? (As you spot too much repetition of certain words, use your software's Edit–Find function to locate them so you can reword for variety.)

Peer Response 👥 Observing a Scene

For general questions for a peer editor, see p. 305.

Let a classmate or friend respond to your draft, suggesting how to use detail to convey your main impression more powerfully. Ask your peer editor to answer questions such as these about writing from observation:

- What main insight or impression do you carry away from this draft?
- Which sense does the writer use particularly well? Are any senses neglected?

- Can you see and feel what the writer experienced? Would more detail be more compelling? Put check marks wherever you want more details.

- How well has the writer used evidence from the senses to build a main impression? Which sensory impressions contribute most strongly to the overall picture? Which seem superfluous?

- If this paper were yours, what is the one thing you would be sure to work on before handing it in?

To see where your draft could need work, consider these questions:

REVISION CHECKLIST

☐ Have you accomplished your purpose — to convey to readers your overall impression of your subject and to share some telling insight about it?

☐ What can you assume your readers know? What do they need to be told?

☐ Have you gathered enough observations to describe your subject? Have you observed with *all* your senses when possible — even smell and taste?

☐ Have you been selective, including details that effectively support your overall impression?

☐ Which observations might need to be checked for accuracy? Which might need to be checked for richness or fullness?

☐ Is your organizational pattern the most effective for your subject? Is it easy for readers to follow? Would another pattern work better?

After you have revised your essay, edit and proofread it. Carefully check the grammar, word choice, punctuation, and mechanics — and then correct any problems. If you have added details while revising, consider whether they have been sufficiently blended with the ideas already there. Here are some questions to get you started:

For more editing and proofreading strategies, see pp. 313–17.

EDITING CHECKLIST

☐ Is your sentence structure correct? Have you avoided writing fragments, comma splices, and fused sentences?   A1, A2

☐ Have you used an adjective when you describe a noun or pronoun? Have you used an adverb when you describe a verb, adjective, or adverb? Have you used the correct form to compare two or more things?   A7

For more help, find the relevant checklists in the Quick Editing Guide beginning on p. A-39. Turn also to the Quick Format Guide beginning on p. A-1.

☐ Is it clear what each modifier in a sentence modifies? Have you **B1** created any dangling or misplaced modifiers?

☐ Have you used parallel structure wherever needed, especially in **B2** lists or comparisons?

Additional Writing Assignments

1. To develop your powers of observation, go for a walk through either an unfamiliar scene or a familiar scene worth a closer look (such as a supermarket, a city street, an open field). Avoid a subject so familiar that you would struggle to take a fresh look (such as a dormitory corridor or a parking lot). Record your observations in two or three detailed paragraphs. Sum up your impression of the place, including any opinion you form through close observation.

2. The perspective of a tourist, an outsider alert to details, often reveals the distinctive character of places and people. Think of a place you've recently visited as an outsider, and jot down details you recall. Or spend a few minutes as a tourist right now. Go to a busy spot on or off campus, and record what you find amusing, surprising, puzzling, or intriguing. Then write an essay on the unique character of the place.

3. Select an observation site that relates to your current or possible career plans. For example, you might choose a medical facility (for nursing or medical school), a school or playground (for education), or an office complex or work site (for business). Observe carefully at this location, noting details that contribute to your main impression of the place and your insight about the site or the work done there. Write an essay to convey these points to an audience interested in the same career path.

4. Observe the details of a specific place on campus as if you were seeing it for the first time. Write about your main impression and insight about it in an essay for campus readers, a letter to a prospective student (who will want to know the relevance of the place), or an entry on your travel blog for foreign tourists (who will want to know why they should stop at this spot). If you wish, include your own photograph of the scene or a standard campus shot; add a caption that expresses its essence.

5. **Source Assignment.** Locate a community tourist guide, a town history or architectural survey, a campus guidebook, or a similar resource; select one of its attractions or locations to visit. Put aside the guide while you inde-

pendently observe and record details about the location. Then present your main impression of the character or significance of the place, supplementing your detailed observations with historical, technical, or other information from your source. Clearly and accurately credit your source so that a reader can easily tell what you observed, what you learned, and where you learned it.

6. **Visual Assignment.** Use one of the photographs below and on page 98 to explore the importance of the observer's point of view. After a preliminary look at the scene, select your vantage point as an observer, and identify the audience your essay will address (for example, readers who would or would not share your perspective). Observe the image carefully, and use its details to support your main impression of the scene from your perspective. Direct your specific insight about it to your audience.

For advice on analyzing an image, refer to Ch. 10.

Comparing and Contrasting

Responding to an Image

The large photograph of the young couple was taken at Woodstock in August 1969 and then featured on the cover for the album and the poster for the movie that recorded the event. The smaller insert, taken before the event's fortieth anniversary, shows the same couple, Nick and Bobbi Ercoline, now married for decades. Examine the two photographs carefully, noting similarities and differences. What does each image convey about its era? What does each convey about the couple, whether age twenty or sixty? What qualities made the original image iconic? What similar or different qualities are captured in the more recent image?

Which city—Dallas or Atlanta—has more advantages or drawbacks for a young single person thinking of settling down to a career? Which of two ads for the same toy appeals more effectively to parents who want to get durability as well as educational value for their money? As singers and songwriters, how are Beyoncé Knowles and Taylor Swift similar and dissimilar? Such questions invite answers that set two subjects side by side.

When you compare, you point out similarities; when you contrast, you discuss differences. When you write about two complicated subjects, usually you need to do both. Considering Mozart and Bach, you might find that each has traits the other has—or lacks. Instead of concluding that one is great and the other inferior, you might conclude that they're two distinct composers, each with an individual style. On the other hand, if your main purpose is to judge between two subjects (such as moving either to Dallas or to Atlanta), you would look especially for positive and negative features, weigh the attractions and faults of each city, and then stick your neck out and make your choice.

Why Comparing and Contrasting Matter

In a College Course

- You compare and contrast to "evaluate" the relative merits of Norman Rockwell and N. C. Wyeth in an art history course or the relative accuracy of two Civil War Web sites for a history course.
- You compare and contrast to "describe" a little-known subject, such as medieval funeral customs, by setting it next to a similar yet familiar subject, such as modern funeral traditions.

In the Workplace

- You compare and contrast your company's products or services with those of competitors, just as your experience, education, and personal attributes were compared and contrasted with those of others before you were hired.

In Your Community

- You compare and contrast your options in choosing a financial aid package, cell phone contract, childcare provider, bike helmet, or new mayor.

❓ What are some instances when you compare or contrast products, services, opportunities, options, solutions, or other things? When might you use comparison, contrast, or both in your writing? What would you expect them to contribute?

Learning from Other Writers

In this chapter you will be asked to write a paper setting two subjects side by side, comparing and contrasting them. Let's see how two other writers have used these familiar habits of thought in writing. To help you begin to analyze the first reading, look at the notes in the margin. They identify features such as the thesis, or main idea, the sequence of the broad subjects considered, and the specific points of comparison and contrast.

As You Read These Comparisons and Contrasts

As you read these essays, ask yourself the following questions:

1. What two (or more) items are compared and contrasted? Does the writer use comparison only? Contrast only? A combination of the two? Why?
2. What is the purpose of the comparison and contrast? What idea does the information support or refute?
3. How does the writer organize the essay? Why?

> To view an infographic that uses comparing and contrasting, go to "Paternity Leave around the World" in Ch. e-1: **bedfordstmartins.com /concisebedguide**.

David Brooks

The Opportunity Gap

In this column from the *New York Times*, David Brooks takes a look at some of the social and political issues that engage him as a commentator and an author of books such as *The Social Animal* (2011).

Over the past few months, writers from Charles Murray° to Timothy Noah° have produced alarming work on the growing bifurcation° of American society. Now the eminent Harvard political scientist Robert Putnam° and his team are coming out with research that's more horrifying. While most studies look at inequality of outcomes among adults and help us understand how America is coming apart, Putnam's group looked at inequality of opportunities among children. They help us understand what the country will look like decades ahead. The quick answer? More divided than ever.

— Introduction to issue

1

Charles Murray: Conservative author of *Coming Apart: The State of White America, 1960–2010* (2012).   **Timothy Noah:** Liberal author of *The Great Divergence: America's Growing Inequality Crisis and What We Can Do about It* (2012).   **bifurcation:** Division into two parts.   **Robert Putnam:** Political scientist, author of *Bowling Alone: The Collapse and Revival of American Community* (2000), and authority on class differences and social mobility.

THESIS —————

Subjects A and
B over time

Point 1 ————

Putnam's data verifies what many of us have seen anecdotally, that the children of the more affluent and less affluent are raised in starkly different ways and have different opportunities. Decades ago, college-graduate parents and high-school-graduate parents invested similarly in their children. Recently, more affluent parents have invested much more in their children's futures while less affluent parents have not. 2

Alternating Subjects
A and B

Point 2 ————

They've invested more time. Over the past decades, college-educated parents have quadrupled the amount of time they spend reading "Goodnight Moon," talking to their kids about their day and cheering them on from the sidelines. High-school-educated parents have increased child-care time, but only slightly. A generation ago, working-class parents spent slightly more time with their kids than college-educated parents. Now college-educated parents spend an hour more every day. This attention gap is largest in the first three years of life when it is most important. 3

Subject A ————

Subject B ————

Point 3 ————

Affluent parents also invest more money in their children. Over the last 40 years upper-income parents have increased the amount they spend on their kids' enrichment activities, like tutoring and extracurriculars, by $5,300 a year. The financially stressed lower classes have only been able to increase their investment by $480, adjusted for inflation. 4

As a result, behavior gaps are opening up. In 1972, kids from the bottom quartile° of earners participated in roughly the same number of activities as kids from the top quartile. Today, it's a chasm.° Richer kids are roughly twice as likely to play after-school sports. They are more than twice as likely to be the captains of their sports teams. They are much more likely to do non-sporting activities, like theater, yearbook and scouting. They are much more likely to attend religious services. 5

It's not only that richer kids have become more active. Poorer kids have become more pessimistic and detached. Social trust has fallen among all income groups, but, between 1975 and 1995, it plummeted among the poorest third of young Americans and has remained low ever since. As Putnam writes in notes prepared for the Aspen Ideas Festival: "It's perfectly understandable that kids from working-class backgrounds have become cynical and even paranoid, for virtually all our major social institutions have failed them — family, friends, church, school and community." As a result, poorer kids are less likely to participate in voluntary service work that might give them a sense of purpose and responsibility. Their test scores are lagging. Their opportunities are more limited. 6

A long series of cultural, economic and social trends have merged to create this sad state of affairs. Traditional social norms were abandoned, meaning more children are born out of wedlock. Their single parents simply have less time and resources to prepare them for a more competitive world. Working-class jobs were decimated,° meaning that many parents are too 7

---

quartile: A one-quarter group (1/4 or 25%) in a statistical study.   **chasm:** A deep divide, like a canyon.   **decimated:** Dramatically reduced (originally meaning by a tenth).

stressed to have the energy, time or money to devote to their children. Affluent, intelligent people are now more likely to marry other energetic, intelligent people. They raise energetic, intelligent kids in self-segregated, cultural ghettoes where they know little about and have less influence upon people who do not share their blessings. The political system directs more money to health care for the elderly while spending on child welfare slides.

Equal opportunity, once core to the nation's identity, is now a tertiary° concern. If America really wants to change that, if the country wants to take advantage of all its human capital rather than just the most privileged two-thirds of it, then people are going to have to make some pretty uncomfortable decisions. Liberals are going to have to be willing to champion norms that say marriage should come before childrearing and be morally tough about it. Conservatives are going to have to be willing to accept tax increases or benefit cuts so that more can be spent on the earned-income tax credit and other programs that benefit the working class. Political candidates will have to spend less time trying to exploit class divisions and more time trying to remedy them — less time calling their opponents out of touch elitists, and more time coming up with agendas that comprehensively address the problem. It's politically tough to do that, but the alternative is national suicide.

8

— Conclusion

Questions to Start You Thinking

Meaning

1. Does Brooks favor one group of parents and children over the other? Which details or statements support your response?

2. Based on the details presented here, why do the groups differ? What has changed over time?

3. What is Brooks's purpose in contrasting the two groups? Is his goal to explain or to convince? Or is it something else?

Writing Strategies

4. In the introduction, Brooks refers to several studies. Is that technique effective? How else might he have begun the essay?

5. Which method of organization does Brooks use to arrange his essay? How effectively does he switch between his two subjects?

6. From reading this essay, what are readers to assume that affluent and less affluent parents and children have in common? Why?

tertiary: Third.

Jacob Griffin   **Student Essay**

Karate Kid vs. Kung Fu Panda: A Race to the Olympics

Student Jacob Griffin compares and contrasts karate and kung fu, asking which of the two deserves to be the first declared an Olympic sport.

About three decades ago, the first Karate Kid waxed on and off, kicking his way   1
into the American sports scene. During the same era, martial arts movies with stars
like Jackie Chan began to popularize kung fu with American audiences. Films such as
the *Karate Kid* trilogy were instant classics, while kung fu has appeared in *Kill Bill*,
the *Matrix* movies, and even the animated *Kung Fu Panda*. Despite the worldwide
popularity of both fighting styles, neither has yet been approved for Olympic
competition. The International Olympic Committee should consider which of these
styles first deserves to be declared an official Olympic sport.

Why do you think the writer raises this issue here?

Besides their shared status in movies and popular culture, these two fighting   2
styles are similar because each is an umbrella term for several different variations.
The World Karate Federation includes four styles on its official list, while hundreds
of kung fu categories are based on types of movement, locations of origin, and
specific characteristics. Additionally, both fighting styles promote more than just
the physical development of those who practice the art. Neither has combat as its
only end. Humility, virtue, and courtesy are all important values in the philosophy
of karate, just as the kung fu idea of *qi*, or *ch'i*, expresses the life energy inside
practitioners. Each emphasizes spiritual growth as well as physical strength and
stamina.

Although both fighting styles have found success in Western pop culture and   3
have encouraged the inner growth of practitioners, karate is the younger of the two.
Karate developed on the island chain between China and Japan, where Okinawa,
Japan, is today. Given the regional politics, geography, and trade routes, Chinese
martial arts probably traveled to Okinawa in the 14th century and then merged with
the local fighting system known as *te*. In contrast, kung fu is a popular term for
many Chinese martial arts, including hand-to-hand combat and wrestling that date
back to the 5th century BC. But, despite this long history, it wasn't until the
founding of the People's Republic of China in 1949 that kung fu became a national
activity with training manuals, academies, and exams. Given kung fu's ancient roots,
karate could be considered an offshoot of Chinese martial arts.

The techniques for each fighting style are also different. Although both use linear   4
and circular movements, karate is usually considered to be more linear than kung fu.
This difference means that karate tends to have more straight lines and more direct
punches, strikes, and kicks in its sequences. Daniel's crane kick in the first *Karate Kid*
film, in which his leg shoots right out in front of him, is the perfect example of
karate's directness. This characteristic style might have been developed by the king's
bodyguards in Okinawa so that they could take quick control of a contest and fend off

multiple attackers. Now the style remains most evident in the short, distinct sets of moves that practitioners must learn and then apply in competition.

In contrast, kung fu is better known for being circular, rather than linear, especially in its hand movements. While just as powerful as karate movements, kung fu's more fluid motions draw their strength from centrifugal° force, as opposed to a direct hit. The movements learned by kung fu practitioners also have more of a flow to them than those in karate, and they tend to be longer, more complicated sets of moves. For these reasons, karate is often considered "hard" and kung fu "soft," although the many kung fu variations have both hard and soft qualities, blurring such distinctions.

5   What other differences between martial arts come to mind? Which matter most?

Finally, karate and kung fu practitioners wear different uniforms and use different weapons. The traditional karate uniform is white with a white kimono top over which a belt is tied. The color of the belt changes with the practitioner's rank, from white, yellow, and orange in the beginning stages, all the way up to purple,

6

centrifugal: Moving away from the center.

Karate

Kung fu

brown, and the famous black belt given to instructors. Karate is also practiced barefoot. When weapons are used in karate, they include the bo staff, a long stick up to six feet, and the *nunchaku*, two shorter sticks connected by a chain.

In contrast, kung fu practitioners may wear a greater variety of uniforms. Their outfits can be black or bold colors (like blue, red, or gold) and made of fabrics such as silk or satin. The tops of kung fu uniforms feature Chinese "frog" buttons, unlike karate's overlapping kimono-style jacket. Colored sashes may be worn as belts are in karate, but this practice of showing rank appears mainly in North American kung fu schools. Kung fu practitioners wear shoes and may use hook swords, butterfly swords, or nine section whips as well as many other weapons.

7

❓ How do you think this question should be decided?

Because both karate and kung fu are now well established in Western pop culture, which of the two fighting styles deserves to be the first approved as an Olympic sport? Although karate has a rich heritage in Okinawa and Japan, the origins of kung fu stretch back even further and point to the influence of Chinese martial arts on karate as it developed. Furthermore, many more variations gather under the umbrella of kung fu than of karate. Kung fu's movements are usually more connected and complex than karate's shorter, more distinct sequences. Thus, if karate is actually an off-shoot of Chinese martial arts, perhaps kung fu deserves to claim Olympic status before karate does. And yet karate's simplified approach—forever memorialized by Mr. Miyagi's wax on, wax off teachings—might be more fit for an international stage.

8

Questions to Start You Thinking

Meaning

1. In what specific ways does Griffin claim that karate and kung fu are similar? In what ways are these two different? Do the similarities outweigh the differences, or vice versa?

2. Can you think of other types of similarities and differences that Griffin might have included?

3. Would you nominate another sport for Olympic status? If so, why?

Writing Strategies

4. Is Griffin's support for his comparison and contrast sufficient and balanced? Explain.

5. What transitional devices does Griffin use to indicate when he is comparing and when he is contrasting?

6. What is Griffin's thesis? Why does Griffin state it where he does?

7. Using highlighters or marginal notes, identify the essay's introduction, thesis, contrasting subjects, points of comparison and contrast, and conclusion. How effective is the organization of this essay?

ⓔ *National Geographic* **Editors**   **Visual Essay**

Hurricane Katrina Pictures: Then & Now, Ruin & Rebirth

National Geographic compiled a series of images showing how New Orleans has recovered since the immediate aftermath of Hurricane Katrina, which hit the area in 2005. To view the photos, go to Chapter 6: **bedfordstmartins .com/concisebedguide**.

Top, children playing on a street in the Ninth Ward in 2010. Below, Amish student volunteers walking down the same street shortly after Hurricane Katrina.

Learning by Writing

The Assignment: Comparing and Contrasting

For an interactive Learning by Doing activity on comparing and contrasting experience of a major event, go to Ch. 6: **bedfordstmartins.com /concisebedguide**.

Write a paper in which you compare and contrast two items to enlighten readers about both subjects. The specific points of similarity and difference will be important, but you will go beyond them to draw a conclusion from your analysis. This conclusion, your thesis, needs to be more than "point A is different from point B" or "I prefer subject B to subject A." You will need to explain why you have drawn your conclusion. You'll also need to provide specific supporting evidence to explain your position and to convince your readers of its soundness. You may choose two people, two kinds of people, two places, two objects, two activities, or two ideas, but be sure to choose two you care about. You might write an impartial paper that distinctly portrays both subjects, or you might show why you favor one over the other.

These students found a clear reason for comparison and contrast:

An American student compared and contrasted her home life with that of her roommate, a student from Nigeria. Her goal was to deepen her understanding of Nigerian society and her own.

A student who was interested in history compared and contrasted civilian responses to the Vietnam and Iraq wars, considering how popular attitudes about military service had changed.

Another writer compared and contrasted facilities at two city parks, making a case for a revised funding formula.

Facing the Challenge   Comparing and Contrasting

The major challenge that writers face when comparing and contrasting two subjects is to determine their purpose. Writers who skip this step run the risk of having readers ask, "So, what's the point?" Suppose you develop brilliant points of similarity and difference between the films of Oliver Stone and those of Stanley Kubrick. Do you want to argue that one director is more skilled than the other? Or perhaps you want to show how they treat love or war differently in their films? Consider the following questions as you determine your primary purpose for comparing and contrasting:

■ Do you want to inform your readers about these two subjects in order to provide a better understanding of the two?

■ Do you want to persuade your readers that one of the two subjects is preferable to the other?

Ask what you want to demonstrate, discover, or prove *before* you begin to draft so you can write a more effective comparison-and-contrast essay.

Generating Ideas

Find Two Subjects. Pick subjects you can compare and contrast purposefully. An examination question may give them to you, ready-made: "Compare and contrast ancient Roman sculpture with that of the ancient Greeks." But suppose you have to find your subjects for yourself. You'll need to choose things that have a sensible basis for comparison, a common element.

For strategies for generating ideas, see Ch. 12.

> moon rocks + stars = no common element
>
> Dallas + Atlanta = cities to consider settling in
>
> Jimmy Fallon + Jimmy Kimmel = television talk-show personalities

Besides having a common element, the subjects should share enough to compare but differ enough to throw each other into sharp relief.

> sports cars + racing cars = common element + telling differences
>
> sports cars + oil tankers = limited common element + unpromising differences

Try generating a list or brainstorming. Recall what you've recently read, discussed, or spotted on the Web. Let your mind skitter around in search of pairs that go together, or play the game of *free association,* jotting down a word and whatever it brings to mind: *Democrats? Republicans. New York? Los Angeles. Facebook? LinkedIn.* Or try the following questions:

DISCOVERY CHECKLIST

- ☐ Do you know two people who are strikingly different in attitude or behavior (perhaps your parents or two brothers, two friends, two teachers)?

- ☐ Can you think of two groups that are both alike and different (perhaps two teams, two clubs, two sets of relatives)?

- ☐ Have you taken two courses that were quite different but both valuable?

- ☐ Do you prefer one of two places where you have lived or visited?

- ☐ Can you recall two events in your life that shared similar aspects but turned out to be quite different (perhaps two sporting events, two romances, two vacations, the births of two children, an event then and now)?

- ☐ Can you compare and contrast two holidays or two family customs?

- ☐ Are you familiar with two writers, two artists, or two musicians who seem to have similar goals but quite different accomplishments?

Once you have a list of pairs, put a star by those that seem promising. Ask yourself what similarities immediately come to mind. What differences?

Can you jot down several of each? Are these striking, significant similarities and differences? If not, move on until you discover a workable pair.

Limit Your Scope. If you want to compare and contrast Japanese literature and American literature in 750 words, your task is probably impossible. But to cut down the size of your subject, you might compare and contrast, say, a haiku of Bashō about a snake with a short poem about a snake by Emily Dickinson. This topic you could cover in 750 words.

Develop Your Pair to Build Support. As you examine your two subjects, your goal is twofold. First, analyze each using a similar approach so you have a reasonable basis for comparison and contrast. Then find the details and examples that will support your points. Consider these sources of support:

■ Two events, processes, procedures	Ask a reporter's questions — 5 *W*'s (who, what, where, when, why) and an *H* (how).
■ Two events from the past	Using the same questions, interview someone present at each event, or read news or other accounts.
■ Two perceptions (public and private)	Interview someone behind the scenes; read or listen to contrasting views.
■ Two approaches or viewpoints	Browse online for Web sites or pages that supply different examples.
■ Two policies or options	Look for articles reporting studies or government statistics.

For advice on finding a few useful sources, turn to B1–B2 in the Quick Research Guide, pp. A-25–A-26. For more on using sources for support, see Ch. 9.

▬▬▬▬

Learning by Doing 🔲 Making a Comparison-and-Contrast Table

After deciding what to compare, write down what you know about subject A and then subject B. Next, divide a page or use your software to create a table with three columns (up and down) and at least half a dozen rows (across). Use the first row to label the columns:

Categories	Subject A	Subject B

Now read over your notes on subject A. When you spot related details, identify a logical category for them. Enter that category name in the left column of the second row. Then add related details for subject A in the middle column. Repeat this process, labeling more rows as categories and filling in corresponding details for subject A. (Draw more lines, or use the menu to add new rows as needed.)

Next, review your notes on subject B. If some details fall into categories already listed in your table, add those details in the subject B column for each category. If new categories emerge, add them in new rows along with the subject B details. After you finish with your notes, round out the table — adding details to fill in empty cells, combining or adding categories. Select the most promising categories from your table as common features for logical comparison and contrast.

Planning, Drafting, and Developing

As you start planning your paper, be prepared to cover both subjects in a similar fashion. Return to your table or make a scratch outline so that you can refine your points of comparison or contrast, consolidate supporting details, and spot gaps in your information. Remind yourself of your goal. What is it you want to show, argue, or find out?

For more on planning and drafting, see Chs. 13 and 14. For more about informal outlines, see pp. 275–79.

State Your Purpose in a Thesis. You need a reason to place two subjects side by side — a reason that you and your audience will find compelling and worthwhile. If you prefer one subject over the other, what reasons can you give for your preference? If you don't have a preference, try instead to understand them more clearly, making a point about each or both. Comparing and contrasting need not be a meaningless exercise. Instead, think clearly and pointedly in order to explain an idea you care about.

For more on stating a thesis, see pp. 263–72.

TWO SUBJECTS	two teaching styles in required biology courses
REASON	to show why one style is better
WORKING THESIS	Although students learn a lot in both of the required introductory biology courses, one class teaches information and the other teaches how to be a good learner.

For help developing and supporting effective thesis statements, go to the interactive "Take Action" charts in Re:Writing at **bedfordstmartins.com /concisebedguide**.

Learning by Doing 📷 Pinpointing Your Purpose

Following the model above on teaching styles, specify your two subjects, identify your reason for comparing, and state your working thesis, making it as pointed as you can. To learn how others react to your purpose, exchange statements with a classmate or small group in person or online. Discuss possibilities for increasing clarity and purposefulness.

Select a Pattern to Help Your Audience. Besides understanding your purpose and thesis, readers also need to follow your supporting evidence — the clusters of details that reveal the nature of each subject you consider. They're likely to expect you to follow one of two ways to organize a comparison-and-contrast essay. Both patterns present the same information, but each has its own advantages and disadvantages.

OPPOSING PATTERN, SUBJECT BY SUBJECT	ALTERNATING PATTERN, POINT BY POINT
Subject A	Point 1
Point 1	Subject A
Point 2	Subject B
Point 3	
	Point 2
Subject B	Subject A
Point 1	Subject B
Point 2	
Point 3	Point 3
	Subject A
	Subject B

Use the Opposing Pattern of Organization. When you use the opposing pattern of subject by subject, you state all your observations about subject A and then do the same for subject B. In the following paragraph from *Whole-Brain Thinking* (New York: William Morrow, 1984), Jacquelyn Wonder and Priscilla Donovan use the opposing pattern of organization to explain the differences in the brains of females and males.

Subject A: Female brain

Point 1: Development
Point 2: Consequences

Shift to subject B:
Male brain
Point 1: Development
Point 2: Consequences

> At birth there are basic differences between male and female brains. The female cortex is more fully developed. The sound of the human voice elicits more left-brain activity in infant girls than in infant boys, accounting in part for the earlier development in females of language. Baby girls have larger connectors between the brain's hemispheres and thus integrate information more skillfully. This flexibility bestows greater verbal and intuitive skills. Male infants lack this ready communication between the brain's lobes; therefore, messages are routed and rerouted to the right brain, producing larger right hemispheres. The size advantage accounts for males having greater spatial and physical abilities and explains why they may become more highly lateralized and skilled in specific areas.

For a single paragraph or a short essay, the opposing pattern can effectively unify all the details about each subject. For a long essay or a complicated subject, it has a drawback: readers might find it difficult to remember all the separate information about subject A while reading about subject B.

Use the Alternating Pattern of Organization. There's a better way to organize most long papers: the *alternating pattern* of *point by point*. Using this method you take up one point at a time, applying it first to one subject and then to the other. Jacob Griffin uses this pattern to lead the reader along clearly and carefully, looking at each subject before moving on to the next point.

For Griffin's complete essay, see pp. 104–6. For more on outlines, see pp. 279–83.

THESIS: The International Olympic Committee should consider which of these styles first deserves to be declared an official Olympic sport.

    I.   Similarities of styles
        A. American popularity through movies
            1. Karate
            2. Kung fu
        B. Variety within styles
            1. Karate
            2. Kung fu
        C. Emphasis on internal values
            1. Karate
            2. Kung fu

   II.   Differences between styles
        A. Age and origins
            1. Karate
            2. Kung fu
        B. Techniques
            1. Karate's linear movement
            2. Kung fu's circular movement
        C. Uniforms and weapons
            1. Karate
            2. Kung fu

Add Transitions. Once your essay is organized, you can bring cohesion to it through effective transitional words and phrases — *on the other hand, in contrast, also, both, yet, although, finally, unlike.* Your choice of wording will depend on the content, but keep it varied and smooth. Jarring, choppy transitions distract attention instead of contributing to a unified essay, each part working to support a meaningful thesis.

For more on transitions, see pp. 295–99.

Learning by Doing 🖉 Building Cohesion with Transitions

Working on paper or in a file, add color highlights to mark each transitional expression already in your draft. Then check any passages without much highlighting to decide whether your audience will need more cues to see how your ideas connect. Next, check each spot where you switch from one subject or point to another to be sure that readers can easily make the shift. Finally, smooth out the wording of your transitions so that they are clear and helpful, not repetitious or mechanical. Test your changes on a reader by exchanging drafts with a classmate.

Revising and Editing

For more on revising and editing strategies, see Ch. 15.

Focus on Your Thesis. Reconsider your purpose when you review your draft. If your purpose is to illuminate two subjects impartially, ask whether you have given readers a balanced view. Obviously it would be unfair to set forth all the advantages of Oklahoma City and all the disadvantages of Honolulu and then conclude that Oklahoma City is superior on every count.

Of course, if you love Oklahoma City and can't stand Honolulu, or vice versa, go ahead: don't be balanced; take a stand. Even so, you will want to include the same points about each city and to admit, in all honesty, that Oklahoma City has its faults. One useful way to check for balance or thoroughness is to outline your draft and give the outline a critical look.

Peer Response 👥 Comparing and Contrasting

For general questions for a peer editor, see p. 305.

You may want a classmate or friend to respond to your draft, suggesting how to present your two subjects more clearly. Ask your peer editor to answer questions like these about comparison and contrast:

- How does the introduction motivate you to read the entire essay?
- What is the point of the comparison and contrast of the two subjects? Is the thesis stated in the essay, or is it implied?
- Is the essay organized by the opposing pattern or by the alternating pattern? Is the pattern appropriate, or would the other one work better?
- Are the same categories discussed for each item? If not, should they be?
- Are there enough details for you to understand the comparison and contrast? Put a check where more details or examples would be useful.
- If this paper were yours, what is the one thing you would be sure to work on before handing it in?

If classmates have made suggestions, perhaps about clearer wording to sharpen distinctions, use their ideas as you rework your thesis.

WORKING THESIS	Although students learn a lot in both of the required introductory biology courses, one class teaches information and the other teaches how to be a good learner.
REVISED THESIS	Although students learn the basics of biology in both of the required introductory courses, one class teaches how to memorize information and the other teaches an invaluable lesson: how to be an active learner.

Vary Your Wording. Make sure, as you go over your draft, that you have escaped a monotonous drone: A does this, B does that; A has these advantages, B has those. Comparison and contrast needn't result in a paper as symmetrical as a pair of sneakers. Revising and editing give you a chance to add lively details, transitions, dashes of color, and especially variety:

> The menu is another major difference between the Cozy Cafe and the Wilton Inn. For lunch, the Cozy Cafe offers sandwiches, hamburgers, and chili. ~~For lunch,~~ *L* *at* the Wilton Inn ~~offers~~ *features* dishes such as fajitas, shrimp salads, and onion soup topped with Swiss cheese. ~~For dinner, the Cozy Cafe continues to serve the lunch menu and~~ *adding* ~~adds~~ home-style comfort foods such as meatloaf, stew, macaroni and cheese, and *after five o'clock* barbecued ribs. ~~By dinner,~~ the Wilton's specialties for the day are posted—perhaps marinated buffalo steak or orange-pecan salmon.

REVISION CHECKLIST

- ☐ Does your introduction present your topic and main point clearly? Is it interesting enough to make a reader want to read the whole essay?

- ☐ Is your reason for doing all the comparing and contrasting unmistakably clear? What do you want to demonstrate, argue for, or find out? Do you need to reexamine your goal?

- ☐ Have you used the same categories for each item so that you treat them fairly? In discussing each feature, do you always look at the same thing?

- ☐ Have you selected points of comparison and supporting details that will intrigue, enlighten, and persuade your audience?

- ☐ What have you concluded about the two? Do you prefer one to the other? If so, is this preference (and your rationale for it) clear?

- ☐ Does your draft look thin at any point for lack of evidence? If so, how might you develop your ideas?

- ☐ Have you used the best arrangement, given your subjects and your point?

- ☐ Are there any spots where you need to revise a boringly mechanical, monotonous style ("On one hand, . . . now on the other hand")?

After you have revised your comparison-and-contrast essay, edit and proofread it. Carefully check the grammar, word choice, punctuation, and mechanics—and then correct any problems you may find.

For more editing and proofreading strategies, see pp. 313–17.

For more help, find the relevant checklists in the Quick Editing Guide beginning on p. A-39. Turn also to the Quick Format Guide beginning on p. A-1.

EDITING CHECKLIST

☐ Have you used the correct comparative forms (for two things) and superlative forms (for three or more) for adjectives and adverbs?   A7

☐ Is your sentence structure correct? Have you avoided writing fragments, comma splices, or fused sentences?   A1, A2

☐ Have you used parallel structure in your comparisons and contrasts? Are your sentences as balanced as your ideas?   B2

☐ Have you used commas correctly after introductory phrases and other transitions?   C1

Additional Writing Assignments

1. Listen to two different recordings of the same piece of music as performed by two different groups, orchestras, or singers. What elements of the music does each stress? What contrasting attitudes toward the music do you detect? In an essay, compare and contrast these versions.

2. In a serious or nonserious way, introduce yourself to your class by comparing and contrasting yourself with someone else. You might choose either a real person or a character in a film, a TV series, a novel, or a comic strip, but you and this other person should have much in common. Choose a few points of comparison (an attitude, a habit, or a way of life), and deal with each in an essay or, if your instructor approves, a mixed-media format.

3. With a classmate or small group, choose a topic, problem, or campus issue about which your views differ to some extent. Agree on several main points of contrast that you want each writer to consider. Then have each person write a paragraph summing up his or her point of view, concentrating on those main points. After your passages are written, collaboratively develop an introduction that outlines the issue, identifies the main points, and previews the contrasting views. Arrange the paragraphs effectively, add transitions, and write a collaborative conclusion. Revise and edit as needed to produce an orderly, coherent collaborative essay.

4. Compare and contrast yourself with a classmate in a collaborative essay. Decide together what your focus will be: Your backgrounds? Your paths to college? Your career goals? Your lives outside class? Your study habits? Your taste in music or clothes? Your politics? Have each writer use this focus to work on a detailed analysis of himself or herself. Then compare analyses, clarify the purpose and thesis of your comparison, and decide how to shape the essay. If your instructor approves, you might prepare a mixed-media presentation or post your essay to introduce yourselves to the class.

5. **Source Assignment.** Write an essay in which you compare and contrast the subjects in any of the following pairs for the purpose of throwing light on both. Turn to readings or essay pairs or e-Pages for this book, a source from the library, an interview with a friendly expert, news coverage, a Web page or image, or another relevant source for details and support. Be sure to credit your sources.

For more on using sources to support a position, see the Quick Research Guide beginning on p. A-20.

> The coverage of a world event on television and in a newspaper
> The experience of watching a film on a DVD and in a theater
> The styles of two athletes playing in the same position (two pitchers, two quarterbacks, two goalies)
> English and another language
> Two differing views of a current controversy
> Northern and southern California (or two other regions)
> Two similar works of architecture (two churches, two skyscrapers, two city halls, two museums, two campus buildings)
> Two articles, essays, or Web sites about the same topic
> Two short stories, two poems, or two literary works about the same theme
> Two articles or other types of sources for an upcoming research paper

6. **Visual Assignment.** The following images are selected from *What the World Eats,* a book that shows families around the world with their food for a week. Compare and contrast two of the images here in an essay, following the advice in this chapter. Be sure that you identify the purpose of your comparison, organize your subjects and points effectively, and support your points with details that you observe in the images.

For other contrasting images of families, see pp. 60, 146, and 222–24.

The Aboubakar family of Darfur province, Sudan, in a refugee camp in Chad with a week's worth of food (cost: $1.22 USD).

The Mendoza family and a servant in their courtyard in Guatemala, with a week's worth of food (cost: $75.70 USD).

The Revis family at home in Raleigh, North Carolina, with a week's worth of food (cost: $341.98 USD).

Taking a Stand

Responding to an Image

The signs in this image identify a group and its position. What issue motivates this group? What concerns might have led to this position? Based on the image, what event do you think it portrays? What might the photographer have wanted to convey?

Both in and outside of class, you'll hear controversial issues discussed — health care costs, immigration policy, bullying, gun legislation, disaster responses, global outsourcing of jobs, copyright issues. Such controversies may be national, regional, or local. Even in academic fields, experts don't always agree, and issues may remain controversies for years. Taking a stand in response to such issues will help you understand the controversy and clarify what you believe. Such writing is common in editorials, letters to the editor, or columns on the op-ed page in print and online news outlets. It is also the foundation of persuasive brochures, partisan blogs, and Web pages that take a stand.

Writing of this kind has a twofold purpose — to state, and to win your readers' respect for, an opinion. What you say might or might not change a reader's opinion. But if you fulfill your purpose, a reader at least will see good reasons for your views. In taking a stand, you do these things:

- You state your opinion or stand.
- You give reasons with evidence to support your position.
- You enlist your readers' trust.
- You consider and respect what your readers probably think and feel.

Why Taking a Stand Matters

In a College Course
- You take a stand in an essay or exam when you respond, pro or con, to a statement such as "The Web, like movable type for printing, is an invention that has transformed human communication."
- You take a stand when you write research papers that support your position on juvenile sentencing, state support for higher education, or tax breaks for new home buyers.

In the Workplace
- You take a stand when you persuade others that your case report supports a legal action that will benefit your clients or that your customer-service initiative will attract new business.

In Your Community
- You take a stand when you write a letter to the editor appealing to voters to support a local bond issue.

❓ When have you taken a stand in your writing? In what circumstances are you likely to do so again?

Learning from Other Writers

In the following two essays, the writers take a stand on issues of importance to them. To help you begin to analyze the first reading, look at the notes in the margin. They identify features such as the thesis, or main idea, and the first of the points that support it in a paper that takes a stand.

As You Read These Essays That Take a Stand

As you read these essays, ask yourself the following questions:

1. What stand does the writer take? Is it a popular opinion, or does it break from commonly accepted beliefs?
2. How does the writer appeal to readers?
3. How does the writer support his or her position? Is the evidence sufficient to gain your respect? Why or why not?

For a multimodal essay that takes a stand, read "Be Cool to the Pizza Dude" by Sarah Adams in Ch. e-5: **bedfordstmartins.com /concisebedguide**.

Suzan Shown Harjo

Last Rites for Indian Dead

As a result of persuasive efforts such as Suzan Shown Harjo's essay, the Native American Graves Protection and Repatriation Act was passed in 1990.

What if museums, universities, and government agencies could put your dead relatives on display or keep them in boxes to be cut up and otherwise studied? What if you believed that the spirits of the dead could not rest until their human remains were placed in a sacred area?

1

Introduction appeals to readers

The ordinary American would say there ought to be a law—and there is, for ordinary Americans. The problem for American Indians is that there are too many laws of the kind that make us the archaeological property of the United States and too few of the kind that protect us from such insults.

2 THESIS
taking a stand

Point 1

Some of my own Cheyenne relatives' skulls are in the Smithsonian Institution today, along with those of at least 4,500 other Indian people who were violated in the 1800s by the U.S. Army for an "Indian Crania Study." It wasn't enough that these unarmed Cheyenne people were mowed down by the cavalry at the infamous Sand Creek massacre; many were decapitated and their heads shipped to Washington as freight. (The Army Medical Museum's collection is now in the Smithsonian.) Some had been exhumed° only hours after being buried. Imagine their grieving families' reaction on finding their loved ones disinterred° and headless.

3 Supporting evidence

---

exhumed: Dug up out of the earth.   **disinterred:** Taken out of a place of burial.

Native Americans march with a truck returning 2,000 skeletal remains of Jemez Pueblo Indian ancestors for reburial in New Mexico. The remains had been in the collections of Harvard University.

Supporting evidence ———

Some targets of the army's study were killed in noncombat situations and beheaded immediately. The officer's account of the decapitation of the Apache chief Mangas Coloradas in 1863 shows the pseudoscientific nature of the exercise. "I weighed the brain and measured the skull," the good doctor wrote, "and found that while the skull was smaller, the brain was larger than that of Daniel Webster."   4

These journal accounts exist in excruciating detail, yet missing are any records of overall comparisons, conclusions, or final reports of the army study. Since it is unlike the army not to leave a paper trail, one must wonder about the motive for its collection.   5

The total Indian body count in the Smithsonian collection is more than 19,000, and it is not the largest in the country. It is not inconceivable that the 1.5 million of us living today are outnumbered by our dead stored in museums, educational institutions, federal agencies, state historical societies, and private collections. The Indian people are further dehumanized by being exhibited alongside the mastodons and dinosaurs and other extinct creatures.   6

Where we have buried our dead in peace, more often than not the sites have been desecrated. For more than two hundred years, relic-hunting has been a popular pursuit. Lately, the market in Indian artifacts has brought this abhorrent activity to a fever pitch in some areas. And when scavengers   7 come upon Indian burial sites, everything found becomes fair game, including sacred burial offerings, teeth, and skeletal remains.

One unusually well-publicized example of Indian grave desecration occurred two years ago in a western Kentucky field known as Slack Farm, the site of an Indian village five centuries ago. Ten men — one with a business card stating "Have Shovel, Will Travel" — paid the landowner $10,000 to lease digging rights between planting seasons. They dug extensively on the forty-acre farm, rummaging through an estimated 650 graves, collecting burial goods, tools, and ceremonial items. Skeletons were strewn about like litter.   8

What motivates people to do something like this? Financial gain is the first answer. Indian relic-collecting has become a multimillion-dollar industry. The price tag on a bead necklace can easily top $1,000; rare pieces fetch tens of thousands.   9   Question used as transition

And it is not just collectors of the macabre° who pay for skeletal remains. Scientists say that these deceased Indians are needed for research that someday could benefit the health and welfare of living Indians. But just how many dead Indians must they examine? Nineteen thousand?   10

There is doubt as to whether permanent curation of our dead really benefits Indians. Dr. Emery A. Johnson, former assistant Surgeon General, recently observed, "I am not aware of any current medical diagnostic or treatment procedure that has been derived from research on such skeletal remains. Nor am I aware of any during the thirty-four years that I have been involved in American Indian . . . health care."   11

Indian remains are still being collected for racial biological studies. While the intentions may be honorable, the ethics of using human remains this way without the full consent of relatives must be questioned.   12

Some relief for Indian people has come on the state level. Almost half of the states, including California, have passed laws protecting Indian burial sites and restricting the sale of Indian bones, burial offerings, and other sacred items. Representative Charles E. Bennett (D-Fla.) and Senator John McCain (R-Ariz.) have introduced bills that are a good start in invoking the federal government's protection. However, no legislation has attacked the problem head-on by imposing stiff penalties at the marketplace, or by changing laws that make dead Indians the nation's property.   13

Some universities — notably Stanford, Nebraska, Minnesota, and Seattle — have returned, or agreed to return, Indian human remains; it is fitting that institutions of higher education should lead the way.   14

Congress is now deciding what to do with the government's extensive collection of Indian human remains and associated funerary objects. The secretary of the Smithsonian, Robert McC. Adams, has been valiantly° attempting to apply modern ethics to yesterday's excesses. This week, he announced that the Smithsonian would conduct an inventory and return all Indian skeletal remains that could be identified with specific tribes or living kin.   15

macabre: Gruesome, ghastly.   **valiantly:** Bravely.

Transition to
concluding proposal
But there remains a reluctance generally among collectors of Indian re- 16
mains to take action of a scope that would have a quantitative impact and
a healing quality. If they will not act on their own—and it is highly unlikely
that they will—then Congress must act.

Conclusion
proposes action
The country must recognize that the bodies of dead American Indian 17
people are not artifacts to be bought and sold as collector's items. It is not
appropriate to store tens of thousands of our ancestors for possible future
research. They are our family. They deserve to be returned to their sacred
burial grounds and given a chance to rest.

The plunder of our people's graves has gone on too long. Let us rebury 18
our dead and remove this shameful past from America's future.

Questions to Start You Thinking

Meaning

1. What is the issue Harjo identifies? How extensive does she show it to be?

2. What is Harjo's position on this issue? Where does she first state it?

3. What evidence does Harjo present to refute the claim that housing
   skeletal remains of Native Americans in museums is necessary for
   medical research and may benefit living Indians?

Writing Strategies

4. What assumptions do you think Harjo makes about her audience?

5. What types of evidence does Harjo use to support her argument? How
   convincing is the evidence to you?

6. How does Harjo use her status as a Native American to enhance her
   position? Would her argument be as credible if it were written by someone of another background?

7. How does she appeal to the emotions of the readers in the essay? In what
   ways do these strategies strengthen or detract from her logical reasons?

8. Why does Harjo discuss what legislatures and universities are doing in
   response to the situation?

Marjorie Lee Garretson   **Student Essay**

More Pros Than Cons in a Meat-Free Life

Marjorie Lee Garretson's opinion piece originally appeared in *The Daily Mississippian*, the
student newspaper of the University of Mississippi, in April 2010.

What would you say if I told you there was a way to improve your overall health, 1
decrease environmental waste, and save animals from inhumane treatment at the
same time? You would probably ask how this is possible. The answer is quite simple:

go vegetarian. Vegetarians are often labeled as different or odd, but if you take a closer look at their actions, vegetarians reap multiple benefits meat eaters often overlook or choose to ignore for convenience.

The health benefits vegetarians acquire lead us to wonder why more people are not jumping on the meat-free bandwagon. On average, vegetarians have a lower body mass index,° significantly decreased cancer rates, and longer life expectancies. In addition, Alzheimer's disease° and osteoporosis° were linked to diets containing dairy, eggs, and meat.

The environment also encounters benefits from vegetarians. It takes less energy and waste to produce vegetables and grains than the energy required to produce meat. Producing one pound of meat is estimated to require 16 pounds of grain and up to 5,000 gallons of water, which comes from adding the water used to grow the grain crop as well as the animal's personal water consumption. Also, according to the Environmental Protection Agency, the runoff of fecal matter from meat factories is the single most detrimental° pollutant to our water supply. In fact, it is said to be the most significant pollutant in comparison to sources of all other industries combined.

The inhumane treatment of animals is common at most animal factories. The living conditions chickens, cows, pigs, and other livestock are forced into are far removed from their natural habitats. The goal of animal agriculture nowadays seems to be minimizing costs without attention to the sacrifices being made to do so. Animals are crammed into small cages where they often cannot even turn around. Exercise is denied to the animals to increase energy toward the production of meat. Female cows are pumped with hormones to allow their bodies to produce triple the amount of milk they are naturally capable of. Chickens are stuffed tightly into wire cages, and conditions are manipulated to increase egg production cycles. When chickens no longer lay eggs and cows cannot produce milk, they are transported to slaughterhouses where their lives are taken from them—often piece by piece.

Animal factory farms do a great job convincing Americans that their industry is vital to our health because of the protein, calcium, and other nutrients available in chicken, beef, and milk. We are bombarded with "Got Milk?" ads featuring various celebrities with white milk mustaches. We are told the egg is a healthy breakfast choice and lean protein is the basis of many good weight loss diets. What all of the ads and campaigns for animal products leave out are all the hormones injected into the animals to maximize production. Also, the tight living conditions allow for feces to contaminate the animals, their environment, and the potential meat they are

2

3 Do you find Garretson's discussion of the health benefits of vegetarianism convincing? Why or why not?

Is it possible to decrease damage to the environment from factory farms without becoming a vegetarian? What other options might there be?

4

5 Do you agree that Americans are hypocritical about the different treatment of household pets and farm animals? Why or why not?

body mass index: A measurement of body fat, based on height and weight.   **Alzheimer's disease:** An incurable brain disorder causing memory loss and dementia.   **osteoporosis:** A disease that increases risk of bone fractures.   **detrimental:** Harmful.

growing. It is ironic how irate° Americans react to puppy mills and the inhumane treatment of household pets, but for our meat and dairy products we look the other way. We pretend it is fine to confine cows, pigs, and chickens to tiny spaces and give them hormones and treat them inhumanely in their life and often in the way they are killed. We then cook and consume them at our dinner tables with our families and friends.

Therefore, I encourage you to consider a meat-free lifestyle not only for the sake   6 of the animals and the environment, but most importantly your personal health. All of your daily nutrients can be found in plant-based sources, and oftentimes when you make the switch to being a vegetarian, your food choices expand because you are willing to use vegetables and grains in innovative ways at the dinner table. Going vegetarian is a life-changing decision and one you can be proud of because you know it is for your own health as well as the greater good.

Questions to Start You Thinking

Meaning

1. What points does Garretson make to support her position that vegetarianism has multiple benefits?

2. What, according to Garretson, are the environmental consequences of meat-eating?

3. In the author's view, why is it especially troubling that we are willing to "look the other way" (paragraph 5) on the inhumane treatment of farm animals?

Writing Strategies

4. What kind of support does Garretson use to back up her claims about the benefits of vegetarianism? Do you find her argument effective? Why or why not?

5. To what extent does Garretson account for other points of view? How does the inclusion (or absence) of opposing views affect your opinion on the issue?

6. This article was written as an editorial for a student newspaper. How might Garretson change the article if she were submitting it as an essay or research paper?

7. Using highlighters or marginal notes, identify the essay's introduction, thesis, major points or reasons, supporting evidence for each point, and conclusion. How effective is the organization of this essay?

irate: Angry.

ⓔ UNICEF Editors   **Video**

Dirty Water Campaign

In 2009, UNICEF's Tap Project bottled the water that millions of people drink worldwide and "sold" it from a Dirty Water vending machine. This campaign garnered media attention and raised money to help people access clean, safe water. To watch a video that documents the project, go to Chapter 7: **bedfordstmartins.com/concisebedguide**.

The Dirty Water vending machine collected donations for the TAP Project.

Learning by Writing

The Assignment: Taking a Stand

Find a controversy that rouses your interest. It might be a current issue, a long-standing one, or a matter of personal concern: military benefits for national guard troops sent to war zones, the contribution of sports to a school's educational mission, or the need for menu changes at the cafeteria to accommodate ethnic, religious, and personal preferences. Your purpose isn't to solve a social or moral problem but to make clear exactly where you stand on an issue and to persuade your readers to respect your

ⓔ For an interactive Learning by Doing activity on writing your representative, go to Ch. 7: **bedfordstmartins.com /concisebedguide**.

position, perhaps even to accept it. As you reflect on your topic, you may change your position, but don't shift positions in the middle of your essay.

Assume that your readers are people who may or may not be familiar with the controversy, so provide relevant background or an overview to help them understand the situation. They also may not have taken sides yet or may hold a position different from yours. You'll need to consider their views and choose strategies to enlist their support.

Each of these students took a clear stand:

> A writer who pays her own college costs disputed the opinion that working during the school year provides a student with valuable knowledge. Citing her painful experience, she maintained that devoting full time to studies is far better than juggling school and work.

> Another writer challenged his history textbook's portrayal of Joan of Arc as "an ignorant farm girl subject to religious hysteria."

> A member of the wrestling team argued that the number of weight categories in the sport should be increased because athletes who overtrain to qualify for the existing categories often damage their health.

e For essays taking different stands on consumer culture, read "The Creation of Discontent" by Juliet Schor and "In Defense of Consumerism" by Llewellyn H. Rockwell Jr. in Ch. e-5: **bedfordstmartins.com /concisebedguide**.

Joan of Arc (1412–1431), heroine, martyr, saint, and cultural icon who boldly led French forces against the English.

Facing the Challenge   Taking a Stand

The major challenge writers face when taking a stand is to gather enough relevant evidence to support their position. Without such evidence, you'll convince only those who agreed with you in the first place. You also won't persuade readers by ranting emotionally about an issue or insulting as ignorant those who hold different opinions. Moreover, few readers respect an evasive writer who avoids taking a stand.

What does work is respect — yours for the views of readers who will, in turn, respect your opinion, even if they don't agree with it. You convey — and gain — respect when you anticipate readers' objections or counterarguments, demonstrate knowledge of these alternate views, and present evidence that addresses others' concerns as it strengthens your argument.

To anticipate and find evidence that acknowledges other views, list groups that might have strong opinions on your topic. Then try putting yourself in the shoes of a member of each group by writing a paragraph on the issue from that point of view.

- What would that person's opinion be?
- On what grounds might he or she object to your argument?
- How can you best address these concerns and overcome objections?

Your paragraph will suggest additional evidence to support your claims.

Generating Ideas

For this assignment, you will need to select an issue, take a stand, develop a clear position, and assemble evidence that supports your view.

Find an Issue. The topic for this paper should be an issue or controversy that interests both you and your audience. Try brainstorming a list of possible topics. Start with the headlines of a newspaper or newsmagazine, review the letters to the editor, check the political cartoons on the opinion page, or watch for stories on demonstrations or protests. You might also consult the library index to *CQ Researcher*, browse news or opinion Web sites, talk with friends, or consider topics raised in class. If you keep a journal, look over your entries to see what has perplexed or angered you. If you need to understand the issue better or aren't sure you want to take a stand on it, investigate by freewriting, reading, or turning to other sources.

For more strategies for generating ideas, see Ch. 12.

Once you have a list of possible topics, drop those that seem too broad or complex or that you don't know much about. Weed out anything that might not hold your—or your readers'—interest. From your new list, pick the issue or controversy for which you can make the strongest argument.

Start with a Question and a Thesis. At this stage, many writers try to pose the issue as a question—one that will be answered through the position they take. Skip vague questions that most readers wouldn't debate, or convert them to questions that allow different stands.

VAGUE QUESTION	Is stereotyping bad?
CLEARLY DEBATABLE	Should we fight gender stereotypes in advertising?

You can help focus your position by stating it in a sentence—a thesis, or statement of your stand. Your statement can answer your question:

WORKING THESIS	We should expect advertisers to fight rather than reinforce gender stereotypes.
OR	Most people who object to gender stereotypes in advertising need to get a sense of humor.

For more on stating a thesis, see pp. 263–69.

Your thesis should invite continued debate by taking a strong position that can be argued rather than stating a fact.

FACT   Hispanics constitute 16 percent of the community but only 3 percent of our school population.

WORKING THESIS   Our school should increase outreach to the Hispanic community, which is underrepresented on campus.

Learning by Doing 🎬 Asking Your Question

Using your list of possible topics, start writing down questions you might want to answer. Then work with a classmate or small group, in person or chatting online, to review everyone's list. Weed out questions that seem vague or difficult to debate. For questions with potential, write out some working thesis statements until you settle on a statement you want to support.

Use Formal Reasoning to Refine Your Position. As you take a stand on a debatable matter, you are likely to use reasoning as well as specific evidence to support your position. A *syllogism* is a series of statements, or premises, used in traditional formal logic to lead deductively to a logical conclusion.

MAJOR STATEMENT   All students must pay tuition.

MINOR STATEMENT   You are a student.

CONCLUSION   Therefore, you must pay tuition.

For a syllogism to be logical, ensuring that its conclusion always applies, its major and minor statements must be true, its definitions of terms must remain stable, and its classification of specific persons or items must be accurate. In real-life arguments, such tidiness may be hard to achieve.

For example, maybe we all agree with the major statement above that all students must pay tuition. However, some students' tuition is paid for them through a loan or scholarship. Others are admitted under special programs, such as a free-tuition benefit for families of college employees or a back-to-college program for retirees. Further, the word *student* is general; it might apply to students at public high schools who pay no tuition. Next, everyone might agree that you are a student, but maybe you haven't completed registration or the computer has mysteriously dropped you from the class list. Such complications can threaten the success of your conclusion, especially if your audience doesn't accept it. In fact, many civic and social arguments revolve around questions such as these: What—exactly—is the category or group affected? Is its definition or consequence stable—or does it vary? Who falls in or out of the category?

Use Informal Toulmin Reasoning to Refine Your Position. A contemporary approach to logic is presented by the philosopher Stephen Toulmin (1922–2009) in *The Uses of Argument* (2nd ed., 2003). He describes an informal way of arguing that acknowledges the power of assumptions in our day-to-day reasoning. This approach starts with a concise statement—the essence of an argument—that makes a claim and supplies a reason to support it.

———— CLAIM ————   ———— REASON ————
Students should boycott the café <u>because</u> the food costs too much.

You develop a claim by supporting your reasons with evidence—your *data* or grounds. For example, your evidence might include facts about the cost of lunches on campus, especially in contrast to local fast-food options, and statistics about the limited resources of most students at your campus.

However, most practical arguments rely on a *warrant*, your thinking about the connection or relationship between your claim and your supporting data. Because you accept this connection and assume that it applies, you generally assume that others also take it for granted. For instance, nearly all students might accept your assumption that a campus café should serve the needs of its customers. Many might also agree that students should take action rather than allow a campus facility to take advantage of them by charging high prices. Even so, you could state your warrant directly if you thought that your readers would not see the connection that you do. You also could back up your warrant, if necessary, in various ways:

- using facts, perhaps based on quality and cost comparisons with food service operations on other campuses
- using logic, perhaps based on research findings about the relationship between cost and nutrition for institutional food as well as the importance of good nutrition for brain function and learning
- making emotional appeals, perhaps based on happy memories of the café or irritation with its options
- making ethical appeals, perhaps based on the college mission statement or other expressions of the school's commitment to students

As you develop your reasoning, you might adjust your claim or your data to suit your audience, your issue, or your refined thinking. For instance, you might *qualify* your argument (perhaps limiting your objections to most, but not all, of the lunch prices). You might also add a *rebuttal* by identifying an *exception* to it (perhaps excluding the fortunate, but few, students without financial worries due to good jobs or family support). Or you might simply reconsider your claim, concluding that the campus café is, after all, convenient for students and that the manager might be willing to offer more inexpensive options without a student boycott.

———— REVISED CLAIM ————┬—— REASON ——
The café should offer less expensive options because most students

can't afford a balanced meal at current prices.

Toulmin reasoning is especially effective for making claims like these:

- Fact — *Loss of polar ice can accelerate ocean warming.*
- Cause — *The software company went bankrupt because of its excessive borrowing and poor management.*
- Value — *Cell phone plan A is a better deal than cell phone plan B.*
- Policy — *Admissions policies at Triborough University should be less restrictive.*

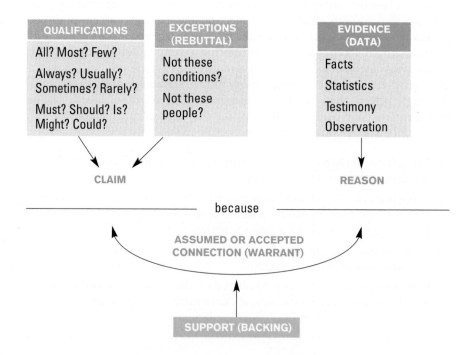

☐ What issue or controversy concerns you? What current debate engages you?

☐ What position do you want to take? How can you state your stand? What evidence might you need to support it?

☐ How might you refine your working thesis? How could you make statements more accurate, definitions clearer, or categories more exact?

☐ What assumptions are you making? What clarification of or support for these assumptions might your audience need?

☐ How might you qualify your thesis? What exceptions should you note? What other views might you want to recognize?

Select Evidence to Support Your Position. When you state your claim, you state your overall position. You also may state supporting claims as topic sentences that establish your supporting points, introduce supporting evidence, and help your reader follow your reasoning. To decide how to support a claim, try to reduce it to its core question. Then figure out what reliable and persuasive evidence might answer the question.

As you begin to look for supporting evidence, consider the issue in terms of the three general types of claims — claims that require substantiation, provide evaluation, and endorse policy.

1. Claims of Substantiation: What Happened?

   These claims require examining and interpreting information in order to resolve disputes about facts, circumstances, causes or effects, definitions, or the extent of a problem.

   Sample Claims:
   a. Certain types of cigarette ads, such as the once-popular Joe Camel ads, significantly encouraged smoking among teenagers.
   b. Despite a few well-publicized exceptions, police brutality in this country is not a major problem.
   c. On the whole, bilingual education programs actually help students learn English more quickly than total immersion programs do.

   Possible Supporting Evidence:
   - Facts and information: parties involved, dates, times, places
   - Clear definitions of terms: *police brutality* or *total immersion*
   - Well-supported comparison and contrast: statistics to contrast "a few well-publicized exceptions" with a majority of instances that are "not a problem"
   - Well-supported cause-and-effect analysis: authoritative information to demonstrate how actions of tobacco companies "significantly encouraged smoking" or bilingual programs "help students learn English faster"

2. Claims of Evaluation: What Is Right?

These claims consider right or wrong, appropriateness or inappropriateness, and worth or lack of worth involved in an issue.

Sample Claims:

a. Research using fetal tissue is unethical in a civilized society.

b. English-only legislation promotes cultural intolerance in our society.

c. Keeping children in foster care for years, instead of releasing them for adoption, is wrong.

Possible Supporting Evidence:

■ Explanations or definitions of appropriate criteria for judging: deciding what's "unethical in a civilized society"

■ Corresponding details and reasons showing how the topic does or does not meet the criteria: details or applications of English-only legislation that meet the criteria for "cultural intolerance" or reasons with supporting details that show why years of foster care meet the criteria for being "wrong"

3. Claims of Policy: What Should Be Done?

These claims challenge or defend approaches for achieving generally accepted goals.

Sample Claims:

a. The federal government should support the distribution of clean needles to reduce the rate of HIV infection among intravenous drug users.

b. Denying children of undocumented workers enrollment in public schools will reduce the problem of illegal immigration.

c. All teenagers accused of murder should be tried as adults.

Possible Supporting Evidence:

■ Explanation and definition of the policy goal: assuming that most in your audience agree that it is desirable to reduce "the rate of HIV infection" or "the problem of illegal immigration" or to try murderers in the same way regardless of age

■ Corresponding details and reasons showing how your policy recommendation would meet the goal: results of "clean needle" trials or examples of crime statistics and cases involving teen murderers

■ Explanations or definitions of the policy's limits or applications, if needed: why some teens should not be tried as adults because of their situations

Consider Your Audience as You Develop Your Claim. The nature of your audience might influence the type of claim you choose to make. For example, suppose that the nurse or social worker at the high school you attended or that your children now attend proposed distributing free condoms to students. The following table illustrates how the responses of different audiences to this proposal might vary with the claim. As you develop your claims, try to put yourself in the place of your audience. For example, if you are a former student, what claim would most effectively persuade you? If you are the parent of a teenager, what claim would best address both your general views and your specific concerns about your own child?

Audience	Type of Claim	Possible Effect on Audience
Conservative parents who believe that free condoms would promote immoral sexual behavior	*Evaluation:* In order to save lives and prevent unwanted pregnancies, distributing free condoms in high school is our moral duty.	Counterproductive if the parents feel that they are being accused of immorality for not agreeing with the proposal
Conservative parents who believe that free condoms would promote immoral sexual behavior	*Substantiation:* Distributing free condoms in high school can effectively reduce pregnancy rates and the spread of STDs, especially AIDS, without substantially increasing the rate of sexual activity among teenagers.	Possibly persuasive, based on effectiveness, if parents feel that their desire to protect their children from harm, no matter what, is recognized and the evidence deflates their main fear (promoting sexual activity)
School administrators who want to do what's right but don't want hordes of angry parents pounding down the school doors	*Policy:* Distributing free condoms in high school to prevent unwanted pregnancies and the spread of STDs, including AIDS, is best accomplished as part of a voluntary sex education program that strongly emphasizes abstinence as the primary preventative.	Possibly persuasive if administrators see that the proposal addresses health and pregnancy issues without setting off parental outrage (by proposing a voluntary program that would promote abstinence, thus addressing concerns of parents)

Assemble Supporting Evidence. Your claim stated, you'll need evidence to support it. That evidence can be anything that demonstrates the soundness of your position and the points you make — facts, statistics, observations, expert testimony, illustrations, examples, and case studies.

For more about forms of evidence, see pp. 40–43.

The three most important sources of evidence are these:

1. *Facts, including statistics.* Facts are statements that can be verified by objective means; statistics are facts expressed in numbers. Facts usually form the basis of a successful argument.

For more about using sources, see Ch. 9 and the Quick Research Guide beginning on p. A-20.

2. *Expert testimony.* Experts are people with knowledge of a particular field gained from study and experience.

3. *Firsthand observation.* Your own observations can be persuasive if you can assure your readers that your account is accurate.

Of course, evidence must be used carefully to avoid defending logical fallacies — common mistakes in thinking — and making statements that lead to wrong conclusions. Examples are easy to misuse (claiming proof by example or too few examples). Because two professors you know are dissatis-

For more on logical fallacies, see pp. 143–44.

fied with state-mandated testing programs, you can't claim that all—or even most—professors are. Even if you surveyed more professors at your school, you could speak only generally of "many professors." To claim more, you might need to conduct scientific surveys, access reliable statistics from the library or Internet, or solicit the views of a respected expert in the area.

Learning by Doing 🎬 Supporting a Claim

Write out, in one complete sentence, the core claim or position you plan to support. Working in a small group, drop all these "position statements" into a hat, with no names attached. Then draw and read each aloud in turn, inviting the group to suggest useful supporting evidence and possible sources for it. Ask someone in the group to act as a recorder, listing suggestions on a separate page for each claim. Finally, match up writers with claims, and share reactions. (If you are working online, follow your instructor's directions, possibly sending your statement privately to your instructor for anonymous posting for a threaded discussion.) If this activity causes you to alter your stand, be thankful: it will be easier to revise now rather than later.

Record Evidence. For this assignment, you will need to record your evidence in written form in a notebook or a computer file. Note exactly where each piece of information comes from. Keep the form of your notes flexible so that you can easily rearrange them as you plan your draft.

Test and Select Evidence to Persuade Your Audience. Now that you've collected some evidence, sift through it to decide which information to use. Evidence is useful and trustworthy when it is accurate, reliable, up-to-date, to the point, representative, appropriately complex, and sufficient and strong enough to back the claim and persuade readers. You may find that your evidence supports a different stand than you intended to take. Might you find facts, testimony, and observations to support your original position after all? Or should you rethink your position? If so, revise your working thesis. Does your evidence cluster around several points or reasons? If so, use your evidence to plan the sequence of your essay.

For more on testing evidence, see section A in the Quick Research Guide, pp. A-21–A-24.

For more on the use of visuals and their placement, see section B in the Quick Format Guide, pp. A-8–A-12.

In addition, consider whether information presented visually would strengthen your case or make your evidence easier for readers to grasp.

- Graphs can effectively show facts or figures.
- Tables can convey terms or comparisons.
- Photographs or other illustrations can substantiate situations.

Test each visual as you would test other evidence for accuracy, reliability, and relevance. Mention each visual in your text, and place the visual close to that reference. Cite the source of any visual you use and of any data you consolidate in your own graph or table.

Most effective arguments take opposing viewpoints into consideration whenever possible. Use these questions to help you assess your evidence from this standpoint.

ANALYZE YOUR READERS' POINTS OF VIEW

- What are their attitudes? Interests? Priorities?
- What do they already know about the issue?
- What do they expect you to say?
- Do you have enough appropriate evidence that they'll find convincing?

FOCUS ON THOSE WITH DIFFERENT OR OPPOSING OPINIONS

- What are their opinions or claims?
- What is their evidence?
- Who supports their positions?
- Do you have enough appropriate evidence to show why their claims are weak, only partially true, misguided, or just plain wrong?

ACKNOWLEDGE AND REBUT THE COUNTERARGUMENTS

- What are the strengths of other positions? What might you want to concede or grant to be accurate or relevant?
- What are the limitations of other positions? What might you want to question or challenge?
- What facts, statistics, testimony, observations, or other evidence supports questioning, qualifying, challenging, or countering other views?

Planning, Drafting, and Developing

Reassess Your Position and Your Thesis. Now that you have looked into the issue, what is your current position? If necessary, revise the thesis that you formulated earlier. Then summarize your reasons for holding this view, and list your supporting evidence.

WORKING THESIS	We should expect advertisers to fight rather than reinforce gender stereotypes.
REFINED THESIS	Consumers should spend their shopping dollars thoughtfully in order to hold advertisers accountable for reinforcing rather than resisting gender stereotypes.

For help developing and supporting effective thesis statements, go to the interactive "Take Action" charts in Re:Writing at **bedfordstmartins.com /concisebedguide**.

Learning by Doing 🗇 Refining Your Plans

Follow the steps outlined in the previous section: update your thesis to match your current view, summarize the reasons behind that position, and list your supporting evidence. Ask a classmate for a second opinion on these plans, and continue reworking them if your exchange generates significant questions or ideas.

Organize Your Material to Persuade Your Audience. Arrange your notes into the order you think you'll follow, perhaps making an outline. One useful pattern is the classical form of argument:

For more on outlines, see pp. 275–83.

1. Introduce the subject to gain the readers' interest.
2. State your main point or thesis.
3. If useful, supply historical background or an overview of the situation.
4. Present your points or reasons, and provide evidence to support them.
5. Refute the opposition.
6. Reaffirm your main point.

When you expect readers to be hostile to your position, stating your position too early might alienate resistant readers or make them defensive. Instead, you may want to refute the opposition first, then replace those views by building a logical chain of evidence that leads to your main point, and finally state your position. Of course, you can always try both approaches to see which one works better. Note also that some papers will be mostly based on refutation (countering opposing views) and some mostly on confirmation (directly supporting your position). Others might even alternate refutation and confirmation rather than separate them.

Define Your Terms. To prevent misunderstanding, make clear any unfamiliar or questionable terms used in your thesis. If your position is "Humanists are dangerous," you will want to give a short definition of what you mean by *humanists* and by *dangerous* early in the paper.

For more on appeals, see pp. 44–45.

Attend to Logical, Emotional, and Ethical Appeals. The logical appeal engages readers' intellect; the emotional appeal touches their hearts; the ethical appeal draws on their sense of fairness and reasonableness. A persuasive argument usually operates on all three levels. For example, you might use all three appeals to support a thesis about the need to curb accidental gunshot deaths, as the following table illustrates.

Type of Appeal	Ways of Making the Appeal	Possible Supporting Evidence
Logical (logos)	■ Rely on clear reasoning and sound evidence to influence a reader's thinking. ■ Demonstrate what you claim, and don't claim what you can't demonstrate. ■ Test and select your evidence.	■ Supply current and reliable statistics about gun ownership and accidental shootings. ■ Prepare a bar graph that shows the number of incidents each year in Lion Valley during the past ten years, using data from the county records. ■ Describe the immediate and long-term consequences of a typical shooting accident.
Emotional (pathos)	■ Choose examples and language that will influence a reader's feelings. ■ Include effective images, but don't overdo them. ■ Complement logical appeals, but don't replace them.	■ Describe the wrenching scenario of a father whose college-age son unexpectedly returns home at 3 A.M. The father mistakes his son for an intruder and shoots him, throwing the family into turmoil. ■ Use quotations and descriptions from newspaper accounts to show reactions of family and friends.
Ethical (ethos)	■ Use a tone and approach that appeal to your reader's sense of fairness and reasonableness. ■ Spell out your values and beliefs, and acknowledge values and beliefs of others with different opinions. ■ Establish your credentials, if any, and the credentials of experts you cite. ■ Instill confidence in your readers so that they see you as a caring, trustworthy person with reliable views.	■ Establish your reasonable approach by acknowledging the views of hunters and others who store guns at home and follow recommended safety procedures. ■ Supply the credentials or affiliation of experts ("Ray Fontaine, public safety director for the town of Lion Valley"). ■ Note ways in which experts have established their authority ("During my interview with Ms. Dutton, she related recent incidents involving gun accidents in the home, testifying to her extensive knowledge of this issue in our community.")

Learning by Doing 🎦 Making Columns of Appeals

Use columns to help you write about your logical, emotional, and ethical appeals. Go to the Format menu in your word processor, select Columns, and click on the preset three-column pattern. (Or draw three columns on paper.) Under "Logical Appeals," write the claims and support that rely on reasoning and sound evidence. Under "Emotional Appeals," note the claims and support that may affect readers' emotions. Under "Ethical Appeals," add your claims and support based on values, both your values and those of opposing points of view as you understand them. As you reread each column, consider how to relate your claims and support across columns, how to organize your ideas persuasively, and how best to merge or separate your logical, emotional, and ethical appeals. Add color coding if you want to identify related ideas.

Logical Appeals	Emotional Appeals	Ethical Appeals

For pointers on integrating and documenting sources, see Ch. 9 and D6 (p. A-31) and E1–E2 (pp. A-32–A-38) in the Quick Research Guide.

Credit Your Sources. As you write, make your sources of evidence clear. One simple way to do so is to incorporate your source into the text: "As analyzed in an article in the October 15, 2012, issue of *Time*" or "According to my history professor, Dr. Harry Cleghorn . . ."

Revising and Editing

For more revising and editing strategies, see Ch. 15.

When you're writing a paper that takes a stand, you may fall in love with the evidence you've gone to such trouble to collect. Taking out information is hard to do, but if it is irrelevant, redundant, or weak, the evidence won't help your case. Play the crusty critic as you reread your paper. Consider outlining what it actually includes so that you can check for missing or unnecessary points or evidence. Pay special attention to the suggestions of friends or classmates who read your draft for you. Apply their advice by ruthlessly cutting unneeded material, as in the following passage:

> The school boundary system requires children who are homeless or whose families move frequently to change schools repeatedly. ~~They often lack clean clothes, winter coats, and required school supplies.~~ As a result, these children struggle to establish strong relationships with teachers, to find caring advocates at school, and even to make friends to join for recess or lunch.

Peer Response 👥 Taking a Stand

For general questions for a peer editor, see p. 305.

Enlist several other students to read your draft critically and tell you whether they accept your arguments. For a paper in which you take a stand, ask your peer editors to answer questions such as these:

- Can you state the writer's claim?
- Do you have any problems following or accepting the reasons for the writer's position? Would you make any changes in the reasoning?

- How persuasive is the writer's evidence? What questions do you have about it? Can you suggest good evidence the writer has overlooked?

- Has the writer provided enough transitions to guide you through the argument?

- Has the writer made a strong case? Are you persuaded to his or her point of view? If not, is there any point or objection that the writer could address to make the argument more compelling?

- If this paper were yours, what is the one thing you would be sure to work on before handing it in?

Use the Take Action chart (p. 142) to help you figure out how to improve your draft. Skim across the top to identify questions you might ask about strengthening support for your stand. When you answer a question with "Yes" or "Maybe," move straight down the column to Locate Specifics under that question. Use the activities there to pinpoint gaps, problems, or weaknesses. Then move straight down the column to Take Action. Use the advice that suits your problem as you revise.

For online Take Action help, go to the interactive "Take Action" charts in Re:Writing at **bedfordstmartins.com /concisebedguide**.

REVISION CHECKLIST

☐ Is your main point, or thesis, clear? Do you stick to it rather than drifting into contradictions?

☐ Where might you need better reasons or more evidence?

☐ Have you tried to keep in mind your readers and what would appeal to them? Where have you answered their likely objections?

☐ Have you defined all necessary terms and explained your points clearly?

☐ Is your tone suitable for your readers? Would any wording alienate them, or, at the other extreme, sound weak or apologetic?

☐ Might your points seem stronger if arranged in a different sequence?

☐ Have you unfairly omitted any evidence that would hurt your case?

☐ In rereading your paper, do you have any excellent, fresh thoughts? If so, where might you make room for them?

After you have revised your argument, edit and proofread it. Carefully check the grammar, word choice, punctuation, and mechanics—and then correct any problems you find. Wherever you have given facts and figures as evidence, check for errors in names and numbers.

For more editing and proofreading strategies, see pp. 313–17.

Take Action Strengthening Support for a Stand

Ask each question at the top of the chart to consider whether your draft might need work on that issue. If so, follow the ASK—LOCATE SPECIFICS—TAKE ACTION sequence to revise.

	Missing Points?	**Missing Supporting Evidence?**	**One-Sided Support?**
1 **ASK**	Did I leave out any main points that I promised in my thesis or planned to include?	Did I leave out evidence needed to support my points—facts, statistics, expert testimony, firsthand observations, details, or examples?	Have I skipped over opposing or alternative perspectives? Have I treated them unfairly, disrespectfully, or too briefly?
2 **LOCATE SPECIFICS**	■ List the main points your thesis states or suggests. ■ List the main points you meant to include. ■ Highlight each point from your lists in your draft.	■ Highlight or color code each bit of supporting evidence. ■ Put a ✓ by any passage without any, without enough, or without specific supporting evidence.	■ Highlight passages in which you recognize other points of view (or copy them into a separate file) so you can look at them on their own. ■ Read these passages to see whether they sound fair and respectful. Jot down notes to yourself about possible revisions.
3 **TAKE ACTION**	■ Add any missing point from your thesis or plan. ■ Express assumptions (points, main ideas, reasons) that are in your head but not your draft. ■ Revise your thesis, adding or dropping points until it promises what you can deliver to readers.	■ Add any missing evidence you meant to include. ■ For each ✓, brainstorm or ask questions (who, what, where, when, why, how) to decide what specific support readers might find convincing. ■ Add the evidence, details, or examples needed to support each main point.	■ Identify or add other points of view if they are expected and you have left them out. ■ Acknowledge credible alternative views, explaining where you agree and differ. ■ Reasonably challenge or counter questionable views. ■ Edit your wording so your tone is respectful of others.

EDITING CHECKLIST

☐ Is it clear what each pronoun refers to? Does each pronoun agree with (match) its antecedent? Do pronouns used as subjects agree with their verbs? Carefully check sentences that make broad claims about *everyone, no one, some, a few,* or some other group identified by an indefinite pronoun.   A6

☐ Have you used an adjective whenever describing a noun or pronoun? Have you used an adverb whenever describing a verb, adjective, or adverb? Have you used the correct form when comparing two or more things?   A7

☐ Have you set off your transitions, other introductory elements, and interrupters with commas, if these are needed?   C1

☐ Have you spelled and capitalized everything correctly, especially names of people and organizations?   D1, D2

☐ Have you correctly punctuated quotations from sources and experts?   C3

For more help, find the relevant checklists in the Quick Editing Guide beginning on p. A-39. Turn also to the Quick Format Guide beginning on p. A-1.

Recognizing Logical Fallacies

Logical fallacies are common mistakes in thinking that may lead to wrong conclusions or distort evidence. Here are a few familiar logical fallacies.

For more on faulty thinking, see pp. A-51–A-52.

Term	Explanation	Example
Non Sequitur	Stating a claim that doesn't follow from your first premise or statement; Latin for "It does not follow"	Jenn should marry Mateo. In college he got all A's.
Oversimplification	Offering easy solutions for complicated problems	If we want to end substance abuse, let's send every drug user to prison for life. (Even aspirin users?)
Post Hoc Ergo Propter Hoc	Assuming a cause-and-effect relationship where none exists, even though one event preceded another; Latin for "after this, therefore because of this"	After Jenny's black cat crossed my path, everything went wrong, and I failed my midterm.
Allness	Stating or implying that something is true of an entire class of things, often using *all, everyone, no one, always,* or *never*	Students enjoy studying. (All students? All subjects? All the time?)

(continued on next page)

Term	Explanation	Example
Proof by Example or Too Few Examples	Presenting an example as proof rather than as illustration or clarification; overgeneralizing (the basis of much prejudice)	Armenians are great chefs. My neighbor is Armenian, and can he cook!
Begging the Question	Proving a statement already taken for granted, often by repeating it in different words or by defining a word in terms of itself	Rapists are dangerous because they are menaces. Happiness is the state of being happy.
Circular Reasoning	Supporting a statement with itself; a form of begging the question	He is a liar because he simply isn't telling the truth.
Either/Or Reasoning	Oversimplifying by assuming that an issue has only two sides, a statement must be true or false, a question demands a yes or no answer, or a problem has only two possible solutions (and one that's acceptable)	What are we going to do about global warming? Either we stop using all of the energy-consuming vehicles and products that cause it, or we just learn to live with it.
Argument from Dubious Authority	Using an unidentified authority to shore up a weak argument or an authority whose expertise lies outside the issue, such as a television personality selling insurance	According to some of the most knowing scientists in America, smoking two packs a day is as harmless as eating oatmeal cookies.
Argument *ad Hominem*	Attacking an individual's opinion by attacking his or her character, thus deflecting attention from the merit of a proposal; Latin for "against the man"	Diaz may argue that we need to save the polar bears, but he's the type who gets emotional over nothing.
Argument from Ignorance	Maintaining that a claim has to be accepted because it hasn't been disproved or that it has to be rejected because it has not been proved	Despite years of effort, no one has proved that ghosts don't exist; therefore, we should expect to see them at any time. No one has ever shown that life exists on any other planet; clearly the notion of other living things in the universe is absurd.
Argument by Analogy	Treating an extended comparison between familiar and unfamiliar items, based on similarities and ignoring differences, as evidence rather than as a useful way of explaining	People were born free as the birds; it's cruel to expect them to work.
Bandwagon Argument	Suggesting that everyone is joining the group and that readers who don't may miss out on happiness, success, or a reward	Purchasing the new Global Glimmer admits you to the nation's most elite group of smartphone users.

Additional Writing Assignments

1. Write a letter to the editor of your newspaper or a newsmagazine in which you agree or disagree with the publication's editorial stand on a current question. Make clear your reasons for holding your view.

2. Write one claim each of substantiation, evaluation, and policy for or against a specific policy or proposal. Indicate an audience each claim might address effectively. Then list reasons and types of evidence you might need to support one of these claims. For the same claim, indicate what opposing viewpoints you would need to consider and how you could best do so.

3. Write a short paper, blog entry, or class posting expressing your view on one of these topics or another that comes to mind. Make clear your reasons for thinking as you do.

Bilingual education	Raising the minimum wage
Nonsmokers' rights	Protecting the gray wolf
Dealing with date rape	Controlling terrorism
Salaries of professional athletes	Prayer in public schools

4. Working with a classmate or a small group online, develop a discussion or collaborative blog to inform your audience about multiple points of view on an issue. Present the most compelling reasons and evidence to support each view. Counter other views as appropriate with reasons and evidence, but avoid emotional outbursts attacking them. Before you begin posting, decide which view each person will present. Considering your purpose and audience, also decide whether the discussion or blog should cover certain points or be organized in a particular way. Before you post your contribution, write it in a location or file where you can save and return to it. Take some time to revise and edit before you send it or paste it in.

   For more on supporting a position with sources, see Ch. 9.

5. **Source Assignment.** Find a letter to the editor, opinion piece, or blog that takes a stand that you disagree with. Write a response to that piece, countering its points, presenting your points, and supporting them with evidence. Be sure to cite the other piece, and identify any quotations or summaries from it. Decide which audience to address: The writer? Readers likely to support the other selection? Readers with interest in the issue but without loyalty to the original publication? Some other group?

6. **Visual Assignment.** Select one of the images on the next two pages. Analyze its argument, noting its persuasive visual elements. Write an essay that first explains its argument, including its topic and its visual appeals to viewers, and then agrees, disagrees, or qualifies that argument.

A young person hospitalized with cancer watches a fundraising walkathon.

A family in Connecticut reads after dinner.

A cell phone tower in Mono Lake, California, from photographer Robert Voit's series, "New Trees."

8 Evaluating and Reviewing

Responding to an Image

In what respects does this photograph of a giant-pumpkin weigh-in capture the essence of such competitions? What overall impression does the image convey? What details contribute to this impression? How does the photograph direct the viewer's eye? In what ways does this image suggest, represent, or comment on a particular set of criteria and process of evaluation?

Evaluating means judging. You do it when you decide what candidate to vote for, pick which camera to buy, or recommend a new restaurant to your friends. All of us pass judgments—often snap judgments—as we move through a day's routine. A friend asks, "How was that movie you saw last night?" and you reply, "Terrific—don't miss it" or maybe "Pretty good, but it had too much blood and gore for me."

But to *write* an evaluation calls for you to think more critically. As a writer you first decide on *criteria,* or standards for judging, and then come up with evidence to back up your judgment. Your evaluation zeroes in on a definite subject that you inspect carefully in order to reach a considered opinion. The subject might be a film, a book, or a performance that you review. Or it might be a sports team, a product, or a body of research that you evaluate. The possibilities are endless.

Why Evaluating and Reviewing Matter

In a College Course

- You evaluate theories and methods in the fields you study, including long-standing controversies such as the dispute about teaching methods raging in education for the deaf.
- You evaluate instructors, courses, and sometimes campus facilities and services to participate in the process of monitoring and improving your college.

In the Workplace

- You evaluate people, projects, goals, and results, just as your potential was evaluated as a job applicant and your performance is evaluated as an employee.

In Your Community

- You evaluate video games for yourself or your children and review films, music, shows, and restaurants as you decide how to spend your money and time.

What have you evaluated within the last few weeks? How have evaluations and reviews been useful for you? How have you incorporated evaluations and reviews into your writing?

Learning from Other Writers

Here are evaluations by a professional and a student. To help you analyze the first reading, look at the notes in the margin. They identify features such as the thesis, or main idea, the criteria for evaluation, and the evidence supporting the writer's judgment, all typical of essays that evaluate.

As You Read These Evaluations

As you read these essays, ask yourself the following questions:

1. Do you consider the writer qualified to evaluate the subject he or she chose? What biases and prejudices might the writer bring to the task?
2. What criteria for evaluation does the writer establish? Are these reasonable standards for evaluating the subject?
3. What is the writer's assessment of the subject? Does the writer provide sufficient evidence to convince you of his or her evaluation?

For another example of evaluation, read "How Computers Change the Way We Think" by Sherry Turkle in Ch. e-4: **bedfordstmartins.com /concisebedguide.**

Scott Tobias

The Hunger Games

Film critic Scott Tobias has reviewed movies for NPR.org, the *Village Voice*, and the *Hollywood Reporter*. As the film editor for the A.V. Club section of the *Onion*, where this review appeared, he evaluates the film version of the popular book, *The Hunger Games*.

If Suzanne Collins's novel *The Hunger Games* turns up on school curricula 50   1
years from now—and as accessible dystopian° science fiction with allusions° to early-21st-century strife, that isn't out of the question—the lazy students of the future can be assured that they can watch the movie version and still get better than a passing grade. But that's a dubious triumph: A book is a book and a movie is a movie, and whenever the latter merely sets about illustrating the former, it's a failure of adaptation, to say nothing of imagination. When the goal is simply to be as faithful as possible to the material—as if a movie were a marriage, and a rights contract the vow—the

THESIS — best result is a skillful abridgment, one that hits all the important marks without losing anything egregious.° And as abridgments go, they don't get much more skillful than this one.

Introduction to criterion 1: adaptation of situation
That such a safe adaptation could come of *The Hunger Games* speaks more   2
to the trilogy's commercial ascent than the book's actual content, which is audacious and savvy in its dark calculations. The opening crawl (and a stirring propaganda movie) informs us that "The Hunger Games" are an annual event

dystopian: Presenting miserable places (as opposed to utopias or perfect places) in fiction.   **allusions:** Indirect or casual references.   **egregious:** Glaring or outrageous.

in Panem, a North American nation divided into 12 different districts, each in service to the Capitol, a wealthy metropolis that owes its creature comforts to an oppressive dictatorship. For the 75 years since a district rebellion was put down, the Games have existed as an assertion of the Capitol's power, a winner-take-all contest that touts heroism and sacrifice—participants are called "tributes"—while pitting the districts against each other. At "The Reaping," a boy and a girl between the ages of 12 and 18 are taken from each district—with odds determined by age and the number of rations they accept throughout the year—and thrown into a controlled arena, where they're forced to kill each other until only one survives.

In District 12, a dirt-poor coal-mining community that looks like a Dorothea Lange° photograph, Katniss Everdeen (Jennifer Lawrence) quietly rebels against the system by hunting game in a forbidden area with her friend Gale (Liam Hemsworth) and trading it on the black market. Katniss prepares her meek younger sister Prim (Willow Shields) for her first Reaping, but the

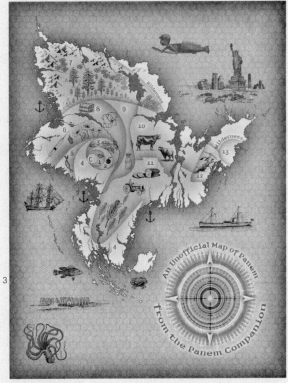

Source: *The Panem Companion,* Smart Pop Books, 2012. © V. Arrow.

odds of a single entry being selected among teenagers with many entries apiece are long. In the film's most affecting scene, those long odds turn against Prim in a shock that Ross renders in agonizing silence, punctuated only by Katniss screaming that she'll volunteer in her sister's place. She's joined, on the boys' side, by Peeta (Josh Hutcherson), a baker's son whose earnestness masks a gift for strategy that Katniss lacks. Together, with the help of the drunkard Haymitch (Woody Harrelson), the only District 12 citizen ever to win the Games, they challenge tributes that range from sadistic volunteers to crafty kids like the pint-sized Rue (Amandla Stenberg) to the truly helpless and soon-to-be-dead.

Director Gary Ross and his screenwriters do well with the unenviable task of setting the table for the series, but with so many characters and subplots to service, they have to ration as stingily as the Capitol. The Reaping is one of the few sequences that's given time to breathe a little, and it makes all the difference—the hushed crowd, neither roused by propaganda nor open in resistance, says everything about the fear and shimmering resentment that stirs in the

3   Introduction to criterion 2: adaptation of characters

4   Introduction to criterion 3: adaptation of plot

Dorothea Lange: Documentary photographer whose images captured the Depression and the Dust Bowl migration.

districts. Once Katniss volunteers, *The Hunger Games* jets from one plot point to another without emphasizing any to great effect. Ross and company deliver on the franchise more effectively than, say, the first *Harry Potter* movie, but there's little evidence that they had any other agenda in mind.

Limitations of adaptation

The primary strength of Collins's book is Katniss herself, a model of steel-spined resourcefulness and power whose internal monologue° roils with daft naiveté and self-doubt, especially when it comes to reading her supposed allies. Absent that monologue, Ross's film mostly has the book's action, and that's enough for a rousing two hours through the surreality of the Capitol — which looks like Dubai meets Nuremberg — and the excitement of the Games themselves, which are sanitized by the PG-13 rating, but nonetheless suspenseful and dread-soaked. And beyond the mayhem are the periodic reminders that the Games are as rigged as any reality show; as with a casino, it's important that the house always wins, even if that means shaking up the rules as it goes along.

Conclusion, returning to thesis

The Hunger Games has its share of standalone payoffs, though some are too sketchily developed to have much of an impact, like Katniss's motherly connection to Rue. Nonetheless, it's the first act in a three-act story, and characters who seem thin now may resonate more down the line. With all the dirty work out of the way, perhaps the sequels will come closer to channeling the revolutionary fervor of Collins's books, and perhaps given the current focus on income inequality, find a populist° edge in the process. Whether the films will take on a life of their own is another matter: As of the first installment, it's stenography° in light.

Questions to Start You Thinking

Meaning

1. How does Tobias categorize *The Hunger Games* film? How does this category influence his review?

2. What does Tobias show in paragraphs 2, 3, and 4? How do the topics of these paragraphs support his overall evaluation?

3. What does Tobias mean when he wonders how well the sequels will convey "the revolutionary fervor of Collins's books" (paragraph 6)? To what extent does he feel that the first film showed met his expectations?

Writing Strategies

4. What is Tobias's overall judgment of the film? What evidence does he use to support this judgment?

5. In your view, how well does he support his judgment? Point to some specific examples in making your case.

---

monologue: One-person speech.   **populist:** Advocating for ordinary people.   **stenography:** Shorthand notes for a copy.

6. Why does Tobias refer to "dystopian science fiction" (paragraph 1) as well as reality shows and casinos (5)? What do such references add to his review?

7. How would you describe Tobias's tone, the quality of his writing that reveals his attitude toward his topic and his readers? Does the tone seem appropriate for his purpose and audience?

Elizabeth Erion   Student Essay

Internship Program Falls Short

Elizabeth Erion drew on two valuable resources for her evaluation: her investigation of the campus internship program and her own experience as an intern. An earlier version of her essay appeared as an editorial in the campus student newspaper.

Since its creation in 1978, the Coram Internship Program has been a mainstay of the Career Development Center. The program matches interested students—usually those entering their junior year—with companies offering paid summer employment. Participating companies vary by year but range from The Guggenheim Museum in New York to the Keck School of Medicine in Los Angeles. In 2011, the program placed thirteen students from the class of 2012 at eleven companies or organizations. While this statistic may at first sound impressive, it accounts for only 2.8% of the class of 2012. Given the popularity of summer internships to lead into one's junior year, it is surprising that a higher percentage of the student body didn't make use of such a seemingly excellent, paid opportunity. But the program's low participation rate may be explained by one of its biggest flaws: its inherently restrictive nature.

By offering funded opportunities at only a certain set of companies, the Coram program limits its utility to a certain set of students—those whose career interests match the industries and whose geographical options match the locations of companies participating during a particular summer. What's more, certain locations and industries are heavily privileged over others. In 2012, nine of the fourteen companies were located in the Boston area. This regionalism is understandable given the college's location in Maine and the high percentage of students and alumni from the Boston area, but it still represents a concerning lack of geographic diversity.

Massachusetts natives probably would find this location far more doable than would students who hail from elsewhere. Local students might have the opportunity to live at home and save significant money (the program stipend does not cover living or travel expenses) or might have an easier time finding roommates or an apartment to sublet due to a strong network of friends and family in the area. They would incur no significant travel costs for a flight, a long train ride, or long-distance

1

? What would you want to gain from an internship program?

2

3

❓ What advice
would you give a
nonlocal student?

gas mileage to arrive and depart from their summer destination. A student from
elsewhere who could not afford such expenses or who could not relocate for a
personal reason—perhaps a family member who is ill—is at a disadvantage. If
students were able to select the locations of their internships, they would be much
more likely to participate in the program.

Similarly, students are restricted to opportunities in a certain set of industries.   4
Four of the participating programs in 2012 were in the financial services sector. Five
were in science and medicine. Only one opportunity was available for students
interested in museum work. The aspiring journalist is out of luck, as the program
offers no journalism internships. So too is the student wishing to gain exposure to
law firm work. These students are forced to look elsewhere, at both paid and unpaid
opportunities. In many sectors—especially the arts—unpaid internships abound,
usually located in prohibitively expensive metropolitan areas. Students who cannot
afford to take unpaid internships are then left with no options, which jeopardizes
their entry into the job market after graduating. Had the Coram program offered
internships in the desired fields of such students, those students could have spent
the summer attaining the experience they needed.

❓ What kinds of
internship
opportunities
would students on
your campus want?

The Coram Internship Program offers an excellent opportunity for the fortunate   5
student who finds a good employment fit with a geographically convenient company.
Unfortunately, the percentage of students who are able to find such a fit is
prohibitively small, as illustrated by the program's low participation rate. The
program's structure denies the chance of obtaining rewarding, paid opportunities to
the majority of the college's students, which is problematic given the importance of
internships in gaining entry-level employment. Ultimately, the Coram Internship
Program proves itself an ineffective career resource for a geographically and
professionally diverse student community.

Questions to Start You Thinking

Meaning

1. Why does Erion feel that evaluating the internship program is
   important? Who might belong to the audience that she would like
   to influence?

2. What does Erion mean when she refers to the internship program's
   major flaw as "its inherently restrictive nature" (paragraph 1)?

3. Based on her evaluation, what changes do you think Erion would want
   the Career Development Center or the internship program to make?

Writing Strategies

4. What criteria does Erion use to judge the internship program? To what
   extent has the program met these criteria, according to Erion?

5. Does Erion provide enough evidence to support her judgment? Why or why not?

6. Do you find Erion's use of statistics effective? Why or why not?

7. Using highlighters or marginal notes, identify the essay's introduction, thesis, criteria for evaluation, supporting evidence, and conclusion. How effective is the organization of the essay?

ⓔ *Consumer Reports* **Editors**   **Video**

Best Buttermilk Pancakes

Consumer Reports is a nonprofit organization dedicated to reviewing products ranging from cars to pancakes. To watch this video review, go to Chapter 8: **bedfordstmartins.com/concisebedguide**.

Source: "Best Buttermilk Pancakes" Copyright 2012 Consumers Union of U.S., Inc. Yonkers, NY 10703-1057, a nonprofit organization. Reprinted with permission from *ConsumerReports.org* for educational purposes only. www.ConsumerReports.org.

Learning by Writing

The Assignment: Writing an Evaluation

Pick a subject to evaluate—one you have personal experience with and feel competent to evaluate. This subject might be a movie, a TV program, a piece of music, an artwork, a new product, a government agency, a campus facility or policy, an essay or reading, or anything else you can think of.

ⓔ For an interactive Learning by Doing activity on evaluating film, go to Ch. 8: **bedfordstmartins.com /concisebedguide**.

Then in a thoughtful essay, analyze your subject and evaluate it. You will need to determine specific criteria for evaluation and make them clear to your readers. In writing your evaluation, you will have a twofold purpose: (1) to set forth your assessment of the quality of your subject and (2) to convince your readers that your judgment is reasonable.

These three students wrote lively evaluations:

Composer and pianist George Gershwin (1898–1937), known for *Rhapsody in Blue, An American in Paris,* and many songs for musical shows and movies.

A music major evaluated works by American composer Aaron Copland, finding him trivial and imitative, "without a tenth of the talent or inventiveness that George Gershwin or Duke Ellington had in his little finger."

A student planning a career in business management evaluated a computer firm in which he had worked one summer. His criteria were efficiency, productivity, appeal to new customers, and employee satisfaction.

A student from Brazil, who had seen firsthand the effects of industrial development in the Amazon rain forest, evaluated the efforts of the U.S. government to protect forests and wetlands, comparing them with the efforts in her own country.

Facing the Challenge   Evaluating and Reviewing

The major challenge writers face when writing evaluations is to make clear to their readers the criteria they have used to arrive at an opinion. While you may not be an expert in any field, you should never underestimate your powers of discrimination. When reviewing a movie, for example, you may begin by simply summarizing its story and saying whether you like it or not. However, for readers who wonder whether to see the movie, you need to go further. For example, you might find its special effects, exotic sets, and unpredictable plot effective but wish that the characters had seemed more believable. Based on these criteria, your thesis might maintain that the movie is not realistic but is entertaining and well worth seeing.

Once you've chosen a topic, clarify your standards for evaluating it:

- What features or aspects will you use as criteria for evaluating?
- How could you briefly explain each of the criteria for a reader?

■ What judgment or evaluation about your topic do the criteria support?

After identifying your criteria, you can examine each in turn. Explaining your criteria will ensure that you move beyond a summary to an opinion or judgment that you can justify to your readers.

Generating Ideas

Find Something to Evaluate. Try *brainstorming* or *mapping* to identify as many possible topics as you can. Test your mastery of each option with potential by concisely describing or summarizing it. Spend enough time investigating possibilities that you can comfortably choose your subject.

For more strategies for generating ideas, see Ch. 12.

Consider Sources of Support. You'll want to spend time finding material to help you develop a judgment. You may recall a program on television or browse for an article to read. You might observe a performance or a sports team. Perhaps you'll want to review several examples of your subject: watching several films or campus plays, listening to several CDs, examining several works of art, testing several products, or interviewing several spectators.

Establish Your Criteria. Jot down criteria, standards to apply to your subject based on the features of the subject worth considering. How well, for example, does a popular entertainer score on musicianship, rapport with the audience, selection of material, originality? In evaluating Portland as a home for a young careerist, you might ask: Does it offer ample entry-level positions in growth firms? Any criterion for evaluation has to fit your subject, audience, and purpose. After all, ample entry-level jobs might not matter to an audience of retirees.

For more on comparing and contrasting, see Ch. 6.

Try Comparing and Contrasting. Often you can readily size up the worth of a thing by setting it next to another of its kind. (When you *compare,* you point to similarities; when you *contrast,* you note differences.) To be comparable, of course, your two subjects need to have plenty in common. The quality of a Harley-Davidson motorcycle might be judged by contrasting it with a Honda but not with a school bus.

Impressionistic set for *The Cabinet of Dr. Caligari* (1920), in which a man investigates the murder of his friend in a mountain village.

For example, if you are writing a paper for a film history course, you might compare and contrast the classic German horror movie *The Cabinet of Dr. Caligari* with the classic Hollywood movie *Frankenstein,* concluding that *Caligari* is more artistic. Then try listing characteristics of each film, point by point:

	CALIGARI	FRANKENSTEIN
SETS	Dreamlike and impressionistic	Realistic, but with heavy Gothic atmosphere
	Sets deliberately angular and distorted	Gothic sets
LIGHTING	Deep shadows that throw figures into relief	Torches highlighting monster's face in night scene

By jotting down each point and each bit of evidence side by side, you can outline your comparison and contrast with great efficiency. Once you have listed them, decide on a possible order for the points.

Try Defining Your Subject. Another technique for evaluating is to define your subject, indicating its nature so clearly that your readers can easily distinguish it from others of its kind. Defining helps readers understand your subject — its structure, habitat, functions. In evaluating a classic television show such as *Roseanne,* you might want to include an *extended* definition of sitcoms over the years, their techniques, views of women, effects on the audience. Unlike a *short definition,* as in a dictionary, an extended definition is intended not simply to explain but to judge: What is the nature of my subject? What qualities make it unique, unlike others of its sort?

Develop a Judgment That You Can Explain to Your Audience. In the end, you will have to come to a decision: Is your subject good, worthwhile, significant, exemplary, preferable — or not? Most writers come to a judgment gradually as they explore their subjects and develop criteria.

DISCOVERY CHECKLIST

☐ What criteria do you plan to use in making your evaluation? Are they clear and reasonably easy to apply?

☐ What evidence can back up your judgments?

☐ Would comparing or contrasting help in evaluating your subject? If so, with what might you compare or contrast your subject?

☐ What qualities define your subject, setting it apart from the rest of its class?

Learning by Doing 🔂 Developing Criteria

With a small group of classmates, meeting in person or online, discuss the subjects each of you plan to evaluate. Make a detailed report about what you're evaluating. If possible, pass around a product, show a photograph of artwork, play a song, or read aloud a short literary work or an idea expressed in a reading. Ask your classmates to explain the reasons for their own evaluations. Maybe they'll suggest criteria or evidence that hadn't occurred to you.

Planning, Drafting, and Developing

Start with a Thesis. Reflect a moment: What is your purpose? What is your main point? Try writing a paragraph that sums up the purpose of your evaluation or stating a thesis that summarizes your main point.

For more on stating a thesis, see pp. 263–69.

TOPIC + JUDGMENT	Campus revival of *South Pacific* — liked the performers featured in it plus the problems the revival raised
WORKING THESIS	Chosen to showcase the achievements of graduating seniors, the campus revival of *South Pacific* also brings up societal problems.

For help developing and supporting effective thesis statements, go to the interactive "Take Action" charts in Re:Writing at **bedfordstmartins.com /concisebedguide**.

Learning by Doing 🔂 Stating Your Overall Judgment

Build your criteria into your working thesis statement by filling in this sentence:

This subject is ＿＿＿＿＿＿ because it ＿＿＿＿＿＿ .
    your judgment   your criteria

With a classmate or small group, compare sentences and share ideas about improving your statement of your judgment and criteria. Use this advice to rework and sharpen your working thesis.

Consider Your Criteria. Many writers find that a list of specific criteria gives them confidence and provokes ideas. Consider filling in a chart with three columns — criteria, evidence, judgment — to focus your thinking.

Develop an Organization. You may want to begin with a direct statement of your judgment: Based on durability, cost, and comfort, the Classic 7 is an ideal campus backpack. On the other hand, you may want to reserve judgment by opening with a question about your subject: How good a film is *Argo*? Each approach suggests a different organization:

Thesis or main point   →   Supporting evidence   →   Return to thesis

Opening question   →   Supporting evidence   →   Overall judgment

Either way, you'll supply lots of evidence — details, examples, maybe comparisons or contrasts — to make your case compelling. You'll also cluster your evidence around your points or criteria for judgment so that readers know how and why you reach your judgment. You might try both patterns of organization to see which works better for your subject and purpose.

Most writers find that an outline — even a rough list — helps them keep track of points to make. If you compare and contrast your subject with something else, one way to arrange the points is *subject by subject*: discuss subject A, and then discuss subject B. For a longer comparison, a better way to organize is *point by point*, applying each point first to one subject and then the other. If approved by your instructor, you also might include a sketch, photograph, or other illustration of your subject or develop a comparative table summarizing the features of similar items you have compared.

Learning by Doing 🌀 Supporting Your Judgments

Consider how well you have linked specific support to your judgments to make your draft interesting and persuasive. Scroll through the file for your draft, and highlight each judgment or opinion in one color. (Look under Format to find Font choices, including color, or use your highlighting options.) Then go back to the beginning, and this time highlight all the facts and evidence in a different color. (If you work on a printed copy, use two highlighters.)

Now observe the flow of color in your draft. Are your judgments followed by evidence that supports them? Do you need to add more support at any points? Should you move sentences around to link support more closely to judgments? Once you have connected judgments and evidence, reread to confirm how well they match. Do you need to modify any judgments or revise any support?

Revising and Editing

For more revising and editing strategies, see Ch. 15.

Focus on Your Thesis. Make your thesis as precise and clear as possible.

WORKING THESIS   Chosen to showcase the graduating seniors, the campus revival of *South Pacific* also brings up societal problems.

REVISED THESIS   The senior showcase, the musical *South Pacific,* spotlights outstanding performers and raises timely societal issues such as prejudice.

Be Fair. Make your judgments reasonable, not extreme. A reviewer can find fault with a film and still conclude that it is worth seeing. There's nothing wrong, of course, with a fervent judgment ("This play is the trashiest excuse for a drama I have ever suffered through"), but consider your readers and their likely reactions. Read some reviews in your local newspaper or online, or watch some movie critics on television to see how they balance their judgments. Because readers will have more confidence in your opinions if you seem fair and reasonable, revise your tone where needed. For example, one writer revised his opening after he realized that he was criticizing the audience rather than evaluating the performance.

The most recent performance by a favorite campus group—Rock Mountain—
was a̶n̶ *incredibly revolting* experience. T̶he̶ outlandish crowd ignored the DJ who
introduced the group/ and a few n̶ameless members of one social group spent
t̶heir time toss̶ing̶ around trash cans in front of the stage/, *the opening number still
announced the group's powerful musical presence.*

[Editorial corrections above text: "disappointing concert" over "incredibly revolting"; "Although t" over "The"; "people" over "nameless members of one social group"; "ed" over "toss"]

Peer Response 👥 Evaluating and Reviewing

For general questions
for a peer editor, see
p. 305.

Enlist the advice of a classmate or friend as you determine your criteria for evaluation and your judgment. Ask your peer editor to answer questions like these about your evaluation:

- What is your overall reaction to this essay? Does the writer persuade you to agree with his or her evaluation?
- When you finish the essay, can you tell exactly what the writer thinks of the subject? Where does the writer express this opinion?
- How do you know what criteria the writer is using for evaluation?
- Does the writer give you sufficient evidence for his or her judgment? Put stars wherever more or better evidence is needed.
- What audience does the writer seem to have in mind?
- Would you recommend any changes in the essay's organization?
- If this paper were yours, what is the one thing you would be sure to work on before handing it in?

REVISION CHECKLIST

☐ Is the judgment you pass on your subject unmistakably clear?

☐ Have you given your readers evidence to support each point you make?

□ Have you been fair? If you are championing something, have you deliberately skipped over its disadvantages or faults? If you are condemning your subject, have you omitted its admirable traits?

□ Have you anticipated and answered readers' possible objections?

□ If you compare two things, do you look at the same points in both?

For more on comparison and contrast, see Ch. 6.

For more editing and proofreading strategies, see pp. 313–17.

After you have revised your evaluation, edit and proofread it. Carefully check grammar, word choice, punctuation, and mechanics—and then correct any problems you find. Make sentences in which you describe the subject of your evaluation as precise and useful as possible. If you have used comparisons or contrasts, make sure these are clear: don't lose your readers in a fog of vague pronouns or confusing references.

EDITING CHECKLIST

For more help, find the relevant checklists in the Quick Editing Guide beginning on p. A-39. Turn also to the Quick Format Guide beginning on p. A-1.

□ Is it clear what each pronoun refers to? Does each pronoun agree with (match) its antecedent?   A6

□ Is it clear what each modifier in a sentence modifies? Have you created any dangling or misplaced modifiers, especially in descriptions of your subject?   B1

□ Have you used parallel structure wherever needed, especially in lists or comparisons?   B2

Additional Writing Assignments

1. Write an evaluation of a college course you have taken or are now taking. Analyze its strengths and weaknesses. Does the instructor present the material clearly, understandably, and engagingly? Are the assignments pointed and purposeful? Is the textbook helpful, readable, and easy to use? Does this course give you your money's worth?

2. Evaluate an unfamiliar magazine, an essay in this textbook, a proposal being considered at work, a source you have read for a college class, an academic Web site about an area that interests you, or a possible source for a

research project. Specify your criteria for evaluation, and identify the evidence that supports your judgments.

3. Evaluate a product that you might want to purchase. Establish criteria that matter to you — and to the other prospective purchasers who might turn to you for a recommendation. Consider, for example, the product's features, construction, utility, beauty, color, cost, or other criteria that matter to purchasers. Make a clear recommendation to your audience: buy or not.

4. Visit a restaurant, museum, or tourist attraction, and evaluate it for others who might consider a visit. Present your evaluation as an essay, an article for a travel or lifestyle magazine, or a travel blog that informs about local sites and evaluates what they offer. Specify your criteria, and include plenty of detail to create the local color your audience will expect.

5. **Source Assignment.** Read these two poems on a similar theme, and decide which seems to you the better poem. In a brief essay, set forth your evaluation. Some criteria to apply might be the poet's choice of concrete, specific words that appeal to the senses and his awareness of his audience. Quote, paraphrase, summarize, and accurately credit supporting evidence from the poems.

Putting in the Seed
ROBERT FROST (1874–1963)

You come to fetch me from my work tonight
When supper's on the table, and we'll see
If I can leave off burying the white
Soft petals fallen from the apple tree
(Soft petals, yes, but not so barren quite,
Mingled with these, smooth bean and wrinkled pea),
And go along with you ere you lose sight
Of what you came for and become like me,
Slave to a springtime passion for the earth.
How Love burns through the Putting in the Seed
On through the watching for that early birth
When, just as the soil tarnishes with weed,
The sturdy seedling with arched body comes
Shouldering its way and shedding the earth crumbs.

Between Our Folding Lips
T. E. BROWN (1830–1897)

Between our folding lips
God slips
An embryon life, and goes;
And this becomes your rose.
We love, God makes: in our sweet mirth
God spies occasion for a birth.
Then is it His, or is it ours?
I know not — He is fond of flowers.

6. **Visual Assignment.** Select one pair of the following images, and examine their features carefully. Write an essay that evaluates the items portrayed in the images or the images themselves. Specify for your audience your criteria for judging. Observe carefully to identify enough visual detail to support your judgments.

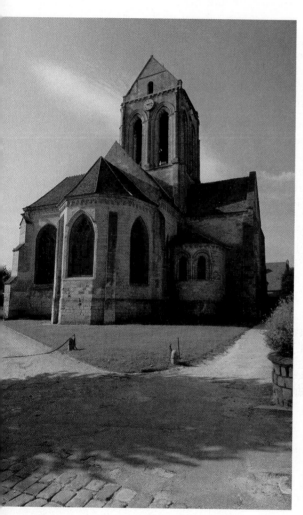

Church at Auvers-sur-Oise, France (2002)

"Church at Auvers-sur-Oise" painted by Vincent van Gogh (1853–1890)

Designers and software engineers at work in a division of Sony Computer Entertainment, 1999.

Technology employees at work in Google Inc.'s seven-story Campus, a "co-working space," 2012.

Supporting a Position with Sources

Responding to an Image

These images show activities that might help a student gather evidence from sources to support a position in a college paper. What does each image suggest about possible sources? What do the images suggest about the process of inquiry? Which activities look most intriguing? What other activities might have appeared in images on this page?

Suppose you surveyed a random group of graduating students about the typical college writing assignment. The odds are good that this assignment might boil down to reading a few texts and writing a paper about them. Simple as this description sounds, it suggests what you probably expect from a college education: an opportunity to absorb and think seriously about provocative ideas. It also suggests the values that lie behind college expectations—a deep respect for the process of inquiry (the academic method of asking and investigating intriguing questions) and for the products of inquiry (the analyses, interpretations, and studies in each academic field).

When you first tackle such assignments, you may wonder "How do I figure out what my instructor really wants?" or "How could I possibly do that?" In response, you may turn to peripheral questions such as "How long does my paper have to be?" or "How many sources do I have to use?" Instead, try to face the central question: "How can I learn the skills I need to use a few sources to develop and support a position in a college paper?"

Unlike a debate or a Super Bowl game, a paper that takes a position generally doesn't have two sides or a single winner. Instead, the writer typically joins the ongoing exchange of ideas about an intriguing topic in the field. Each paper builds on the exchanges of the past—the articles, essays, reports, and books that convey the perspectives, research findings, and conclusions of others. Although reading such sources may seem daunting, you are not expected to know everything yourself but simply to work hard at learning what others know. Your paper, in turn, advances the exchange to convey your well-grounded point of view or to defend your well-reasoned interpretation.

Why Supporting with Sources Matters

In a College Course

- You support a position with sources when you write a history paper about an event, synthesizing a first-person account, contemporary newspaper story, and scholarly article.
- You support a position with sources when you write an analysis after reading a short story along with several critical essays about it.

In the Workplace

- You support a position with sources when you write a report pulling together multiple accounts and records to support your recommendation.

In Your Community

- You support a position with sources when you write a well-substantiated letter to the editor.

When have you used sources to support a position in your writing? What source-based writing might you do at work or in your community?

Learning from Other Writers

The selections here illustrate how two different writers draw on evidence from sources to substantiate their points. The notes in the margin of the first reading will help you begin to analyze features such as the thesis, or main idea, and the variety of methods used to introduce and integrate information from sources.

For another essay that supports a position with sources, read "Dead Men *Do* Tell Tales" by Timothy J. Bertoni and Patrick D. Nolan in Ch. 9: **bedfordstmartins.com /concisebedguide**.

As You Read These Essays That Support a Position with Sources

As you read these essays, ask yourself the following questions:

1. What thesis, or main idea, expresses the position supported by the essay? How does the writer try to help readers appreciate the importance of this position?

2. How does the writer use information from sources to support a thesis? Do you find this information relevant and persuasive?

3. How does the writer vary the way each source is introduced and the way information is drawn from it?

Jake Halpern

The Popular Crowd

Works by author and radio producer Jake Halpern include *Braving Home* (2003), a study of people who live in extreme places, and *Dormia* (2009), a fantasy novel. The selection here comes from *Fame Junkies* (2007), Halpern's analysis of celebrity worship. Its references to sources have been adapted to illustrate MLA style.

Americans now appear to be lonelier than ever. In his book *The Loss of Happiness in Market Democracies,* the Yale political scientist Robert Lane notes that the number of people who described themselves as lonely more than quadrupled in the past few decades (85). We have increasingly become a nation of loners — traveling salesmen, Web designers, phone-bank operators, and online day traders who live and work in isolation. According to the U.S. Census Bureau, we also marry later in life. In 1956 the median age for marriage was 22.5 for men and 20.1 for women; by 2004 it was 27.4 for men and 25.8 for women (Russell). This helps to explain something else the Census Bureau has noted: Americans are increasingly living alone. The share of American households including seven or more people dropped from 35.9 percent in 1790, 5.8 percent in 1950, and 1.2 percent in 2004. Meanwhile, the number of households consisting of just one person rose from 3.7 percent in 1790 to 9.3 percent in 1950 and 26.4 percent in 2004. Nowadays, one out of four

Background information including facts and statistics

American households consists of a single person. In recent years this trend has been especially discernible° among young people (Cushman 599; U.S. Census Bureau). Since 1970 the number of youths (ages fifteen to twenty-five) living alone has almost tripled, and the number of young adults (ages twenty-five to thirty-four) living alone has more than quadrupled (Russell).

The combination of loneliness and our innate° desire to belong may be fueling our interest in celebrities and our tendency to form para-social relationships° with them. Only a few research psychologists have seriously explored this possibility, among them Lynn McCutcheon and Dianne Ashe. McCutcheon and Ashe compared results from 150 subjects who had taken three personality tests—one measuring shyness, one measuring loneliness, and one measuring celebrity obsession, on something called the Celebrity Attitudes Scale, or CAS. The CAS asks subjects to rate the veracity° of statements such as "I am obsessed by details of my favorite celebrity's life" and "If I were lucky enough to meet my favorite celebrity, and he/she asked me to do something illegal as a favor, I would probably do it." McCutcheon and Ashe found a correlation among scores on loneliness, shyness, and the CAS (Ashe and McCutcheon 129). Their results led McCutcheon to observe in a subsequent paper, "Perhaps one of the ways [we] cope with shyness and loneliness is to cultivate a 'safe,' non-threatening relationship with a celebrity" (McCutcheon et al. 503).

Another investigation, led by Jacki Fitzpatrick, of Texas Tech University, looked at the correlation° between para-social relationships and actual romantic relationships. Fitzpatrick asked forty-five college students to complete a questionnaire containing several psychological measures, including one that gauged para-social relationships (the Para-social Interaction Scale) and another that gauged romantic relationships (the Multiple Determinants of Relationship Commitment Inventory). She and her colleague, Andrea McCourt, discovered that subjects who were less invested in their romantic relationships were more involved in para-social relationships. They concluded, "It makes sense that individuals may use para-social relationships as one way to fulfill desires or address needs (e.g., for attention, companionship) that are unmet in their romances" (Fitzpatrick and McCourt).

The Rochester survey,* too, provides evidence that lonely teenagers are especially susceptible to forming para-social relationships with celebrities. Boys who described themselves as lonely were almost twice as likely as others to endorse the statement "My favorite celebrity just helps me feel good and forget about all of my troubles." Girls who described themselves as lonely were almost three times as likely as others to endorse that statement.

2 THESIS presenting position

Supporting evidence, including description of psychological study

Examples quoted from survey

Point 1

Direct quotation

Et al. ("and others") used for source with four or more authors

3

Paraphrase

Point 2

4 Author's position based on study

---

discernible: Distinguishable, noticeable. **innate:** Inborn from birth. **para-social relationships:** One-sided friendships, based on the illusion of interaction and mutual knowledge. **veracity:** Truthfulness. **correlation:** Agreement, parallelism.

*The Rochester, NY, survey of 653 fifth to eighth grade students, conducted by Jake Halpern and Carol M. Liebler, is discussed in full in *Fame Junkies* (New York: Houghton Mifflin 2007). [Editor's note]

Another survey question asked teens whom they would most like to meet   5
for dinner: Jesus Christ, Albert Einstein, Shaquille O'Neal, Jennifer Lopez,
50 Cent, Paris Hilton, or the President. Among boys who said they were not
lonely, the clear winner was Jesus Christ; but among those who described
themselves as lonely, Jesus finished last and 50 Cent was the clear winner.
Similarly, girls who felt appreciated by their parents, friends, and teachers
tended to choose dinner with Jesus, whereas those who felt underappreciated
were likely to choose Paris Hilton. One possible interpretation of these results is that lonely and underappreciated teens particularly want to befriend
the ultimate popular guy or girl. Regardless of who exactly this figure is at a
given time, it's clear that many of us—lonely people in particular—yearn to
belong to the popular crowd.

Paraphrase

Analysis

*Conclusion
synthesizing sources*

Works Cited

Ashe, D. D., and Lynn McCutcheon. "Shyness, Loneliness, and Attitude Toward
Celebrities." *Current Research in Social Psychology* 6.9 (2001): 124–33. Print.

Cushman, Philip. "Why the Self Is Empty: Toward a Historically Situated
Psychology." *American Psychologist* 45.5 (1990): 599–612. Print.

Fitzpatrick, Jacki, and Andrea McCourt. "The Role of Personal Characteristics and Romantic Characteristics in Para-social Relationships: A Pilot
Study." *Journal of Mundane Behavior* 2.1 (2001): n. pag. Web. [Author's date
of access not known.]

Lane, Robert E. *The Loss of Happiness in Market Democracies*. New Haven: Yale
UP, 2000. Print.

McCutcheon, Lynn, Mara Aruguete, Vann B. Scott, Jr., and Kristen L.
VonWaldner. "Preference for Solitude and Attitude Toward One's Favor-
ite Celebrity." *North American Journal of Psychology* 6.3 (2004): 499–505.
Print.

Russell, Cheryl. *newstrategist.com*. New Strategist Publications, n.d. Web.
[Author's date of access not known.]

United States Census Bureau. Fertility and Family Branch. *HH-4: Households
by Size: 1960 to Present*. 15 Sept. 2004. *U.S. Census Bureau*. Web. [Author's
date of access not known.]

*Each source cited in
Halpern's essay listed
alphabetically by
author, with full
publication information*

*First line of entry
placed at left margin;
with subsequent lines
indented ½″*

Questions to Start You Thinking

Meaning

1. What position does Halpern take in this essay?

2. In paragraph 1, Halpern refers to America as "a nation of loners." What
does he mean by this statement, and how does he see the problem
changing in recent decades?

3. How does Halpern suggest that following and watching a celebrity
could help people cope with shyness?

4. How has Halpern arranged the main points of his essay? How do these
points develop his thesis in paragraph 2 and lead up to paragraph 5?

Writing Strategies

5. What types of evidence does Halpern use to support his position? How convincing is this evidence to you?

6. Halpern alternates between stating some source information in his own words and quoting some directly. What are the advantages and disadvantages of these two approaches?

7. How would you describe Halpern's tone, the quality of his writing that reveals his attitude toward his topic and his readers? What specific words, phrases, or sentences contribute to his tone? Does the tone seem appropriate for his purpose and audience?

8. Compare this selection, excerpted from a book, with an article written for a newspaper (see, for example, "The Opportunity Gap," p. 101). What differences in formatting, style, and presentation do you notice between the two selections?

Abigail Marchand   **Student Essay**

The Family Dynamic

Abigail Marchand wrote this essay in response to a reading assigned in her composition class. She used MLA style to cite and list sources.

Children are resilient creatures, and often adults underestimate their vast emotional capabilities, their compassion, and their ability to find the good in everything. When babies are brought home from the hospital, they don't care if their parents are same sex or not. They only want to feel safe, to be held, and most of all to be loved. It is unfortunate that we as a human race allow our own petty ideals to interfere with these simple needs.   1

The notion that a child can thrive only in a "nuclear" family has long been dispelled. With the increase in the divorce rate and the number of children born to single mothers, many children are not raised in that traditional family. Thus, the idea of a child being raised by a same-sex couple really shouldn't seem that foreign. According to a 2011 U.S. Census Bureau report, only about 1% of couples are of the same sex (1), but over 115,000 of their households include children (3). Anna Quindlen very directly sums up this situation: "Evan has two moms. This is no big thing" (501).   2   What does a "nuclear" family mean to you?

For a variety of reasons, many children today are growing up in a completely different environment than that of their grandparents of the 1950s and 1960s. However, as Quindlen says, "the linchpin of family has commonly been a loving commitment between two adults" (501). Even though a family might have two mothers or two fathers or even one single parent, what should matter is not the quantity of love a child receives but the quality of that love.   3

A child's development will neither be hurt nor helped by a same-sex family. Frankly, the makeup of the family and specifically the absence of an opposite-sex partner have   4 little impact on the day-to-day lives of most children. As two sociologists who reviewed past research studies on parenting concluded, "The gender of parents correlates in novel ways with parent-child relationships but has minor significance for children's psychological adjustment and social success" (Biblarz and Stacey 3). Many same-sex households involve members of the opposite sex in some capacity, whether as friend, aunt, uncle, or cousin. In addition, as children from same-sex families attend schools, they encounter any number of people, both male and female. The argument that the child would interact only with one gender is ludicrous.

How do you view parenting responsibilities — as your parents' child or as your children's parent?

The advantages of a same-sex household would be similar to those of a standard father-and-mother household: Two people are there to help raise the children. Compared to a single mother raising a child alone, the same-sex household would benefit from having another person to shoulder some of the responsibilities. As a parent of four sons, I know the benefits of having a second person to help with transportation to various events, dinner preparation, or homework. Navigating the treacherous landscape of child rearing is far easier with an ally.   5

On a developmental level, a same-sex household would not affect the child's ability to grow and become a productive member of society. Certainly most children can adapt to any situation, and in the case of same-sex relationships, a child usually is brought into the home as a baby, so that environment is all he or she would know. The absence of an opposite-sex parent would never come into question since most children don't concern themselves with the gender of their family members. Instead, they view their caregivers as any other child would—as mommy or daddy.   6

The only disadvantage to same-sex households rests with the concerned citizens bent on "explaining" to the children how their parental unit is somehow doing something wrong. These naysayers pose the greatest risk to the children because they cannot look beyond the surface of the same-sex partners to see that most of these households function better than many "normal" ones. In a recent collection of interviews, seventeen-year-old Chris echoes this sentiment: "The hardest part about having a gay dad is that no matter how okay you are with it, there's always going to be someone who will dislike you because of it" (Snow 3). Garner's interviews with grown-up children of gay parents also raise the same theme, "the personal impact of a public issue" (15).   7

In fact, most people are unlikely to recognize a child being raised in a same sex household unless they specifically know the child's parents. My son attends daycare with two brothers who have two mothers. I never would have known this if I hadn't personally met both mothers. Their children are well-adjusted little boys who are fortunate to have two caring women in their lives.   8

What do you think that children need from parents and from society?

The real focus should be on whether all of the child's needs are met. It shouldn't matter if those needs are met by a mother and father, two mothers, or two fathers. Children should feel loved and cared for above all else. Unfortunately, in the case of same-sex households, external pressures can potentially shatter a child's well-being when "well-meaning" people attempt to interfere with something they know nothing about. It is amazing that people are more focused on the bedroom activities,   9 activities that never enter a child's consciousness anyway, than on the run-of-the-mill activities that most same-sex couples encounter in the rearing of a child. The only real disadvantage to these households lies solely with the closed minds of intolerance.

Works Cited

Biblarz, Timothy J., and Judith Stacey. "How Does the Gender of Parents Matter?" *Journal of Marriage and Family* 72.1 (2010): 3–22. Print.

Garner, Abigail. *Families Like Mine: Children of Gay Parents Tell It Like It Is*. New York: Harper Perennial, 2005. Print.

Quindlen, Anna. "Evan's Two Moms." *The Bedford Guide for College Writers*. 10th ed. Ed. X. J. Kennedy, Dorothy M. Kennedy, and Marcia F. Muth. Boston: Bedford/St. Martin's, 2014. 501–02. Print.

Snow, Judith E. *How It Feels to Have a Gay or Lesbian Parent: A Book by Kids for Kids of All Ages*. New York: Harrington Park, 2004. 1–3. Print.

United States. Dept. of Commerce. Census Bureau. *Same-Sex Couple Households*. 2011. *American Community Survey Briefs*. Web. 27 Sept. 2012.

For more on MLA citation style, see E1–E2 in the Quick Research Guide, pp. A-32–A-38. For a sample paper in MLA style, see pp. A-59–A-67.

Questions to Start You Thinking

Meaning

1. What position does Marchand support in this essay?

2. What reasons for her view does Marchand supply?

3. How does Marchand see children? What does she expect of families?

Writing Strategies

4. What types of evidence does Marchand use to support her position? How convincing is this evidence to you?

5. Has Marchand considered alternative views? How does the inclusion (or lack) of these views contribute to or detract from the essay?

6. Marchand uses specific examples in several places. Which of these seem most effective to you? Why?

7. Using highlighters or marginal notes, identify the essay's introduction, thesis, major points, supporting evidence for each point, and conclusion. How effective is the organization of this essay?

e Research Cluster   Text, Audio, and Video

Celebrity Culture

Most of us interact with celebrity culture, whether hunting for photos of a favorite actor's wedding or scanning headlines at the cash register, but few of us question this interaction. This cluster offers varying viewpoints on why people are interested in celebrities' lives and how that interest affects them. The cluster includes four selections: Cary Tennis's "Why Am I Obsessed with Celebrity Gossip?" [advice column]; Karen Sternheimer's "Celebrity Relationships: Why Do We Care?" [video]; Tom Ashbrook and Ty Burr's "The Strange Power of Celebrity" [audio]; and Timothy J. Bertoni and Patrick D. Nolan's "Dead Men *Do* Tell Tales" [academic paper]. To access the selections, go to Chapter 9: **bedfordstmartins.com/concisebedguide**.

Learning by Writing

The Assignment: Supporting a Position with Sources

For an interactive Learning by Doing activity on finding credible sources, go to Ch. 9: **bedfordstmartins.com /concisebedguide**.

For the contents of *A Writer's Reader*, see pp. xxvi– xxvii or go to **bedfordstmartins.com /concisebedguide**.

Identify a cluster of readings about a topic that interests you. For example, choose related readings from this book and its e-Pages or from other readings assigned in your class. If your topic is assigned and you don't begin with much interest in it, develop your intellectual curiosity. Look for an angle, an implication, or a vantage point that will engage you. Relate the topic in some way to your experience. Read (or reread) the selections, considering how each supports, challenges, or deepens your understanding of the topic.

Based on the information in your cluster of readings, develop an enlightening position about the topic that you'd like to share with an audience of college readers. Support this position — your working thesis — using quotations, paraphrases, summaries, and syntheses of the information in the readings as evidence. Present your information from sources clearly, and credit your sources appropriately.

Three students investigated topics of great variety:

One student examined local language usage that combined words from English and Spanish, drawing on essays about language diversity to analyze the patterns and implications of such usage.

Another writer used a cluster of readings about technology to evaluate the privacy issues on a popular Web site for student profiles.

A third, using personal experience with a blended family and several essays on families, challenged misconceptions about today's families.

Facing the Challenge   Finding Your Voice

The major challenge that writers face when using sources to support a position is finding their own voice. You create your voice as a college writer through your choice of language and angle of vision. You probably want to present yourself as a thoughtful writer with credible insights, someone a reader will want to hear from.

Finding your own voice may be difficult in a source-based paper. After all, you need to read carefully and then capture information to strengthen your discussion by quoting, paraphrasing, or summarizing. You need to introduce it, feed it into your draft, and credit it. By this time, you may worry that your sources have taken over your paper. You may feel there's no room left for your own voice and, even if there were, it's too quiet to jostle past the powerful words of your sources. That, however, is your challenge.

As you develop your voice as a college writer and use it to guide your readers' understanding, you'll restrict sources to their proper role as supporting evidence. Don't let them get pushy or dominate your writing. Use these questions to help you strengthen your voice:

For more on evidence, see pp. 40–45 and pp. 133–38.

- Can you write a list or passage explaining what you'd like readers to hear from your voice? Where could you add more of this in your draft?

- Have you used your own voice, not quotations or paraphrases from sources, to introduce your topic, state your thesis, and draw conclusions?

- Have you generally relied on your own voice to open and conclude paragraphs and to reinforce your main ideas in every passage?

- Have you alternated between your voice and the voices of sources? Can you strengthen your voice if it gets trampled by a herd of sources?

- Have you used your voice to identify and introduce source material before you present it? Have you used your voice to explain or interpret source material after you include it?

- Have you used your voice to tell readers why your sources are relevant, how they support your points, and what their limits might be?

- Have you carefully created your voice as a college writer, balancing passion and personality with rock-solid reasoning?

Whenever you are uncertain about the answers to these questions, make an electronic copy of your file or print it out. Highlight all of the wording in your own voice in a bright, visible color. Check for the presence and prominence of this highlighting, and then revise the white patches (the material drawn from sources) as needed to strengthen your voice.

Generating Ideas

For more strategies for generating ideas, see Ch. 12.

Pin Down Your Working Topic and Your Cluster of Readings. Specify what you're going to work on. This task is relatively easy if your instructor has assigned the topic and the required set of readings. If not, figure out what limits your instructor has set and which decisions are yours.

- Carefully follow any directions about the number or types of sources that you are expected to use.

- Instead of hunting only for sources that share your initial views about the topic, look for a variety of reliable and relevant sources so that you can broaden, even challenge, your perspective.

For advice about finding and evaluating academic sources, turn to sections B and C in the Quick Research Guide, pp. A-24–A-28.

Consider Your Audience. You are writing for an academic community that is intrigued by your topic (unless your instructor specifies another group). Your instructor's broad goal probably includes making sure that you are prepared to succeed when you write future assignments, including full research papers. For this reason, you'll be expected to quote, paraphrase, and summarize information from sources. You'll also need to introduce—or launch—such material and credit its source, thus demonstrating that you have mastered the essential skills for source-based writing.

In addition, your instructor will want to see your own position emerge from the swamp of information that you are reading. You may feel that your ideas are like a prehistoric creature, dripping as it struggles out of the bog. If so, encourage your creature to wade toward dry land. Jot down your own ideas whenever they pop into mind. Highlight them in color on the page or on the screen. Store them in your writing notebook or a special file so that you can find them, watch them accumulate, and give them well-deserved prominence in your paper.

e For clusters of readings on this topic and others, see the contents of *A Writer's Reader* on pp. xxvi–xxvii or go to **bedfordstmartins.com /concisebedguide**.

One Student Thinking through a Topic

General Subject: Men and Women

Assigned topic: State and support a position about differences in the behavior of men and women.

What do I know about?

What do I care about?

RECALL PERSONAL EXPERIENCES: Friends at school? Competition for jobs? Pressure on parents to be good role models?

CONSIDER READINGS: Razdan? Jensen? Zeilinger? Staples? Brady?

· Stereotypes of women — emotional and caring
· Stereotypes of men — tough and aggressive
· What aboout me? I'm a woman in training to be a police officer — and I'm a mother. I'm emotional, caring, aggressive, and tough.

I bet that men and women are more alike than different. What do the readings say? What evidence do they present?

· **RETURN TO THE READINGS.**
· **TEST AND REFINE YOUR WORKING THESIS.**
· **LOOK FOR EVIDENCE.**

Take an Academic Approach. Your experience and imagination remain your own deep well, an endless reservoir from which you can draw ideas whenever you need them. For an academic paper, this deep well may help you identify an intriguing topic, raise a compelling question about it, or pursue an unusual slant. For example, you might recall talking with your cousin about her expensive prescriptions and decide to investigate the controversy about importing low-cost medications from other countries.

You'll also be expected to investigate your topic using authoritative sources. These sources — articles, essays, reports, books, Web pages, and other reliable materials — are your second deep well. When one well runs dry for the moment, start pumping the other. As you read critically to tap your second reservoir, you join the academic exchange. This exchange is the flow of knowledge from one credible source to the next as writers and researchers raise questions, seek answers, evaluate information, and advance knowledge. As you inquire, you'll move from what you already know to deeper knowledge. Welcome sources that shed light on your inquiry from varied perspectives rather than simply agree with a view you already hold.

For more on generating ideas, see Ch. 12.

For more on reading critically, see Ch. 2.

To see how the academic exchange works, turn to pp. 182–83.

Learning by Doing 🖳 Selecting Reliable Sources

When you choose your own sources, evaluate them to be sure they are reliable choices that your audience will respect. When your sources are assigned, assess their strengths, weaknesses, and limitations to use them effectively. Bring your articles, essays, and other sources to a small-group evaluation session. Using the checklist in C3 in the Quick Research Guide (pp. A-27–A-28), discuss your common sources or a key source selected by each writer in the group. Look for points that you might mention in a paper to bolster a source's credibility with readers (for example, the author's professional affiliation). Look as well for limitations that might restrict what a source can support.

Skim Your Sources. When you work with a cluster of readings, you'll probably need to read them repeatedly. Start out, however, by skimming—quickly reading only enough to find out what direction a selection takes.

- Leaf through the reading; glance at any headings or figure labels.
- Return to the first paragraph; read it in full. Then read only the first sentence of each paragraph. At the end, read the final paragraph in full.
- Stop to consider what you've already learned.

Do the same with your other selections, classifying or comparing them as you begin to think about what they might contribute to your paper.

DISCOVERY CHECKLIST

☐ What topic is assigned or under consideration? What ideas about it emerge as you brainstorm, freewrite, or use another strategy to generate ideas?

☐ What cluster of readings will you begin with? What do you already know about them? What have you learned about them simply by skimming?

For more on stating a thesis, see pp. 263–69.

☐ What purpose would you like to achieve in your paper? Who is your primary audience? What will your instructor expect you to accomplish?

☐ What clues about how to proceed can you draw from the two sample essays in this chapter or from other readings identified as useful models?

For help developing effective thesis statements, go to the interactive "Take Action" charts in Re:Writing at **bedfordstmartins.com /concisebedguide**.

Planning, Drafting, and Developing

Start with a Working Thesis. Sometimes you start reading for a source-based paper with a clear position in mind; other times, you begin simply with your initial response to your sources. Either way, try to state your main idea as a working thesis even if you expect to rewrite it — or replace it — later on. Once your thesis takes shape in words, you can assess the richness and relevance of your reading based on a clear main idea.

FIRST RESPONSE TO SOURCES	Joe Robinson, author of "Four Weeks Vacation," and others say that workers need more vacation time, but I can't see my boss agreeing to this.
WORKING THESIS	Although most workers would like longer vacations, many employers do not believe that they would benefit, too.

Once your thesis takes shape in words, you can analyze its parts and use them to guide your search for reliable information. Of course you'll want to support your view, but often material that questions it proves more valuable, prompting you to rethink your thesis, refine it, or counter more effectively whatever challenges it. For example, the working thesis above breaks into two parts: workers and employers. Each might benefit from, or suffer from, longer vacations. Instead of looking for a perfect source to prove your thesis, you're now ready to look for the light each source can shed on either view (benefit or suffer) held by either party (worker or employer) you've identified.

Learning by Doing 🎯 Connecting Evidence and Thesis

State your working thesis, no matter how shaky it seems. List the parties or components it mentions, the views they might hold, or whatever else your evidence from sources might support, qualify, or challenge. Keep your working thesis and your evidence list handy as you read.

Read Each Source Thoughtfully. Before you begin copying quotations, scribbling notes, or highlighting a source, simply read, slowly and carefully. After you have figured out what the source says, you are ready to decide how you might use its information to support your ideas. Read again, this time sifting and selecting what's relevant to your thesis.

- How does the source use its own sources to support its position?
- Does it review major sources chronologically (by date), thematically (by topic), or by some other method?
- Does it use sources to supply background for its own position? Does it compare its position or research findings with those of other studies?
- What audience does the source address? What was its author's purpose?
- How might you want to use the source?

Join the Academic Exchange. A well-researched article that follows academic conventions will identify its sources for several reasons. It gives honest credit to the work on which it relies—work done by other researchers and writers. They deserve credit because their information contributes to the article's credibility and substantiates its points. The article also informs you about its sources so you, or any other reader, could find them yourself.

The visual on pages 182–83 illustrates how this exchange of ideas and information works and how you join this exchange from the moment you begin to use sources in your college writing. The middle of the visual shows the opening of a sample article about a global health problem: obesity. Because this article appears online, it credits its sources by providing a link to each one. A comparable printed article might identify its sources by supplying brief in-text citations (in parentheses in MLA or APA style), footnotes, numbers keyed to its references, or source identifications in the text itself. To the left of and below the source article are several of its sources. (They, in turn, also supply information about their sources.) The column to the right of the source article illustrates ways that you might capture information from the source.

For more on plagiarism, see D1 in the Quick Research Guide, pp. A-28–A-29.

For help avoiding plagiarism, go to the interactive "Take Action" charts in Re:Writing at **bedfordstmartins.com /concisebedguide**.

For more on citing and listing sources, see E1 and E2 in the Quick Research Guide, pp. A-32–A-38.

Capture Information and Record Source Details. Consider how you might eventually want to capture each significant passage or point from a source in your paper—by quoting the exact words of the source, by paraphrasing its ideas in your own words, or by summarizing its essential point. Keeping accurate notes and records as you work with your sources will help you avoid accidental plagiarism (using someone else's words or ideas without giving the credit due). Accurate notes also help to reduce errors or missing information when you add the source material to your draft.

As you capture information, plan ahead so that you can acknowledge each source following academic conventions. Record the details necessary to identify the source in your discussion and to list it with other sources at the end of your paper. The next sections illustrate how to capture and credit your sources, using examples for a paper that connects land use and threats to wildlife. Compare the examples with the original passage from the source.

Identify Significant Quotations. When an author expresses an idea so memorably that you want to reproduce those words exactly, quote them word for word. Direct quotations can add life, color, and authority; too many can drown your voice and overshadow your point.

ORIGINAL   The tortoise is a creature that has survived virtually unchanged since it first appeared in the geologic record more than 150 million years ago. The species became threatened, however, when ranchers began driving their herds onto Mojave Desert lands for spring grazing, at the very time that the tortoise awakens from hibernation and emerges from its burrows to graze on the greening desert shrubs and grasses. As livestock trampled the burrows and monopolized the scarce desert vegetation, tortoise populations plummeted. (page 152)

Babbitt, Bruce. *Cities in the Wilderness: A New Vision of Land Use in America*. Washington: Island Press-Shearwater, 2005. Print.

TOO MUCH QUOTATION   When "tortoise populations plummeted," a species "that has survived virtually unchanged since it first appeared in the geologic record more than 150 million years ago" (Babbitt 152) had losses that helped to justify setting workable boundaries for the future expansion of Las Vegas.

MEMORABLE QUOTATION   When "tortoise populations plummeted" (Babbitt 152), an unlikely species that has endured for millions of years helped to establish workable boundaries for the future expansion of Las Vegas.

The Mojave Desert

Writers often begin by highlighting or copying too many quotations as they struggle to master the ideas in the source. The better you understand the reading and your own thesis, the more effectively you'll choose quotations. After all, a quotation in itself is not necessarily effective evidence; too many quotations suggest that your writing is padded or lacks originality.

HOW TO QUOTE
- Select a quotation that is both notable and pertinent to your thesis.
- Record it accurately, writing out exactly what it says. Include its punctuation and capitalization. Avoid abbreviations that might later be ambiguous.
- Mark both its beginning and ending with quotation marks.
- Note the page or other location (such as an electronic paragraph) where the quotation appears. If the quotation begins on one page but ends on another, mark where the switch occurs so that the credit in your draft will be accurate no matter how much of the quotation you eventually use.
- Double-check the accuracy of each quotation as you record it.

For more on quotations, see D3 in the Quick Research Guide, p. A-29.

Use an ellipsis mark—three spaced dots (. . .) within a sentence or four dots (. . . .), a period and three spaced dots, concluding a sentence—to show where you leave out any original wording. You may omit wording that doesn't relate to your point, but don't distort the original meaning. For example, if a

For more on punctuating quotations and using ellipsis marks, see C3 in the Quick Editing Guide, pp. A-55–A-56.

THE ACADEMIC EXCHANGE Suppose that you used the center article to support a position. In turn, your source drew on other writings, some of which are shown to the left of and below the center article. The various ways you might use this source are shown on the right-hand page.

Sources Cited in Your Source

Your Source <www.slate.com>

Source: U.S. Department of Agriculture

<www.usda.gov>

AREI Chapter 3.5: Global Resources and Productivity

Keith Wiebe

Abstract—*Global food production has grown faster than population in recent decades, due largely to improved seeds and increased use of fertilizer and irrigation. Soil degradation which has slowed yield growth in some areas, depends on farmers' incentives to adopt conservation practices, but does not threaten food security at the global level.*

Introduction

Increased resource use and improvements in technology and efficiency have increased global food production more rapidly than population in recent decades, but 800 million people remain food insecure (fig. 3.5.1). . . . .

Source: World Bank

<web.worldbank.org>

Poverty Analysis: Overview

Trends in poverty over time: Living Standards have improved...

Living standards have risen dramatically over the last decades. The proportion of the developing world's population living in extreme economic poverty -- defined as living on less than $1 per day ($1.08 in 1993 dollars, adjusted to account for differences in purchasing power across countries) -- has fallen from 28 percent in 1990 to 21 percent in 2001.

Substantial improvements in social indicators have accompanied growth in average incomes. Infant mortality rates in low- and middle-income countries have fallen from 86 per 1,000 live births in 1980 to 60 in 2002. Life expectancy in these countries has risen from 60 to 65 between 1980 and 2002. For more health, nutrition and population statistics, see the HNPStats database. . . . .

Please Do Not Feed the Humans

THE GLOBAL EXPLOSION OF FAT.

By William Saletan

Posted Saturday, Sept. 2, 2006, at 8:22 AM ET

In 1894, Congress established Labor Day to honor those who "from rude nature have delved and carved all the grandeur we behold." In the century since, the grandeur of human achievement has multiplied. Over the past four decades, global population has doubled, but food output, driven by increases in productivity, has outpaced it. Poverty, infant mortality, and hunger are receding. For the first time in our planet's history, a species no longer lives at the mercy of scarcity. We have learned to feed ourselves.

We've learned so well, in fact, that we're getting fat. Not just the United States or Europe, but the whole world. Egyptian, Mexican, and South African women are now as fat as Americans. Far more Filipino adults are now overweight than underweight. In China, one in five adults is too heavy, and the rate of overweight in children is 28 times higher than it was two decades ago. In Thailand, Kuwait, and Tunisia, obesity, diabetes, and heart disease are soaring.

Hunger is far from conquered. But since 1990, the global rate of malnutrition has declined an average of 1.7 percent a year. Based on data from the World Health Organization and the U.N. Food and Agriculture Organization, for every two people who are malnourished, three are now overweight or obese. Among women, even in most African countries, overweight has surpassed underweight. The balance of peril is shifting.

Indirect Source: U.S. Department of Labor

<www.dol.gov/opa/aboutdol/laborday.htm>

The History of Labor Day

Labor Day: How it Came About; What it Means

"Labor Day differs in every essential way from the other holidays of the year in any country," said Samuel Gompers, founder and longtime president of the American Federation of Labor. "All other holidays are in a more or less degree connected with conflicts and battles of man's prowess over man, of strife and discord for greed and power, of glories achieved by one nation over another. Labor Day...is devoted to no man, living or dead, to no sect, race, or nation."

Labor Day, the first Monday in September, is a creation of the labor movement and is dedicated to the social and economic achievements of American workers. It constitutes a yearly national tribute to the contributions workers have made to the strength, prosperity, and well-being of our country.

Founder of Labor Day

More than 100 years after the first Labor Day observance, there is still some doubt as to who first proposed the holiday for workers.

Some records show that Peter J. McGuire, general secretary of the Brotherhood of Carpenters and Joiners and a cofounder of the American Federation of Labor, was first in suggesting a day to honor those "who from rude nature have delved and carved all the grandeur we behold."

182

Information Captured from Your Source

Sample Working Thesis

A clear thesis statement establishes a framework for selecting source material as useful evidence and for explaining its relevance to readers.

> WORKING THESIS   In order to counter national and worldwide trends toward obesity, agricultural communities like Grand Junction need to apply their expertise as food producers to the promotion of healthy food products.

Quotation from an Indirect Source

A quotation from an indirect source captures the exact words of an author quoted within the source.

> An 1894 action by Congress created a holiday to recognize workers who "delved and carved" to produce what Americans enjoy (qtd. in Saletan).

If possible, go to the original source to be sure that the quotation is accurate and that you are using it appropriately. (See the bottom of the left-hand page.)

> Credit, though disputed, has gone to labor leader Peter McGuire for promoting the recognition of those who "delved and carved all the grandeur we behold" (US Dept. of Labor).

Quotation from a Source

A quotation captures the author's exact words directly from the source.

> As Saletan observes, "We have learned to feed ourselves," but the success of agricultural enterprise and technology does not guarantee that well-fed people are healthy.

Paraphrase of a Source

A paraphrase captures an author's specific ideas fully and accurately, restating them in your own words and sentences.

> Though the number of hungry people drops nearly 2 percent annually, more people, including African women, are now overfed by a ratio of 3 to 2 and thus have traded the health risks of malnutrition for those of obesity (Saletan).

Summary of a Source

A summary reduces an author's main point to essentials, using your own words and sentences.

> Given that a worldwide shift in food security has led to an obesity epidemic (Saletan), consumers need lighter, healthier food options, a goal that the Grand Junction agricultural community can actively support.

MLA Works Cited Entry

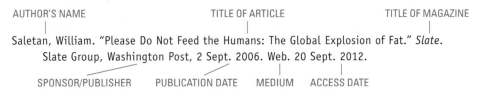

AUTHOR'S NAME   TITLE OF ARTICLE   TITLE OF MAGAZINE

Saletan, William. "Please Do Not Feed the Humans: The Global Explosion of Fat." *Slate*.
   Slate Group, Washington Post, 2 Sept. 2006. Web. 20 Sept. 2012.

SPONSOR/PUBLISHER   PUBLICATION DATE   MEDIUM   ACCESS DATE

reviewer calls a movie "a perfect example of poor directing and inept acting," don't quote this comment as "perfect . . . directing and . . . acting."

Paraphrase Specific Information. Paraphrasing involves restating an author's ideas in your own language. A paraphrase is generally about the same length as the original. It conveys the ideas and emphasis of the original in your words and sentences, thus bringing your own voice to the fore. A fresh and creative paraphrase expresses your style without awkwardly jumping between it and your source's style. Be sure to name the source so that your reader knows exactly where you move from one to the other.

Here, again, is the original passage by Bruce Babbitt, followed by a sloppy paraphrase. The paraphrase suffers from a common fault, slipping in too many words from the original. (The borrowed words are underlined in the paraphrase.) Those words need to be expressed in the writer's own language or identified as direct quotations with quotation marks.

ORIGINAL

The tortoise is a creature that has survived virtually unchanged since it first appeared in the geologic record more than 150 million years ago. The species became threatened, however, when ranchers began driving their herds onto Mojave Desert lands for spring grazing, at the very time that the tortoise awakens from hibernation and emerges from its burrows to graze on the greening desert shrubs and grasses. As livestock trampled the burrows and monopolized the scarce desert vegetation, tortoise populations plummeted. (page 152)

Babbitt, Bruce. *Cities in the Wilderness: A New Vision of Land Use in America*. Washington: Island Press-Shearwater, 2005. Print.

SLOPPY PARAPHRASE

Babbitt says that the tortoise is a creature in the Mojave that is virtually unchanged over 150 million years. Over the millennia, the tortoise would awaken from hibernation just in time for spring grazing on the new growth of the region's shrubs and grasses. In recent years the species became threatened. When cattle started to compete for the same food, the livestock trampled the tortoise burrows and monopolized the desert vegetation while the tortoise populations plummeted (152).

To avoid picking up language from the original as you paraphrase, state each sentence afresh instead of just changing a few words in the original. If possible, take a short break, and then check each sentence against the original. Highlight any identical words or sentence patterns, and rework your paraphrase again. Proper nouns or exact terms for the topic (such as *tortoise*) do not need to be rephrased.

The next example avoids parroting the original by making different word choices while reversing or varying sentence patterns.

> PARAPHRASE   As Babbitt explains, a tenacious survivor in the Mojave is the 150-million-year-old desert tortoise. Over the millennia, the hibernating tortoise would rouse itself each spring just in time to enjoy the new growth of the limited regional plants. In recent years, as cattle became rivals for this desert territory, the larger animals destroyed tortoise homes, ate tortoise food, and thus eliminated many of the tortoises themselves (152).

A common option is to blend paraphrase with brief quotation, carefully using quotation marks to identify any exact words drawn from the source.

> BLENDED   Babbitt describes a tenacious survivor in the Mojave, the 150-million-year-old desert tortoise. Over the millennia, the hibernating tortoise would rouse itself each spring just in time to munch on the new growth of the sparse regional plants. As cattle became rivals for the desert food supply and destroyed the tortoise homes, the "tortoise populations plummeted" (152).

Even in a brief paraphrase, be careful to avoid slipping in the author's words or closely shadowing the original sentence structure. If a source says, "President Obama called an emergency meeting of his cabinet to discuss the crisis," and you write, "The president called his cabinet to hold an emergency meeting to discuss the crisis," your words are too close to those of the source. One option is to quote the original, though it doesn't seem worth quoting word for word. Or, better, you could write, "Summoning his cabinet to an immediate session, Obama laid out the challenge before them."

HOW TO PARAPHRASE

- Select a passage with detailed information relevant to your thesis.
- Reword the passage: represent it accurately but use your own language.
- Change both its words and its sentence patterns. Replace its words with different expressions. Begin and end sentences differently, simplify long sentences, and reorder information.
- Note the page or other location (such as an electronic paragraph) where the original appears in your source. If the passage runs from one page

For more on paraphrases, see D4 in the Quick Research Guide, pp. A-29–A-30.

onto the next, record where the page changes so that your credit will be accurate no matter how much of the paraphrase you use.

- After a break, recheck your paraphrase against the original to be certain that it does not repeat the same words or merely replace a few with synonyms. Revise as needed, placing fresh words in fresh arrangements.

Summarize an Overall Point. Summarizing is a useful way of incorporating the general point of a whole paragraph, section, or work. You briefly state the main sense of the original in your own words and also identify the source. Like a paraphrase, a summary uses your own language. However, a summary is shorter than the original; it expresses only the most important ideas — the essence — of the original. This example summarizes the section of Babbitt's book containing the passage quoted on pages 180–81 and 184.

SUMMARY   According to Bruce Babbitt, former Secretary of the Interior and governor of Arizona, the isolated federal land in the West traditionally has been open to cattle and sheep ranching. These animals have damaged the arid land by grazing too aggressively, and the ranchers have battled wildlife grazers and predators alike to reduce competition with their stock. Protecting species such as the gray wolf and the desert tortoise has meant limiting grazing, an action supported by the public in order to conserve the character and beauty of the public land.

HOW TO SUMMARIZE

For more on summaries, see D5 in the Quick Research Guide, p. A-30.

- Select a passage, an article, a chapter, or an entire book whose main idea bears on your thesis.

- Read the selection carefully until you have mastered its overall point.

- Write a sentence or a series of sentences that states its essence in your own words.

- Revise your summary until it is as concise, clear, and accurate as possible. Replace any vague generalizations with precise words.

For more on plagiarism, see D1 in the Quick Research Guide, pp. A-28–A-29.

- Name your source as you begin your summary, or identify it in parentheses.

Credit Your Sources Fairly. As you quote, paraphrase, or summarize, be certain to note which source you are using and exactly where the material appears in the original. Carefully citing and listing your sources will give credit where it's due as it enhances your credibility as a careful writer.

For help avoiding plagiarism, go to the interactive "Take Action" charts in Re:Writing at **bedfordstmartins.com /concisebedguide**.

Although academic fields prefer specific formats for their papers, MLA style is widely used in composition, English, and other humanities courses.

Methods of Capturing Information from Sources

	Quotation	Paraphrase	Summary
Format for Wording	Use exact words from the source, and identify any additions, deletions, or other changes	Use your words and sentence structures, translating the content of the original passage	Use your words and sentence structures, reducing the original passage to its core
Common Use	Capture lively and authoritative wording	Capture specific information while conserving its detail	Capture the overall essence of an entire source or a passage in brief form
Advantages	Catch a reader's attention Emphasize the authority of the source	Treat specifics fully without shifting from your voice to the source's	Make a broad but clear point without shifting from your voice to the source's
Common Problems	Quoting too much Quoting inaccurately	Slipping in the original wording Following the original sentence patterns too closely	Losing impact by bogging down in too much detail Drifting into vague generalities
Markers	Identify source in launch statement or text citation and in final list of sources Add quotation marks to show the source's exact words Use ellipses and brackets to mark any changes	Identify source in launch statement or text citation and in final list of sources	Identify source in launch statement or text citation and in final list of sources

In MLA style, you credit your source twice. First, identify the author's last name (and the page number in the original) in the text as you quote, paraphrase, summarize, or refer to the source. Often you will simply mention the author's name (or a short version of the title if the author is not identified) as you introduce the information from the source. If not, note the name and page number of the original in parentheses after you present the material: (Walton 88). Next, fully identify the source in an alphabetical list at the end of your paper.

Right now, the methods for capturing information and crediting sources may seem complicated. However, the more you use them, the easier they become. Experienced writers also know some time-tested secrets. For example, how can you save time, improve accuracy, and avoid last-minute stress about sources? The answer is easy. Include in your draft, even your very first one, both the source identification and the location. Add them at the very moment when you first add the material, even if you are just dropping it in so you don't forget it. Later on, you won't have to hunt for the details.

For sample source citations and lists, see the readings on pp. 168–73 and the MLA and APA examples in E in the Quick Research Guide, pp. A-32–A-38, and in A in the Quick Format Guide, pp. A-1–A-7. For sample papers in MLA and APA style, see pp. A-59–A-76.

Let Your Draft Evolve. No matter how many quotations, paraphrases, and summaries you assemble, chunks of evidence captured from sources do not — on their own — constitute a solid paper. You need to interpret and explain that evidence for your readers, helping them to see exactly why, how, and to what extent it supports your position.

For help supporting a thesis, go to the interactive "Take Action" charts in Re:Writing at **bedfordstmartins.com /concisebedguide**.

To develop a solid draft, many writers rely on one of two methods, beginning either with the evidence or with the position they wish to support.

METHOD 1 Start with your evidence. Use one of these strategies to arrange quotations, paraphrases, and summaries in a logical, compelling order.

- Cut and paste the chunks of evidence, moving them around in a file until they fall into a logical order.
- Print each chunk on a separate page, and arrange the pages on a flat surface like a table, floor, or bed until you reach a workable sequence.
- Label each chunk with a key word, and use the key words to work out an informal outline.

Once your evidence is organized logically, add commentary to connect the chunks for your readers: introduce, conclude, and link pieces of evidence with your explanations and interpretations. (Ignore any leftovers from sources unless they cover key points that you still need to integrate.) Let your draft expand as you alternate evidence and interpretation.

METHOD 2 Start with your position or your conclusion, selecting a way to focus on how you want your paper to present it.

- You can state your case boldly and directly, explaining your thesis and supporting points in your own words.
- If you feel too uncertain to take that step, you can write out directions, telling yourself what to do in each part of the draft (in preparation for actually doing it).

Either way, use this working structure to identify where to embed the evidence from your sources. Let your draft grow as you pull in your sources and expand your comments.

For more on quotations, paraphrases, and summaries, see D3, D4, and D5 in the Quick Research Guide, pp. A-29–A-30.

DEVELOPMENT CHECKLIST

☐ Have you quoted only notable passages that add support and authority?

☐ Have you checked your quotations for accuracy and marked where each begins and ends with quotation marks?

- ☐ Have you paraphrased accurately, reflecting both the main points and the supporting details in the original?

- ☐ Does each paraphrase use your own words without repeating or echoing the words or the sentence structure of the original?

- ☐ Have you briefly stated supporting ideas that you wish to summarize, sticking to the overall point without bogging down in details or examples?

- ☐ Has each summary remained respectful of the ideas and opinions of others, even if you disagree with them?

- ☐ Have you identified the source of every quotation, paraphrase, summary, or source reference by noting in parentheses the last name of the writer and the page number (if available) where the passage appears in the source?

- ☐ Have you ordered your evidence logically and effectively?

- ☐ Have you interpreted and explained your evidence from sources with your own comments in your own voice?

Revising and Editing

As you read over the draft of your paper, remember what you wanted to accomplish: to develop an enlightening position about your topic and to share this position with a college audience, using sources to support your ideas.

For more on revising and editing strategies, see Ch. 15.

Strengthen Your Thesis. As you begin revising, you may decide that your working thesis is ambiguous, poorly worded, hard to support, or simply off the mark. Revise it so that it clearly alerts readers to your main idea.

WORKING THESIS	Although most workers would like longer vacations, many employers do not believe that they would benefit, too.
REVISED THESIS	Despite assumptions to the contrary, employers who increase vacation time for workers also are likely to increase creativity, productivity, and the bottom line.

Launch Each Source. Whenever you quote, paraphrase, summarize, or refer to a source, launch it with a suitable introduction. An effective launch sets the scene for your source material, prepares your reader to accept it, and marks the transition from your words and ideas to those of the source. As you revise, confirm that you launch all of your source material well.

In a launch statement, often you will first identify the source — by the author's last name or by a short version of the title when the author isn't named — in your introductory sentence. If not, identify the source in parentheses, typically to end the sentence. Then try to suggest why you've mentioned this source at this point, perhaps noting its contribution, its credibility, its vantage point, or its relationship to other

For more about launching sources, see D6 in the Quick Research Guide, p. A-31.

sources. Vary your launch statements to avoid tedium and to add emphasis. Boost your credibility as a writer by establishing the credibility of your sources.

Here are some typical patterns for launch statements:

As Yung demonstrates, . . .

Although Zeffir maintains . . . , Matson suggests . . .

Many schools educated the young but also unified the community (Hill 22). . . .

In *Forward March*, Smith's study of the children of military personnel, . . .

Another common recommendation is . . . ("Safety Manual").

Making good use of her experience as a travel consultant, Lee explains . . .

When you quote or paraphrase from a specific page (or other location, such as a paragraph numbered on a Web page), include that exact location.

The classic definition of . . . (Bagette 18) is updated to . . . (Zoe par. 4).

Benton distinguishes four typical steps in this process (248–51).

These examples follow MLA style. For more about how to capture, launch, and cite sources in your text using either MLA or APA style, see D6 and E in the Quick Research Guide, pp. A-31–A-38.

Learning by Doing 🎙 Launching Your Sources

Make a duplicate file of your draft or print it. Add highlights in one color to mark all your source identifications; use another color to mark source material:

> The problem of unintended consequences is well illustrated by many environmental changes over recent decades. For instance, if using the Mojave Desert for cattle grazing seemed efficient to ranchers, it also turned out to be destructive for long-time desert residents such as tortoises (Babbitt 152).

Now examine your draft. How do the colors alternate? Do you find color globs where you simply list sources without explaining their contributions? Do you find material without source identification (typically the author's name) or without a location in the original (typically a page number)? Fill in whatever gaps you discover.

Synthesize Several Sources. Often you will compare, contrast, or relate two or three sources to deepen your discussion or to illustrate a range of views. When you synthesize, you pull together several sources in the same passage to build a new interpretation or reach a new conclusion. You go beyond the separate contributions of the individual sources to relate the sources to each other and to connect them to your thesis. A synthesis should be easy to follow and use your own wording.

HOW TO SYNTHESIZE

- Summarize (see pp. 186–87) each of the sources you want to synthesize. Boil down each summary to its essence.
- Write a few sentences that state in your own words how the sources are linked. For example, are they similar, different, or related? Do they share assumptions and conclusions, or do they represent alternatives, opposites, or opponents? Do they speak to chronology, influence, logical progression, or diversity of opinion?
- Write a few more sentences stating what the source relationships mean for your thesis and the position you develop in your paper.
- Refine your synthesis statements until they are clear and illuminating for your audience. Embed them as you move from one source summary to the next and as you reach new interpretations or conclusions that go beyond the separate sources.

Use Your Own Voice to Interpret and Connect. By the time your draft is finished, you may feel that you have found relevant evidence in your sources but that they now dominate your draft. As you reread, you may discover passages that simply string together ideas from sources.

DRAFT

Easterbrook <u>says</u> in "In Search of the Cause of Autism: How about Television?" that television may injure children who are susceptible to autism. The Centers for Disease Control and Prevention <u>says</u> that autism trails only mental retardation among disabilities that affect children's development. The Kaiser Family Foundation study <u>says</u> that parents use television and other electronic entertainment "to help them manage their household and keep their kids entertained" (Rideout, Hamel, and Kaiser Family Foundation 4).

Whole passage repeats "says"

Repeats sentence pattern opening with author

Jumps from one source to the next without transitions

When your sources overshadow your thesis, your explanations, and your writing style, revise to restore balance. Try strategies such as these to regain control of your draft:

- Add your explanation and interpretation of the source information so that your ideas are clear.
- Add transitions, and state the connections that you assume are obvious.
- Arrange information in a logical sequence, not in the order in which you read it or recorded notes about it.

- Clarify definitions, justify a topic's importance, and recognize alternative views to help your audience appreciate your position.
- Reword to vary your sentence openings, and avoid repetitive wording.

Thoughtful revision can help readers grasp what you want to say, why you have included each source, and how you think that it supports your thesis.

REVISION

Connects two sources

Adds transitions

Two major studies take very different looks at the development of children in our society. First, a research study sponsored by the Kaiser Family Foundation examines how parents use television and other electronic options "to help them manage their household and keep their kids entertained" (Rideout, Hamel, and Kaiser Family Foundation 4). Next, based on statistics about how often major developmental disabilities occur in children, the Centers for Disease Control and Prevention reports that autism currently trails only mental retardation among

Identifies author's experience to add credibility

disabilities that affect children's development. Journalist and book author Gregg Easterbrook pulls together these two views, using the title of his article to raise his unusual question: "In Search of the Cause of Autism: How about Television?" He urges

Defines issue and justifies concern

study of his speculation that television may injure children who are vulnerable to autism and joins an ongoing debate about what causes autism, a challenging disability that interferes with children's ability to communicate and interact with other people.

List Your Sources as College Readers Expect. When you use sources in a college paper, you'll be expected to identify them twice: briefly when you draw information from them and fully when you list them at the end of your paper, following a conventional system. The list of sources for the draft and revision in the previous section would include these entries.

Centers for Disease Control and Prevention. "Frequently Asked Questions—
   Prevalence." *Autism Information Center.* CDC, 30 Jan. 2006. Web. 12 Sept. 2006.

Easterbrook, Gregg. "In Search of the Cause of Autism: How about Television?" *Slate*.
Washington Post, 5 Sept. 2006. Web. 12 Sept. 2006.

Rideout, Victoria, Elizabeth Hamel, and Kaiser Family Foundation. *The Media Family:
Electronic Media in the Lives of Infants, Toddlers, Preschoolers and Their Parents*.
Menlo Park: Henry J. Kaiser Family Foundation, 2006. *Kaiser Family Foundation*.
Web. 12 Sept. 2006.

Learning by Doing 🎦 Checking Your Presentation of Sources

Use your software to help you improve the presentation of source materials in your draft. For example, search for all the quotation marks in your paper. Make sure that each is one of a pair surrounding every quotation in your paper. At the same time, be sure that the source and location are identified for each quotation. Try color highlighting in your final list of sources to help you spot and refine details, especially any common personal errors. For instance, if you forget periods after names of authors or mix up semicolons and colons, highlight those marks in color so you slow down and focus on them. Then correct or add marks as needed. After you check your entries, restore the passage to the usual black color.

Use the Take Action chart (p. 194) to help you figure out how to improve your draft. Skim across the top to identify questions you might ask about integrating sources in your draft. When you answer a question with "Yes" or "Maybe," move straight down the column to Locate Specifics under that question. Use the activities there to pinpoint gaps, problems, or weaknesses. Then move straight down the column to Take Action. Use the advice that suits your problem as you revise.

For online Take Action help, visit **bedfordstmartins.com /concisebedguide** and go to Re:Writing.

Peer Response 👥 Supporting a Position with Sources

Have several classmates read your draft critically, considering how effectively you have used your sources to support a position. Ask your peer editors to answer questions such as these:

- Can you state the writer's position on the topic?
- Do you have any trouble seeing how the writer's points and the supporting evidence from sources connect? How might the writer make the connections clearer?
- How effectively does the writer capture the information from sources? Would you recommend that any of the quotations, paraphrases, or summaries be presented differently?

For general questions for a peer editor, see p. 305.

Take Action Integrating Source Information Effectively

Ask each question at the top of the chart to consider whether your draft might need work on that issue. If so, follow the
ASK—LOCATE SPECIFICS—TAKE ACTION sequence to revise.

	Weak Launch Statements?	Too Little Voice?	Too Few Source Credits?
1 **ASK**	Have I tossed in source material without preparing my audience for it? Do I repeat the same words in my launch statements?	Have I lost my own voice? Have I allowed my sources to take over my draft? Have I strung together too many quotations?	Have I identified any source only once or twice even though I use it throughout a section?
2 **LOCATE SPECIFICS**	■ Underline each launch statement (the sentence or its part that introduces source material). Decide if it assures readers that the source is credible, logical, and relevant to your thesis. ■ Highlight any repeated words (*says*, *states*) or transitions (*also*, *then*).	■ Highlight the material from sources in one color and your own commentary in another. ■ Check the color balance in each paragraph. If the source color dominates, consider how to restore your own voice.	■ Select a passage that relies on sources. Highlight your ideas in one color and those from sources in a different color. ■ Add a slash to mark each switch between two sources or between your ideas and a source.
3 **TAKE ACTION**	■ Sharpen underlined launch statements, perhaps noting (a) an author's credentials significant to readers, (b) a source's historical or current contributions, or (c) its relationship to other sources. ■ Edit the highlighted words (and any other repeated expressions) for variety and precision. For *says*, try *emphasizes*, *suggests*, *reviews*, *presents*, or *explains*. For *also*, try *in addition*, *furthermore*, or *similarly*.	■ Restore your voice in each paragraph by adding a topic sentence in your own words that links to your thesis and a conclusion that sums up. ■ Add transitions (*further*, *in contrast*, *as a result*) and explanations where you move point to point or source to source. ■ Reduce what you quote to focus on striking words. Sum up, or drop the rest. ■ Weave in your ideas until they, not your sources, dominate.	■ At each slash marking a source switch, add a launch statement for the second source. ■ At each slash (or color change) marking a switch to your ideas, phrase your comment so that it does not sound like more of the source. ■ At each slash (or color change) marking a switch from your ideas, identify the source again. ■ When you quote and then continue with the same source, identify it again.

194

- Are any of the source citations unclear? Can you tell where source information came from and where quotations and paraphrases appear in a source?

- Is the writer's voice clear? Do the sources drown it out in any spots?

- If this paper were yours, what is the one thing you would be sure to work on before handing it in?

REVISION CHECKLIST

☐ Is your thesis, or main idea, clear? Is it distinguished from the points made by your sources?

☐ Do you speak in your own voice, interpreting and explaining your sources instead of allowing them to dominate your draft?

☐ Have you moved smoothly back and forth between your explanations and your source material?

☐ Have you credited every source in the text and in a list at the end of your paper? Have you added each detail expected in the format for listing sources?

☐ Have you been careful to quote, paraphrase, summarize, and credit sources accurately and ethically? Have you hunted up missing details, double-checked quotations, and rechecked the accuracy of anything prepared hastily?

After you have revised your paper, edit and proofread it. Carefully check the grammar, word choice, punctuation, and mechanics — and then correct any problems you find. Be certain to check the punctuation with your quotations, making sure that each quotation mark is correctly placed and that you have used other punctuation, such as commas, correctly.

For more help, find the relevant checklists in the Quick Editing Guide beginning on p. A-39. Turn also to the Quick Format Guide beginning on p. A-1.

EDITING CHECKLIST

☐ Do all the verbs agree with their subjects, especially when you switch from your words to those of a source?   A4

☐ Do all the pronouns agree with their antecedents, especially when you use your words with a quotation from a source?   A6

☐ Have you used commas correctly, especially where you integrate material from sources?   C1

☐ Have you punctuated all your quotations correctly?   C3

Additional Writing Assignments

1. **Source Assignment.** Read several sources about the same topic. Instead of using them as evidence to support your ideas on the topic, analyze how well they function as sources. State your thesis about them, and evaluate their strengths and weaknesses, using clear criteria. (See, for example, the criteria in C3 in the Quick Research Guide, pp. A-27–A-28.)

2. **Source Assignment.** Locate several different accounts of a notable event in newspapers, magazines, published letters or journals, books, blogs, or other sources, depending on the time when the event occurred. State and support a thesis that explains the differences among the accounts. Use the accounts as evidence to support your position.

3. **Source Assignment.** Browse in your library's new book and periodical areas (on site or online) or in specialty search engines to identify a current topic of interest to you. (Adding the current or previous year's date to a search is one way to find recent publications or acquisitions.) Gather and evaluate a cluster of resources on your topic. Write an essay using those readings to support your position about the new development.

For more on reviewing and evaluating, see Ch. 8.

4. **Source Assignment.** Following the directions of your instructor, use several types of sources to support your position in an essay. One option might be to select paired or related readings (from this book or its e-Pages), and also to interview someone with the background or experience to act as another valuable source of information. A second option might be to view and evaluate a film, television program, radio show, blog, Web site, art exhibit, performance, or other event. Then supplement your review by reading several articles that review the same event, evaluate a different or related production, or discuss criteria for similar types of items or events.

5. **Source Assignment.** Create a concise Web site that addresses a question of interest to you. Select and read a few reliable sources about that question, and then create several screens or short pages to explain what you have learned. For example, you might want to define or explain aspects of the question, justify the conclusion you have reached, or evaluate alternative answers as well as your own. Credit all of your sources, and supply links when appropriate.

6. **Visual Assignment.** Examine the following images, and analyze one (or more) of them. Use the image to support your position in an essay, perhaps a conclusion about the image or about what it portrays. Point out relevant detail to persuade your audience of your view. Cite the images correctly, using the style your instructor specifies.

10 Responding to Visual Representations

Images are a constant and persistent presence in our lives. The sign atop a taxi invites us to try the new ride at a local tourist attraction. A celebrity sporting a milk mustache smiles from the side of a city bus, accompanied by the familiar question, "Got milk?" The lettering on a pickup truck urges us to call for a free landscaping estimate. During campaign season, politicians beam at us from brochures, billboards, and screens. On television, video, and the Web, advertising images surround us, trying to shape our opinions about everything from personal hygiene products to snack foods to political issues.

Besides ads, all sorts of cartoons, photos, drawings, paintings, logos, graphics, and other two-dimensional media work to evoke responses. The critical skills you develop for analyzing these still images also apply to other visual representations, including television commercials, films, and stage productions. Whether visual images provoke a smile or a frown, one thing is certain: visuals help to structure our views of reality.

Why Responding to Visuals Matters

In a College Course

- You respond to images of people and places in class discussions and papers for sociology, foreign language, and international business classes.
- You write reports on digital images during your health-sciences lab or clinical experience.

In the Workplace

- You evaluate the values conveyed by proposed images for a new Web page.

In Your Community

- You gather recent newspaper images of local teens to document the need for a community sports program.

❓ When have you responded to visuals in your writing? In what situations might you analyze images in future writing?

Using Strategies for Visual Analysis

Just as you annotate or respond to a written text, do the same to record your observations and interpretations of images. Include a copy of the image, if available, when you solicit peer review or submit your essay. Begin your visual analysis by conducting a *close reading* of the image. Like a literal and critical reading of a written text, a close reading of an image involves careful, in-depth examination of the advertisement, photograph, cartoon, artwork, or other visual on three levels:

- **What is the big picture?** What is the source of the image? What is its purpose? What audience does it address? What prominent element in the image stands out? What focal point draws the eye?

- **What characteristics of the image can you observe?** What story does the image tell? What people or animals appear in the image? What are the major elements of the image? How are they arranged?

- **How can you interpret what the image suggests?** What feeling or mood does it create? What is its cultural meaning? What are the roles of any signs, symbols, or language that it includes? What is its theme?

As you analyze visuals, you may discover that your classmates respond differently than you do to some images, just as they might to a written text. Your personal cultural background and your experiences may influence how you see the meaning of an image. As a result, your thesis interpreting the meaning of an image or analyzing its effectiveness will be your own — shaped by your responses and supported by your observations.

For an interactive Learning by Doing activity on analyzing the Web site for your campus, go to Ch. 10: **bedfordstmartins.com /concisebedguide**.

For more on literal and critical reading of texts, see Ch. 2. For checklists for analyzing images, see pp. 204, 210–11, and 215–16.

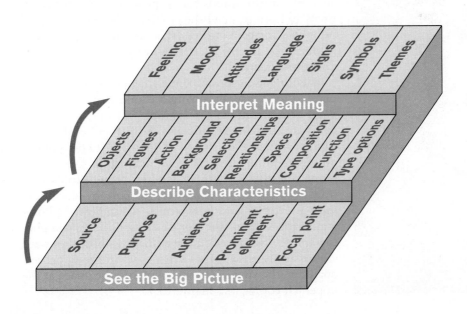

Level One: Seeing the Big Picture

For more on crediting sources of visuals, see B in the Quick Format Guide, pp. A-8–A-12.

Begin your close reading of an image by discovering what you can about its origins and overall composition. If you include the image in a paper, you will need to cite the source and its "author" or artist, just as you would if you were including text from a reading, an article, or a literary work.

Source, Purpose, and Audience

Identifying the background of an image is sometimes complicated. For example, an image may appear in its original context or in a different situation, used seriously, humorously, or allusively.

- What is the context for the image? If it is an ad, when and where did it run? If it is a photograph, painting, or other work of art, who is the artist? Where and how has it been published, circulated, or exhibited?
- What is the purpose of the image?
- What audience does it aim to attract? How does it appeal to viewers?

Prominent Element

Next, examine the overall composition of the image. Ask yourself, "Is there one prominent element—object, person, background, writing—in the image that immediately attracts my attention?"

Answering that question is easy for a visual that showcases a single object or person, as in Figure 10.1. There, the child is the obvious prominent element. Her dark eyes, framed by her dark hair, draw the viewer to her alert, intent expression. That expression suggests her capacity to learn from all she observes. The text above and below her image reinforces this message as it cautions adults to be careful what they teach children through their own conduct.

Identifying the prominent element can be more complicated for a visual showing a whole scene or inviting many interpretations. For example, what draws your eye in Figure 10.2? Many people would first notice the neon sign on the left. The sign is bright, colorful (in a photo otherwise dominated by black and white tones), and framed neatly by the first window panel. People who read from left to right and top to bottom—including most Americans and Europeans—typically read photographs in the same way. For this reason, artists and photographers often position key elements—those they want viewers to see right away—somewhere in the upper left quadrant, drawing the viewer's eye into the image at the upper left corner. (See Figure 10.3.)

Figure 10.1 Public Service Announcement with One Prominent Element. *Source:* Act Against Violence.org/Ad Council

EVERY TIME YOU SCREAM AT A DRIVER, SHE LEARNS A LESSON.

You're always teaching. *Teach carefully.*

www.ACTAgainstViolence.org

Ad Council

MetLife Foundation

act

Figure 10.2 (top) Photograph by Ian Pool

Figure 10.3 (above left) Photograph Divided into Quarters

Figure 10.4 (above right) Z Pattern Often Used to Read Images

Figure 10.5 (right) Close-Up Detail of Photograph

Focal Point

There is another reason the reader's eye might be drawn first to the neon sign on the left in Figure 10.2. This simple yet bold sign communicates much about the place as a whole, announcing it to be an inexpensive, down-to-earth restaurant, offering simple fare. It probably opens early and stays open late, maybe even all night, serving average people of modest means. As a focal point, therefore, this sign sets up an important point of contrast with the unusual customer seated at the right. Because of the left-to-right and top-to-bottom reading pattern, most of us view photographs in a Z pattern, as shown in Figure 10.4. Thus, the bottom right corner of an image is a second important position that a skilled photographer can use to hold viewers' attention. When you look at the "big picture," you can see an image's overall composition, identify its prominent element, and determine its focal point.

VISUAL ANALYSIS CHECKLIST
Seeing the Big Picture

☐ What is the source of the image? What is its purpose and audience?

☐ What prominent element in the image immediately attracts your attention? How and why does it draw you into the image?

☐ What is the focal point of the image? How does the image direct your attention to this point? What path does your eye follow as you observe the image?

Learning by Doing 🎦 Seeing the Big Picture

Working with a classmate or a small group, select another image in this book such as one that opens or closes a chapter. Consider the image's purpose and audience (in its original context or in this book), but concentrate on its prominent element, which draws the viewer's eye, and its focal point, which suggests the center of its action or moment. Share analyses in a class discussion, or report or post yours for another group.

Level Two: Observing the Characteristics of an Image

As you read a written text literally, you become aware of what it presents, what it means, and how it applies in other situations. Similarly, your close reading of an image includes observing its *denotative* or literal characteristics. At this stage, you focus on exactly what the image depicts — observing it objectively — rather than probing what it means or signifies.

Cast of Characters

Objects. Examine the condition, colors, sizes, functions, and positions of the objects included in the image. In Figure 10.2, for example, the main object outside is a luxurious black car, parked at the far right. Though little of the car is visible, its sleek design, wide tire, and position near the Batman figure mark it as the iconic Batmobile. In contrast, the objects inside the restaurant are mundane and predictable: a trash can, three potted plants, a narrow blue cash machine, tables and chairs, stainless steel food-service machines, a napkin dispenser, and stacks of empty cups.

Figures. Look closely at any figures (people, animals) in the image. Consider facial expressions, poses, hairstyles and colors, ages, sexes, ethnicity, possible education or occupation, apparent relationships, and so on.

Figure 10.2 shows a lone, seated man, framed by the window panel and silhouetted against the white floor-to-ceiling blinds. The man wears a black cape, a close-fitting, rubberized suit, wide gold belt, gloves, and boots, an outfit that accentuates his muscled physique. A mask hides all but the lower part of his face. Like no other detail, the mask's large, pointy ears identify the figure as the comic-book superhero Batman.

Story of the Image

Action. The action shown in an image suggests its "plot" or story, the events surrounding the moment it captures. Figure 10.2 shows Batman eating a quick dinner or late-night snack. It suggests his earlier actions driving to the place, parking outside, ordering his food, and taking a seat at a small corner table.

Background. The background in an image shows where and when the action takes place. In Figure 10.2, the background is a bagel and donut shop on a winter night. This eatery—well lit and ordinary—sharply contrasts with its only customer, the figure of Batman, who is dark and mysterious, both in costume and mission. Because he is usually engaged in dangerous and high-minded crime-fighting crusades, the background seems designed to surprise viewers, who might ask, "What is the Dark Knight doing in a place like this?" Beyond the physical details of the photograph's background, fans will know that Batman is the secret disguise of the billionaire industrialist-playboy Bruce Wayne, a man traumatically orphaned who has vowed to devote his life to bringing criminals to justice. For anonymity, he does his crime-fighting and detective work clothed in the mystique and costume of Batman, a creature of the night. Throughout all his comic-book exploits, he is known for his intelligence, athleticism, command of technology, sense of justice—and damaged psyche.

Design and Arrangement

Selection of Elements. When you look at the design of an image, reflect on both the elements included and their organization.

- What are the major colors and shapes? How are they arranged?
- Does the image look balanced? Are light and dark areas symmetrical?
- Does the image appear organized or chaotic?
- Is one area darker (heavier) or brighter (lighter) than other areas?
- What emotion, historical period, or memory does the image evoke?

In Figure 10.2, the shapes and colors are arranged so that the building's interior looks like daytime—bright, safe, warm, and cozy—which accentuates the cold, dark, and dangerous night outside. The bright areas in the middle of the photograph are surrounded by shadowy spaces with Batman sitting on the edge between the two. In this way, the image balances light and dark. Batman has come in for a few moments, but the photo's organization still connects him with the inhospitable world outside.

Relationship of Elements. Visual elements may be related to one another or to written text that appears with them. In Figure 10.2, for instance, the sign identifies a familiar, everyday location. However, the four big plate glass window panels, stretching across the front of the shop, suggest the way that drawings in a comic book march across a page, separated into neat rectangular frames. But here, no "thought balloon" emerges from Batman's head, allowing viewers to share his thoughts and learn why he is out of context. The photograph is arranged to raise, not answer, the question of what Batman is doing here. It invites viewers to interpret what is happening, to insert their own thought balloons over Batman's head. At the same time, it makes the point that we rarely know other people's stories, thoughts, and interior lives. When we see strangers in public settings, they are essentially unknowable, as this figure is.

Use of Space. An image may be surrounded by "white space"—empty space without text or graphics—or it may be "busy," filled with visual and written elements. Effective white space provides relief from a busy layout or directs the reader's eye to key elements. The image in Figure 10.2 uses the white-tiled wall above the counter and the white blinds to set off the shadowy darkness. Figure 10.6 specifically uses empty white space to call attention to the Volkswagen's small size. When this advertisement was produced back in 1959, many American cars were large and heavy. The VW, a German import, provided consumers with an alternative, and the advertising emphasized this contrast.

Artistic Choices

Whatever the form of an image, the person who composes it considers its artistic effect, function, and connection to related text.

Composition Decisions. Aesthetic or artistic choices may vary with the designer's preferences and the characteristics of the medium. A photographer might use a close-up, medium, or wide-angle shot—and also determine the

Figure 10.6 Volkswagen Advertisement, about 1959

angle of the shot, the lighting, and the use of color. Compare Figures 10.2 and 10.5 to see how a close-up may leave out context but accent detail, such as Batman's white cup. On the other hand, in the Volkswagen ad (Figure 10.6), the white space creates the effect of a long shot taken from below with a telephoto lens. We see the car as it might appear through the wrong end of a pair of binoculars. This vantage point shrinks the car so that the small vehicle looks even smaller.

Figure 10.7 Chevrolet Advertisement, 1955

For sample tables and figures, see B (pp. A-8–A-12) in the Quick Format Guide. For sample photographs, turn to the images opening Chs. 4–9, as well as the e-Pages.

Function Decisions. An image that illustrates a point needs to serve the overall purpose of the document. In other words, form should follow function. Of the many illustrations available—photographs, drawings, charts, graphs, tables—certain types are especially suited to certain functions. For example, the 1955 Chevrolet ad, Figure 10.7, shows people having a good time enjoying a summer day near the shore. This illustration suggests that Chevrolet purchasers will enjoy life, a notion that undoubtedly suits the advertiser's goals. Likewise, a pie chart effectively conveys parts of a whole, while a photograph captures the drama and intensity of the moment—a child's rescue, a family's grief, an earthquake's toll. When you look at visuals in publications, consider how they function and why the writer might have chosen them.

Typeface Options. Many images, especially advertisements, combine image and text, using the typeface to set a mood and convey an impression. For example, **Times New Roman** is a common typeface, easy to read and somewhat conservative, whereas **Comic Sans MS** is considered informal—almost playful—and looks handwritten. Any printed element in an image may be trendy or conservative, large or small, in relation to the image as a whole. Further, it may inform, evoke emotion, or decorate the page.

Look back at Figure 10.6, the 1959 Volkswagen ad. The words "Think small" are printed in a sans serif typeface, one "without serifs," the small tails at the ends of the letters. This type is spare and unadorned, just like the VW itself. The ad also includes significant text across the bottom of the page. While this text is difficult to read in the reproduction in this book, it humorously points out the benefits of driving a small imported vehicle instead of one of the large, roomy cars common at the time.

In contrast to the VW ad campaign, the 1955 Chevrolet marketing strategy promoted big vehicles, as Figure 10.7 illustrates. Here the cars are shown in medium to close-up view to call attention to their length. Happy human figures in and beside the cars emphasize their size, and the cars are painted in bright colors, unlike the VW's serviceable black. The primary text below the scene is large enough to be read in the reproduction here. It asks which sporty Chevy would be most fun for the reader—the Bel Air convertible, the Handyman Station Wagon, or the stylish Sport Coupe. Then some "fine print"—difficult to read in the reproduction—notes other features of each car, such as its top, interior, and power.

Other images besides ads use type to set a mood or convey feelings and ideas. Figure 10.8 is a design student's response to an assignment that called for using letters to create an image. The simple typeface and stairlike arrangement help viewers "experience" the word *stairway*. Figure 10.9 illustrates how certain typefaces have become associated with countries—even to the point of becoming clichés. In fact, designers of travel posters and brochures often draw on

Figure 10.8 Stairway.
Source: Design for Communication: Conceptual Graphic Design Basics

Figure 10.9 Type as Cultural Cliché.
Source: From *Publication Design*, 3/e,
by Roy Paul Nelson, © 1983 McGraw-
Hill Education.

Figure 10.10 Type that Contributes to Meaning. *Source:* Andrew Dillon Bustin, Boston,
Massachusetts, 2011

predictable choices like these to suggest a mood — for example, boldness, tradition adventure, history. Similarly, the plain, slanted type in Figure 10.10 suggests movement toward the future, reinforcing the message of the words.

VISUAL ANALYSIS CHECKLIST
Observing the Characteristics of an Image

☐ What objects are included in the image?

☐ What figures (people or animals) appear in the image?

☐ What action takes place in the image? What is its "plot" or story?

☐ What is in the background? In what place does the action take place?

☐ What elements, colors, and shapes contribute to the design? How are they arranged or balanced? What feeling, memory, or association is evoked?

☐ How are the pictorial elements related to one another? How are they related to any written material? What do these relationships tell you as a viewer?

☐ Does the image include white space, fill its space, or seem busy?

☐ What composition decisions has the designer or artist made? What type of shot, shot angle, lighting, or color is used?

☐ What is the function of the image? How does form support function?

☐ What typefaces are used? What impressions do they convey?

Learning by Doing 📷 Observing Characteristics

Working with a classmate or small group, continue analyzing the image you selected for the activity on page 204. Examine a major characteristic—such as characters, story, design, or artistic choices—to determine exactly what it shows. Report or post your conclusions for your class or another group.

Level Three: Interpreting the Meaning of an Image

When you read a written text analytically, you examine its parts from different angles, synthesize the material by combining it with related information, and finally evaluate or judge its significance. When you interpret an image, you do much the same, actively examining what the image *connotes* or suggests, speculating about what it means.

Because interpretation is more personal than observation, this process can reveal deep-seated individual and cultural values. In fact, interpreting an image is sometimes emotional or difficult because it may require you to examine beliefs that you are unaware of holding. You may even feel that too much is being read into the image because the process takes patience.

Like learning to read critically, learning to interpret images is a valuable skill. When you give an image a close, patient, in-depth examination, you can often deepen your understanding of its creator's artistic, political, economic, or other motives. You can also become more aware of the cultural values and personal views you bring to an image and gain a better sense of why you respond to it as you do.

General Feeling or Mood

To begin interpreting an image, consider what feeling or mood it creates and how it does so. In Figure 10.2, the mood created by the photo of Batman is one of loneliness and isolation without even the companionship of someone working behind the counter. Yet the campy humor in the photo leads one to wonder whether the figure is an actor, a guest from a costume party, or somehow, improbably, the Caped Crusader himself. Is he waiting to meet someone? Has he stopped to relax after battling evildoers all night? Is he a regular or a one-time visitor?

Whatever the story, the image shrinks a superhero down to human size, simply having a snack. From the perspective of the photograph, the Batman figure looks relatively small and vulnerable, despite his imposing costume. He looks like someone who is resting and recharging his energy level but will soon go back out into the night. He suggests a policeman taking a break from his beat, or a worker or student on a coffee break. The image might be suggesting that in the real world, the superheroes are regular people, like us. Indeed, we all might be on heroic missions, just by going about our daily work, getting an education, raising children, and participating in community life.

Another image might capture or represent a different version of this feeling or mood. As Figure 10.11 illustrates, people take many kinds of breaks, finding carefree moments of escape in various ways. Perhaps Batman unwinds at a late-night donut shop while the silhouetted people in Figure 10.11 ride a Ferris wheel at an amusement park, lifted up on a short, circular detour from their normal routine. Here, a lighthearted mood of family fun or romance predominates. The seated figures are not alone; they are paired off on the ride's gondola benches, with sneakered or sandaled feet dangling. The fiery reds and oranges of the sunset infuse the scene with warmth although the ride's heavy triangular shapes, octopus arms, and burned out

Figure 10.11 Photograph Conveying a Mood. *Source:* Ben Kleppinger, Bryantsville, Kentucky

bulbs might suggest a slightly menacing mechanical contraption. Although the mood of Figure 10.2 is wintery, and the mood of this photo is summery, both invite reflection on what it means to take a break.

Sociological, Political, Economic, or Cultural Attitudes

On the surface, the Volkswagen ad in Figure 10.6 (p. 207) is simply an attempt to sell a car. But its message might be interpreted to mean "scale down"—lead a less consumer-oriented lifestyle. If Volkswagen had distributed this ad in the 1970s, it would have been unremarkable—faced with the first energy crisis that adversely affected American gasoline prices, many advertisers used ecological consciousness to sell cars. In 1959, however, energy conservation was not really a concern. Contrasted with other automobile ads of its time, the Volkswagen ad seems somewhat eccentric, making the novel suggestion that larger cars are excessively extravagant.

Whereas the Volkswagen ad suggests that "small" refers to both size and affordability, the Chevrolet ad in Figure 10.7 (p. 208) depicts a large vehicle, "stealing the thunder from the high-priced cars." Without a large price tag, the Chevrolet still offers a large lifestyle, cruising in a convertible or vacationing at the shore. Figure 10.12 deliberately contrasts presence and absence, projecting a possible future scene—without the bear—to bring home its message about the need to protect our national parks and their residents. What's missing also may be more subtle, especially for viewers who wear the blinders of their own times, circumstances, or expectations. For example, viewers of today might readily notice the absence of people of color in the 1955 Chevrolet ad. An interesting

Figure 10.12 Photograph Using a Missing Element to Convey a Message.
Source: Public Service Announcement, Americans for National Parks

Figure 10.13 Public-Service Advertisement Showing Wordplay. *Source:* Design for Communication: Conceptual Graphic Design Basics

study might investigate what types of magazines originally carried this ad, whether their readers recognized what was missing, and whether (and how) Chevrolets were also advertised in publications aimed at Asian, African, or Spanish-speaking Americans.

Language

Just as you examine figures, colors, and shapes in an image, so you need to examine its words, phrases, and sentences to interpret what it suggests. Does its language provide information, generate an emotional response, or do both? Do its words repeat a sound or concept, signal a comparison (such as a "new, improved" product), carry sexual overtones, issue a challenge, or offer a philosophy of life? The words in the center of the Chevrolet ad in Figure 10.7 (p. 208) associate the car with a sporty, fun-filled lifestyle. On the other hand, VW's "Think small" ad in Figure 10.6 turns compactness into a goal, a desirable quality in a car and, by extension, in life.

Frequently advertisements employ wordplay—lighthearted or serious—to get their messages across. Consider the public-service advertisement in Figure 10.13, created by a graphic-design student. This ad features a play on the word *tolerance*, which is scrambled on the chalkboard so that the letters in the center read *learn*. The chalkboard, a typical classroom feature, suggests that tolerance is a basic lesson to be learned. Also, the definition of tolerance at the bottom of the ad is much like other definitions students might look up in a dictionary. (It reads, "The capacity for, or practice of, recognizing or respecting the behavior, beliefs, opinions, practices, or rights of others, whether agreeing with them or not.")

Wordplay can also challenge viewers' preconceptions about an image. The billboard in Figure 10.14 shows a romantic—indeed, a seductive—scene. The sophisticated couple gaze deeply into each other's eyes as the man kisses the woman's hand. However, the verbal exchange undermines that intimate

Figure 10.14 Billboard Showing Wordplay. *Source:* Photograph by Bill Aron, PhotoEdit

scene and viewers' expectations about what happens next. Instead of a similar compliment in response to "Your scent is intoxicating," the billboard makes plain its antismoking position with the reply: "Yours is carcinogenic." In just seven words, the billboard counters the suave, romantic image of smoking with the reality of smelly, cancer-causing tobacco smoke.

Signs and Symbols

Signs and symbols, such as product logos, are images or words that communicate key messages. In the Chevrolet ad in Figure 10.7 (p. 208), the product logo concludes the ad, promoting "motoramic" fun and power. Sometimes a product logo alone may be enough, as in the Hershey chocolate company's holiday ads with little more than a single Hershey's Kiss.

Themes

The theme of an image is not the same as its plot. When you identify the plot, you identify the story that is told by the image. When you identify the theme, you explain what the image is about. An ad for a diamond ring may tell the story of a man surprising his wife with a ring on their twenty-fifth wedding anniversary, but the advertisement's theme could be sex, romance, commitment, or another concept. Similarly, the theme of a soft-drink ad might be competition, community, compassion, or individualism.

Through close reading, you can unearth details to support your interpretation of the theme and convince others of its merit. For example, the image in Figure 10.15, appears to illustrate a recipe for a tasty margarita. However, the list of ingredients suggests a tale of too many drinks and a drunk-driving accident after running a red light. Instead of promoting an alcoholic beverage or promising relaxing fun, this public-service announcement challenges the assumption that risky behavior won't carry consequences. Its text reminds viewers of its theme: well-being comes not from alcohol-fueled confidence but from responsible choices.

Figure 10.15 Poster Conveying a Theme. *Source:* U.S. Department of Transportation/Ad Council

---

VISUAL ANALYSIS CHECKLIST
Interpreting the Meaning of an Image

☐ What general feeling do you get from looking at the image? What mood does it create? How does it do so?

☐ What sociological, political, economic, or cultural attitudes are reflected?

☐ What language is included in the image? How does the language function?

☐ What signs and symbols can you identify? What role do these play?

☐ What theme or themes can you identify in the image?

Learning by Doing 🖼 Interpreting Meaning

Working with a classmate or small group, continue analyzing the image you selected for the activity on page 204. Examine one of its major characteristics— feeling or mood, attitude, language, signs or symbols, or theme—to interpret what the image might mean. Share your conclusions with your class or another group in a brief oral report or an online posting.

Learning from Another Writer: Visual Analysis

For visual essays and help analyzing them, go to **bedfordstmartins.com /concisebedguide**.

Because visual images surround us, you may be asked to respond to them and to analyze them, concentrating on persuasive, cultural, historical, sociological, or other qualities. Rachel Steinhaus analyzed a television commercial to investigate how advertisements persuade us to buy.

Rachel Steinhaus   **Student Analysis of an Advertisement**

"Life, Liberty, and the Pursuit"

The television commercial for the 2008 Cadillac CTS, featuring the star Kate   1
Walsh, epitomizes a car advertisement that focuses not on the vehicle itself, but on the ideas that the company wants to associate with its product. Rather than focusing on the power and features of the car, the commercial emphasizes the ideas of sex, social status, freedom, and Americanism, wrapping the car in a shroud of social contradictions and ideals. Viewers are enticed to see the car as more than a means of transportation. This other image of the car as a sexual object is what resonates most clearly with viewers as it illustrates how the ad manipulates their emotions and ideas in order to sell the product.

This commercial begins with the word *Cadillac* scrawled across a view of a city   2
with the lights creating long stretches across the screen, as though the viewer is in a car traveling quickly down the street. This effect, the illusion of fast motion, is maintained throughout the commercial. Kate Walsh, star of the television shows *Private Practice* and *Grey's Anatomy*, then lists a number of the car's optional features, from a pop-up navigation system to sunroofs and 40G hard drives, saying that those

opportunities are not what are important "in today's luxury game" (Cadillac). The ad continues to show different aspects of the car as Kate Walsh reveals what she presumably believes is the most important quality in a car: "When you turn your car on, does it return the favor?" (Cadillac). A few more images show the sleek car driving through the city and a tunnel, and then the name of the car, the phrase "Life, Liberty, and the Pursuit," and the Cadillac logo appear on the screen sequentially.

3 The most prominent aspect of this ad is its focus on the automobile as a sex symbol, which is most blatantly expressed by the line in the commercial, "When you turn it on, does it return the favor?" (Cadillac). This colloquial phrase clearly sends the message that cars that are not sexy are inferior to the 2008 CTS. The phrase also personifies the vehicle itself, giving it the capability to turn someone on, which is generally a human action. This use of personification fits with the idea presented in "The New Citroen," where Barthes describes the automobile as "humanized art" (89). The car may be a product with a particular function, but it is designed to look appealing while also having human qualities that allow people to be more emotionally attached to their car than the average product.

4 Kate Walsh reinforces the sexual ideas connected to the car in this commercial. Her attire, a dress and heels, is clearly chosen to provide sex appeal. The camera shots, angled to show her looking over the steering wheel as she delivers the end of the line and to show her foot as she hits the accelerator in her strappy heels, objectify her as a source of sex appeal (Garfield). Her celebrity status also influences the viewer's idea of what it would mean to own the car. Although the car's available features are casually listed, making Cadillac appear modest about its technology and luxury embellishments, Kate Walsh places the focus on the prospective owner's status. Simply attaching the name of a celebrity to a car is enough to raise interest for some viewers as they imagine themselves owning something that a rich and successful star also enjoys. The combination of Walsh's stardom and her sex appeal becomes the main focus of this advertisement.

5 In addition to these strong sexual and status connotations, the commercial emphasizes the idea that this car is a solid American product. The tagline at the end of the commercial, "Life, Liberty, and the Pursuit" (Cadillac) is a reference to the well-known line of the Declaration of Independence, automatically connecting the Cadillac CTS to patriotism. Even without finishing the phrase, this added plug connects supporting one's country to buying an American-made Cadillac 2008 CTS. The ad assumes that the typical American viewer will automatically insert the words "of happiness" to complete the phrase and also connect buying a CTS with furthering their own "pursuit of happiness." The context of the phrase within the Declaration of Independence is also important because it describes our inalienable rights, therefore connecting the thought that buying this car is the right of an American.

6 The open-ended phrase, however, also lends itself to interpretation as a literal statement, alluding to the idea that the Cadillac CTS will give one the freedom to

pursue whatever one wishes. In a physical sense, the driver can use the CTS horsepower to pursue other, "lesser" cars. On the other hand, the emotional message is that the driver can pursue different dreams and lifestyles because of the reputation and self-image that the CTS affords. This second interpretation relates well to the celebrity power that Kate Walsh brings to the ad.

The freedom to follow one's dreams goes hand in hand with the freedom of the road that this advertisement conveys. As Walsh goes speeding down a tunnel, nothing inhibits her progress. However, Böhm and the other authors of "Impossibilities of Automobility" see things in a much more realistic light. Both the congestion created by the infrastructure required to support automobiles and our reliance on cars make driving far from pleasurable, according to the article. Driving is often marked by frustration and danger, rather than absolute freedom. Cadillac's commercial, however, ignores these facts, instead showing off speed by the blurred lights as the car flies by and giving Kate Walsh the freedom to go wherever she wishes.   7

Cadillac's commercial promotes the 2008 CTS without much focus on the car's actual features. Instead, the ad uses appeals to sex, celebrity, freedom, and Americanism. Cadillac is proud to attach its name to a car that could mean so much to the life of the viewer, and the Cadillac logo appears in the commercial no less than six times. Even this constant repetition of the brand name takes away from the car itself, as its name, CTS, is mentioned only once. Despite a lack of focus on the actual vehicle, the advertiser assumes that our culture responds well to the appeals to sex, status, freedom, and patriotism that the automobile industry chooses to show in ads like this one.   8

Works Cited

Barthes, Roland. "The New Citroen." *Mythologies*. Trans. Annette Lavers. 1957. New York: Hill-Farrar, 2001. 88–90. Print.

Böhm, Steffen, Campbell Jones, Chris Land, and Matthew Paterson. "Impossibilities of Automobility." *Against Automobility*. Ed. Böhm, Jones, Land, and Paterson. Oxford: Wiley-Blackwell, 2006. 1–16. Print.

Cadillac. Advertisement. Web. 8 Mar. 2009. http://www.youtube.com/watch?v=jkEw1rsBUak.

Garfield, Bob. "Taking Cadillac from Stodgy to Sexy: Kate Walsh." *Advertising Age* 1 Oct. 2007. Web. 8 Mar. 2009.

Questions to Start You Thinking

Meaning

1. How does Steinhaus say that the Cadillac ad sells cars?

2. What selling points does Kate Walsh add to the commercial? What does the wording from the Declaration of Independence add?

Writing Strategies

3. Where does Steinhaus introduce her thesis and her major supporting points?

4. How does Steinhaus ensure that readers know enough about the advertisement to follow her discussion?

5. How does Steinhaus help her audience follow her paper?

6. What different kinds of support does Steinhaus draw from her sources?

Learning by Writing

The Assignment: Analyzing a Visual Representation

Find a print or online advertisement that uses an image to promote a product, service, or nonprofit group. Study the ad carefully, using the three Visual Analysis checklists (pp. 204, 210–11, and 215–16) to observe the characteristics of the image and interpret meaning. Write an essay analyzing how the ad uses visual elements to persuade viewers to accept its message. Include a copy of the ad with your essay or supply a link to it. If your instructor approves, you may select a brochure, flyer, graphic, photo essay, art work, sculpture, campus landmark, or other visual option for analysis.

Facing the Challenge   Analyzing an Image

The major challenge that writers face when analyzing an image is to state a clear thesis about how the image creates its impact and then to support that thesis with relevant detail. Although you may analyze the many details that an image includes, you need to select and group those that support your thesis in order to develop a successful essay. If you try to pack in too many details, you are likely to distract your audience and bury your main point. On the other hand, if you include too few, your case may seem weak. In addition, you need to select and describe your details carefully so that they persuasively, yet fairly, confirm your points about the image.

Generating Ideas

Browse through print or online publications to gather several possibilities — ads that make clear appeals to viewers. Look for ads that catch your eye and promise rich detail for analysis.

As you consider how an ad tries to attract a viewer's attention, try several approaches. For example, think about the purpose of the ad and the audience likely to view it where it is published or circulated. Consider the same appeals you might identify in written or spoken texts: its logical appeal to the mind, its emotional appeal to the heart, and its ethical appeal, perhaps to trust the product or sponsor. Look also for the specific visual components analyzed in this chapter — elements that guide a viewer's attention, develop the ad's persuasive potential, and convey its meaning.

DISCOVERY CHECKLIST

☐ What is the overall meaning and impact of the ad?

☐ What main points about the ad seem most important? Which details support each point most clearly and fairly?

☐ How do the ad's visual elements contribute to its persuasiveness? Which elements appeal most strongly to viewers?

Planning, Drafting, and Developing

Begin working on a thesis that states how the advertisement tries to attract and influence viewers. For example, you might identify a consistent persuasive appeal used in major components of the ad, or you might show how several components work together to persuade particular viewers.

WORKING THESIS	The dog food ad has photos of puppies to interest animal lovers.
IMPROVED	The Precious Pooch dog food advertisement uses photos of cuddly puppies to appeal to dog owners.
MORE PRECISE	The Precious Pooch dog food advertisement shows carefully designed photos of cuddly puppies to soften the hearts and wallets of devoted dog owners.

Point Out the Details. Identify details — and explain their significance — to guide readers through your supporting evidence. Help them see exactly which visual elements create an impression, solidify an appeal, or connect with a viewer as you say that they do. Avoid general description for its own sake, but supply enough relevant description to make your points clear.

Organize Support for Your Thesis. As you state your thesis more precisely, break down the position it expresses into main points. Then list the relevant supporting detail from the ad that can clarify and develop each point.

Open and Conclude Effectively. Begin by introducing to your audience both the ad and your thesis about it. Describe the ad briefly but clearly so that your readers start off with an overall understanding of its structure and primary features. State your thesis equally clearly so that your readers know how you view the ad's persuasive strategy. Use your conclusion to pull together your main points and confirm your thesis.

Revising and Editing

Exchange drafts with your peers to learn what is — or isn't — clear to someone else who is not immersed in your ad. Then revise as needed.

REVISION CHECKLIST

- ☐ Have you briefly described the ad as you open your essay?

- ☐ Have you stated your thesis about how the ad persuades its audience?

- ☐ Have you identified visual features and details that support your view?

- ☐ Do you need more detail about the ad's figures, action, or design?

- ☐ Do you need more on the feeling, attitude, theme, or meaning conveyed?

- ☐ Have you moved smoothly between each main point about the effectiveness of the ad and the detail from the ad that demonstrates the point?

After you have revised your visual analysis, check the grammar, word choice, punctuation, and mechanics — then correct any problems you find.

EDITING CHECKLIST

- ☐ Have you used adjectives and adverbs correctly to present the ad?   A7

- ☐ Have you placed modifiers correctly so that your descriptions are clear?   B1

- ☐ Have you used correct manuscript format for your paper?

For more help, find the relevant checklists in the Quick Editing Guide beginning on p. A-39. Turn also to the Quick Format Guide beginning on p. A-1.

Learning from Another Writer: Visual Essay

Besides responding to visual representations designed by others, you might have opportunities to create your own series of images and text. Visual essays can record an event or situation, or they can support an observation, interpretation, or position, usually through a combination of image and text or a multimedia text incorporating sound or video.

:e Shannon Kintner   **Student Visual Essay**

Charlie Living with Autism

In this excerpt from a photo essay, we are given a glimpse into the life of Charlie, a five-year-old boy diagnosed with nonsevere autism. Shannon Kintner took this series while a student at the University of Texas, though not for a class nor as part of her job at *The Daily Texan*. She did the project on her own to learn more about autism, to gain experience, and to develop her portfolio, a collection of work that demonstrates one's interests and abilities. To view the rest of the slideshow, read a brief article about Charlie, and complete more activities, go to Chapter 10: **bedfordstmartins.com/concisebedguide**.

Mindy Minto, Charlie's mother, wipes pizza sauce off Charlie's shoulder during dinner one night. Charlie has echolalia, which means he repeats certain phrases to apply to all scenarios; he often says "popcorn, please" to indicate that he is hungry.

A behavioral therapist guides Charlie's hand while writing his name. Charlie just wrote his name by himself for the first time in mid-April.

Charlie plays with his dog, Lola, before dinner. Both of Charlie's parents have described the two as best friends.

Kari Hughes, a behavioral therapist, asks Charlie to point out certain objects pictured on flashcards. His at-home therapy balances between a few minutes of playtime for every five achievements he makes, such as identifying flashcards or completing a puzzle.

Questions to Start You Thinking

Meaning

For more Questions to Start You Thinking, go to Ch. 10: **bedfordstmartins.com /concisebedguide**.

1. What story does the selection of images tell?

2. The photographer shows Charlie eating with his family, learning with his teacher, and playing with his dog. How does this variety enhance the viewer's experience?

3. Autism is a complex condition that can affect language ability, intellectual functioning, and behavioral patterns. Some symptoms often generally linked to autism include repetitive behavior, restricted interests, trouble having easy-flowing, "back-and-forth"-style communications, and difficulty with social interactions, which depend on the ability to read facial expressions and other cues. However, autism, as expressed in individuals, varies a great deal from person to person and from setting to setting, and it changes as a person with autism grows and develops. How does this photo essay help us to better understand — and to put a human face on — a word one often hears: "autism"?

Writing Strategies

4. How would you describe the nature of Kintner's written text? Why do you think that she uses this approach?

5. What is the effect of Kintner's title for her photo essay?

Additional Writing Assignments

1. **Visual Activity.** Select an image such as an advertisement, a visual from a magazine or image database, or a CD or album cover. Make notes on its "literal" characteristics (see pp. 204–11). Then, bring your image and notes to class. In small groups of three to five students, share your images and discuss your literal readings.

2. **Visual Activity.** In a small group, pick one or two of the images analyzed for activity 1. Ask each group member, in turn, to suggest possible interpretations of the images. (For guidance, see pp. 211–16.) What different interpretations do group members suggest? How do you account for the differences? Share your findings with the rest of the class.

3. **Visual Assignment.** Find a Web page that draws a strong emotional response. Study the page closely, observing its characteristics and interpreting its meaning. Write an essay in which you explain the techniques by which the page evokes your emotional response. If appropriate, you also may want to define a standard for its type of Web page and evaluate the site in terms of that standard. Include a link to the page with your essay.

4. **Visual Assignment.** Volkswagen continues to produce thought-provoking advertisements like the one shown in Figure 10.6 on page 207. Search online for some of the company's recent ads (try VW or Volkswagen commercials). View one or two ads, considering such features as their stories or "plots"; the choice of figures, settings, and images; the angles from which subjects are filmed; and any text messages included. Based on your analysis, decide what message you think that the company wants to communicate about its cars. In your essay, describe this message, the audience that Volkswagen seems to aim for, and the artistic choices in the ads that appeal to this audience.

5. **Visual Assignment.** Compile a design notebook. Over several weeks, collect ten or twelve images that appeal to you. Your teacher may assign a genre or theme, or you may wish to choose examples of a genre such as snack food ads, portraits, photos of campus landmarks, or landscape paintings. On the other hand, your collection might revolve around a theme, such as friendship, competition, community, or romance. "Read" each image closely, and write short responses explaining your reactions. At the end of the collection period, choose two or three images. Write an essay to compare or contrast them, perhaps analyzing how they illustrate the same genre, convey a theme, or appeal to different audiences.

6. **Visual Assignment.** Prepare your own visual essay on a topic that engages or concerns you. Decide on the purpose and audience for your essay. Take, select, and arrange photographs that will help to achieve this purpose. (Use the guidelines in this chapter to help you evaluate your own photos.) Add concise complementary text to the photos. Ask your classmates to review your essay to help you reach the clearest and most effective final form.

For criteria for visual analysis, review this chapter. For more on comparison and contrast (Ch. 6), evaluation (Ch. 8), or other relevant situations, go to the previous chapters in Part 2.

7. **Visual Assignment.** Find a CD cover whose design interests you. Make notes about design choices such as its prominent element and focal point and its use of color, imagery, and typography. Based on the design, try to predict what kind of music is on the CD, and then listen to a track or two. Did the music match your expectations based on the CD design? If you had been the CD designer, would you have made any different artistic choices? Write a brief essay discussing your observations, and try to attach a copy of the CD cover (perhaps printed from the Web). As an alternative assignment, listen to some music that's new to you, and design a CD cover for it, applying the elements discussed in this chapter. Describe in a brief paper the visual elements you would include on your CD cover. If you wish, sketch your cover design.

For sample essays responding to films, see Ch. 8.

8. **Visual Assignment.** Using the advice in this chapter, analyze an episode in a television series, a film, a multimodal blog, a YouTube or other video, a television or video commercial, or a campus theater, dance, or other production. Analyze the visual elements of your selection, and also evaluate it in terms of criteria that you explain to your audience.

Writing Online

Perhaps you are an experienced online writer — texting friends, chatting with family, updating your social-network page, and commenting on YouTube videos. On the other hand, perhaps you need help from co-workers or from younger or more experienced classmates to master new online tasks. Either way, you — like most college students — are increasingly likely to be an online academic writer. Many college classes are now offered in three formats, all likely to expect online writing:

- **face-to-face classes,** meeting at a set time and place but possibly with online communication and paper submissions
- **online classes** with synchronous (scheduled at the same time) or asynchronous (unscheduled, but available when convenient) virtual meetings, discussions, activities, paper exchanges, and submissions
- **hybrid (or blended) classes** with both in-person and online meetings, discussions, activities, paper exchanges, and submissions

In addition, any of these three class formats may rely on the campus course or learning management system (CMS or LMS), a Web-accessible environment where class participants can access information, communicate with each other, and post papers or other assignments. This chapter will review likely online activities in your current course, whatever its format.

Why Writing Online Matters

In a College Course

- You need to take a course offered only online, so you want to be ready to meet deadlines, manage files, and contribute to online discussions.
- You want to improve your online discussion contributions so that they sound more academic and professional.

In the Workplace

- You need to help online customers in a friendly yet efficient manner.

In Your Community

- You design an online tenant newsletter to unify your neighbors and help motivate your apartment manager.

(?) When have you done academic or professional writing online? How effective was this writing? In what situations might you need to do such writing in the future?

Getting Started

Many schools provide an orientation program for new or returning students as well as directions for using online campus resources. Whatever the format of your course, you are expected to have or to gain technical skills sufficient to meet course requirements. Find out how to tap campus resources for immediate crises, self-help tutorials, and technology consultation. In addition, your instructors will supply a syllabus, course policies, assignments, assessment criteria, and other information for each course. Especially for online work, remember these two essential survival skills: read first, and then ask questions.

e For interactive Learning by Doing activities on tracking your time online and exploring your CMS or LMS, go to Ch. 11: **bedfordstmartins.com /concisebedguide**.

Learning by Doing ✍ Identifying Online Writing Expectations

Review your course syllabus and assignments. List each type of online writing that you will need to do. Write down any problems or questions you can anticipate. Then map out a plan to begin solving or answering those issues.

Class Courtesy

All of your classes—face-to-face, online, or hybrid—have expectations for conduct and procedures. Some rules, such as keeping food and beverages out of a computer lab or laptop-cart classroom, obviously protect the equipment for everyone's benefit. Although explicit rules may vary by campus or instructor, conduct yourself in ways that demonstrate your attentiveness, courtesy, and consideration for others. During a face-to-face class, avoid texting or taking mobile phone calls. When technology problems inevitably arise, ask about solutions instead of blaming the online environment for snags. Online, consider both your tone and level of formality. Use the relative anonymity of online participation to advance your intellectual growth, not to make negative comments at the expense of others. Think twice before you post each message so you don't regret a hasty attack, a bad joke, a personal revelation, or an emotional rant. If you are uncertain about what is appropriate, ask your instructor for guidelines, and observe the conventions of professional communication. Strive to be

Common Interactive CMS or LMS Options

CMS or LMS Options	Typical Functions	Components Your Class Might Use
Course Materials	Handy essential information, available online for reference anytime during the course	Course syllabus and calendar, required and background readings, online reserve readings coordinated with the library, optional sources and links, reading or writing assignments, directions for activities, class and lecture notes, study guides, assessment criteria, online tutorials, podcasts, videos, and Webliographies
Course Communication	Convenient and varied systems for course messages and discussions, limited to class members	Convenient e-mail (to the whole class, a small group, or an individual), notices about changes or cancellations, text messaging, social networking, chats, threaded discussions, paper exchanges, a comment system, and a whiteboard for graphics or drawings
Class Profiles	Individual introductions posted for all the class to read, establishing each person's online personality and presence	Descriptions of the individual's background, interests, or expectations of the class, possibly with a photo or other personal representation; possibly CMS or LMS reports on whole-class patterns to allow for timely improvements
Threaded Discussions	Series of related exchanges focused on a specific course topic, question, or issue (open to all classmates or only to a group)	Questions and comments exploring and thinking critically about a topic along with any subthreads that evolve during discussion
Text Exchanges and Responses	Drafts and final papers posted for response from other students or for assessment by the instructor	Overall responses to the strengths, weaknesses, and effectiveness of the paper as well as detailed comments noted in the file; possibly options for feedback requests

a thoughtful learner who treats others respectfully as colleagues in a learning community.

Online Ethics

Respect class or campus guidelines for online text exchanges with other students. Treat each other courteously and respectfully, address others in an appropriate classroom manner, and follow directions designed to protect each other's privacy and hard work. Your instructor may provide cautions about sharing personal or confessional information, especially because your CMS, LMS, or campus may retain indefinite access to class materials.

In addition, find out whether your papers might be routinely or randomly submitted to a plagiarism-detection site. Be certain that you understand your campus rules about plagiarism and your instructor's directions about online group exchanges so that you do not confuse individual and collaborative work. Further, use sources carefully as you do online research:

Common Interactive Online Options

Online Options	Typical Functions	Applications Your Class Might Use
Class Blogs	Individual or collaborative Web logs or journals for a sequence of public (whole class) or private (small group or instructor) comments on a topic or theme	Regular comments to encourage writing, reflecting, exploring, analyzing, and sharing ideas that could evolve into more fully developed written pieces
Class Wiki	An encyclopedia of collaborative entries explaining terms relevant to a course topic or issue	An existing or evolving set of essential key terms, activities, concepts, issues, or events
Class Ning	Private social network for class members (as a whole or in special-interest groups) to share information and exchange ideas	List of relevant campus or community events, participant profiles, and a forum or blog to comment on key topics
Text Exchanges	Texts submitted for response from others through messages with attached files (to use software to add comments) or a real-time document-sharing Web site (to use its comment system)	Overall comments on strengths, weaknesses, and effectiveness; suggestions noted in the file (perhaps color coded by respondent); one-on-one exchanges, such as questions and answers, about a draft
Audio Applications	Recorded spoken comments, including responses to drafts, in-person group discussions, presentation or podcast practices, podcasts, course lectures, or interviews	Verbal comments to strengthen personal connections, recorded by the instructor or peers for one student or a group; class interviews of content or research experts (authors, librarians, faculty)
Visual Applications	Organized and archived photos, videos, Web shots, or other images	Visual materials to prompt, inform, illustrate texts, or add to presentation software
Course Resources	Public social-network page, department Web page, program resources, library Web site, open-source materials, online writing lab (OWL), Web pages	Opportunities for building a supportive online academic group and accessing recommended course resources

For more about using sources, see the Quick Research Guide beginning on p. A-20.

- Distinguish your writing and your ideas from those of sources so that you avoid blurring or confusing the two.
- Keep track of sources so that you can credit their words and ideas accurately, following the style expected by your instructor.
- Respect intellectual property rights by asking permission and crediting sources if you integrate someone else's images or media in your paper.

Learning by Doing Making Personal Rules

Using brainstorming or mapping, develop the list of rules only you know that you need—rules to bring out your best as an online student or writer. For example, do you need a personal "rule" about checking for your USB drive, card, or portable hard drive after every computer session on campus so you don't lose your work? Or do you need a "rule" about backing up files? List your rules in an e-mail message to yourself. Then sum up the most important points, using your software's word count tool to limit this statement to the 140 characters allowed by Twitter for a "tweet." If you wish, also note your "rules" in your cell phone notepad for quick reference along with your online course PIN number, if needed. Return to standard English—correct grammar, punctuation, capitalization, and complete words, not abbreviations—for material submitted to your instructor.

Common Online Writing Situations

The expectations for your college writing may be the same whether you hand in a printed paper during class, send the file to your instructor, or post your work in a CMS or LMS. Some assignments might specify required, encouraged, or accepted online features such as links for references or multimedia components. For other online writing, consider the conventions—accepted practices readers are likely to expect—and the class directions.

Messages to Your Instructor

Learning online requires a lot of communication. Because you aren't meeting—and communicating—face-to-face, you need to engage actively in other types of exchanges. First, welcome available communication by reading posted assignments and directions that advise you about how to meet expectations successfully. Next, initiate communication, asking specific questions online about what to do and how to do it.

When you e-mail your instructor with a question, practice respectful professional communication. Think about your audience—a hard-working teacher who probably posts many class materials and responds to many questions from students in different courses. You can guess that a busy instructor appreciates a direct question from a motivated student who wants help. Ask specific questions well before deadlines, and give your instructor plenty of time to reply. Consider your tone so that you sound polite, interested, and clear about what you need to know.

VAGUE I don't know how to start this assignment.

SPECIFIC I've listed my ideas in a scratch outline, but I'm not sure what you mean by . . .

If your class uses a CMS or LMS, send your message through that system (unless your instructor asks you to use his or her campus e-mail address). Right away your instructor will know which class you're in and, in a small composition class, recognize you by your first name. If you e-mail outside the CMS, send the message from your campus account, and use the subject line to identify the course name or number and your problem: Deadline for Comp 101 Reading or Question about Math 110 Study Guide.

If you are unsure how to address your instructor, begin with "Hello, Professor Welton" or "Hi, Ms. Welton," following the instructor's preference if known. Avoid too much informality, such as greeting your instructor with "Yo, Prof" or "Hiya, Chief," asking "Whatzup with the paper?" or closing with "Later." Conclude with your name (including your last name and a section number if the class is large).

Proofread and spell-check your message before you send it so that your writing does not look hasty or careless. Consider setting it to return an automatic "read" confirmation when the recipient opens it so that you do not need to e-mail again to check its arrival. Avoid e-mailing from a personal account that might be mistaken for spam and blocked from the campus system. Remember that your instructor's relationship with you is professional, not social; do not send social-networking invitations or forward humorous stories or messages about politics, religion, or other personal topics.

Learning by Doing 🔘 Finding a College Voice

Working with a small group in person or online, list at least a dozen popular greetings, closings, and other expressions currently part of your (or your friends') informal voice in text messaging, social networking, or other informal electronic communication. Translate each expression into a clear, polite version without abbreviations, shortcuts, or unconventional grammar—in short, a version appropriate for a message to an instructor in your "college" voice.

Learning from Other Writers: Messages to Your Instructor

Here are two requests sent to the students' instructor in an online composition class, one asking about how to cite an assigned reading and the other about the instructor's comments on a draft.

STUDENT QUESTION ABOUT AN ASSIGNMENT

From: Heather Church

Subject: Reading Response

Hi, Ms. Beauchene,

I want to make sure I am doing this assignment correctly. Is the source an online newspaper article? Also, I can't find out how to cite part of a sentence included in my response. If I quote "binge drinking," for example, do I have to say the page number next to it? I thought that I would cite this as if it is an article with no author. Is that correct?

Thank you.

Heather

STUDENT QUESTION ABOUT COMMENTS ON A DRAFT

From: Arthur Wasilewski

Subject: Comments on Last Paper

Hello, Professor Beauchene,

I would like to ask you a question about your corrections. You changed the last sentence of the last paragraph. I was wondering if you could explain the change. Is it something structural or grammatical? Or was it changed for the sake of style or flow?

Arthur

Questions to Start You Thinking

Meaning

1. Why is Heather Church contacting the instructor? What does she want to know?

2. Why is Arthur Wasilewski contacting the instructor? What does he want to know?

Writing Strategies

3. What impression on their instructor do you think that the students wanted to make? What features of their messages indicate this?

e **Portland State University Writing Center**   **Video Tutorial**

Sample E-mail to an Instructor

The Portland State University Writing Center created an online tutorial about how to use the appropriate tone and language when e-mailing an instructor. To watch the video, go to Chapter 11: **bedfordstmartins/concisebedguide**.

> Subject: my grade
>
> yo prentice!!!
>
> i just got my paper back and i'm a little upset about my grade. ☹ i worked really hard on it, i went to the writing center, i didn't miss the workshop, and still i got a B. i feel that i deserved a better grade because of the reasons i listed above. i worked harder on this than on any of my other classes. i have to get an A in this class for my financial aid. also, i may not have told you this, but i have been sort of sick this month and had a hard time writing the paper, so if it's not very good, that's why. ☺

Learning by Doing 🎤 Contacting Your Instructor

Write an e-mail to your instructor requesting information. For example, you might have a question about requirements, assessment criteria for your first essay, procedures for activities such as timed quizzes, or policies such as penalties for late work. Clearly and briefly specify what you want to know. As you ask your question, also try to show your instructor that you are a thoughtful, hard-working learner. Exchange drafts with classmates to learn what they would suggest to make your question clearer or your tone more appropriate.

Online Profile

Because you may never meet your online classmates in person, you may be asked to post a brief online profile introducing yourself to the class. You also might be asked to interview a classmate so that each of you can post an introduction of the other. Such assignments are intended to increase online camaraderie. However, if you feel shy or wish to retain anonymity, cover suggested topics such as academic interests or writing experiences, but stick to general background with limited personal detail. If you prefer not to post a photograph of yourself, consider an image or icon of a pet, possession, or favorite place. If the class already has much in common—for example, all in the same discipline or program—you might include your career plans. Avoid overly personal revelations, gushing enthusiasm, and clipped brevity.

The following profiles, illustrating a personal post and an interview, combine some personal background with academic and career interests.

From: LaTanya Nash

Subject: My Profile as a Future Nurse

After almost a month in the hospital when I was six, I knew that I wanted to be a nurse. That's when I found out how important nurses are to patients and how much they can add to a patient's recovery. I've had after-school and summer jobs in an assisted living center for seniors and a center for children with disabilities. Now that I'm starting college, I'm ready to work on my nursing degree. I'm glad to have this writing class because I've learned from my jobs how important it is for nurses to write clearly.

Learning by Doing 🎤 Posting a Personal Profile

Write a brief personal profile introducing yourself to your instructor and classmates. Provide enough information about your college interests, background, or goals to give your audience a clear impression about you as a member of the class online learning community. (Avoid any confessional or overly personal revelations.) Consider adding a photo or an image representing you or your interests.

From: Lainie Costas

Subject: Interview of Tomas

After interviewing Tomas online, I want to introduce a classmate who has just started college this semester. He has been working since high school—doing everything from washing dishes to making pizzas. Now he's planning on getting a business degree to help him start his own restaurant. He already knows what employees need to do, but he wants to learn about things like business plans, finances, and advertising. Like me, he's a little worried about starting with a writing class, but I know from his messages that he has plenty of interesting things to say.

Learning by Doing 📷 Introducing a Classmate

E-mail, chat, schedule an online video call, or talk in person with a classmate to learn about each other's background, interests, and expectations of the course. (If your instructor assigns pairs or topics, follow those directions.) Using what you learn, write and post a professional message to introduce your classmate.

Online Threaded Discussions or Responses

When you add your response to a topic in a threaded discussion, an interactive forum, or a class reading blog, follow your instructor's directions, and also read responses from classmates to clarify how to meet the assignment. Because everyone participating already understands the writing situation, you don't need to write a full introduction as you would in an essay. Instead, simply dive in as requested—for example, add your thoughtful comments on a reading, identify and explain a key quotation from it, or reflect on your own reading or writing processes. If you comment on a previous post, do so politely; clarify how your ideas differ without any personal criticism. Follow length guidelines, and be sure to proofread and spell-check your post.

Learning from Other Writers: Threaded Discussion

The following string of messages begins with the instructor's explanation of the assignment—responding to an assigned reading in one of two specific ways—followed by a few responses of students. Notice how each writer responds personally but sticks to the focus by extending the "thread." Directions for other discussions might emphasize different ways to extend the thread — for example, responding specifically to a preceding comment, summarizing several comments and adding to them, synthesizing and then advancing ideas, raising a different but relevant line of consideration, comparing or contrasting possible responses, tracing possible causes and effects, or other paths that apply your critical thinking skills.

STUDENT ONLINE THREADED DISCUSSION

Instructor Kathleen Beauchene and Students Cristina Berrios, Joshua Tefft, Leah Threats, Arthur Wasilewski, and Joel Torres

Discussion of Writing Processes

Message no. 2706

Author: Kathleen Beauchene (ENGL1010_600_Beauchene)

Date: Saturday, October 10, 2:37pm

In the attached file, you will read about one author's writing process. In your post, you may either comment on a point he makes or share your own writing process, what works or doesn't work for you.

Message no. 2707

Author: Cristina Berrios

Date: Saturday, October 10, 4:02pm

I find that the author's writing process is similar in many ways to how most write, but I do not always have time to write and rewrite and organize and write and so on. . . . Of course I can see if you are a professional writer rewriting and making sure that your work can be produced to sell, but in my eyes I only need to make sure that my story is interesting, consecutive and progressive, and grammatically correct to the best of my ability. . . . Luckily I work in an office where I can interact closely with colleagues who are willing to listen to my "draft" (some of them are college students as well) and give me feedback.

Message no. 2708

Author: Joshua Tefft

Date: Saturday, October 10, 4:43pm

My writing process, like most people's, is similar to what the author does, given I have a lot of time anyway. I really have trouble with not erasing initial drafts, that is, incomplete drafts. I always find myself too critical of my work before it is anywhere near the final stages. But I've begun to learn to receive outside criticism before I put my own on it; this usually gives me a more open-minded perspective on my writing. But I've realized it's a long process to get the results one wants.

Message no. 2709

Author: Leah Threats

Date: Saturday, October 10, 11:49pm

My writing process includes a lot of thought process before I go anywhere near writing a first draft. Then I begin to write and reread it a few times while in the first paragraph, change wording, cut and paste all over the paper. Then I will move on to the middle of the paper, make sure my introduction has enough to it, and the mid section is full of "beef." Then in the ending, I try to make sure I don't leave the writer thinking, What else? . . . I do take the time to make sure I am not shortchanging my reader. As a person who LOVES to read, I want to be able to draw the reader into whatever it is I am writing to them.

Message no. 2711

Author: Arthur Wasilewski

Date: Sunday, October 11, 1:41pm

I approach the writing process with a shoot-from-the hip mentality. Whatever comes to my head first is usually the right idea. I'll think about the idea throughout the whole day or week, and transcribe it to paper after I've gone through a few mental iterations of my original idea.

Message no. 2713

Author: Joel Torres

Date: Sunday, October 11, 8:21pm

After reading this attachment I realize there are some things I sort of start to do in my own writing process, but stop halfway or do not go through thoroughly. I have used the outline idea from time to time. I should go into more depth and organize the ideas in my papers better in the future though. The whole concept of sleeping between drafts does not sit well with me. I find that when I sit down and write a paper, it is best when I dedicate a couple of hours and get into the "zone" and let the ideas flow through me. If the paper is a research paper, I usually do best when I type it directly onto a word processor. When the assignment is an essay or something along the lines of a written argument or a literary work, I like to handwrite and then go back and type it after. Distractions for me are a huge issue; TV, other Web sites, and just lack of focus definitely hurt my writing and are obstacles I must overcome every time a written assignment is due.

Questions to Start You Thinking

Meaning

1. What did the instructor ask the class to do in the discussion?
2. Highlight or jot down a few key words to sum up the approach of each student in the threaded discussion.

Writing Strategies

3. In what ways do the students show that they are focused on the "thread" that connects their contributions to the discussion?

Learning by Doing 🔄 Joining a Threaded Discussion

Read the preceding sample online discussion of writing processes. Write your addition to the string, explaining your process—what works or doesn't work.

File Management

Electronic submission of papers is convenient, saving trees as well as time. Writing online has immediacy—potentially a 24/7 audience, ready to read and respond to your writing. On the other hand, online college writing requires longer-term planning, especially to organize and manage files in classes that encourage revising drafts or developing a portfolio.

For sample pages, see the Quick Format Guide (pp. A-1–A-19). For sample source citations in MLA and APA style, see the Quick Research Guide, pp. A-20–A-38.

Using File Templates. No matter how you submit an essay or research paper, instructors generally expect you to use MLA, APA, or another academic style accepted in the field. These styles specify page layout, font style and size, paragraph indentations, formats for citations, and many other details that determine both the look and the approach of the paper.

Instead of treating each paper as a separate item, set up a template for any style you are required to use in a specific class or field of study. Check your software menu for Tools, File, or Format, or go to Help for directions on making a template, a basic paper format with built-in design features. Refine the details, using samples and checklists in this book as well as your instructor's directions and comments on the format of your drafts. When you begin a new draft, call up your template, and start writing. The template will automatically format the features you have customized. If you need several templates, keep them clearly labeled in a template folder.

Learning by Doing 🔄 Preparing a Template

Set up a template for your papers for your composition class or your portfolio. Follow your instructor's directions about the academic style to follow and any special features to add. Turn to the campus computer lab or writing center if you need help preparing the template or figuring out what it should include.

Naming and Organizing Files. Check your syllabus or assignments to find out whether you need to follow a certain system or pattern for naming your files. Such systems help an instructor to see at a glance who wrote which assignment for which class: Lopez Recall 101Sec2. If you are expected to save or submit your drafts or build a portfolio, you will want to add a draft number, draft code (noting a first draft or a later revision), or a date: Lopez Recall 3, Lopez Recall Dft, Lopez Recall Rev, or Lopez Recall 9-14-13. Remember that your downloaded essay will be separated from your e-mail message; be certain that the file label alone will be clear.

Even if you are not required to submit your drafts, it's a good idea to save each major stage as you develop the paper instead of always reworking the same file. If you set up a folder for your course, perhaps with subfolders for each assignment, your writing records will be organized in a central location. Then you can easily go back to an earlier draft and restore something you cut or show your development to your instructor if asked to do so. You also have a handy backup if you lose a draft or forget to save it to your flash drive (or forget the flash drive itself).

Learning by Doing 🎥 Organizing Your Files

Outline the principles behind your system for managing files. If your system is random or disorganized, figure out a system that makes sense to you and keeps your writing for several courses well organized. Compare your ideas with those of a few classmates, and help each other to improve your plans. Then move your existing files into your new or refined system. Maintain your system by storing files where they belong and sticking to the pattern for naming and dating them.

Inserting Comments. When you need to exchange files with other students for peer responses, use your software menu (Tools, Options, or Inserts), try its Help feature, or find a tutorial on the class comment system — track-and-comment word-processing tools, CMS or LMS posts, or a document-sharing site with comment options. If the directions seem complicated, print the Help page, and refer to it as you learn the system.

A comment system typically allows you to use color to show cross-outs and additions or to add initials or color to identify comments in "balloons" in the margin. Less formal options include adding comments or a note at the end of a paragraph, highlighted in yellow. Be sure to send your peer response file on time with helpful suggestions.

COMMENT CHECKLIST

☐ How do you post or send a draft for peer or instructor review?

☐ How do you access Help or a tutorial about adding comments?

☐ What do you do to turn the Comment function on and off?

☐ How do you add comments in the text and in balloons or boxes in the margins using the color that identifies you as a reader?

☐ What do you need to do to read, print, save, or delete comments?

☐ How do you access the file-exchange site your class uses?

☐ How do you record and identify your comments on other writers' papers?

☐ How do you retrieve your own draft with the comments of others?

Polishing Electronically. As you revise and edit a draft, use all your re-sources, online and off. Call up the assignment or syllabus. Review what is required and how it will be assessed. Reread any comments from your peers or instructor. Use the Find or Search menu to hunt for repeated errors or too many repetitions of a favorite word or transition. Use the spelling and grammar checkers in your software, CMS, or LMS, even for short messages, so that you always present careful work. If your concentration slips, go offline: print out your draft and read it aloud.

Submitting Papers Online. It's usually easy to walk into a face-to-face class and hand in a printed paper. Online, you might hit snags — problems with a transmittal message if your CMS, LMS, or e-mail system is down; prob-lems with a drop box or forum that closes early due to an error or power outage; problems with a file, attaching or remembering to attach yours or opening someone else's. Try to avoid sending an assignment two minutes before the deadline because a time crunch may increase problems.

Many instructors will see "the computer ate my homework" as a prob-lem you should have solved, not an acceptable excuse for late work. If you have trouble transmitting a file, send a short separate message to your in-structor to explain how you are solving the problem, or ask your instructor to confirm the file's safe arrival. (Instructors are likely to prefer that you keep explanations to a minimum, concentrate on solutions, and use an au-tomatic "read" reply to confirm receipt.) If your computer has a problem, you are responsible for going to the lab or using another computer to sub-mit your work on time. If your campus system is temporarily down, you are responsible for submitting your work as soon as access is restored.

No matter what software you use, "translate" your file to the required for-mat — maybe Word (.doc or .docx) but often Rich Text Format (.rtf), a general format most word-processing software can read. Check your File menu for two different commands: Save (to save the file to the location where you rou-tinely store class files) and Save As (to save the file in a different format, to a different location, or with a different name). If you consistently add the date at the end of the file name, you will simplify finding and sending the most current version. If you use the same name or same date for duplicate files in different formats, you also will know that they correspond. Once the correct file is properly formatted, attach it to your message. If your file is returned with comments from your instructor or classmates, give it a new name and date so it does not replace your original.

Backing Up Your Files. No matter how tired or rushed you are, always save and back up your work, preferably using several methods. Use a backup card, portable drive, flash drive, smart stick, file storage site, or whatever is available and efficient for you. Label or identify your equipment with your name so that you could pull your drive out of the lost-and-found basket at the library or someone could arrange to return it to you.

If you are working on a campus computer, carry your drive with you on a neck strap or clipped to your backpack so that your current work is always with you. If you are working on a major project with a tight deadline, attach major drafts to an e-mail to yourself. If you back up your files at home or in your room, do so every day. Then, if a file is damaged or lost, your hard drive fails during finals week, or you leave your drive at the library, you can still finish your writing assignments on time.

FILE CHECKLIST

☐ What academic style and paper format is expected in your class? Have you prepared a template or file format in this style?

☐ Have you saved the files that show your paper's development during several drafts? Have you named or dated them so that the sequence is clear?

☐ Have you named a file you are submitting as directed? Have you used Save As to convert it to the required file format?

☐ Have you developed a file storage system so that you have a folder for each course and a subfolder for all related files for a specific paper?

☐ Do you carry a flash drive or other storage device with you so that you can work on your papers in the computer lab or library whenever you have time?

☐ Do you consistently back up your files every time you write using a flash drive, portable drive, or other device?

☐ If a CMS or LMS is new to you, do you know — exactly — when your assignment is due? Do you know how to submit the file, confirm its arrival, and download your paper when it is returned with comments?

Additional Writing Assignments

1. Begin a reflective electronic journal. Add entries daily or several times each week to record ideas, observations, thoughts, and reactions that might enrich your writing. Use your file as a resource as you write assigned essays. Post selections, if you wish, for class or small-group discussion.

2. Write a comparison-and-contrast essay based on your experiences with face-to-face, online, or hybrid courses. Consider starting with a table with columns to help you systematically compare features of the class formats, the learning requirements or priorities they encourage, any changes in your priorities or activities as a student, or other possible points of comparison.

3. Keep a blog about your writing experience. (If this will be your first blog, begin by looking for tips or tutorials on the CMS, LMS, or site where your class will establish their blogs.) Post regular entries as you work on a specific essay or writing project, commenting on the successes, challenges, and surprises that the college writer meets.

4. Establish a collaborative blog with others in your class about a key course topic or possible sources or ideas for your writing or research projects. Decide on a daily or weekly schedule for blogging.

5. Start a threaded discussion about resources for your course topic, current assignment, research project, or other class project. Ask contributors to identify a resource, explain how to locate or access it, evaluate its strengths, and describe any limitations.

6. Set up a small-group or class Wiki, encouraging everyone to identify terms, concepts, strategies, activities, or events of significance to the course, a common academic program, or a shared writing interest. Write and edit collaboratively to arrive at clear, accurate, and useful explanations of these items to help everyone master the course (or program) material.

7. Set up a class Help Board on your CMS or LMS, a place where a student can post an immediate problem while working on the course reading or writing. Ask participants to respond to at least two or three questions for each that they post. Ask your instructor to add advice as needed.

8. Working with a small group, use a document-sharing system to draft an essay or other project, giving all group members and your instructor access to the process. Work collaboratively through simultaneous or sequential drafting, using chat or other electronic messaging to discuss your work. When your draft is complete, have all participants (including your instructor, if possible) share reflections about both the process and the outcome.

9. Use an available communication system (for example, for a Web-based telephone call, conference call, or video call; for a real-time online meeting; or for an audio chat) for a conversation with a classmate or small group. Set a specific time for the meeting, and circulate any materials ahead of time. The purpose of the conversation might be discussing a reading, responding

to each other's current draft, reviewing material before an exam, or a similar group activity. After the conversation, write an evaluation of the experience, including recommendations for the next time you use the technology.

10. **Source Assignment.** Conduct some research using your college's online catalog. Look up several courses that you must or might take during the next few terms. What formats — face-to-face, online, or hybrid — are available for these courses? In what ways would the courses differ, based on the catalog or a linked description? How might each format appeal to your strengths, learning preferences, and educational circumstances? Write a short report that summarizes what you learn and then uses that information to explain which choices might best suit you.

11. **Visual Assignment.** Prepare graphics, take photographs, or identify images (credited appropriately) that contribute to one of the other assignments for this chapter.

A WRITER'S
STRATEGIES

A Writer's Strategies Contents

12 **Strategies for Generating Ideas**   248

13 **Strategies for Stating a Thesis and Planning**   262

14 **Strategies for Drafting**   284

15 **Strategies for Revising and Editing**   300

Introduction: Expanding Your Resources

Part Three shows how a paper evolves from idea to final form. Its chapters are packed with tips and activities that you can use to generate ideas, find your purpose, sharpen your point, draft, revise, edit, and carry to the future what you have learned as a writer. These chapters offer in-depth advice on writing stages and strategies—techniques you can learn, methods you can follow, and good practices you can observe. As you apply their suggestions in the Learning by Doing activities, you will develop your own ideas and get feedback from classmates. As you return to these chapters while you are writing, their checklists will help you thoughtfully develop and critique your own ideas.

In Part 2, each stage was covered for each assignment. Here, four major stages get their own full chapters, and the strategies for each are explained and illustrated more fully. Of course, no strategy will appeal to every writer, and no writer uses every one for every writing task. Consider this part of the book a reference guide or instruction manual. Turn to it when you need more help, when you're curious, or when you'd like to enlarge your repertoire of writing skills. Try the ideas here when you get stuck, when you need to solve problems, when you want to make improvements, or when you wish to challenge yourself to develop new strategies. We can't tell you which of the ideas and techniques covered in these pages will work for you, but we can promise that if you try some of them you'll be rewarded.

For information and journal questions about the Part Three photograph, see the last two pages of the Appendices.

12 Strategies for Generating Ideas

For most writers, the hardest part of writing comes first—confronting a blank page. Fortunately, you can prepare for that moment by finding ideas and getting ready to write. All the tested techniques here have worked for writers—professionals and students—and some may work for you.

Finding Ideas

When you begin to write, ideas may appear effortlessly on the paper or screen, perhaps triggered by resources around you—something you read, see, hear, discuss, or think about. (See the top half of the graphic below.) But at other times you need idea generators, strategies to try when your ideas dry up. If one strategy doesn't work for your task, try another. (See the lower half of the graphic.)

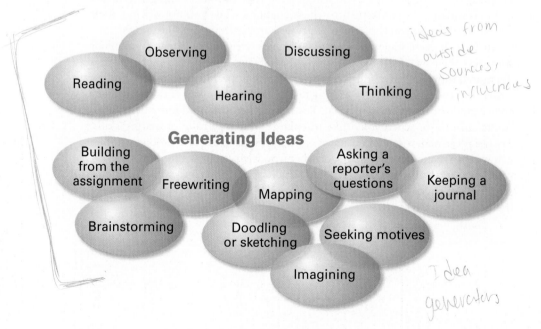

Observing   Discussing   *ideas from outside sources/influences*

Reading   Hearing   Thinking

Generating Ideas

Building from the assignment   Freewriting   Mapping   Asking a reporter's questions   Keeping a journal

Brainstorming   Doodling or sketching   Seeking motives

Imagining   *Idea generators*

✳ Building from Your Assignment

Learning to write is learning what questions to ask yourself. Your assignment may trigger this process, raising some questions and answering others. For example, Ben Tran jotted notes in his book as his instructor and classmates discussed his first assignment—recalling a personal experience.

The assignment clarified what audience to address and what purpose to set. Ben's classmates asked about length, format, and due date, but Ben saw three big questions: Which experience should I pick? How did it change me? Why was it so important for me? Ben still didn't know what he'd write about, but he had figured out the questions to tackle first.

For more detail about this assignment, turn to p. 69 in Ch. 4.

What event? What consequences?

Write about one specific experience that changed how you acted, thought, or felt. Use your experience as a springboard for reflection. Your purpose is not merely to tell an interesting story but to show your readers—your instructor and your classmates—the importance of that experience for you.

What readers? class + prof.

What purpose? 2 parts!

Tell the story but do more—reflect & show importance.

Sometimes assignments assume that you already know something critical—how to address a particular audience or what to include in some type of writing. When Amalia Blackhawk read her argument assignment, she jotted down questions to ask her instructor.

Anything OK? Or only newspaper type of issue?

Editor of what?

What's my purpose? Persuading readers to respect my view or to agree?

Select a campus or local issue that matters to you, and write a letter to the editor about it. Be certain to tell readers what the issue is, why it is important, and how you propose to address it. Assume that your letter will appear in a special opinion feature that allows letters longer than the usual word-count limits.

My classmates? The publication's readers?

How long is the usual letter? How long should mine be? Anything else letters like this should do?

Try these steps as you examine an assignment:

1. *Read through the assignment once* to discover its overall direction.

2. *Read it again,* marking information about your situation as a writer. Does the assignment identify or suggest your audience, your purpose in writing, the type of paper expected, the parts typical of that kind of writing, or the format required?

3. *List the questions that the assignment raises for you.* Exactly what do you need to decide—the type of topic to pick, the focus to develop, the issues or aspects to consider, or other guidelines to follow?

4. *Finally, list any questions that the assignment doesn't answer or ask you to answer.* Ask your instructor about these questions.

Learning by Doing 🎥 Building from Your Assignment

Select an assignment from this book, another textbook, or another class, and make notes about it. What questions does it answer? Which questions or decisions does it direct to you? What other questions might you want to ask your instructor? Then exchange assignments with a classmate; make notes about that assignment, too. With your partner, compare responses to both.

For an interactive Learning by Doing activity on brainstorming from a video, go to Ch. 12: **bedfordstmartins.com /concisebedguide**.

Brainstorming

A *brainstorm* is a sudden insight or inspiration. As a writing strategy, brainstorming uses free association to stimulate a chain of ideas, often to personalize a topic and break it down into specifics. Start with a word or phrase, and spend a set period of time simply listing ideas as rapidly as possible. Write down whatever comes to mind with no editing or going back.

As a group activity, brainstorming gains from varied perspectives. At work, it can fill a specific need — finding a name for a product or an advertising slogan. In college, you can brainstorm with a few others or your entire class. Sit facing one another. Designate one person to record on paper, screen, or chalkboard whatever the others suggest. After several minutes of calling out ideas, look over the recorder's list for useful results. Online, toss out ideas during a chat or post them for all to consider.

On your own, brainstorm to define a topic, generate an example, or find a title for a finished paper. Angie Ortiz brainstormed after her instructor assigned a paper ("Demonstrate from your experience how electronic technology is changing our lives"). She wrote *electronic technology* on the page, set her alarm for fifteen minutes, and began to scribble.

> Electronic technology
> iPod, cell phone, laptop, tablet. Plus TV, cable, DVDs. Too much?!
> Always on call — at home, in car, at school. Always something playing.
> Spend so much time in electronic world — phone calls, texting, tunes. Cuts into time really hanging with friends — face-to-face time.
> Less aware of my surroundings outside of the electronic world?

When her alarm went off, Angie took a break. After returning to her list, she crossed out ideas that did not interest her and circled her final promising question. A focus began to emerge: the capacity of the electronic world to expand information but reduce awareness.

When you want to brainstorm, try this advice:

1. *Launch your thoughts with a key word or phrase.* If you need a topic, try a general term (*computer*); if you need an example for a paragraph in progress, try specifics (*financial errors computers make*).

2. *Set a time limit.* Ten minutes (or so) is enough for strenuous thinking.

3. *Rapidly list brief items.* Stick to words, phrases, or short sentences that you can quickly scan later.

4. *Don't stop.* Don't worry about spelling, repetition, or relevance. Don't judge, and don't arrange: just produce. Record whatever comes to mind, as fast as you can. If your mind goes blank, keep moving, even if you only repeat what you've just written.

When you finish, circle or check anything intriguing. Scratch out whatever looks useless or dull. Then try some conscious organizing: Are any thoughts related? Can you group them? Does the group suggest a topic?

Learning by Doing 🏷 Brainstorming

From the following list, choose a subject that interests you, that you know something about, and that you'd like to learn more about—in other words, that you might like to write on. Then brainstorm for ten minutes.

travel	fear	exercise
dieting	dreams	automobiles
family	technology	sports
advertisements	animals	education

Now look over your list, and circle any potential paper topic. If you wish, pass around a list of three or four options, asking each classmate to check the most engaging idea.

Freewriting

To tap your unconscious by *freewriting,* simply write sentences without stopping for about fifteen minutes. The sentences don't have to be grammatical, coherent, or stylish; just keep them flowing to unlock an idea's potential.

For Ortiz's brainstorming, see p. 250.

Generally, freewriting is most productive if it has an aim—for example, finding a topic, a purpose, or a question you want to answer. Angie Ortiz wrote her topic at the top of a page—and then explored her rough ideas.

> Electronic devices — do they isolate us? I chat all day online and by phone, but that's quick communication, not in-depth conversation. I don't really spend much time hanging with friends and getting to know what's going on with them. I love listening to my iPod on campus, but maybe I'm not as aware of my surroundings as I could be. I miss seeing things, like the new art gallery that I walk by every day. I didn't even notice the new sculpture park in front! Then, at night, I do assignments on my computer, browse the Web, and watch some cable. I'm in my own little electronic world most of the time. I love technology, but what else am I missing?

Angie's result wasn't polished prose. Still, in a short time she produced a paragraph to serve as a springboard for her essay.

If you want to try freewriting, here's what you do:

1. *Write a sentence or two at the top of your page or file* — the idea you plan to develop by freewriting.

2. *Write without stopping for at least ten minutes.* Express whatever comes to mind, even "My mind is blank," until a new thought floats up.

3. *Explore without censoring yourself.* Don't cross out false starts or grammar errors. Don't worry about connecting ideas or finding perfect words. Use your initial sentences as a rough guide, not a straitjacket. New directions may be valuable.

4. *Prepare yourself* — if you want to. While you wait for your ideas to start racing, you may want to ask yourself some questions:

   What interests you about the topic? What do you know about it that the next person doesn't? What have you read, observed, or heard about it?

   How might you feel about this topic if you were someone else (a parent, an instructor, a person from another country)?

5. *Repeat the process, looping back to expand a good idea if you wish.* Poke at the most interesting parts to see if they will further unfold:

   What does that mean? If that's true, what then? So what?

   What other examples or evidence does this statement call to mind?

   What objections might a reader raise? How might you answer them?

Learning by Doing 🖉 Freewriting

Select an idea from your current thinking or a brainstorming list. Write it at the top of a page or file, and freewrite for fifteen minutes. Share your freewriting with your classmates. If you wish, loop back to repeat this process.

Doodling or Sketching

If you fill the margins of your notebooks with doodles, harness this artistic energy to generate ideas for writing. Elena Lopez began to sketch her collision with a teammate during a soccer tournament (Figure 12.1). She added stick figures, notes, symbols, and color as she outlined a series of events.

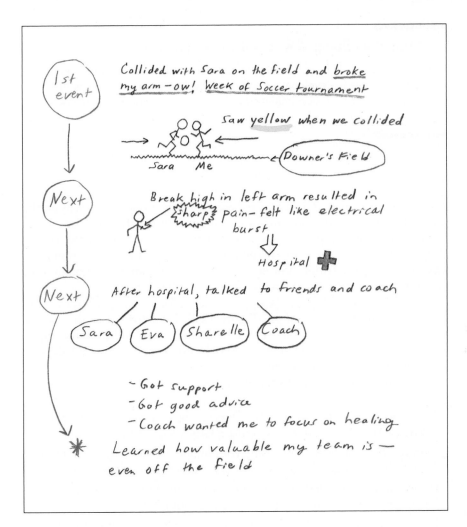

Figure 12.1 Doodling or sketching to generate ideas

Try this advice as you develop ideas by doodling or sketching:

1. *Give your ideas room to grow.* Open a new file using a drawing program, doodle in pencil on a blank page, or sketch on a series of pages.

2. *Concentrate on your topic, but welcome new ideas.* Begin with a key visual in the center or at the top of a page. Add sketches or doodles as they occur to you to embellish, expand, define, or redirect your topic.

3. *Add icons, symbols, colors, figures, labels, notes, or questions.* Freely mix visuals and text, recording ideas without stopping to refine them.

4. *Follow up on your discoveries.* After a break, add notes to make connections, identify sequences, or convert visuals into descriptive sentences.

Learning by Doing 📷 Doodling or Sketching

Start with a doodle or sketch that illustrates your topic. Add related events, ideas, or details to develop your topic visually. Share your material with classmates; use their observations to help you refine your direction as a writer.

Mapping

Mapping taps your visual and spatial creativity as you position ideas on the page, in a file, or with cloud software to show their relationships or relative importance. Ideas might radiate outward from a key term in the center, drop down from a key word at the top, sprout upward from a root idea, branch out from a trunk, flow across page or screen in a chronological or causal sequence, or follow a circular, spiral, or other form.

Andrew Choi used mapping to gather ideas for his proposal for revitalizing the campus radio station (Figure 12.2). He noted ideas on colored sticky notes—blue for problems, yellow for solutions, and pink for implementation details. Then he moved the sticky notes around on a blank page, arranging them as he connected ideas.

Here are some suggestions for mapping:

1. *Allow space for your map to develop.* Open a new file, try posterboard for arranging sticky notes or cards, or use a large page for notes.
2. *Begin with a topic or key idea.* Using your imagination, memory, class notes, or reading, place a key word at the center or top of a page.
3. *Add related ideas, examples, issues, or questions.* Quickly and spontaneously place these points above, below, or beside your key word.
4. *Refine the connections.* As your map evolves, use lines, arrows, or loops to connect ideas; box or circle them to focus attention; add colors to relate points or to distinguish source materials from your own ideas.

After a break, continue mapping to probe one part more deeply, refine the structure, add detail, or build an alternate map from a different viewpoint. Also try mapping to develop graphics that present ideas in visual form.

Learning by Doing 📷 Mapping

Start with a key word or idea that you know about. Map related ideas, using visual elements to show how they connect. Share your map with classmates, and then use their questions or comments to refine your mapping.

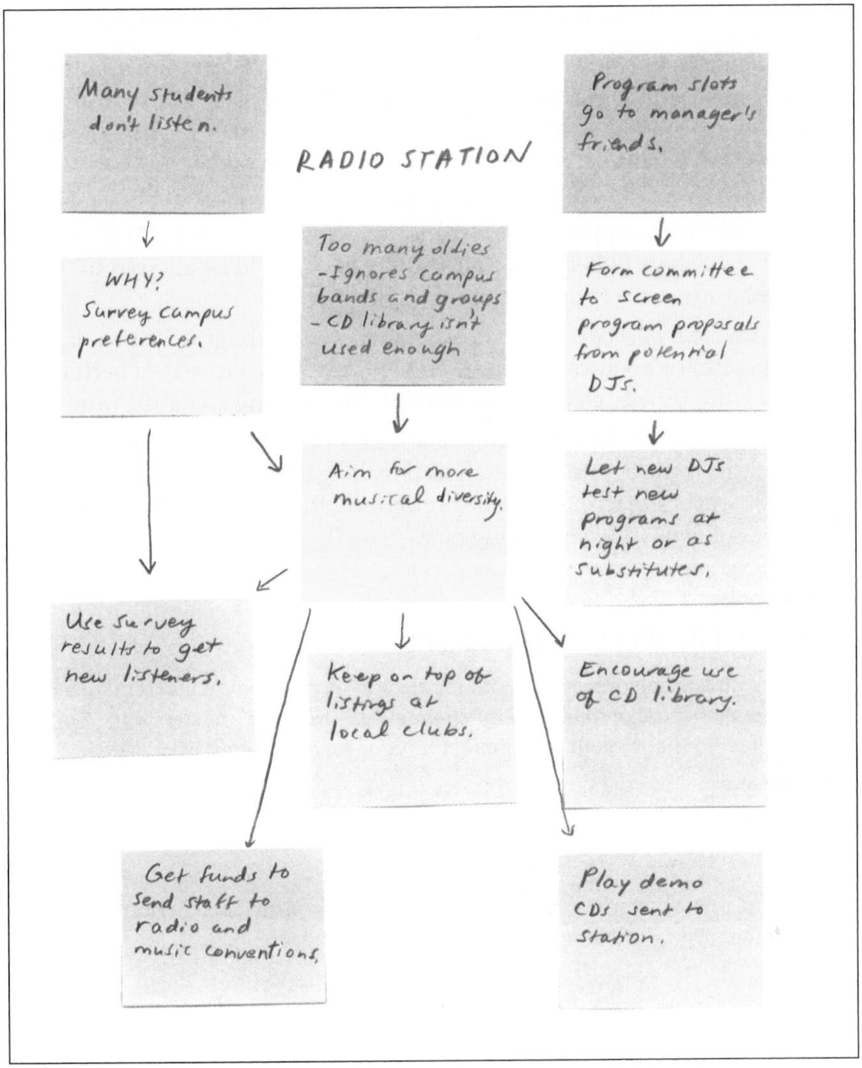

Figure 12.2 Mapping to generate ideas

The map contains the following handwritten notes:

- Many students don't listen.
- RADIO STATION
- Program slots go to manager's friends.
- WHY? Survey campus preferences.
- Too many oldies — Ignores campus bands and groups — CD library isn't used enough
- Form committee to screen program proposals from potential DJs.
- Aim for more musical diversity.
- Let new DJs test new programs at night or as substitutes.
- Use survey results to get new listeners.
- Keep on top of listings at local clubs.
- Encourage use of CD library.
- Get funds to send staff to radio and music conventions.
- Play demo CDs sent to station.

Imagining

Your imagination is a valuable resource for exploring possibilities—analyzing an option, evaluating an alternative, or solving a problem—to discover surprising ideas, original examples, and unexpected relationships.

Suppose you asked, "What if the average North American lived more than a century?" No doubt many more people would be old. How would that shift affect doctors, nurses, and medical facilities? How might city planners respond? What would the change mean for shopping centers? For television programming? For leisure activities? For Social Security?

Use some of the following strategies to unleash your imagination:

1. *Speculate about changes, alternatives, and options.* What common assumption might you question or deny? What deplorable condition would you remedy? What changes in policy, practice, or attitude might avoid problems? What different paths in life might you take?

2. *Shift perspective.* Experiment with a different point of view. How would someone on the opposing side respond? A plant, an animal, a Martian? Shift the debate (whether retirees, not teens, should be allowed to drink) or the time (present to past or future).

3. *Envision what might be.* Join the others who have imagined a utopia (an ideal state) or an anti-utopia by envisioning alternatives — a better way of treating illness, electing a president, or ordering a chaotic jumble.

4. *Synthesize.* Synthesis (generating new ideas by combining previously separate ideas) is the opposite of analysis (breaking ideas down into component parts). Synthesize to make fresh connections, fusing materials — perhaps old or familiar — into something new.

Learning by Doing 🔘 Imagining

Begin with a problem that cries out for a solution, a condition that requires a remedy, or a situation that calls for change. Ask "What if?" or start with "Suppose that" to trigger your imagination. Share ideas with your classmates.

For more about analysis and synthesis, see pp. 25–27.

Asking a Reporter's Questions

Journalists, assembling facts to write a news story, ask themselves six simple questions — the five *W*'s and an *H*:

Who?	Where?	Why?
What?	When?	How?

In the *lead,* or opening paragraph, of a good news story, the writer tries to condense the whole story into a sentence or two, answering all six questions.

> A giant homemade fire balloon [*what*] startled residents of Costa Mesa [*where*] last night [*when*] as Ambrose Barker, 79, [*who*] zigzagged across the sky at nearly 300 miles per hour [*how*] in an attempt to set a new altitude record [*why*].

Later in the news story, the reporter will add details, using the six basic questions to generate more about what happened and why.

For your college writing, use these questions to generate details. They can help you explore the significance of a childhood experience, analyze what happened at a moment in history, or investigate a campus problem. Don't worry if some go nowhere or are repetitious. Later you'll weed out irrelevant points and keep those that look promising.

For a topic that is not based on your personal experience, you may need to do reading or interviewing to answer some of the questions. Take, for example, the topic of the assassination of President John F. Kennedy, and notice how each question can lead to further questions.

- *Who* was John F. Kennedy? What kind of person was he? What kind of president? Who was with him when he was killed? Who was nearby?
- *What* happened to Kennedy? What events led up to the assassination? What happened during it? What did the media do? What did people across the country do? What did someone who remembers this event do?
- *Where* was Kennedy assassinated — city, street, vehicle, seat? Where was he going? Where did the shots likely come from? Where did they hit him? Where did he die?
- *When* was he assassinated — day, month, year, time? When did Kennedy decide to go to this city? When — precisely — were the shots fired? When did he die? When was a suspect arrested?
- *Why* was Kennedy assassinated? What are some of the theories? What solid evidence is available? Why has this event caused controversy?
- *How* was Kennedy assassinated? How many shots were fired? Specifically what caused his death? How can we get at the truth of this event?

Learning by Doing 🎙 Asking a Reporter's Questions

Choose one of the following topics, or use one of your own:

A memorable event in history or in your life
A concert or other performance that you have attended
An accomplishment on campus or an occurrence in your city
An important speech or a proposal for change
A questionable stand someone has taken

Answer the six reporter's questions about the topic. Then write a sentence or two synthesizing the answers to the six questions. Incorporate that sentence into an introductory paragraph for an essay that you might write later.

Seeking Motives

In much college writing, you will try to explain motives behind human behavior. In a history paper, you might consider how George Washington's conduct shaped the presidency. In a literature essay, you might analyze the motives of Hester Prynne in *The Scarlet Letter*. Because people, including characters in fiction, are so complex, this task is challenging.

To understand any human act, according to philosopher-critic Kenneth Burke, you can break it down into five components, a *pentad*, and ask questions about each one. Burke's pentad overlaps the reporter's questions but also can show how components of a human act affect one another, taking you deeper into motives. Suppose you are writing a political-science paper on President Lyndon Baines Johnson (LBJ), sworn in as president right after President Kennedy's assassination in 1963. A year later, he was elected to the post by a landslide. By 1968, however, he had decided not to run for a second term. You use Burke's pentad to investigate why.

1. *The act*: What was done?

   Announcing the decision to leave office without standing for reelection.

2. *The actor*: Who did it?

   President Johnson.

3. *The agency*: What means did the person use to make it happen?

   A televised address to the nation.

4. *The scene*: Where, when, and under what circumstances did it happen?

   Washington, DC, March 31, 1968. Protesters against the Vietnam War were gaining influence. The press was increasingly critical of the war. Senator Eugene McCarthy, an antiwar candidate for president, had made a strong showing against LBJ in the New Hampshire primary.

5. *The purpose or motive for acting*: What could have made the person do it?

   LBJ's motives might have included avoiding probable defeat, escaping further personal attacks, sparing his family, making it easier for his successor to pull out of the war, and easing dissent among Americans.

Next, you can pair Burke's five components and ask about the pairs:

actor to act	act to scene	scene to agency
actor to scene	act to agency	scene to purpose
actor to purpose	act to purpose	agency to purpose

PAIR	actor to agency
QUESTION	What did LBJ [actor] have to do with his televised address [agency]?
ANSWER	Commanding the attention of a vast audience, LBJ must have felt in control—though his ability to control the situation in Vietnam was slipping.

Not all the paired questions will prove fruitful; some may not even apply. But one or two might reveal valuable connections and start you writing.

Learning by Doing 🔧 Seeking Motives

Choose a puzzling action—perhaps something you, a family member, or a friend has done; a decision of a political figure; something in a movie, on television, or in a book. Apply Burke's pentad to seek motives for the action.

If you wish, also pair up components. When you believe you understand the individual's motivation, write a paragraph explaining the action, and share it with classmates.

Keeping a Journal

Journal writing richly rewards anyone who engages in it regularly. You can write anywhere or anytime: all you need is a few minutes to record an entry and the willingness to set down what you think and feel. Your journal will become a mine studded with priceless nuggets — thoughts, observations, reactions, and revelations that are yours for the taking. As you write, you can rifle your well-stocked journal for topics, insights, examples, and other material. The best type of journal is the one that's useful to *you*.

For ideas about keeping a reading journal, see p. 23.

Reflective Journals. When you write in your journal, put less emphasis on recording what happened, as you would in a diary, than on *reflecting* about what you do or see, hear or read, learn or believe. An entry can be a list or an outline, a paragraph or an essay, a poem or a letter you don't intend to send. Describe a person or a place, set down a conversation, or record insights into actions. Consider your pet peeves, fears, dreams, treasures, or moral dilemmas. Use your experience as a writer to nourish and inspire your writing, recording what worked, what didn't, and how you reacted to each.

Responsive Journals. Sometimes you *respond* to something in particular — your assigned reading, a classroom discussion, a movie, a conversation, or an observation. Faced with a long paper, you might assign *yourself* a focused response journal so you have plenty of material to use.

For more on responding to reading, see Ch. 2.

For responsive journal prompts, see the end of each selection in *A Writer's Reader:* **bedfordstmartins.com /concisebedguide**.

Warm-Up Journals. To prepare for an assignment, you can group ideas, scribble outlines, sketch beginnings, capture stray thoughts, record relevant material. Of course, a quick comment may turn into a draft.

E-Journals. Once you create a file and make entries by date or subject, you can record ideas, feelings, images, memories, and quotations. You will find it easy to copy and paste inspiring e-mail, quotations from Web pages, or images and sounds. Always identify the source of copied material so that you won't later confuse it with your original writing.

Blogs. Like traditional journals, "Web logs" aim for frank, honest, immediate entries. Unlike journals, they often explore a specific topic and may be available publicly on the Web or privately by invitation. Especially in an online class, you might blog about your writing or research processes.

Learning by Doing 🔊 Keeping a Journal

Keep a journal for at least a week. Each day record your thoughts, feelings, observations, and reactions. Reflect on what happens, and respond to what you read, including selections from this book or its e-Pages. Then bring your journal to class, and read aloud to your classmates the entry you like best.

Getting Ready

Once you have generated a suitable topic and some ideas related to that topic, you are ready to get down to the job of actually writing.

Setting Up Circumstances

If you can write only with your shoes off or with a can of soda nearby, set yourself up that way. Some writers need to hear blaring rap music; others need quiet. Create an environment that puts you in the mood for writing.

Devote One Special Place to Writing. Your place should have good lighting and space to spread out. It may be a desk in your room, the dining room table, or a quiet library cubicle — someplace where no one will bother you, where your mind and body will settle in, and preferably where you can leave projects and keep handy your computer and materials.

Establish a Ritual. Some writers find that a ritual relaxes them and helps them get started. You might open a soda, straighten your desk, turn music on (or off), and create a new file on the computer.

Relocate. If you're stuck, try moving from library to home or from kitchen to bedroom. Try an unfamiliar place — a restaurant, an airport, park.

Reduce Distractions. Most of us can't prevent interruptions, but we can reduce them. If you expect your boyfriend to call, call him before you start writing. If you have small children, write when they are asleep or at school. Turn off your phone, and concentrate hard. Let others know you are serious about writing; allow yourself to give it full attention.

Write at Your Best Time. Some think best early in the morning; others favor the small hours when their stern self-critic might be asleep, too. Either time can also reduce distractions from others.

Write on a Schedule. Writing at a predictable time of day worked marvels for English novelist Anthony Trollope, who would start at 5:30 A.M., write 2,500 words before 8:30 A.M., and then go to his job at the post office. (He wrote more than sixty books.) Even if you can't set aside the same time every day, it may help to decide, "Today from four to five, I'll write."

Preparing Your Mind

Ideas, images, or powerful urges to write may arrive like sudden miracles. Even if you are taking a shower or heading to a movie, yield to impulse and write. Encourage such moments by opening your mind to inspiration.

Talk about Your Writing. Discuss ideas in person, by phone, or online with a classmate or friend, encouraging questions, comments, and suggestions. Or talk to yourself, using a voice-activated recorder, while you sit through traffic jams, walk your dog, or ride your stationary bike.

Lay Out Your Plans. Tell a nearby listener—your next-door neighbor, spouse, parent, friend—why you want to write this paper, what you'll put in it, how you'll lay it out. If you hear "That sounds good," you'll be encouraged. If you see a yawn, you'll still have ideas in motion.

Keep a Notebook or Journal Handy. Always keep some paper in your pocket or backpack or on the night table to write down good ideas that pop into your mind. Imagination may strike in the grocery checkout line, in the doctor's waiting room, or during a lull on the job.

Read. The step from reading to writing is a short one. Even when you're reading for fun, you're involved with words. You might hit on something for your paper. Or read purposefully: set out to read and take notes.

DISCOVERY CHECKLIST

- ☐ Is your environment organized for writing? What changes might help you reduce distractions and procrastination?

- ☐ Have you scheduled enough time to get ready to write? How might you adjust your schedule or your expectations to encourage productivity?

- ☐ Is your assignment clear? What additional questions might you want to ask about what you are expected to do?

- ☐ Have you generated enough ideas that interest you? What might help you expand, focus, or deepen your ideas?

Learning by Doing Reflecting on Generating Ideas

Select one method of generating ideas that you find to be a productive or enjoyable way to begin writing. Reflect on your success using the method itself to generate ideas about why it works for you. In a pair or a team, have each person advocate for his or her preferred method, presenting its benefits, acknowledging its limitations, and trying to persuade others to give it a try.

13 Strategies for Stating a Thesis and Planning

Starting to write often seems a chaotic activity, but the strategies in this chapter can help create order. For most papers, you will want to consider your purpose and audience and then focus on a central point by discovering, stating, and improving a thesis. To help you arrange your material, the chapter also includes advice on grouping ideas and outlining.

Shaping Your Topic for Your Purpose and Your Audience

For critical questions about audience and more about purpose, see p. 263. For more about both, see pp. 11–15.

As you work on your college papers, you may feel as if you're juggling — selecting weighty points and lively details, tossing them into the air, keeping them all moving in sequence. Busy as you are juggling, however, your performance almost always draws a crowd — your instructor, classmates, or other readers. They'll expect your attention, too, as you try to achieve your purpose — probably informing, explaining, or persuading.

Think carefully about your audience and purpose as you plan. If you want to show your classmates and instructor the importance of an event, start by deciding how much detail they need. If most of them have gotten speeding tickets, they'll need less information about that event than city commuters might. However, to achieve your purpose, you'll need to go beyond what happened to why the event mattered to you. No matter how many tickets your readers have gotten, they won't know what that experience means to you unless you share that information. They may incorrectly assume that you worried about being late to class or having to pay higher

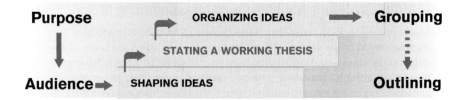

insurance rates. In fact, you had suddenly realized your narrow escape from an accident like your cousin's, a recognition that motivated you to change.

Similarly, if you want to persuade county officials to change the way absentee ballots are distributed to college students, you'll need to support your idea with reasons and evidence—drawing on state election laws and legal precedents familiar to these readers as well as experiences of student voters. You may need to show how your proposal would solve existing problems and also why it would do so better than other proposals.

Plan for your purpose and audience using questions such as these:

- *What is your general purpose?* What do you want to accomplish? Do you want readers to smile, think, or agree? To learn, accept, respect, care, change, or reply? How might your writing accomplish your aims?

- *Who are your readers?* If they are not clearly identified by your assignment or situation, what do you assume about them? What do they know or want to know? What opinions do they hold? What do they find informative or persuasive? How might you appeal to them?

- *How might you narrow and focus your ideas about the topic,* given what you know or assume about your purpose and audience? Which slant would best achieve your purpose? What points would appeal most strongly to your readers? What details would engage or persuade them?

- *What qualities of good writing have been discussed in your class,* explained in your syllabus, or identified in readings? What criteria have emerged from exchanges of drafts with classmates or comments from your instructor? How might you demonstrate these qualities to readers?

Learning by Doing Considering Purpose and Audience

Think back to a recent writing task—a college essay, a job application, a report or memo at work, a letter to a campus office, or some other piece. Write a brief description of your situation as a writer at that time. What was your purpose? Who—exactly—were your readers? How did you account for both as you planned? How might you have made your writing more effective?

Stating and Using a Thesis

Most pieces of effective writing are unified around one main point. That is, all the subpoints and supporting details are relevant to that point. Generally, after you have read an essay, you can sum up the writer's main point in a sentence, even if the author has not stated it explicitly. We call this summary statement a *thesis*.

Explicit Thesis. Often a thesis will be explicit, plainly stated, in the selection itself. In "The Myth of the Latin Woman: I Just Met a Girl Named

For an interactive Learning by Doing activity on analyzing a thesis, go to Ch. 13: **bedfordstmartins.com /concisebedguide**.

María" from *The Latin Deli* (Athens: University of Georgia Press, 1993), Judith Ortiz Cofer states her thesis at the end of the first paragraph: "You can leave the Island, master the English language, and travel as far as you can, but if you are a Latina, especially one like me who so obviously belongs to Rita Moreno's gene pool, the Island travels with you." This clear statement, strategically placed, helps readers see her point.

Implicit Thesis. Sometimes a thesis is implicit, indirectly suggested rather than directly stated. In "The Niceness Solution," a selection from Bruce Bawer's *Beyond Queer* (New York: Free Press, 1996), Paul Varnell describes an ordinance "banning rude behavior, including rude speech," passed in Raritan, New Jersey. After discussing a 1580 code of conduct, he identifies four objections to such attempts to limit free speech. He concludes with this sentence: "Sensibly, Raritan Police Chief Joseph Sferro said he would not enforce the new ordinance." Although Varnell does not state his main point in one concise sentence, readers know that he opposes the Raritan law and any other attempts to legislate "niceness."

The purpose of most academic and workplace writing is to inform, to explain, or to convince. To achieve any of these purposes, you must make your main point crystal clear. A thesis sentence helps you clarify your idea and stay on track as you write. It also helps your readers see your point and follow your discussion. Sometimes you may want to imply your thesis, but if you state it explicitly, you ensure that readers cannot miss it.

Learning by Doing 🔊 Identifying Theses

If you select the essays yourself, choose them from Chs. 4–9 in Part 2.

Working in a small group, select and read five essays from this book (or read those your instructor has chosen). Then, individually, write out the thesis for each essay. Some thesis statements are stated outright (explicit), but others are indirect (implicit). Compare and contrast the thesis statements you identified with those your classmates found. How do you account for differences? Try to agree on a thesis statement for each essay.

Look for specific advice under headings that mention a thesis in Chs. 4–9. Watch for the red labels that identify thesis examples.

How to Discover a Working Thesis

It's rare for a writer to develop a perfect thesis statement early in the writing process and then to write an effective essay that fits it exactly. What you should aim for is a *working thesis*—a statement that can guide you but that you will ultimately refine. Ideas for a working thesis are probably all around you.

Your topic identifies the area you want to explore. To convert a topic to a thesis, you need to add your own slant, attitude, or point. A useful thesis contains not only the key words that identify your *topic* but also the *point* you want to make or the *attitude* you intend to express.

Topic   +   Slant or Attitude or Point   =   Working Thesis

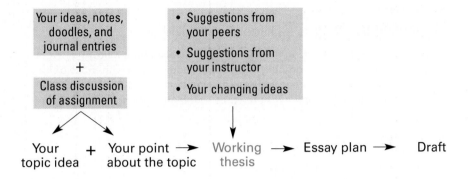

Suppose you want to identify and write about a specific societal change.

TOPIC IDEA   old-fashioned formal courtesy

Now you experiment, testing ideas to make the topic your own.

TRIAL   Old-fashioned formal courtesy is a thing of the past.

Although your trial sentence emphasizes change, it's still circular, repeating rather than advancing a workable point. It doesn't say anything new about old-fashioned formal courtesy; it simply defines *old-fashioned*. You still need to state your own slant — maybe why things have changed.

TOPIC IDEA + SLANT   old-fashioned formal courtesy + its decline as gender roles have changed

WORKING THESIS   As the roles of men and women have changed in our society, old-fashioned formal courtesy has declined.

With this working thesis, you could focus on how changing societal attitudes toward gender roles have caused changes in courtesy. Later, when you revise, you may refine your thesis further — perhaps restricting it to courtesy toward the elderly, toward women, or, despite stereotypes, toward men. The chart on page 267 suggests ways to develop a working thesis.

For advice about revising a thesis, see pp. 269–71.

Once you have a working thesis, be sure its point accomplishes the purpose of your assignment. Suppose your assignment asks you to compare and contrast two local newspapers' coverage of a Senate election. Ask yourself what the point of that comparison and contrast is. Simply noting a difference won't be enough to satisfy most readers.

NO SPECIFIC POINT   The *Herald*'s coverage of the Senate elections was different from the *Courier*'s.

WORKING THESIS   The *Herald*'s coverage of the Senate elections was more thorough than the *Courier*'s.

Learning by Doing 🎬 Discovering a Thesis

Write a sentence, a working thesis, that unifies each of the following groups of details. Then compare and contrast your theses with those of your classmates. What other information would you need to write a good paper on each topic? How might the thesis statement change as you write the paper?

1. Cigarettes are expensive.
   Cigarettes can cause fires.
   Cigarettes cause unpleasant odors.
   Cigarettes can cause health problems for smokers.
   Secondhand smoke from cigarettes can cause health problems.

2. Clinger College has a highly qualified faculty.
   Clinger College has an excellent curriculum in my field.
   Clinger College has a beautiful campus.
   Clinger College is expensive.
   Clinger College has offered me a scholarship.

3. Crisis centers report that date rape is increasing.
   Most date rape is not reported to the police.
   Often the victim of date rape is not believed.
   Sometimes the victim of date rape is blamed or blames herself.
   The effects of date rape stay with a woman for years.

How to State a Thesis

Once you have a notion of a topic and main point, use these pointers to state or improve a thesis to guide your planning and drafting.

■ *State the thesis sentence exactly.* Replace vague or general wording with concise, detailed, and down-to-earth language.

TOO GENERAL   There are a lot of troubles with chemical wastes.

Are you going to deal with all chemical wastes, throughout all of history, all over the world? Will you list all the troubles they can cause?

MORE SPECIFIC   Careless dumping of leftover paint is to blame for a recent outbreak of skin rashes in Atlanta.

For an argument, you need to take a stand on a debatable issue that would allow others to take different positions. State yours exactly.

SPECIFIC STAND   The recent health consequences of carelessly dumping leftover paint require Atlanta officials both to regulate and to educate.

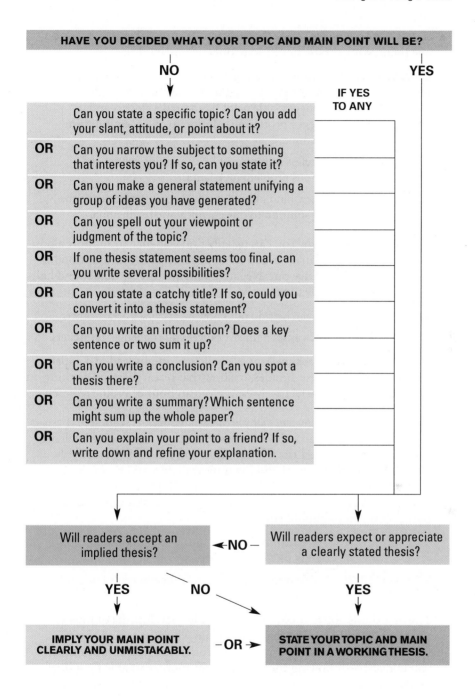

HAVE YOU DECIDED WHAT YOUR TOPIC AND MAIN POINT WILL BE?

NO   YES

IF YES TO ANY

Can you state a specific topic? Can you add your slant, attitude, or point about it?

OR Can you narrow the subject to something that interests you? If so, can you state it?

OR Can you make a general statement unifying a group of ideas you have generated?

OR Can you spell out your viewpoint or judgment of the topic?

OR If one thesis statement seems too final, can you write several possibilities?

OR Can you state a catchy title? If so, could you convert it into a thesis statement?

OR Can you write an introduction? Does a key sentence or two sum it up?

OR Can you write a conclusion? Can you spot a thesis there?

OR Can you write a summary? Which sentence might sum up the whole paper?

OR Can you explain your point to a friend? If so, write down and refine your explanation.

Will readers accept an implied thesis? ◄—NO— Will readers expect or appreciate a clearly stated thesis?

YES NO   YES

IMPLY YOUR MAIN POINT CLEARLY AND UNMISTAKABLY. –OR→ STATE YOUR TOPIC AND MAIN POINT IN A WORKING THESIS.

- *State just one central idea in the thesis sentence.* If your paper is to focus on one point, your thesis should state only one main idea.

TOO MANY IDEAS	Careless dumping of leftover paint has caused a serious problem in Atlanta, and a new kind of biodegradable paint has been developed, and it offers a promising solution to one chemical waste dilemma.
ONE CENTRAL IDEA	Careless dumping of leftover paint has caused a serious problem in Atlanta.
OR	A new kind of biodegradable paint offers a promising solution to one chemical waste dilemma.

- *State your thesis positively.* You can usually find evidence to support a positive statement, but you'd have to rule out every possible exception in order to prove a negative one. Negative statements also may sound half-hearted and seem to lead nowhere.

NEGATIVE	Researchers do not know what causes breast cancer.
POSITIVE	The causes of breast cancer still challenge researchers.

Presenting the topic positively as a "challenge" might lead to a paper about an exciting quest. Besides, to show that researchers are working on the problem would be relatively easy, given an hour of online research.

- *Limit your thesis to a statement that you can demonstrate.* A workable thesis is limited so that you can support it with sufficient convincing evidence. It should stake out just the territory that you can cover thoroughly within the length assigned and the time available, and no more. The shorter the essay, the less development your thesis should promise or require. Likewise, the longer the essay, the more development and complexity your thesis should suggest.

DIFFICULT TO SHOW	For centuries, popular music has announced vital trends in Western society.
DIFFICULT TO SHOW	My favorite piece of music is Beethoven's Fifth Symphony.

The first thesis above could inform a whole encyclopedia of music; the second would require that you explain why that symphony is your favorite, contrasting it with all the other musical compositions you know. The following thesis sounds far more workable for a brief essay.

POSSIBLE TO SHOW	In the past two years, a rise in the number of preteenagers has resulted in a comeback for heavy metal on the local concert scene.

Unlike a vague statement or a broad, unrestricted claim, a limited thesis narrows and refines a topic, restricting your essay to a reasonable scope.

TOO VAGUE	Native American blankets are very beautiful.
TOO BROAD	Native Americans have adapted to cultural shifts.
POSSIBLE TO SHOW	For some members of the Apache tribe, working in high-rise construction has allowed both economic stability and cultural integrity.

If the suggestions in this chapter have helped you draft a working thesis — even an awkward or feeble one — you'll find plenty of advice about improving it in the next few pages and more later about revising it. But what if you're freezing up because your thesis simply won't take shape? First, relax. Your thesis will emerge later on — as your thinking matures and you figure out your paper's true direction, as peer readers spot the idea in your paper you're too close to see, as you talk with your instructor and suddenly grasp how to take your paper where you want it to go. In the meantime, plan and write so that you create a rich environment that will encourage your thesis to emerge.

For more on revising a thesis, see pp. 269–71.

Learning by Doing 🖋 Examining Thesis Statements

Discuss each of the following thesis sentences with your classmates. Answer these questions for each: •

Is the thesis stated exactly?
Does the thesis state just one idea?
Is the thesis stated positively?
Is the thesis sufficiently limited for a short essay?
How might the thesis be improved?

1. Teenagers should not get married.
2. Cutting classes is like a disease.
3. Students have developed a variety of techniques to conceal inadequate study from their instructors.
4. Older people often imitate teenagers.
5. Violence on television can be harmful to children.
6. I don't know how to change the oil in my car.

How to Improve a Thesis

Simply knowing what a solid working thesis *should* do may not help you improve your thesis. Whether yours is a first effort or a refined version, turn to the Take Action chart (p. 270) to help you figure out how to improve

Take Action Building a Stronger Thesis

Ask each question at the top of the chart to consider whether your draft might need work on that issue. If so, follow the ASK—LOCATE SPECIFICS—TAKE ACTION sequence to revise.

	Unclear Topic?	Unclear Slant?	Broad Thesis?
1 **ASK**	Could I define or state my topic more clearly?	Could I define or state my slant more clearly?	Could I limit my thesis to develop it more successfully?
2 **LOCATE SPECIFICS**	■ Write out your current working thesis. ■ Circle the words in it that identify your topic. WORKING THESIS (Adaptability) is essential for World Action volunteers. [What, exactly, does the topic *adaptability* mean?]	■ Write out your current working thesis. ■ Underline the words that state your slant, attitude, or point about your topic. WORKING THESIS Volunteering is an invaluable experience. [Why or in what ways is volunteering invaluable?]	■ Write out your current working thesis. ■ Decide whether it establishes a task that you could accomplish given the available time and the expected length. WORKING THESIS Rock and roll has evolved dramatically since the 1950s. [Tracing this history in a few pages would be impossible.]
3 **TAKE ACTION**	■ Rework the circled topic. State it more clearly, and specify what it means to you. ■ Define or identify the topic in terms of your purpose and the likely interests of your audience. REVISED THESIS An ability to adjust to, even thrive under, challenging circumstances is essential for World Action volunteers.	■ Rework your underlined slant. Jot down ideas to sharpen it and express an engaging approach to your topic. ■ Refine it to accomplish your purpose and appeal to your audience. REVISED THESIS Volunteering builds practical skills while connecting volunteers more fully to their communities.	■ Restrict your thesis to a slice of the pie, not the whole pie. ■ Focus on one part or element, not several. Break it apart, and pick only a chunk. ■ Reduce many ideas to one point, or convert a negative statement to a positive one. REVISED THESIS The music of the alternative-rock band Wilco continues to evolve as members experiment with vocal moods and instrumentation.

your thesis. Skim across the top to identify questions you might ask about your working thesis. When you answer a question with "Yes" or "Maybe," move straight down the column to Locate Specifics under that question. Use the activities there to pinpoint gaps, problems, or weaknesses. Then move straight down the column to Take Action. Use the advice that suits your problem as you revise.

How to Use a Thesis to Organize

Often a good, clear thesis will suggest an organization for your ideas.

WORKING THESIS	Despite the disadvantages of living in a downtown business district, I wouldn't live anywhere else.
FIRST ¶S	Disadvantages of living in the business district
NEXT ¶S	Advantages of living there
LAST ¶	Affirmation of your preference for downtown life

For more on using a thesis to develop an outline, see pp. 276–78.

Just putting your working thesis into words can help organize you and keep you on track. A clear thesis can guide you as you select details and connect sections of the essay.

In addition, your thesis can prepare your readers for the pattern of development or sequence of ideas that you plan to present. As a writer, you look for key words (such as *compare, propose,* or *evaluate*) when you size up an assignment. Such words alert you to what's expected. When you write or revise your thesis, you can use such terms or their equivalents (such as *benefit* or *consequence* instead of *effect*) to preview for readers the likely direction of your paper. Then they, too, will know what to expect.

For more on key terms in college assignments, see p. 37.

WORKING THESIS	Expanding the campus program for energy conservation would bring welcome financial and environmental benefits.
FIRST ¶S	Explanation of the campus energy situation
NEXT ¶S	Justification of the need for the proposed expansion
NEXT ¶S	Financial benefits for the college and students
NEXT ¶S	Environmental benefits for the region and beyond
LAST ¶	Concluding assertion of the value of the expansion

As you write, however, you don't have to cling to a thesis for dear life. If further investigation changes your thinking, you can change your thesis.

WORKING THESIS	Because wolves are a menace to people and farm animals, they ought to be exterminated.
REVISED THESIS	The wolf, a relatively peaceful animal useful in nature's scheme of things, ought to be protected.

You can restate a thesis any time: as you write, revise, or revise again.

Learning by Doing 🔘 Using a Thesis to Preview

Each of the following thesis statements is from a student paper in a different field. With your classmates, consider how each one previews the essay to come and how you would expect the essay to be organized into sections.

1. Although the intent of inclusion is to provide the best care for all children by treating both special- and general-education students equally, some people in the field believe that the full inclusion of disabled children in mainstream classrooms may not be in the best interest of either type of student. (From "Is Inclusion the Answer?" by Sarah E. Goers)

2. With ancient Asian roots and contemporary European influences, the Japanese language has continued to change and to reflect cultural change as well. (From "Japanese: Linguistic Diversity" by Stephanie Hawkins)

3. *Manifest destiny* was an expression by leaders and politicians in the 1840s to clarify continental extension and expansion and in a sense revitalize the mission and national destiny for Americans. (From ethnic studies examination answer by Angela Mendy)

4. By comparing the *Aeneid* with *Troilus and Criseyde*, one can easily see the effects of the code of courtly love on literature. (From "The Effect of the Code of Courtly Love: A Comparison of Virgil's *Aeneid* and Chaucer's *Troilus and Criseyde*" by Cindy Keeler)

5. The effects of pollutants on the endangered Least Tern entering the Upper Newport Bay should be quantified so that necessary action can be taken to further protect and encourage the species. (From "Contaminant Residues in Least Tern [*Sterna antillarum*] Eggs Nesting in Upper Newport Bay" by Susanna Olsen)

Organizing Your Ideas

When you organize an essay, you select an order for the parts that makes sense and shows your readers how the ideas are connected. Often your organization will not only help a reader follow your points but also reinforce your emphases by moving from beginning to end or from least to most significant, as the table on page 273 illustrates.

Grouping Your Ideas

While exploring a topic, you will usually find a few ideas that seem to belong together — two facts on New York traffic jams, four actions of New York drivers, three problems with New York streets. But similar ideas seldom appear together in your notes because you did not discover them all at the same time. For this reason, you need to sort your ideas into groups and arrange them in sequences. Here are six ways to work:

Organization	Movement	Typical Use	Example
Spatial	Left to right, right to left, bottom to top, top to bottom, front to back, outside to inside	■ Describing a place, a scene, or an environment ■ Describing a person's physical appearance	Describe an ocean vista, moving from the tidepools on the rocky shore to the plastic buoys floating offshore to the sparkling water meeting the sunset sky.
Chronological	What happens first, second, and next, continuing until the end	■ Narrating an event ■ Explaining steps in a procedure ■ Explaining the development of an idea or a trend	Narrate the events that led up to an accident: leaving home late, stopping for an errand, checking messages while rushing along the highway, racing up to the intersection.
Logical	General to specific (or the reverse), least important to most, cause to effect, problem to solution	■ Explaining an idea ■ Persuading readers to accept a stand, a proposal, or an evaluation	Analyze the effects of last year's storms by selecting four major consequences, placing the most important one last for emphasis.

1. *Rainbow connections.* List the main points you're going to express. Highlight points that go together with the same color. When you write, follow the color code, and integrate related ideas at the same time.

2. *Emphasizing ideas.* Make a copy of your file of ideas or notes. Use your software tools to highlight, categorize, and shape your thinking by grouping or distinguishing ideas. Mark similar or related ideas in the same way; call out major points. Then move related materials into groups.

   Highlighting

   Boxing

   Showing color

   Using **bold**, *italics*, underlining

   • Adding bullets

   1. Numbering

   Changing fonts

   Varying print sizes

3. *Linking.* List major points, and then draw lines (in color if you wish) to link related ideas. Figure 13.1 illustrates a linked list for an essay on Manhattan driving. The writer has connected related points, numbered their sequence, and supplied each group with a heading. Each heading will probably inspire a topic sentence to introduce a major division of the essay. Because one point, chauffeured luxury cars, failed to relate to any other, the writer has a choice: drop it or develop it.

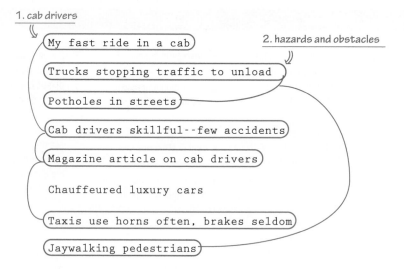

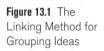

Figure 13.1 The Linking Method for Grouping Ideas

4. *Solitaire.* Collect notes and ideas on roomy (5-by-8-inch) file cards, especially to write about literature or research. To organize, spread out the cards; arrange and rearrange them. When each idea seems to lead to the next, gather the cards into a deck in this order. As you write, deal yourself a card at a time, and turn its contents into sentences.

5. *Slide show.* Use presentation software to write your notes and ideas on "slides." When you're done, view your slides one by one or as a collection. Sort your slides into the most promising order.

6. *Clustering.* Clustering is a visual method for generating as well as grouping ideas. In the middle of a page, write your topic in a word or a phrase. Then think of the major divisions into which you might break your topic. For an essay on Manhattan drivers, your major divisions might be *types* of drivers: (1) taxi drivers, (2) bus drivers, (3) truck drivers, (4) New York drivers of private cars, and (5) out-of-town drivers of private cars. Arrange these divisions around your topic, circle them, and draw lines out from the major topic. You now have a rough plan for an essay. (See Figure 13.2.)

   Around each division, make another cluster of details you might include — examples, illustrations, facts, statistics, opinions. Circle each specific item, connect it to the appropriate type of driver, and then expand the details into a paragraph. This technique lets you know where you have enough specific information to make your paper clear and interesting — and where you don't. If one subtopic has no small circles around it (such as "Bus Drivers" in Figure 13.2), either add specifics to expand it or drop it.

Figure 13.2 The Clustering Method for Grouping Ideas

My fastest taxi ride

My talks with drivers

Chauffeurs I have seen

Taxi Drivers

Drivers of Private Cars (New Yorkers)

Statistic: low accident rate

Talk with my friend Sam

Manhattan Drivers

Truck Drivers

Memory: I was scared!

Observation: they unload, stop traffic

Article in *New York* magazine

Drivers of Private Cars (Visitors)

Bus Drivers

Learning by Doing Clustering

Generate clusters for three of the following topics. With your classmates, discuss which one of the three would probably help you write the best paper.

teachers	fast food	civil rights
Internet sites	leisure activities	substance abuse
my favorite restaurants	musicians	technology

Outlining

A familiar way to organize is to outline. A written outline, whether brief or detailed, acts as a map that you make before a journey. It shows where to leave from, where to stop along the way, and where to arrive. If you forget where you are going or what you want to say, you can consult your outline to get back on track. When you turn in your essay, your instructor may re-quest an outline as both a map for readers and a skeletal summary.

For more on thesis statements, see pp. 263–72.

For more on using outlining for revision, see pp. 303–4.

- Some writers like to begin with a working thesis. If it's clear, it may sug-gest how to develop or expand an outline, allowing the plan for the paper to grow naturally from the idea behind it.
- Others prefer to start with a loose informal outline—perhaps just a list of points to make. If readers find your papers mechanical, such an out-line may free up your writing.
- Still others, especially for research papers or complicated arguments, like to lay out a complex job very carefully in a detailed formal outline. If readers find your writing disorganized and hard to follow, this more detailed plan might be especially useful.

Thesis-Guided Outlines. Your working thesis may identify ideas you can use to organize your paper. (If it doesn't, you may want to revise your the-sis and then return to your outline or vice versa.) Suppose you are as-signed an anthropology paper on the people of Melanesia. You focus on this point:

> Working Thesis: Although the Melanesian pattern of family life may look strange to Westerners, it fosters a degree of independence that rivals our own.

If you lay out your ideas in the same order that they follow in the two parts of this thesis statement, your simple outline suggests an essay that naturally falls into two parts—features that seem strange and admirable results.

1. Features that appear strange to Westerners
   - A woman supported by her brother, not her husband
   - Trial marriages common
   - Divorce from her children possible for any mother
2. Admirable results of system
   - Wives not dependent on husbands for support
   - Divorce between mates uncommon
   - Greater freedom for parents and children

When you create a thesis-guided outline, look for the key element of your working thesis. This key element can suggest both a useful question to consider and an organization, as the table on page 277 illustrates.

Informal Outlines. For in-class writing, brief essays, and familiar topics, a short or informal outline, also called a *scratch outline,* may serve your needs. Jot down a list of points in the order you plan to make them. Use this outline, for your eyes only, to help you get organized, stick to the point, and remember ideas under pressure. The following example outlines a short paper explaining how outdoor enthusiasts can avoid

Sample Thesis Statement	Type of Key Element	Examples of Key Element	Question You Might Ask	Organization of Outline
A varied personal exercise program has four main *advantages*.	Plural word	Words such as *benefits*, *advantages*, *teenagers*, or *reasons*	What are the types, kinds, or examples of this word?	List outline headings based on the categories or cases you identify.
Wylie's *interpretation* of Van Gogh's last paintings unifies aesthetics and psychology.	Key word identifying an approach or vantage point	Words such as *claim*, *argument*, *position*, *interpretation*, or *point of view*	What are the parts, aspects, or elements of this approach?	List outline headings based on the components that you identify.
Preparing a pasta dinner for surprise guests can be an easy process.	Key word identifying an activity	Words such as *preparing*, *harming*, or *improving*	How is this activity accomplished, or how does it happen?	Supply a heading for each step, stage, or element that the activity involves.
Although the new wetland preserve will protect only some wildlife, it will bring several long-term benefits to the region.	One part of the sentence subordinate to another	Sentence part beginning with a qualification such as *despite*, *because*, *since*, or *although*	What does the qualification include, and what does the main statement include?	Use a major heading for the qualification and another for the main statement.
When Sandie Burns arrives in her wheelchair at the soccer field, other parents soon see that she is a *typical* soccer mom.	General evaluation that assigns a quality or value to someone or something	Evaluative words such as *typical*, *unusual*, *valuable*, *notable*, or other specific qualities	What examples, illustrations, or clusters of details will show this quality?	Add a heading for each extended example or each group of examples or details you want to use.
In spite of these tough economic times, the student senate *should* strongly recommend extended hours for the computer lab.	Claim or argument advocating a certain decision, action, or solution	Words such as *should*, *could*, *might*, *ought to*, *need to*, or *must*	Which reasons and evidence will justify this opinion? Which will counter the opinions of others who disagree with it?	Provide a heading for each major justification or defensive point; add headings for countering reasons.

illnesses carried by unsafe drinking water. It simply lists the methods for treating potentially unsafe water that the writer plans to explain.

Working Thesis: Campers and hikers need to ensure the safety of the water that they drink from rivers or streams.

Introduction: Treatments for potentially unsafe drinking water

1. Small commercial filter
   –Remove bacteria and protozoa including salmonella and E. coli
   –Use brands convenient for campers and hikers
2. Chemicals
   –Use bleach, chlorine, or iodine
   –Follow general rule: 12 drops per gallon of water
3. Boiling
   –Boil for 5 minutes (Red Cross) to 15 minutes (National Safety Council)
   –Store in a clean, covered container

Conclusion: Using one of three methods of treating water, campers and hikers can enjoy safe water from natural sources.

This simple outline could easily fall into a five-paragraph essay or grow to eight paragraphs—introduction, conclusion, and three pairs of paragraphs in between. You won't know how many you'll need until you write.

An informal outline can be even briefer than the preceding one. To answer an exam question or prepare a very short paper, your outline might be no more than an *outer plan*—three or four phrases jotted in a list:

Isolation of region
Tradition of family businesses
Growth of electronic commuting

The process of making an informal outline can help you figure out how to develop your ideas. Say you plan a "how-to" essay analyzing the process of buying a used car, beginning with this thesis:

Working Thesis: Despite traps that await the unwary, preparing yourself before you shop can help you find a good used car.

The key word here is *preparing*. Considering *how* the buyer should prepare before shopping for a used car, you're likely to outline several ideas:

–Read car blogs, car magazines, and Consumer Reports.
–Check craigslist, dealer sites, and classified ads.
–Make phone calls to several dealers.
–Talk to friends who have bought used cars.
–Know what to look and listen for when you test-drive.
–Have a mechanic check out any car before you buy it.

After some horror stories about people who got taken by car sharks, you can discuss, point by point, your advice. You can always change the sequence, add or drop an idea, or revise your thesis as you go along.

Learning by Doing 🎯 Moving from Outline to Thesis

Based on each of the following informal outlines, write a possible thesis statement expressing a possible slant, attitude, or point (even if you aren't sure that the position is entirely defensible). Compare thesis statements with classmates. What similarities and differences do you find? How do you account for these?

1. Smartphones
   Get the financial and service plans of various smartphone companies.
   Read the phone contracts as well as the promotional offers.
   Look for the time period, flexibility, and cancellation provisions.
   Check the display, keyboard, camera, apps, and other features.

2. Popular Mystery Novels
   Both Tony Hillerman and Margaret Coel have written mysteries with Native American characters and settings.
   Hillerman's novels feature members of the Navajo Tribal Police.
   Coel's novels feature a female attorney who is an Arapaho and a Jesuit priest at the reservation mission who grew up in Boston.
   Hillerman's stories take place mostly on the extensive Navajo Reservation in Arizona, New Mexico, and Utah.
   Coel's are set mostly on the large Wind River Reservation in Wyoming.
   Hillerman and Coel try to convey tribal culture accurately, although their mysteries involve different tribes.
   Both also explore similarities, differences, and conflicts between Native American cultures and the dominant culture.

3. Downtown Playspace
   Downtown Playspace has financial and volunteer support but needs more.
   Statistics show the need for a regional expansion of options for children.
   Downtown Playspace will serve visitors at the Children's Museum and local children in Head Start, preschool, and elementary schools.
   It will combine an outdoor playground with indoor technology space.
   Land and a building are available, but both require renovation.

Formal Outlines. A *formal outline* is an elaborate guide, built with time and care, for a long, complex paper. Because major reports, research papers, and senior theses require so much work, some professors and departments ask a writer to submit a formal outline at an early stage and to include one in the final draft. A formal outline shows how ideas relate one to another—which ones are equal and important (*coordinate*) and which are less important (*subordinate*). It clearly and logically spells out where you are going. If you outline again after writing a draft, you can use the revised outline to check your logic then as well, perhaps revealing where to revise.

When you make a full formal outline, follow these steps:

- Place your thesis statement at the beginning.
- List the major points that support and develop your thesis, labeling them with roman numerals (I, II, III).
- Break down the major points into divisions with capital letters (A, B, C), subdivide those using arabic numerals (1, 2, 3), and subdivide those using small letters (a, b, c). Continue until your outline is fully developed. If a very complex project requires further subdivision, use arabic numerals and small letters in parentheses.
- Indent each level of division in turn: the deeper the indentation, the more specific the ideas. Align like-numbered or -lettered headings under one another.
- Cast all headings in parallel grammatical form: phrases or sentences, but not both in the same outline.

For more on parallelism, see B2 (p. A-52) in the Quick Editing Guide.

CAUTION: Because an outline divides or analyzes ideas, some readers and instructors disapprove of categories with only one subpoint, reasoning that you can't divide anything into one part. Let's say that your outline on earthquakes lists a 1 without a 2:

> D. Probable results of an earthquake include structural damage.
>   1. House foundations crack.

Logically, if you are going to discuss the *probable results* of an earthquake, you need to include more than one result:

> D. Probable results of an earthquake include structural damage.
>   1. House foundations crack.
>   2. Road surfaces are damaged.
>   3. Water mains break.

Not only have you now come up with more points, but you have also emphasized the one placed last.

A *formal topic outline* for a long paper might include several levels of ideas, as this outline for Linn Bourgeau's research paper illustrates. Such an outline can help you work out both a persuasive sequence for the parts of a paper and a logical order for any information from sources.

Crucial Choices: Who Will Save the Wetlands If Everyone Is at the Mall?

Working Thesis: Federal regulations need to foster state laws and educational requirements that will help protect the few wetlands that are left, restore as many as possible of those that have been destroyed, and take measures to improve the damage from overdevelopment.

I. Nature's ecosystem
   A. Loss of wetlands nationally
   B. Loss of wetlands in Illinois
      1. More flooding and poorer water quality
      2. Lost ability to prevent floods, clean water, and store water
   C. Need to protect humankind
II. Dramatic floods
   A. Midwestern floods in 1993 and 2011
      1. Lost wetlands in Illinois and other states
      2. Devastation in some states
   B. Cost in dollars and lives
      1. Deaths during recent flooding
      2. Costs in millions of dollars a year
   C. Flood prevention
      1. Plants and soil
      2. Floodplain overflow
III. Wetland laws
   A. Inadequately informed legislators
      1. Watersheds
      2. Interconnections in natural water systems
   B. Water purification
      1. Wetlands and water
      2. Pavement and lawns
IV. Need to save wetlands
   A. New federal laws
   B. Re-education about interconnectedness
      1. Ecology at every grade level
      2. Education for politicians, developers, and legislators
   C. Choices in schools, legislature, and people's daily lives

Learning by Doing 🖐 Responding to an Outline

Discuss the formal topic outline above with a small group or the entire class, considering the following questions:

- Would this outline be useful in organizing an essay?
- How is the organization logical? Is it easy to follow? What are other possible arrangements for the ideas?
- Is this outline sufficiently detailed for a paper? Can you spot any gaps?
- What possible pitfalls would the writer using this outline need to avoid?

A topic outline may help you work out a clear sequence of ideas but may not elaborate or connect them. Although you may not be sure how everything will fit together until you write a draft, you may find that a *formal sentence outline* clarifies what you want to say. It also moves you a step closer to drafting topic sentences and paragraphs even though you would still need to add detailed information. Notice how this sentence outline for Linn Bourgeau's research paper expands her ideas.

Crucial Choices: Who Will Save the Wetlands If Everyone Is at the Mall?

Working Thesis: Federal regulations need to foster state laws and educational requirements that will help protect the few wetlands that are left, restore as many as possible of those that have been destroyed, and take measures to improve the damage from overdevelopment.

I.   Each person, as part of nature's ecosystem, chooses how to interact with nature, including wetlands.

 A. The nation has lost over half its wetlands since Columbus arrived.

 B. Illinois has lost even more by legislating and draining them away.

  1. Destroying wetlands creates more flooding and poorer water quality.

  2. The wetlands could prevent floods, clean the water supply, and store water.

 C. The wetlands need to be protected because they protect and serve humankind.

II. Floods are dramatic and visible consequences of not protecting wetlands.

 A. The midwestern floods of 1993 and 2011 were disastrous.

  1. Illinois and other states had lost their wetlands.

  2. Those states also suffered the most devastation.

 B. The cost of flooding can be tallied in dollars spent and in lives lost.

  1. Nearly thirty people died in floods between 1995 and 2011.

  2. Flooding in 2011 cost Illinois about $216 million.

 C. Preventing floods is a valuable role of wetlands.

  1. Plants and soil manage excess water.

  2. The Mississippi River floodplain was reduced from 60 days of water overflow to 12.

III. The laws misinterpret or ignore the basic understanding of wetlands.

 A. Legislators need to know that an "isolated wetland" does not exist.

  1. Water travels within an area called a watershed.

  2. The law needs to consider interconnections in water systems.

 B. Wetlands naturally purify water.

  1. Water filters and flows in wetlands.

  2. Pavement and lawns carry water over, not through, the soil.

IV. Who will save the wetlands if everyone is at the mall?

    A. Federal laws should require implementing what we know.

    B. The vital concept of interconnectedness means reeducating everyone from legislators to fourth graders.

       1. Ecology must be incorporated into the curriculum for every grade.

       2. Educating politicians, developers, and legislators is more difficult.

    C. The choices people make in their schools, legislative systems, and daily lives will determine the future of water quality and flooding.

Learning by Doing 🎯 Outlining

1. Using one of your groups of ideas from the activities in Chapter 12, construct a formal topic outline that might serve as a guide for an essay.
2. Now turn that topic outline into a formal sentence outline.
3. Discuss both outlines with your classmates and instructor, bringing up any difficulties you met. If you get better notions for organizing, change the outline.

For help organizing support effectively, go to the interactive "Take Action" charts in Re:Writing at **bedfordstmartins.com /concisebedguide**.

Learning by Doing 🎯 Reflecting on Planning

Reflect on the purpose and audience for your current paper. Then return to the thesis, outline, or other plans you have prepared. Will your plans accomplish your purpose? Are they directed to your intended audience? Make any needed adjustments. Exchange plans with a classmate or small group, and discuss ways to continue improving them.

14 Strategies for Drafting

Learning to write well involves learning what key questions to ask yourself: How can I begin this draft? What should I do if I get stuck? How can I flesh out the bones of my paper? How can I end effectively? How can I keep my readers with me? In this chapter we offer advice to get you going and keep you going, drafting the first paragraph to the last.

Making a Start Enjoyable

A playful start may get you hard at work before you know it.

- **Time Yourself.** Set your watch, alarm, or egg timer, and vow to draft a page before the buzzer sounds. Don't stop for anything. If you're writing nonsense, just push on. You can cross out later.

- **Slow to a Crawl.** If speed quotas don't work, time yourself to write with exaggerated laziness, maybe a sentence every fifteen minutes.

- **Scribble on a Scrap.** If you dread the blank paper or screen, try starting on scrap paper, the back of a list, or a small notebook page.

- **Begin Writing What You Find Most Appetizing.** Start in the middle or at the end, wherever thoughts come easily to mind. As novelist Bill Downey observes, "Writers are allowed to have their dessert first."

- **State Your Purpose.** Set forth what you want to achieve: To tell a story? To explain something? To win a reader over to your ideas?

- **Slip into a Reader's Shoes.** Put yourself in your reader's place. Start writing what you'd like to find out from the paper.

- **Nutshell It.** Summarize the paper you want to write. Condense your ideas into one small, tight paragraph. Later you can expand each sentence until the meaning is clear and all points are adequately supported.

- **Shrink Your Immediate Job.** Break the writing task into small parts, and tackle only the first, perhaps just two paragraphs.

- **Seek a Provocative Title.** Write down a dozen possible titles for your paper. If one sounds strikingly good, don't let it go to waste!

- **Record Yourself.** Talk a first draft into a recorder or your voice mail. Play it back. Then write. Even if it is hard to transcribe your spoken words, this technique may set your mind in motion.
- **Speak Up.** On your feet, before an imaginary cheering crowd, spontaneously utter a first paragraph. Then — quick! — record it or write it out.
- **Take Short Breaks.** Even if you don't feel tired, take a break every half hour or so. Get up, walk around the room, stretch, or get a drink of water. Two or three minutes should be enough to refresh your mind.

Restarting

When you have to write a long or demanding essay that you can't finish in one sitting, you may return to it only to find yourself stalled. You crank your starter and nothing happens. Your engine seems reluctant to turn over. Try the following suggestions for getting back on the road.

- **Leave Hints for How to Continue.** If you're ready to quit, jot down what might come next or the first sentence of the next section. When you return, you will face not a blank wall but rich and suggestive graffiti.
- **Pause in Midstream.** Try breaking off in midsentence or midparagraph. Just leave a sentence trailing off into space, even if you know its closing words. When you return, you can start writing again immediately.
- **Repeat.** If the next sentence refuses to appear, simply recopy the last one until that shy creature emerges on the page.
- **Reread.** When you return to work, spend a few minutes rereading what you have already written or what you have planned.
- **Switch Instruments.** Do you compose on a laptop? Try longhand. Or drop your pen to type. Write on note cards or colored paper.
- **Change Activities.** When words won't come, turn to something quite different. Run, walk your dog, cook a meal, or nap. Or reward yourself — after you reach a certain point — with a call to a friend or a game. All the while, your unconscious mind will work on your writing task.

Paragraphing

An essay is written not in large, indigestible lumps but in *paragraphs* — small units, each more or less self-contained, each contributing some new idea in support of the essay's thesis. Writers dwell on one idea at a time, stating it, developing it, illustrating it with examples or a few facts — *showing* readers, with detailed evidence, exactly what they mean.

Paragraphs can be as short as one sentence or as long as a page. Sometimes length is governed by audience, purpose, or medium. Journalists expect newspaper readers to gobble up facts like popcorn, quickly skimming short one- or two-sentence paragraphs. College writers, in contrast, should assume their readers expect to read well-developed paragraphs.

When readers see a paragraph indentation, they interpret it as a pause, a chance for a deep breath. After that signpost, they expect you to concentrate on a new aspect of your thesis for the rest of that paragraph. This chapter gives you advice on guiding readers through your writing — using opening paragraphs to draw them in, topic sentences to focus and control body paragraphs, and concluding paragraphs to wrap up the discussion.

Using Topic Sentences

For an interactive Learning by Doing activity on identifying topic sentences, go to Ch. 14: **bedfordstmartins.com/concisebedguide**.

A *topic sentence* spells out the main idea of a paragraph in the body of an essay. It guides you as you write, and it hooks your readers as they discover what to expect and how to interpret the paragraph. As the topic sentence establishes the focus of the paragraph, it also relates the paragraph to the topic and thesis of the essay as a whole. (Much of the advice on topic sentences for paragraphs also extends to thesis statements for essays.) To convert an idea to a topic sentence, add your own slant, attitude, or point.

Main Idea   +   Slant or Attitude or Point   =   Topic Sentence

For more on thesis statements, see pp. 263–72.

How do you write a good topic sentence? Make it interesting, accurate, and limited. The more pointed and lively it is, the more it will interest readers. Even a dull, vague start is enlivened once you zero in on a specific point.

MAIN IDEA + SLANT	television + everything that's wrong with it
DULL START	There are many things wrong with television.
POINTED TOPIC SENTENCE	Of all the disappointing television programming, what I dislike most is melodramatic news.
¶ PLAN	Illustrate the point with two or three melodramatic news stories.

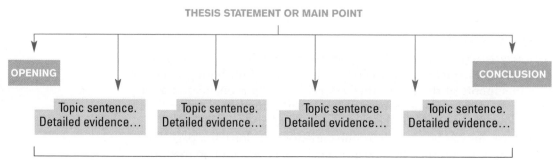

A topic sentence also should be an accurate guide to the rest of the paragraph so that readers expect just what the paragraph delivers.

INACCURATE GUIDE	All types of household emergencies can catch people off guard. [The paragraph covers steps for emergency preparedness — not the variety of emergencies.]
ACCURATE TOPIC SENTENCE	Although an emergency may not be a common event, emergency preparedness should be routine at home.
¶ PLAN	Explain how a household can prepare for an emergency with a medical kit, a well-stocked pantry, and a communication plan.

Finally, a topic sentence should be limited so you don't mislead or frustrate readers about what the paragraph covers.

MISLEADING	Seven factors have contributed to the increasing obesity of the average American. [The paragraph discusses only one — portion size.]
LIMITED TOPIC SENTENCE	Portion size is a major factor that contributes to the increasing obesity of average Americans.
¶ PLAN	Define healthy portion sizes, contrasting them with the large portions common in restaurants and in packaged foods.

Open with a Topic Sentence. Usually the topic sentence appears first in the paragraph, followed by sentences that clarify, illustrate, and support what it says. It is typically a statement but can sometimes be a question, alerting the reader to the topic without giving away the punchline. This example from "The Virtues of the Quiet Hero," Senator John McCain's essay about "honor, faith, and service," was presented on October 17, 2005, in the "This I Believe" series on National Public Radio's *All Things Considered*. Here, as in all the following examples, we have put the topic sentence in *italics*.

> *Years later, I saw an example of honor in the most surprising of places.* As a scared American prisoner of war in Vietnam, I was tied in torture ropes by my tormentors and left alone in an empty room to suffer through the night. Later in the evening, a guard I had never spoken to entered the room and silently loosened the ropes to relieve my suffering. Just before morning, that same guard came back and retightened the ropes before his less humanitarian comrades returned. He never said a word to me. Some months later on a Christmas morning, as I stood alone in the prison courtyard, that same guard walked up to me and stood next to me for a few moments. Then with his sandal, the guard drew a cross in the dirt. We stood wordlessly there for a minute or two, venerating the cross, until the guard rubbed it out and walked away.

This paragraph moves from the general to the specific. The topic sentence clearly states at the outset what the paragraph is about. The second sentence introduces the situation McCain recalls. Then the next half-dozen sentences supply two concrete, yet concise, illustrations of his central point.

Place a Topic Sentence near the Beginning. Sometimes the first sentence of a paragraph acts as a transition, linking what is to come with what has gone before. Then the *second* sentence might be the topic sentence as illustrated in the following paragraph from *Tim Gunn's Fashion Bible: The Fascinating History of Everything in Your Closet* by Tim Gunn with Ada Calhoun (New York: Gallery Books, 2012, p. 190). The paragraph immediately before this one summarizes how the early history of shoe design often tried to balance competing desires for modesty, alluring beauty, and practicality. This prior paragraph begins, "Modesty got the better of the shoe industry in the seventeenth century" and concludes, "It wasn't until the late 1930s that sling-backs and open-toed heels gave us another glimpse at the toes and heels."

> Heel height has fluctuated ever since, as have platforms. One goal of a high shoe is to elevate the wearer out of the muck. Before there was pavement (asphalt didn't even appear until 1824, in Paris), streets were very muddy. People often wore one kind of shoe indoors, like a satin slipper, and another outside, perhaps with some kind of overshoe. One type of overshoe was called pattens, which were made of leather, wood, or iron, and lifted the wearer up a couple of inches or more from the sidewalk to protect the sole of the shoe from grime. Men and women wore these from the fourteenth- to the mid-nineteenth century, when street conditions started to become slightly less disgusting.

End with a Topic Sentence. Occasionally a writer, trying to persuade the reader to agree, piles detail on detail. Then, with a dramatic flourish, the writer *concludes* with the topic sentence, as student Heidi Kessler does.

> A fourteen-year-old writes to an advice columnist in my hometown newspaper that she has "done it" lots of times and sex is "no big deal." At the neighborhood clinic where my aunt works, a hardened sixteen-year-old requests her third abortion. A girl-child I know has two children of her own, but no husband. A college student in my dorm now finds herself sterile from a "social disease" picked up during casual sexual encounters. Multiply these examples by thousands. *It seems clear to me that women, who fought so hard for sexual freedom equal to that of men, have emerged from the battle not as joyous free spirits but as the sexual revolution's walking wounded.*

This paragraph moves from particular to general — from four examples about individuals to one large statement about American women. By the time you finish, you might be ready to accept the paragraph's conclusion.

Imply a Topic Sentence. It is also possible to find a perfectly unified, well-organized paragraph that has no topic sentence at all, like the following from "New York" (*Esquire* July 1960) by Gay Talese:

> Each afternoon in New York a rather seedy saxophone player, his cheeks blown out like a spinnaker, stands on the sidewalk playing "Danny Boy" in such a sad, sensitive way that he soon has half the neighborhood peeking out of windows tossing nickels, dimes, and quarters at his feet. Some of the coins roll under parked cars, but most of them are caught in his outstretched hand. The saxophone player is a street musician named Joe Gabler; for the past thirty years he has serenaded every block in New York and has sometimes been tossed as much as $100 a day in coins. He is also hit with buckets of water, empty beer cans and eggs, and chased by wild dogs. He is believed to be the last of New York's ancient street musicians.

No one sentence neatly sums up the writer's idea. Like most effective paragraphs that do not state a topic sentence, this one contains something just as good — a *topic idea*. The author doesn't wander aimlessly. He knows exactly what he wants to achieve — a description of how the famous Joe Gabler plies his trade. Because Talese keeps this purpose firmly in mind, the main point — that Gabler meets both reward and abuse — is clear to the reader as well.

Learning by Doing 🎬 Shaping Topic Sentences

In a small group, answer these questions about each topic sentence below:

> Will it catch readers' attention? Is it accurate? Is it limited?
> How might you develop the idea in the rest of the paragraph?
> Can you improve it?

1. Television commercials stereotype people.
2. Living away from home for the first time is hard.
3. It's good for a child to have a pet.
4. A flea market is a good place to buy jewelry.
5. Pollution should be controlled.
6. Everybody should recycle wastes.

Writing an Opening

Even writers with something to say may find it hard to begin. Often they are so intent on a brilliant opening that they freeze. They forget even the essentials — set up the topic, stick to what's relevant, and establish a thesis. If you feel like a deer paralyzed by headlights, try these ways of opening:

- Start with your thesis statement, with or without a full opening paragraph. Fill in the rest later.
- Write your thesis statement — the one you planned or one you'd now like to develop — in the middle of a page. Go back to the top, and concisely add the background a reader needs to see where you're going.
- Write a long beginning for your first draft; then cut it down to the most dramatic, exciting, or interesting essentials.
- Simply set down words — any words — on paper, without trying to write an arresting opening. Rewrite later.
- Write the first paragraph last, after you know where your essay goes.
- Move your conclusion to the beginning, and write a new ending.
- Write a summary for yourself and your readers.

Your opening should intrigue readers — engaging their minds and hearts, exciting their curiosity, drawing them into the world set forth in your writing.

DISCOVERY CHECKLIST

- ☐ What vital background might readers need?
- ☐ What general situation might help you narrow down to your point?
- ☐ What facts or statistics might make your issue compelling?
- ☐ What powerful anecdote or incident might introduce your point?
- ☐ What striking example or comparison would engage a reader?
- ☐ What question will your thesis — and your essay — answer?
- ☐ What lively quotation would set the scene for your essay?
- ☐ What assertion or claim might be the necessary prelude for your essay?
- ☐ What points should you preview to prepare a reader for what will come?
- ☐ What would compel someone to keep on reading?

Begin with a Story. Often a simple anecdote can capture your readers' interest and thus serve as a good beginning. Here is how Nicholas Kulish opens his essay "Guy Walks into a Bar" (*New York Times* 5 Feb. 2006):

> Recently my friend Brandon and I walked along Atlantic Avenue in Brooklyn looking for a place to watch a football game and to quench our thirst for a cold brew. I pushed open the door and we were headed for a pair of empty stools when we both stopped cold. The bar was packed with under-age patrons.

Most of us, after an anecdote, want to read on. What will the writer say next? How does the anecdote launch the essay? Here, Kulish sets the stage for his objections to parents bringing babies and toddlers to bars.

Comment on a Topic or Position. Sometimes a writer expands on a topic, bringing in vital details, as David Morris does to open his article "Rootlessness" (*Utne Reader* May/June 1990):

> Americans are a rootless people. Each year one in six of us changes residences; one in four changes jobs. We see nothing troubling in these statistics. For most of us, they merely reflect the restless energy that made America great. A nation of immigrants, unsurprisingly, celebrates those willing to pick up stakes and move on: the frontiersman, the cowboy, the entrepreneur, the corporate raider.

After stating his point baldly, Morris supplies statistics to support his contention and briefly explains the phenomenon. This same strategy can be used to present a controversial opinion, then back it up with examples.

Ask a Question. An essay can begin with a question and answer, as James H. Austin begins "Four Kinds of Chance," in *Chase, Chance, and Creativity: The Lucky Art of Novelty* (New York: Columbia UP, 1978):

> What is chance? Dictionaries define it as something fortuitous that happens unpredictably without discernible human intention. Chance is unintentional and capricious, but we needn't conclude that chance is immune from human intervention. Indeed, chance plays several distinct roles when humans react creatively with one another and with their environment.

Beginning to answer the question in the first paragraph leads readers to expect the rest of the essay to continue the answer.

End with the Thesis Statement. Opening paragraphs often end by stating the essay's main point. After capturing readers' attention with an anecdote, gripping details, or examples, you lead readers in exactly the direction your essay goes. In response to the question "Should Washington stem the tide of both legal and illegal immigration?" ("Symposium."

For more on thesis statements, see pp. 263–72.

Insight on the News 11 Mar. 2002), Daniel T. Griswold uses this strategy to begin his answer:

> Immigration always has been controversial in the United States. More than two centuries ago, Benjamin Franklin worried that too many German immigrants would swamp America's predominantly British culture. In the mid-1800s, Irish immigrants were scorned as lazy drunks, not to mention Roman Catholics. At the turn of the century a wave of "new immigrants" — Poles, Italians, Russian Jews — were believed to be too different ever to assimilate into American life. *Today the same fears are raised about immigrants from Latin America and Asia, but current critics of immigration are as wrong as their counterparts were in previous eras.*

Writing a Conclusion

The final paragraphs of an essay linger longest for readers, as in E. B. White's "Once More to the Lake" from *One Man's Meat* (Gardiner, ME: Tilbury House, 1941). White describes his return with his young son to a vacation spot he had loved as a child. As the essay ends in an unforgettable image, he realizes the inevitable passing of generations.

> When the others went swimming my son said he was going in, too. He pulled his dripping trunks from the line where they had hung all through the shower and wrung them out. Languidly, and with no thought of going in, I watched him, his hard little body, skinny and bare, saw him wince slightly as he pulled up around his vitals the small, soggy, icy garment. As he buckled the swollen belt, suddenly my groin felt the chill of death.

White's classic ending opens with a sentence that points back to the previous paragraph as it also looks ahead. Then White leads us quickly to his final, chilling insight. And then he stops.

It's easy to say what *not* to do at the end of an essay: don't leave your readers half expecting you to go on. Don't restate all you've just said. Don't introduce a brand-new topic that leads away from your point. And don't signal that the end is near with an obvious phrase like "As I have said." For some answers to "How *do* you write an ending, then?" try this checklist.

DISCOVERY CHECKLIST

☐ What restatement of your thesis would give readers satisfying closure?

☐ What provocative implications of your thesis might answer "What now?" or "What's the significance of what I've said?"

☐ What snappy quotation or statement would wrap up your point?

☐ What closing facts or statistics might confirm the merit of your point?

☐ What final anecdote, incident, or example might round out your ideas?

☐ What question has your essay answered?

☐ What assertion or claim might you want to restate?

☐ What summary might help a reader pull together what you've said?

☐ What would make a reader sorry to finish such a satisfying essay?

End with a Quotation. An apt quotation can neatly round out an essay, as literary critic Malcolm Cowley shows in *The View from Eighty* (New York: Viking, 1980), his discussion of the pitfalls and compensations of old age.

For more on punctuating quotations, see C3 (pp. A-55–A-56) in the Quick Editing Guide.

> "Eighty years old!" the great Catholic poet Paul Claudel wrote in his journal. "No eyes left, no ears, no teeth, no legs, no wind! And when all is said and done, how astonishingly well one does without them!"

State or Restate Your Thesis. In a sharp criticism of American schools, humorist Russell Baker in "School vs. Education" ends by stating his main point, that schools do not educate.

> Afterward, the former student's destiny fulfilled, his life rich with Oriental carpets, rare porcelain, and full bank accounts, he may one day find himself with the leisure and the inclination to open a book with a curious mind, and start to become educated.

End with a Brief Emphatic Sentence. For an essay that traces causes or effects, evaluates, or argues, a pointed concluding thought can reinforce your main idea. If you use Twitter, sending messages limited to 140 characters, apply those skills in a paragraph. Stick to academic language, but craft a concise, pointed sentence, maybe with a twist. In "Don't Mess with Mother" (*Newsweek* 19 Sept. 2005), Anna Quindlen ends her essay about the environmental challenges of post-Katrina New Orleans this way:

> New Orleans will be rebuilt, but rebuilt how? In the heedless, grasping fashion in which so much of this country has been built over the past fifty years, which has led to a continuous loop of floods, fires and filth in the air and water? Or could the new New Orleans be the first city of a new era, in which the demands of development and commerce are carefully balanced against the good of the land and, in the long run, the good of its people? We have been crummy stewards of the Earth, with a sense of knee-jerk entitlement that tells us there is always more where this came from.
>   There isn't.

Stop When the Story Is Over. Even a quiet ending can be effective, as long as it signals clearly that the essay is finished. Journalist Martin Gansberg simply stops when the story is over in his true account of the fatal stabbing of a young woman, Kitty Genovese, in full view of residents of a Queens, New York, apartment house. The residents, unwilling to become involved, did nothing to interfere. Here is the last paragraph of "Thirty-eight Who Saw Murder Didn't Call Police" (*New York Times* 17 Mar. 1964):

> It was 4:25 A.M. when the ambulance arrived to take the body of Miss Genovese. It drove off. "Then," a solemn police detective said, "the people came out."

Learning by Doing 🎥 Opening and Concluding

Openings and conclusions frame an essay, contributing to the unity of the whole. The opening sets up the topic and main idea; the conclusion reaffirms the thesis and rounds off the ideas. Discuss the following with your classmates.

1. Here are two possible opening paragraphs from a student essay on the importance of teaching children how to swim.

   A. Humans inhabit a world made up of over 70 percent water. In addition to these great bodies of water, we have built millions of swimming pools for sports and leisure activities. At one time or another most people will be faced with either the danger of drowning or the challenge of aquatic recreation. For these reasons, it is essential that we learn to swim. Being a competitive swimmer and a swimming instructor, I fully realize the importance of knowing how to swim.

   B. Four-year-old Carl, curious like most children, last spring ventured out onto his pool patio. He fell into the pool and, not knowing how to swim, helplessly sank to the bottom. Minutes later his uncle found the child and brought him to the surface. Because Carl had no pulse, his uncle administered CPR until the paramedics arrived. Eventually the child was revived. During his stay in the hospital, his mother signed him up for beginning swimming classes. Carl was a lucky one. Unlike thousands of other children and adults, he got a second chance.

   1. Which introduction is more effective? Why?
   2. What would the body of this essay consist of? What kinds of evidence would be included?
   3. Write a suitable conclusion for this essay.

2. If you were to read each of the following introductions from professional essays, would you want to read the entire essay? Why?

   A. During my ninth hour underground, as I scrambled up a slanting tunnel through the powdered gypsum, Rick Bridges turned to me and said, "You know, this whole area was just discovered Tuesday." (David Roberts, "Caving Comes into Its Golden Age: A New Mexico Marvel," *Smithsonian* Nov. 1988: 52)

B. From the batting average on the back of a George Brett baseball card to the interest rate fluctuations that determine whether the economy grows or stagnates, Americans are fascinated by statistics. (Stephen E. Nordlinger, "By the Numbers," *St. Petersburg Times* 6 Nov. 1988: 11)

C. "What does it look like under there?"

It was always this question back then, always the same pattern of hello and what's your name, what happened to your eye and what's under there. (Natalie Kusz, "Waiting for a Glass Eye," *Road Song* [New York: Farrar, 1990], rpt. in *Harper's* Nov. 1990)

3. How effective are these introductions and conclusions from student essays? Could they be improved? If so, how? If they are satisfactory, explain why. What would be a catchy yet informative title for each essay?

A. Recently a friend down from New York astonished me with stories of several people infected—some with AIDS—by stepping on needles washed up on the New Jersey beaches. This is just one incident of pollution, a devastating problem in our society today. Pollution is increasing in our world because of greed, apathy, and Congress's inability to control this problem. . . .

Wouldn't it be nice to have a pollution-free world without medical wastes floating in the water and washing up on our beaches? Without cars and power plants spewing greenhouse gases? With every corporation abiding by the laws set by Congress? In the future we can have a pollution-free world, but it is going to take the cooperation of everyone, including Congress, to ensure our survival on this Planet Earth.

B. The divorce rate rose 700 percent in the last century and continues to rise. More than one out of every two couples who are married end up divorcing. Over one million children a year are affected by divorce in the family. From these statistics it is clear that one of the greatest problems concerning the family today is divorce and the adverse effects it has on our society. . . .

Divorce causes problems that change people for life. The number of divorces will continue to exceed the 700 percent figure unless married couples learn to communicate, to accept their mates unconditionally, and to sacrificially give of themselves.

4. Using a topic that you generated in Chapter 12, write at least three different introductions with conclusions. Ask classmates which is most effective.

Adding Cues and Connections

Effective writing proceeds in some sensible order, each sentence following naturally from the one before it. Yet even well-organized prose can be hard to read unless it is *coherent* and smoothly integrates its elements. Readers need cues and connections—devices to tie together words in a sentence, sentences in a paragraph, paragraphs in an essay.

For an interactive Learning by Doing activity on identifying transitions, go to Ch. 14: **bedfordstmartins.com /concisebedguide**.

Add Transitional Words and Sentences. Many words and phrases specify connections between or within sentences and paragraphs. In fact, you use transitions every day as cues or signals to help others follow your train of thought. For example, you might say to a friend, "Well, *on the one hand,* a second job would help me save money for tuition. *On the other hand,* I'd have less time to study." But some writers rush through, omitting links between thoughts or mistakenly assuming that connections they see will automatically be clear to readers. Often just a word, phrase, or sentence of transition inserted in the right place transforms a disconnected passage into a coherent one. In the chart on page 297, *transitional markers* are grouped by purpose or the kind of relation or connection they establish.

Occasionally a whole sentence serves as a transition. The opening of one paragraph may hark back to the last one while revealing a new or narrower direction. The next excerpt came from "Preservation Basics: Why Preserve Film?" a Web page of the National Film Preservation Foundation (NFPF) at filmpreservation.org. The first paragraph introduces the organization's mission; the next two each open with transitional sentences (italics ours) that introduce major challenges to that mission.

> Since Thomas Edison's invention of the kinetoscope in 1893, Americans have traveled the world using motion pictures to tell stories, document traditions, and capture current events. Their work stands as the collective memory of the first century witnessed by the moving image. By saving and sharing these motion pictures, we can illuminate our common heritage with a power and immediacy unique to film.
>
> *Preservationists are working against the clock.* Made on perishable plastic, film decays within years if not properly stored.
>
> *Already the losses are high.* The Library of Congress has documented that fewer than 20 percent of U.S. feature films from the 1920s survive in complete form in American archives; of the American features produced before 1950, only half still exist. For shorts, documentaries, and independently produced works, we have no way of knowing how much has been lost.

The first paragraph establishes the value of "saving and sharing" the American film legacy. The next two paragraphs use key words related to preservation and its absence (*perishable, decays, losses, lost*) to clarify that what follows builds on what has gone before. Each also opens with a short, dramatic transition to one of the major problems: time and existing loss.

Supply Transition Paragraphs. Transitions may be even longer than sentences. In a long and complicated essay, moving clearly from one idea to the next will sometimes require a short paragraph of transition.

Common Transitions

TO MARK TIME	then, soon, first, second, next, recently, the following day, in a little while, meanwhile, after, later, in the past, finally
TO MARK PLACE OR DIRECTION	in the distance, close by, near, far away, above, below, to the right, on the other side, opposite, to the west, next door
TO SUMMARIZE OR RESTATE	in other words, to put it another way, in brief, in simpler terms, on the whole, in fact, in a word, to sum up, in short, in conclusion, to conclude, therefore
TO RELATE CAUSE AND EFFECT OR RESULT	therefore, accordingly, hence, thus, for, so, consequently, as a result, because of, due to, eventually, inevitably
TO ADD OR AMPLIFY OR LIST	and, also, too, besides, as well, moreover, in addition, furthermore, in effect, second, in the second place, again, next
TO COMPARE	similarly, likewise, in like manner, in the same way
TO CONCEDE	whereas, on the other hand, with that in mind, still, and yet, even so, in spite of, despite, at least, of course, no doubt, even though
TO CONTRAST	on the other hand, but, or, however, unlike, nevertheless, on the contrary, conversely, in contrast, instead, counter to
TO INDICATE PURPOSE	to this end, for this purpose, with this aim
TO EXPRESS CONDITION	although, though
TO GIVE EXAMPLES OR SPECIFY	for example, for instance, in this case, in particular, to illustrate
TO QUALIFY	for the most part, by and large, with few exceptions, mainly, in most cases, generally, some, sometimes, typically, frequently, rarely
TO EMPHASIZE	it is true, truly, indeed, of course, to be sure, obviously, without doubt, evidently, clearly, understandably

So far, the physical and psychological effects of driving nonstop for hundreds of miles seem clear. The next consideration is why drivers do this. What causes people to become addicted to their steering wheels?

Use a transition paragraph only when you sense that your readers might get lost if you don't patiently lead them by the hand. If your essay is short, one question or statement beginning a new paragraph will be enough.

A transition paragraph also can help you move between one branch of argument and your main trunk or between a digression and your main direction. In this excerpt from *The Film Preservation Guide: The Basics for Archives, Libraries, and Museums* (San Francisco: NFPF, 2004; http://www.filmpreservation.org/userfiles/image/PDFs/fpg_3.pdf), the writer introduces the importance of inspecting film and devotes the next paragraph to a digression—referring readers to an inspection sheet in the appendix.

> Inspection is the single most important way to date a film, identify its technical characteristics, and detect damage and decay. Much can be learned by examining your film carefully, from start to finish.
>
> A standardized inspection work sheet (see appendix B) lists things to check and helps organize notes. This type of written report is the foundation for future preservation actions. Collecting the information during inspection will help you make informed decisions and enable you to document any changes in film condition over time.
>
> Signs of decay and damage may vary across the length of the film. . . .

The second paragraph acts as a transition, guiding readers to specialized information in the appendix and then drawing them back to the overall purpose of inspection: assessing the extent of damage to a film.

Select Repetition. Another way to clarify the relationship between two sentences, paragraphs, or ideas is to repeat a key word or phrase. Such purposeful repetition almost guarantees that readers will understand how all the parts of a passage fit together. Note the word *anger* in the following paragraph (italics ours) from *Of Woman Born* (New York: Norton, 1976), poet Adrienne Rich's exploration of her relationship with her mother.

> And I know there must be deep reservoirs of *anger* in her; every mother has known overwhelming, unacceptable *anger* at her children. When I think of the conditions under which my mother became a mother, the impossible expectations, my father's distaste for pregnant women, his hatred of all that he could not control, my *anger* at her dissolves into grief and *anger* for her, and then dissolves back again into *anger* at her: the ancient, unpurged *anger* of the child.

Strengthen Pronouns. Because they always refer back to nouns or other pronouns, pronouns serve as transitions by making readers refer back as well. Note how certain pronouns (in italics) hold together the following paragraph from "Misunderstood Michelle" by columnist Ellen Goodman in *At Large* (New York: Summit Books, 1981):

> I have two friends who moved in together many years ago. *He* looked upon this step as a trial marriage. *She* looked upon it as, well, moving in together. *He* was sure that in a matter of time, after *they* had built up trust and confidence, *she* would agree that marriage was the next logical step. *She*, on the other hand, was thrilled that here at last was a man *who* would never push *her* back to the altar.

The paragraph uses other transitions, too: time markers (*many years ago, in a matter of time, after*), *on the other hand* to show a contrast, and repetition of words related to marriage (*trial marriage, marriage, the altar*). All serve the main purpose of transitions — keeping readers on track.

Learning by Doing Identifying Transitions

Go over one of the papers you have already written for this course, and circle all the transitional devices you can detect. Then exchange papers with a classmate. Can you find additional transitions in the other's paper? Or would you recommend transitions where there aren't any?

Learning by Doing Reflecting on Drafting

Think about how you wrote your last successful draft. What did you do? How did you shape your paragraphs? How did you manage transitions to guide readers? What was your secret for success? Write out drafting directions for yourself — ready for your next assignment. Compare directions with a classmate or small group, and exchange any useful advice.

15 Strategies for Revising and Editing

Good writing is rewriting. In this chapter we provide strategies for revising and editing—ways to rethink muddy ideas and emphasize important ones, to rephrase obscure passages and restructure garbled sentences. Our advice applies not only to rewriting whole essays but also to rewriting, editing, and proofreading sentences and paragraphs.

Re-viewing and Revising

Revision means "seeing again"—discovering again, conceiving again, shaping again. It may occur at any and all stages of the writing process, and most writers do a lot of it. *Macro revising* is making large, global, or fundamental changes that affect the overall direction or impact of writing—its

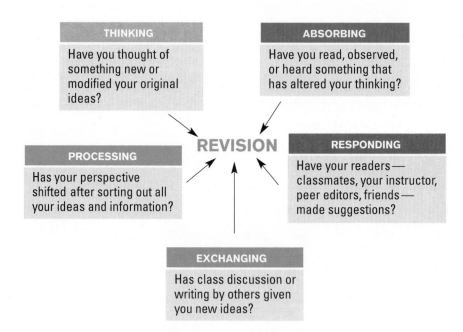

THINKING
Have you thought of something new or modified your original ideas?

ABSORBING
Have you read, observed, or heard something that has altered your thinking?

REVISION

PROCESSING
Has your perspective shifted after sorting out all your ideas and information?

RESPONDING
Have your readers— classmates, your instructor, peer editors, friends— made suggestions?

EXCHANGING
Has class discussion or writing by others given you new ideas?

purpose, organization, or audience. Its companion is *micro revising,* paying attention to sentences, words, punctuation, and grammar—including ways to create emphasis and eliminate wordiness.

MACRO REVISING	MICRO REVISING
• **PURPOSE:** Have you refined what you want to accomplish? • **THESIS:** Could you state your main point more accurately? • **AUDIENCE:** Should you address your readers differently? • **STRUCTURE:** Should you reorganize any part of your writing? • **SUPPORT:** Do you need to add, drop, or rework your support?	• **EMPHASIS:** Can you position your ideas more effectively? • **CONCISENESS:** Can you spot extra words that you might cut? • **CLARITY:** Can you make any sentences and words clearer?

Revising for Purpose and Thesis

When you revise for purpose, you make sure that your writing accomplishes what you want it to do. If your goal is to create an interesting profile of a person, have you done so? If you want to persuade your readers to take a certain course of action, have you succeeded? When your project has evolved or your assignment grown clearer to you, the purpose of your final essay may differ from your purpose when you began. To revise for purpose, try to step back and see your writing as other readers will.

Concentrate on what's actually in your paper, not what you assume is there. Create a thesis sentence (if you haven't), or revise your working thesis statement (if you've developed one). Reconsider how it is worded:

For more on stating and improving a working thesis, see pp. 263–72.

- Is it stated exactly in concise yet detailed language?
- Is it focused on only one main idea?
- Is it stated positively rather than negatively?
- Is it limited to a demonstrable statement?

Then consider how accurately your thesis now represents your main idea:

- Does each part of your essay directly relate to your thesis?
- Does each part of your essay develop and support your thesis?
- Does your essay deliver everything your thesis promises?

If you find unrelated or contradictory passages, you have several options: revise the thesis, revise the essay, or revise both.

If your idea has deepened, your topic become more complex, or your essay developed along new lines, refine or expand your thesis accordingly.

WORKING THESIS	The *Herald*'s coverage of the Senate elections was more thorough than the *Courier*'s.
REVISED THESIS	The *Herald*'s coverage of the Senate elections was less timely but more thorough and more impartial than the *Courier*'s.
WORKING THESIS	As the roles of men and women have changed in our society, old-fashioned formal courtesy has declined.
REVISED THESIS	As the roles of men and women have changed in our society, old-fashioned formal courtesy has declined not only toward women but also toward men.

REVISION CHECKLIST

☐ Do you know exactly what you want your essay to accomplish? Can you put it in one sentence: "In this paper I want to . . ."?

☐ Is your thesis stated outright in the essay? If not, have you provided clues so that your readers will know precisely what it is?

☐ Does every part of the essay work to achieve the same goal?

☐ Have you tried to do too much? Does your coverage seem too thin? If so, how might you reduce the scope of your thesis and essay?

☐ Does your essay say all that needs to be said? Is everything—ideas, connections, supporting evidence—on paper, not just in your head?

☐ In writing the essay, have you changed your mind, rethought your assumptions, made a discovery? Does anything now need to be recast?

☐ Have you developed enough evidence? Is it clear and convincing?

For an interactive Learning by Doing activity on editing sentences, go to Ch. 15: **bedfordstmartins.com /concisebedguide**.

Revising for Audience

What works with one audience can fall flat with another. Your organization, selection of details, word choice, and tone all affect your particular readers. Visualize one of them poring over the essay, reacting to what you have written. What expressions do you see on that reader's face? Where does he or she have trouble understanding? Where have you hit the mark?

☐ Who will read this essay?

☐ Will your readers think you have told them something worth knowing?

☐ Are there any places where readers might fall asleep? If so, can you shorten, delete, or liven up such passages?

☐ Does the opening of the essay mislead your readers by promising something that the essay never delivers?

☐ Do you unfold each idea in enough detail to make it clear and interesting?

☐ Have you anticipated questions your audience might ask?

☐ Where might readers raise objections? How might you answer them?

☐ Have you used any specialized or technical language that your readers might not understand? If so, have you worked in brief definitions?

☐ What is your attitude toward your audience? Are you chummy, angry, superior, apologetic, preachy? Should you revise to improve your attitude?

Revising for Structure and Support

When you revise for structure and support, you make sure that the order of your ideas, your selection of supporting material, and its arrangement are as effective as possible. You may have all the ingredients of a successful essay — but they may be a confusing mess.

In a well-structured essay, each paragraph, sentence, and phrase serves a clear function. Are your opening and closing paragraphs relevant, concise, and interesting? Is everything in each paragraph on the same topic? Are all ideas adequately developed? Are the paragraphs arranged in the best possible order? Finally, do you lead readers from one idea to the next with clear and painless transitions?

For more on paragraphs, topic sentences, and transitions, see Ch. 14.

An outline can help you discover what you've succeeded in getting on paper. Find the topic sentence of each paragraph in your draft (or create one, if necessary), and list them in order. Label the sentences *I., II., A., B.,* and so on, to show the logical relationships of ideas. Do the same with the supporting details under each topic sentence, labeling them also with letters and numbers and indenting appropriately. Now look at the outline. Does it make sense on its own, without the essay to explain it? Would a different order or arrangement be more effective? Do any sections look thin and need more evidence? Are the connections between parts on paper, not just in your head? Maybe too many ideas are jammed into too few paragraphs. Maybe

For more on using outlining for planning, see pp. 275–83.

you need more specific details and examples—or stronger ones. Strengthen the outline and then rewrite to follow it.

REVISION CHECKLIST

- ☐ Does your introduction set up the whole essay? Does it both grab readers' attention and hint at what is to follow?

- ☐ Does the essay fulfill all that you promise in your opening?

- ☐ Would any later passage make a better beginning?

- ☐ Is your thesis clear early in the essay? If explicit, is it positioned prominently?

- ☐ Do the paragraph breaks seem logical?

- ☐ Is the main idea of each paragraph clear? Is it stated in a topic sentence?

- ☐ Is the main idea of each paragraph fully developed? Where might you need more or better evidence? Should you omit or move any stray bits?

- ☐ Is each detail or piece of evidence relevant to the topic sentence of the paragraph and the main point of the essay?

- ☐ Would any paragraphs make more sense in a different order?

- ☐ Does everything follow clearly? Does one point smoothly lead to the next? Would transitions help make the connections clearer?

- ☐ Does the conclusion follow logically or seem tacked on?

Learning by Doing 🎥 Tackling Macro Revision

Select a draft that would benefit from revision. Then, based on your sense of its greatest need, choose one of the revision checklists to guide a first revision. Let the draft sit for a while. Then work with one of the remaining checklists.

Working with a Peer Editor

There's no substitute for having someone else read your draft. Whether you are writing for an audience of classmates or for a different group (the town council or readers of *Time*), having a classmate go over your essay is a worthwhile revision strategy. To gain all you can as a writer from a peer review, you need to play an active part:

- ■ Ask your reader questions. (See page 305 for ideas.) Or bring a "Dear Editor" letter or memo, written ahead, to your meeting.

Questions for a Peer Editor

First Questions for a Peer Editor

What is your first reaction to this paper?

What is this writer trying to tell you?

What are this paper's greatest strengths?

Does it have any major weaknesses?

What one change would most improve the paper?

Questions on Meaning

Do you understand everything? Is the draft missing any information that you need to know?

Does this paper tell you anything you didn't know before?

Is the writer trying to cover too much territory? Too little?

Does any point need to be more fully explained or illustrated?

When you come to the end, has the paper delivered what it promised?

Could this paper use a down-to-the-ground revision?

Questions on Organization

Has the writer begun in a way that grabs your interest and quickly draws you into the paper's main idea? Or can you find a better beginning at some later point?

Does the paper have one main idea, or does it juggle more than one?

Would the main idea stand out better if anything were removed or added?

Might the ideas in the paper be more effectively arranged? Do any ideas belong together that now seem too far apart?

Can you follow the ideas easily? Are transitions needed? If so, where?

Does the writer keep to one point of view—one angle of seeing?

Does the ending seem deliberate, as if the writer meant to conclude, not just run out of gas? How might the writer strengthen the conclusion?

Questions on Writing Strategies

Do you feel that this paper addresses you personally?

Do you dislike or object to any statement the writer makes or any wording the writer uses? Is the problem word choice, tone, or inadequate support to convince you? Should the writer keep or change this part?

Does the draft contain anything that distracts you or seems unnecessary?

Do you get bored at any point? How might the writer keep you reading?

Is the language of this paper too lofty and abstract? If so, where does the writer need to come down to earth and get specific?

Do you understand all the words used? Do any specialized words need clearer definitions?

- Be open to new ideas — for focus, organization, or details.
- Use what's helpful, but trust yourself as the writer.

Be a helpful peer editor: offer honest, intelligent feedback, not judgment.

See specific checklists in the "Revising and Editing" sections in Chs. 4 to 9.

- Look at the big picture: purpose, focus, thesis, clarity, coherence, organization, support.
- When you spot strengths or weaknesses, be specific: note examples.
- Answer the writer's questions, and also use the questions supplied throughout this book to concentrate on essentials, not details.

Meeting with Your Instructor

Prepare for your conference on a draft as you prepare for a peer review. Reread your paper; then write out your questions, concerns, or current revision plans. Whether you are meeting face-to-face, online, or by audio or video phone, arrive on time. Even if you feel shy or anxious, remember that you are working with an experienced reader who wants to help you improve your writing.

- If you already have received comments from your instructor, ask about anything you can't read, don't understand, or can't figure out how to do.
- If you are unsure about comments from peers, get your instructor's view.
- If you have a revision plan, ask for suggestions or priorities.
- If more questions arise after your conference, especially about comments on a draft returned there, follow up with a call, e-mail message, question after class, or second conference (as your instructor prefers).

Decoding Your Instructor's Comments

Many instructors favor two kinds of comments:

- Summary comments — sentences on your first or last page — that may compliment strengths, identify recurring issues, acknowledge changes between drafts, make broad suggestions, or end with a grade
- Specific comments — brief notes or questions added in the margins — that typically pinpoint issues in the text

Although brief comments may seem like cryptic code or shorthand, they usually rely on key words to note common, recurring problems that probably are discussed in class and related to course criteria. They also may act as reminders, identifying issues that your instructor expects you to look up in your book and solve. A simple analysis — tallying up the repeated comments in one paper or several — can quickly help you set priorities for revision and editing. Some sample comments follow with translations, but turn to your instructor if you need a specific explanation.

COMMENTS ON PURPOSE	Thesis? Vague Broad Clarify What's your point? So? So what?
POSSIBLE TRANSLATION	You need to state your thesis more clearly and directly so that a reader knows what matters. Concentrate on rewording so that your main idea is plain.
COMMENTS ON ORGANIZATION	Hard to follow Logic? Sequence? Add transitions? Jumpy
POSSIBLE TRANSLATION	You need to organize more logically so your paper is easy for a reader to follow without jumping from point to point. Add transitions or other cues to guide a reader.
COMMENTS ON SENTENCES AND WORDS	Unclear Clarify Awk Repetition Too informal
POSSIBLE TRANSLATION	You need to make your sentence or your wording easier to read and clearer. Rework awkward passages, reduce repetition, and stick to academic language.
COMMENTS ON EVIDENCE	Specify Focus Narrow down Develop more Seems thin
POSSIBLE TRANSLATION	You need to provide more concrete evidence or explain the relevance or nature of your evidence more clearly. Check that you support each main point with plenty of pertinent and compelling evidence.
COMMENTS ON SOURCES	Likely opponents? Source? Add quotation marks? Too many quotes Summarize? Synthesize? Launch source?
POSSIBLE TRANSLATION	You need to add sources that represent views other than your own. You include wording or ideas that sound like a source, not like you, so your quotation marks or citation might be missing. Instead of tossing in quotations, use your critical thinking skills to sum up ideas, relate them to each other, and introduce them more effectively.
COMMENTS ON CITATIONS	Cite? Author? Page? MLA? APA?
POSSIBLE TRANSLATION	Add missing source citations in your text and use the expected academic format to present them.
COMMENTS ON FINAL LIST OF SOURCES	MLA? APA? Comma? Period? Cap? Space?
POSSIBLE TRANSLATION	Your entries do not follow the expected format. Check the model entries in this book. Look for the presence, absence, or placement of the specific detail noted.

Revising for Emphasis, Conciseness, and Clarity

After you've revised for the large issues in your draft — purpose, thesis, audience, structure, and support — you're ready to turn your attention to micro revising. Now is the time to look at your language, to emphasize what matters most, and to communicate it concisely and clearly.

Stressing What Counts

An effective writer decides what matters most and shines a bright light on it using the most emphatic positions in an essay, a paragraph, or a sentence — the beginning and the end.

Stating It First. In an essay, you might start with what matters most. For an economics paper on import quotas (such as the number of foreign cars allowed into a country), student Donna Waite summed up her conclusion.

> Although an import quota has many effects, both for the nation imposing the quota and for the nation whose industries must suffer from it, I believe that the most important effect is generally felt at home. A native industry gains a chance to thrive in a marketplace of lessened competition.

To take a stand or make a proposal, you might open with your position.

> Our state's antiquated system of justices of the peace is inefficient.

> The United States should orbit a human observer around Mars.

In a single sentence, as in an essay, you can stress things at the start. Consider the following unemphatic sentence:

> When Congress debates the Hall-Hayes Act removing existing protections for endangered species, as now seems likely to occur on May 12, it will be a considerable misfortune if this bill should pass, since the extinction of many rare birds and animals would certainly result.

The debate and its probable timing consume the start of the sentence. Here's a better use of this emphatic position:

> The extinction of many rare birds and animals would certainly follow passage of the Hall-Hayes Act.

Now the writer stresses what he most fears — the dire consequences of the act. (A later sentence might add the date and his opinion about passage.)

Stating It Last. To place an idea last can throw weight on it. Emphatic order, proceeding from least important to most, is dramatic: it builds up and up. In a paper on import quotas, however, a dramatic buildup might look contrived. Still, in an essay on how city parks lure visitors to the city, the thesis sentence—summing up the point of the essay—might stand at the very end: "For the urban core, improved parks could bring about a new era of prosperity." Giving evidence first and leading up to the thesis at the end is particularly effective in editorials and informal persuasive essays.

A sentence that uses climactic order, suspending its point until the end, is a *periodic* sentence as novelist Julian Green illustrates.

> Amid chaos of illusions into which we are cast headlong, there is one thing that stands out as true, and that is—love.

Cutting and Whittling

Like pea pickers who throw out dirt and pebbles, good writers remove needless words that clog their prose. One of the chief joys of revising is to watch 200 paunchy words shrink to a svelte 150. To see how saving words helps, let's look at some strategies for reducing wordiness.

Cut the Fanfare. Why bother to announce that you're going to say something? Cut the fanfare. We aren't, by the way, attacking the usefulness of transitions that lead readers along.

For more on transitions, see pp. 295–99.

WORDY	As far as getting ready for winter is concerned, I put antifreeze in my car.
REVISED	To get ready for winter, I put antifreeze in my car.
WORDY	The point should be made that . . . Let me make it perfectly clear that . . . In this paper I intend to . . . In conclusion I would like to say that . . .

Use Strong Verbs. Forms of the verb *be* (*am, is, are, was, were*) followed by a noun or an adjective can make a statement wordy, as can *There is* or *There are*. Such weak verbs can almost always be replaced by active verbs.

WORDY	The Akron game was a disappointment to the fans.
REVISED	The Akron game disappointed the fans.
WORDY	There are many people who dislike flying.
REVISED	Many people dislike flying.

Use Relative Pronouns with Caution. When a clause begins with a relative pronoun (*who, which, that*), you often can whittle it to a phrase.

WORDY	Venus, which is the second planet of the solar system, is called the evening star.
REVISED	Venus, the second planet of the solar system, is called the evening star.

Cut Out Deadwood. The more you revise, the more shortcuts you'll discover. Phrases such as *on the subject of, in regard to, in terms of,* and *as far as . . . is concerned* often simply fill space. Try reading the sentences below without the words in *italics*.

> Howell spoke for the sophomores, and Janet *also spoke* for the seniors.
>
> He is *something of* a clown but *sort of the* lovable *type*.
>
> As a major in *the field of* economics, I plan to concentrate on *the area of* international banking.
>
> *The decision as to* whether *or not* to go is up to you.

Cut Descriptors. Adjectives and adverbs are often dispensable.

WORDY	Johnson's extremely significant research led to highly important major discoveries.
REVISED	Johnson's research led to major discoveries.

Be Short, Not Long. While a long word may convey a shade of meaning that a shorter synonym doesn't, in general favor short words over long ones. Instead of *the remainder,* write *the rest;* instead of *activate, start* or *begin;* instead of *adequate* or *sufficient, enough*. Look for the right word — one that wraps an idea in a smaller package.

WORDY	Andy has a left fist that has a lot of power in it.
REVISED	Andy has a potent left.

By the way, it pays to read. From reading, you absorb words like *potent* and set them to work for you.

Keeping It Clear

Recall what you want to achieve — clear, direct communication with your readers using specific, unambiguous words arranged in logical order.

WORDY	He is more or less a pretty outstanding person in regard to good looks.
REVISED	He is strikingly handsome.

Read your draft with fresh eyes. Return, after a break, to passages that have been a struggle; heal any battle scars by focusing on clarity.

UNCLEAR	Thus, after a lot of thought, it should be approved by the board even though the federal funding for all the cow-tagging may not be approved yet because it has wide support from local cattle ranchers.
CLEAR	In anticipation of federal funding, the Livestock Board should approve the cow-tagging proposal widely supported by local cattle ranchers.

MICRO REVISION CHECKLIST

☐ Have you positioned what counts at the beginning or the end?

☐ Are you direct, straightforward, and clear?

☐ Do you announce an idea before you utter it? If so, consider chopping out the announcement.

☐ Can you substitute an active verb where you use a form of *be* (*is, was, were*)?

☐ Can you recast any sentence that begins *There is* or *There are*?

☐ Can you reduce to a phrase any clause beginning with *which, who,* or *that*?

☐ Have you added deadwood or too many adjectives and adverbs?

☐ Do you see any long words where short words would do?

☐ Have you kept your writing clear, direct, and forceful?

Learning by Doing 🖊 Tackling Micro Revision

Think over the revisions you've already made and the advice you've received from peers or other readers. Is your paper more likely to seem bland (because it lacks emphasis), wordy (because it needs a good trimming), or foggy (because it needs to be more direct and logical)? Focus on one issue: adding emphasis, cutting extra words, or expressing ideas clearly.

For his composition class, Daniel Matthews was assigned a paper using a few sources. He was to write about an "urban legend," a widely accepted and emotionally appealing — but untrue — tale about events. The following selection from his paper, "The Truth about 'Taps,'" introduces his topic, briefly explaining the legend and the true story about it. The first draft illustrates macro revisions (highlighted in the margin) and micro revisions (marked in the text); the clear and concise final version follows.

FIRST DRAFT

Anyone who has ever

As you know, whenever you have attended the funeral services for a fallen   *— Avoid "you" in case*
                                                                                  readers have not shared
                                                                                  this experience.
                                has
veteran of the United States of America, you have stood fast as a lone bugler filled

the air with the mournful and sullenly appropriate last tribute to a defender of the

nation   *T*
United States of America. As most of us know, the name of the bugle call is "Taps,"

legend   *has*   *ed*
and the story behind its origin is one that is gaining a popularity of its own as it

Rework paragraph to summarize legend when first mentioned.

INSERT:
According to this story, Union Captain Robert Ellicombe discovered that a Confederate casualty was, in fact, his son, a music student in the South. The father found "Taps" in his son's pocket, and the tune was first played at a military burial as his son was laid to rest (Coulter).

Group all the discussion of the versions in one place.

Divide long sentence to keep it clear.

Strengthen paragraph conclusion by sticking to its focus.

has
~~is more and more frequently being~~ circulated in this time of war and terror. Although ~~it is clear that~~ this tale ~~of the origin~~ of a beautiful ode to a fallen warrior is heartfelt ~~and full of purposeful intent~~, it is an "urban legend." *As such, i*~~It~~ fails to provide due justice to the memories of the men responsible for the true origin of "Taps."

    General Daniel Butterfield is the *true* originator of the bugle call "Taps~~,~~" ⊙ ~~formerly known as "Lights Out."~~ Butterfield served ~~as a general~~ in the Union army during the Civil War and was awarded the Medal of Honor for actions during that time. One of his most endearing claims to fame is the bugle call "Taps," which he composed at Harrison's Landing in 1862 (Warner 167). ~~The bugle call~~ "Taps" originates from another call named "Lights Out"~~;~~ ~~this call was~~ used by the Army to signal the end of the day~~.~~ Butterfield, wanting a new and original call unique to his command, summoned bugler Oliver Willcox Norton to his tent one night~~. and~~ *R* ~~father~~ than compose an altogether new tune, he instead modified the notes to the call "Lights Out" (US Military District of Washington). ~~Then~~ *Shortly thereafter* this call could be heard ~~being used~~ up and down the Union lines as the other commanders ~~who had~~ heard the call ~~liked it and adapted it for their own use. This call, the modified version of "Lights Out" is~~ *and itself* also ~~in a way~~ a derivative of ~~the~~ British bugle call *"Tattoo," a* ~~"Tattoo" which is very~~ similar in both sound and purpose ~~to "Lights Out,"~~ (Villanueva)~~. notes this as well in his paper "24 Notes That Tap Deep Emotion."~~

REVISED DRAFT

Anyone who has ever attended the funeral services for a fallen veteran of the United States of America has stood fast as a lone bugler filled the air with a mournful last tribute to a defender of the nation. The name of the bugle call is "Taps," and the legend behind its origin has gained popularity as it has circulated in this time of war and terror. According to this story, Union Captain Robert Ellicombe discovered that a Confederate casualty was, in fact, his son, a music student in the South. The father found "Taps" in his son's pocket, and the tune was first played at a military burial as his son was laid to rest (Coulter). Although this tale of a beautiful ode to a fallen warrior is heartfelt, it is an "urban legend." As such, it fails to provide due justice to the memories of the men responsible for the true origin of "Taps."

General Daniel Butterfield is the true originator of the bugle call "Taps." Butterfield served in the Union army during the Civil War and was awarded the Medal of Honor for actions during that time. One of his most endearing claims to fame is the bugle call "Taps," which he composed at Harrison's Landing in 1862 (Warner 167). "Taps" originates from another call named "Lights Out," used by the army to signal the end of the day and itself a derivative of "Tattoo," a British bugle call similar in both sound and purpose (Villanueva). Butterfield, wanting a new and original call unique to his command, summoned bugler Oliver Willcox Norton to his tent one night. Rather than compose an altogether new tune, he instead modified the notes to the call "Lights Out" (US Military District of Washington). Shortly thereafter this call could be heard up and down the Union lines as other commanders heard the call and adapted it for their own use.

Editing and Proofreading

Editing means correcting and refining grammar, punctuation, and mechanics. Proofreading means taking a final look to check correctness and to catch spelling or word-processing errors. Don't edit and proofread too soon. As you draft, don't fret over spelling an unfamiliar word; it may be revised out in a later version. Wait until you have revised to refine and correct. In college, good editing and proofreading can make the difference between a C and an A. On the job, it may help you get promoted. Readers, teachers, and bosses like careful writers who take time to edit and proofread.

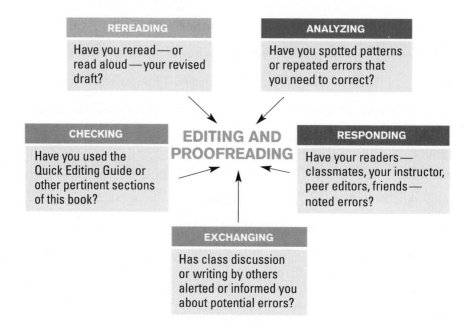

Editing

As you edit, whenever you question whether a word or construction is correct, consult a good reference handbook. Learn the grammar conventions you don't understand so you can spot and eliminate problems in your own writing. Practice until you easily recognize major errors such as fragments and comma splices. Ask for assistance from a peer editor or a tutor in the writing center if your campus has one.

EDITING	PROOFREADING
• **GRAMMAR:** Are your sentences and their parts correct?	• **SPELLING:** Have you spell-checked and reread your work attentively?
• **SENTENCES:** Are your sentences clear and effective?	• **INCORRECT WORDS:** Have you mistakenly picked any wrong words?
• **WORD CHOICE:** Are your words correct and well selected?	• **MISSING WORDS:** Have you left out any words?
• **PUNCTUATION:** Do you need to add, correct, or drop any marks?	• **MINOR ERRORS:** Can you see any small mistakes?
• **MECHANICS:** Do you need to correct capitals, italics, or other matters?	• **MINOR DETAILS:** Do you need to correct any details?
• **FORMAT:** Do you need to adjust margins, spacing, or headings?	

Use the "Quick Editing Guide" (beginning on p. A-39) to review grammar, style, punctuation, and mechanics problems typically found in college writing. Look for definitions, examples, and a checklist to help you tackle each one. Here is an editing checklist for these problems:

EDITING CHECKLIST
Common and Serious Problems in College Writing

The following cross-references refer to the Quick Editing Guide section at the back of this book.

Grammar Problems   *Section Number*

☐ Have you avoided writing sentence fragments?   A1

☐ Have you avoided writing comma splices or fused sentences?   A2

☐ Have you used the correct form for all verbs in the past tense? A3

☐ Do all verbs agree with their subjects?   A4

☐ Have you used the correct case for all pronouns?   A5

☐ Do all pronouns agree with their antecedents?   A6

☐ Have you used adjectives and adverbs correctly?   A7

Sentence Problems

☐ Does each modifier clearly modify the appropriate sentence element? B1

☐ Have you used parallel structure where necessary?   B2

Punctuation Problems

☐ Have you used commas correctly?   C1

☐ Have you used apostrophes correctly?   C2

☐ Have you punctuated quotations correctly?   C3

Mechanics Problems

☐ Have you used capital letters correctly?   D1

☐ Have you spelled all words correctly?   D2

For help documenting any sources in your paper, turn to sections D6 and E1–E2 in the Quick Research Guide (pp. A-31–A-38).

Proofreading

All writers make mistakes as they put ideas on paper. Because the mind works faster than the pencil (or the computer), a moment's break in concentration—when someone talks or your phone rings—can lead to errors. Making such mistakes isn't bad—you simply need to take the time to find and correct them.

- Let a paper sit several days, overnight, or at least a few hours before proofreading so that you allow time to gain perspective.
- Budget enough time to proofread thoroughly. For a long essay or complex research paper with a list of sources, schedule several sessions.
- Ask someone else to read your paper and tell you if it is free of errors. But take pride in your own work. *Don't* let someone else do it for you.
- Use a dictionary or a spell-checker, but remember that a spell-checker recognizes only correct spelling, not correct choices.
- Keep a list of your habitual errors, especially those your instructor has already pointed out. Double-check for these errors (such as leaving off -*s* or -*ed* endings or putting in unnecessary commas).

Proofreading does take patience but is a skill you can develop. For instance, when you simply glance at the spelling of *environment,* you may miss the second *n.* When you read normally, you usually see only the shells of words—the first and last letters. You fix your eyes on the print only three or four times per line or less. When you proofread, try to look at the letters in each word and the punctuation marks between words. Slow down and concentrate.

PROOFREADING CHECKLIST

☐ Have you read your draft very slowly, looking at every word and letter? Have you tried to see what is actually written, not what you think is there?

☐ Have you read your paper aloud so you can see and hear mistakes?

☐ Have you read the essay backward so that you look at each word instead of getting caught up in the flow of ideas?

☐ Have you read your essay several times, focusing each time on a specific area of difficulty? (For example, read once for spelling, once for punctuation, and once for a problem that recurs in your writing.)

Learning by Doing 🎦 Editing and Proofreading

1. Read the following passage carefully. Assume that the organization of the paragraph is satisfactory, but find and correct fifteen errors in sentence structure, grammar, spelling, punctuation, and capitalization. After you have corrected the passage, discuss with your classmates the changes you have made and your reasons for making those changes.

   Robert Frost, one of the most poplar American poets. He was born in San Francisco in 1874, and died in Boston in 1963. His family moved to new

England when his father died in 1885. There he completed highschool and attended colledge but never graduate. Poverty and problems filled his life. He worked in a woll mill, on a newspaper, and at varous odd jobs. Because of ill health he settled on a farm and began to teach school to support his wife and children. Throughout his life he dedicated himself to writing poetry, by 1915 he was in demand for public readings and speaking engagements. He was awarded the Pulitzer Prize for poetry four times—in 1924, 1931, 1937, and 1943. The popularity of his poetry rests in his use of common themes and images. everyone can relate to his universal poems, such as "Birches" and "Stopping by Woods on a Snowy Evening." Students read his poetry in school from seventh grade through graduate school, so almost everyone recognize lines from his best-loved poems. America is proud of it's son, the homespun poet Robert Frost.

2. Select a passage, from this textbook or elsewhere, that is about one hundred words long. Type up the passage, intentionally adding ten errors in grammar, spelling, punctuation, or capitalization. Swap passages with a classmate; proofread, then check each other's work against the originals. Share your proofreading strategies.

Learning by Doing 🎯 Reflecting on Revising and Editing

Think back on your process for finishing your last paper. In what ways did you revise that paper well, working on both macro and micro changes? How might you plan to revise your next paper? In what ways did you edit your last paper well? How might you plan to edit your next paper? Working with a classmate or small group, share your successful approaches face-to-face or online.

A WRITER'S RESEARCH MANUAL

PART FOUR

A Writer's Research Manual Contents

16 **Planning Your Research Project** 322

17 **Working with Sources** 333

18 **Finding Sources** 351

19 **Evaluating Sources** 368

20 **Integrating Sources** 376

Introduction: Investigating Questions

How does fan violence affect sporting events?

What steps can law enforcement take to help prevent stalking?

Is it true that about a million children in the United States are homeless?

Why is cyberbullying so widespread?

You may ask questions like these, discuss them with friends, or read about them. If so, you are conducting informal research to satisfy your curiosity. Just as *revision* means "seeing again," so *research* means "seeking or hunting again"—reconsidering information to revise and deepen what you know. In day-to-day life, you conduct practical research to solve problems and make decisions. You may want to buy a digital camera, consider an innovative medical procedure, or plan a vacation. To become better informed, you may talk with friends, search the Internet, request product information, compare ads and prices, and read articles. You pull together and weigh all this information to make a well-informed decision based on available evidence.

When a college professor assigns a research paper, you won't be expected to solve the problem of world hunger, but you will be expected to do more than merely paste together information and opinions from others. The key is to start your investigation as professional researchers do—with a research question that you truly want to learn more about. The excitement lies in using research to draw conclusions and arrive at your own fresh view. Like a detective, you will need to plan your work but remain flexible, backtracking, jumping ahead, or going sideways if you meet an obstacle. To help you do so, this research manual provides effective, efficient strategies and procedures.

For information and journal questions about the Part Four photograph, see the last two pages of the Appendices.

16 Planning Your Research Project

Conducting research is a lifelong skill, valuable in college, at work, and in your personal life. Yet this skill is increasingly complex. You must actively engage, inquire, search, access, evaluate, integrate, and synthesize information from moving, not fixed, targets. Electronic databases are fluid, sources may change, and details may shift over time.

As a result, a research project requires information literacy — the capacity to handle information — as well as critical reading and thinking as you join the academic exchange. The graphic on page 323 identifies major stages in a typical research process, moving from the exploration of a topic to the evaluation, analysis, and synthesis that eventually evolve into a final paper with well-integrated sources.

Why Planning a Research Project Matters

In a College Course

- You plan ahead to finish — on time and on target — the research project assigned in your writing class.
- You apply your planning experience to your capstone research project for your major.

In the Workplace

- You organize your work group to investigate a potential client base, using available demographic data.

In Your Community

- You arrange the needs assessment necessary to justify a new recreation center.

❓ When have you planned a research project? In what situations do you expect to do so again?

THE RESEARCH PROCESS

Engage: Explore a topic that intrigues you, following your assignment (see pp. 324–26).

Inquire: State your research question (see pp. 326–29).

Organize: Manage your project (see pp. 330–32).

• Plan a method of recording information.

• Organize a research archive, and create a schedule.

Investigate: Work with your sources (see Ch. 17).

• Start a working bibliography, and draw the details from sources.

• Quote, paraphrase, and summarize to capture information in your notes (see pp. 345–48).

Search: Seek and evaluate reliable sources that might help to answer your question (see Chs. 18 and 19).

• Use the Internet, library catalog, databases, and reference materials.

• Develop search strategies for print and electronic resources.

• Analyze and evaluate the reliability and relevance of each source.

Synthesize: Integrate reliable information and evidence to support your answer to your research question.

• Use sources ethically to avoid plagiarism (see Chs. 17 and 20).

• Quote, paraphrase, summarize, and synthesize to capture and integrate source materials in your paper (see Chs. 17 and 20).

• Clarify the thesis that answers your question, and support it as you write your paper (see Ch. 13).

• Cite and list your sources (see pp. 336–43, sections D6 and E in the Quick Research Guide, and the sample MLA and APA papers in the Appendix).

Beginning Your Inquiry

A research paper is often the most engaging and complex assignment in a course. This chapter will help you plan and manage your project by developing the skills and tools you will need to accomplish even the most formidable research task.

The Assignment: Writing from Sources

Find a topic that intrigues you, and develop a focused research question about it. After conducting whatever research is necessary, synthesize the information you assemble to develop your own reasonable answer to the research question. Then write a paper, persuasively using a variety of source material to convey your conclusions.

Because your final paper answers your research question, you are writing for a reason, not just stacking up facts. Reading and digesting the ideas of others is just the first step. You'll also analyze, evaluate, and synthesize, thinking critically to achieve your purpose. Answering your question will probably require you to return to writing situations you addressed earlier — perhaps comparing, taking a stand, evaluating, or supporting a position. You also may turn to field methods such as observing or interviewing.

Aim to persuade your audience to consider, respect, accept, or act on the answer to your question. If possible, use this project to benefit your college, employer, local community, or campus cause. Having a real audience will help you select what to include or exclude as you write your paper.

Learning by Doing 🔲 Reflecting on Research

Reflect on your past research experience. Have you written a research paper in the past? Do you feel confident that you can handle a college research assignment? Or does even the word *research* make you feel anxious? Sum up your past experience. Then list the skills you have already developed in this class that might help you begin your current research project.

Asking a Research Question

What assistance most effectively helps members of the military return to civilian life after a stressful tour of duty?

How accurately do standardized tests measure learning?

What can be done to aid hungry children in your community?

To define a narrow research question, start with your interests and research goals. Choose a territory — a research topic that stimulates your curiosity. If you need ideas, listen to the academic exchanges around you.

Perhaps the reading, writing, or discussion in your geography course alerts you to global environmental threats. Then target your research, maybe narrowing "global threats to forests" to "farming practices that threaten rain forests."

- ☐ What experience can you recall that raises intriguing questions or creates unusual associations in your mind?

- ☐ What have you observed recently—at school or work, online, or on television today—that you could more thoroughly investigate?

- ☐ What new perspectives on issues or events have friends, classmates, instructors, commentators, bloggers, or others offered?

- ☐ What have you read or heard about lately that you would like to pursue?

- ☐ What problem would you like to solve?

Exploring Your Territory

Like explorers in new territory, research writers first take a broad look at promising viewpoints, changes, and trends. Then they zero in on a small area.

Go Online. You may start out by searching for your topic; *families*, for instance, turned up about 739 million Google entries. In our search, the first two came from Wikipedia, the collaborative online encyclopedia which may orient you to key words and subtopics. (Be cautious, however. Because users can edit entries on this site, instructors may or may not consider it reliable for deeper research.) Next came organizations with *families* in their names — nonprofit, government, religious, for-profit groups, all jumbled together. Similarly, Google Scholar's first item covered plant (not human) families, while Google Groups led to more personal family interests. A vast Internet search can produce many sources but little focus.

For more on electronic searches, see Ch. 18.

Browse the Library. For more focused, academic sources, visit your campus library or its Web site. The library probably subscribes to many general databases (such as Academic Search Premier, Academic OneFile, and Gale Virtual Reference), as well as field-specific resources. Ask a reference librarian (electronically or in person) where to start investigating a topic.

Talk with Experts. If you're curious about America's fascination with cars, meet with a professor, such as a sociologist or a journalist, who specializes in the area. Talk with friends who are passionate about their cars. Or go to an auto show, observing and talking with people who attend.

For more on purpose
and audience, see
pp. 11–15 and 301–3.

Revisit Your Purpose and Audience. Refine your purpose and your audience analysis in light of your discoveries thus far. Consider what goal you'd like your research to accomplish — whether in your personal life, for a college class, or on the job.

Satisfy curiosity	Analyze a situation
Take a new perspective	Substantiate a conclusion
Make a decision	Support a position
Solve a problem	Advocate for change

Suppose your survey of campus programs leads you to a proposal by the International Students Office for matching first-year students with host families during holidays. You wonder what such programs cost, how they work, what they offer students and host families. At first, you think that your purpose is to persuade the community to participate. Then you see that the real challenge is to gain the activity director's support.

Turning a Topic into a Question

As you explore, move from broad to specific by asking more precise questions. Ask exactly what you want to learn; your task will leap into focus.

BROAD OVERVIEW	Family structures
TOPIC	Blended families
SPECIFIC QUESTION	How do blended families today differ from those a century ago?
BROAD OVERVIEW	Contemporary architecture
TOPIC	Landscape architecture
SPECIFIC QUESTION	In what ways have the principles of landscape architecture shaped the city's green design?

For more on
generating ideas,
see Ch. 12.

Generate Ideas. Freewrite, map, or brainstorm, and then select a question that appears promising. Your instructor may have suggestions, but you will probably be more motivated investigating a question you choose.

Size Up Your Question. If your question is too broad, you'll be swamped with information. If it has been overdone, you'll struggle to sound fresh. Focus to find a workable research question:

- Is it interesting to you? Will your discoveries interest your readers?
- Is it debatable? Does it allow for a range of opinions? Will you be able to support your own view rather than explain what's generally known and accepted?

■ Is it narrow enough for a productive investigation in the few weeks you have? Would a background search supply the vocabulary you need to stick to a single focus?

BROAD QUESTION	How is the climate of the earth changing?
NARROWER QUESTION	How will El Niño affect climate changes in California during the next decade?
BROAD QUESTION	Who are the world's best living storytellers?
NARROWER QUESTION	How is Irish step dancing a form of storytelling?
BROAD QUESTION	Why are people homeless?
NARROWER QUESTION	What housing programs succeed in our region?

Although you should restrict your topic, a question can be too narrow or too insignificant. If so, it may be difficult to find relevant sources.

TOO NARROW	How did John F. Kennedy's maternal grandfather influence the decisions JFK made during his first month as president?

A question may also be so narrow that it's uninteresting. Avoid questions that can be answered with a simple yes or no or with a few statistics.

TOO NARROW	Are there more black students or white students in the entering class this year?
BETTER	How does the racial or ethnic diversity of students affect campus relations at our school?

Shape a question that leads you into the heart of a lively controversy. The best research questions ask about issues and problems that others take seriously and debate, matters of real interest to you and your readers.

Hone Your Question. Make your question specific and simple: identify one thing to find out, not several. The very phrasing of a well-crafted question can suggest keywords — and useful synonyms — for searches.

QUESTION	What has caused a shortage of affordable housing in northeastern cities?
POSSIBLE SEARCH TERMS	Housing shortage, affordable urban housing

Refine Your Question. Until you start your research, you can't know how fruitful your first question will be. At least it establishes a starting point. If it doesn't lead you to definite facts or reliable opinions, if it doesn't start you thinking critically, reword it or throw it out and ask a new question.

RESEARCH CHECKLIST
Questioning Your Question

☐ Does your question probe an issue that engages you personally?

☐ Is its scope appropriate — neither huge nor puny? Will you be able to answer it given the time and length limits for your paper?

☐ Can you find both current and background information about it?

☐ Have you worded your question concretely and specifically, so that it states exactly what you are looking for?

Learning by Doing 🎦 Polling Your Peers

On a blank page, list your three most interesting ideas with a brief description of each topic's research potential. Working with a small group or whole class, pass your page to the person next to you. On the page you receive, mark a check by the idea that you find most intriguing. Repeat this process until everyone has responded to each page, and your page returns to you. Taking into account the group's check marks, turn one topic into a research question, and then outline your tentative approach to it. Decide whether you've found the question you want to explore. Repeat the process if the group wants more response.

For more on stating and using a thesis, see pp. 263–69.

Predict an Answer in a Working Thesis. Some writers find a project easier to tackle if they have in mind not only a question but also a possible answer, even a working thesis. However, be flexible, ready to change either answer or question as your research progresses.

RESEARCH QUESTION	How does a nutritious lunch benefit students?
WORKING THESIS	Nutritious school lunches can improve students' classroom performance.

Use Your Working Thesis to Guide Your Research. You probably will revise or replace your working thesis before you finish, but it can guide you now.

- Identify terms to define and subtopics or components to explore.
- List or informally outline points you might develop.
- Note opposing views, alternatives, or solutions likely to emerge.

This early exploration will help you pursue the sources and information you need but avoid any wild goose chase that might distract you.

However, if all you find is support for what you already think, your working thesis may be too dominant. You may be simply defending your

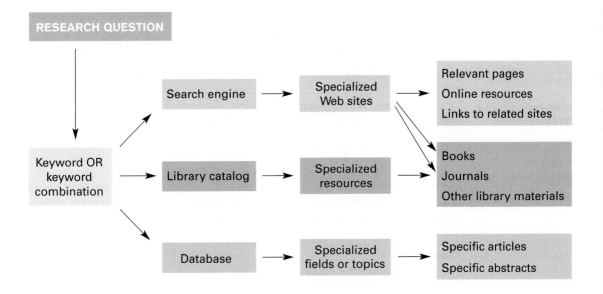

view, not conducting true research. For this reason, some writers delay stating a thesis until they've done substantial research or even begun drafting.

Surveying Your Resources

Test whether your question is likely to lead to an ample research paper with a fast search at the library site. You'll need enough ideas, opinions, facts, statistics, and expert testimony to address your question. If you turn up a skimpy list, change search terms. For hundreds of sources, refine your question. Aim for a question that is the focus of a dozen or twenty available sources. If you need help, talk to a reference librarian.

Also decide which types of sources to target. Some questions require a wide range, others a narrower range, restricted by date or discipline.

- Opinions on controversies? Turn to newspaper editorials, opinion columns, issue-oriented sites, and partisan groups for diverse views.

- News and analysis? Look for stories from newsmagazines, newspapers, news services, and public broadcasting.

- Statistics and facts? Try census or other government data, library databases, annual fact books, and almanacs.

- Professional or workforce information? Turn to reports and surveys with academic, government, and corporate sponsors to reduce bias.

- Research-based analysis? Try scholarly or well-researched nonfiction, government reports, specialized references, and academic databases.

- Original records or images? Check archives, online historical records, and materials held by institutions such as the Library of Congress.

To review the types of evidence, see pp. 41–42.

For an interactive Learning by Doing activity on narrowing online research, go to Ch. 16: **bedfordstmartins .com/concisebedguide**.

Using Keywords and Links

For help using keywords, go to the interactive "Take Action" charts in Re:Writing at **bedfordstmartins.com /concisebedguide**.

Keywords are terms or phrases that identify topics discussed in a research source. When you enter keywords into an electronic search engine (whether in a library catalog, database, or Web site), the engine returns to you a list of all the sources it can find with those words. Finding the best keywords for a topic and search engine is essential. Start with the main terms in your research question. Record the keywords you try, noting whether they produce too few or too many results.

For Internet and library search strategies, see Ch. 18.

As keywords lead to Web sites compiled by specialists or people with a shared interest, browse through the information, resources, and *links* — lists of related sites. These links, in turn, often contain their own lists of related Web pages. Follow these connections systematically to expand your knowledge rapidly, but avoid only supporting a preconceived notion.

For advice on creating a working bibliography, see pp. 334–35.

Learning by Doing 📷 Proposing Your Project

Assemble and review your research materials — topic ideas, research question, any working thesis, notes on resources and keywords, and anything else you've planned or gathered. Then write a short informal proposal that sums up what you want to discover and how you plan to proceed. In a small group, present your proposals, and exchange ideas about how to continue your inquiry.

Managing Your Project

No matter what your question or where you plan to look for material, you will want to keep track of where you've been and where you need to go.

Recording Information

Plan ahead to produce what you need: relevant evidence from reliable sources to develop and support your answer to your research question. Avoid two extremes — collecting everything or counting only on memory.

For advice on working with sources, see Ch. 17; for advice on integrating sources, see Ch. 20.

Use Time-Honored Methods for Depth. Selective copying (photocopying or saving to a file) helps you accumulate material, but copying whatever you find wastes time. Instead, take notes, annotate, highlight, quote, paraphrase, and summarize — all time-honored methods for absorbing, evaluating, and selecting information from a source. Such methods help you identify potentially useful materials and, later, integrate them smoothly into your paper.

Innovate for Efficiency. Develop efficient techniques such as these:

- Write a summary on the first page of a printout or photocopy.
- Add a paraphrase in the margin next to a key section of a printout.

- Identify a lively or concrete quotation with a highlighter.
- E-mail information from a library database to yourself so that it is easy to move into an electronic folder or file.
- Bookmark useful Web sites; save productive searches and results to a folder.
- Record key quotations in a computer file so that you can easily reorganize them. (Note source details, including database name, access date, URL, and any page number.)
- Summarize sources on sticky notes or cards so that you can quickly rearrange them in various orders on your wall, desk, or bed.
- Use a concept mapping program or poster board to sketch a "storyboard" for the main "events" that you want to cover in your paper.

Many researchers use word-processing files with clearly separate entries, $4'' \times 6''$ card format, or color coding; some stick to traditional note cards (with one note on each). Both are more flexible than notebook pages. When the time comes to organize, it's easy to reshuffle cards, print electronic notes, or sort them into a logical order.

Read as a Skeptical Critic. Distinguish what's significant for answering your research question and what's only slightly related. If you wish, add your own ratings (*, +, !! or – , ??) at the top or in the margin.

For more on critical reading, see Ch. 2.

Take Accurate and Thorough Notes. Read the entire article or section of a book before beginning to take notes. Then decide what — and how much — to record so you dig out the useful nuggets without distorting the meaning. Double-check all statistics and lists. Record enough notes and citations that, once they're written, you are independent of the source.

Starting a Research Archive

Organize your information from sources by creating a research archive. An *archive* is a place where information is systematically stored for later use. Clearly distinguish sources you save from your own notes. Use highlighting and other markers to make key passages easy to find in any format.

Save Computer Files. Save Web pages, e-mails, posts to newsgroups and lists, transcripts of chats, and database records to a drive or other storage device. Note URLs or search paths, dates of access, and similar details. Give each file a descriptive name so that you can find the information quickly later on. You can also organize the files in different electronic folders or directories, clearly named. Back up all electronic records.

Save Favorites and Bookmarks. Save the locations of Web sites in your browser so that you can easily return to your *favorites* or *bookmarks*. Annotate and organize them into folders.

Save Search Results. If a database or Internet search is productive, note where you searched and what keywords you used. Then you can easily repeat the search later, print out the results, or save them to a file.

File Paper Copies. If you prefer a paper format, photocopy book passages and articles, print out electronic sources (noting the database and date of access), and keep field material. File these using a separate folder for each source, labeled with title or subject and author. Attach sticky notes to mark key passages, or highlight them. Be sure the author (or title) and page number appear on each page so you can credit your source.

RESEARCH CHECKLIST
Getting Organized

☐ Have you identified and stated an intriguing research question?

☐ What has your quick survey of library and online sources revealed? Can you find enough information—but not too much—to answer your question?

☐ Which types of sources might be best for beginning your research?

☐ Have you created a realistic schedule based on your deadlines? Have you allowed plenty of time for research while meeting other commitments?

☐ Have you tested your method of recording research information? Will it be easy to keep up? Will it help you compile useful and accurate information?

☐ Have you begun organizing your research archive—opening files, setting up electronic folders, or buying file folders for paper copies?

Learning by Doing 🖻 Interviewing a Researcher

Pair up with a classmate, and interview each other as researchers. Ask about your classmate's interest in the topic, research question, investigative approach, and project concerns. After your classmate has interviewed you, write out any advice for yourself as a researcher.

Working with Sources 17

As you turn to sources, gather complete information.

- First, in a source entry, record the details that identify each source so you can find it and eventually credit it correctly in your paper. Assemble these entries in a working bibliography.
- Second, in source notes, capture information of value to your inquiry as quotations, paraphrases, or summaries ready for use in your paper.
- Finally, if required or useful to you as a researcher, combine a source entry with a summary to build an annotated bibliography.

Why Working with Sources Matters

In a College Course
- You read case studies, theories, industry projections, and much more for your economics class, so you need to capture information efficiently.
- You combine what you learn from clinic observations with information about your own child's diagnosis to direct your paper to an audience of parents.

In the Workplace
- You use company sales data, but you want to develop an annotated list of industry and government sources to expand available statistics.

In Your Community
- You agree to write a brief history of your campus social group, presenting the old records accurately but not offending potential contributors on alumni day.

When have you quoted, paraphrased, summarized, or credited sources? In what situations do you expect to do so again?

Drawing the Details from Your Sources

For more examples, see the sample MLA paper on pp. A-59–A-67, the sample APA paper on pp. A-68–A-76, and the Quick Research Guide, beginning on p. A-20.

The Source Navigators on pages 336–43 show how to find the details needed to identify several types of sources you are likely to use. Each source is keyed to a menu to show where you might look for the details you need to record in a source entry, ready to be copied from a working bibliography to the list of sources ending the paper. Each entry also is accompanied by sample source notes.

The sample source entries show two common academic styles: MLA (Modern Language Association) and APA (American Psychological Association). Because MLA and APA entries differ, stick to the style your instructor expects. However, both require much the same information, as do academic styles for other fields. The chart on page 344 summarizes what you'll need to record, both the basics—details nearly always required to identify each type of source—and common additions or likely complications. When in doubt, record more than you're likely to need so you won't have to return to a source later on.

Starting a Working Bibliography

Your working bibliography is a detailed and evolving list of articles, books, Web sites, and other resources that may contribute to your research. It guides your research by recording the sources you plan to consult and adding notes about those you do examine. Each entry in your working bibliography eventually needs to follow the format your instructor expects, generally either MLA or APA style.

Choose a Method. Pick the method you can use most efficiently.

- Note cards, recording one source per card
- Small notebook, writing on one side of the page
- Word-processor file
- Citation management software or other database

Keep Careful Records. The more carefully you record possible sources, the more time you'll save later when you list the works you actually used and cited. At that point, you'll be grateful to find all the necessary titles, authors, dates, page numbers, and other details at your fingertips—and you'll avoid a frantic, last-minute database search or library trip.

When you start a bibliographic entry for a source, your information may be incomplete: "Find bionic ears article—maybe last year in science magazine." Start with whatever clues you can gather—keywords, partial titles, authors, relevant publications, rough dates. Once you locate the source, you can fill in the detail. Eventually each entry should include everything you need to find the source as well as to prepare the list of sources at the end of your paper.

As your working bibliography develops, your circumstances may favor different methods of recording information. For example, when you find that science magazine with the article on bionic ears, you may read a printed copy or print the full text from a database. Either way, you can easily take notes using your usual method: on paper or in an electronic file. For field research, you might simply start with the name of a possible contact: "Dr. Edward Denu — cardiologist — interview about drug treatments." Should you interview Dr. Denu or someone from his staff about medication for heart patients, you might record the conversation (with that person's permission) or jot notes in a handheld electronic storage tool as you talk, later adding the information to your notes.

For a table on types of information to record, see p. 344.

Learning by Doing 🔲 Teaming Up for Source "Warm-Ups"

Working with a partner or team, do some source citation warm-ups, just as you might do push-ups or run a lap before a game or meet. Using this book, write a sentence that mentions a chapter, a reading, or the book as a whole. Use samples from the Source Navigators (pp. 336–43) or the Quick Research Guide (pp. A-20–A-38) to help you figure out how to identify that item in the list of sources at the end of your paper. Then add a sentence and a reference for a second source, such as a related reading, an e-Page, or a complementary Web page. Work together to cross-check and improve all your source references.

For an interactive Learning by Doing activity on practicing with online sources, go to Ch. 17: **bedfordstmartins.com /concisebedguide**.

Capturing Information in Your Notes

Read critically to decide what each source offers. If you cannot understand a source that requires specialized background, don't take notes or use it in your paper. On the other hand, if a source seems accurate, logical, and relevant, consider exactly how you want to record it in your notes.

For more examples of capturing information from sources, see pp. 178–89, pp. 379–84, and D in the Quick Research Guide, pp. A-28–A-31.

Identify What's from Where. Clearly identify the author of the source, a brief title if needed, and the page number (or other location) where a reader could find the information. These details connect each source note to your corresponding bibliography entry. Adding a keyword at the top of each note will help you cluster related material in your paper.

Article in a Print Magazine

Record this information in your notes about each source:

1 The complete name of the author

2 The title and any subtitle of the article

3 The title and any subtitle of the magazine

4 The full date of the issue

5 The article's page numbers

6 The periodical's volume number and issue number if available (for APA), sometimes found on title or contents page

7 The medium of publication (for MLA)

CITIES

SCIENTIFIC AMERICAN

Volume 305, Number 3

Cynthia Rosenzweig is a senior research scientist at the NASA Goddard Institute for Space Studies and at Columbia University's Earth Institute.

All Climate Is Local

Mayors are often better equipped than presidents to cut greenhouse gases

By Cynthia Rosenzweig

FOR YEARS SCIENTISTS HAVE URGED national leaders to tackle climate change, based on the assumption that prevention efforts would require the coordinated actions of entire nations to be effective. But as anyone who has watched the past 15 years of international climate negotiations can attest, most countries are still reluctant to take meaningful steps to lower their production of greenhouse gases, much less address issues such as how to help developing countries protect themselves from the extreme effects of climate change. Frustrated by the ongoing diplomatic stalemate, a number of urban leaders have decided to take mat-

severe. Most of the world's major metropolises were originally built on rivers or coastlines and are therefore subject to flooding from rising seas and instances of heavier rainfall.

Many civic leaders point to Hurricane Katrina and the devastation it visited on New Orleans in 2005 as their moment of awakening. They saw how the multiple failures of an aging and inadequate infrastructure, plus indifferent planning, sharply increased the death toll of a catastrophe that had long been predicted. Indeed, two major alliances of city mayors to combat climate change formed within months after Hurricane Katrina's landfall. The organization now known as the C40 Cities Climate Leadership Group launched in London in October

70 Scientific American, September 2011

Photograph by Dan Saelinger

336

Create a source entry out of the information you collect:

Source entry in MLA style

Rosenzweig, Cynthia. "All Climate Is Local." *Scientific American*
Sept. 2011: 70-73. Print.

Source note with a general summary of the article

Discusses the benefits of tackling climate change at the local level as opposed to the national level.

Source entry in APA style

Rosenzweig, C. (2011, September). All climate is local. *Scientific American*, *305*(3), 70-73.

Source note with a technical summary of the article

Reviews climate-change research and conferences on temperature shifts, weather events, emission rates, and other issues that help mayors and urban planners develop innovative responses.

Source Navigator

Article in a Scholarly Journal from a Database

Record this information in your notes about each source:

1. The complete name of the author(s)
2. The title and any subtitle of the article
3. The title and any subtitle of the journal
4. The journal volume and issue numbers
5. The year of the issue
6. The printed article's original page numbers if available
7. The name of the database, subscriber service, or library service (for MLA)
8. DOI (digital object identifier) if available or URL for journal's home page (for APA)
9. The medium of publication (for MLA)
10. The access date when you used the source (for MLA)

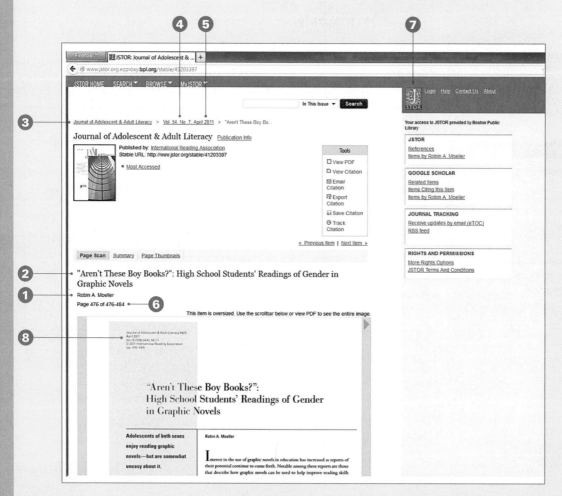

Create a source entry out of the information you collect:

MLA

Source entry in MLA style, e-mailed from database and recorded in a computer file

① **②**
Moeller, Robin A. "'Aren't These Boy Books?': High School Students'

③
Readings of Gender in Graphic Novels." *Journal of Adolescent*

④ **⑤** **⑥** **⑦** **⑨** **⑩**
& Adult Literacy 54.7 (2011): 476–84. *JSTOR*. Web. 29 Nov. 2012.

Source note with a paraphrase of one paragraph in the article

Many professional associations promote graphic novels as a tool for encouraging reading because high school students are drawn to the genre, which in turn can increase literary appreciation as well as literacy (p. 476).

APA

Source entry in APA style, e-mailed from database and recorded in a computer file

① **⑤** **②**
Moeller, R. A. (2011). "Aren't these boy books?": High school students'

③
readings of gender in graphic novels. *Journal of Adolescent*

④ **⑥** **⑧**
& Adult Literacy, 54(7), 476–484. doi: 10.1598/JAAL54.7.1

Source note with a summary of the article's conclusion and recommendations

Because of the level of engagement that boys, and to a lesser degree girls, showed while reading sophisticated graphic fiction, the format successfully encouraged their media literacy and therefore should be considered for inclusion in the high school curriculum.

Source Navigator

Book

Record this information in your notes about each source:

1. The complete name of the author
2. The title and any subtitle of the book
3. The place of publication, using the first city listed, and the state (for APA)
4. The name of the publisher, in short form
5. The latest date of publication (from the front or back of the title page)
6. The medium of publication (for MLA)
7. The call number or library location (for your future use)
8. Keyword or author (for your filing system)

② THINKING, FAST AND SLOW

Front of title page

① DANIEL KAHNEMAN

④ FARRAR, STRAUS AND GIROUX / NEW YORK ③

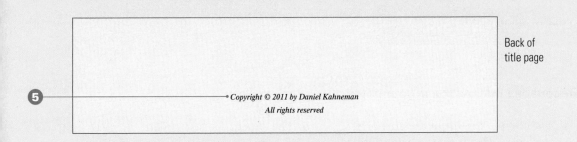

Back of
title page

Create a source entry out of the information you collect:

MLA

Source entry in MLA style, recorded on a card

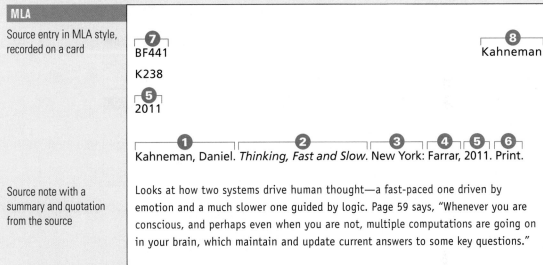

7 BF441

K238

5 2011

1 Kahneman, Daniel. **2** *Thinking, Fast and Slow*. **3** New York: Farrar, **4** 2011. **5** Print. **6**

8 Kahneman

Source note with a summary and quotation from the source

Looks at how two systems drive human thought—a fast-paced one driven by emotion and a much slower one guided by logic. Page 59 says, "Whenever you are conscious, and perhaps even when you are not, multiple computations are going on in your brain, which maintain and update current answers to some key questions."

APA

Source entry in APA style, recorded on a card

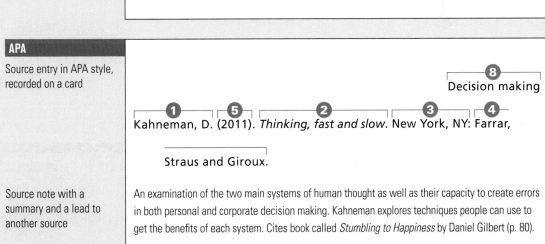

8 Decision making

1 Kahneman, D. **5** (2011). **2** *Thinking, fast and slow*. **3** New York, NY: Farrar, **4**

Straus and Giroux.

Source note with a summary and a lead to another source

An examination of the two main systems of human thought as well as their capacity to create errors in both personal and corporate decision making. Kahneman explores techniques people can use to get the benefits of each system. Cites book called *Stumbling to Happiness* by Daniel Gilbert (p. 80).

Source Navigator

Page from a Web Site

Record this information in your notes about each source:

1 The complete name of the author, if available, often from the beginning or end of the page

2 The title of the page

3 The name of the site

4 The name of any sponsoring organization

5 The date of the last update

6 The medium of publication (for MLA)

7 The access date when you used the source

8 The Internet address (URL) (for APA)

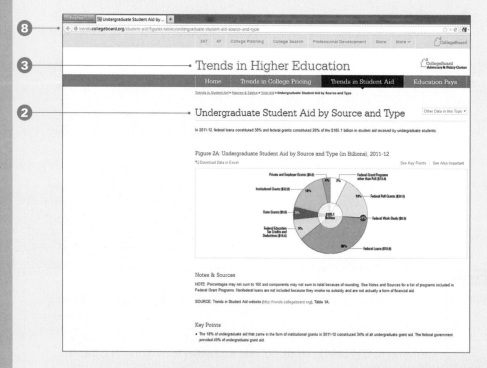

Create a source entry out of the information you collect:

MLA

Source entry in MLA style, recorded in a computer file

"Undergraduate Student Aid by Source and Type." *Trends in Higher Education.* College Board, 2012. Web. 29 Nov. 2012.

Source note summarizes topic of pie chart

Chart breaks down the types of financial aid undergraduate students received in 2011–2012 as well as the sources from which the aid came.

APA

Source entry in APA style, recorded in a computer file

College Board. (2012). *Trends in Higher Education.* Retrieved from

http://trends.collegeboard.org/student-aid/figures-tables

/undergraduate-student-aid-source-and-type

[Access dates are not required for sources whose content is not expected to change.]

Source note records specifics from table; retrieval URL simplifies return to source.

Federal work-study funds accounted for less than 1% of the financial aid distributed to undergraduate students in 2011–2012. See figure 2A: Undergraduate Student Aid by Source and Type.

Types of Information to Record

	The Basics	Common Additions
Names	■ Complete name of the author, as supplied in the source, unless not identified	■ Names of coauthors, in the order listed in the source ■ Names of any editor, compiler, translator, or contributor
Titles	■ Title and any subtitle of an article, Web page, or posting (in quotation marks for MLA) ■ Title and any subtitle of a journal, magazine, newspaper, book, or Web site (italicized)	■ Title of a journal special issue ■ Title of a series of books or pamphlets and any item number
Publication Details for Periodicals	■ Volume and issue numbers for a journal (and a magazine for APA) ■ DOI (digital object identifier) article number (for APA) ■ Section number or letter for a newspaper	■ Any edition of a newspaper (for MLA)
Publication Details for Books	■ City of publication, using the first city listed (for MLA) with state or country (for APA) ■ Name of the publisher	■ Edition number (4th) or description (revised) ■ Volume number and total volumes, if more than one ■ Names and locations of copublishers ■ Publisher's imprint (for MLA)
Publication Details for Electronic Sources	■ Name (italicized) of the database, subscriber service, or library service (for MLA) ■ Name of any site sponsor or publisher	■ Details of any original or alternate print publication ■ Document numbers
Dates	■ Year of publication, full date (periodical), or date of creation or last update (electronic source) ■ Your access date for an electronic source as printed or written on your hard copy (for MLA) or only for documents that change (for APA)	■ Original date of publication for a literary work or classic
Location of Information	■ Article's opening and concluding page numbers and any page for citing exact location of material in source	■ Paragraph, screen, chapter, or section numbers if supplied or section names, as in electronic sources
Location of Source	■ Internet address (URL, or uniform resource locator) for a hard-to-find source or, for APA, publication or publisher home page if no DOI	■ Call number, library area, or electronic address (to simplify your future use)
Medium of Publication	■ Medium of publication or reception such as Web, Print, CD, Film (for MLA) or of material reviewed (Motion picture, Book) or type of source (Computer software) (for APA)	

Also identify which ideas are yours and which are your source's. For example, you might mark your source notes with these labels:

"...": quotation marks to set off all the exact words of the source

para: your paraphrase, restatement, or translation of a passage from the source into your own words and sentences

sum: your overall summary of the source's main point

paste: your cut-and-paste, quoting a passage moved electronically

JN (your initials) or [ ]: your own ideas, connections, or reactions

A system like this helps you develop your ideas, distinguish them from your paraphrase or cut-and-paste, and avoid accidental plagiarism, using another writer's words or ideas without appropriate credit.

Decide What You Need. When it comes time to draft your paper, you will incorporate your source material in three basic ways:

- *Quoting:* transcribing the author's exact words directly from the source
- *Paraphrasing:* fully rewording the author's ideas in your own words
- *Summarizing:* reducing the author's main point to essentials

Your notes, too, should use these three forms. Weighing each source carefully and guessing how you might use it—even as you are reading—is part of the dynamic process of research.

Quoting

If you intend to use a direct quotation, capture it carefully, copying by hand or pasting electronically. Reproduce the words, spelling, order, and punctuation exactly, even if they're unusual. Put quotation marks around the material in your notes so you'll remember that it's a direct quotation.

RECORDING A GOOD QUOTATION

1. Quote sparingly, selecting only strong passages that might add support and authority to your assertions.
2. Mark the beginning and the ending with quotation marks.
3. Carefully write out or copy and paste each quotation. Check your copy— word by word—for accuracy. Check capitals and punctuation.
4. Record the page number where the quotation appears in the source. If it falls on two pages, note both; mark where the page turns.

Sometimes it doesn't pay to copy a long quotation word for word. If you take out one or more irrelevant words, indicate the omission with an ellipsis mark (...). If you need to add wording, especially so that a selection makes sense, enclose your addition in brackets [like this].

Sample Quotations, Paraphrase, and Summary (MLA Style)

Passage from Original Source

Obesity is a major issue because (1) vast numbers of people are affected; (2) the prevalence is growing; (3) rates are increasing in children; (4) the medical, psychological, and social effects are severe; (5) the behaviors that cause it (poor diet and inactivity) are themselves major contributors to ill health; and (6) treatment is expensive, rarely effective, and impractical to use on a large scale.

   Biology and environment conspire to promote obesity. Biology is an enabling factor, but the obesity epidemic, and the consequent human tragedy, is a function of the worsening food and physical activity environment. Governments and societies have come to this conclusion very late. There is much catching up to do.

Sample Quotations from Second Paragraph

Although human biology has contributed to the pudgy American society, everyone now faces the powerful challenge of a "worsening food and physical activity environment" (Brownell and Horgen 51). As Brownell and Horgen conclude, "There is much catching up to do" (51).

Sample Paraphrase of First Paragraph

The current concern with increasing American weight has developed for half a dozen reasons, according to Brownell and Horgen. They attribute the shift in awareness to the number of obese people and the increase in this number, especially among youngsters. In addition, excess weight carries harsh consequences for individual physical and mental health and for society's welfare. Lack of exercise and unhealthy food choices worsen the health consequences, especially because there's no cheap and easy cure for the effects of eating too much and exercising too little (51).

Sample Paraphrase Mixed with Quotation

Lack of exercise and unhealthy food choices worsen the health consequences, especially because they remain "major contributors to ill health" (Brownell and Horgen 51).

Sample Summary

After outlining six reasons why obesity is a critical issue, Brownell and Horgen urge Americans to eat less and become more active (51).

Sample Summary Mixed with Quotation

After outlining six reasons why obesity is a critical issue, Brownell and Horgen urge Americans to remedy "the worsening food and physical activity environment" (51).

Works Cited Entry (MLA Style)

Brownell, Kelly D., and Katherine Battle Horgen. *Food Fight: The Inside Story of the Food Industry, America's Obesity Crisis, and What We Can Do about It.* Chicago: Contemporary-McGraw, 2004. Print.

Paraphrasing

When paraphrasing, express an author's ideas, fairly and accurately, in your own words and sentences. Avoid judging, interpreting, or merely echoing the original. A good paraphrase may retain the organization, emphasis, and details of the original, so it may not be much shorter. Even so, paraphrasing is useful to walk your readers through the points made in the original.

For more on quotations and ellipsis marks, see C3 in the Quick Editing Guide, pp. A-55–A-56.

ORIGINAL	"In staging an ancient Greek tragedy today, most directors do not mask the actors."
TOO CLOSE TO THE ORIGINAL	Most directors, in staging an ancient Greek play today, do not mask the actors.
A GOOD PARAPHRASE	Few contemporary directors of Greek tragedy insist that their actors wear masks.

WRITING A GOOD PARAPHRASE

1. Read the entire passage through several times.
2. Divide the passage into its most important ideas or points, either in your mind or by highlighting or annotating the passage.
3. Look away from the original, and restate the first idea in your own words. Sum up the support for this idea. Review the section if necessary.
4. Go on to the next idea, and do the same. Continue in this way.
5. Go back and reread the original passage one more time, making sure you've conveyed its ideas faithfully without repeating its words or sentence structure. Revise your paraphrase if necessary.

Summarizing

Sometimes a paraphrase uses up too much space or disrupts the flow of your own ideas. Instead, you simply want to capture the main ideas of a source "in a nutshell." A summary can save space, distilling detailed text into one or two succinct sentences in your own words. Be careful as you reduce a long passage not to distort the original meaning or emphasis.

WRITING A GOOD SUMMARY

1. Read the original passage several times.
2. Without looking back, recall and state its central point.
3. Reread the original passage one more time, making sure you've conveyed its ideas faithfully. Revise your summary if necessary.

Mixing Methods

Sometimes you paraphrase for precision or summarize for brevity but want to include notable wording from your source. In this situation, add quotation marks to identify what is directly quoted. Whatever your method, identify your source, and note the page where the quotation or paraphrase originates.

For help quoting, paraphrasing, and summarizing, go to the interactive "Take Action" charts in Re:Writing at **bedfordstmartins.com /concisebedguide**.

RESEARCH CHECKLIST
Taking Notes with Quotations, Paraphrases, and Summaries

☐ For each source note, have you identified the source (by the author's last name or a keyword from the title) and the exact page? Have you added a keyword heading to each note to help you group ideas?

☐ Have you added a companion entry to your bibliography for each new source?

☐ Have you remained true to the meaning of the original source?

☐ Have you quoted sparingly — selecting striking, short passages?

☐ Have you quoted exactly? Do you use quotation marks around significant words, phrases, and passages from the original sources? Do you use ellipsis marks or brackets to show where any words are omitted or added?

☐ Are most notes in your own words — paraphrasing or summarizing?

☐ Have you avoided paraphrasing too close to the source?

For help incorporating sources, go to the interactive "Take Action" charts in Re:Writing at **bedfordstmartins.com /concisebedguide**.

Learning by Doing 🖾 Capturing Information from Sources

Identify a substantial paragraph or passage from a source you might use for your research paper or from a reading in this book (selected by you, your small group, or your instructor). Study this passage until you understand it thoroughly. Then use it as you respond to the following activities.

1. Quoting
   Identify one notable quotation from the passage you selected. Write a brief paragraph justifying your selection, explaining why you find it notable and why you might want to use it in a paper. Share your paragraph with classmates. In what ways were your reasons for selection similar or different?

2. Paraphrasing
   Write a paraphrase of your passage. Use your own language to capture what it says without parroting its words or sentence patterns. Share your paraphrase with classmates. What are its strengths and weaknesses? Where might you want to freshen the language?

3. Summarizing
   In one or two sentences, summarize the passage you selected. Capture its essence in your own words. Share your summary with classmates. What are its strengths and weaknesses? Where might you want to simplify or clarify?

4. Reflecting and Exchanging
   After completing 1, 2, and 3 above, decide which method of working with a passage proved most challenging. Write out specific tips for yourself about how to make that task easier, faster, and more successful. Compare your tips with those of your classmates so that you all gain fresh ideas about how to quote, paraphrase, and summarize.

Developing an Annotated Bibliography

An annotated bibliography is a list of your sources — read to date or credited in your final paper — that includes a short summary or annotation for each entry. This common assignment quickly informs a reader about the direction of your research. It also shows your mastery of two major research skills: identifying a source and writing a summary.

To develop an annotated bibliography, find out which format you are expected to use to identify sources and what your annotations should do — summarize only, add evaluation, or meet a special requirement (such as interpretation). A summary is a brief, neutral explanation in your own words of the source's thesis or main points. In contrast, an evaluation is a judgment of the source's accuracy, reliability, or relevance.

Summary with Source Identification and Proposed Use. Several drafts of Schyler Martin's annotated bibliography were due as he identified possible sources for his MLA-style essay, "Does Education Improve Social Ills in Native American Communities?" He identified each source as primary (a firsthand or eyewitness account) or secondary (a secondhand analysis based on primary material), summarized it, and described how he expected it to support his position.

For more on the MLA and APA formats, see the MLA sample paper on pp. A-59–A-67 and the sample APA paper on pp. A-68–A-76.

> Loew, Patty. *Indian Nations of Wisconsin: Histories of Endurance and Renewal.* Madison: Wisconsin Historical Society Press, 2001. Print.
>
> Secondary source. Professor Loew, a member of the Ojibwe tribe, presents Wisconsin history from a Native point of view. I will be using Loew's interviews to support my claims of education changing lives.

> Wildcat, Daniel R. "Practical Professional Indigenous Education." *Power and Place: Indian Education in America.* Comp. Vine Deloria, Jr., and Daniel R. Wildcat. Golden: Fulcrum, 2001. 113-21. Print.
>
> Secondary source. This book compares and contrasts the "Western" idea of education with Native American beliefs, showing where the "holes" are in today's educational policies. I will use Wildcat's chapter to demonstrate the argument of education only being useful when it is applied.

For her history paper, Shari O'Malley summed up relevance:

> Goodman, Phil. "Patriotic Femininity: Women's Morals and Men's Morale During the Second World War." *Gender & History* 10.2 (1998): 278-93. Print.
>
> Goodman examines British attitudes about women replacing men in the workplace and related wartime issues.

Summary with Evaluation. As Stephanie Hawkins worked on the annotated bibliography for her APA-style paper "Japanese: Linguistic Diversity," she wanted to show her critical thinking. Besides summarizing her sources, she evaluated their contributions, relationships, or usefulness to her study.

Abe, H. N. (1995). From stereotype to context: The study of Japanese women's speech. *Feminist Studies, 21*(3), 647-671.

Abe discusses the roots of Japanese women's language, beginning in ancient Japan and continuing into modern times. I was able to use this peer-reviewed article to expand on the format of women's language and the consequences of its use.

Kristof, N. (1995, September 24). On language: Too polite for words. *New York Times Magazine,* pp. SM22-SM23.

Kristof, a regular columnist for the *New York Times Magazine,* briefly describes the use of honorifics as an outlet for sarcasm and insults. Although the article discusses cultures other than Japanese, it provides insight into the polite vulgarity of the Japanese language.

Summary with Interpretation. Often an annotated bibliography includes unfamiliar materials, and your readers can benefit from extra explanation, background, or context. Examples include primary sources, interviews, oral histories, music, images, artistic works, texts from other times or cultures, or translations. In such cases, you may want to summarize the source and also interpret it for your readers, as this MLA-style entry and annotation illustrates.

Virginia Slims Lights. Advertisement. *Family Circle.* 26 Dec. 1985: 34–35. Print.

This advertisement for cigarettes, one of five in this issue of a popular women's magazine, illustrates how advertisers appealed to women smokers during this era. The ad's heading, "Introducing the LONGEST Slims of all," runs across two pages with a long-legged woman smoker lying on her side, also stretched across both pages. She is dressed not in alluring evening wear but in a blue-flowered sweater and woolly gold slacks. Both her attire and her wholesome look suit the issue's date and holiday features which include read-aloud stories, cookie recipes, and holiday decorating. Her head is thrown back and she smiles, holding her cigarette, which apparently promises enjoyment and relaxation at a busy time of the year for the magazine's readers.

Learning by Doing 🔲 Writing an Annotation

Select one of your sources (or a reading from this book), and write a few sentences to describe what the source covers and why it is relevant to your project. If your instructor has specified a particular approach, tailor your annotation to follow those directions. Exchange annotation drafts with a classmate or small group, and discuss ways to clarify contents or relevance.

Finding Sources

Although research begins with an intriguing question or issue, it quickly becomes a fast-paced hunt, moving among electronic, print, and human resources. Time is always limited, so you need efficient search strategies to help you find substantial, relevant sources. Should you begin your search for sources on the Internet? Or should you first log onto the campus library site?

Many instructors advocate beginning your research through the campus library. They are confident that you will be able to identify and access reliable information there, especially "peer-reviewed" or "refereed" articles—those whose scholarship and research methods have been assessed by experts in the field before being accepted for publication. Because college papers are built through an academic exchange, you need to rely on high-quality sources and strive to draw solid, well-grounded conclusions for your audience.

However, instructors also know that most of us spend a lot of time on the Internet, so you—and they—can easily browse for ideas or run a quick search for key terms. For news-oriented topics or opinions on trending social issues, you also can find up-to-the-minute, though not necessarily reliable, information. Where you begin your research may depend on your experience and the nature of your topic. Even if you start looking for a topic on the Web, turn to your campus library for focus and depth.

Why Finding Sources Matters

In a College Course

- You need to support your paper for the most demanding professor in the entire nursing school, so you know that means more than Google and Wikipedia.
- Your annotated bibliography is a third of your grade in history, so you need to find books and articles by reliable historians as well as original documents from the time period.

In the Workplace

- You want to organize objectives for the next decade, using available projections for your profession.

For more on the Academic Exchange, see pp. 180 and 182–83.

In Your Community

■ You organize focus groups for a community grant proposal, identifying sources to inform participants.

❓ When have you needed to find specific types of sources? In what situations do you expect to do so again?

Searching the Internet

The Internet contains an ever-growing number of resources that vary greatly in quality and purpose. A quick search may turn up intriguing topic ideas or slants, but it also will turn up thousands—maybe millions—of Web pages of uncertain relevance. These pages are far more likely to be motivated by the desire to sell something, to promote an opinion, to socialize, or to attract you to an advertising platform than to meet your academic research needs. They also will not necessarily be grouped by academic field or be designed to meet any academic standards. And even if you believe that a Web search with millions of returns has located everything that exists, it will not include the thousands of private, corporate, or government sites from the "deep" or "hidden" Web that requires passwords, limits access, or simply has not yet been indexed. The sheer bulk of this information makes searching for relevant research materials both too easy and too difficult, but a few basic principles can help.

Finding Recommended Internet Resources

Go first to online resources recommended by your instructor, department, or library. Their recommendations save search time, avoid random sites, and can take you directly to respected resources prepared by experts (scholars or librarians) for academic researchers (like you). Your college library, on campus or online, will offer many more resources such as these.

■ Research Web sites sponsored by another library, academic institution, or consortium such as ipl2, the Internet Public Library at ipl.org, the Michigan eLibrary at mel.org, InfoMine at infomine.ucr.edu, or the authoritative World Wide Web Virtual Library at vlib.org

■ Self-help guides or Internet databases organized by area (social sciences or business), topic (literary analysis), or type of information, such as the extensive Auraria Library *Statistics and Facts* guide at guides.auraria.edu /statistics

■ Other research centers or major libraries with their own collections of links, such as the Library of Congress online catalog at catalog2.loc.gov or its "Newspaper & Current Periodical Reading Room" at loc.gov/rr /news

■ Specialty search engines for government materials and agencies at FedWorld.ntis.gov and usa.gov

For a checklist for finding recommended sources, see B1 in the Quick Research Guide on p. A-25.

For more on campus library resources, see pp. 356–60.

For more on evaluating sources, see Ch. 19 and C in the Quick Research Guide, pp. A-26–A-28.

- Specialty search engines for specific materials such as Google Images at images.google.com, including the *Life* magazine photo archive, or Creative Commons at search.creativecommons.org
- Collections of sources such as those gathered in the New York University LibGuides at nyu.libguides.com
- Collections of e-books, including reference books and literary texts now out of copyright, such as Bartleby.com at bartleby.com/ and Project Gutenberg at gutenberg.org
- Web databases with "unrestricted access" (not online subscription services restricted to campus users) as varied as the United Nations databases at un.org/en/databases, the extensive health resources of MedlinePlus at nlm.nih.gov/medlineplus, and controversies at ProCon.org.
- Community resources or organizations, often useful for local research and service learning reports

Selecting Search Engines

Unlike a library, the Internet has no handy catalog, and search engines are not objective searchers. Each has its own system of locating material, categorizing it, and establishing the sequence for reporting results. One search site, patterned on a library index, might be selective. Another might separate advertising from search results, while a third pops up "sponsors" that pay advertising fees first, even though sites listed later might be better matches.

The best search engine is one you select and learn to use well. If you have a favorite, check its search practices. As you work out a combination of search terms relevant to your research question, think of your wording as a zoom lens. Tinker with it to search as narrowly as possible, finding relevant sites but avoiding endless options. Then try the identical search with another search engine to compare the results.

RESEARCH CHECKLIST
Comparing Search Engine Results

☐ What does the search engine's home page suggest its typical users want — academic information, business news, sports, shopping, or music?

☐ What does the search engine gather or index — information from and about a Web page (Google), each word on a Web page (Yahoo!), academic sources (Google Scholar), a collection of other search engines (Metacrawler), or returns compared for several engines (TurboScout)?

☐ What can you learn from a search engine's About, Search Tips, or Help?

☐ How does the advanced search work? Does it improve your results?

☐ Does the search engine take questions (Ask, Wolfram Alpha), categorize by source type (text, images, news), or group by topic (About)?

☐ How well does the search engine target your query — the words that define your specific search?

☐ How can you distinguish results (responses to your query), sponsors (advertisers who pay for priority placement), and other ads by placement, color, or other markers?

For an interactive Learning by Doing activity on comparing Google and database searches, go to Ch. 18: **bedfordstmartins.com /concisebedguide**.

Learning by Doing 🖼 Comparing Web Searches

Working with some classmates, agree on the topic and terms for a test search. (Or agree to test terms each of you selects.) Have everyone conduct the same search using different search engines, and then compare the results. Use the checklist above to suggest features for comparison. If possible, sit together, using your tablets, laptops, or campus computers so that you can easily see, compare, and evaluate the search engine results. Report your conclusions to the class.

Conducting Advanced Electronic Searches

Search engines contain millions of records on Web sites, much as a database or library catalog contains records on books, periodicals, or other materials found in a library. Generally, search engines can be searched by broad categories such as *education* or *health* or by more specific keywords.

For sample keyword searches, see p. 355 and p. 361.

Limit the Search. When you limit your search to keywords and broad categories, you may be overwhelmed with information. For example, Figure 18.1 illustrates a keyword search for sources on *foster care* on Google that produced more than 200 million entries. A keyword search may be ideal for a highly specialized term or topic, such as training for distance runners. For a more general topic — such as *foster care* — limit your search to find more relevant results. As Figure 18.2 shows, an advanced search produced fewer sources on one aspect of foster care — placing teenagers.

Select Limitations for Advanced Searches. Google and Metacrawler, for example, allow you to limit searches to all, exactly, any, or none of the words you enter. Look for directions for limitations such as these:

- a phrase such as "elementary school safety," requested as a unit (exactly these words) or enclosed in quotation marks to mark it as a unit

- a specific language (human or computer) such as English or Spanish

- a specific format or type of software such as a PDF file

- a date range (before, after, or between creation, revision, or indexing)

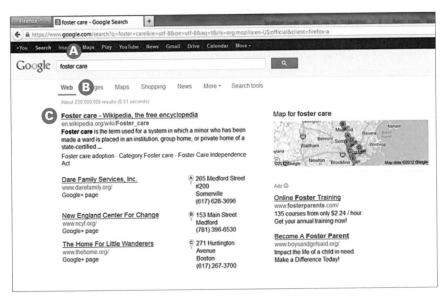

Figure 18.1 Results of a keyword search for *foster care* using Google, reporting more than 200 million entries

A. Search terms
B. Total number of entries located
C. Highlighted search terms found in entries

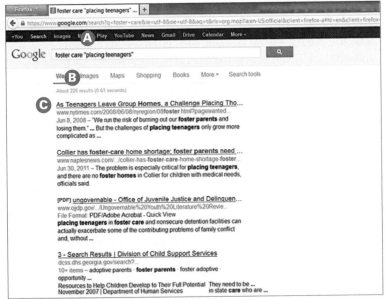

Figure 18.2 Advanced search results on *foster care + "placing teenagers"* using Google, reporting 226 entries

Google and the Google logo are registered trademarks of Google, Inc., used with permission.

A. Search terms
B. Total number of entries located
C. Highlighted search terms found in entries

- a domain such as .edu (educational institution), .gov (government), .org (organization), or .com (commercial site or company), which indicates the type of group sponsoring the site
- a part of the world, such as North America or Africa
- the location (such as the title, the URL, or the text) of the search term
- the audio or visual media enhancements
- the file size

Finding Specialized Online Materials

You can locate a variety of material online, ranging from e-zines (electronic magazines) to blogs (Web logs) to conversations among people. Be careful to distinguish expertise from opinion and speculation.

Look for Electronic Publications. Wide public access to the Internet has given individuals and small interest groups an economical publication option. Evaluate and use such texts cautiously.

Browse the Blogs. Globe of Blogs at globeofblogs.com provides access to the personal, political, and topical commentaries of individuals around the globe. Google features blog searches by topic at google.com/blogsearch. You may want to use RSS (often expanded as "Real Simple Syndication") software to alert you to breaking news or to sample blogging on a current topic.

Keep Up with the News. Using Google, select "News" to call up "Top Stories" and national or international coverage categories or to personalize your news search. Also visit the Web sites for news organizations (NBC, BBC, NPR, PBS Newshour, Reuters, the *Wall Street Journal*) to compare coverage and depth or to track recent stories. RSS feeds and mailing lists are available for news as well as specialized topics, such as daily quotes, biographies, and historical events on the current date from Britannica Online at http://newsletters.britannica.com/toolbox.

Searching the Library

What would you pay for access to a 24/7 Web site designed to make the most of your research time? What if it also screened and organized reliable sources for you—and tossed in free advice from information specialists? Whatever your budget, you've probably already paid—through your tuition—for these services. To get your money's worth, simply use your student ID to access your college library, online or on campus.

Visit the library home page for an overview of resources such as these:

- the online catalog for finding the library's own books, journals, newspapers, and materials you can read or check out on campus

- databases (with subscription fees paid) for electronic access to scholarly or specialized citations, abstracts, articles, and other resources
- access to the resources of the state, region, or nation through Interlibrary Loan (ILL), a regional consortium, or a trip to a nearby library
- links for finding specialized campus libraries, archives, or collections
- pages, tutorials, and tours for advice on using the library productively

To introduce you to the campus library, your instructor may arrange a class orientation. If not, visit the library Web site and campus facility yourself.

RESEARCH CHECKLIST
Accessing Library Resources

☐ What services, materials, and information does the home page present?

☐ How do you gain online access to the library from your own computer? What should you do if you have trouble logging in?

☐ How can you get live help from library staff: by drop-in visit, appointment, phone, e-mail, text message, chat, or other technology?

☐ What resources — such as the library catalog and databases — can you search in the library, on campus, or off campus?

☐ How can you identify databases useful for your project? What tutorials from the library or database provider show how to use them efficiently?

☐ How are print books, journals, magazines, or newspapers organized?

☐ How do you find resources such as government documents, maps, legal records, statistics, videos, images, recordings, or local historical archives?

☐ Where can you study individually or meet with a group in the library?

☐ What links or no-fee access to reliable Web sites, search engines such as Google Scholar, or academic style guides does the library provide?

☐ What other services — copying, printing, computer access — are available at your library?

For links to free reliable research resources, go to Re:Writing at **bedfordstmartins.com /concisebedguide**.

Learning by Doing 🔟 Reflecting on Your Library Orientation Session

After visiting the library for your class orientation, list the most useful things you have learned — such as directions for access, advice about off-campus use, ways to get search advice, specific resources for your likely project or major, types of materials new to you, the name of a reference librarian, or helpful tricks for doing faster research. Then list your current questions about your own research project, and figure out where to start looking for the best and fastest answers.

Target Your Search. Your campus library may surprise you with its sophisticated technology and easy access to an overwhelming array of resources. Identify and hunt for what you want to find.

- Do you need a mixture of sources? Use the catalog to find specialized books or journals, databases to identify individual articles, reference books to look up definitions or overviews, or government sites or indexes to find reports. If your library offers WorldCat Local or a mega search system, you can search all types of resources at one time.

- Do you need current or historical information? Look for articles in periodicals (regularly published newspapers, magazines, and journals) for news of the day, week, or year — now or in the past. Turn to scholarly books for well-seasoned discussions.

Figure 18.3 Sample home page from the Tuskegee University Libraries

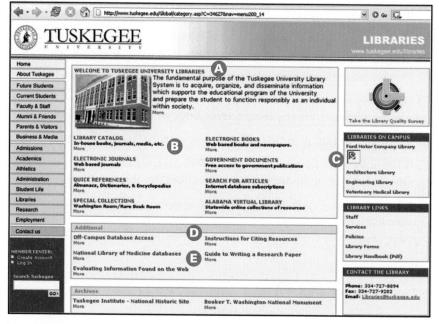

A. Overview of libraries and their purpose
B. Access to library holdings and resources
C. Information on specific campus libraries
D. Off-campus access
E. Other research resources

- Does your instructor require articles from peer-reviewed or refereed journals? Use *Ulrich's Periodicals Directory* or databases to screen for journals that rely on expert reviewers to assess articles considered for publication.

- Do you need opinions about current issues? Search databases for newspapers or magazines that carry opinion pieces, issue-oriented or investigative articles, or contrasting regional, national, or international views.

- Do you need the facts? Check state or federal agencies or nonprofit groups for statistics about people such as those in your zip code, including education, employment, or health.

Search the Library Catalog Creatively. Electronic catalogs may allow many search options, as the chart below illustrates. Consult a librarian or follow the prompts to find out which searches your catalog allows.

For help using keywords, go to the interactive "Take Action" charts in Re:Writing at **bedfordstmartins.com /concisebedguide**.

Type of Search	Explanation	Examples	Search Tips
Keyword	Terms that identify topics discussed in the source, including works by or about an author, but may generate long lists of relevant and irrelevant sources	■ workplace mental health ■ geriatric home health care ■ Creole cookbook ■ Jane Austen novels	Use a cluster of keywords to avoid broad terms (whale, nursing) or to reduce irrelevant topics using the same terms (people of color, color graphics)
Subject	Terms assigned by library catalogers, often following the Library of Congress Subject Headings (LCSH)	■ motion pictures (not films) ■ developing countries (not Third World) ■ cooking (not cookbooks)	Consult the online LCSH or note the linked subject headings with search results to find the exact phrasing used
Author	Name of individual, organization, or group, leading to list of print (and possibly online) works by author (or editor)	■ Hawthorne, Nathaniel ■ Colorado School of Mines ■ North Atlantic Treaty Organization	Begin as directed with an individual's last name or first; for a group, first use a keyword search to identify its exact name
Title	Name of book, pamphlet, journal, magazine, newspaper, video, CD, or other material	■ *Peace and Conflict Studies* ■ *Los Angeles Times* ■ *Nursing Outlook*	Look for a separate search option for titles of periodicals (journals, newspapers, magazines)
Identification Numbers	Library or consortium call numbers, publisher or government publication numbers	■ MJ BASI, local call number for recordings by Count Basie	Use the call number of a useful source to find related items online or shelved nearby
Dates	Publication or other dates used to search (or limit searches) for current or historical materials	■ Elizabeth 1558 (when she became queen of England) ■ science teaching 2013	Add dates to keyword or other searches to limit the topics or time of publication

Learning by Doing 🎛 Brainstorming for Search Terms

Start with a class topic or your rough ideas for a research question. Working with a classmate or small group, brainstorm in class or online for keywords or synonyms that might be useful search terms for each person's topic. Test your terms by searching several places — the library catalog, a subject-area database, a newspaper database, a reliable consumer Web page, a relevant government agency, or other library resources. Compare search results in terms of type, quantity, quality, and relevance of sources. Note which terms work best in which situations. Then refine your search terms — add limitations, change key words, narrow the ideas, and so forth. Search again, trying to increase the relevance of what you find.

Sort Your Search Results. When your search produces a list of possible sources, click on the most promising items to learn more about them. See Figure 18.4 for a sample keyword search and Figure 18.5 for the online record for one source. Besides the call number or shelf location, the record will identify the author, title, place of publication, date, and often the book's contents, length, scope, and search terms that may help focus your search. Use these clues to help you select options wisely.

Sample the Field. Many libraries supply Library Guides or lists of well-regarded starting points for research within a field. These valuable short-cuts help you quickly find a cluster of useful resources. The chart on page 362 supplies only a small sampling of the specialized indexes, dictionaries, encyclopedias, handbooks, yearbooks, and other resources available.

Browse the Shelves. A call number, like a building's address, tells where a book "resides." College libraries generally use the Library of Congress system with letters and numbers rather than the numerical Dewey Decimal system, but both systems group items by subject. With a call number from an online record, follow the library map and section signs to the shelf with a promising book. Once there, browse through its intriguing neighbors, which will treat the same subject.

Use the Resources. Your campus library can help you become a more efficient and productive student. Try its wide variety of resources, advice, and tools: e-books, audio books, podcasts, videos, tutorials, workshops, citation managers, source organizers, and apps for academic tasks (note takers, time managers, project schedules, group organizers, file hosting services).

For help using databases, go to the interactive "Take Action" charts in Re:Writing at **bedfordstmartins.com /concisebedguide**.

Searching Library Databases

Databases gather information. Your library may subscribe to dozens or hundreds to give you easy access to current, screened resources, including hard-to-find fee-based Web sources. Check the library site for its database

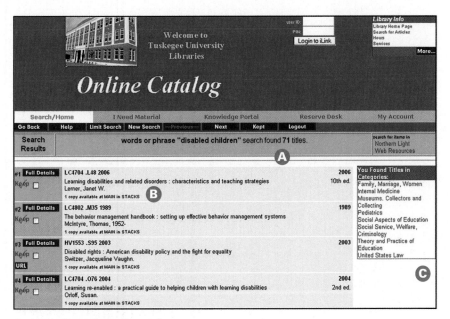

Figure 18.4 General results of a keyword search on "disabled children" using an online library catalog

A. Number of search results
B. Results screen (linked to full entries) with call numbers, titles, authors, and availability
C. Topic areas where results were found

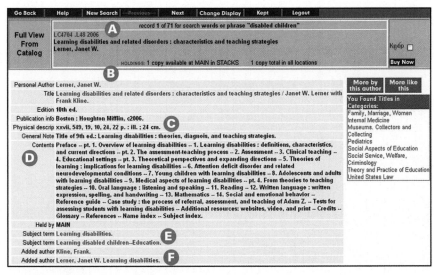

Figure 18.5 Specific record selected from keyword search results

A. Call number, title, and author
B. Availability and location
C. Number of pages, illustrations, and height of book
D. Contents by part and chapter
E. Alternate subject heading (often hyperlinked)
F. Additional author

Field

Field	Specialized Indexes	Reference Works	Government Resources	Internet Resources
Humanities	Essay and General Literature Index; JSTOR	The Humanities: A Selective Guide to Information Sources	EDSITEment at edsitement.neh.gov	Voice of the Shuttle at vos.ucsb.edu
Film and Theater	Film & Television Literature Index / Films on Demand	McGraw-Hill Encyclopedia of World Drama	Smithsonian Archives Center: Film, Video, and Audio Collections at amhistory.si.edu/archives/d-4.htm	Performing Arts links at tla-online.org/links/libraries.html
History	Historical Abstracts / America: History and Life	Dictionary of Concepts in History	The Library of Congress: American Memory at memory.loc.gov/ammem/index.html	WWW Virtual Library: History Central Catalogue at vlib.iue.it/history/index.html
Literature	MLA International Bibliography	Encyclopedia of the Novel	National Endowment for the Humanities at neh.gov	American Studies Journals at theasa.net/journals
Social Sciences	Social Sciences Citation Index	International Encyclopedia of the Social and Behavioral Sciences	Fedstats at fedstats.gov	Intute: Social Sciences at intute.ac.uk/socialsciences/
Education	Education Abstracts	International Encyclopedia of Education	National Center for Education Statistics at nces.ed.gov	ERIC: Education Resources Information Center at eric.ed.gov
Political Science	Worldwide Political Science Abstracts	State Legislative Sourcebook: A Resource Guide to Legislative Information in the 50 States	Fedworld at fedworld.ntis.gov/	Political Resources on the Net at politicalresources.net / National Security Archive at gwu.edu/~nsarchiv
Women's Studies	Women's Studies International	Women in World History: A Biographical Encyclopedia	U.S. Department of Labor Women's Bureau at dol.gov/wb/	Institute for Women's Policy Research at iwpr.org/index.cfm
Science and Technology	General Science Abstracts / Web of Science	McGraw-Hill Encyclopedia of Science and Technology	National Science Foundation at nsf.gov	EurekAlert! at eurekalert.org
Earth Sciences	Bibliography and Index of Geology	Facts on File Dictionary of Earth Science	USGS (U.S. Geological Survey): Science for a Changing World at usgs.gov	Center for International Earth Science Information Network at ciesin.org
Environmental Studies	Environmental Abstracts	Encyclopedia of Environmental Science	EPA: U.S. Environmental Protection Agency at epa.gov	EnviroLink at envirolink.org
Life Sciences	Biological Abstracts	Encyclopedia of Human Biology	National Agricultural Library at nal.usda.gov	CAPHIS Top 100 List at caphis.mlanet.org/consumer

descriptions and lists by topic or field. A librarian can help match your research question to the databases likely to provide what you need.

- **General databases** with citations, abstracts, or full-text articles from many fields: Academic Search Premier, General OneFile, LexisNexis, OmniFile Full Text

- **General-interest databases** with news and culture of the time: Reader's Guide Full-Text or Retrospective (popular periodicals); New York Times Historical, America's Newspapers, LexisNexis (news)

- **Specialized databases by type of material:** JSTOR, Project Muse, Sage (scholarly journals); Biological Abstracts (summaries of sources); WorldCat (books), American Periodical Series Online (digitized magazines from 1741 to 1900)

- **Specialized databases by field:** MedlinePlus, ScienceDirect, Green-FILE (biology, medicine, health); ABI/Inform (business), AGRICOLA (agriculture)

- **Issue-oriented databases:** PAIS International (public affairs), CQ Researcher (featured issues), Opposing Viewpoints in Context (debatable topics)

- **Reference databases:** Gale Virtual Reference Library, Oxford Reference, Credo Reference

For specific information, select a database that covers the exact field, scholarly level, type of source, or time period that you need. Databases identify sources only in publications they analyze and only for dates they cover. Take tricky problems to a librarian who may suggest a different database or older print or CD-ROM indexes for historical research.

Keywords. Start your search with the keywords in your research question:

| college costs | campus budgets | wetlands |

If your first search produces too many sources, narrow your terms:

| college tuition increases | state campus budget cuts | Illinois wetlands and Great Midwestern Flood |

Or add specifics, such as an author, title, or date.

Advanced Searches. Fill in the database's advanced search screen to restrict by date or other options, or try common search options. For example, a database might allow wildcard or truncation symbols to find all forms of a term, often * for multiple or ? for individual characters:

| child* | children, childcare, childhood |
| Colorad* | Colorado, Coloradan, Coloradans |

A database also might allow Boolean searches that combine or rule out terms:

AND (narrows: all terms must appear in a result)   Colorado and River

OR (expands: any one of the terms must appear)   Colorado or River

NOT (rules out: one term must not appear)   Colorado not River

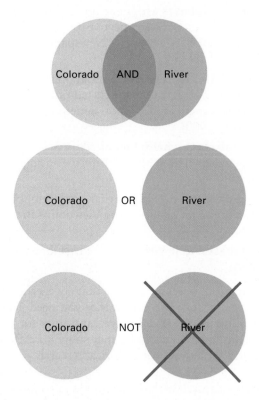

Search Returns. Your search calls up a list of records or entries that include your search terms. Click on one of these for specifics about the item (title, author, publication information, date, other details) and possibly a description or summary (often called an abstract) or a link to the full text of the item. When you find a useful item, read, take notes, print, save, or e-mail the citation or article to yourself, as your system allows. If the database supplies only an abstract, read it to decide whether you need to track down the full article elsewhere.

RESEARCH CHECKLIST
Selecting Periodical Articles from a Database

☐ What does the periodical title suggest about its audience, interest area, and popular or scholarly orientation? How likely are its articles to supply what you need?

☐ Have the periodical articles been peer-reviewed (evaluated by other scholars prior to acceptance for publication), edited and fact-checked by journalists, or accepted for publication based on popular appeal?

☐ Does the title or description of the article suggest that it will answer your research question? Or does the entry sound intriguing but irrelevant?

☐ Does the date of the article fit your need for current, contemporary, eyewitness, or classic material?

☐ Does the length of the article suggest that it is a short review, a concise overview, or an exhaustive discussion? How much detail will you need?

☐ Does the database offer the full text of the article in direct-scan pdf or reformatted html? If not, is the periodical likely to be available from another database, its Web site, or your library's shelves?

Learning by Doing 🔳 Comparing Databases

Work with others interested in a particular subject or field. Pick at least three databases in that area. For each, investigate what type of response it provides (source references, abstracts, summaries, full-text articles), which dates it covers, how extensive its collection might be, and how you can most successfully use it. Report back to your group or to the entire class.

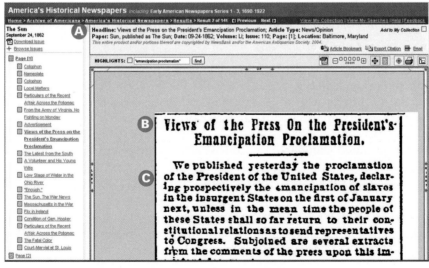

Figure 18.6 Search result from *America's Historical Newspapers*

A. Publication name, date, volume number, page number
B. Article title (and author, if available)
C. Text of article

Learning by Doing 🔀 Comparing Google and Database Searches

Work in pairs or a small group, using your tablets or laptops in class or online. Agree on a few search terms relevant for topics that interest you individually or collectively. Search for each term twice — first using Google and then using your library's general academic database. Compare and contrast the results based on quantity, relevance, usefulness, status (as peer-reviewed or refereed academic sources), or other criteria. If you wish, expand your comparisons to include Google Scholar, a different Internet search engine, a library database for a specific field, or other options.

Using Specialized Library Resources

Many other library resources are available to you beyond what you can access from your library's home page. If you need help locating or using materials, consult a librarian.

Encyclopedias. Multivolume general references, such as the *New Encyclopaedia Britannica* and *Encyclopedia Americana,* can help you survey a topic. Specialized encyclopedias cover a field in much greater depth. You can also conduct "reverse research" — reading a useful reference entry first to inform you and then to follow its bibliography to reliable sources.

Dictionary of American History	*Encyclopedia of Psychology*
Encyclopedia of Human Biology	*Encyclopedia of Sociology*
Gale Encyclopedia of Science	*Encyclopedia of World Cultures*

Dictionaries. Specialized dictionaries cover foreign languages, abbreviations, and slang as well as the terminology of a particular field, as in *Black's Law Dictionary, Stedman's Medical Dictionary,* or the *Oxford Dictionary of Natural History.* After you read a definition in a specialty dictionary, look for terms that might narrow your database searches.

Handbooks and Companions. Concise articles survey terms and topics on a specific subject.

Bloomsbury Guide to Women's Literature   *Dictionary of the Vietnam War*

Government Documents. The U.S. government, the most prolific publisher in the world, makes an increasing number of documents available for all citizens on the Web, along with indexes like these:

- *Monthly Catalog of United States Government Publications,* which is the most complete index to federal documents available
- *CIS Index,* which specializes in congressional documents with a handy legislative history index

- *Congressional Record Index,* which indexes daily reports on Congress

The government also compiles valuable statistics:

- *Statistical Abstract of the United States,* which may be the most useful single compilation of statistics, with hundreds of tables relating to population, social issues, economics, and so on
- *census.gov,* which collects an extraordinary amount of statistical data and releases much of it on the Web

Atlases. For a geographical angle, use maps of countries and regions as well as history, natural resources, ethnic groups, and other topics.

Biographical Sources. Directories list basic information about prominent people. Tools such as *Biography Index* and the *Biography and Genealogy Master Index* locate resources like *American Men and Women of Science, The Dictionary of American Biography, The Dictionary of Literary Biography, The Dictionary of National Biography, Who's Who in Politics,* and *Who's Who in the United States.*

Bibliographies. A bibliography lists a wide variety of sources on a specific subject, research others have already done. Every time you find a good book or article, look at the sources the author draws on; some of these may be useful to you and can lead to sources that you wouldn't otherwise find. For example, *The Essential Shakespeare: An Annotated Bibliography of Major Modern Studies* lists the best books and articles published on each of Shakespeare's works, a wonderful shortcut when you're looking for worthwhile criticism. If you're lucky, adding the word *bibliography* to a subject or keyword search on your topic will turn up a similarly helpful list of sources with annotations.

Special Materials. Your library is likely to have other collections of materials, especially on regional or specialized topics, but you may need to ask what's available. For example, firsthand diaries, letters, speeches, and interviews are increasingly available in searchable databases. Your library also may collect pamphlets and reports distributed by companies, trade groups, and professional organizations.

RESEARCH CHECKLIST
Managing Your Project

☐ Are you on schedule? Do you need to adjust your timetable to give yourself more or less time for any of the stages?

☐ Are you using your research question to stay on track and avoid digressions?

☐ Are you keeping your materials up-to-date — listing new sources in your working bibliography and storing new material in your archives?

☐ Do you have a clear idea of where you are in the research process?

---

19 Evaluating Sources

For more on critical reading and thinking, see Chs. 2 and 3.

After you locate and collect information, you need to think critically and evaluate — in other words, judge — your sources.

- Which of your sources are reliable?
- Which of these sources are relevant to your topic?
- What evidence from these sources is most useful for your paper?

Why Evaluating Sources Matters

In a College Course

- You have found half a dozen sources about your topic, but they wildly disagree; you have to decide what to do next.
- You found a Web site without any author, a testimonial by a TV star you dimly remember, and a boring article by a professor, but you don't know which one to believe.

In the Workplace

- You have to prepare a recommendation for a client after deciding what data and field reports to provide.

In Your Community

- You disagree with the mayor's decision to ban urban gardening, so you want to find current, substantial information that will change her mind.

When have you decided which sources to use and which to skip? In what situations do you expect to evaluate sources again?

Evaluating Library and Internet Sources

Not every source you locate will be equally reliable or equally useful. Sites recommended by your library have been screened by professionals, but each has its own point of view or approach, often a necessary bias to restrict its focus. Sources from the Web require special care. Like other firsthand materials, postings, blogs, and sites reflect the biases, interests, or information gaps of their writers or sponsors. Commercial and organizational sites may supply useful material, but they provide only what supports their goals—selling their products, serving their clients, enlisting new members, or persuading others to accept their activities or views. See Figure 19.1 for a sample evaluation of a Web site that provides both informative and persuasive materials.

How can you simplify evaluation? Begin with your selection of sources. Suppose you draw information from an article in a print or online peer-reviewed journal. The evaluation of that article actually began when the journal editors first read it and then asked expert reviewers to evaluate whether it merited publication. Similarly, a serious book from a major publishing company or university press probably has been submitted to knowledgeable reviewers. Such reviewers may be asked to assess whether the book or article seems well reasoned, logically presented, and competently researched. However, they can't decide if the work is pertinent to your research question or contains evidence useful for your paper.

How do you know what evidence is best? Do what experienced researchers do—ask key questions. Use the time-tested journalist's questions—who, what, when, where, why, how—to evaluate each of your sources.

RESEARCH CHECKLIST
Evaluating Sources

Who?

- ☐ Who is the author of the source? What are the author's credentials and profession? What might be the author's point of view?

- ☐ Who is the intended audience of the source? Experts in the field? Professionals? General readers? People with a special interest? In what ways does the source's tone or evidence appeal to this audience?

- ☐ Who is the publisher of the source or the sponsor of the site? Is it a corporation, a scholarly organization, a professional association, a government agency, or an issue-oriented group? Have you heard of this publisher or sponsor before? Is it well regarded? Does it seem reputable and responsible? Is it considered academic or popular?

- ☐ Who has reviewed the source prior to publication? Only the author? Peer reviewers who are experts in the area? An editorial staff?

What?

- ☐ What is the purpose of the publication or Web site? Is it to sell a product or service? To entertain? To supply information? To publish new research? To shape opinion about an issue or a cause?

- ☐ What bias or point of view might affect the reliability of the source?

☐ What kind of information does the source supply? Is it a primary source (a firsthand account) or a secondary source (an analysis of primary material)? If it is a secondary source, does it rely on sound evidence from primary sources?

☐ What evidence does the source present? Does it seem accurate and trustworthy? Is it sufficient and relevant given what you know? Does its argument or analysis seem logical and complete, or does it leave questions unanswered? Does it identify and list its sources or supply active links?

When?

☐ When was the source published or created? Is its information current?

☐ When was it last revised or updated? Is its information up-to-date?

Where?

☐ Where did you find the source? Is it available through your campus library's site? Is it on a Web site that popped up in a general search?

☐ Where has the source been recommended? On an instructor's syllabus or Web page? On a library list? In another reliable source? During a conference with an instructor or a librarian?

Why?

☐ Why should you use this source rather than others?

☐ Why is its information directly relevant to your research question?

How?

☐ How does the selection of evidence in the source reflect the interests and expertise of its author, publisher or sponsor, and intended audience? How might you need to qualify its use in your paper?

☐ How would its information add to your paper? How would it help answer your research question and provide evidence to persuade your readers?

For an interactive Learning by Doing activity on evaluating online sources, go to Ch. 19: **bedfordstmartins** **.com/concisebedguide**.

Learning by Doing 🎦 Evaluating Your Sources

Select a source that you expect to be useful for your paper. Using the preceding checklist, jot down notes as you examine the source for reliability and relevance. Working with a classmate or group, present your evaluations to each other. Then discuss strategies for dealing with the strengths and limitations of the sources you have evaluated. (Use the next sections to help you deepen your evaluation.)

Figure 19.1
Evaluating the
purpose, audience,
and bias of a Web
site offering infor-
mative and persua-
sive materials

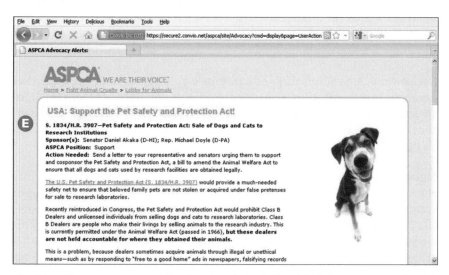

A. Identifies group as organization (.org), not school (.edu) or company (.com)
B. Uses engaging animal graphics
C. Appeals for support
D. Explains purpose of group and provides toolbar link to contact information
E. Links to information and recommends action about issues that concern
animal lovers

Who Is the Author?

Learn about each author's credentials, affiliations, and reputation so that any author who shapes or supports your ideas is reliable and trustworthy.

Print Credentials. Check for the author's background in any preface, introduction, or concluding note in an article or a book. National newsmagazines (for example, *The Economist* or *Time*) usually identify experts before or next to their contributions. However, most of their articles are written by reporters who try to substantiate facts and cover multiple views, perhaps compiling regional contributions. In contrast, some other magazines select facts to mirror editorial opinions.

Internet Credentials. For a Web site, look for a hyperlinked author's name leading to other articles, a link to author information, or an e-mail address so you could contact the author about his or her background. If your source is a posting to a newsgroup or a mailing list, deduce what you can from the writer's e-mail address and any signature file. Try a Web search for the person's name, looking for associated sites or links to or from the author's site. If you can't find out about the author, treat the information as background for you, not as evidence in your paper.

Field Credentials. For field research, you may be able to select your sources. Consider their backgrounds, credentials, and biases. To investigate safety standards for infant car seats, a personal interview with a local pediatrician will probably produce different information than an interview with a sales representative.

Reputation. A good measure of someone's expertise is the regard of other experts. Do others cite the work of your source's author? Does your instructor or a campus expert recognize or recommend the author? Is the author listed in a biographical database? Does a search for the author on Google Scholar produce other sources that cite the author?

Material with No Author Identified. If no author is given, try to identify the sponsor, publisher, or editor. On a Web site, check the home page or search for a disclaimer, contact information, or an "About This Site" page. If a print source doesn't list an author, consider the publication: Is the article in a respected newspaper like the *Wall Street Journal* or a supermarket tabloid? Is the source a news story, an opinion piece, or an ad? Is the brochure published by a leader in its field?

Who Else Is Involved?

Intended Audience. A source written for authorities in a field is likely to assume that readers already have plenty of background. Such sources typically skip overviews and tailor their details for experts. In contrast, sources for general audiences usually define terms and supply background. Instead of beginning your paper on HIV treatments with an article in a well-known medical journal for physicians that discusses the most favorable chemical composition for a protease inhibitor drug, turn first to a source that defines *protease inhibitor* and explains how it helps HIV patients.

Publisher or Sponsor. The person, organization, agency, or corporation that prints or sponsors a source also may shape its content. Like authors, publishers often hold a point of view. Critically question what might motivate a publisher. Is a Web site created for commercial (.com) purposes, such as selling a product or service? Is it sponsored by an organization devoted to a cause (.org, as in Figure 19.1) or a government agency (.gov)? Is it the work of an individual with strong opinions but little expertise? Is a newsgroup or list limited to a particular interest? Is a publisher noted for works in a specific field or with a political agenda? Does a periodical have a predictable point of view? A faith-based publication will take a different view than a newsmagazine, just as a conservative publication will differ from a liberal one. For a Web site sponsor, look for a mission statement or an "About" page. Consult a librarian if you need help with these difficult questions.

For an example showing how a URL identifies a publisher, see A on p. 371.

Reviewers before Publication. Consider whether a publisher has an editorial staff, an expert editor, or an advisory board of experts. Does it rely on peer reviewers to critique articles or books under consideration? Does it expect research to meet professional standards? Does it outline such standards in its advice for prospective authors or its description of its mission? Does a sponsor have a solid reputation as a professional organization?

What Is the Purpose?

A library reference book serves a different purpose from a newspaper editorial, a magazine ad, or a Web site that promotes a service. To understand the purpose or intention of a source, ask critical questions: Is its purpose to explain or inform? To report new research? To persuade? To add a viewpoint? To sell a product? Does the source acknowledge its purpose in its preface, mission statement, or "About Us" or FAQ (Frequently Asked Questions) page?

Bias. A *bias* is a preference for a particular side of an issue. Because most authors and publishers have opinions on their topics, there's little point in asking whether they are biased. Instead, ask how that viewpoint affects the presentation of information and opinion. What are the author's or sponsor's allegiances? Does the source treat one side of an issue more favorably than another? Is that bias hidden or stated? A strong bias does not invalidate a source. However, if you spot such bias early, you can look for other viewpoints to avoid lopsided analyses.

Primary or Secondary Information. A *primary source* is a firsthand account written by an eyewitness or a participant. It contains raw data and immediate impressions. A *secondary source* is an analysis of information in one or more primary sources. Primary sources for investigating the Korean War might include diaries or letters written by military personnel, accounts of civilian witnesses, articles by journalists on the scene, and official military reports. If a historian used those accounts as evidence in a study of military strategy or if a peace activist used them in a book on consequences of warfare for civilians, the resulting works would be secondary sources.

Most research papers benefit from both primary and secondary sources. If you repeatedly cite a fact or an authority quoted in someone else's analysis, try to go to the primary source. After all, a bombing raid that spared 70 percent of a village also leveled 30 percent of it. The original research (published as a primary source) can help you learn where facts end and interpretation begins.

When Was the Source Published?

In most fields, new information and discoveries appear every year, so a source needs to be up-to-date or at least still timely. New information may appear first in Web postings, media broadcasts, newspapers, and eventually magazines, though such sources may not allow time to consider information thoughtfully. Later, as material is more fully examined, it may appear in scholarly articles and books. For this reason, older materials can supply a valuable historical, theoretical, or analytical focus.

Where Did You Find the Source?

Is it recommended by your instructor? Is it in the library's collection? When instructors or academic units direct you to sources, you benefit from both their subject-matter and teaching expertise. On the other hand, when you find a Web source while randomly browsing or pick up a magazine at the dentist's office, you'll need to do all the source evaluation yourself. Begin by asking where the source got its information.

Why Would You Use This Source?

For more on selecting sources, see section B in the Quick Research Guide, pp. A-24–A-26.

For more on testing evidence, see pp. 43–44.

Why use one source rather than another? Is its information useful for your purposes? Would its strong quotations or hard facts be effective? Does it tackle the topic in a relevant way? For one paper, you might appropriately rely on a popular magazine; for another, you might need the scholarly findings on which the magazine relied. Look for the best sources for your purpose, asking not only "Will this do?" but also "Would something else be better?"

How Would This Source Contribute to Your Paper?

The evidence in a source—its ideas, facts, and expert or other opinions—can tell you about its reliability and usefulness for your project. Is its evidence complete, up-to-date, and carefully assembled? Is there enough convincing evidence to support its claims? Does visual material enhance the source, not distract from its argument or information? Does the source identify its own sources in citations and a bibliography? Even a highly reliable source needs to be relevant to your research question and your ideas about how to answer that question. An interesting fact or opinion could be just that—interesting. Instead, you need facts, expert opinions, information, and quotations that relate directly to your purpose and audience.

Learning by Doing 🔲 Adding Useful Sources

Writers often use common organizational patterns to review a group of solid sources. For example, you might arrange sources chronologically to trace history or development, compare and contrast sources to present alternatives, or trace cause and effect through several sources. Examine the contributions of your current sources to your argument. Do you need to complete a chronology with an established view or a current one? Do you need to fill out a comparison or a causal analysis? Add relevant sources as needed for balance or depth.

For more on using time order, see Ch. 4; for more on comparison and contrast, see Ch. 6.

Reconsidering Purpose and Thesis

Once you have gathered and evaluated a reasonable collection of sources, it's time to step back and consider them as a group.

- Have you found enough relevant and credible sources to satisfy the requirements of your assignment? Have you found enough to suggest sound answers to your research question?

- Are your sources thought provoking? Can you tell what is generally accepted, controversial, or possibly unreliable? Have your sources enlightened you while substantiating, refining, or changing your ideas?

- Are your sources varied? Have they helped you achieve a reasonably complete view of your topic, including other perspectives, approaches, alternatives, or interpretations? Have they deepened your understanding and helped you reach well-reasoned, balanced conclusions?

- Are your sources appropriate? Do they answer your question with evidence your readers will find persuasive? Do they have the range and depth necessary to achieve your purpose and satisfy your readers?

Use these questions to check in with yourself. Make sure that you have a clear direction for your research—whether it's the same direction you started with or a completely new one. Perhaps you are ready to answer your research question, refine your thesis, and begin a draft that pulls together your ideas and those of your sources. On the other hand, you may want to find other sources to support or challenge your assumptions, to counter strong evidence against your position, or to pursue a tantalizing new direction.

20 Integrating Sources

For more on using sources in your writing, see Ch. 9 and D1–D6 in the Quick Research Guide, pp. A-28–A-31.

Your paper should project your own voice and showcase your ideas—your thesis and main points about your research question. It also should marshal compelling support, using the evidence that you have quoted, paraphrased, and summarized from sources. Add this support responsibly, identifying both the sources and the ideas or exact words captured from them.

Why Integrating Sources Matters

In a College Course
- You have read and read for your sociology paper, but now you need to fit your sources into your paper very efficiently so you finish on time.
- You need to integrate your class projects and reading log into your capstone portfolio to complete the final requirement for your credential.

In the Workplace
- You must synthesize materials from three rival departments in a collaborative report.

In Your Community
- You know that parents exchange information about autism, but the school board wants academic sources to identify best practices for teachers.

When have you integrated a jumble of sources? In what situations do you expect to do so again?

Using Sources Ethically

The complex, lively process of research is enriched by the exchange of ideas. However, discussions of research ethics sometimes reduce that topic to one issue: plagiarism. Plagiarism is viewed especially seriously in college because it shows a deep disrespect for the work of the academic world—investigating, evaluating, analyzing, interpreting, and synthesizing ideas. And it may have

Plagiarism Problem	Remedy
You have dawdled. Someone tells you about a site that sells papers, but you know this is wrong. Plus their topics don't sound like your assignment, and you need to hand in drafts and an annotated bibliography, too.	Don't buy the paper. Ask your instructor for more time, even with a penalty. Cancel your social life for the week, and hunt for recommended sources. Be proud that you showed integrity and didn't risk your college career.
You've fully investigated a serious research question about a problem affecting your family, but now you're mixing up what you've quoted, summed up, and thought up yourself. You're afraid your disorganization will look like plagiarism.	Stop and get organized. Link every note or file to its source with the author's last name (or brief title) and page number. Treat unidentified leftover notes as background. Don't add what you can't credit.
You found a great book in the library but had only a minute to record the basics. Later you found these notes: InDfCult, HUP, Cambridge, Carol Padden, Tom Humphries, 5 122 For Df voice/technol = issue Relates to cult def	Go back to the library, and get help finding the book. Spell out clear information about *Inside Deaf Culture* by Carol Padden and Tom Humphries, published in Cambridge, MA, by Harvard University Press in 2005. Turn back to p. 122. Decide what to do: quote (exact words with quotation marks) or paraphrase (your own words, not "parroting").
You've never read a book with hard words like *transmogrify* and *heuristic*. You can't restate them because you don't understand them. You're afraid your instructor will think you're a cheater who just copied, not an embarrassed student who can't read well enough.	Don't use a source you can't understand. Look for others shelved nearby or listed under the same keywords. If the source is required, reread and sum up each passage in turn to master it. Spend time improving your reading using campus or community support services.
You're struggling to start writing. Finally you're creating sentences, then pasting in notes. You suddenly wonder how you'll figure out where to add your source citations. What if you didn't identify a few sources or add the page numbers for quotations?	Backtrack fast. Add notes (color, brackets, or comments) to mark exactly where you need to add a source citation later. For yourself, note the basics—author and page. Add quotation marks for words directly from the source at the moment you integrate them.
In your home country, you and your friends worked together to state the answer the teacher expected. Everyone handed it in, so nobody was left out. Here your teacher wants different papers, and you are afraid yours will be wrong.	Different cultures have different expectations. Research papers here often are explorations, not right answers. Think about ideas of classmates or sources, but write down your own well-reasoned thoughts. Get advice from the ESL or writing center.

serious consequences—failing a paper, failing a course, or being dismissed from the institution.

Plagiarists intentionally present someone else's work as their own—whether they dishonestly submit as their own a paper purchased from the Web, pretend that passages copied from an article are their own writing, present the ideas of others without identifying their sources, or paste in someone else's graphics without acknowledgment or permission.

Although college writers may not intend to plagiarize, most campus policies look at the outcome, not the intent. Working carefully with sources and treating ideas and expressions of others respectfully can build the skills necessary to avoid mistakes. Educating yourself about the standards of your campus, instructor, and profession also can protect you from ethical errors with heavy consequences. The chart on page 377 illustrates how to avoid or remedy common situations that can generate problems.

Careful researchers acknowledge intellectual obligations and responsibilities, showing respect for all engaged in the academic exchange:

■ researchers whose studies provide a sturdy foundation

■ readers curious about discoveries, reasons, and evidence

■ themselves as they gain experience with credible research practices

---

RESEARCH CHECKLIST
Learning How to Conduct Research Ethically

☐ Have you accepted the responsibility of reviewing your campus standards for ethical academic conduct? Have you checked your syllabus for any explanation about how those standards apply in your course?

☐ If you feel ill prepared for doing research, have you sought help from your instructor or staff at the library, writing center, or computer lab?

☐ Are you regularly recording source entries in your working bibliography?

☐ Are you carefully distinguishing your own ideas from those of your sources when you record notes or gather material for your research archive? Have you tried putting source notes in one column on a page and your thoughts in a second column?

☐ Are you sticking to your research schedule to avoid a deadline crisis?

☐ Have you analyzed your paper-writing habits to identify any, such as procrastination, that might create ethical problems for you? How do you plan to change such habits to avoid problems?

☐ Have you used this book to practice and improve research skills (such as quoting, paraphrasing, or summarizing)?

☐ Have you found the chapter in this book that explains the documentation style you'll use in your paper? If not, find it now.

☐ Have you identified and followed campus procedures for conducting field research involving other people?

☐ Have you recorded contact information so that you can request permission to include any visual materials from sources in your paper?

☐ If your research is part of a group project, have you honored your agreements, meeting your obligations in a timely manner?

☐ Have you asked your instructor's advice about any other ethical issues that have arisen during your research project?

Capturing, Launching, and Citing Evidence

Sources alone do not make for an effective research paper. Instead, the ideas, explanations, and details from your sources need to be integrated — combined and mixed — with your own thoughts and conclusions about the question you have investigated. Together they eventually form a unified whole that conveys your perspective and the evidence that logically supports it. To make sure that your voice isn't drowned out by your sources, keep your research question and working thesis — maybe still evolving — in front of you as you integrate information. On the other hand, identify and credit your sources appropriately, treating them with the respect they deserve.

For more on stating a thesis, see pp. 363–72.

Once you have recorded a source note, you may be tempted to include it in your paper at all costs. Resist. Include only material that answers your research question and supports your thesis. A note dragged in by force always sticks out like a pig in the belly of a boa constrictor.

When material does fit, consider how to incorporate it effectively and ethically. Quoting reproduces an author's exact words. Paraphrasing restates an author's ideas in your own words and sentences. Summarizing extracts the essence of an author's meaning. You also need to launch captured material by introducing it to readers and to cite it by crediting its source.

For more about how to quote, paraphrase, and summarize, see pp. 178–89 and 345–48.

Quoting and Paraphrasing Accurately

To illustrate the art of capturing source material, let's first look at a passage from historian Barbara W. Tuchman. In *A Distant Mirror: The Calamitous Fourteenth Century* (New York: Knopf, 1978), Tuchman sets forth the effects of the famous plague known as the Black Death. In her foreword, she admits that any historian dealing with the Middle Ages faces difficulties. For one, large gaps exist in the records. Here is her original wording:

Capture	Launch	Cite
■ Quote	■ Identify authority	■ Credit the source in your draft
■ Paraphrase	■ Provide credentials for credibility	■ Link the citation to your final list of sources
■ Summarize	■ Usher in the source	■ Specify the location of the material used
■ Synthesize	■ Connect support to your points	

For an interactive Learning by Doing activity on quoting and paraphrasing accurately, go to Ch. 20: **bedfordstmartins .com/concisebedguide**.

ORIGINAL

    A greater hazard, built into the very nature of recorded history, is overload of the negative: the disproportionate survival of the bad side — of evil, misery, contention, and harm. In history this is exactly the same as in the daily newspaper. The normal does not make news. History is made by the documents that survive, and these lean heavily on crisis and calamity, crime and misbehavior, because such things are the subject matter of the documentary process — of lawsuits, treaties, moralists' denunciations, literary satire, papal Bulls. No Pope ever issued a Bull to approve of something. Negative overload can be seen at work in the religious reformer Nicolas de Clamanges, who, in denouncing unfit and worldly prelates in 1401, said that in his anxiety for reform he would not discuss the good clerics because "they do not count beside the perverse men."

    Disaster is rarely as pervasive as it seems from recorded accounts. The fact of being on the record makes it appear continuous and ubiquitous whereas it is more likely to have been sporadic both in time and place. Besides, persistence of the normal is usually greater than the effect of disturbance, as we know from our own times. After absorbing the news of today, one expects to face a world consisting entirely of strikes, crimes, power failures, broken water mains, stalled trains, school shutdowns, muggers, drug addicts, neo-Nazis, and rapists. The fact is that one can come home in the evening — on a lucky day — without having encountered more than one or two of these phenomena.

    Although you might highlight this passage as you read it, it is too long to include in your paper. Quoting it directly would let your source overshadow your own voice. Instead, you might quote a striking line or so and paraphrase the rest by restating the details in your own words. Here, the writer puts Tuchman's ideas into other words but retains her major points and credits her ideas.

PARAPHRASE WITH QUOTATION

Tuchman points out that historians find some distortion of the truth hard to avoid, for more documentation exists for crimes, suffering, and calamities than for the events of ordinary life. As a result, history may overemphasize the negative. The author reminds us that we are familiar with this process in our news coverage, which treats bad news as more interesting than good news. If we believed that news stories told all the truth, we would feel threatened at all times by technical failures, crime, and violence—but we are threatened only some of the time, and normal life goes on. The good, dull, ordinary parts of our lives do not make the front page, and the praiseworthy tend to be ignored. "No Pope," says Tuchman, "ever issued a Bull to approve of something." But in truth, social upheaval did not prevail as widely as we might think from the surviving documents of medieval life (xviii).

In this reasonably complete paraphrase, about half as long as the original, most of Tuchman's points are spelled out. The writer doesn't interpret or evaluate Tuchman's ideas — she only passes them on. Paraphrasing helps her emphasize ideas important to her research. It also makes readers more aware of them as support for her thesis than quoting the passage would. The writer has directly quoted Tuchman's remark about papal Bulls because it would be hard to improve on that short, memorable statement.

Often you paraphrase to emphasize one point. This passage comes from Evelyn Underhill's classic study *Mysticism* (New York: Doubleday, 1990):

ORIGINAL

In the evidence given during the process for St. Teresa's beatification, Maria de San Francisco of Medina, one of her early nuns, stated that on entering the saint's cell whilst she was writing this same "Interior Castle" she found her [St. Teresa] so absorbed in contemplation as to be unaware of the external world. "If we made a noise close to her," said another, Maria del Nacimiento, "she neither ceased to write nor complained of being disturbed." Both these nuns, and also Ana de la Encarnacion, prioress of Granada, affirmed that she wrote with immense speed, never stopping to erase or to correct, being anxious, as she said, to write what the Lord had given her before she forgot it.

Suppose that the names of the witnesses do not matter to a researcher who wishes to emphasize, in fewer words, the renowned mystic's writing habits. That writer might paraphrase the passage (and quote it in part) like this:

PARAPHRASE WITH QUOTATION

Underhill has recalled the testimony of those who saw St. Teresa at work on *The Interior Castle*. Oblivious to noise, the celebrated mystic appeared to write in a state of complete absorption, driving her pen "with immense speed, never stopping to erase or to correct, being anxious, as she said, to write what the Lord had given her before she forgot it" (242).

Summarizing Concisely

For Tuchman's original passage, see p. 380.

To illustrate how summarizing can serve you, this example sums up the passage from Tuchman:

SUMMARY

Tuchman reminds us that history lays stress on misery and misdeeds because these negative events attracted notice in their time and so were reported in writing; just as in news stories today, bad news predominates. But we should remember that suffering and social upheaval didn't prevail everywhere all the time (xviii).

This summary merely abstracts from the original. Not everything is preserved — not Tuchman's thought about papal Bulls, not examples such as neo-Nazis. But the gist—the summary of the main idea—echoes Tuchman faithfully.

Before you write a summary, an effective way to sense the gist of a passage is to pare away examples, details, modifiers, and nonessentials. Here is the quotation from Tuchman as one student marked it up on a photocopy, crossing out elements she decided to omit from her summary.

> ~~A greater hazard,~~ built into the ~~very~~ nature of recorded history, is ~~overload of the negative:~~ the disproportionate survival of the bad side—~~of evil, misery, contention, and harm. In history~~ this is exactly the same as in the daily newspaper. ~~The normal does not make news. History is made by the~~ documents that survive, ~~and these~~ lean heavily on crisis and calamity, crime and misbehavior, because such things are the subject matter of the documentary process ~~—of lawsuits, treaties, moralists' denunciations, literary satire, papal Bulls. No Pope ever issued a Bull to approve of something. Negative overload can be seen at work in the religious reformer Nicolas de Clamanges, who, in denouncing unfit and worldly prelates in 1401, said that in his anxiety for reform he would not discuss the good clerics because "they do not count beside the perverse men."~~
>
> Disaster is rarely as pervasive as it seems from recorded accounts. ~~The fact of being on the record makes it appear continuous and ubiquitous whereas~~ it is more likely to have been sporadic both in time and place. Besides, persistence of the normal is usually greater than the effect of disturbance, as we know from our own times. ~~After absorbing the news of today, one expects to face a world consisting entirely of strikes, crimes, power failures, broken water mains, stalled trains, school shutdowns, muggers, drug addicts, neo Nazis, and rapists. The fact is that one can come home in the evening—on a lucky day—without having encountered more than one or two of these phenomena.~~

Rewording what was left, she wrote the following condensed version:

SUMMARY

History, like a morning newspaper, reports more bad than good. Why? Because the documents that have come down to us tend to deal with upheavals and disturbances, which are seldom as extensive and long-lasting as history books might lead us to believe (Tuchman xviii).

For more on avoiding plagiarism and using accepted methods of adding source material, see Ch. 9 and D1 in the Quick Research Guide, pp. A-28–A-29.

In writing her summary, the student could not simply omit the words she had deleted. The result would have been less readable and still long. She knew she couldn't use Tuchman's very words: that would be plagiarism. To make a compact, honest summary that would fit smoothly into her paper, she had to condense the passage into her own words.

Avoiding Plagiarism

Never lift another writer's words or ideas without giving that writer due credit and transforming them into words of your own. If you do use words or ideas without giving credit, you are plagiarizing. When you honestly summarize and paraphrase, clearly show that the ideas are the originator's, here Tuchman or Underhill. In contrast, the next examples are unacceptable paraphrases of Tuchman's passage that use, without thanks, her ideas and even her very words. Finding such gross borrowings in a paper, an instructor might hear the ringing of a burglar alarm. The first example lifts both thoughts and words, underlined here with the lines in the original noted in the margin.

For Tuchman's original passage, see p. 380.

PLAGIARIZED THOUGHTS AND WORDS

Sometimes it's difficult for historians to learn the truth about the everyday lives

of people from past societies because of <u>the disproportionate survival of the bad</u> —— Quoted from line 2

<u>side of things.</u> Historical documents, like today's newspapers, tend to lean rather

heavily on <u>crisis, crime, and misbehavior.</u> Reading the newspaper could lead <u>one</u> —— Close to lines 5–6

<u>to expect a world consisting entirely of strikes, crimes, power failures, muggers,</u> —— Close to line 19

<u>drug addicts, and rapists.</u> In fact, though, <u>disaster is rarely so pervasive as</u> —— Lists from lines 19–21

<u>recorded accounts can make it seem.</u> ———————————————— Close to ¶ 2 opening

This writer did not understand the passage well enough to put Tuchman's ideas in his or her own words. If you allow enough time to read, think, and write, you are likely to handle sources more effectively than those who procrastinate or rush through their research. The next example is a more subtle theft, lifting thoughts but not words.

For more on planning a research project, see Ch. 16.

PLAGIARIZED THOUGHTS

It's not always easy to determine the truth about the everyday lives of people from past societies because bad news gets recorded a lot more frequently than good news does. Historical documents, like today's news channels, tend to pick up on malice and disaster and ignore flat normality. If I were to base my opinion of the world on what is on the news, I would expect death and destruction around me all the time. Actually, I rarely come up against true disaster.

By using the first-person pronoun *I*, this student suggests that Tuchman's ideas are his own. That is just as dishonest as quoting without using quotation marks, as reprehensible as not citing the source of ideas.

The next example fails to make clear which ideas belong to the writer and which to Tuchman.

For a tutorial
on avoiding
plagiarism, go to the
interactive "Take
Action" charts in
Re:Writing at
**bedfordstmartins.com
/concisebedguide**.

For more on working
with sources, see
Chs. 9 and 17 as well
as the Quick Research
Guide, beginning on
p. A-20. For more on
quotation marks,
ellipses, and brackets,
see C3 in the Quick
Editing Guide,
pp. A-55–A-56.

PLAGIARIZED WITH FAULTY CREDIT

Barbara Tuchman explains that it can be difficult for historians to learn about
the everyday lives of people who lived long ago because historical documents
tend to record only bad news. Today's news is like that, too: disaster, malice,
and confusion take up a lot more room than happiness and serenity. Just as the
ins and outs of our everyday lives go unreported, we can suspect that upheavals
do not play as important a part in the making of history as they seem to.

After rightly attributing ideas in the first sentence to Tuchman, the writer
makes a comparison to today's world in sentence 2. In sentence 3, she returns to Tuchman's ideas without giving Tuchman credit. The placement
of sentence 3 suggests that this last idea is the student's, not Tuchman's.

As you write, use ideas and words from your sources carefully, and credit
those sources. Supply introductory and transitional comments to launch
and attribute quotations, paraphrases, and summaries to the original source
("As Tuchman observes . . ."). Rely on quotation marks and other punctuation to show exactly which words come from your sources.

RESEARCH CHECKLIST
Avoiding Plagiarism

☐ Have you identified the author of material you quote, paraphrase, or
summarize? Have you credited the originator of facts and ideas you use?

☐ Have you clearly shown where another writer's ideas stop and yours begin?

☐ Have you checked each paraphrase or summary against the original for
accuracy? Do you use your own words? Do you avoid words and sentences
close to those in the original? Do you avoid distorting the original meaning?

☐ Have you checked each quotation against the original for accuracy? Have
you used quotation marks for both passages and significant words taken
directly from your source? Have you noted the page in the original?

☐ Have you used an ellipsis mark (. . .) to show your omissions from the
original? Have you used brackets ([ ]) to indicate your changes or additions
in a quotation? Have you avoided distorting the original meaning?

Launching Source Material

You need to write a launch statement to identify the source of each detail
and each idea—whether a quotation, summary, or paraphrase. Whenever
possible, help readers see why you have selected particular sources, why you
find their evidence pertinent, or how they support your conclusions. Select
the verb that conveys to readers each source's contribution: says, claims,
agrees, challenges, argues, discusses, interprets, describes, and so forth. Use

your launch statements to show not only that you have read your sources but also that you have absorbed and applied what they say about your research question. Try the following strategies to strengthen launch statements.

For more on the format for source citations in the text, see D6 in the Quick Research Guide, p. A-31.

- Name the author in the sentence that introduces the source:

  As Wood explains, the goal of American education continues to fluctuate between gaining knowledge and applying it (58).

- Add the author's name in the middle of the source material:

  In *Romeo and Juliet,* "That which we call a rose," Shakespeare claims, "By any other word would smell as sweet" (2.2.43–44).

- Note the professional title or affiliation of someone you've interviewed to add authority and increase the credibility of your source:

  According to Jan Lewis, a tax attorney at Sands and Gonzales, . . .

  Briefly noting relevant background or experience can do the same:

  Recalling her tour of duty in Iraq, Sergeant Nelson noted . . .

- Identify information from your own field research:

  When interviewed about the campus disaster plan, Natalie Chan, Director of Campus Services, confirmed . . .

- Name the author only in the source citation in parentheses if you want to keep your focus on the topic:

  A second march on Washington followed the first (Whitlock 83).

- Explain for the reader why you have selected and included the material:

  As Serrano's three-year investigation of tragic border incidents shows, the current policies carry high financial and human costs.

- Interpret what you see as the point or relevance of the material:

  Stein focuses on stem-cell research, but his discussion of potential ethical implications (18) also applies to other medical research.

- Relate the source clearly to the thesis or point it supports:

  Although Robinson analyzes workplace interactions, her conclusions (289–92) suggest the need to look at the issues in schools as well.

- Compare or contrast the point of view or evidence of two sources:

  While Desmond emphasizes the European economic disputes, Lewis turns to the social stresses that also set the stage for World War II.

Adding transitional expressions to guide readers can strengthen your launch statements by relating one source to another (*in addition, in contrast, more recently, in a more favorable view*) or particular evidence to your line of reasoning (*next, furthermore, in addition, despite, on the other hand*). However, transitions alone are not enough. Your analysis and your original thought need to introduce and follow from source information.

Take Action Integrating and Synthesizing Sources

Ask each question at the top of the chart to consider whether your draft might need work on that issue. If so, follow the ASK — LOCATE SPECIFICS — TAKE ACTION sequence to revise.

	Weak Group of Sources?	Unclear Connections?	No New Ideas?
1 ASK	Do I need to reexamine the group of sources that I plan to synthesize?	Do I need to relate my sources more deeply and clearly to each other?	Do I need to deepen my synthesis so it goes beyond my sources to my own ideas?
2 LOCATE SPECIFICS	■ List the sources you're synthesizing. ■ Write out principles you have used (or could use) to select and group them—chronology to show change over time, theme to show aspects of a topic, comparison to show similarities, or another system. ■ Eliminate any fudging about your sources: pin down your guesses; summarize or paraphrase quotes; specify rather than generalize.	■ For each source, review your notes so you can sum up its focus. ■ Highlight connective statements or transitions already used in your draft to link the sources. ■ Mark any jumps from source to source without transitions. ■ Read your draft out loud to yourself, marking any weak or incomplete synthesis of sources. ■ Ask a peer to mark any unclear passages.	■ Schedule several blocks of time so that you can concentrate on your intellectual task. ■ Mark a check by any part of your synthesis that reads like a grocery list (bread, eggs, milk or Smith, Jones, Chu). ■ Star each spot where you repeat the source's point without relating it to your point or adding your interpretation.
3 TAKE ACTION	■ Write down how each source develops your principles. ■ Redefine your principles or your ideas about what each source shows, as needed. ■ Revise your group: drop or add sources; move some if they don't fit well. If a source fits at several places, pick the best spot or fill a gap.	■ If a connection is missing, review the focus for the source; add a statement to connect it to the source before or after it. ■ Brainstorm or jot notes to refine, restate, or expand connections. ■ Use your notes to deepen connections as you refine your synthesis.	■ Generate ideas to build a cache of notes about how you want to relate your sources to your ideas and what they collectively suggest. Be creative; let your original ideas emerge. ■ For each check or star, use your own voice and ideas to fill gaps, deepen connections, or state relationships.

Learning by Doing 📷 Connecting Your Sources

Work on a chunk of your draft that pulls together multiple sources. In your file or on a printout, highlight each connection that you have stated in that passage. Look for transitional words, transitional sentences, repeated key words or synonyms, and significant pronouns that refer back to key words or terms. (Use one highlighting color for all these types of transitions, or use a separate color for each common type.) Now look for any gaps in your transitions — sections without any highlighting where you need to connect ideas. Also look for too much highlighting, places where you might thin out wordy transitions that obscure your point.

For more on connections and transitions, see pp. 295–99.

Citing Each Source Clearly

Often your launch statement does double duty: naming a source as well as introducing the quotation, paraphrase, or summary from it. Naming, or citing, each source both credits it and helps locate it at the end of your paper in the list of sources called Works Cited (MLA) or References (APA). There you provide full publication information so that readers could find your original sources if they wished.

For examples of citations, see the sample MLA paper on pp. A-59–A-67 and the sample APA paper on pp. A-68–A-76.

To make this connection clear, identify each source by mentioning the author (or the title if no author is identified) as you add information from the source to your paper. (In APA style, also add the date.) You can emphasize this identification by including it in your launch statement, or you can tuck it into parentheses after the information. Then, supply the specific location of any quotation or paraphrase (usually the page number in the original) so that a reader could easily turn to the exact material you have used. Check your text citations against your concluding list of sources to be sure that the two correspond.

Learning by Doing 📷 Launching and Citing Your Sources

Work on a section of your draft that mentions several sources. In your file or on a printout, highlight each launch statement. First check each highlighted passage to be sure that you have named the author or source and stated the page number for a quotation or paraphrase. (Also add the date in APA style.) Next check each passage to be sure that you have clearly conveyed to a reader the value or contribution of each source — what it adds to your understanding, how it supports your conclusion, or why you have included it. Exchange drafts with a classmate to benefit from a second opinion.

Synthesizing Ideas and Sources

Regardless of how you launch sources, you need to figure out how to integrate and synthesize them effectively. Use the Take Action chart (p. 386) for this purpose. Skim across the top to identify questions you might ask about your draft. When you answer a question with "Yes" or "Maybe," move straight down the column to Locate Specifics under that question. Use the activities there to identify gaps or weaknesses. Then move straight down to Take Action. Use the advice that suits your problem as you revise.

For more on synthesizing, see pp. 190–92. To Take Action on synthesizing, see chart on p. 386.

Integrating source notes into your paper generally requires positioning materials in a sequence, fitting them in place, and then reworking and interpreting them to convert them into effective evidence that advances your case. Synthesizing sources and evidence weaves them into a unified whole.

Build your synthesis on critical reading and thinking: pulling together what you read and think, relating ideas and information, and drawing conclusions that go beyond those of your separate sources. If you have a sure sense of your paper's direction, you may find this synthesis fairly easy. On the other hand, if your research question or working thesis has changed or you have unearthed persuasive information at odds with your original direction, consider these questions:

- Taken as a whole, what does all this information mean?
- What does it actually tell you about the answer to your research question?
- What's the most important thing you've learned?
- What's the most important thing you can tell your readers?

Learning by Doing 🎦 Synthesizing Your Sources

Working with a classmate or small group, exchange sections of your drafts where you want or need to pull ideas together. Explain to your peers what you are trying to say or do in that section. Then ask them for ideas about how to synthesize more clearly and forcefully in your draft.

Guide to the Appendices

Quick Format Guide   A-1

Quick Research Guide   A-20

Quick Editing Guide   A-39

A Sample MLA Research Paper   A-59

A Sample APA Research Paper   A-68

Introduction: Turning to References

Though your college papers present your own thinking and learning, you'll probably need resources to find out what's correct or what's conventional. Here, three guides provide quick answers to common questions. The Quick Format Guide illustrates how to present an academic paper following the guidelines of either MLA (Modern Language Association) or APA (American Psychological Association). The Quick Research Guide reviews essentials of academic research — accomplishing your purpose by capturing, presenting, and crediting information from well-regarded sources, using either MLA or APA style. Finally the Quick Editing Guide reviews common problems with grammar, sentences, punctuation, and mechanics. It also advises you about writing more clearly and stylishly.

In the first of two sample research papers, Candace Rardon uses MLA style for "Meet Me in the Middle: The Student, the State, and the School" as she investigates responses of schools to the rising costs of a college education. Her paper adds an outline, as required by the instructor. Next, in APA-style "Sex Offender Lists: A Never-Ending Punishment," Jenny Lidington explores the intention and functional problems of the sex offender registry. Her scholarly approach helps readers grasp the complexities of a difficult societal issue that often generates strong feelings. She tackles the topic thoughtfully, establishing the basis for her questions, defining terms, making distinctions, reviewing history, and tracing consequences. Although these papers are presented for easy reading in a textbook, your paper should use the type style and size that both MLA and APA suggest: Times New Roman font, 12-point size, with one-inch margins on all four sides, double-spaced lines, and no automatic hyphenation.

Quick Format Guide

A | Following the Format for an Academic Paper A-1

B | Integrating and Crediting Visuals A-8

C | Preparing a Document Template A-13

D | Solving Common Format Problems A-13

E | Designing Other Documents for Your Audience A-14

F | Organizing a Résumé and an Application Letter A-17

When you think about a newspaper, a specific type of publication comes to mind because the newspaper is a familiar *genre*, or form. Almost all printed newspapers share a set of defined features: a masthead, headlines, pictures with captions, graphics, and articles arranged in columns of text. Even if the details vary, you can still recognize a newspaper as a newspaper. Popular magazines, academic journals, letters of recommendation, corporate annual reports, and many other types of writing can be identified and distinguished by such features.

Readers also have expectations about how a college paper should look, sometimes including the presentation of visual material such as graphs, tables, photographs, or other illustrations, depending on the field and the assignment. How can you find out what's expected? Check your course materials. Look for directions about format, advice about common problems, requirements for a specific academic style — or all three.

A | Following the Format for an Academic Paper

You can easily spot the appealing features of a magazine, newspaper, or Web site with bold headlines, colorful images, and creative graphics. These lively materials serve their purpose, attracting your attention and promoting the interests of the publication's owners, contributors, or sponsors. In contrast, academic papers may look plain, even downright dull. However, their aim is not to entertain you but to engage your mind.

(continued on p. A-7)

MLA FIRST PAGE

Running head with writer's last name, one space, and the page number on every page

Writer's name

Instructor's name

Course

Date

Title, centered but not in quotes or italics

Double-spaced 12-point Times New Roman font recommended

Right margin uneven with no automatic hyphenation

Thesis previews paper's development

Launch statement names publication and author

Long quotation (5 prose or 4 poetry lines or more) indented without quotation marks

Ellipses show omissions, and brackets show additions within a quotation

Page number locates information in source

Electronic sources without page numbers cited only by author or by title with organization as author

1″

½″

Williams 1

Christopher Williams

Professor Smith

Composition I

12 May 2013

½″ indent or 5 spaces

Watercoolers of the Future

The traditional office environment includes many challenges such as commuting in rush-hour traffic, spending long hours in a cubicle, and missing family events due to strict work hours. These challenges are all changing, however, now that technology is altering how and where people work. With more and more freelance and home-based possibilities, a trend known as co-working has led to the development of shared workspaces. As technology changes the traditional office workspace, new co-working cooperatives are creating the watercoolers of the future, positive gathering spots where working people can meet and share ideas.

1″

New technology is leading the shift away from corporate offices. In *The Future of Work,* Malone explains this move away from the physical office with four walls:

1″

Dispersed physically but connected by technology, workers are now able . . . to make their own decisions using information gathered from many other people and places. . . . [They] gain the economic benefits of large organizations, like economies of scale and knowledge, without giving up the human benefits of small ones, like freedom, creativity, motivation, and flexibility. (4)

Working at a distance or from home can take a toll on workers, however. Loneliness and lack of social opportunities are some of the largest problems for people who do not work in a traditional office (Miller). This is where co-working comes in. Independent workers such as freelancers, people starting their own businesses, and telecommuters share office space. They often pay a monthly fee in exchange for use of the rented area and whatever it provides, such as desk space, meeting rooms,

1″

MLA WORKS CITED

1"

½"

Williams 7

Works Cited

Butler, Kiera. "Works Well with Others." *Mother Jones* Jan./Feb.
     2008: 66-69. Print.

1"

Cetron, Marvin J., and Owen Davies. "Trends Shaping Tomorrow's
     World: Economic and Social Trends and Their Impacts." *The*
     Futurist 44.3 (2010): 35-51. *Academic OneFile*. Web. 1 May
     2013.

1"

Citizen Space. "Our Philosophy." *Citizen Space*. Citizen Space,
     n.d. Web. 1 May 2013.

Donkin, Richard. *The Future of Work*. Hampshire: Palgrave
     Macmillan, 2009. Print.

Godin, Seth. "The Last Days of Cubicle Life." *Time*. Time, 14 May
     2009. Web. 30 Apr. 2013.

Goetz, Kaomi. "Co-working Offers Community to Solo Workers."
     National Public Radio. Natl. Public Radio, 6 Jan. 2010. Web.
     7 May 2013.

---. "For Freelancers, Landing a Workspace Gets Harder." *National*
     Public Radio. Natl. Public Radio, 10 Apr. 2012. Web.
     7 May 2013.

Malone, Thomas W. *The Future of Work: How the New Order of*
     Business Will Shape Your Organization, Your Management
     Style and Your Life. Boston: Harvard Business, 2004. Print.

McConville, Christine. "Freelancers Bag Cheap Office Space."
     Boston Herald. Boston Herald and Herald Media, 15 Aug.
     2009. Web. 30 Apr. 2013.

Miller, Kerry. "Where the Coffee Shop Meets the Cubicle."
     Bloomberg Businessweek. Bloomberg, 26 Feb. 2007. Web.
     30 Apr. 2013.

1"

List of Works Cited on a
separate page

Running head continues

List alphabetized by last
names of authors or by
titles (when no author is
named)

First line of entry at
left margin

Additional lines
indented ½"

Double-spaced
throughout

Three hyphens show
same author continues

For a sample MLA
paper, see pp.
A-59–A-67.

APA TITLE PAGE AND ABSTRACT

Running head with short title in capital letters on left and page number on right

Double-spaced 12-point Times New Roman font recommended

Title, centered

Author

School

Running head continues on following pages

Heading, centered

No paragraph indentation

Double-spaced

Main ideas summed up, usually in less than 250 words

Key words, common for journal articles, also may be expected by your instructor

1"

Running head: PET HEALTH INSURANCE   1

Limitations of Pet Health Insurance
Jennifer Miller
Springfield Community College

PET HEALTH INSURANCE   2

Abstract

In recent years, the amount of money spent annually in the United States on veterinary care for the millions of household pets has risen into the billions of dollars. One option for owners is to buy a pet health insurance policy. Policies currently available have both advantages and disadvantages. Benefits can include coverage of increasingly complicated treatments. Drawbacks to coverage include the exclusion of pre-existing conditions and hidden fees. In the end, interest-bearing savings accounts may be a better option than policy premiums for most pet owners.

Key words: pet health insurance, pet ownership

APA FIRST PAGE OF TEXT

PET HEALTH INSURANCE

½" (or 5–7 spaces)

3

1"

½"

Limitations of Pet Health Insurance

The Humane Society of the United States (2012) reports in *U.S. Pet Ownership Statistics* that over 78 million dogs and 84 million cats are owned as household pets. However, only 3% of household pets are insured. Furthermore, in 2007, "only 850,000 pet insurance policies [were] in effect . . . according to the National Commission on Veterinary Economic Issues" (Weston, 2010). Recent studies suggest that, despite the growing availability of insurance plans for pet health care, these policies may not be the cheapest way to care for a household pet. Pet owners need to consider a number of factors before buying a policy, including the pet's age, any preexisting diseases that an insurance carrier might decide not to cover, and a policy's possible hidden fees.

1"

1"

Types of Pet Health Insurance Currently Available

Pet ownership is important to many people, and pets can do a great deal to improve the mental health and quality of life for their owners (McNicholas et al., 2005, p. 1252). However, paying for a pet's own health care can be stressful and expensive. Mathews (2009) reported on the costs in the *Wall Street Journal:*

½" This year, pet owners are expected to spend around $12.2 billion for veterinary care, up from $11.1 billion last year and $8.2 billion five years ago, according to the American Pet Products Association. Complex procedures widely used for people, including chemotherapy and dialysis, are now available for pets, and the potential cost of treating certain illnesses has spiked as a result. (Introduction section, para. 4)

Many providers currently offer plans to insure household pets. The largest of the providers is the long-standing Veterinary Pet Insurance (VPI), holding over two-thirds of the country's market (Weston, 2010). Other companies include ASPCA Pet Health Insurance, Petshealth Care Plan, and AKC Pet Healthcare Plan. All offer plans for dogs and cats, yet VPI is one of only a

1"

Running head continues

Title centered

Launch statement names organization as author with date added in parentheses

Double-spaced throughout

Brackets show additions, and ellipses show omissions within a quotation

Electronic source without page cited only by author and date

Thesis previews paper's development

First-level heading in bold type and centered

Citation identifies authors, date, and location in the source (required for quotation and preferred for paraphrase)

Long quotation (40 words or more) indented without quotation marks

Section name and paragraph number locate quotation in electronic source without page numbers

Right margin uneven with no automatic hyphenation

APA REFERENCES

Running head with page numbering continues

Heading, centered

List alphabetized by last names of authors or by titles (when no author is named)

First line of entry at left margin

Additional lines indented ½"

Double-spaced throughout

No period after URL

As many as seven authors named in References

No period after DOI (digital object identifier) for article

Long URL divided before period, slash, or other punctuation mark

For a sample APA paper, see pp. A-68–A-76.

PET HEALTH INSURANCE   12

References

Barlyn, S. (2008, March 13). Is pet health insurance worth the price? *The Wall Street Journal,* p. D2.

Busby, J. (2005). *How to afford veterinary care without mortgaging the kids.* Bemidji, MN: Busby International.

Calhoun, A. (2008, February 8). What I wouldn't do for my cat. *Salon.* Retrieved from http://www.salon.com

Darlin, D. (2006, May 13). Vet bills and the priceless pet: What's a practical owner to do? *The New York Times.* Retrieved from http://www.nytimes.com

Humane Society of the United States. (2012). U.S. pet ownership statistics. Retrieved from http://www.humanesociety.org/issues /pet_overpopulation/facts/pet_ownership_statistics.html

Kenney, D. (2009). *Your guide to understanding pet health insurance.* Memphis, TN: PhiloSophia.

Mathews, A. W. (2009, December 9). Polly want an insurance policy? *Wall Street Journal.* Retrieved from http://online.wsj.com

McNicholas, J., Gilbey, A., Rennie, A., Ahmedzai, S., Dono, J., & Ormerod, E. (2005). Pet ownership and human health: A brief review of evidence and issues. *British Medical Journal, 331,* 1252-1254. doi:10.1136/bmj.331.7527.1252

Price, J. (2010, April 9). Should you buy pet health insurance? *Christian Science Monitor.* Retrieved from http://www.csmonitor .com

Weston, L. P. (2010, November 4). Should you buy pet insurance? *MSN Money.* Retrieved from http://money.msn.com/insurance /should-you-buy-pet-insurance-weston.aspx

(continued from p. A-1)

The conventions — the accepted expectations — for college papers vary by field but typically support core academic values: to present ideas, reduce distractions, and integrate sources. A conventional format reassures readers that you respect the values behind the guidelines.

Common Academic Values	Common Paper Expectations and Format
Clear presentation of ideas, information, and research findings	■ Word-processed text on one side of a white sheet of paper, double-spaced, one-inch margins ■ Paper printed in crisp, black, 12-point Times New Roman type with numbered pages
Investigation of an intriguing issue, unanswered question, unsolved puzzle, or unexplored relationship	■ Title and running head to clarify focus for reader ■ Abstract in social sciences or sciences to sum up ■ Opening paragraph or section to express thesis, research question, or conclusions ■ Closing paragraph or section to reinforce conclusions
Academic exchange of ideas and information, including evidence from reliable authorities and investigations	■ Quotations from sources identified by quotation marks or block format ■ Paraphrase, summary, and synthesis of sources ■ Citation of each source in the text when mentioned ■ Well-organized text with transitions and cues to help readers make connections ■ Possibly headings to identify sections
Identification of evidence to allow a reader to evaluate its contribution and join the academic exchange	■ Full information about each source in a concluding list ■ Specific format used for predictable, consistent arrangement of detail

MLA (Modern Language Association) style, explained in the *MLA Handbook for Writers of Research Papers,* Seventh Edition (New York: MLA, 2009), is commonly used in the humanities. APA (American Psychological Association) style, explained in the *Publication Manual of the American Psychological Association,* Sixth Edition (Washington, D.C.: American Psychological Association, 2010), is commonly used in the social and behavioral sciences. Both MLA and APA, like other academic styles, specify how a page should look and how sources should be credited. (See pp. A-2–A-6.)

For examples showing how to cite and list sources in MLA and APA styles, see E in the Quick Research Guide, pp. A-32–A-38. For sample papers, see A-59–A-76.

B | Integrating and Crediting Visuals

Visuals in your text can engage readers, convey information, and reinforce your words. The MLA and APA style guides divide visuals into two groups:

- **Tables** are grids that clearly report numerical data or other information in columns (running up and down) and rows (running across).

- **Figures** include charts, graphs, diagrams, drawings, maps, photographs, or other images.

Much of the time you can create pie charts, bar graphs, or tables in your text file using your software, spreadsheet, or presentation options. Try a drawing program for making diagrams, maps, or sketches or an image editor for scanning print photographs or adding your own digital shots.

When you add visuals from other sources, you can photocopy or scan printed material, pick up online graphics, or turn to the computer lab for sophisticated advice. For a complex project, get help well ahead of your deadline, and allow plenty of time to learn new techniques.

Select or design visuals that are clear, easy to read, and informative.

- To present statistical information, use graphs, charts, or tables.

- To discuss a conflict in a certain geographical area, supply a map.

- To illustrate a reflective essay, scan an image of yourself or an event.

- To clarify stages, steps, or directions for a process, add a diagram.

B1 Position visuals and credit any sources.

Present each visual: provide a context for it, identify its purpose, explain its meaning, and help a reader see how it supports your point. Following your style guide, identify and number it as a table or figure. Place the visual near the related text discussion so readers can easily connect the two.

Solve any layout problems in your final draft as you arrange text and visual on the page. For instance, align an image with the left margin to continue the text's forward movement. Use it to balance and support, not overshadow, text. Let the visual draw a reader's eye with an appropriate—not excessive—share of the page. To present a long table or large photograph on its own page, simply add page breaks before and after it. To include tables or figures for reference, such as your survey forms, place them in an appendix or collect them in an electronic supplement, as APA suggests.

Acknowledge visual sources as carefully as textual sources. Credit material from a source, printed or electronic, as you present the visual. Ask permission, if required, to use an image from a copyrighted source, including most printed books, articles, and other resources; credit the owner of the copyright. If you download an image from the Web, follow the site guidelines for the use of images. If you are uncertain about whether you can use an image from a source, ask your teacher's advice.

B2 Prepare tables using MLA or APA format.

If you conduct a small survey, use the insert or table menu to create a simple table to summarize responses. Supply a label and a title or caption before the table. (Italicize its name if you are using APA style.) Double-space, add lines to separate sections, and use letters to identify any notes.

TABLE FORMAT FOR PRESENTING YOUR SURVEY FINDINGS

Table 1

Sources of Financial Support Reported by Survey Participants[a]

Type of Support	First-Year Students (n = 20)	Other Undergraduates (n = 30)
Scholarship or Campus Grant	25%	20%
Student Loans	40%	57%
Work Study	20%	7%
Family Support	50%	40%
Part-Time or Full-Time Job	25%	57%
Employer or Military Contribution	10%	17%
Other	5%	7%

a. Percentages based on the total number of respondents (n) were calculated and rounded to the nearest whole number.

Label with number

Title or caption

Letter keyed to note

Column headings

Pair of rules or lines to enclose heading

Rule or line to mark end

Note of explanation if needed

If your results came from only a few students at one campus, you might compare them with state or national findings, as in the next sample table. When you include a table or an image from a source, credit it, and identify it as a source (MLA) or as adapted (APA) if you have modified it.

TABLE FORMAT FOR MLA AND APA SOURCE CREDITS

Label with number

Table 2

Title or caption

Percentages of Undergraduates Receiving Selected Types of Financial Aid, by Type of Institution, Attendance Pattern, Dependency Status, and Income Level: 2007-08

Column headings

Spanner heading (for all rows) centered

Institution Characteristics	Any Grants	Any Student Loans	Work-Study	Veterans Benefits
Public				
2-year	39.6	13.2	3.3	2.0
4-year (non-doctorate)	52.5	43.4	7.3	2.4
4-year (doctorate)	53.1	47.8	8.0	2.0

MLA source credit

Source: United States, Dept. of Educ., Inst. of Educ. Statistics, Natl. Center for Educ. Statistics; *2007-08 National Postsecondary Student Aid Study;* US Dept. of Educ., Apr. 2009; Web; 1 Dec. 2012; table 1.

The credit above follows MLA style; the credit below follows APA. At the end, add the date and name as any copyright holder requests.

APA source credit

Note. Adapted from U.S. Department of Education, Institute of Education Sciences, National Center for Education Statistics. 2009. *2007-08 National Postsecondary Student Aid Study* (NCES Publication No. NPSAS:08), Table 1.

B3 Add diagrams, graphs, charts, and other figures.

Select or design figures purposefully. Consider your readers' needs as you decide which types might convey information effectively. A diagram can help readers see the sequence of steps in a process. A graph can show how different groups of people behave over time. A sketch of an old building can illustrate the style of its era. Add a clear caption or title to identify what you are illustrating as well as labels for readers to note key elements, add numerical or textual detail, and use visual elements — size, shape, direction, color — to emphasize, connect, or contrast.

- A diagram can simplify a complex process and clarify its stages. Figure A.1 shows the stages in wastewater treatment.
- A comparative line graph can show how trends change over time. Figure A.2 compares trends in food allergies over a decade, marking percentages on the vertical line and years on the horizontal line.

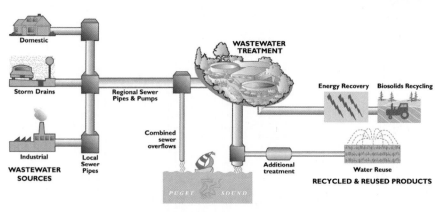

Figure A.1 A Diagram Showing the Process of Wastewater Treatment in King County, Washington. Source: King County, Washington, Department of Natural Resources Wastewater Treatment Division

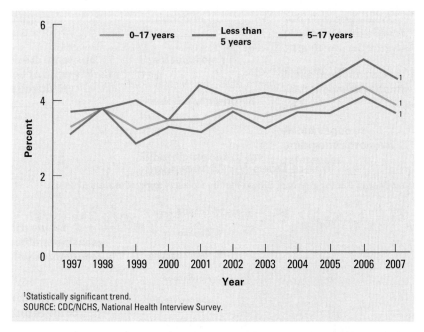

Figure A.2 A Comparative Line Graph Showing the Percentage of Children with a Reported Food or Digestive Allergy from 1997 through 2007 by Age Group. Source: The Centers for Disease Control and Prevention

- A column or bar graph can compare relative values. Figure A.3 illustrates the relative levels of alcohol usage among different age groups.
- A pie chart can compare components with each other and the whole. Figure A.4 shows how the total energy bill (100%) for a single family home is spent on various uses.

For a tutorial on preparing effective graphs and charts, go to Re:Writing at **bedfordstmartins.com /concisebedguide**.

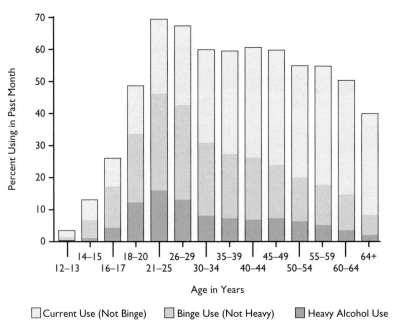

Figure A.3 A Bar Chart Presenting Numerical Comparisons. Source: U.S. Department of Health and Human Services, Substance Abuse and Mental Health Services Administration, Office of Applied Studies

Where Does My Money Go?

Annual Energy Bill for a typical Single Family Home is approximately $2,200.

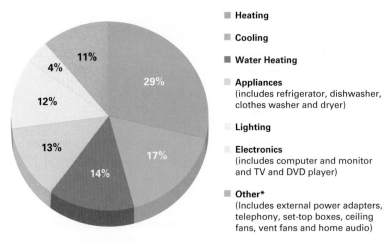

Figure A.4 Pie Chart Showing Energy Consumption for a Typical Single Family Home in 2009. Source: ENERGYSTAR, The U.S. Environmental Protection Agency, The U.S. Department of Energy

C | Preparing a Document Template

Unless your teacher encourages creative formatting, avoid experimenting with a college paper. Follow the assigned format and style; check your draft against your instructor's directions and against examples (such as the MLA and APA samples here). Use your software's Help function to learn how to set font, page, format, or template features such as these:

- placement of information on the first page
- margin widths for the top, bottom, and sides of the page (such as 1″)
- name of font (Times New Roman), style (regular roman, italics, or bold), and size of type (12 point)
- running head with automatic page numbering
- double spacing (without extra space between paragraphs)
- text alignment, even on the left but not on the right (left alignment, not centered text, with automatic hyphenation of words turned off)
- width of the paragraph indentation and special "hanging" indentation for your final list of sources
- any other features of the required format

A template simplifies using expected features every time you write a paper with the same specifications. If you have trouble setting features or saving the template, get help from your instructor, a classmate, the writing center, or the computer lab. Follow these steps to create your template:

1. Format your paper the way you want it to look.
2. Create a duplicate copy of your formatted file.
3. Delete all of the text discussion in the duplicate document.
4. Use the Save As feature to save the file as a document template.
5. Give the template a clear name ("Comp paper" or "MLA form").
6. To open a new file, select this template from your template folder.

D | Solving Common Format Problems

Software programs differ, as do versions of the same software. Watch for default settings or format shifts that do not match an academic format.

- When you find unconventional features, such as extra lines between paragraphs or automatic hyphenation, reset these features.
- Use your software's Help function to look up the feature by naming it (paragraph), identifying the issue (paragraph spacing), or specifying what you want to do (troubleshoot paragraph spacing).
- Print Help screens for a complicated path or confusing directions.

Other problems can arise because academic style guides make their own assumptions about the texts their users are likely to write. For example, MLA style assumes you will write an essay, simply separate items in a list with commas, and probably limit additions to tables and illustrations. On the other hand, APA style assumes you probably need section headings, lists (numbered, bulleted, or lettered within a sentence), and appendices, especially for research materials such as sample questionnaires. In addition, your instructor might require an outline or links for online sources. Follow your instructor's advice if your paper requires formatting that the style you are using (MLA or APA) does not recognize.

Readers appreciate your consideration of their practical problems, too. A clear, neat, readable document is one that readers can readily absorb. For example, your instructor might ask you to reprint a paper if your toner cartridge is nearly empty. Clear papers in a standard format are easier on the eyes than those with faint print or unusual features. In addition, such papers have margin space for comments so they are easy to grade. If you submit an electronic file, pay attention to online formatting conventions.

E | Designing Other Documents for Your Audience

Four key principles of document design can help you prepare effective documents in and out of the classroom: know your audience, satisfy them with the features and format they expect, consider their circumstances, and remember your purpose.

DISCOVERY CHECKLIST

- ☐ Who are your readers? What matters to them? How might the format of your document acknowledge their values, goals, and concerns?

- ☐ What form or genre do readers expect? Which of its features and details do they see as typical? What visual evidence would they find appropriate?

- ☐ What problems or constraints will your readers face as they read your document? How can your design help to reduce these problems?

- ☐ What is the purpose of your document? How can its format help achieve this purpose? How might it enhance your credibility as a writer?

- ☐ What is the usual format of your document? Find and analyze a sample.

E1 Select type font, size, and face.

Typography refers to the appearance of letters on a page. You can change typeface or font, style from roman to bold or italics, or type size for a passage by highlighting it and clicking on the appropriate toolbar icon. Selecting Font in the Home, Format, or Page Layout menu usually leads to options such as superscript, shadows, or small capitals.

Most college papers and many other documents use Times New Roman in a 12-point size. Signs, posters, and visuals such as slides for presentations might require larger type (with a larger number for the point size). Test such materials for readability by printing samples in various type sizes and standing back from them at the distance of your intended audience. Size also varies with different typefaces because they occupy different amounts of horizontal space on the page. Figure A.5 shows the space required for the same sentence written in four different 12-point fonts.

Times New Roman	An estimated 40 percent of young children have an imaginary friend.
Courier New	An estimated 40 percent of young children have an imaginary friend.
Arial	An estimated 40 percent of young children have an imaginary friend.
Comic Sans MS	An estimated 40 percent of young children have an imaginary friend.

Figure A.5 Space Occupied by Different Typefaces

Fonts also vary in design. Times New Roman and Courier New are called *serif* fonts because they have small tails, or serifs, at the ends of the letters. Arial and the more casual Comic Sans MS are *sans serif*—without serifs—and thus have solid, straight lines without tails at the tips of the letters.

Times New Roman (serif) K k P p

Arial (sans serif) K k P p

Sans serif fonts have a clean look, desirable for headlines, ads, "pull quotes" (in larger type to catch the reader's eye), and text within APA-style figures. More readable serif fonts are used for article (or "body") text. Times New Roman, the common word-processor default font preferred for MLA and APA styles, was developed for the *Times* newspaper in London. As needed, use light, slanted *italics* (for certain titles) or dark **bold** (for APA headings).

E2 Organize effective lists.

The placement of material on a page—its layout—can make information more accessible for readers. MLA style recognizes common ways of integrating a list within a sentence: introduce the list with a colon or dash (or set it off with two dashes); separate its items with commas, or use semicolons if the items include commas. APA style adds options, preceding each item in a sentence with a letter enclosed by parentheses: (a), (b), and (c) or using display lists — set off from text — for visibility and easy reading.

One type of displayed list, the numbered list, can emphasize priorities, conclusions, or processes such as steps in research procedures, how-to advice, or instructions, as in this simple sequence for making clothes:

NUMBERED LIST

1. Lay out the pattern and fabric you have selected.
2. Pin the pattern to the fabric, noting the arrows and grain lines.
3. Cut out the fabric pieces, following the outline of the pattern.
4. Sew the garment together using the pattern's step-by-step instructions.

Another type of displayed list sets off a bit of information with a bullet, most commonly a small round mark (•) but sometimes a square (■), from the Home or Symbol menu. Bulleted lists are common in résumés and business documents but not necessarily in academic papers, though APA style now recognizes them. Use them to identify steps, reasons, or items when you do not wish to suggest any order of priority, as in this list of tips for saving energy.

BULLETED LIST

- Let your hair dry without running a hair dryer.
- Commute by public transportation.
- Turn down the thermostat by a few degrees.
- Unplug your phone charger and TV during the day.

E3 Consider adding headings.

In a complex research report, business proposal, or Web document, headings can show readers how the document is structured, which sections are most important, and how parts are related. Headings also name sections so readers know where they are and where they are going. Headings at the same level should be consistent and look the same; headings at different levels should differ from each other and from the main text in placement and style, making the text easy to scan for key points.

For academic papers, MLA encourages writers to organize by outlining their essays but does not recommend or discuss text headings. In contrast, APA illustrates five levels of headings beginning with these two:

First-Level Heading Centered in Bold

Second-Level Heading on the Left in Bold

Besides looking the same, headings at the same level in your document should be brief, clear, and informative. They also should use consistent parallel phrasing. If you write a level-one heading as an *-ing* phrase, do the same for all the level-one headings that follow. Here are some examples of four common patterns for phrasing headings.

For more on parallel structure, see section B2 in the Quick Editing Guide, p. A-52.

-*ING* PHRASES	**QUESTIONS**
Using the College Catalog	What Is Hepatitis C?
Choosing Courses	Who Is at Risk?
Declaring a Major	How Is Hepatitis C Treated?

NOUN PHRASES	**IMPERATIVE SENTENCES**
E-Commerce Benefits	Initiate Your IRA Rollover
E-Commerce Challenges	Balance Your Account
Online Shopper Profiles	Select New Investments

Web pages—especially home pages and site guides—are designed to help readers find information quickly, within a small viewing frame. For this reason, they generally have more headings than other documents. If you design a Web page or post your course portfolio, consider what different readers might want to find. Then design your headings and content to meet their needs.

F | Organizing a Résumé and an Application Letter

When your reader is a prospective employer, present a solid, professional job application, preferably a one-page résumé and application letter (see pp. A-18–A-19). Both should be clearly organized to show why you are a strong candidate for the position. The purpose of your résumé is to organize the details of your education and experience (usually by category and by reverse chronology) so they are easy to review. Wording matters, so use action verbs and parallel structure to convey your experience and enthusiasm. The purpose of your application letter is to highlight your qualifications and motivate the reader to interview and eventually hire you. A follow-up letter might thank your interviewer, confirm your interest, and supply anything requested. Write clearly, and use a standard format; a sloppy letter might suggest that you lack the communication skills employers value.

Your campus career center may provide sample application letters and résumés so you can compare layout variations, evaluate their impact, and effectively design your own. To apply for a professional program, internship, or other opportunity, simply adapt your letter and résumé. For an electronic job application form, select relevant information from your résumé and embed as many key words as possible that might be used to sort or rank applications.

Splits heading with
contact information

Joseph Cauteruccio, Jr.

65 Oakwood Ave. Apt. #105
Somerville, MA 02144
Mobile 617-555-5555
jcjr@comnet.com

Experience

Places current
information first

Research Analyst   *June 2012 – Present*
Industrial Economics, Incorporated — Cambridge, MA

Develop profit estimation model, adopted as practice area standard, for petroleum bulk
stations
Create and implement valuation methodology for a major privately held forestry
company

Intern, Global Treasury — Investment Management Team   *June 2011 – August 2011*
State Street Corporation — Boston, MA

Specifies activities

Research and analyze corporate bonds, including economic and industry analyses

Education

Bachelor of Arts — Bates College, Lewiston, ME   *September 2008 – May 2012*

Major: Economics   Related courses: Calculus; Advanced Statistics and Econometrics
Minor: Japanese

Skills & Competencies

Uses bold type to
highlight categories

Statistical Packages: SAS, STATA, R
Programming Languages & Related: VBA, Python, SQL, LINUX/UNIX, Scripting
(KSH/BASH), DOS
Microsoft Office: Advanced Excel, PowerPoint
Other: Cloud Computing (PaaS, AWS, shell interaction, batch processing), Hadoop
Ecosystem
Languages and Music: Conversational Japanese, Guitar, Saxophone, Banjo

Labels sections and
uses dividers

Leadership & Involvement

Analytic Pro Bono Work (present)
Leverage data mining skills to assist nonprofit organizations
Consult on data collection and management
Improve donation volume and donor retention

Boston Data Science Community
Participate actively in industry groups, Boston Predictive Analytics, Boston R Users

Alpine Climbing (2007-present)
Organize route finding and equipment logistics
Lead trips throughout California, Canadian Rockies, and New England

65 Oakwood Ave. Apt. #105
Somerville, MA 02144
15 May 2013

Ross Landon
Denver Strategists
8866 Larimer Street, Suite 404
Denver, CO 80217

Dear Mr. Landon:

Josh Greenway, formerly a data analyst with Denver Strategists, recommended that I contact you about the upcoming expansion of your Marketing Analysis Group. I am looking for an opportunity to combine my college major in economics with my long-standing interest in statistics. Because your expansion promises an excellent opportunity to do so, I wish to apply for one of your openings for a data analyst.

As my résumé indicates, my college internship with the Investment Management Team at Global Treasury introduced me to the many processes involved in industry analyses. Since graduation, I have worked as a research analyst at Industrial Economics, estimating valuation and profits for clients in diverse industries. In addition, as a pro bono consultant with Boston nonprofit organizations, I have expanded my expertise with statistics packages. For these groups, I have directed my skills to improving data mining and data management in order to help them cultivate and retain contributors more effectively.

I am now looking forward to designing and conducting more complex data mining and data analysis projects. Joining your expansion team would offer me a welcome opportunity to develop my analytic skills, expand my experience with various statistical methods, and gain sophistication working with team colleagues as well as a variety of clients. For me, data analysis is a challenging and rewarding way to combine my skills in math, statistics, and technology with the creativity data science requires. Both my education and my experience have prepared me to address a company's problems or change a client's perspective through data-based analysis.

I would be happy to meet with you to learn more about your plans for the Marketing Analysis Group. Please call me at 617-555-5555, e-mail me at jcjr@comnet.com, or write to me at the address above. I appreciate your consideration and look forward to hearing from you.

Sincerely,

Joe Cauteruccio

Joseph Cauteruccio

Enclosure: Résumé

Follows standard letter format

Addresses specific person

Identifies job sought and describes interests

Explains qualifications

Confirms interest

Supplies contact information

Includes résumé with letter

Quick Research Guide

A | Defining Your Quest A-21

B | Searching for Recommended Sources A-24

C | Evaluating Possible Sources A-26

D | Capturing, Launching, and Citing Evidence Added from Sources A-28

E | Citing and Listing Sources in MLA or APA Style A-32

When you begin college, you may feel uncertain about what to say and how to speak up. As you gain experience, you will join the academic exchange around you by reading, thinking, and writing with sources. You will turn to articles, books, and Web sites for evidence to support your thesis and develop your ideas, advancing knowledge through exchange.

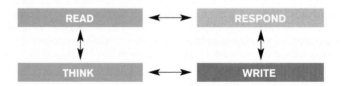

Conducting research requires time to explore, to think, and to respond. However, efficient and purposeful research can produce greater success in less time than optimistic browsing. Maybe you need more confidence or good advice fast: you've procrastinated, you're overwhelmed, or you're uncertain about how to succeed. To help you, this Quick Research Guide concentrates on five key steps.

TURNING TO SOURCES FOR SUPPORTING EVIDENCE

A | Defining Your Quest

Especially when your research goals are specific and limited, you're more likely to succeed if you try to define the hunt in advance.

PURPOSE CHECKLIST

☐ What is the thesis you want to support, point you want to show, question you want to answer, or problem you want to solve?

For more about stating and using a thesis, see pp. 263–272.

☐ Does the assignment require or suggest certain types of supporting evidence, sources, or presentations of material?

☐ Which ideas do you want to support with good evidence?

☐ Which ideas might you want to check, clarify, or change?

☐ Which ideas or opinions of others do you want to verify or counter?

☐ Do you want to analyze material yourself (for example, comparing different articles or Web sites) or to find someone else's analysis?

☐ What kinds of evidence do you want to use — facts, statistics, or expert testimony? Do you also want to add your own firsthand observation?

For more about types of evidence, see pp. 40–44.

TWO VIEWS OF SUPPORTING EVIDENCE

COLLEGE WRITER	COLLEGE READER
• Does it answer my question and support my thesis?	• Is it relevant to the purpose and assignment?
• Does it seem accurate?	• Is it reliable, given academic standards?
• Is it recent enough?	• Is it current, given the standards of the field?
• Does it add enough detail and depth?	• Is it of sufficient quantity, variety, and strength?
• Is it balanced enough?	• Is it typical and fair?
• Will it persuade my audience?	• Does the writer make a credible case?

For evidence checklists, see pp. 43–44 and p. A-24.

A1 Decide what supporting evidence you need.

When you want to add muscle to college papers, you need reliable resources to supply facts, statistics, and expert testimony to back up your claims. You may not need comprehensive information, but you will want to hunt — quickly and efficiently — for exactly what you do need. That evidence should satisfy you as a writer and meet the criteria of your college readers — instructors and possibly classmates. Suppose you want to propose solutions to your community's employment problem.

WORKING THESIS

Many residents of Aurora need more — and more innovative — higher education to improve their job skills and career alternatives.

Because you already have ideas based on your firsthand observations and the experiences of people you know, your research goals are limited. First, you want to add accurate facts and figures that will show why you believe a compelling problem exists. Next, you want to visit the Web sites of local educational institutions and possibly locate someone to interview about existing career development programs.

A2 Decide where you need supporting evidence.

As you plan or draft, you may tuck in notes to yourself — figure that out, find this, look it up, get the numbers here. Other times, you may not know exactly what or where to add. One way to determine where you need supporting evidence is to examine your draft, sentence by sentence.

- What does each sentence claim or promise to a reader?
- Where do you provide supporting evidence to demonstrate the claim or fulfill the promise?

The answers to these questions — your statements and your supporting evidence — often fall into a common alternating pattern:

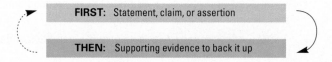

FIRST: Statement, claim, or assertion

THEN: Supporting evidence to back it up

For more about arguments based on claims of substantiation, evaluation, or policy, see pp. 133–36.

When you spot a string of assertions without much support, you have found a place where you might need more evidence. Select reliable evidence so that it substantiates the exact statement, claim, or assertion that precedes it. Likewise, if you spot a string of examples, details, facts, quotations, or other evidence, introduce or conclude it with an interpretive statement that explains the point the evidence supports. Make sure your general statement connects and pulls together all of the particular evidence.

When Carrie Williamson introduced her cause-and-effect paper, "Rain Forest Destruction," she made a general statement and then supported it by quoting facts from a source. Then she repeated this statement-support pattern, backing up her next statement in turn. By using this pattern from the very beginning, Carrie reassured her readers that she was a trustworthy writer who would try to supply convincing evidence throughout her paper.

For the source entries from Carrie Williamson's MLA list of works cited, see pp. A-35–A-36.

The tropical rain forests are among the most biologically diverse communities in the world. According to the Rainforest Alliance, "The forests of the Neotropics are the habitat for tens of thousands of plant and wildlife species," as in "a single square mile of tropical forest in Rondonia, Brazil," which is home to "1,200 species of butterflies—twice the total number found in the United States and Canada" ("Conservation"). These amazing communities depend on each part being intact in order to function properly but are being destroyed at an alarming rate. Over several decades, even in protected areas, only 2% increased while 85% "suffered declines in surrounding forest cover" (Laurance et al. 291). Many rain forest conservationists debate the leading cause of deforestation. Regardless of which is the major cause, logging, slash-and-burn farming, and resource exploitation are destroying more of the rain forests each year.

Statement

Supporting evidence: Information and statistics about species

Statement

Supporting evidence: Facts about destruction

Statement identifying cause-and-effect debate

Statement previewing points to come

The table below shows some of the many ways this common statement-support pattern can be used to clarify and substantiate your ideas.

First: Statement, Claim, or Assertion	Then: Supporting Evidence
Introduces a topic	Facts or statistics to justify the importance or significance of the topic
Describes a situation	Factual examples or illustrations to convey reality or urgency
Introduces an event	Accurate firsthand observations to describe an event that you have witnessed
Presents a problem	Expert testimony or firsthand observation to establish the necessity or urgency of a solution
Explains an issue	Facts and details to clarify or justify the significance of the issue
States your point	Facts, statistics, or examples to support your viewpoint or position
Prepares for evidence that follows	Facts, examples, observations, or research findings to develop your case
Concludes with your recommendation or evaluation	Facts, examples, or expert testimony to persuade readers to accept your conclusion

Use the following checklist to help you decide whether—and where—you might need supporting evidence from sources.

EVIDENCE CHECKLIST

☐ What does your thesis promise that you'll deliver? What additional evidence would ensure that you effectively demonstrate your thesis?

☐ Are your statements, claims, and assertions backed up with supporting evidence? If not, what evidence might you add?

☐ What evidence would most effectively persuade your readers?

☐ What criteria for useful evidence matter most for your assignment or your readers? What evidence would best meet these criteria?

☐ Which parts of your paper sound weak or incomplete to you?

☐ What facts or statistics would clarify your topic?

☐ What examples or illustrations would make the background or the current circumstances clearer and more compelling for readers?

☐ What does a reliable expert say about the situation your topic involves?

☐ What firsthand observation would add authenticity?

☐ Where have peers or your instructor suggested more or stronger evidence?

B | Searching for Recommended Sources

When you need evidence, you may think first of the Internet. However, random Web sites require you to do extra work—checking what's presented as fact, looking for biases or financial motives, and searching for what's not stated rather than accepting what is. Such caution is required because anyone—expert or not—can build a Web site, write a blog entry, post an opinion, or send an e-mail. Repetition does not ensure accuracy, reliability, or integrity because the Internet has no quality controls.

On the other hand, when your college library buys books, subscribes to scholarly journals, and acquires resources, print or electronic, these publications are expected to follow accepted editorial practices. Well-regarded publishers and professional groups turn to peer reviewers—experts in the field—to assess articles or books before they are selected for publication. These quality controls bring readers material that meets academic or professional standards. When you need to search efficiently, begin with reliable sources, already screened by professionals.

B1 Seek advice about reliable sources.

Although popular search engines can turn up sources on nearly any topic, will those sources meet your criteria and those of your readers? After all, your challenge is not simply to find any sources but to find solid sources with reliable evidence. The following shortcuts can help you find solid sources fast — ideally already screened, selected, and organized for you.

RESOURCE CHECKLIST

☐ Have you talked with your instructor after class, during office hours, or by e-mail to ask for advice about resources for your topic? Have you checked the assignment, syllabus, handouts, or class Web site?

☐ Have your classmates recommended useful academic databases, disciplinary Web sites, or similar resources?

☐ Does the department offering the course have a Web site with lists of library resources or links to sites well regarded in that field?

☐ Does your textbook Web site provide links to additional resources?

☐ Which search strategies and library databases does the librarian at the reference desk recommend for your course and topic?

☐ Which databases or links on your library's Web site lead to government (federal, state, or local) resources or articles in journals and newspapers?

☐ Which resources are available through the online library catalog or in any periodicals or reference area of your campus library?

B2 Select reliable sources that meet readers' criteria.

If you planned to investigate common Internet hoaxes for a paper about online practices, you might deliberately turn to sources that are, by definition, unreliable. However, in most cases, you want to turn right away to reliable sources. For some assignments, you might be expected to use varied sources: reports from journalists, advice from practitioners in the field, accounts of historical eyewitnesses, or opposing opinions on civic policy. For other assignments, you might be expected to turn only to scholarly sources—also identified as peer-reviewed or refereed sources—with characteristics such as these:

- in-depth investigation or interpretation of an academic topic or problem
- discussion of previous studies, which are cited in the text and listed at the end for easy reference by readers
- use of research methods accepted in a discipline or several fields

- publication by a reputable company or sponsoring organization
- acceptance for publication based on the author's credentials and reviews by experts (peer reviewers) who assess the quality of the study
- preparation for publication supervised by academic or expert editors or by authors and professional staff

Your instructors are likely to favor these quality controls. Your campus librarian can help you limit your searches to peer-reviewed journals or check the scholarly reputation of sources that you find.

C | Evaluating Possible Sources

Like the perfect wave or the perfect day, the perfect source is hard to come by. Instead of looking for perfect sources, evaluate sources on the basis of practicality, standards, and evidence.

C1 Evaluate sources as a practical researcher.

Your situation as a writer may determine how long or how widely you can search or how deeply you can delve into the sources you find. If you are worried about finishing on time or about juggling several assignments, you will need to search efficiently, using your own practical criteria.

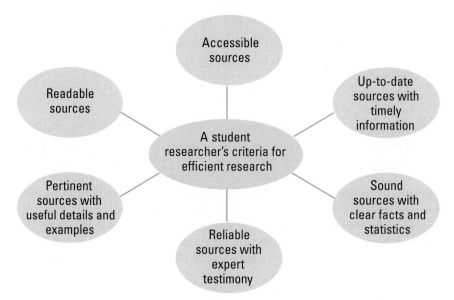

C2 Evaluate sources as your readers would.

If you are uncertain about college requirements, start with recommended sources that are easily accessible, readable, and up-to-date. Look for sources that are chock-full of reliable facts, statistics, research findings, case studies, observations, examples, and expert testimony to persuade your readers.

• Where do you need to add evidence?
• What evidence might support your thesis?
• What evidence is likely to persuade a reader?

$\longrightarrow$

• Which solid sources supply what you need?
• Which sources meet your needs as a researcher?
• Which sources meet the expectations of readers?

C3 Evaluate sources for reliable and appropriate evidence.

When you use evidence from sources to support your points, both you and your readers are likely to hold two simple expectations:

- that your sources are reliable so you can trust their information
- that the information you select from them is appropriate for your paper

After all, how could an unreliable source successfully support your ideas? And what could unsuitable or mismatched information contribute? The difficulty, of course, is learning how to judge what is reliable and appropriate. The following checklist suggests how you can use the time-tested journalist's questions to evaluate print or electronic sources.

EVALUATION CHECKLIST

Who?

☐ Who is the author? What are the author's credentials and experience?

☐ Who is the intended audience? Is it general or academic?

☐ Who publishes or sponsors the source? Is this publisher well regarded?

☐ Who has reviewed the source before publication? Only the author? Expert peer reviewers or referees? An editorial staff?

What?

☐ What is the purpose of the publication or Web site? Is it trying to sell, inform, report, or shape opinion?

☐ What bias or point of view might affect the reliability of the source?

☐ What evidence does the source present? Does the source seem trustworthy and logical? Does it identify its sources or supply active links?

When?

☐ When was the source published or created? When was it revised?

☐ When has it been cited by others in the field?

Where?

☐ Where did you find the source?

☐ Where is the source recommended? Has your library supplied it?

Why?

☐ Why would you use this source rather than others?

☐ Why is its information relevant to your research question?

How?

☐ How would it support your thesis and provide persuasive evidence?

☐ How does the source reflect its author, publisher or sponsor, and audience? How might you need to qualify its use in your paper?

For help incorporating source material, go to the interactive "Take Action" charts in Re:Writing at **bedfordstmartins.com /concisebedguide**.

For examples in both MLA and APA style, see E1–E2.

For a tutorial on avoiding plagiarism, go to Re:Writing at **bedfordstmartins.com /concisebedguide**.

D | Capturing, Launching, and Citing Evidence Added from Sources

Sometimes researchers concentrate so hard on hunting for reliable sources that they forget what comes next. The value of every source remains potential until you successfully capture its facts, statistics, expert testimony, examples, or other information in a form that you can incorporate into your paper. Then, you need to launch — or introduce — the information in order to identify its source or its contribution to your paper. Finally, you must accurately cite, or credit, both in the text of your paper and in a final list of sources, each source whose words or ideas you use.

D1 Avoid plagiarism.

Allow enough time to add information from sources skillfully and correctly. Find out exactly how your instructor expects you to credit sources. Even if you do not intend to plagiarize — to use another writer's words or ideas without appropriately crediting them — a paper full of sloppy or careless shortcuts can look just like a paper deliberately copied from unacknowledged sources. Instead, borrow carefully and honestly.

Identify the source of information, any idea, summary, paraphrase, or quotation, right away, as soon as you add it to your notes. Carry that acknowledgment into your first draft and all the drafts that follow. You generally do not need to identify a source if you use what is called "common knowledge"—quotations, expressions, or information widely known and widely accepted. If you are uncertain about the need for a citation, ask your instructor, or simply provide the citation.

D2 Read your source critically.

Before you pop outside material into your paper, read critically to evaluate its reliability and suitability. If you cannot understand a source that requires specialized background, don't use it. If its ideas, facts, claims, or viewpoint seem unusual, incorporate only what you can substantiate in unrelated sources. If its evidence seems accurate, logical, and relevant, decide exactly how you might want to add it to your paper. Carefully distinguish it from your own ideas, whether you quote, paraphrase, or summarize.

For more on critical reading, see Ch. 2. For more on evaluating evidence, see pp. 40–44. For more on logical fallacies, see pp. 51–52, and 143–44.

D3 Quote accurately.

As you take notes, record as many quotations as you want if that process helps you master the material. When you add quotations to your paper, be selective. A quotation in itself is not necessarily effective evidence, and too many quotations will suggest that your writing is padded or lacks original thought. Quote exactly, and credit your source using the format expected.

For more on punctuating quotations and using ellipsis marks, see C3 in the Quick Editing Guide, pp. A-55–A-56.

QUOTATION CHECKLIST

☐ Have you quoted only a notable passage that adds support and authority?

☐ Have you checked your quotation word by word, for accuracy?

☐ Have you marked the beginning and the ending with quotation marks?

☐ Have you used ellipses (. . .) to mark any spot where you have left out words in the original?

☐ Have you identified the source of the quotation in a launch statement (see D6) or in parentheses?

☐ Have you recorded in parentheses the page number where the quotation appears in the source?

D4 Paraphrase carefully.

A paraphrase presents a passage from a source in your own words and sentences. It may include the same level of detail as the original, but it should not slip into the original wording (unless you identify those

For more about how to quote, paraphrase, and summarize, see pp. 180–87.

snippets with quotation marks). Credit the original source as you do when you quote.

PARAPHRASE CHECKLIST

☐ Have you read the passage critically to be sure you understand it?

☐ Have you paraphrased accurately, reflecting both the main points and the supporting details in the original?

☐ Does your paraphrase use your own words without repeating or echoing the words or the sentence structure of the original?

☐ Does your paraphrase stick to the ideas of the original?

☐ Have you revised your paraphrase so it reads smoothly and clearly?

☐ Have you identified the source of the paraphrase in a launch statement (see D6) or in parentheses?

☐ Have you recorded in parentheses the page number where the passage appears in the source?

D5 Summarize fairly.

A summary clearly identifies the source and reduces its ideas to their essence. Using your own words, your summary may boil a book, a chapter, an article, or a section down to a few sentences that accurately and clearly sum up the sense of the original.

SUMMARY CHECKLIST

☐ Have you read critically to be sure you understand the source?

☐ Have you fairly stated the author's main point in your own words?

☐ Have you briefly stated any supporting ideas that you wish to sum up?

☐ Have you stuck to the overall point without bogging down in details?

☐ Is your summary respectful of others, even if you disagree with them?

☐ Have you revised your summary so it reads smoothly and clearly?

☐ Have you identified the source of the summary in a launch statement (see D6) or in parentheses?

☐ Have you recorded in parentheses the page number where any specific passage appears in the source?

D6 Launch and cite each quotation, paraphrase, summary, and synthesis.

Weave ideas from sources into your paper so that they effectively support the point you want to make. As you integrate each idea, take three steps.

1. Capture. Begin with the evidence you have captured from your source. Refine this material so that it will fit smoothly into your paper. Reduce your quotation to its most memorable words, freshen the wording of your paraphrase, or tighten your summary. Synthesize by pulling together your own ideas and those of your sources to reach new insights. Position the evidence where it is needed to support your statements.

2. Launch. Launch, or introduce, the material captured from each source. Avoid tossing stand-alone quotations into your paper or stacking up a series of paraphrases and summaries. Instead, use your launch statement to lead smoothly into your source information. Try to draw on the authority of the source, mention the author's credentials, or connect the material to other sources or to your points. Let readers know why you have selected this evidence and what you think it adds to your paper.

> Dalton, long an advocate of "green" construction, recommends . . . (18).
>
> As a specialist in elder law, attorney Tamara Diaz suggests . . .
>
> Like Westin, regional director Neil urges that ". . ." (308). Brown, however, takes an innovative approach to local conservation practices and recommends . . . (108).
>
> Another policy analyst, arguing from principles expressed in the Bill of Rights, maintains . . . (Frank 96).
>
> While Congress pits secure borders against individual liberties, immigration analyst Smith proposes a third option that . . . (42).

For more on launch statements, see pp. 189–90.

For more on punctuating quotations, see C3 in the Quick Editing Guide, pp. A-55–A-56.

3. Cite. Identify each source briefly yet accurately. Follow MLA, APA, or another academic format.

For examples showing how to cite and list sources in your paper, see section E.

- Name the author in parentheses (unless named in your launch statement).
- In APA style, add the date of the source.
- Add an exact page number to locate the original passage.
- If a source does not name its author, begin the citation with the first words of the title.
- Add a full entry for each source to a list at the end of your paper.

E | Citing and Listing Sources in MLA or APA Style

For practice citing and listing sources in MLA style, go to the interactive "Take Action" charts in Re:Writing at **bedfordstmartins.com /concisebedguide**.

MLA style is the format for crediting sources that is recommended by the Modern Language Association and often required in English classes. APA style, the format recommended by the American Psychological Association, is often used in social sciences, business, and some composition classes. These two styles are widely used in college papers, but your specialized courses may require other academic styles, depending on the field. Because instructors expect you to credit sources carefully, follow any directions or examples supplied, or refer to the style manual required. Although academic styles all credit sources, their details differ. Stick to the one expected.

In both the MLA and APA styles, your sources need to be identified twice in your paper: first, briefly, at the very moment you draw upon the source material and later, in full, at the end of your paper. The short reference includes the name of the author of the source (or a short form of the title if the source does not name an author), so it's easy for a reader to connect that short entry in your text with the related full entry in the final alphabetical list.

E1 Cite and list sources in MLA style.

If you need to find formats for other types of sources, consult the current *MLA Handbook for Writers of Research Papers,* often available in the library, or check your research manual or research guide for more information.

Cite in the text. At the moment you add a quotation, paraphrase, or summary, identify the source. Citations generally follow a simple pattern: name the author, and note the page in the original where the material is located.

> (Last Name of Author ##)   (Talia 35)   (Smitt and Gilbert 152–53)

Place this citation immediately after a direct quotation or paraphrase.

> When "The Lottery" begins, the reader thinks of the "great pile of stones" (Jackson 260) as children's entertainment.

If you name the author in your launch, the citation is even simpler.

> As Hunt notes, the city faced "a decade of deficits and drought" (54).

For quotations from poems, plays, or novels, supply line, act and scene, or chapter numbers rather than page numbers.

> The speaker in Robinson's poem describes Richard Cory as "richer than a king" (line 9), an attractive man who "fluttered pulses when he said,/ 'Good-morning'" (7–8).

If you use only one source, identify it as your essay begins. Then just give page or line numbers in parentheses after each quote or paraphrase.

CITATION CHECKLIST

☐ Have you placed your citation right after your quotation, paraphrase, or summary?

☐ Have you enclosed your citation with a pair of parenthesis marks?

☐ Have you provided the last name of the author either in your launch statement or in your citation?

☐ Have you used a short title for a work without an identified author?

☐ Have you added any available page or other location number (such as a Web paragraph, poetry line, novel chapter, or play act and scene), as numbered in the source, to identify where the material appears?

List at the end. For each source mentioned in the text, supply a corresponding full entry in a list called Works Cited at the end of your paper.

WORKS CITED CHECKLIST

☐ Have you figured out what type of source you have used? Have you followed the sample pattern for that type as exactly as possible?

☐ Have you used quotation marks and italics correctly for titles?

☐ Have you used correct punctuation — periods, commas, colons, parentheses?

☐ Have you checked the accuracy of numbers: pages, volumes, dates?

☐ Have you accurately recorded names: authors, titles, publishers?

☐ Have you correctly typed or copied in the address of an electronic source that a reader could not otherwise find or that your instructor requires?

☐ Have you correctly arranged your entries in alphabetical order?

☐ Have you checked your final list against your text citations so that every source appears in both places?

☐ Have you double-spaced your list just like your paper, without any extra space between entries?

☐ Have you begun the first line of each entry at the left margin and indented each additional line (the same space you would indent a paragraph)?

For format examples, see the Quick Format Guide, pp. A-2–A-3, and the sample MLA paper, pp. A-59–A-67.

Follow MLA patterns. Use the following examples as patterns for your entries. For each type of source, supply the same information in the same order, using the same punctuation or other features.

Book
TEXT CITATION

(Blyth 37)

WORKS CITED ENTRY

Author's name   Period   Title of book, in italics   Period   City of publication

Blyth, Mark. *Austerity: The History of a Dangerous Idea*. New York:

Oxford UP, 2013. Print. —— Period

Publisher   Year of   Period   Medium
publication   of publication

Essay, Story, or Poem from a Book
TEXT CITATION

(Brady 532)

WORKS CITED ENTRY

Author of   Title of selection,   Original date   Title of book or
selection   in quotation marks   (optional)   anthology, in italics

Brady, Judy. "I Want a Wife." 1971. *The Bedford Guide for College*

Writers. 10th ed. Ed. X. J. Kennedy, Dorothy M. Kennedy, —— Authors or
editors of
and Marcia F. Muth. Boston: Bedford, 2014. 532-33. Print.   book

City of   Publisher   Year of   Page numbers   Medium   Period
publication   of book   publication   of the selection   of publication

Online e-Pages Selection in a Book
TEXT CITATION

(Consumer Reports)

WORKS CITED ENTRY

Organization as   Medium of   Title of book,
author of selection   Title of selection   selection   in italics

Consumer Reports. *Best Buttermilk Pancakes*. Video. *The Bedford Guide*

for College Writers. 10th ed. Bedford, 2014. Web. 15 Feb. 2014.

Edition   Publisher   Year of   Medium   Date of visit
of book   publication   of publication

Popular Magazine Article

The author's name and the title generally appear at the beginning of an article. If the author is not identified, simply begin your entry with the title.

Typically, the magazine name, the date, and page numbers appear at the bottom of pages. Arrange the date in this order: 4 Oct. 2013.

TEXT CITATION

(Freedman 10)

WORKS CITED ENTRY

Title of article,
in quotation marks

Title of magazine,
in italics

Author's name

Freedman, David H. "The Happiness App." *Discover* Jan.-Feb. 2013: 10-11.

Print.

Date of publication   Page numbers
of the article

Medium of
publication

Scholarly Journal Article

TEXT CITATION

(Goodin and Rice 903)

WORKS CITED ENTRY

Authors' names   Title of article, in quotation marks

Goodin, Robert E., and James Mahmud Rice. "Waking Up in the Poll

Booth." *Perspectives on Politics* 7.4 (2009): 901-10. Print.

Title of journal,   Volume   Year   Page   Medium of
in italics   and issue   Colon   numbers   publication
                   numbers   of the article

Article from a Library Database

In databases, the print publication details often appear at the top of the online entry. A printout usually records this information plus your date of access. Select the paginated pdf format, or follow the first page number of the print source by a hyphen if the page range is not known.

TEXT CITATION

Omit the page number when it is not available online.

(Laurance et al. 291)

See p. A-23 for the text reference from Carrie Williamson's paper.

WORKS CITED ENTRY

Author's
name

Title of article,
in quotation marks

Page numbers in
print version

Laurance, William F., et al. "Averting Biodiversity Collapse in Tropical

Forest Protected Areas." *Nature* 489.7415 (13 Sept. 2012): 290-94.

Academic OneFile. Web. 6 Dec. 2012.

Name of database   Medium of   Date of   Title of magazine,   Volume and   Date   Colon
in italics   publication   visit   in italics   issue numbers

Page from a Web Site

The page title and site title often appear at the top of a given page. The date when a site was posted or last updated often appears at the bottom, as does the name of the sponsor (which also may appear as a link). A printout of the page will record this information as well as the date you visited.

TEXT CITATION

See p. A-23 for the text reference from Carrie Williamson's paper.

A site is identified by title if it does not name an author. Page or paragraph numbers may not be available for a Web page.

According to the Rainforest Alliance, . . .

WORKS CITED ENTRY

No author identified   Title of page, in quotation marks   Title of site, in italics   Sponsor name

"Conservation in the Neotropics." *Rainforest-alliance.org.* Rainforest

Alliance, 2012. Web. 6 Dec. 2012.

Date posted or updated   Medium of publication   Date of visit

E2 Cite and list sources in APA style.

Cite in the text. After the author's last name, add the date. Use p. (for "page") or pp. (for "pages") before the page numbers.

If you need to find formats for other types of sources, consult the current *Publication Manual of the American Psychological Association,* often available in the library, or check your research manual or research guide for more information.

(Last Name of Author, Date, p. ##)   (Talia, 2013, p. 35)
(Smith & Gilbert, 2012, pp. 152–153)

List at the end. Call your list of sources References. Include all the sources cited in your text except for personal communications and classics.

Follow APA patterns. Use the following examples as patterns for your entries. For each type of source, supply the same information in the same order using the same punctuation or other features.

Book
TEXT CITATION

(Blyth, 2013, p. 37)

REFERENCES ENTRY

Blyth, M. (2013). *Austerity: The history of a dangerous idea.* New York, NY: Oxford University Press.

Work or Section in a Book
TEXT CITATION

(Brady, 1971/2014, p. 532)

REFERENCES ENTRY

Brady, J. (2014). I want a wife. In X. J. Kennedy, D. M. Kennedy, & M. F. Muth (Eds.), *The Bedford guide for college writers* (10th ed., pp. 532-533). Boston, MA: Bedford/St. Martin's. (Original work published 1971)

Online e-Pages Selection in a Book

TEXT CITATION

(Consumer Reports, 2014)

REFERENCES ENTRY

Consumer Reports. (Producer). (2014). *Best buttermilk pancakes* [Video file]. In X. J. Kennedy, D. M. Kennedy, & M. F. Muth (Eds.), *The Bedford guide for college writers* (10th ed.). Retrieved from http://www.bedfordstmartins.com/bedguide/epages

Popular Magazine Article

TEXT CITATION

(Freedman, 2013, p. 11)

REFERENCES ENTRY

Freedman, D. H. (2013, January-February). The happiness app. *Discover, 34*(1), 10-11.

Scholarly Journal Article

For a magazine or journal article, add any volume number in italics and any issue number in parentheses, without a space or italics.

TEXT CITATION

(Goodin & Rice, 2009, p. 903)

REFERENCES ENTRY

Goodin, R. E., & Rice, J. M. (2009). Waking up in the poll booth. *Perspectives on Politics, 7,* 901-910. doi:10.1017/S1537592709991873

Article from a Library Database

IN-TEXT CITATION

No exact page or paragraph number may be available for an online article.

(Laurance et al., 2012, p. 291)

REFERENCES ENTRY

The database does not need to be named unless a reader would have trouble finding the item without the URL.

Laurance, W. F., Useche, D. C., Rendeiro, J., Kalka, M., Bradshaw, C. J. A., Sloan, S. P., Laurance, S. G., et al. (2012). Averting biodiversity collapse

in tropical forest protected areas. *Nature, 489,* 290-294. doi:10.1038
/nature11318

Page from a Web Site

TEXT CITATION

For APA format
examples, see the
Quick Format Guide,
pp. A-4–A-6, and the
sample APA paper,
pp. A-68–A-76.

Because the Web site does not name an author, the citation identifies the
site's sponsor.

According to the Rainforest Alliance (2012) . . .

REFERENCES ENTRY

Your access date is not needed unless the material is likely to change.

Rainforest Alliance. (2012). Conservation in the neotropics. Retrieved
from http://www.rainforest-alliance.org/adopt/conservation

Quick Editing Guide

A | **Editing for Common Grammar Problems** A-40

B | **Editing to Ensure Effective Sentences** A-49

C | **Editing for Common Punctuation Problems** A-53

D | **Editing for Common Mechanics Problems** A-56

This Quick Editing Guide provides an overview of grammar, style, punctuation, and mechanics problems typical of college writing.

EDITING CHECKLIST
Common and Serious Problems in College Writing

Grammar Problems

☐ Have you avoided writing sentence fragments?   A1

☐ Have you avoided writing comma splices or fused sentences?   A2

☐ Have you used the correct form for all verbs in the past tense?   A3

☐ Do all verbs agree with their subjects?   A4

☐ Have you used the correct case for all pronouns?   A5

☐ Do all pronouns agree with their antecedents?   A6

☐ Have you used adjectives and adverbs correctly?   A7

Sentence Problems

☐ Does each modifier clearly modify the appropriate sentence element?   B1

☐ Have you used parallel structure where needed?   B2

Punctuation Problems

☐ Have you used commas correctly?   C1

☐ Have you used apostrophes correctly?   C2

☐ Have you punctuated quotations correctly?   C3

Mechanics Problems

☐ Have you used capital letters correctly?   D1

☐ Have you spelled all words correctly?   D2

For editing and
proofreading
strategies, see
pp. 313–17.

Editing and proofreading are needed at the end of the writing process because writers — *all* writers — find it difficult to write error-free sentences the first time they try. Once you are satisfied that you have expressed your ideas, you should make sure that each sentence and word is concise, clear, and correct. Certain common errors in Standard Written English are like red flags to careful readers: they signal that the writer is either ignorant or careless. Use the editing checklist on page A–39 to check your paper for these problems; then use the editing checklists in each section to help you correct specific errors. Concentrate on any problems likely to reappear in your writing.

Your grammar checker or software can help you catch some errors, but not others. Always consider the grammar checker's suggestions carefully before accepting them and continue to edit on your own.

- A grammar checker cannot always correctly identify the subject or verb in a sentence; it may question whether a sentence is complete or whether its subject and verb agree, even when the sentence is correct.

- Grammar checkers are likely to miss misplaced modifiers, faulty parallelism, possessives without apostrophes, or incorrect commas.

- Most grammar checkers do a good job of spotting problems with adjectives and adverbs, such as confusing *good* and *well*.

- Keep track of your mistakes to develop an "error hit list." Use your software's Find capacity (try the Home or Edit menu) to check for searchable problems such as instances of *each* (always singular) or *few* (always plural) to see if all the verbs agree.

A | Editing for Common Grammar Problems

A1 Check for any sentence fragments.

A complete sentence has a subject, has a predicate, and can stand on its own. A **sentence fragment** cannot stand on its own as a sentence because it lacks a subject, a predicate, or both, or for some other reason fails to convey a complete thought. Though common in ads and fiction, fragments are not usually effective in college writing because they do not express coherent thoughts.

To edit for fragments, check that each sentence has a subject and a verb and expresses a complete thought. To correct a fragment, complete

At-A-Glance Guide

Irregular Verbs at a Glance   A-43

Forms of *Be* and *Have* at a Glance   A-44

Personal Pronoun Cases at a Glance   A-46

Indefinite Pronouns at a Glance   A-47

Irregular Adjectives and Adverbs at a Glance   A-48

Possessive Personal Pronouns at a Glance   A-54

Capitalization at a Glance   A-57

it by adding a missing part, dropping an unnecessary subordinating conjunction, or joining it to a nearby sentence, if that would make more sense.

FRAGMENT	Roberto has two sisters. Maya and Leeza.
CORRECT	Roberto has two sisters, Maya and Leeza.
FRAGMENT	The children going to the zoo.
CORRECT	The children were going to the zoo.
CORRECT	The children going to the zoo were caught in a traffic jam.
FRAGMENT	Last night when we saw Viola Davis's most recent movie.
CORRECT	Last night we saw Viola Davis's most recent movie.

EDITING CHECKLIST
Fragments

☐ Does the sentence have both a subject and a predicate?

☐ If the sentence contains a subordinate clause, does it contain a clause that is a complete sentence too?

☐ If you find a fragment, can you link it to an adjoining sentence, eliminate its subordinating conjunction, or add any missing element?

A2 Check for any comma splices or fused sentences.

A complete sentence has a subject and a predicate and can stand on its own. When two sentences are combined as one sentence, each sentence within the larger one is called a *main clause*. However, writers need to

subject: The part of a sentence that names something—a person, an object, an idea, a situation—about which the predicate makes an assertion: The *king* lives.

predicate: The part of a sentence that makes an assertion about the subject involving an action (Birds *fly*), a relationship (Birds *have feathers*), or a state of being (Birds *are warm-blooded*)

subordinating conjunction: A word (such as *because, although, if, when*) used to make one clause dependent on, or subordinate to, another: *Unless* you have a key, we are locked out.

main clause: A group of words that has both a subject and a verb and can stand alone as a complete sentence: *My friends like baseball.*

coordinating conjunction: A one-syllable linking word (*and, but, for, or, nor, so, yet*) that joins elements with equal or near-equal importance: Jack *and* Jill, sink *or* swim

subordinating conjunction: A word (such as *because, although, if, when*) used to make one clause dependent on, or subordinate to, another: *Unless* you have a key, we are locked out.

follow the rules for joining main clauses to avoid serious sentence errors. A **comma splice** is two main clauses joined with only a comma. A **fused sentence** (or **run-on**) is two main clauses joined with no punctuation at all.

COMMA SPLICE	I went to the shop, I bought a new coat.
FUSED SENTENCE	I went to the shop I bought a new coat.

To find these errors, examine the main clauses in each sentence to make sure they are joined correctly. Correct a comma splice or fused sentence in one of these four ways, depending on which makes the best sense:

ADD A PERIOD	I went to the shop. I bought a new coat.
ADD A COMMA AND A COORDINATING CONJUNCTION	I went to the shop, and I bought a new coat.
ADD A SEMICOLON	I went to the shop; I bought a new coat.
ADD A SUBORDINATING CONJUNCTION	I went to the shop, where I bought a new coat.

EDITING CHECKLIST
Comma Splices and Fused Sentences

☐ Can you make each main clause a separate sentence?

☐ Can you link the two main clauses with a comma and a coordinating conjunction?

☐ Can you link the two main clauses with a semicolon or, if appropriate, a colon?

☐ Can you subordinate one clause to the other?

A3 Check for correct past tense verb forms.

The **form** of a verb, the way it is spelled and pronounced, can change to show its **tense** — the time when its action did, does, or will occur (in the past, present, or future). A verb about something in the present will often have a different form than a verb about something in the past.

verb: A word that shows action (The cow *jumped* over the moon) or a state of being (The cow *is* brown)

PRESENT	Right now, I *watch* only a few minutes of television each day.
PAST	Last month, I *watched* television shows every evening.

Regular verbs are verbs whose forms follow standard rules; they form the past tense by adding *-ed* or *-d* to the present tense form:

watch/watched   *look/looked*   *hope/hoped*

Check all regular verbs in the past tense for one of these endings.

FAULTY	I *ask* my brother for a loan yesterday.
CORRECT	I *asked* my brother for a loan yesterday.

FAULTY	Nicole *race* in the track meet last week.
CORRECT	Nicole *raced* in the track meet last week.

TIP: If you say the final -*d* sound when you talk, you may find it easier to add the final -*d* or -*ed* when you write past tense regular verbs.

Because **irregular verbs** do not have standard forms, their unpredictable past tense forms must be memorized. In addition, the past tense may differ from the past participle. Check a dictionary for these forms.

FAULTY	My cat *laid* on the tile floor to take her nap.
CORRECT	My cat *lay* on the tile floor to take her nap.

FAULTY	I *have swam* twenty laps every day this month.
CORRECT	I *have swum* twenty laps every day this month.

participle: A form of a verb that cannot function alone as a main verb, including present participles ending in -*ing* (*dancing*) and past participles often ending in -*ed* or -*d* (*danced*)

TIP: In college papers, follow convention by using the present tense, not the past, to describe the work of an author or the events in a literary work.

FAULTY	In "The Lottery," Jackson *revealed* the power of tradition. As the story *opened,* the villagers *gathered* in the square.
CORRECT	In "The Lottery," Jackson *reveals* the power of tradition. As the story *opens,* the villagers *gather* in the square.

Irregular Verbs at a Glance

INFINITIVE (BASE)	PAST TENSE	PAST PARTICIPLE
begin	began	begun
burst	burst	burst
choose	chose	chosen
do	did	done
eat	ate	eaten
go	went	gone
lay	laid	laid
lie	lay	lain
speak	spoke	spoken

Past Tense Verb Forms

☐ Have you identified the main verb in the sentence?

☐ Is the sentence about past, present, or future? Does the verb show this time?

☐ Is the verb regular or irregular? Have you used its correct form?

A4 Check for correct subject-verb agreement.

The **form** of a verb, the way it is spelled and pronounced, can change to show **number**—whether the subject is singular (one) or plural (more than one). It can also show **person**—whether the subject is *you* or *she*, for example.

SINGULAR	Our instructor *grades* every paper carefully.
PLURAL	Most instructors *grade* tests using a standard scale.
SECOND PERSON	You *write* well-documented research papers.
THIRD PERSON	She *writes* good research papers, too.

A verb must match (or *agree with*) its subject in terms of number and person. Regular verbs (whose forms follow a standard rule) are problems only in the present tense. There they have two forms: one that ends in *-s* or *-es* and one that does not. Only the subjects *he, she, it,* and singular nouns use the verb form that ends in *-s* or *-es.*

I like	we like
you like	you like
he/she/it/Dan/the child like<u>s</u>	they like

The verbs *be* and *have* are irregular, so their present tense forms must be memorized. The verb *be* is also irregular in the past tense.

---

verb: A word that shows action (The cow *jumped* over the moon) or a state of being (The cow *is* brown)

subject: The part of a sentence that names something—a person, an object, an idea, a situation—about which the predicate makes an assertion: The *king* lives.

Forms of *Be* and *Have* at a Glance

THE PRESENT TENSE OF *BE*		THE PAST TENSE OF *BE*	
I am	we are	I was	we were
you are	you are	you were	you were
he/she/it is	they are	he/she/it was	they were

THE PRESENT TENSE OF *HAVE*		THE PAST TENSE OF *HAVE*	
I have	we have	I had	we had
you have	you have	you had	you had
he/she/it has	they have	he/she/it had	they had

Problems in agreement often occur when the subject is hard to find, is an indefinite pronoun, or is confusing. Make sure that you include any *-s* or *-es* endings and use the correct form for irregular verbs.

FAULTY	Jim *write* at least fifty e-mails a day.
CORRECT	Jim *writes* at least fifty e-mails a day.
FAULTY	The students *has* difficulty with the assignment.
CORRECT	The students *have* difficulty with the assignment.
FAULTY	Every one of the cakes *were* sold at the fundraiser.
CORRECT	Every one of the cakes *was* sold at the fundraiser.

indefinite pronoun: A pronoun standing for an unspecified person or thing, including singular forms (*each, everyone, no one*) and plural forms (*both, few*): *Everyone* is soaking wet.

EDITING CHECKLIST
Subject-Verb Agreement

☐ Have you correctly identified the subject and the verb in the sentence?

☐ Is the subject singular or plural? Does the verb match?

☐ Have you used the correct form of the verb?

A5 Check for correct pronoun case.

Depending on the role a pronoun plays in a sentence, it is said to be in the **subjective case, objective case,** or **possessive case.** Use the subjective case if the pronoun is the subject of a sentence, the subject of a subordinate clause, or a subject complement (after a linking verb). Use the objective case if the pronoun is a direct or indirect object of a verb or the object of a preposition. Use the possessive case to show possession.

SUBJECTIVE	*I* will argue that our campus needs more parking.
OBJECTIVE	This issue is important to *me*.
POSSESSIVE	*My* argument will be quite persuasive.

Writers often use the subjective case when they should use the objective case—sometimes trying to sound formal and correct. Instead, choose the correct form based on a pronoun's function in the sentence. If the sentence pairs a noun and a pronoun, try the sentence with the pronoun alone.

FAULTY	My company gave my husband and *I* a trip to Hawaii.
PRONOUN ONLY	My company gave *I* a trip?
CORRECT	My company gave my husband and *me* a trip to Hawaii.
FAULTY	My uncle and *me* had different expectations.
PRONOUN ONLY	*Me* had different expectations?
CORRECT	My uncle and *I* had different expectations.

pronoun: A word that stands in place of a noun (*he, him,* or *his* for *Nate*)

subject: The part of a sentence that names something—a person, an object, an idea, a situation—about which the predicate makes an assertion: The *king* lives.

subject complement: A noun, an adjective, or a group of words that follows a linking verb (*is, become, feel, seem,* or another verb that shows a state of being) and that renames or describes the subject: This plum tastes *ripe*.

object: The target or recipient of the action of a verb: Some geese bite *people*.

Personal Pronoun Cases at a Glance

SUBJECTIVE	OBJECTIVE	POSSESSIVE
I	me	my, mine
you	you	your, yours
he	him	his
she	her	hers
it	it	its
we	us	our, ours
they	them	their, theirs
who	whom	whose

FAULTY	Jack ran faster than my brother and *me*.
PRONOUN ONLY	Jack ran faster than *me* ran?
CORRECT	Jack ran faster than my brother and *I*.

A second common error with pronoun case involves gerunds. Whenever you need a pronoun to modify a gerund, use the possessive case.

FAULTY	Our supervisor disapproves of *us* talking in the hallway.
CORRECT	Our supervisor disapproves of *our* talking in the hallway.

EDITING CHECKLIST
Pronoun Case

gerund: A form of a verb, ending in *-ing,* that functions as a noun: Lacey likes *playing* in the steel band.

☐ Have you identified all the pronouns in the sentence?

☐ Does each one function as a subject, an object, or a possessive?

☐ Given the function of each, have you used the correct form?

A6 Check for correct pronoun-antecedent agreement.

The **form** of a pronoun, the way it is spelled and pronounced, can change to show **number**—whether the subject is singular (one) or plural (more than one). It also can change to show **gender**—masculine or feminine, for example—or **person:** first (*I, we*), second (*you*), or third (*he, she, it, they*).

pronoun: A word that stands in place of a noun (*he, him,* or *his* for *Nate*)

SINGULAR	My brother took *his* coat and left.
PLURAL	My brothers took *their* coats and left.
MASCULINE	I talked to Steven before *he* had a chance to leave.
FEMININE	I talked to Stephanie before *she* had a chance to leave.

A pronoun refers to its **antecedent**, usually a specific noun or pronoun nearby. The connection between the two must be clear so that readers know what the pronoun means in the sentence. The two need to match (or *agree*) in number and gender.

A common error is using a plural pronoun to refer to a singular antecedent. This error often crops up when the antecedent is difficult to find, is an indefinite pronoun, or is confusing for another reason. First, find the antecedent, and decide whether it is singular or plural. Then make the pronoun match its antecedent.

FAULTY   Neither Luz nor Pam received approval of *their* financial aid.

CORRECT   Neither Luz nor Pam received approval of *her* financial aid.

[*Neither Luz nor Pam* is a compound subject joined by *nor*. Any pronoun referring to it must agree with only the nearer part of the compound: *her* agrees with *Pam*, which is singular.]

Indefinite pronouns are troublesome antecedents when they are grammatically singular but create a plural image in the writer's mind. Fortunately, most indefinite pronouns are always singular or always plural.

FAULTY   Each of the boys in the club has *their* own custom laptop.

CORRECT   Each of the boys in the club has *his* own custom laptop.

[The word *each*, not *boys*, is the antecedent. *Each* is an indefinite pronoun and is always singular. Any pronoun referring to it must be singular as well.]

FAULTY   Everyone in the meeting had *their* own cell phone.

CORRECT   Everyone in the meeting had *his or her* own cell phone.

[*Everyone* is an indefinite pronoun that is always singular. Any pronoun referring to it must be singular as well.]

indefinite pronoun:
A pronoun standing for an unspecified person or thing, including singular forms (*each, everyone, no one*) and plural forms (*both, few*): *Everyone* is soaking wet.

Indefinite Pronouns at a Glance

ALWAYS SINGULAR			ALWAYS PLURAL
anybody	everyone	nothing	both
anyone	everything	one (of)	few
anything	much	somebody	many
each (of)	neither (of)	someone	several
either (of)	nobody	something	
everybody	no one		

Pronoun-Antecedent Agreement

☐ Have you identified the antecedent for each pronoun?

☐ Is the antecedent singular or plural? Does the pronoun match?

☐ Is the antecedent masculine, feminine, or neuter? Does the pronoun match?

☐ Is the antecedent first, second, or third person? Does the pronoun match?

modifier: A word (such as an adjective or adverb), phrase, or clause that provides more information about other parts of a sentence: Plays *staged by the drama class* are *always successful.*

A7   Check for correct adjectives and adverbs.

Adjectives and **adverbs** describe or give information about (*modify*) other words. Many adverbs are formed by adding *-ly* to adjectives: *simple, simply; quiet, quietly.* Because adjectives and adverbs resemble one another, writers sometimes mistakenly use one instead of the other. To edit, find the word that the adjective or adverb modifies. If that word is a noun or pronoun, use an adjective (to describe which or what kind). If that word is a verb, adjective, or another adverb, use an adverb (to describe how, when, where, or why).

FAULTY	Kelly ran into the house *quick.*
CORRECT	Kelly ran into the house *quickly.*
FAULTY	Gabriela looked *terribly* after her bout with the flu.
CORRECT	Gabriela looked *terrible* after her bout with the flu.

Adjectives and adverbs with similar comparative and superlative forms can also cause trouble. Always ask whether you need an adjective or an adverb in the sentence, and then use the correct word.

FAULTY	His scar healed so *good* that it was barely visible.
CORRECT	His scar healed so *well* that it was barely visible.

Good is an adjective; it describes a noun or pronoun. *Well* is an adverb; it modifies or adds to a verb (*heal*, in this case) or an adjective.

Irregular Adjectives and Adverbs at a Glance

POSITIVE ADJECTIVES	COMPARATIVE ADJECTIVES	SUPERLATIVE ADJECTIVES
good	better	best
bad	worse	worst
little	less, littler	least, littlest
many, some, much	more	most
POSITIVE ADVERBS	COMPARATIVE ADVERBS	SUPERLATIVE ADVERBS
well	better	best
badly	worse	worst
little	less	least

EDITING CHECKLIST
Adjectives and Adverbs

☐ Have you identified which word the adjective or adverb modifies?

☐ If the word modified is a noun or pronoun, have you used an adjective?

☐ If the word modified is a verb, adjective, or adverb, have you used an adverb?

☐ Have you used the correct comparative or superlative form?

B | Editing to Ensure Effective Sentences

B1 Check for any misplaced or dangling modifiers.

For a sentence to be clear, the connection between a modifier and the thing it modifies must be obvious. Usually a modifier should be placed just before or just after what it modifies. If the modifier is too close to some other sentence element, it is a **misplaced modifier.** If the modifier cannot logically modify anything in the sentence, it is a **dangling modifier.** Both errors can confuse readers—and sometimes create unintentionally humorous images. As you edit, place a modifier directly before or after the word modified and clearly connect the two.

modifier: A word (such as an adjective or adverb), phrase, or clause that provides more information about other parts of a sentence: Plays *staged by the drama class* are *always successful.*

MISPLACED	Dan found the leftovers when he visited in the refrigerator.
CORRECT	Dan found the leftovers in the refrigerator when he visited.
	[In the faulty sentence, *in the refrigerator* seems to modify Dan's visit. Obviously the leftovers, not Dan, are in the refrigerator.]
DANGLING	Looking out the window, the clouds were beautiful.
CORRECT	Looking out the window, I saw that the clouds were beautiful.
CORRECT	When I looked out the window, the clouds were beautiful.
	[In the faulty sentence, *Looking out the window* should modify *I*, but *I* is not in the sentence. The modifier dangles without anything logical to modify until *I* is in the sentence.]

EDITING CHECKLIST
Misplaced and Dangling Modifiers

☐ What is each modifier meant to modify? Is the modifier as close as possible to that sentence element? Is any misreading possible?

☐ If a modifier is misplaced, can you move it to clarify the meaning?

☐ What noun or pronoun is a dangling modifier meant to modify? Can you make that word or phrase the subject of the main clause? Or can you turn the dangling modifier into a clause that includes the missing noun or pronoun?

Take Action Improving Sentence Style

Ask each question at the top of the chart to consider whether your draft might need work on that issue. If so, follow the ASK—LOCATE SPECIFICS—TAKE ACTION sequence to revise.

	Passive Voice?	**Faulty Parallelism?**	**Repetitive Sentence Patterns?**
1 ASK	Have I relied on sentences in the passive voice instead of the active voice?	Have I missed opportunities to emphasize comparable ideas by stating them in comparable ways?	Do my sentences sound alike because they repeat the same opening, pattern, or length?
2 LOCATE SPECIFICS	■ Reread your sentence. If its subject also performs the action, it is in the active voice. (Underline the performer; double underline the action.) ■ If the sentence subject does not perform the action, your sentence is in the passive voice. You have tucked the performer into a *by* phrase or have not identified the performer.	■ Read your sentences, looking for lists or comparable items. ■ Underline items in a series to compare the ways you present them. **Draft:** Observing primates can reveal <u>how they cooperate</u>, <u>their tool use</u>, and <u>building</u> secure nests.	■ Add a line break at the end of every sentence in a passage so you can easily compare sentence openings, patterns, or lengths. ■ Use your software (or yourself) to count the words in each sentence. ■ Search for variations such as colons (:) and semicolons (;) to see how often you use them.
3 TAKE ACTION	■ Consider changing passive voice to active. Make the performer of the action the sentence subject (which reduces extra words by dropping the *by* phrase). **Passive:** The primate play area <u>was arranged by the zookeeper</u>. (9 words; emphasizes object of the action) **Active:** <u>The zookeeper arranged</u> the primate play area. (7 words; emphasizes zookeeper who performed the action)	■ Rework so that items in a series all follow the same grammatical pattern. ■ Select the common pattern based on the clarity and emphasis it adds to your sentence. **Parallel:** Observing primates can reveal how they <u>cooperate</u>, <u>use</u> tools, and <u>build</u> secure nests.	■ Rewrite for variety if you repeat openings (*During, Because, After, Then, And*). ■ Rewrite for directness if you repeat indirect openings (*There are, There is, It is*). ■ Rewrite to vary sentence lengths. Tuck in a few short sentences. Combine choppy sentences. Add a complicated sentence to build up to your point. ■ Try some colons or semicolons for variety.

Take Action Improving Sentence Clarity

Ask each question at the top of the chart to consider whether your draft might need work on that issue. If so, follow the ASK—LOCATE SPECIFICS—TAKE ACTION sequence to revise.

	Disconnected or Scattered Ideas?	Wordy Sentences?	Any Other Improvements in Sentence Style?
1 **ASK**	Have I tossed out my ideas without weighting or relating them?	Have I used more words than needed to say what I mean?	After a final look at the sentences in my draft, should I do anything else to improve them?
2 **LOCATE SPECIFICS**	■ Highlight the transitional words (*first, second, for example, however*). ■ Star all the sentences or sentence parts in a passage that seem to be of equal weight.	■ Read your draft out loud. Put a check by anything that sounds long-winded, repetitive, chatty, or clichéd. ■ Use past papers to help you list your favorite wordy expressions (such as *a large number of* for *many*) or extra words (such as *very* or *really*).	■ Read your draft out loud. Mark any sentences that sound incomplete, awkward, confusing, boring, or lifeless. ■ Ask your peer editors how you might make your sentences stronger and more stylish.
3 **TAKE ACTION**	■ Review passages with little highlighting; add more transitions to relate ideas. ■ In your starred sentences, strengthen the structure. Introduce less significant parts with subordinating words (*because, although*). Use *and* or *but* to coordinate equal parts.	■ At each check, rephrase with simpler or more exact words. ■ Search with your software for wordy expressions; replace or trim them. ■ Highlight a passage; use the Tools or Review menu to count its words. See how many extra words you can drop.	■ Return to each mark to make weak sentences clear, emphatic, interesting, and lively. ■ Consider the useful suggestions of your peers. ■ Review sections A and B of this guide, and edit until your sentences express your ideas as you wish.

B2 Check for parallel structure.

correlative conjunction: A pair of linking words (such as *either/or, not only/ but also*) that appear separately but work together to join elements of a sentence: *Neither* his friends *nor* hers like pizza.

A series of words, phrases, clauses, or sentences with the same grammatical form is said to be **parallel.** Using parallel form for elements that are parallel in meaning or function helps readers grasp the meaning of a sentence more easily. A lack of parallelism can distract, annoy, or even confuse readers.

To use parallelism, put nouns with nouns, verbs with verbs, and phrases with phrases. Parallelism is particularly important in a series, with correlative conjunctions, and in comparisons using *than* or *as*.

FAULTY	I like to go to Estes Park for skiing, ice skating, and to meet interesting people.
CORRECT	I like to go to Estes Park to ski, to ice skate, and to meet interesting people.
FAULTY	The proposal is neither practical, nor is it innovative.
CORRECT	The proposal is neither practical nor innovative.
FAULTY	Teens need a few firm rules rather than having many flimsy ones.
CORRECT	Teens need a few firm rules rather than many flimsy ones.

Edit to reinforce parallel structures by repeating articles, conjunctions, prepositions, or lead-in words as needed.

AWKWARD	His dream was that he would never have to give up his routine but he would still find time to explore new frontiers.
PARALLEL	His dream was that he would never have to give up his routine but *that* he would still find time to explore new frontiers.

EDITING CHECKLIST
Parallel Structure

☐ Are all the elements in a series in the same grammatical form?

☐ Are the elements in a comparison parallel in form?

☐ Are the articles, conjunctions, prepositions, or lead-in words for elements repeated as needed rather than mixed or omitted?

Use the Take Action charts (pp. A-50 and A-51) to help you figure out how to improve your draft. Skim across the top to identify questions you might ask about the sentences in your draft. When you answer a question with "Yes" or "Maybe," move straight down the column to Locate Specifics under that question. Use the activities there to pinpoint gaps, problems, or weaknesses. Then move straight down the column to Take Action. Use the advice that suits your problem as you revise.

C | Editing for Common Punctuation Problems

C1 Check for correct use of commas.

The **comma** is a punctuation mark indicating a pause. By setting some words apart from others, commas help clarify relationships. They prevent the words on a page and the ideas they represent from becoming a jumble.

1. Use a comma before a coordinating conjunction (*and, but, for, or, so, yet, nor*) joining two main clauses in a compound sentence.

   The discussion was brief, *so* the meeting was adjourned early.

2. Use a comma after an introductory word or word group unless it is short and cannot be misread.

   After the war, the North's economy developed rapidly.

3. Use commas to separate the items in a series of three or more items.

   The chief advantages will be *speed, durability,* and *longevity.*

4. Use commas to set off a modifying clause or phrase if it is nonrestrictive — if it can be taken out of the sentence without significantly changing the essential meaning of the sentence.

   Good childcare, *which is hard to find,* should be available at work.

   Good childcare *that is reliable and inexpensive* is every employee's hope.

5. Use commas to set off a nonrestrictive appositive, an expression that comes directly after a noun or pronoun and renames it.

   Sheri, my sister, has a new job as an events coordinator.

6. Use commas to set off parenthetical expressions, conjunctive adverbs, and other interrupters.

   The proposal from the mayor's commission, however, is not feasible.

appositive: A word or group of words that adds information about a subject or object by identifying it in a different way: Terry, *the drummer,* manages the band.

parenthetical expression: An aside to readers or a transitional expression such as *for example* or *in contrast*

conjunctive adverb: A linking word that can connect independent clauses and show a relationship between two ideas: Jen studied hard; *consequently,* she passed the exam.

EDITING CHECKLIST

Commas

☐ Have you added a comma between two main clauses joined by a coordinating conjunction?

☐ Have you added commas needed after introductory words or word groups?

☐ Have you separated items in a series with commas?

☐ Have you avoided commas before the first item in a series or after the last?

☐ Have you used commas before and after each nonrestrictive (nonessential) word, phrase, or clause?

☐ Have you avoided using commas around a restrictive word, phrase, or clause that is essential to the meaning of the sentence?

☐ Have you used commas to set off appositives, parenthetical expressions, conjunctive adverbs, and other interrupters?

C2 Check for correct use of apostrophes.

An **apostrophe** is a punctuation mark that either shows possession (*Sylvia's*) or indicates that one or more letters have intentionally been left out to form a contraction (*didn't*). An apostrophe is never used to create the possessive form of a pronoun; use the possessive pronoun form instead.

FAULTY	*Mikes* car was totaled in the accident.
CORRECT	*Mike's* car was totaled in the accident.
FAULTY	*Womens'* pay is often less than *mens'*.
CORRECT	*Women's* pay is often less than *men's*.
FAULTY	Che *did'nt* want to stay at home and study.
CORRECT	Che *didn't* want to stay at home and study.
FAULTY	The dog wagged *it's* tail happily. [it's = it is? No.]
CORRECT	The dog wagged *its* tail happily.
FAULTY	*Its* raining.
CORRECT	*It's* raining. [it's = it is]

Possessive Personal Pronouns at a Glance

PERSONAL PRONOUN	POSSESSIVE CASE
I	my, mine
you	your, yours (*not* your's)
he	his
she	her, hers (*not* her's)
it	its (*not* it's)
we	our, ours (*not* our's)
they	their, theirs (*not* their's)
who	whose (*not* who's)

EDITING CHECKLIST

Apostrophes

☐ Have you used an apostrophe when letters are left out in a contraction?

☐ Have you used an apostrophe to create the possessive form of a noun?

☐ Have you used the possessive case — not an apostrophe — to show that a pronoun is possessive?

☐ Have you used *it's* correctly (to mean *it is*)?

C3 Check for correct punctuation of quotations.

When you quote the exact words of a person you have interviewed or a source you have read, enclose those words in quotation marks. Notice how student Betsy Buffo presents the words of her subject in this passage from her essay "Interview with an Artist":

> Derek is straightforward when asked about how his work is received in the local community: "My work is outside the mainstream. Because it's controversial, it's not easy for me to get exposure."

She might have expressed and punctuated this passage in other ways:

> Derek says that "it's not easy" for him to find an audience.

> Derek struggles for recognition because his art falls "outside the mainstream."

If your source is quoting someone else (a quotation within a quotation), put your subject's words in quotation marks and the words he or she is quoting in single quotation marks. Always put commas and periods inside the quotation marks; put semicolons and colons outside. Include all necessary marks in the correct place or sequence.

> As Betsy Buffo explains, "Derek struggles for recognition because his art falls 'outside the mainstream.'"

Substitute an ellipsis mark (. . .) — three spaced dots — for any words you have omitted from the middle of a direct quotation. If you are following MLA style, you may place the ellipses inside brackets ([. . .]) when necessary to avoid confusing your ellipsis marks with those of the original writer. If the ellipses come at the end of a sentence, add another period to conclude the sentence. You don't need an ellipsis mark to show the beginning or ending of a quotation that is clearly incomplete.

In this selection from "Overworked!" student Melissa Lamberth identifies quotations and an omission. (She cites Joe Robinson's essay from the reader in her *Bedford Guide*):

In his essay "Four Weeks Vacation," Robinson writes, "The health implications of sleep-deprived motorists weaving their way to the office . . . are self-evident" (481).

For more about quotations from sources, see D3 in the Quick Research Guide, p. A-29.

EDITING CHECKLIST
Punctuation with Quotations

☐ Are the exact words quoted from your source enclosed in quotation marks?

☐ Are commas and periods placed inside closing quotation marks?

☐ Are colons and semicolons placed outside closing quotation marks?

☐ Do ellipses show where you omit words from the middle of a quote?

D | Editing for Common Mechanics Problems

D1 Check for correct use of capital letters.

Capital letters begin a new sentence; names of specific people, nationalities, places, dates, and things (proper nouns); and main words in titles.

FAULTY	During my Sophomore year in College, I took World Literature, Biology, American History, Psychology, and French—courses required for a Humanities Major.
CORRECT	During my sophomore year in college, I took world literature, biology, American history, psychology, and French—courses required for a humanities major.

EDITING CHECKLIST
Capitalization

☐ Have you used a capital letter at the beginning of each complete sentence, including sentences that are quoted?

☐ Have you used capital letters for proper nouns and pronouns?

☐ Have you avoided using capital letters for emphasis?

☐ Have you used a capital letter for the first, last, and main words in a title? (Main words exclude prepositions, coordinating conjunctions, and articles.)

preposition: A transitional word (such as *in, on, at, of, from*) that leads into a phrase
coordinating conjunction: A one-syllable linking word (*and, but, for, or, nor, so, yet*) that joins elements with equal or near-equal importance
article: The word *a, an,* or *the*

For a list of commonly confused words, see p. A-58.

D2 Check spelling.

Misspelled words are difficult to spot in your own writing. You usually see what you think you wrote. Spell checkers offer a handy alternative to the dictionary, but you need to know their limitations. A spell checker compares the words in your text with the words in its dictionary, and it highlights words that do not appear there, including most proper nouns. Spell checkers will not highlight words misspelled as different words, such as *except* for *accept, to* for *too,* or *own* for *won.*

Capitalization at a Glance

THE FIRST LETTER OF A SENTENCE, INCLUDING A QUOTED SENTENCE

She called out, "Come in! The water's warm."

PROPER NAMES AND ADJECTIVES MADE FROM THEM

Smithsonian Institution   a Freudian reading   Marie Curie

RANK OR TITLE BEFORE A PROPER NAME

Ms. Olson   Professor Santocolon   Dr. Frost

FAMILY RELATIONSHIP ONLY WHEN IT SUBSTITUTES FOR OR IS PART OF A PROPER NAME

Grandma Jones   Father Time

RELIGIONS, THEIR FOLLOWERS, AND DEITIES

Islam   Orthodox Jew   Buddha

PLACES, REGIONS, GEOGRAPHIC FEATURES, AND NATIONALITIES

Palo Alto   the Berkshire Mountains   Egyptians

DAYS OF THE WEEK, MONTHS, AND HOLIDAYS

Wednesday   July   Labor Day

HISTORICAL EVENTS, PERIODS, AND DOCUMENTS

the Boston Tea Party   the Middle Ages   the Constitution

SCHOOLS, COLLEGES, UNIVERSITIES, AND SPECIFIC COURSES

Temple University   Introduction to Clinical Psychology

FIRST, LAST, AND MAIN WORDS IN TITLES OF PAPERS, BOOKS, ARTICLES, WORKS OF ART, TELEVISION SHOWS, POEMS, AND PERFORMANCES

The Decline and Fall of the Roman Empire   "The Lottery"

EDITING CHECKLIST
Spelling

☐ Have you checked for the words you habitually misspell?

☐ Have you checked for commonly confused or misspelled words?

☐ Have you checked a dictionary for any words you are unsure about?

☐ Have you run your spell checker? Have you read your paper carefully for errors that it would miss such as a stray letter?

COMMONLY CONFUSED HOMONYMS

accept (v., receive willingly); **except** (prep., other than)

Mimi could *accept* all of Lefty's gifts *except* his ring.

affect (v., influence); **effect** (n., result)

If the new rules *affect* us, what will be their *effect*?

capital (adj., uppercase; n., seat of government); **capitol** (n., government building)

The *Capitol* building in our nation's *capital* is spelled with a *capital C.*

cite (v., refer to); **sight** (n., vision or tourist attraction); **site** (n., place)

Did you *cite* Aunt Peg as your authority on which *sites* feature the most interesting *sights*?

complement (v., complete; n., counterpart); **compliment** (v. or n., praise)

For Lee to say that Sheila's beauty *complements* her intelligence may or may not be a *compliment.*

desert (v., abandon; n., hot, dry region); **dessert** (n., end-of-meal sweet)

Don't *desert* us by leaving for the *desert* before *dessert.*

elicit (v., bring out); **illicit** (adj., illegal)

By going undercover, Sonny should *elicit* some offers of *illicit* drugs.

led (v., past tense of *lead*); **lead** (n., a metal)

Gil's heart was heavy as *lead* when he *led* the mourners to the grave.

principal (n. or adj., chief); **principle** (n., rule or standard)

The *principal* problem is convincing the media that the high school *principal* is a person of high *principles.*

stationary (adj., motionless); **stationery** (n., writing paper)

Hubert's *stationery* shop stood *stationary* until a flood swept it away.

their (pron., belonging to them); **there** (adv., in that place); **they're** (contraction of *they are*)

Sue said *they're* going over *there* to visit *their* aunt.

to (prep., toward); **too** (adv., also or excessively); **two** (n. or adj., numeral: one more than one)

Let's not take *two* cars *to* town — that's *too* many unless Hal comes *too.*

who's (contraction of *who is*); **whose** (pron., belonging to whom)

Who's going to tell me *whose* dog this is?

your (pron., belonging to you); **you're** (contraction of *you are*)

You're not getting *your* own way this time!

A Sample MLA Research Paper

For more on MLA paper format, see the Quick Format Guide beginning on p. A-1.

In her paper "Meet Me in the Middle: The Student, the State, and the School," Candace Rardon investigates the rising costs of a college education and how schools have responded to the problem. Besides incorporating many features of effective research papers, this paper also illustrates the conventions for citing and listing sources in MLA style.

No cover page is needed for an MLA paper. Because an outline was required by the instructor, it precedes the paper. Although this sample paper is presented for easy reading in a textbook, your paper should use the type style and size that MLA suggests: Times New Roman font, 12-point size. Set one-inch margins on all four sides, double-space all the lines, and turn off automatic hyphenation. Use your software's Help feature or visit the campus computer lab for help setting up this format for your file.

As you read Candace Rardon's paper, watch for the notes in its margins that alert you to common features of MLA papers. Use the following checklist to improve your own paper.

RESEARCH CHECKLIST
Citing Sources in MLA Style

☐ Have you placed your citation right after your quotation, paraphrase, summary, or other reference to the source?

☐ Have you identified the author of each source in your text or in parentheses?

☐ Have you used the first few words of the title for a work without an identified author?

☐ Have you noted a page number or other location when needed?

Listing Sources in MLA Style

☐ Have you begun each entry with the author's name?

☐ Have you followed the right pattern for each type of source?

☐ Have you accurately recorded names (author, title, publisher) and numbers (pages, volumes, dates)?

☐ Have you identified the medium of publication, reception, or delivery?

☐ Have you arranged your entries in alphabetical order?

☐ Have you checked your list against your text citations so every source appears in both places?

☐ Have you checked any entry from a citation management system as carefully as your own entries?

Writer's last name, followed by page number in small roman numerals, on upper right corner of all pages of outline

"Outline" centered, one inch from top

Main idea stated in thesis

Double-spacing throughout

Sentence outline providing a skeleton of the research paper

For more on outlines, see pp. 275–83.

Rardon i

Outline

Meet Me in the Middle:

The Student, the State, and the School

Thesis: By taking steps such as practicing cost containment, using technological advancements, and exploring new revenue streams, many schools have been able to keep tuition costs down.

I. Among the various factors to consider when choosing a college, cost is increasingly becoming the most important and, for many, a barrier.

A. Prices for undergraduate tuition at both public and private institutions have steadily increased over the past decades.

B. Students have increasingly taken on more debt in paying for college.

II. State governments have been forced to decrease their funding to public colleges and universities.

A. In the current economic situation, states have been forced to cut budgets and reduce their levels of funding.

B. In 2009 and 2010, thirty-nine states cut the amount budgeted to higher education.

III. With students accepting record debt and states forced to cut their budgets, public colleges and universities have a unique opportunity—even responsibility—to change.

A. Cost containment can decrease a school's budget and reliance on state funds.

B. Operational changes can result in savings through the use of online and technological resources.

C. Schools can explore alternative revenue streams such as grants, patents, and real estate opportunities.

Conclusion: By cutting past costs, thinking differently about present operations, and looking to new future revenues, schools are ensuring their own vitality and their students' success.

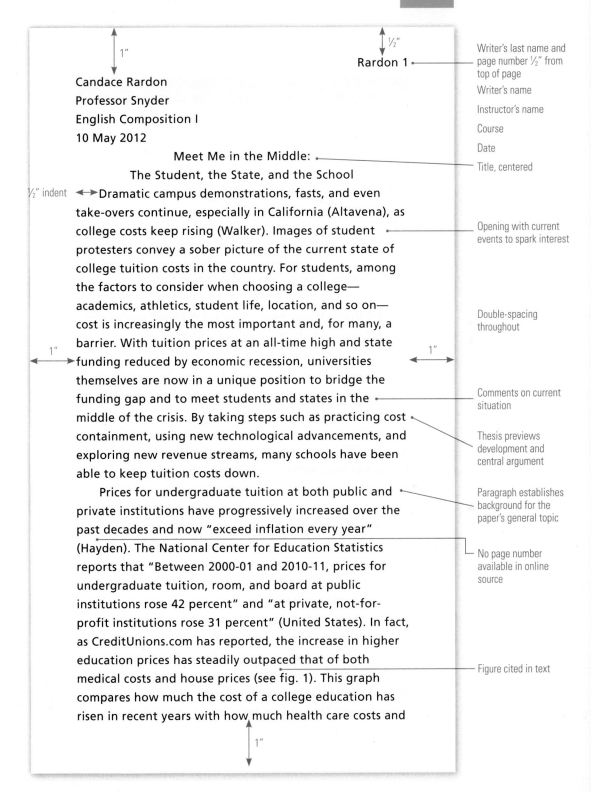

Rardon 1

Writer's last name and page number ½" from top of page

Candace Rardon
Professor Snyder
English Composition I
10 May 2012

Writer's name

Instructor's name

Course

Date

Meet Me in the Middle:
The Student, the State, and the School

Title, centered

½" indent ⟷ Dramatic campus demonstrations, fasts, and even take-overs continue, especially in California (Altavena), as college costs keep rising (Walker). Images of student protesters convey a sober picture of the current state of college tuition costs in the country. For students, among the factors to consider when choosing a college— academics, athletics, student life, location, and so on— cost is increasingly the most important and, for many, a barrier. With tuition prices at an all-time high and state funding reduced by economic recession, universities themselves are now in a unique position to bridge the funding gap and to meet students and states in the middle of the crisis. By taking steps such as practicing cost containment, using new technological advancements, and exploring new revenue streams, many schools have been able to keep tuition costs down.

Opening with current events to spark interest

Double-spacing throughout

Comments on current situation

Thesis previews development and central argument

Prices for undergraduate tuition at both public and private institutions have progressively increased over the past decades and now "exceed inflation every year" (Hayden). The National Center for Education Statistics reports that "Between 2000-01 and 2010-11, prices for undergraduate tuition, room, and board at public institutions rose 42 percent" and "at private, not-for-profit institutions rose 31 percent" (United States). In fact, as CreditUnions.com has reported, the increase in higher education prices has steadily outpaced that of both medical costs and house prices (see fig. 1). This graph compares how much the cost of a college education has risen in recent years with how much health care costs and

Paragraph establishes background for the paper's general topic

No page number available in online source

Figure cited in text

1" (margin indicators: top, left, right, bottom)

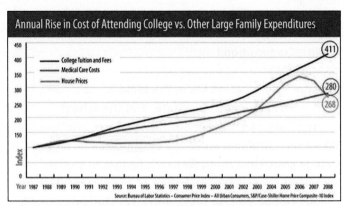

Fig. 1. Annual Rise in Cost of Attending College.
Source: Bureau of Labor Statistics, Consumer Price Index,
and All Urban Consumers, Standard & Poor/Case-Schiller
Home Price Composite-10 Index (Hoffman).

Figure labeled in caption; source information provided

Source presents and credits findings of another study

Key term is defined

house prices have gone up over the same period. While
the cost of all three has gone up, the expense of college
has increased the most.

As the graph shows, the prices of tuition, medical
care, and houses are plotted against both time and the
Consumer Price Index. Computed by the Department of
Labor's Bureau of Labor Statistics, the Consumer Price
Index is a calculation generally used to measure inflation
over a period of time, based on how the prices of
common goods and services change. From 1989 to 2008,
the price of higher education has consistently risen more
than the prices of medical care and houses, a burden that
often falls on the student.

Trends in student borrowing point to a crisis in the
amount of debt that students and families have to
shoulder to afford an education. *Trends in Student Aid
2012,* a College Board report, states that in 2010-11, only
43% of students who graduated with a bachelor's degree
from a public four-year institution did so without

Rardon 3

education debt (Baum and Payea). The rest graduated with debt averaging $23,800. Despite a recent 4% drop in borrowing, the first in two decades, these numbers demonstrate the rising financial burden placed on college students. Many continue "making decisions and trade-offs among schools, living arrangements, work, and finances" (Bozick 278). Economist Richard Vedder has summed up the situation: "What we have now is an unsustainable trend" (qtd. in Sandler 199).

Due to the economic recession, states have been forced to cut their budgets and reduce their funding to higher education. The Center on Budget and Policy Priorities reports that in 2009 and 2010, thirty-nine states decreased their budgets for higher education, leading to "reductions in faculty and staff in addition to tuition increases" (Johnson, Oliff, and Williams 6). Like California, the state of Florida was forced to raise tuition by 15% in 2009-10. The tuition increases that result from a lack of state funds have become a nationwide threat.

With students accepting record debt and states forced to cut their budgets, public colleges and universities have a unique opportunity—even responsibility—to change. Instead of raising tuition to make up for lost state funds, many schools have begun to cut costs. Through cost containment, schools can decrease their operating budgets and their reliance on state funds. In an article for *Time*, Sophia Yan outlines reductions on more than twenty campuses. For instance, Harvard University saved $900,000 by cutting hot breakfasts during the week in the dining halls. Western Washington University saved $485,000 by cutting its football team, and Whittier College saved $50,000 by cutting first-year orientation by a day. On the theory that "every little bit helps," schools are finding ways to save money.

Only one citation needed for material in sequence in a paragraph and clearly from the same source

Facts and statistics support main point

For an explanation of statistics as evidence, see pp. 41–42.

Page numbers provided for quotations

Original quote from another source

Paper continues to lay out background of argument

Transition from background to central argument

First way to avoid raising tuition is explained

Specific examples provide evidence for point

For more on integrating sources, see Ch. 20.

Rardon 4

Going beyond cutbacks in services, schools have also considered operational changes that will result in even more savings. The Delta Project on Postsecondary Education Costs, Productivity, and Accountability, a nonprofit group that analyzes college costs and spending trends, recommends ways to increase productivity:

> Make investments in course redesign and other curricula changes that will make for a more cost-effective curriculum. . . . This includes redesigning large undergraduate courses, creating cost-effective developmental education modules that can be delivered statewide; and redesigning the general education curriculum to enhance community college transfer. (4)

Other suggestions include making buildings more energy efficient and creating work opportunities for jobless students as interns or research assistants (4). Such changes can lead to substantial savings and help schools across the country.

Another alternative to raising tuition is for schools to embrace technological advances. As Kamenetz observes, "Whether hybrid classes, social networks, tutoring programs, games, or open content, technology provides speed skates for students and teachers, not crutches." Specific models have come from the National Center for Academic Transformation, a nonprofit organization that uses information technology to raise student performance and lower costs. Its six course redesign models vary in the amount of in-class instruction replaced by technology (Natl. Center, "Six Models" 1). When the University of Alabama adopted the emporium model for Intermediate Algebra and replaced lectures with an online learning resource center (3), the redesign increased student success, met individual needs, and saved 30% of costs (Natl. Center, "Program"). Of course, such course redesign cannot always be applied across the curriculum, but schools giving serious

Point from last paragraph used for transition to new point

Launch statement refers to organization as author

Direct quotation longer than four lines set off from text without quotation marks, followed by page number in parentheses

1"

Transition leads to second way to avoid raising tuition

Quotation and source clearly identified but pages are not numbered in source

Short title added to distinguish two sources by the same author

Basic models are explained before giving a specific example

Statistics support claims

Rardon 5

thought to current technology can transform the classroom, saving money and helping students.

Finally, schools can supplement income from student tuition by considering additional sources of revenue. *Business Week* writer Francesca Di Meglio reports that many schools already look to grants, patents, real estate, and popular graduate courses to "protect [their] bottom line from fiscal and demographic trends that are making the college business more challenging." As early as the 1950s, three Indiana University researchers patented Crest toothpaste, and its returns went on to fund an on-campus dental research institute. Similarly, in 2004 Emmanuel College in Boston allowed Merck, a large pharmaceuticals company, to build a research facility on an acre of land with a 75-year lease for $50 million. Di Meglio's examples show how schools can tap into these alternative income streams and reduce some of the pressure on tuition.

Rising tuition costs, growing student borrowing, and shrinking government funding have endangered widespread access to a college education. As President Obama himself said in the 2010 State of the Union Address, "in the United States of America, no one should go broke because they chose to go to college. . . . it's time for colleges and universities to get serious about cutting their own costs—because they, too, have a responsibility to help solve this problem." In an era of economic strain, schools can embrace this chance to think creatively about the way they operate. By cutting costs where they spent money in the past, thinking differently about how they operate in the present, and looking to new ways of bringing in revenue in the future, schools can ensure their own vitality and their students' success. When public colleges and universities take such steps to ensure that a college education is available to everyone, meeting students and states in the middle with innovative ideas, students can stop protesting and start welcoming in an era of increased college access.

Third way to avoid raising tuition is introduced

Launch statement names publication and author

Brackets identify words added to original text

Paraphrase of original source

Final sentence in paragraph connects examples from source with overall argument

Ellipses show where words are omitted

Conclusion emphasizes critical points in argument

Conclusion returns to events in opening

List of works cited on a separate page

List alphabetized by names of authors or by titles (when no author is named); names match source citations in text

First line of entry at left margin, additional lines indented ½"

All lines double spaced, within and between entries

Appropriate abbreviations used if no information given for publisher or date

No URLs for accessible Internet sources unless required by instructor

Works Cited

Altavena, Lily. "California State Students Protest by Fasting." *The Choice: Demystifying College Admissions and Aid. New York Times.* New York Times, 7 May 2012. Web. 8 May 2012.

Baum, Sandy, and Kathleen Payea. *Trends in Student Aid 2012.* Washington: College Board, 2012. *Trends in Higher Education Series.* Web. 20 Apr. 2012.

Bozick, Robert. "Making It through the First Year of College: The Role of Students' Economic Resources, Employment, and Living Arrangements." *Sociology of Education* 80.3 (2007): 216-84. *JSTOR.* Web. 23 Apr. 2012.

Delta Project on Postsecondary Education Costs, Productivity, and Accountability. "Postsecondary Education Spending Priorities for the American Recovery and Reinvestment Act of 2009." Washington: Delta Project, Feb. 2009. Web. 20 Apr. 2012.

Di Meglio, Francesca. "Colleges Explore Alternative Revenue Streams." *BusinessWeek.com.* Bloomberg, 7 Aug. 2008. Web. 2 May 2012.

Hayden, Tom. "Rising Cost of College? We Can't Afford to Be Quiet." *Chronicle of Higher Education* 28 Mar. 2010: n. pag. *Academic OneFile.* Web. 20 Apr. 2012.

Hoffman, Teri. "Graph of the Week: Annual Rise in Cost of Attending College vs. Other Large Family Expenditures." *CreditUnions.com.* Callahan & Associates, 27 July 2009. Web. 2 May 2012.

Johnson, Nicholas, Phil Oliff, and Erica Williams. "An Update on State Budget Cuts." *Center on Budget and Policy Priorities.* Washington: CBPP, 19 Apr. 2010. Web. 26 Apr. 2012.

Kamenetz, Anya. "The Virtual University." *American Prospect* 21.4 (2010): 22+. *LexisNexis Academic.* Web. 2 May 2012.

Rardon 7

National Center for Academic Transformation. "Program
in Course Redesign: The University of Alabama." *The
National Center for Academic Transformation.* NCAT,
2005. Web. 2 May 2012.

---. "Six Models for Course Redesign." *The National
Center for Academic Transformation.* NCAT, 2008.
Web. 2 May 2012.

Obama, Barack. "Remarks by the President in State of
the Union Address." United States Capitol,
Washington. 27 Jan. 2010. Address.

Sandler, Corey. *Cut College Costs Now! Surefire Ways to
Save Thousands of Dollars.* Avon: Adams Media,
2006. Print.

United States. Dept. of Education. National Center for
Education Statistics. "Fast Facts: Tuition Costs of
Colleges and Universities." 2012. *Digest of Education
Statistics,* 2011. Web. 26 Apr. 2012.

Walker, Brianne. "UC, CSU Tuition Increases: The Causes
and Consequences." *Neon Tommy: Annenberg
Digital News.* USC Annenberg, 13 Dec. 2011. Web. 20
Apr. 2012.

Yan, Sophia. "Colleges Find Creative Ways to Cut Back."
Time 21 Sept. 2009: 81. Print.

Three hyphens replace
repeating exact name
from previous entry

A Sample APA Research Paper

For more on APA format, see the Quick Format Guide, beginning on p. A-1.

In "Sex Offender Lists: A Never-Ending Punishment," Jenny Lidington explores the intention of the sex offender registry and its many functional problems.

Her scholarly approach is designed to help readers grasp the complexities of a difficult societal issue that often generates strong feelings. Notice how thoughtfully she tackles the topic: defining terms, making distinctions, reviewing history, tracing consequences, distinguishing differences, and establishing the basis for her questions. Her paper illustrates APA paper format and the APA conventions for citing and listing sources.

Although this sample paper is presented for easy reading in a textbook, your paper should use the type style and size that APA suggests: Times New Roman font, 12-point size. Set one-inch margins on all four sides, double-space all the lines, and turn off automatic hyphenation. Use your software's Help feature or visit the campus computer lab for help setting up this format for your file.

As you read Jenny Lidington's paper, watch for the notes in its margins that alert you to common features of APA papers. Use the following checklist to improve your own paper.

RESEARCH CHECKLIST
Citing Sources in APA Style

☐ Have you identified the author of each source in your text or in parentheses?

☐ Have you noted the date (or "n.d." for "no date") for each source?

☐ Have you added a page number or other location when needed?

Listing Sources in APA Style

☐ Have you started each entry with the author? Have you left spaces between the initials? Have you used "&" (not "and") to add the last coauthor's name?

☐ Have you included the date in each entry?

☐ Have you used capitals and italics correctly for different types of titles?

☐ Have you typed or pasted in the DOI or URL? Have you split a long URL before a punctuation mark?

☐ Have you arranged your entries in alphabetical order?

☐ Have you checked your final list of references against your text citations so every source appears in both places?

☐ Have you checked any entry from a citation management system as carefully as your own entries?

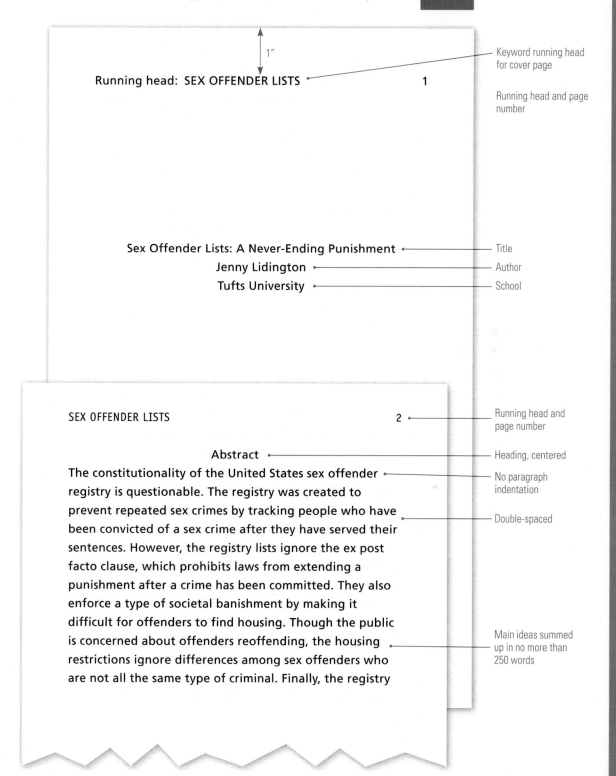

1"

Keyword running head
for cover page

Running head and page
number

Sex Offender Lists: A Never-Ending Punishment
Jenny Lidington
Tufts University

Title

Author

School

Running head and
page number

Abstract

The constitutionality of the United States sex offender registry is questionable. The registry was created to prevent repeated sex crimes by tracking people who have been convicted of a sex crime after they have served their sentences. However, the registry lists ignore the ex post facto clause, which prohibits laws from extending a punishment after a crime has been committed. They also enforce a type of societal banishment by making it difficult for offenders to find housing. Though the public is concerned about offenders reoffending, the housing restrictions ignore differences among sex offenders who are not all the same type of criminal. Finally, the registry

Heading, centered

No paragraph
indentation

Double-spaced

Main ideas summed
up in no more than
250 words

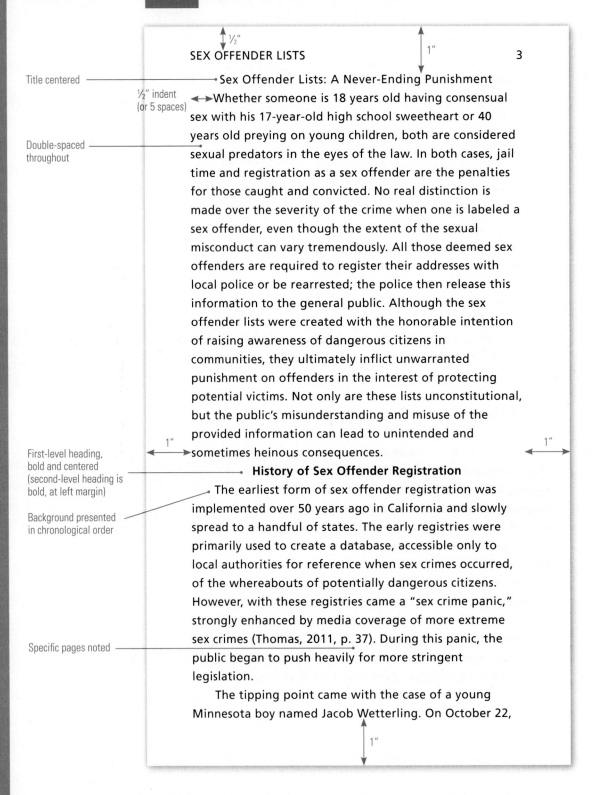

½"

1"

Title centered

½" indent
(or 5 spaces)

Double-spaced
throughout

Sex Offender Lists: A Never-Ending Punishment

Whether someone is 18 years old having consensual sex with his 17-year-old high school sweetheart or 40 years old preying on young children, both are considered sexual predators in the eyes of the law. In both cases, jail time and registration as a sex offender are the penalties for those caught and convicted. No real distinction is made over the severity of the crime when one is labeled a sex offender, even though the extent of the sexual misconduct can vary tremendously. All those deemed sex offenders are required to register their addresses with local police or be rearrested; the police then release this information to the general public. Although the sex offender lists were created with the honorable intention of raising awareness of dangerous citizens in communities, they ultimately inflict unwarranted punishment on offenders in the interest of protecting potential victims. Not only are these lists unconstitutional, but the public's misunderstanding and misuse of the provided information can lead to unintended and sometimes heinous consequences.

First-level heading,
bold and centered
(second-level heading is
bold, at left margin)

Background presented
in chronological order

1"   1"

History of Sex Offender Registration

The earliest form of sex offender registration was implemented over 50 years ago in California and slowly spread to a handful of states. The early registries were primarily used to create a database, accessible only to local authorities for reference when sex crimes occurred, of the whereabouts of potentially dangerous citizens. However, with these registries came a "sex crime panic," strongly enhanced by media coverage of more extreme sex crimes (Thomas, 2011, p. 37). During this panic, the public began to push heavily for more stringent legislation.

Specific pages noted

The tipping point came with the case of a young Minnesota boy named Jacob Wetterling. On October 22,

1"

1989, Jacob was bicycling with his brother and a friend when a masked gunman intercepted them and kidnapped Jacob. Though Jacob and his attacker were never found, it is believed that Jacob was sexually assaulted and murdered. In light of this tragedy, the Jacob Wetterling Act was established in 1994, requiring states to create and maintain sex offender registries. Notably, the information on the registries was accessible only to appropriate authorities. While this policy had monumental implications, it did not satisfy the public as communities wanted access to records of sex offenders' residences (Thomas, 2011, p. 42).

On July 29, 1994, another horrific and highly publicized incident occurred, which substantiated the argument for public notification and would significantly impact sex offenders' quality of life. Megan Kanka, a 7-year-old girl from New Jersey, was raped and murdered by her neighbor, Jesse Timmenequas. Jesse, unbeknownst to the community, was a repeat sex offender. This event spurred legislators to create the registry reforms the public desired by passing Megan's Law. This legislation amended the Jacob Wetterling Act by requiring community notification of nearby sex offenders' residences. Along with publishing the registration information, other methods of notification were encouraged. Louisiana, for example, required sex offenders "to post signs at their homes declaring their status as sex offenders" (Thomas, 2011, p. 45).

Constitutional Questions about Sex Offender Registries

Overlooking the rights of perpetrators of abominable crimes can be easy; however, the constitutionality of sex offender registration is entirely questionable. Whatever the crime, the rights of the convicted should be upheld. Because the registration process occurs after an offender is released from incarceration, these lists fail to comply

Figures (not words) used for pages, dates, ages, and numbers with more than one digit

SEX OFFENDER LISTS 5

with the ex post facto clause, which prohibits the creation of laws that add punishments after a crime has been committed. These lists have been taken to court on grounds of retrospection, though rulings have not favored the offenders (Pattis, 2011), and also on grounds of due process, as offenders have no opportunity to argue against community notification.

A third constitutional issue is whether the residential restrictions imposed by the lists constitute banishment, an illegal form of punishment under the constitution. In many states, sex offenders are not allowed within a few blocks of schools, daycare centers, or playgrounds. Particularly in communities with many facilities, acceptable livable areas for registered offenders may be limited or nonexistent. "I never realized how many schools and parks there were until I had to stay away from them," a registered sex offender conceded in Levenson and Cotter's 2005 survey (as cited in Thomas, 2011, p. 129). Essentially, these restrictions, intended to make given areas safer, create potentially dangerous sex-offender communities. This was the case in Broward County, Florida, where 95 registered sex offenders lived within a five-block tract (Thomas, 2011, p. 129). Those who cannot find housing or afford available housing are left homeless though commonly banished from homeless shelters and hostels, too (Thomas, 2011, p. 129).

Public Misconceptions

Those who argue that sex offender registries are constitutional often maintain that the lists are not punitive and provide the public with vital information that can prevent future sex crimes. Even those who admit that the lists may infringe upon offenders' rights argue that any minor violations are outweighed by the contribution to public safety. This argument might be the case if the critically flawed information in sex offender

---

Multiple authors joined by and *in text*

Additional source cited in source where it was mentioned

SEX OFFENDER LISTS   6

lists was not subject to public misinterpretation. One
shortcoming is a lack of specificity: A person who urinated
in public is on the same list as one who repeatedly raped
young children. In California, one of each 375 adults is
registered as a sex offender, a testament to this loose
definition of sex crimes (Leon, 2011, p. 119). Although
offenders are ranked on a scale of one to three (the
worst) in terms of likelihood of reoffending, people tend
to ignore these distinctions. As a police officer stated for
the *Seattle Times*, "People look at them in a bucket. They
say 'Any kind of sex offender is a sex offender, and always
will be a sex offender'" (Farley, 2011, para. 13).

Paragraph number
supplied for online
article without
numbered pages

Another flaw lies in the accuracy of the rankings.
Most crimes require a post-incarceration evaluation to
determine whether the criminal is still a threat to society,
but sex offenders have no follow-up. When they are
released from prison, their names go into a sex offender
registry, no matter how much time has passed since the
crime. The "threat level" classification represents the level
at the time of the crime, not the offender's current risk
level. Therapy sessions both during and after prison could
result in the offender no longer posing a threat to the
community. Studies show that within three years of being
released from prison, only 5.3 percent of sex offenders are
rearrested for another sex crime (Smith, 2003; U.S.
Department of Justice, 2003, p. 1), which further suggests
that the sex offender lists are extremely questionable.

In addition, due to the potentially inaccurate
classifications, offenders may be assigned inappropriate
punishments for their given crime. For example, many sex
offenders whose crimes were not against children (or who
may be children themselves) are given the same living
restrictions as child rapists. The man imprisoned for
having sex with his girlfriend days before she was legally
old enough to give consent does not pose enough risk to

restrict him from living near playgrounds and schools. Although some states such as New Jersey and Washington are working to assess risks more accurately, they are the exceptions (Leon, 2011, pp. 141–142).

Consequences of a Lack of Privacy

These major flaws in the sex offender registry system can have counterproductive and tragic effects. When sex offenders must register, their personal information is not given on a need-to-know basis; it is blazoned across the community where they live. Their names, photographs, license plate numbers, and home and work addresses are posted online for the world to view. They may struggle to find housing, to avoid public disapproval or embarrassing exposure of their pasts, and to pass background checks necessary to find work. Because these offenders are often shunned by the adult world, they may seek companionship with children, which potentially tempts some to offend again. With their faces plastered on local bulletin boards or e-mail alerts, offenders can grow increasingly aggravated, which also may lead them to new crimes (Chen, 2009).

This lack of privacy also makes offenders vulnerable to public vigilantes who can inflict harsh punishments. According to a Los Angeles County study by Gallo et al.,

> A number of judges felt that although the avowed purpose of the registration statute is to facilitate the process of law enforcement by providing a list of suspects . . . the information obtained under section 290 is subject to some abuse—either through police harassment or by indiscriminate revelation to unauthorized persons. (as cited in Leon, 2011, pp. 68–69)

Tragically, public harassment can lead to suicides and murders of registered sex offenders, as was the case for 24-year-old William Elliot. At age 20, Elliot was sentenced

Long quotation (40 words or longer) indented ½" without quotation marks

to four months in jail for having sex with his girlfriend who was two weeks away from turning 16 (the legal age of consent in Maine). Four years later, a young man named Stephen Marshall found Elliot's residential information on an online sex-offender database. Marshall used this information to stalk Elliot and shoot him to death in his own home (Ahuja, 2006). This incident is a horrific example of the unintended effects of public misinterpretation of sex offender lists, but it also calls into question whether these lists can be considered nonpunitive.

Violations of Rights of Citizens

Perceived as monsters, fiends, and psychopaths, sex offenders are not easily seen as victims; however, as American citizens, they have the same right to life, liberty, and the pursuit of happiness as anyone else. Although the sex registry laws were created with the best of intentions, they violate these constitutional rights and can have gruesome unintended consequences. Most importantly, they are not especially effective.

Many people believe that the typical sex crime is child rape when in reality most sex crimes are much more benign. The dramatic cases encourage regulation that far exceeds what is necessary for most offenders, placing those who have urinated publicly in the same category as pedophiles (Bonnar-Kidd, 2010, p. 416). However, the sex-crime taboos make it difficult for the public to override emotionally charged ideas of the misconduct that the lists represent and then to see the critical flaws in the current registry system. If these lists are to continue to exist, they should no longer serve as dehumanizing blacklists for the public to use at its own discretion.

Page numbering continues

Heading, centered

First line of entry at left margin, additional lines indented ½"

List alphabetized by names of authors

All author names begin with last name

No period after URL

First word in title and after colon and all proper nouns capitalized

References

Ahuja, G. (2006, April 18). Sex offender registries: Putting lives at risk? ABC News. Retrieved from http://abcnews .go.com

Bonnar-Kidd, K. K. (2010). Sexual offender laws and prevention of sexual violence or recidivism. *American Journal of Public Health*, 100, 412-419. doi: 10.2105 /AJPH.2008.153254

Chen, S. (2009, February 19). After prison, few places for sex offenders to live. *The Wall Street Journal*. Retrieved from http://wsj.com

Farley, J. (2011, January 1). Sex-offender rankings: Is there room for gray areas? *The Seattle Times*. Retrieved from http://seattletimes.com

Leon, C. S. (2011). *Sex fiends, perverts, and pedophiles: Understanding sex crime policy in America*. New York, NY: New York University Press.

Pattis, N. (2011, February 7). Time to revisit ex post facto clause for sex offenders [Web log post]. Retrieved from http://www.pattisblog.com/index.php?article =Time_To_Revisit_Ex_Post_Facto_Clause_For_Sex _Offenders_2983

Smith, S. (2003, November 16). Five percent of sex offenders rearrested for another sex crime. [Press release]. Retrieved from U.S. Department of Justice, Office of Justice Programs, Bureau of Justice Statistics website: http://bjs.ojp.usdoj.gov/content /pub/press/rsorp94pr.cfm

Thomas, T. (2011). *The registration and monitoring of sex offenders: A comparative study*. New York, NY: Routledge.

U.S. Department of Justice, Office of Justice Programs, Bureau of Justice Statistics. (2003). *Recidivism of sex offenders released from prison in 1994* (NCJ 198281). Retrieved from http://bjs.ojp.usdoj.gov/content/pub /pdf/rsorp94.pdf

Acknowledgments *(continued from p. vi)*

Adams, Sarah. "Be Cool to the Pizza Dude." Copyright © 2005 by Sarah Adams. From the book *This I Believe: The Personal Philosophies of Remarkable Men and Women* edited by Jay Allison and Dan Gediman. Copyright © 2006 by This I Believe, Inc. Reprinted by arrangement with Henry Holt and Company, LLC.

Baker, Russell. "The Art of Eating Spaghetti." Reprinted by permission of Don Congdon Associates, Inc. © 1982 by Russell Baker.

Brooks, David. "The Opportunity Gap." From *The New York Times*, July 9, 2012 © 2012 *The New York Times*. All rights reserved. Used by permission and protected by the Copyright Laws of the United States. The printing, copying, redistribution, or retransmission of this Content without express written permission is prohibited.

Conklin, Jed. "Boxing Beauties." Courtesy of Jed Conklin.

Copeland, Libby. "Is Facebook Making Us Sad?" From *Slate*. © 2011, The Slate Group. All rights reserved. Used by permission and protected by the Copyright Laws of the United States. The printing, copying, redistribution, or retransmission of the Material without express written permission is prohibited.

Foster, Brent. "Highway Angel." Courtesy of Brent Foster/ *www.brentfostercinema.com.*

GOOD/Column Five. "Paternity Leave around the World" infographic. Originally appeared on *www.good.is* on June 7, 2012. Reprinted with permission from GOOD.

Halpern, Jake. Excerpt from *Fame Junkies: The Hidden Truths Behind America's Favorite Addiction* by Jake Halpern. Copyright © 2007 by Jake Halpern. Reprinted by permission of Houghton Mifflin Harcourt Publishing Company. All rights reserved.

Harjo, Suzan Shown. "Last Rites for Indian Dead." First published in the *Los Angeles Times*, September 16, 1989. Copyright © 1989 by Suzan Shown Harjo. Reprinted with the permission of the author.

Jensen, Robert. "The High Cost of Manliness." Reprinted by permission of the author.

Jones, Gerard. "Violent Media Is Good For Kids." © 2000, Foundation for National Progress. Reprint courtesy of *Mother Jones* magazine.

King, Stephen. "Why We Crave Horror Movies." Reprinted With Permission. © Stephen King. All rights reserved. Originally appeared in *Playboy*, 1982.

Klosterman, Chuck. "My Zombie, Myself." From *The New York Times*, December 5, 2010. © 2010, *The New York Times*. All rights reserved. Used by permission and protected by the Copyright Laws of the United States. The printing, copying, redistribution, or retransmission of this Content without express written permission is prohibited.

Liu, Eric. "The Chinatown Idea," from *The Accidental Asian: Notes of a Native Speaker* by Eric Liu. Copyright © 1998 by Eric Liu. Used by permission of Random House, Inc. Any third party use of this material, outside of this publication, is prohibited. Interested parties must apply directly to Random House, Inc. for permission.

McCain, John. Excerpt from "The Virtues of the Quiet Hero." Copyright © 2005 by John McCain. From the book *This I Believe: The Personal Philosophies of Remarkable Men and Women*, edited by Jay Allison and Dan Gediman. Copyright © 2006 by This I Believe, Inc. Reprinted by arrangement with Henry Holt and Company, LLC.

Off Book. "Generative Art–Computers, Data, and Humanity." Courtesy of Kornhaber Brown and PBS Digital Studios.

Rockwell, Llewellyn H. "In Defense of Consumerism." Reprinted by permission of the author.

Rodriguez, Richard. "Public and Private Language." *Hunger of Memory* by Richard Rodriguez. Copyright © 1982 by Richard Rodriguez. Reprinted by permission of Georges Borchardt, Inc., on behalf of the author.

Rothkopf, David. "A Proposal to Draft America's Elderly." Reprinted by permission of the author.

Saletan, William. Excerpt from "Please Do Not Feed the Humans" from *Slate*. © September 2, 2006, The Slate Group. All rights reserved. Used by permission and protected by the Copyright Laws of the United States.

Schor, Juliet. "The Creation of Discontent." Copyright © 1992 by Juliet B. Schor. Reprinted by permission of Basic Books, a member of the Perseus Books Group.

Shermer, Michael. "The Science of Righteousness." Reproduced with permission. Copyright © 2012, *Scientific American*, a division of Nature America, Inc. All rights reserved.

Shoup, Brad. "'Harlem Shake' vs. History: Is the YouTube Novelty Hits Era That Novel?" Reprinted by permission of Atlantic Media Company.

Stone, Elizabeth. "Grief in the Age of Facebook." Reprinted by permission of the author.

StrategyOne. "Once a Mother, Always a Mother" infographic. Courtesy of Edelman Berland.

Tan, Amy. "Mother Tongue." Copyright © 1990 by Amy Tan. First appeared in *The Threepenny Review*. Reprinted by permission of the author and the Sandra Dijkstra Literary Agency.

Tannen, Deborah. "Who Does the Talking Here?" *The Washington Post*, July 15, 2007. Copyright by Deborah Tannen. Adapted from *You Just Don't Understand: Women and Men in Conversation*, HarperCollins. Reprinted with Permission.

Tobias, Scott. Review of *The Hunger Games*. Reprinted with permission of THE AV CLUB. Copyright © 2013 by ONION, INC. www.avclub.com.

Turkle, Sherry. "How Computers Change the Way We Think." Reprinted by permission of the author.

White, E. B. Excerpt from "Once More to the Lake" from *One Man's Meat*, text copyright © 1941, 1944 by E. B. White. Copyright renewed. Reprinted by permission of Tilbury House, Publishers, Gardiner, Maine, and International Creative Management. All rights reserved.

Zeilinger, Julie. "Guys Suffer from Gender Roles Too." From *A Little F'd Up: Why Feminism Is Not a Dirty Word* by Julie Zeilinger. Reproduced with permission of Publishers Group West in a book/e-book via Copyright Clearance Center.

Art Credits (in order of appearance):

Pages 2–3: Fountain and bathers. David L. Ryan/*The Boston Globe* via Getty Images.

Page 14: *works & conversation* photo: R. Whittaker.

Page 18: Hansel & Gretel. Private Collection/©Look and Learn/Bridgeman Art Library.

Page 32: Michael Shermer. Photo by David Patton.

Page 34: Heat maps of Web pages from eye-tracking studies. Copyright Nielsen Norman Group. All rights reserved.

Page 42: Candy bar. iStockphoto.

Page 53: David Rothkopf. Photo by Christopher Leaman.

Pages 56–57: Rowboats tied to dock. David L. Ryan/*The Boston Globe* via Getty Images.

Page 60: Photo collage of recalled experiences. Clockwise from top left: Michael Schwarz/The Image Works; Mario Tama/Getty Images; Lawrence Migdale/Science Source; D. Miller/Classicstock/Aurora Photos.

Page 62: Russell Baker. Yvonne Hemsey/Getty Images.

Page 63: Lady Macbeth. Tristram Kenton/Lebrecht/The Image Works.

Page 71: Soccer goalie. Robert Llewellyn/Aurora Photos.

Page 77: Group of women sharing dinner. Veer/Corbis Photography.

Page 78: Hikers in silhouette. © Andrew Dillon Bustin.

Page 78: Times Square crowd. Photo by Bojune Kwon, from The Neurosis in the City.

Page 79: Concert crowd and airport. © Andrew Dillon Bustin.

Page 80: Baseball player making catch. Jared Wickenham/Getty Images.

Page 82: Eric Liu. Photo by Alan Alabastro.

Page 84: Market in New York City's Chinatown. Dorling Kindersley/Getty Images.

Page 88: The *Titanic* 1912. © The Mariners' Museum/Corbis.

Page 89: Emergency room. David Joel/Getty Images.

Page 91: Elvis impersonators. Chris Jackson/Getty Images.

Page 97: View from bicycle. Robert van Waarden/Getty Images.

Page 98: Server at party. Doug Mills/*The New York Times*/Redux Pictures.

Page 98: Climbers on Mt. Rushmore. Kevin Steele/Aurora Photos.

Page 99: Couple at Woodstock, 1969. © Burk Uzzle, Laurence Miller Gallery.

Page 99: Couple at Woodstock, 2009. *N.Y. Daily News.*

Page 101: David Brooks. Brendan Smialowski/Getty Images.

Page 105: Karate. helenved/Shutterstock.com.

Page 105: Kung fu. © IMAGEMORE Co., Ltd./Alamy.

Page 107: Hurricane Katrina aftermath. Mario Tama/Getty Images. Caption: NG Staff/*National Geographic* Stock.

Pages 117–18: Families with a week's worth of food. © Peter Menzel/menzelphoto.com.

Page 119: Protestors. © Alex Milan Tracy/Demotix/Corbis.

Page 121: Suzan Shown Harjo. AP Photo/Manuel Balce Ceneta.

Page 122: Native Americans returning ancestral remains. AP Photo/*The Albuquerque Journal*, Eddie Moore.

Page 127: Dirty Water campaign. Casanova-Pendrill.

Page 128: Joan of Arc. Imagno/Getty Images.

Page 146: Boy in hospital. Suzanne Kreiter/*The Boston Globe* via Getty Images.

Page 146: Family reading. Nicole Bengiveno/*The New York Times*/Redux Pictures.

Page 147: Cell phone tower disguised as tree. © Robert Voit.

Page 148: Judging giant pumpkins. Justin Sullivan/Getty Images.

Page 150: Scott Tobias. Courtesy of Scott Tobias.

Page 151: Map of Panem. *The Panem Companion*, Smart Pop Books, 2012. © V. Arrow.

Page 155: Still from *Consumer Reports* pancakes video. "Best Buttermilk Pancakes" Copyright 2012 Consumers Union of U.S., Inc. Yonkers, NY 10703-1057, a nonprofit organization. Reprinted with permission from ConsumerReports.org for educational purposes only. www.ConsumerReports.org.

Page 156: George Gershwin. Hulton Archive/Getty Images.

Page 157: Still from *The Cabinet of Dr. Caligari*. Photofest.

Page 164: Photo of church at Auvers-sur-Oise. Pierre-Franck Colombier/Getty Images.

Page 164: *The Church at Auvers-sur-Oise* by Vincent van Gogh. Buyenlarge/Getty Images.

Page 165: Sony office, 1999. © TWPhoto/Corbis.

Page 165: Google Campus, 2012. Bloomberg via Getty Images.

Page 166: Photo collage of source usage. Clockwise from top left: Scott Bauer/USDA; © Mika/Corbis; © Journal-Courier/Steve Warmowski/The Image Works; Jeff Greenberg/The Image Works.

Page 168: Jake Halpern. Courtesy of Jake Halpern.

ABOUT THE PHOTOGRAPHS THAT OPEN PARTS 1–4

A Series of Aerial Photographs by David L. Ryan

A long-time staff photographer at the *Boston Globe*, David L. Ryan is well known for his distinctive aerial photography. His witty and moving images often show familiar scenes from fresh perspectives and reveal beautiful patterns hidden among commonplace, everyday realities. Like a writer, he keeps his audience close in his thoughts as he works, with the goal of sharing his curiosity, knowledge, and enthusiasm with those who see his images. As he puts it, "I've been in Boston all my life. I've gone around here by boat, helicopter, plane, train, bicycle, and walking. I want to make people say, '*How did you get that*?'" In another parallel with writing, he finds an open-minded, "learning by doing" approach to be beneficial: "I'm still experimenting with it," he says of his work. "Everything is an experiment."

Part 1: Fountain and bathers (pages 2–3)

It's obvious that a photographer must choose a point of view. He or she must literally choose a place to stand and an angle from which to view a scene. So must a writer.

In this image, what effects are created by the photographer's chosen point of view? What effect does his elevated perspective have on how the scene appears? What is gained and lost by photographing from this distance? What observations do you think the photographer is making about what he is seeing?

Part 2: Rowboats tied to dock (pages 56–57)

If you were to take something you have written and rewrite it from an entirely different point of view, the two versions would likely have different meanings and might accomplish different purposes. You convey meaning and purpose, in part, through your choice of perspective. Similarly, for a photographer, a change in perspective can create a feeling of strangeness, make a point, or offer a commentary. From the air things might look like something else for a second.

In this image, what point or points do you think the photographer is making? Is his focus the season, sport, recreation, equipment, place, person, state of mind, or some other subject? How does his point of view help to convey that meaning?

Part 3: Trains (pages 244–45)

Before a photographer takes a picture, he or she has to decide how much of the scene to include. Will the image be a close-up of a face or an aerial view? Does the image give the viewer specific information about a specific individual or show more general patterns? Writers, too, must make decisions about how much of a topic or a discussion to include and how to define the boundaries of a topic.

What does this photograph include? What does it leave out? What can you tell about the people — either as individuals or as groups — shown in this photo? What does the image communicate that might be less apparent from ordinary photographs taken of people at ground level? How does the image find interest and import in the routine?

Part 4: Flooded baseball fields (pages 318–19)

Photographers and writers are both alert to rhythms and correspondences as well as to patterns and meanings below the surface. Writers can express rhythm by selecting

their words, by controlling the length of sentences and paragraphs, and by creating a structure that helps the reader follow an unfolding essay. Ryan makes his work compelling by conveying a sense of rhythm through geometry.

What is the mood of this photograph? What does this image of flooded fields say to you, the viewer? How does it balance ordinary and extraordinary elements against each other?

INDEX

Academic exchange, 180, 182–83, 182 (fig.)

Academic paper, format for, A-1–7

Academic problems, critical thinking processes applied to, 39–40

accept/except, A-58

Ad hominem argument, 144

Adjectives
editing, A-48–49
irregular, A-48

Advanced searches for Internet resources, 354–56, 355 (fig.)

Adverbs
editing, A-48–49
irregular, A-48

Advertisements, 207, 208 *See also* Public service announcements

affect/effect, A-58

Allness, 143

Alternating pattern of organization, 113

Analysis
in critical reading, 26, 26 (fig.)
in critical thinking processes, 37–38, 40, 52–54
of readers' points of view, 137
of writing strategies, 29

Annotated bibliography, 349–50

Annotation
of critical reading, 21–23
writing, 350

Antecedent, A-46–48

APA style, 334–44, A-36–38
academic paper format, 389, A-4–6
annotated bibliography entries, 349–50
for books, 342, A-36
citing sources in text, A-31, A-36–38
for headings, A-16
for journals, A-37
for library database articles, A-37–38
listing sources in References, A-36–38
for magazines, 337, A-37
for online e-Pages, A-37
sample headings in, A-16

sample list formats, A-15–16

sample research paper in, A-68–76

for scholarly journal citations, 339

for Web pages, 343, A-38

for work or section in a book, A-36–37

Apostrophes, A-54–55

Appeals
in critical thinking, 44–45
emotional appeal *(pathos),* 44–45
ethical appeal *(ethos),* 45
logical appeal *(logos),* 44
making columns of, 139–40
in taking a stand, 138–39

Application letter, format for, A-17–19

Applying, in cognitive activity, 26

Appositives, A-53

Archives, research, 331–32
bookmarks in, saving, 331
computer files in, saving, 331
favorites in, saving, 331
paper copies in, filing, 332
search results in, saving, 332

Argument, fallacies in, 143–44

Articles, A-56

"Art of Eating Spaghetti, The" (Baker), 62–65

as, A-52

Atlases, 367

Attitudes in images, analyzing, 213–14

Audience
characteristics and expectations of, 13
college, targeting, 15
in comparing and contrasting, 112
considering, 134–35
in evaluating and reviewing, 158
evaluating intended, 371 (fig.), 372–73
evidence in critical thinking to appeal to, 44–45
for image, 202
in observing a scene, 93
organizing material to persuade, 138
in recalling an experience, 73, 74

Audience (continued)
  for research project, 326
  revising for, 302–3
  in supporting a position with sources, 176
  testing and selecting evidence to persuade,
    136–37
  topic for, 262–63, 262 (fig.)
  writing for, 12–15, 14 (fig.)
Audio applications for online writing, 230
Austin, James H., 291
Authors
  credentials of, 372
  evaluating, 372
  reputation of, 372
  unidentified, 372

Babbitt, Bruce, 181, 184–85, 186, 190
Background
  for critical reading, gaining, 19–20
  in image, 202, 205
Backing up files, 241
Baker, Russell, 62–65, 70, 293
Bandwagon argument, 144
Bar graphs, 139, A-8, A-11, A-12 (fig.)
Bawer, Bruce, 264
be, forms of, A-44
Begging the question, 144
"Best Buttermilk Pancakes" (*Consumer Reports*), 155
Beston, Henry, 92
"Between Our Folding Lips" (Brown), 163
Beyond Queer (Bawer), 264
Bias
  defined, 373
  of sources, 373
  of Web sites, 368, 371 (fig.)
Bibliographies, 367
Biographical sources, 367
Blogs
  class, 230
  Internet resources found on, 356
Bloom, Benjamin S., 25–27, 26 (fig.)
Boldface type, 273, A-13–16, A-18
Book citations
  APA style for, 342, A-36
  MLA style for, 342, A-34
  recording source information, in notes,
    340–41

Bookmarks in research archives, saving, 331
Book publication details, recording in notes, 344
Boolean searches, 364, 364 (fig.)
Brainstorming
  for evaluating and reviewing, 157
  for generating ideas, 70, 250–51
  for observing a scene, 90
  for recalling an experience, 70
  for research project, 326
  for search terms in library, 360
Brooks, David, 101–3
Brown, T. E., 163
Building from ideas, 249–50
Bullets, 273, A-14, A-16
Burke, Kenneth, 257–58
Busy space in images, 206

Cabinet of Dr. Caligari, The, 157–58
Calhoun, Ada, 288
capital/capitol, A-58
Capital letters, A-56, A-57
Capturing source material, 379–84
  paraphrasing and quoting, 379–81
  plagiarism and, avoiding, 383–84
  summarizing concisely, 381–83
Catalog, electronic, 356, 359, 360, 361 (fig.)
Cause and effect
  in logical patterns, 50 (fig.), 51
  responding to an image, 138
"Celebrity Culture" (research cluster), 173–74
Census.gov, 367
Chackowicz, Howie, 68
"Charlie Living with Autism" (Kintner), 222–24
Charts
  for function decisions, 208–9
  in MLA and APA style, A-8, A-10–12
  pie, 209, A-8, A-11, A-12 (fig.)
Checklists. *See also* Editing
  for audience, 13–14, 15, 303
  for citation, A-33
  for citing and listing sources in APA style,
    A-68
  for citing and listing sources in MLA style,
    A-59
  for college audience, 15
  for comments, 239–40
  for comparing and contrasting, 109, 115, 116

for conclusions, 292–93
for critical reading, 28–29
for development, 188–89
for document design, A-14
for drafting strategies, 290, 292–93
for editing, 315, A-39–40
for ethical research, 378–79
for evaluating and reviewing, 158, 161–62,
    A-27–28
for evidence, 43, A-24, A-27–28
for files, 241
for generating ideas, 28–29, 70, 261
for grammar problems, 315, A-39
for library resources, 357
for logical reasoning, 52
for mechanics problems, 315, A-40
for micro revision, 311
for note taking, 348
for observing a scene, 90, 95–96
for openings, 290
for paraphrasing, A-30
for periodical articles from database,
    364–65
for plagiarism, 384
for project management, 367–68
for proofreading, 316
for punctuation, 315, A-39
for purpose, 302, A-21
for quotations, A-29, A-56
for reasoning, 52
for recalling experience, 70, 75, 76
for research question, 325, 328, 332
for resources, A-25
for revision, 302, 303
for search engine results, 353–54
for sentence problems, 315, A-39
for source evaluation, 369–70
for structure and support, 304
for summary, A-30
for supporting a position with sources, 178,
    188–89, 195
for taking a stand, 133, 141, 143
for thesis, 302
for visual analysis, 204, 210–11, 215–16, 220,
    221
for works cited, A-33
for writers, 6–7

for writing problems, A-39–40
for writing strategies, 29
"Chinatown Idea, The" (Liu), 82–85
Chronological sequence, 73, 273
Circular reasoning, 144
CIS Index, 366
cite/sight, A-58
Claims
    appeals and, 139–40
    considering audience, 134–35
    of evaluation, 134, 135
    evidence to support, 135–36
    of policy, 134, 135
    of substantiation, 133, 135
Clarity, revising for, 310
Clauses, commas to set off, A-53
Close reading of images, 201–4
Clustering, 274, 275 (fig.)
Cognitive activity, levels of, 25–27, 26 (fig.)
College assignments, critical thinking for, 40
Collins, Suzanne, 150, 152
Commas, editing, A-53–54
Comma splices, editing, A-41–42
Comments, inserting, 239
Comparing and contrasting, 99–118
    assignment in, 108
    challenge in, 108
    comparison-and-contrast table in, 110–11
    in evaluating and reviewing, 157–58
    examples of, 101–7
    generating ideas for, 109–11
    importance of, 100
    peer response in, 114
    planning, drafting, and developing in, 111–14
    responding to an image, 118–19
    revising and editing in, 114–16
    writing assignments in, 116–18
Comparison-and-contrast table, 110–11
complement/compliment, A-58
Comprehending, in cognitive activity, 26, 26
    (fig.)
Computer files in research archives, saving,
    331
Conciseness, revising for, 309–10
Conclusions
    state or restate thesis in, 293
    writing, 292–95

Congressional Record Index, 367
Conjunctive adverbs
　commas to set off, A-53
　defined, A-53
Consumer Reports, 155
Coordinating conjunctions
　commas with, A-53
　defined, A-42, A-56
Correlative conjunctions, defined, A-50
Course management system (CMS), 227, 229,
　　231, 239, 240
Course resources, 230
Cowley, Malcolm, 293
Credentials of author, 372
Criteria
　defined, 149
　in evaluation and reviewing, 149, 157, 159
Critical reading, 17–35
　analysis, 20–25, 29–33
　generating ideas from, 27–29
　getting started in, 18–19
　on literal and analytical levels, 25–27, 26 (fig.)
　of multimodal texts, 33–35
　of online texts, 33–35
　preparing for, 19–20
　processes, 17–23
　responding to, 20–25, 29–33
　writing activities and, 35–36
Critical thinking, 37–55
　for college assignments, 40
　evidence in, 40–45
　faulty, avoiding, 52
　presenting, 47–51
　processes, 37–40
　rhetorical analysis and, 45–47
　writing activities in, 54–55
Cues and connections, 295–99. *See also* Transi-
　tions

-d, A-42–43
Dangling modifiers, editing, A-49
Databases. *See also* Library database
　comparing, 365
　searches on, *vs.* Google searches, 366
Dates, recording in notes, 344

Deductive reasoning in critical thinking, 48,
　　48 (fig.)
Denotative characteristics, 204
desert/dessert, A-58
Details
　drawn from sources, 334
　in observing a scene, 92, 93 (fig.), 94
　in recalling an experience, 72–73
　in supporting a position with sources, 180
　in taking a stand, 137–40
　in visual analysis, 220
Developing
　in comparing and contrasting, 111–14
　in evaluating and reviewing, 159–60
　in observing a scene, 92–93
　in recalling an experience, 72–73
　in supporting a position with sources,
　　178–89
　in taking a stand, 137–40
　in visual analysis, 220–21
　in writing processes, 9–10, 9 (fig.)
Dewey Decimal system, 360
Diagrams, A-8, A-10, A-11 (fig.). *See also*
　　Figures
Dictionaries, 366
Digital living in responding to an image, 573
"Dirty Water Campaign" (UNICEF), 127
Discovery
　in generating ideas, 7–8, 8 (fig.)
　of material, 8
　what to write about, 7–8
　of working thesis, 264–66, 265 (fig.)
Distant Mirror: The Calamitous Fourteenth Century,
　　A (Tuchman), 379–84
Document design and template, A-13–17
Documenting sources. *See also* Listing sources
　APA style for, A-36–38
　diagrams, graphs, charts, tables, and other
　　figures, A-9–12
　MLA style for, A-32–36
"Does Education Improve Social Ills in Native
　　American Communities?" (Martin), 349
Dominant impression. *See* Main impression
Donovan, Priscilla, 112
"Don't Mess with Mother" (Quindlen), 293

Doodling
    for generating ideas, 70, 252–54, 253 (fig.)
    for recalling an experience, 70
Drafting. *See also* Revising
    chronology in, 73
    in comparing and contrasting, 111–14
    of conclusions, 292–95
    of cues and connections, 295–99
    in evaluating and reviewing, 159–60
    in observing a scene, 92–93
    of openings, 290–92
    paragraphing and, 285–86
    in recalling an experience, 72–73
    starting or restarting, 285
    strategies for, 284–99
    in supporting a position with sources, 178–89
    in taking a stand, 137–40, 142
    of topic sentences, 286–89
    in visual analysis, 220–21
    in writing processes, 9, 9 (fig.), 10

-ed, A–42–43
Editing, A–39–A–58
    in comparing and contrasting, 114–16
    in evaluating and reviewing, 160–62
    for grammar problems, A–40–49
    for mechanics problems, A-56-58
    in observing a scene, 94–96
    for punctuation problems, A-53–56
    in recalling an experience, 75–76
    for sentence problems, A-49–52
    strategies for, 314–15, 314 (fig.)
    in supporting a position with sources, 189–95
    in taking a stand, 140–43
    in visual analysis, 221
    in writing processes, 10 (fig.), 11
effect/affect, A-58
Either/or reasoning, 144
E-journals, 259
Electronic catalogs, 356, 359–61, 361 (fig.)
Electronic publications
    details of, recording in notes, 344
    finding, 356
Electronic writing space, 72
elicit/illicit, A-58

Ellipses in quotations, 181, 184, A-55
E-mail to instructor, sample, 233
Emotional appeal *(pathos)*
    in critical thinking, 44–45
    in taking a stand, 138–40
Emphasis
    of ideas, 273
    revising for, 308–9
Encyclopedias, 366
Ercoline, Nick and Bobbi, 99
Erion, Elizabeth, 153–55
-es, verb tense and, A-44–45
Essays
    citations, MLA style for, A-34
    concluding, in literary analysis, 221
    introducing, in literary analysis, 221
Ethical appeal *(ethos)*
    in critical thinking, 45
    in taking a stand, 138–40
Ethical use of sources, 376–79. *See also* Plagiarism
Ethos. See Ethical appeal *(ethos)*
Evaluating and reviewing, 148–65
    challenge in, 156–57
    in cognitive activity, 26 (fig.), 27
    examples of, 150–55
    generating ideas for, 157–59
    importance of, 149
    peer response in, 161
    planning, drafting, and developing in,
        159–60
    responding to an image, 206–7
    revising and editing in, 160–62
    writing assignments in, 155–56, 162–65
Evaluating sources, 368–75
    age of source material, 374
    audience, 371 (fig.), 372–73
    author, 372
    contributions of source material, 374–75
    importance of, 368–75
    of Internet, 368–75
    of library, 368–75
    location of source material, 374
    publisher, 373
    purpose, 371 (fig.), 373–74, 375
    reviewer, 373

Evaluating sources (continued)
  sponsor, 373
  thesis and, reconsidering, 375
  use of source material, 374
  Web sites, 368–69, 371 (fig.)
Evaluation
  claims of, 134, 135
  in critical thinking processes, 37–38, 40
  of sources, 368–75, A-26–28
Evidence. *See also* Evidence in critical thinking
  adding, A-28–31
  critical thinking and, 40–42
  in evaluating and reviewing, 149, 158, 160, 161
  in integrating sources, 379–87
  in literary analysis, 220
  placement of, A-22–24
  recording, 136
  supporting, 179, 188, 191, A-23
  in supporting a position with sources, 179, 188, 191
  taking a stand and, 133–37
  views of supporting, A-21 (fig.)
Evidence in critical thinking
  to appeal to audience, 44–45
  emotional appeal *(pathos)* and, 44–45
  ethical appeal *(ethos)* and, 45
  expert testimony, 42
  facts, 41
  firsthand observation, 42
  logical appeal *(logos)* and, 44
  statistics, 41–42
  to support critical thinking, 40–43
  testing, 43–44
  types of, 41–42
except/accept, A-58
Experiences, recalling. *See* Recalling an experience
Expert sources, 325
Expert testimony as evidence, 42, 135
Explicit thesis, 263–64
Eyre, Alea, 85–87

Face-to-face classes, 227, 228, 231, 240
Facts as evidence, 41, 135
Fallacies, 143–44

"Family Dynamic, The" (Marchand), 171–73
Faulty thinking, avoiding, 52
Favorites in research archives, saving, 331
Fields, in library searches, 360, 362
Figures
  analyzing, 205
  in MLA and APA style, A-8, A-10–12, A-11 (fig.), A-12 (fig.)
  software for creating, A-8
File management, 238–41
  backing up files, 241
  inserting comments, 239
  naming and organizing files, 239
  polishing electronically, 240
  submitting papers online, 240–41
  templates in, 238
Film Preservation Guide: The Basics for Archives, Libraries, and Museums, The (NFPF), 298
Finishing, in writing processes, 11
Firsthand observation as evidence, 42, 135
Flashback, 73
Follow-up, for critical reading, 19
Fonts, A-14–15
Form
  of pronoun, A-46
  of verbs, A-42
Formal outlines, 279–81, 282–83
Formal reasoning to refine position, 130–31
Format, A-1–19
  for academic paper, A-1–7
  for application letter, A-17–19
  for document design, A-14–17
  document template for, A-13
  problems with, A-13–14
  for résumé, A-17–19
  for visuals, A-8–12
"Four Kinds of Chance" (Austin), 291
Free association, 109
Freewriting
  for generating ideas, 251–52
  for recalling an experience, 70
  of research project information, 326
Frost, Robert, 163
Fused sentences, editing, A-41–42

"Game Ain't Over 'til the Fatso Man Sings, The"
   (Chackowicz), 68
Gansberg, Martin, 294
Garretson, Marjorie Lee, 124–26
Gender, of pronoun, A-46
General databases, 363
General-interest databases, 363
Generalizations in critical thinking, 47–48
Generating ideas, 248 (fig.)
   by analyzing writing strategies, 29
   by asking reporter's questions, 71, 256–57
   by brainstorming, 70, 90, 157, 250–51
   by building from assignment, 249–50
   for comparing and contrasting, 109–11
   by considering audience, 134–35
   by considering sources of support, 71–72
   from critical reading, 27–29
   discovery in, 7–8, 8 (fig.)
   by doodling, 70, 252–54, 253 (fig.)
   for evaluating and reviewing, 157–59
   by finding an issue, 129
   finding ideas and, 248–60
   by freewriting, 70, 251–52
   getting ready to write and, 260–61
   by imagining, 255–56
   by keeping journal, 259–60
   by logging reading, 28
   by mapping, 70–71, 157, 254, 255 (fig.)
   for observing a scene, 90–92
   by paraphrasing, 28
   by questions, 129–30
   by reading critically, 28
   for recalling an experience, 70–72
   by recalling past readings, 28
   to refine position, 130–32
   for research project, 326
   by searching for topics, 27–28
   by seeking motives, 257–59
   by sketching, 70, 252–54, 253 (fig.)
   strategies for, 248–61
   by summarizing, 28
   for supporting a position with sources, 176–78
   for taking a stand, 129–37
   by thesis, 129–30
   by using images, 92

in visual analysis, 219–20
in writing processes, 7–8, 260–61
Gerunds, pronoun case and, A-46
Getting started
   in critical reading, 18–19
   in critical thinking, 38–39, 39 (fig.)
   in online writing, 228–31
   in writing processes, 7, 260–61
Globe of Blogs, 356
Goodman, Ellen, 298–99
good vs. well, A-40
Google Images, 353
Google Scholar, 366
Google searches
   advanced, 354, 355 (fig.), 356
   blog, 356
   vs. database searches, 366
   keyword, 354, 355 (fig.)
   news, 356
Government documents, 366–67
Grammar checkers, A-40
Grammar problems, editing for, A-40–49
   adjectives, A-48–49
   adverbs, A-48–49
   comma splices, A-41–42
   fused sentences, A-41–42
   past tense verb forms, A-42–44
   pronoun-antecedent agreement, A-46–48
   pronoun case, A-45–46
   sentence fragments, A-40–41
   subject-verb agreement, A-44–45
Griswold, Daniel T., 292
Growing Up (Baker), 62–65
"Guy Walks into a Bar" (Kulish), 291

Halpern, Jake, 168–71
Handbooks and companions, 366
Harjo, Suzan Shown, 121–24
have, forms of, A-44
Hawkins, Stephanie, 349–50
Headings
   of academic papers, A-4, A-6
   in document design, A-16–17
   MLA and APA style for, A-16
   of résumés, A-18

"High Cost of Manliness, The" (Jensen), 24–25,
Highlighting of research project information, 330
Homonyms, commonly confused, A-58
"How Mobile Devices Are Changing Community Information Environments", 22–23
"Hunger Games, The" (Tobias), 150–53
Hunger of Memory (Rodriguez), 73
"Hurricane Katrina Pictures" (*National Geographic*), 107
Hybrid (or blended) classes, 227, 228

Ideas. *See also* Generating ideas
    finding, 248–60
    grouping, 272–75
    organizing and outlining, 272–83
    plagiarism and, 345
    synthesizing, 388
illicit/elicit, A-58
Images. *See also* Images, responding to
    action shown in, 205
    analyzing, 216–19
    attitudes in, 213–14, 213 (fig.)
    audience for, 202
    background in, 202, 203 (fig.), 205
    characteristics of, 204–11
    close reading of, 201–4
    composition decisions in, 203 (fig.), 206–7, 207 (fig.)
    composition of, 202–3, 206–7
    design of, 205–6, 206 (fig.)
    feeling or mood of, 211–13, 212 (fig.)
    of figures, 205
    focal point of, 203 (fig.), 204
    function decisions in, 208–9, 208 (fig.)
    language in, 214–15, 214 (fig.)
    meaning of, interpreting, 211–16
    of objects, 205
    prominent element of, 202, 203 (fig.)
    purpose for, 202
    signs and symbols in, 208 (fig.), 215
    source of, 202
    space in, 203 (fig.), 206
    typeface options in, 209–10, 209 (fig.), 210 (fig.)

Images, responding to
    in comparing and contrasting, 99–100
    in evaluating and reviewing, 148–49
    in observing a scene, 80
    in recalling an experience, 60
    in supporting a position with sources, 166
    in taking a stand, 119
Imagining, 255–56
Implicit thesis, 263–64
Indefinite pronouns, A-45, A-47
Inductive reasoning in critical thinking, 48, 48 (fig.)
Informal outlines, 276, 278–79
Informal Toulmin reasoning, 131–32
Instructors
    decoding comments of, 306–7
    meeting, 306
    messages to, 231–34
Integrating sources, 376–88
    capturing source material and, 379–84
    citing evidence and, 387
    ethics in, 376–79 (*See also* Plagiarism)
    importance of, 376
    launching source material and, 384–85
    synthesizing ideas and sources, 388
    Take Action chart for, 386
Interactive online options, 230
Interlibrary Loan (ILL), 357
Internet sources, 352–56
    advanced searches for, 354–56, 355 (fig.)
    author credentials in, 372
    evaluating, 368–75
    search engines for, 353
"Internship Program Falls Short" (Erion), 153–55
Interpretation, summary with, 350
Introductory clauses, comma after, A-53
Investigation, in research process, 323 (fig.)
Irregular verbs, A-43
Issue-oriented databases, 363
Italics, 273, 287, A-13–15
    in APA style, A-15, A-37
    in MLA style, A-2, A-34–35, A-36

"Japanese: Linguistic Diversity" (Hawkins), 349–50
Jensen, Robert, 24–25
Journal citations
    APA style for, 339, A-37
    MLA style for, 339, A-35
    recording, in notes, 338–39
Journals for generating ideas, 259–60
Judgment, in evaluating and reviewing, 158–61

"Karate Kid vs. Kung Fu Panda" (Griffin), 104–6
Keywords, in research project, 330
Keyword searches
    on Internet, 354, 355 (fig.)
    of library catalog, 360, 361 (fig.)
    of library database, 363
Kintner, Shannon, 222–24
Knowing, in cognitive activity, 26, 26 (fig.)
Kulish, Nicholas, 291

"Last Rites for Indian Dead" (Harjo), 121–24
Latin Deli, The, 263–64
Launch statements, 384–85
Learning management system (LMS), 227, 229, 231, 239, 240
led/lead, A-58
Letter format, A-17–19
Library
    call numbers, 360
    catalog, electronic, 356, 359, 360, 361 (fig.)
    evaluating sources from, 368–75
    fields in, 360, 362
    home page, example of, 358 (fig.)
    orientation session, 357–58
    as research project source, 325
    searches in, 358-60, 361 (fig.)
    services offered by, overview of, 356–57
    sources in, finding, 356–67
    specialized resources in, 365–67
    using resources in, 360
Library database, 357, 360, 361 (fig.), 363–66
    APA style for, 339, A-37–38
    MLA style for, 339, A-35
    searches of, 363–64, 365 (fig.)

Library of Congress system, 360
Lidington, Jenny, A-68–76
"Life, Liberty, and the Pursuit" (Steinhaus), 216–19
Line graphs, A-10, A-11 (fig.)
Line numbers, MLA stlye for, A-32
Linking, 273, 274 (fig.)
Links, in research project, 330
Listing sources. See also Documenting sources
    APA style for, A-36
    MLA style for, A-33
Lists
    APA style for, A-16
    bulleted, A-16
    MLA style for, A-15–16
    numbered, A-16
Liu, Eric, 82–85
Living well, responding to an image, 599
Logging reading for generating ideas, 28
Logical appeal (logos)
    in critical thinking, 44
    in taking a stand, 138–40
Logical fallacies, 143–44
Logical organization, 273
Logical patterns
    in critical thinking, 49–51, 50 (fig.)
    testing, 51
Logos. See Logical appeal (logos)
-ly, A-48

Macro revisions, 300–301, 301 (fig.)
Magazine articles
    APA style for, 337, A-37
    MLA style for, 337, A-34–35
    recording, in notes, 336–37
Main clauses, defined, A-41–42
Main idea. See Thesis
Main impression, in observing a scene, 82, 89, 92, 93, 94, 95
Mapping
    for evaluation and reviewing, 157
    for generating ideas, 254, 255 (fig.)
    for recalling an experience, 70–71
Marchand, Abigail, 171–73

Martin, Schyler, 349

Material, organizing to persuade audience, 138

Matthews, Daniel, 311–13

McCain, John, 287–88

Mechanics, editing for, A-56–58

Medium of publication, recording in notes, 344

"Meet Me in the Middle: The Student, the State, and the School" (Rardon), A-59–67

Metacrawler, 354

Micro revisions, 301, 301 (fig.), 311–13

Misplaced modifiers, editing, A-49

"Misunderstood Michelle" (Goodman), 298–99

MLA style, 180–87, 334–44, 346, A-32–36
    academic paper format, 389, A-2–3
    annotated bibliography entries, 349–50
    for books, 342
    citing sources in text, 186–87, A-31, A-32–36
    for essays, stories, or poems, A-34
    for headings, A-16
    for journals, 339, A-35
    for library database articles, A-35
    listing sources in Works Cited, A-33–36
    for lists, A-15–16
    for magazines, 337, A-34–35
    for online e-Pages, A-34
    for paraphrases, 346
    for quotations, 346
    sample list formats in, A-15–16
    sample research paper in, A-59–67
    sample table format in, A-9–10
    for summaries, 346
    for Web pages, 343, A-36

Modifiers, 39, A-48–49
    dangling, A-49
    misplaced, A-49

Monthly Catalog of United States Government Publications, 366

"More Pros Than Cons in a Meat-Free Life" (Garretson), 124–26

Morris, David, 291

Motives for generating ideas, 257–59

Multimodal texts, reading, 33–35

Mysticism (Underhill), 381

"Myth of the Latin Woman, The" *(Latin Deli, The)*, 263–64

Names, recording in notes, 344

Narration, 73

National Geographic, 107

"New Literacy, The," 29–31

News organizations, Web sites for, 356

"New York" (Talese), 289

NFPF, 296, 298

"Niceness Solution, The" (Varnell), 264

Ning, class, 230

Nonrestrictive words, A-53

Non sequitur, 143

Northern Farm (Beston), 92

Notes
    author of source in, 335
    example of source notes, 340–43
    information in, 335–48
    page number of source in, 335
    plagiarism and, avoiding, 345
    for research project, 331

Note taking for research project, 331

Numbering
    to emphasize ideas, 273
    of lists, A-16
    of pages (*See* Page numbers)

Number(s)
    of pronouns, A-46
    of verbs, A-44

Objective case, A-45

Objects, 205, A-45

Observing a scene, 80–98
    details in, 92, 93 (fig.), 94
    examples of, 82–88
    generating ideas for, 90–92
    importance of, 81
    organization in, 93, 93 (fig.)
    peer response in, 94–95
    planning, drafting, and developing in, 92–93
    responding to an image, 80
    revising and editing in, 94–96
    writing assignments in, 96–98

"Observing the *Titanic*", 87–88

Of Woman Born (Rich), 298

"Once More to the Lake" (White), 292

Online classes, 227, 228, 240
Online e-Pages
    APA style for, A-37
    MLA style for, A-34
Online profile, 234–35
Online sources, for research, 325
Online texts, critical reading of, 33–35
Online writing, electronic writing space and, 72
Online writing classes, 227–43. *See also* File
        management
    college voice in, finding, 232
    courtesy and ethics in, 228, 229, 230
    face-to-face classes, 227, 228, 231, 240
    file management in, 238–41
    getting started in, 228–31
    hybrid (or blended) classes, 227, 228
    interactive options in, 230
    introducing classmates and, 235
    management systems and, 227, 229, 231, 239,
        240
    messages to instructors in, 231–34
    online profile and, 234–35
    threaded discussions or responses and, 235–38
    writing assignments in, 242–43
Openings
    with comment on topic or position, 291
    drafting, 290–92
    ending with thesis statement, 291–92
    with question, 291
    with story, 291
    with topic sentences, 287–88
    writing, 290–92
"Opportunity Gap, The" (Brooks), 101–3
Opposing pattern of comparing and contrast-
        ing, 112
Organization
    chronological, 273
    in evaluating and reviewing, 159–60
    of ideas, 271–75
    of images, 205–6
    logical, 273
    in observing a scene, 93, 93 (fig.)
    of online files, 239
    outlining used in, 275–83
    patterns of, 112–13

of research process, 323 (fig.)
    spatial, 273
Outline
    in evaluating and reviewing, 158, 160
    formal, 279–81, 282–83
    informal, 276, 278–79
    responding to, 281
    of thesis, 275–83
Oversimplification, 143

Page numbers, A-13, A-34
    APA style for, A-6
    MLA style for, A-2
    in source notes, 338, 344
Paper copies in research archives, filing, 332
Paragraphs
    drafting, 285–86
    as transitions, 296, 297–98
Parallel structure, A-50, A-52
Paraphrasing
    blending with quotation, 185
    for generating ideas, 28
    integrating, 379–81
    in notes, 345, 346, 347
    plagiarism and, 345
    of research project information, 330
    in supporting a position with sources, 184–86
Parenthetical expressions
    commas to set off, A-53
    defined, A-53
Participles, defined, A-43
Particulars in critical thinking, 47–48
Passive voice
    Take Action advice for, A-50
Past tense verb forms, editing, A-42–44
Pathos. See Emotional appeal *(pathos)*
Patterns
    in comparing and contrasting, 112–13
    to help audience, 112
    logical, in critical thinking, 49–51
    of organization, 112–13
Peer editors, working with, 304–6
Peer response
    in comparing and contrasting, 114
    in evaluating and reviewing, 161

Peer response (continued)
  in observing a scene, 94–95
  in recalling an experience, 74
  in taking a stand, 140–41
Pentad, Burke's, 257–58
Periodicals, recording publication details in
    notes, 344
Person
  pronoun and, A-46
  verbs and, A-44
Pie charts, 209, A-11, A-12 (fig.)
Plagiarism
  avoiding, 180, 383–84, A-28–29
  campus rules about, 229
  intentional, 377
  remedies for, 377
  unintentional, 378
Plagiarism-detection site, 229
Planning
  in comparing and contrasting, 111–14
  in evaluating and reviewing, 159–60
  in observing a scene, 92–93
  in recalling an experience, 72–73
  of research project, 322
  in supporting a position with sources, 178–89
  in taking a stand, 137–40
  in visual analysis, 220–21
  in writing processes, 8–9, 9 (fig.)
Poems, MLA style for, A-34
Point-by-point organization
  alternating pattern of, 113
  in comparing and contrasting, 112
  in evaluating and reviewing, 160
Policy, claims of, 134, 135
"Popular Crowd, The" (Halpern), 168–71
Popular culture, responding to an image, 547
Portland State University Writing Center, tuto-
    rial, 233
Position
  formal reasoning to refine, 130–31
  informal Toulmin reasoning to refine, 131–32
  supporting (See Sources, supporting a posi-
    tion with)
Possession, apostrophes for, A-54
Possessive case, A-45

Possessive pronoun case, A-54
Post hoc ergo propter hoc, 143
Predicates, defined, A-41
Preparing for critical reading, 19–20
Prepositions, defined, A-56
Presenting critical thinking, 47–51
  deductive reasoning in, 48, 48 (fig.)
  generalizations in, 47–48
  inductive reasoning in, 48, 48 (fig.)
  logical patterns in, developing, 49–51, 50 (fig.)
  particulars in, 47–48
  sequences and scaffolding in, 49
"Preservation Basics: Why Preserve Film?"
    (NFPF), 296
Primary sources, 374
principal/principle, A-58
Print credentials, 372
Print size, varying, 273, A-15
Pronoun
  defined, A-45, A-46
  form of, A-46
  gender of, A-46
  number of, A-46
  person and, A-46
Pronoun-antecedent agreement, A-46–48
Pronoun case, A-45–46
Pronouns, A-45
  indefinite, A-47
  personal, A-46
  relative, 309
  as transitions, 298–99
Proof by example or too few examples, 144
Proofreading
  in evaluating and reviewing, 162
  in observing a scene, 94
  in recalling an experience, 75–76
  strategies for, 314 (fig.), 315–17
  in supporting a position with sources, 195
  in writing processes, 10 (fig.), 11
"Proposal to Draft America's Elderly, A" (Roth-
    kopf), 53–54
Publication details, recording in notes, 344
Publication medium, recording in notes, 344
Public service announcements, 202 (fig.), 213
    (fig.), 214 (fig.), 215 (fig.)

Publishers, evaluating, 373
Punctuation, editing
  apostrophes, A-54–55
  commas, A-53–54
  quotation marks, A-55–56
Purpose
  bias in, 373
  in comparing and contrasting, 100, 108, 109,
    111, 114
  for critical reading by thinking about, 19
  in critical thinking, 40
  evaluating, 371 (fig.), 373–74, 375
  in observing a scene, 81, 89, 93
  in recalling an experience, 69, 74
  for research project, 326
  revising for, 301–2
  in taking a stand, 120, 127–28
  topic for, 262–63, 262 (fig.)
  writing for, 11–12
"Putting in the Seed" (Frost), 163

Questions
  Burke's pentad and, 257–58
  to generate ideas, 71, 129–30
  honing, 327
  opening with, 291
  for peer editor, 305
  phrasing headings with, A-17
  predicting answers for, 328
  reporter's, 71
  sizing up, 326–27
  topics for research project turned into,
    326–29
Quick Editing Guide, A-39–58
Quick Format Guide, A-1–19
Quick Research Guide, A-20–38
Quindlen, Anna, 293
Quotation marks, A-55–56
Quotations
  accuracy of, A-29
  capturing, A-31
  citing, A-31
  editing, A-55–56
  ellipses in, 181, 184, A-55
  ending conclusions with, 293

integrating, 379–81
launching, A-31
in notes, 345, 346
paraphrase blended with, 185
of research information, 330
for supporting a position with sources,
  180–81, 184

Rainbow connections, 273
Rardon, Candace, A-59–67
Reading critically. See Critical reading
Reading deeply for responding to critical reading, 20–21
Reading journal, for responding to critical reading, 23
Recalling an experience, 60–79
  assignment in, 69
  challenge in, 69
  details in, 74
  editing in, 75–76
  examples of, 62–68
  generating ideas for, 70–72
  importance of, 61
  peer response in, 74
  planning, drafting, and developing in, 72–73
  proofreading in, 75–76
  responding to an image, 60
  revising in, 74–75
  writing assignments in, 76–77
Recalling past readings for generating ideas, 28
Reference databases, 363
Reflective journals, 259
Repetition, 298–99
Reporter's questions
  for evaluating evidence, A-27–28
  for evaluating sources, 369–70
  for generating ideas, 256–57
  for recalling an experience, 71
Research, A-20–38. See also Sources
  APA style for, A-36–38
  defining quest in, A-21–24
  evaluating sources in, A-26–28
  evidence added from sources in, A-28–31
  MLA style for, A-32–36
  process, 323 (fig.)

Research (continued)
   question, 324–30, 329 (fig.)
   searching for sources in, A-24–26
Research project, 322–32
   assignment in, writing from sources, 324
   beginning, 324
   collaborative research for, 332
   information for, recording, 330–31
   keywords and links in, 330
   managing, 330–32
   planning, importance of, 322
   proposing, 330
   research archives for, 331–32
   research questions in, asking, 324–30,
      329 (fig.)
   resources for, surveying, 329
   topics for, 325–26
Responding to critical reading. *See* Critical read-
      ing analysis
Responding to visual representations. *See* Visual
      analysis
Responsive journals, 259
Restarting, drafting, 285
Résumés, format for, A-17–19
Retelling experiences. *See* Narration
Reviewers, evaluating, 373
Revising
   for audience, 302–3
   for clarity, 310
   in comparing and contrasting, 114–16
   for conciseness, 309–10
   for emphasis, 308–9
   in evaluating and reviewing, 160–62
   instructor and, 306–7
   macro revisions and, 300–301, 301 (fig.)
   micro revisions and, 301, 301 (fig.), 311–13
   in observing a scene, 94–96
   peer editors and, working with, 304–6
   for purpose, 301–2
   in recalling an experience, 74–75
   strategies for, 300–313
   for structure, 303–4
   for support, 303–4
   in supporting a position with sources, 189–95
   in taking a stand, 140–43

   for thesis, 301–2
   in visual analysis, 221
   in writing processes, 10, 10 (fig.)
Rhetorical analysis, critical thinking and,
      45–47
Rich, Adrienne, 298
"Rootlessness" (Morris), 291
Rothkopf, David, 53–54
Run-on sentences, editing. *See* Fused sentences,
      editing

-*s*, A-44–45
Sans serif fonts, A-15
Scaffolding in critical thinking, 49
Scholarly journal citations. *See* Journal
      citations
"School *vs.* Education" (Baker), 293
Schreiner, Robert G., 65–68, 73
"Science of Righteousness, The" (Shermer),
      32–33
Search
   in research process, 323 (fig.)
   results, saving in research archives, 332
Secondary sources, 374
Sentence fragments, editing, A-40–41
Sentence problems, editing, A-49–52
   dangling modifiers, A-49
   misplaced modifiers, A-49
   parallel structure, A-50
   sentence clarity, improving, A-52
   sentence style, improving, A-51
Sentences as transitions, 296
Sequence
   in critical thinking, 49
   in observing a scene, 93 (fig.)
   in recalling an experience, 75
Series, comma to separate items in, A-53
Serif fonts, A-15
"Sex Offender Lists: A Never-Ending Punish-
      ment" (Lidington), A-68–76
Shermer, Michael, 32–33
sight/cite, A-58
Signs, analyzing, 208 (fig.), 215
Sketching for generating ideas, 70, 252–54,
      253 (fig.)

Skimming
  of sources, for supporting a position, 178
  text, for critical reading, 20
Slide show, 274
Software
  file management and, 239
  formatting and, 240–41
  polishing online submissions and, 240
  templates and, 238
Solitaire, 274
Source information. *See also* Capturing source
    material
  capturing, 348
  integrating effectively, 194
  location of, recording in notes, 344
  in notes, 335–48
  for research project, recording, 330–31
  in supporting a position with sources, 187
Sources, 351–67. *See also* Sources, supporting a
    position with
  academic exchange for, 180, 182–83, 182 (fig.)
  annotated bibliography, 349–50
  capturing information from, 348
  citing and listing in APA style, A-36–38
  citing and listing in MLA style, A-32–36
  credit given to, 186, 187
  details drawn from, 334
  editing, in taking a stand, 140
  evaluating, A-26–28
  evidence added from, A-28–31
  importance of, 333, 351–52
  incorporating, methods of, 345–48
  Internet, 352–56
  launching, 189–90
  library, 356–674
  in library, finding, 356–674
  location of, recording in notes, 344
  methods of capturing information from, 187
    (*See also* Paraphrasing; Quotations;
    Summary)
  in notes, 335–48
  primary, 374
  reading thoughtfully, 179
  reliable, selecting, 177–78, A-25–26
  for research project, 324, 325, 329
  in research quest, A-21–24
  searching for, A-24–26
  secondary, 374
  skimming, 178
  supporting a position with, assignment in,
    174–75
  synthesizing, 386, 388
  in taking a stand, editing, 140
  warm-ups for, 335
  working bibliography and, 334–35
  working with, 333–50
Sources, supporting a position with, 166–99. *See
    also* Sources
  academic approach to, 177
  details in, 238
  in evaluation and reviewing, 157
  examples of, 168–74
  finding your voice and, challenge in, 175–76
  generating ideas for, 71–72, 176–78
  importance of, 167
  planning, drafting, and developing in, 178–89
  responding to an image, 224
  revising and editing in, 189–95
  writing assignments in, 196–99
Spatial organization, 273
Specialized materials and resources
  databases, 363
  on Internet, finding, 356
  in library, 366–367
Spell checkers, A-57
Spelling, editing, A-56–58
Sponsors, evaluating, 373
Stand, taking. *See* Taking a stand
Starting, drafting, 284–85
stationary/stationery, A-58
statistical Abstract of the United States, 367
Statistics as evidence, 41–42
Steinhaus, Rachel, 216–19
"Stockholm" (Eyre), 85–87
Stories, MLA style for, A-34
Story, opening with, 291
Strategies
  for drafting, 284–99
  for editing, 313–15
  for generating ideas, 248–61

Strategies (continued)
  for proofreading, 315–17
  for revising, 300–313
  for stating a thesis and planning, 262–83
Structure, revising for, 303–4
Subject
  defined, A-41, A-44, A-45
  in evaluating and reviewing, defining, 158
Subject-by-subject organization
  in comparing and contrasting, 112
  in evaluating and reviewing, 160
  opposing pattern of, 112
Subject complement, defined, A-45
Subjective case, A-45
Subject-verb agreement, A-44–45
Submitting papers online, 240–41
Subordinating conjunction, defined, A-41,
    A-42
Substantiation, claims of, 133, 135
Summary
  capturing, A-31
  citing, A-31
  with evaluation, 349–50
  fairness in, A-30
  for generating ideas from reading, 28
  integrating, 381–83
  with interpretation, 350
  in notes, 345, 346, 347
  of overall point in supporting a position with
    sources, 186
  of research project information, 330
  in responding to critical reading, 24–25, 28
Support, revising for, 303–4
Synthesis
  in cognitive activity, 26 (fig.), 27
  in critical thinking processes, 37–38, 40
  of ideas and sources, 388
  in research process, 323 (fig.)
  in supporting a position with sources, 166–99

Tables
  comparison-and-contrast, 110–11
  for function decisions, 208
  in MLA and APA style, A-8, A-9–10
  software for creating, A-8

Take Action
  for building a stronger thesis, 270
  for improving sentence clarity, A-51
  for improving sentence style, A-50
  for integrating and synthesizing sources, 386
  for integrating source information, 194
  for strengthening support for a stand, 142
Taking a stand, 119–47
  assignment in, 127–28
  challenge in, 128–29
  examples of, 121–27
  generating ideas for, 129–37
  importance of, 120
  logical fallacies in, recognizing, 143–44
  peer response in, 140–41
  planning, drafting, and developing in, 137–40
  responding to an image, 119
  revising and editing in, 140–43
  writing assignments in, 145–47
Talese, Gay, 289
Tap Project (UNICEF), 127
Templates in file management, 238
Terms
  defining, 138
  in research paper, 330
Text exchanges, 230
their/there/they're, A-58
Thesis, 262–83
  in comparing and contrasting, 111, 114
  evaluating, 375
  in evaluating and reviewing, 159, 160
  explicit, 263–64
  identifying, 264
  implicit, 263–64
  improving, 269–71
  in interviewing a subject, 92, 94
  in observing a scene, 92, 94
  to organize ideas, 271–75
  outlining, 275–83
  to preview, 272
  in recalling an experience, 72, 74
  in responding to visual analysis, 220, 221
  revising for, 301–2
  statements, examining, 269
  stating and using, 266–69, 267 (fig.)

stating or restating, to conclude, 293

in supporting a position with sources, 178–79, 183, 189

in taking a stand, 129–30, 137

topic for, 262–63, 262 (fig.)

working, discovering, 264–66, 265 (fig.)

in writing a conclusion, 293

in writing an opening, 291–92

Thesis-guided outlines, 276, 277

"Thirty-eight Who Saw Murder Didn't Call Police" (Gansberg), 294

This American Life, 68

Thompson, Clive, 29–31

Threaded discussions, 235–38

Tim Gunn's Fashion Bible, 288

Titles, recording in notes, 344

Tobias, Scott, 150–53

Topics

finding, 325–26

idea, 289

searching, for generating ideas, 27–28

in supporting a position with sources, 176–77

for thesis, 262–63

turning into a question, 326–29

Topic sentences

defined, 286

drafting, 286–89

elements of, 286–87

ending with, 288–89

implying, 289

opening with, 287–88

placement of, 288

shaping, 289

to/too/two, A-58

Toulmin reasoning to refine position, 131–32

Transitional expressions to launch source material, 385

Transitional markers, 296, 297

Transitions

building cohesion with, 113–14

common, 297

in comparing and contrasting, 113–14

identifying, 299

paragraphs as, 296, 297–98

pronouns as, 298–99

repetition and, 298–99

words and sentences as, 296

"Truth about 'Taps,' The" (Matthews), 311–13

Tuchman, Barbara W., 379–84

two/to/too, A-58

Typeface options in images, 209–10, 209 (fig.), 210 (fig.)

Underhill, Evelyn, 381, 383

Underlining, 194, 270, 273

UNICEF, 127

Varnell, Paul, 264

Verbs

defined, A-42, A-44

forms of, A-42

irregular, A-43

number of, A-44

past tense, A-42–44

person and, A-44

regular, A-42–43

subject-verb agreement and, A-44–45

tenses of, A-42

View from Eighty, The (Cowley), 293

"Virtues of the Quiet Hero, The" (McCain), 287–88

Visual analysis, 200–226. *See also* Images

assignment in, 219

challenge in, 219

details in, 311

examples of, 216–19

generating ideas in, 219–20

importance of, 200

planning, drafting, and developing in, 220–21

revising and editing in, 221

strategies for, 201–16

visual essay and, examples of, 222–24

writing assignments in, 225–26

Visual applications for online writing, 230

Visual essay, examples of, 222–24

Visual representations, responding to. *See* Visual analysis

Visuals

acknowledging, A-9

format for, A-8–12

Visuals (continued)
  graphs, A-8
  in online writing, applications for, 230
  positioning, A-8
  responding to (*See* Visual analysis)
  tables, A-8, A-9–10
Voice
  in college, finding, 232
  in supporting a position with sources, finding, 175–76

Warm-up journals, 259
Web logs, 259
Web sites
  APA style for, 343, A-38
  credentials of, 372
  evaluating, 368–69, 371 (fig.)
  MLA style for, 343, A-36
  reading, 35
  recording source information from, 342–43
"What Is a Hunter?" (Schreiner), 65–68
White, E. B., 292
White space in images, 206
Whole-Brain Thinking (Wonder and Donovan), 112
who's/whose, A-58
Wiki, class, 230
Wonder, Jacquelyn, 112
Word group, comma after, A-53
Wordiness, 309–10, A-51
Words as transitions, 296
Working bibliography, starting, 334–35
Working thesis. *See also* Thesis
  discovering, 264–66, 265 (fig.)
  as research guide, 328–29

would, in conditional sentence
  in reading process, 35–36
  in writing processes, 12–15
Writing, 6–16
  approach to, 7
  for audience, 12–15, 14 (fig.)
  generating ideas in, 7–8
  purpose for, 11–12
Writing activities
  in critical thinking, 54–55
  in reading process, 35–36
  in writing processes, 12–15
Writing assignments
  in comparing and contrasting, 116–18
  in evaluating and reviewing, 155–56, 162–65
  in observing a scene, 96–98
  in online writing, 242–43
  in taking a stand, 145–47
  in visual analysis, 225–26
Writing from recall. *See* Recalling an experience
Writing online. *See* Online writing classes
Writing processes, 7–11, 9 (fig.)
  finishing, 11
  generating ideas in, 7–8
  getting started in, 7
  planning, drafting, and developing in, 8–9, 9 (fig.)
  proofreading in, 10 (fig.), 11
  revising and editing in, 10–11, 10 (fig.)
Writing space, electronic, 72

"Young Americans' Indifference to Media Coverage of Public Affairs" (Bennett), 46–47
your/you're, A-58

CORRECTION SYMBOLS

Many instructors use these abbreviations and symbols to mark errors in
student papers. Refer to this chart to find out what they mean.

Abbreviation or Symbol	Meaning	For more information in Quick Editing Guide
abbr	abbreviation	
adj	misuse of adjective	A7 (p. A-48)
adv	misuse of adverb	A7 (p. A-48)
agr	faulty agreement	A4 (p. A-44), A6 (p. A-46)
awk	awkward	Take Action (p. A-51)
cap	capital letter	
case	error in case	A5 (p. A-45)
coord	faulty coordination	
cs	comma splice	A2 (p. A-41)
dm	dangling modifier	B1 (p. A-49)
f	format (see Quick Format Guide)	
frag	fragment	A1 (p. A-40)
fs	fused sentence	A2 (p. A-41)
hyph	error in use of hyphen	
inc	incomplete construction	
irreg	error in irregular verb	A3 (p. A-42)
ital	italics	
lc	use lowercase letter	D1 (p. A-56)
mixed	mixed construction	
mm	misplaced modifier	B1 (p. A-49)
mood	error in mood	
num	error in the use of numbers	
p	error in punctuation	C (p. A-53)
pass	ineffective passive voice	Take Action (p. A-50)
ref	error in pronoun reference	A6 (p. A-46)
rep	careless repetition	Take Action (p. A-50)
rev	revise	
run-on	comma splice or fused sentence	A2 (p. A-41)
sp	misspelled word	D2 (p. A-56)
sub	faulty subordination	
t or *tense*	error in verb tense	A3 (p. A-42)
v	voice	Take Action (p. A-50)
vb	error in verb form	A3 (p. A-42)
wc	word choice	D2 (p. A-58)
w	wordy	Take Action (p. A-51)
— ( ) [ ] …	dash, parentheses, brackets, ellipses	
//	faulty parallelism	B2 (p. A-52)
x	obvious error	

PROOFREADING SYMBOLS

Use these standard proofreading marks when making minor corrections in your final draft. If extensive revision is necessary, type or print out a clean copy.

∾	Transpose (reverse order)
≡	Capitalize
/	Lowercase
#	Add space
⌒	Close up space
℘	Delete
⎯℘	Stet (undo deletion)
∧	Insert
⊙	Insert period
⋏	Insert comma
;/	Insert semicolon
:/	Insert colon
∨	Insert apostrophe
⟦ ⟧	Insert quotation marks
⎮=⎮	Insert hyphen
¶	New paragraph
no ¶	No new paragraph

Add your instructor's own abbreviations below:

Active Learning and Transferable Skills

Learning by Doing

A Selected List of Activities

From *A College Writer's Processes*
Considering Purpose   12
Considering Audience   14
Reading a Web Site   35
Identifying Types of Appeals   45

From *A Writer's Situations*
Making a Comparison-and-Contrast Table   110
Building Cohesion with Transitions   113
Supporting a Claim   136
Launching Your Sources   190

From *A Writer's Strategies*
Opening and Concluding   294
Tackling Macro Revision   304
Tackling Micro Revision   311

From *A Writer's Research Manual*
Proposing Your Project   330
Comparing Web Searches   354
Evaluating Your Sources   370
Synthesizing Your Sources   388

Take Action

Self-Assessment Flowcharts for Improving Your Writing

Strengthening Support for a Stand   142
Integrating Source Information Effectively   194
Building a Stronger Thesis   270
Integrating and Synthesizing Sources   386
Improving Sentence Style   A-50
Improving Sentence Clarity   A-51

Resources for Building Transferable Skills

Finding Your Voice in a Source-Based Paper   175
Joining the Academic Exchange   182
Analyzing a Visual   201
Writing Online Course Messages   231
Formatting Your Paper   A-1
Capturing Evidence from Sources   A-28
Checklists for Quoting, Paraphrasing, and Summarizing   A-29, A-30
Fixing Common Problems   A-39
Sample MLA Paper   A-59
Sample APA Paper   A-68